The Kenyon Review, 1939–1970

The Kenyon Review

1939-1970

A Critical History

Marian Janssen

Louisiana State University Press
Baton Rouge and London

Designer: Patricia Douglas Crowder
Typeface: Linotron 202 Bembo
Typesetter: G & S Typesetters, Inc.
Printer: Thomson-Shore, Inc.
Binder: John H. Dekker & Sons, Inc.

Library of Congress Cataloging-in-Publication Data
Janssen, Marian, 1953–
     The Kenyon Review, 1939–1970 : a critical history / Marian
Janssen.
        p. cm.
     Includes index.
     ISBN 0-8071-1522-3
     1. Kenyon Review.   I. Title.
PN4900.K46J36   1989
051—dc20   89-30981
                                              CIP

To my mother
and the memory of my father

Contents

Author's Note   ix

Acknowledgments   xi

Abbreviations   xv

Prologue: The American Literary Review   1

1. Toward the First Issue   10

2. A Multiplicity of Interests, 1939–1942   46

3. A Flowering of Criticism, 1942–1947   91

4. Poetry, Fiction, and Other Interests, 1942–1947   122

5. Recognition and New Directions, 1947–1955   153

6. A Second Flowering of Criticism, 1947–1955   180

7. Literature and the Arts, 1947–1955   223

8. Decline, 1955–1960   265

Aftermath: Ransom's Review in Perspective   312

Index   353

Author's Note

Quotations from manuscript sources reproduce the original unless, for clarity's sake, corrections have been made in square brackets. With respect to references to *The Kenyon Review,* it should be noted that only numbers of volumes, and not of years, have been given. For more complete, if not always accurate, bibliographical information concerning the *Kenyon*'s first twenty-five years, the reader is referred to Elizabeth Browne (comp.), *Kenyon Review Index: 25 Year Cumulative Compilation, 1939–1963* (New York, 1964).

Acknowledgments

In the writing of this study, I have been helped in many ways by individuals and institutions.

First of all, I am indebted to Helen Ransom Forman, literary executrix of the John Crowe Ransom estate, and her daughter, Elizabeth, for granting me permission to consult and quote the Ransom correspondence, and for talking to me about *The Kenyon Review* in its Ransom days. My thanks also go to Evan Rice, Philip Blair Rice's son, for making his father's correspondence available and for sharing his remembrances.

I am very grateful to Robie Macauley, George Lanning, and Ellington White for answering, during long interviews, my many questions about their editorial intentions and about other matters concerning *The Kenyon Review*. Eric Bentley, Cleanth Brooks, Kenneth Burke, and Robert Penn Warren, all important contributors, also were most gracious and freely exchanged views with me about literary criticism and literary magazines. David McDowell recalled for me the *Kenyon*'s early days, when he helped Ransom and Rice to get out the magazine. George Core and Thomas Daniel Young, experts in the field of southern literature and literary magazines, shared some of that expertise with me. Irving Kreutz, Monroe K. Spears, and Peter Taylor patiently answered my question-filled letters.

I also wish to thank Isabel Bayley, Literary Trustee for the Estate of Katherine Anne Porter; Paula Deitz; Kate Donahue; Beatrice Roethke

Lushington; Ann Leslie Moore; and William Phillips for permission to quote letters and other documents.

Ronald Sharp and Frederick Turner, the founders and first editors of the second series of *The Kenyon Review* (1979–), talked with me about their editorial views and retrieved from their archives in Gambier, Ohio, boxes full of material mainly dealing with business matters concerning the first series. Others at Kenyon College were equally helpful. Kenyon's president, Philip H. Jordan, Jr.; its head librarian, William T. Dameron; and its archivist, Thomas B. Greenslade, made all correspondence, memos, and other original materials about *The Kenyon Review* available to me. Gerrit and Janet Roelofs and the late Robert Daniel were among the many friendly people in Gambier who talked to me about *The Kenyon Review*.

After Kenyon College, I acknowledge the assistance of over fifty institutions in making letters and documents in their collections available to me. For brevity's sake, I cite here only those institutions that have provided me with material, specifically designated in the notes, from which I have quoted in the text: University of Arkansas Libraries; Boston University Library; Brown University Library; Bancroft Library, University of California at Berkeley; Butler Library, Columbia University; Cornell University Library; East Texas State University Library; Houghton Library, Harvard University; *Hudson Review* Office; Harry Ransom Humanities Research Center, University of Texas; Lilly Library, Indiana University; University of Iowa Library; Library of Congress; University of Maryland College Park Libraries; University of Minnesota Libraries; Newberry Library; New York Public Library; Van Pelt Library, University of Pennsylvania; Pattee Library, Pennsylvania State University; Princeton University Library; Rockefeller Archive Center; *Sewanee Review* Office; Tennessee State Library and Archives; Jean and Alexander Heard Library, Vanderbilt University; University of Virginia Library; University of Washington Library; Olin Library, Washington University; Washington and Lee University Library; and Beinecke Library, Yale University.

I am most grateful to Professor T. A. Birrell and Professor Harry Finestone, who read an incomplete version of my manuscript; their suggestions have greatly furthered its growth toward healthy maturity.

I owe special thanks to my friends Frits van Heekesen, Els Nelissen, and Roos van Rooij for their practical assistance and mental support.

The debt I owe to G. A. M. Janssens, teacher and friend, cannot be fully acknowledged. Without his expert advice and encouragement, this book could not have been written.

Abbreviations

Throughout the footnotes, the following abbreviations, for publications and then for manuscript collections, have been used.

AS   *American Scholar*
HR   *The Hudson Review*
KC   *Kenyon Collegian*
KR   *The Kenyon Review*
PR   *Partisan Review*
SoR   *The Southern Review*
SR   *The Sewanee Review*
SRL   *Saturday Review of Literature*
TLS   *The Times Literary Supplement*

Barzun Papers: Jacques Barzun Papers, Butler Library, Columbia University, New York

Berryman Papers: John Berryman Papers, Manuscripts Division, University of Minnesota Libraries, Minneapolis

Bishop Papers: John Peale Bishop Papers, published with permission of Princeton University Library

Blackmur Papers: Richard Blackmur Papers, published with permission of Princeton University Library

Van Wyck Brooks Papers: The Van Wyck Brooks Collection, Department of Special Collections, Van Pelt Library, University of Pennsylvania, Philadelphia

Burke Papers: Kenneth Burke Papers, Pattee Library, Pennsylvania State University, University Park

Cairns Papers: Huntington Cairns Papers, Library of Congress, Washington, D.C.

Carter Papers: Thomas Henry Carter Papers, Washington and Lee University Library, Lexington, Virginia

Chase Papers: Richard Chase Papers, Butler Library, Columbia University, New York

Corman Papers: Cid Corman Papers, Harry Ransom Humanities Research Center, The University of Texas at Austin

Cowley Papers: Malcolm Cowley Papers, The Newberry Library, Chicago

Davidson Papers: Donald Davidson Papers, Jean and Alexander Heard Library, Vanderbilt University, Nashville

Deutsch Papers: Babette Deutsch Papers, Rare Books and Manuscripts Division, The New York Public Library, Astor, Lenox and Tilden Foundations, New York

Duncan Papers: Robert Duncan Papers, Olin Library, Washington University, St. Louis

East Texas Papers: Oral History Papers, East Texas State University Library, Commerce

Engle Papers: Paul Engle Papers, University of Iowa Library, Iowa City

Fletcher Papers: John Gould Fletcher Papers, Special Collections, University of Arkansas Libraries, Fayetteville

C. H. Ford Papers: Charles Henri Ford Papers, Harry Ransom Humanities Research Center, The University of Texas at Austin

F. M. Ford Papers: Ford Madox Ford Papers, Department of Rare Books, Cornell University Library, Ithaca

Garrigue Papers: Jean Garrigue Papers, Henry W. and Albert A. Berg Collection, The New York Public Library, Astor, Lenox and Tilden Foundations, New York

GF Papers: Grants for France Papers (R.G. 1.1. 500 R France; box 19), Rockefeller Archive Center, Tarrytown, New York

Ginsberg Papers: Allen Ginsberg Papers, Butler Library, Columbia University, New York

Hillyer Papers: Robert Hillyer Papers, Brown University Library, Providence

HR Papers: *Hudson Review* Papers, *Hudson Review* Office, New York

Jarrell Papers: Randall Jarrell Papers, Henry W. and Albert A. Berg Collection, The New York Public Library, Astor, Lenox and Tilden Foundations, New York

KC Collection: Kenyon College Collection (R.G. 1.2. 200 R Kenyon College; boxes 358/9), Rockefeller Archive Center, Tarrytown, New York

KC Papers: Kenyon College Papers, Kenyon College Archives and President's Office, Kenyon College, Gambier, Ohio

KR Papers: *Kenyon Review* (1939–70) Papers, Olin Library and Gordon Keith Chalmers Memorial Library, Kenyon College, Gambier, Ohio

KRns Papers: *Kenyon Review,* new series (1979–) Papers, *Kenyon Review* Office, Kenyon College, Gambier, Ohio

LMS Papers: Literary Magazines Study Papers (R.G. 1.1. 200 R Literary

Magazines Study; box 243), Rockefeller Archive Center, Tarrytown, New York

Lowell Papers: Robert Lowell Papers, by permission of the Houghton Library, Harvard University, Cambridge, Mass.

Lytle Papers: Andrew Lytle Papers, Jean and Alexander Heard Library, Vanderbilt University, Nashville

Matthiessen Papers: F. O. Matthiessen Papers, Collection of American Literature, Beinecke Rare Book and Manuscript Library, Yale University, New Haven

Miles Papers: Josephine Miles Papers, The Bancroft Library, University of California, Berkeley

Mizener Papers: Arthur Mizener Papers, Jean and Alexander Heard Library, Vanderbilt University, Nashville

Moore Papers: Merrill Moore Papers, Library of Congress, Washington, D.C.

O'Donnell Papers: George Marion O'Donnell Papers, Olin Library, Washington University, St. Louis

PR Papers: *Partisan Review* Papers, Boston University Library, Boston

Porter Papers: Katherine Anne Porter Papers, Special Collections, University of Maryland College Park Libraries

Random House Papers: Random House Papers, Butler Library, Columbia University, New York

Ransom Papers: Ransom Family Papers, Tennessee State Library and Archives, Nashville

Rexroth Papers: Kenneth Rexroth Papers, Olin Library, Washington University, St. Louis

Rice Papers: Philip Blair Rice Papers, Olin Library and Gordon Keith Chalmers Memorial Library, Kenyon College, Gambier, Ohio

Roethke Papers: Theodore Roethke Papers, University of Washington Library, Seattle

Schwartz Papers: Delmore Schwartz Papers, Collection of American Literature, Beinecke Rare Book and Manuscript Library, Yale University, New Haven

Scott Papers: Winfield Townley Scott Papers, Brown University Library, Providence

Shapiro Papers: Karl Shapiro Papers, Library of Congress, Washington, D.C.

SoR Papers: *Southern Review* (1935–42) Papers, Collection of American Literature, Beinecke Rare Book and Manuscript Library, Yale University, New Haven

SR Papers: *Sewanee Review* Papers, *Sewanee Review* Office, University of the South, Sewanee, Tennessee

Stallknecht Papers: Newton P. Stallknecht Papers, Lilly Library, Indiana University, Bloomington

Stallman Papers: Robert Wooster Stallman Collection (acc. no. 6778), Barrett Library, University of Virginia Library, Charlottesville

Stewart Papers: Randall Stewart Papers, Jean and Alexander Heard Library, Vanderbilt University, Nashville

Tate Papers: Allen Tate Papers, published with permission of Princeton University Library

Van Doren Papers: Mark Van Doren Papers, Butler Library, Columbia University, New York

Van Duyn Papers: Mona Van Duyn Papers, Olin Library, Washington University, St. Louis

VQR Papers: *Virginia Quarterly Review* (acc. no. 292), Manuscripts Department, University of Virginia Library, Charlottesville

Warren Papers: Robert Penn Warren Papers, Collection of American Literature, Beinecke Rare Book and Manuscript Library, Yale University, New Haven

Watkins Papers: Vernon Watkins Papers, Harry Ransom Humanities Research Center, The University of Texas at Austin

Zabel Papers: Morton Dauwen Zabel Papers, The Newberry Library, Chicago

The Kenyon Review, 1939–1970

Prologue
The American Literary Review

The birth of *The Kenyon Review* in 1939, its life, and its death in 1970 escaped the attention of the majority of the American reading public. Yet it was this review, with its circulation of six thousand at most, that to an important degree shaped the literary sensibility of a generation. As G. A. M. Janssens has shown in his exemplary study, *The Kenyon Review* belongs to the tradition of the twentieth-century American literary review that came into being in New York City in January, 1920, when the old Chicago *Dial* was reconstructed by Scofield Thayer and James Sibley Watson. The new *Dial* (1920–1929) was modeled on *La Nouvelle Review Française,* established in France in 1909; and it felt affinity, as did its successors, with T. S. Eliot's *Criterion,* edited in Great Britain from 1922 to 1939. These successors constitute a group of similarly serious and intellectual magazines, which were closely patterned after *The Dial,* though they all possessed distinctive personal characteristics. They are the lively, youthful *Hound & Horn* (1927–1934), which emphasized literary criticism and a topical coverage of the arts, with special attention given to the American scene; the disinterested *Symposium* (1930–1933), which crossed between literary criticism and philosophy, had a theoretical slant, and was internationally oriented; and, most comprehensive of all, the personable *Southern Review* (1935–1942), which stressed literary criticism—as a creative pursuit and as an academic discipline—and cultural and political debate, and was interested in national, international, and regional issues.[1]

1. G. A. M. Janssens, *The American Literary Review: A Critical History 1920–1950* (The Hague, 1968). The only other standard work about literary reviews is Frederick J. Hoffman *et*

These short-lived highbrow magazines are the immediate predecessors of the leading literary reviews of the malleable 1940s and
1950s, *The Kenyon Review,* the reconstructed *Sewanee Review, Partisan Review,* and a newcomer in 1948, *The Hudson Review.* Each of
these reviews has its own distinctive character and its own specific
history determined by internal, editorial and external, cultural fac-
tors. Still, their common parentage and the way in which they presented themselves to the public warrant grouping them into one family. Crudely categorizing their common traits, we find that they were
manifestly and proudly highbrow and that they published, first of
all, serious, searching criticism, mainly of literature but also of the
other arts. They also published poetry and fiction, which were usually selected according to the same criteria as the criticism and, consequently, complemented and highlighted it. These literary reviews
refused to bow down to the people who regarded them as futile un-
dertakings read only by those few writing for them; in their heyday,
they often published critical and creative writing that would be generally accepted only years later.

"The ideal task of the critical quarterly is not to give the public
what it wants, or what it thinks it wants but what—through the medium of its most intelligent members—it ought to have," Allen Tate,
the power behind many literary reviews, asserted unhesitatingly in
1936; only in 1944, when he had become the editor of *The Sewanee
Review,* did he discover the chasm between aspiration and achievement, between ideals and reality. Still, the editors of the main reviews in the 1940s and 1950s were driven by a sense of mission as
revealed in Tate's words; and it is precisely this missionary zeal that

---

al., in *The Little Magazine: A History and a Bibliography* (Princeton, 1946). More recent works
are E. Anderson and M. Kinzie (eds.), *The Little Magazine in America: A Modern Documentary
History* (Yonkers, 1978); and Bill Henderson (ed.), *The Art of Literary Publishing: Editors on
Their Craft* (Wainscott, N.Y., 1980). These two books are compilations of impressions and remi-
niscences of different editors and, if generally interesting, are not profound investigations into
the functions of literary magazines and as such of only minor use for this study. Useful and
important articles about literary magazines are Monroe K. Spears, "The Present Function of
the Literary Quarterlies," *Texas Quarterly,* III (1960), 33–50; and George Core, "*The Sewanee
Review* and the Editorial Performance," *Yearbook of English Studies,* X (1980), 101–15. Of a
much earlier date, but essential to any investigation of literary reviews, are T. S. Eliot, "The
Idea of a Literary Review," *Criterion,* IV (1926), 1–6; Allen Tate, "The Function of the Critical
Quarterly," *Essays of Four Decades* (London, 1970), 45–55 (this essay was first published in
1936); and Lionel Trilling, "The Function of the Literary Magazine," *The Liberal Imagination: Essays on Literature and Society* (New York, 1950), 93–103 (this essay was first published
in 1946).

made their magazines into the literary legislators of their times. These editors cared so passionately for and were so fervent in their defense of a certain conception of literature that their reviews became nuclei toward which like-minded contributors gravitated naturally. It was soon a common charge that the literary reviews published and discussed the same writers time and again—but then, as Cleanth Brooks and Robert Penn Warren, the editors of *The Southern Review,* remarked, it "is only natural that when an affinity is discovered between a magazine and a writer the work of that writer will appear there rather often."[2] Besides, while the critical cultivation of a core of writers the editors believed in gave each magazine its individual character, these literary reviews in their heyday were not house organs for only one kind of criticism. They were open to other sorts of superior criticism, aiming for the perfect balance between cliquishness and catholicity.

Charges of partisanship—and of an overemphasis on criticism—brought against the reviews were often fed by nostalgia for the little magazines that had flourished from World War I until the 1930s. In the 1960s a new wave of little magazines, also designed to shock, challenge, and change, flooded the literary landscape.[3] Wedged between these two ages of expansion and experimentation, the 1940s and 1950s were an age of concentration and introspection; they have come to be called, usually derogatively, the age of criticism. But the editors of the literary reviews, which filled the void the littles had left, were only a little less passionate, if more solemn, than the editors of the little magazines had been. They set out to explore and explain the new literature that had sprung up and that they themselves had sometimes helped to blossom. Simultaneously, they set out to show that literature has its own unique value, that it is not just a propagandist means to political ends, and therefore deserves, even demands, its own unique attention.

In bracketing *Partisan Review* with the *Kenyon, Sewanee,* and *Hudson* reviews, we have done some violence to, but have not violated, literary history. The *Kenyon, Sewanee,* and, later, *Hudson* reviews had

2. Tate, "The Function of the Critical Quarterly," 55; Allen Tate, "The State of Letters," *SR,* LII (1944), 608–14; Cleanth Brooks and Robert Penn Warren, "Introduction," in Brooks and Warren (eds.), *Stories from the "Southern Review"* (Baton Rouge, 1953), xiv.
3. An example of nostalgia for the littles of the 1920s is Beverly Gross, "Culture and Anarchy: What Ever Happened to Lit Magazines?" *Antioch Review,* XXIX (1969), 43–75.

modeled themselves on *The Dial, The Hound & Horn, The Southern Review,* and each other; what is more, the editors of the first two were a group of friends united by background and literary beliefs. *Partisan Review* had started out quite differently. It began in New York City in 1934 as a publication of the John Reed Club and so was initially committed to the Party line in critical and creative writing. Within a few years, however, after its turn against Stalinism, the propagandist emphasis of this magazine decreased, whereas its literary value increased. In 1943, Dwight Macdonald, one of its editors, resigned in disgust because *Partisan* had left "the thorny fields of politics" and had become too "exclusively 'literary.'"[4] Yet, during the early years, *Partisan Review* kept its leftist orientation, and the bulk of the criticism it printed was imbued with the notion that writers are influenced by the politics of their times.

With ongoing time and, perhaps, the aging of *Partisan*'s editors and contributors, their writings, which once had been radically informed, became liberally informed. Meanwhile, though *The Kenyon Review* was being stereotyped as politically conservative, mainly because of the Agrarian background of John Crowe Ransom, its principal editor, Ransom's political convictions had become liberal. What is more to the point, however, is that *The Kenyon Review* had always eschewed political debate and from the first had explicitly and particularly dissociated itself from southern patriotism. At any rate, by the mid-1950s, *Partisan Review* had exchanged its putative proletarian reading public for an intellectual elite and its political ideological criteria for aesthetic ones. In its emphasis on distinguished writing, *Partisan* had come to resemble the *Kenyon, Sewanee,* and *Hudson* reviews so closely that they were often lumped together under some such title as "The American Big Four."[5]

The great influence of the literary reviews in the 1940s and 1950s, as Monroe K. Spears has written, "need not be argued, for no one denies that they have a considerable influence; the common tendency, in fact, is to exaggerate this influence and hold the quarterlies responsible for whatever is wrong in the literary world." There is also general agreement about the predominance of the *Kenyon* and *Partisan*

4. Dwight Macdonald, "Letters," *PR,* X (1943), 382.
5. Derwent May, "The Little Magazine—VII: The American Big Four," *TLS,* April 25, 1968, p. 434.

among these reviews. The role *Partisan Review* has played has been given extensive attention: directly, in a book, *Writers and Partisans* (1968) by James Gilbert, in a dissertation, "'Partisan Review'" (1980) by Herbert Eugene Shapiro, and in numerous articles; indirectly, in the spate of publications about the New York intellectuals, including the memoirs of such members of the *Partisan* family as Lionel Abel, William Barrett, Irving Howe, Alfred Kazin, William Phillips, and Norman Podhoretz. Although, indeed, some of those most intimately connected with *The Kenyon Review*—John Crowe Ransom, Allen Tate, and Robert Penn Warren—have also been discussed extensively, their relationship to the *Kenyon* has usually been neglected. "[W]ith the founding of the *Kenyon Review* [Ransom] entered upon his time of greatest influence in criticism and poetry," Louis D. Rubin, Jr., remarked in a review of *Gentleman in a Dustcoat* (1976) by Thomas Daniel Young. In this long biography, however, the account of Ransom's twenty-one years as the editor of the *Kenyon* is surprisingly short. Moreover, in the few articles in which *The Kenyon Review* is treated individually and not as just one of the "Four Reviews," the *Kenyon* is often misconceived as a narrowly New Critical magazine dominated by a coterie of reactionary southerners. With the possible exception of Donald Lloyd Clarke's dissertation, "John Crowe Ransom: Editor" (1972), dealing superficially with the first twelve years of Ransom's editorship of the *Kenyon*, hardly anyone has seriously attempted to demythicize this imaginary *Kenyon Review*. Therefore, to right the record and to give this magazine the place it deserves, a history of *The Kenyon Review*, concentrating on its content and taking into account the American literary situation at large, is a useful undertaking.[6]

6. Spears, "The Present Function of the Literary Quarterlies," 40; James Gilbert, *Writers and Partisans: A History of Literary Radicalism in America* (New York, 1968); Herbert Eugene Shapiro, "'Partisan Review': The Forging of a Jewish-American Literary Aesthetic" (Ph.D. dissertation, University of Rochester, 1980). Examples of articles dealing directly with *Partisan Review* are: Frederick Crews, "The Partisan," *New York Review of Books*, November 23, 1978, pp. 3–10; Leslie A. Fiedler, "'Partisan Review': Phoenix or Dodo?" *Perspectives USA*, XV (1956), 82–97; S. A. Longstaff, "*Partisan Review* and the Second World War," *Salmagundi*, XLIII (1979), 108–29 (Longstaff is at work on a history of *Partisan Review*); and Ian Hamilton, "Family Feuds," *The Little Magazines: A Study of Six Editors* (London, 1976), 99–124. Examples of books and memoirs about the New York intellectuals are: Alexander Bloom, *Prodigal Sons: The New York Intellectuals & Their World* (New York, 1986); Maarten van Rossem, *Het Radicale Temperament: De Dubbele Politieke Bekering van een Generatie Amerikaanse Intellectuelen* (Utrecht, 1983); Lionel Abel, *The Intellectual Follies: A Memoir of the Literary Venture in New York and Paris*

A literary magazine is a complex organism, and the analyst who would do justice to all its aspects and nuances must not be tempted by a *parti pris*. In his "Little Magazines," Alan Wall stresses the importance of beginning "from the magazines themselves, from their own unique mode of production, if false accordances are not to be established after the fact."[7] This study starts from no preconceived notions about *The Kenyon Review*. It quantifies and analyzes the relation between critical and creative writing in the magazine, the different approaches to criticism and their prominence, and the balance and shifts between different editorial interests such as literature, philosophy, and the arts. It tries to assess the particularity and place of the individual contribution in the ongoing editorial concern for significance and continuity. While this study does discuss maverick contributors and incidental editorial discoveries and firsts in all fields, the lineaments of the magazine can be best traced in the impact of the regular circle of *Kenyon* contributors.

The final estimate of the place and the importance of a literary review rests in its bound volumes, but much of the interest of a critical history of its coming-to-be and its influence derives from the extent to which it is possible to recreate its daily life. Private editorial intentions and ambitions are often but dimly reflected in the periodic installments offered to the world at large, and the only way to recapture these intentions and ambitions is by interviews and, most illuminatingly, from original unpublished sources. This study makes extensive use of such sources. Wherever possible, informing the analysis of the *Kenyon*'s content are insights about editorial considera-

---

(New York, 1984); William Barrett, *The Truants: Adventures among the Intellectuals* (Garden City, N.Y., 1982); Irving Howe, *A Margin of Hope: An Intellectual Autobiography* (New York, 1982); Alfred Kazin, *Starting Out in the Thirties* (Boston, 1965), and *New York Jew* (New York, 1978); William Phillips, *A Partisan View: Five Decades of the Literary Life* (New York, 1983); and Norman Podhoretz, *Making It* (New York, 1967). Among the publications in book form that became available after the completion of this manuscript are: Terry A. Cooney, *The Rise of the New York Intellectuals: Partisan Review and Its Circle, 1934–1945* (Madison, Wis., 1986); and Alan M. Wald, *The New York Intellectuals: The Rise and Decline of the Anti-Stalinist Left from the 1930's to the 1980's* (Chapel Hill, 1987); Louis D. Rubin, Jr., Review of Thomas Daniel Young's *Gentleman in a Dustcoat: A Biography of John Crowe Ransom*, in *New Republic*, February 12, 1977, p. 23; and Donald Lloyd Clarke, "John Crowe Ransom: Editor" (Ph.D. dissertation, Texas Christian University, 1972).

7. Alan Wall, "Little Magazines: Notes towards a Methodology," in Francis Barker *et al.* (eds.), *Literature, Society and the Sociology of Literature: Proceedings of the Conference Held at the University of Essex, July 1976* (Colchester, 1977), 105.

tions, the authors' intentions, and readers' reactions, culled from private correspondence or gained from interviews. The use of these original materials, which deal with everything from lowly but crucial financial matters to splendid but unrealistic editorial dreams, has clarified much about what went into the making of a most influential literary review.

This critical history argues, then, that during the first decade, at a time when a new and serious approach to literature was desperately needed, *The Kenyon Review* was the magazine that most frequently and most consistently published creative, impassioned New Criticism, without closing its pages to other kinds of imaginative, serious criticism. Contrary to common opinion, the cultural criticism by such New York intellectuals as Philip Rahv, Isaac Rosenfeld, and, particularly, the *Kenyon's* advisory editor from 1942 to 1963, Lionel Trilling, was not only not repulsed but was, indeed, welcomed warmly; this was mainly thanks to Philip Blair Rice, Ransom's versatile, indispensable associate editor. Besides criticism, philosophical and, during its first few years, pedagogical concerns made up a generous part of its content. But political and regional issues were avoided; reading the *Kenyon* of the early 1940s, one has virtually no sense that World War II was being fought. From the first, poetry was an essential and glorious feature, and the *Kenyon* inspired and helped to advance many of the most distinguished mid-century American poets, among them Randall Jarrell, Robert Lowell, and Karl Shapiro. When *The Southern Review* expired in 1942, it left its emphasis on fiction to its rightful heir, *The Kenyon Review,* and talented short-story writers, in much greater number and diversity than is commonly assumed, began to frequent the *Kenyon's* pages.

These important creative aspects of the *Kenyon* have been grossly neglected because the brave spirit of its criticism has overshadowed the excellence of its record in poetry and, to a lesser degree, in fiction. Within a decade of the *Kenyon's* birth, the vibrant originality of its critical articles had made criticism the order of the day. With the other literary reviews in its wake, *The Kenyon Review,* which had been the demon of the academy when criticism was suspect, had become its darling. By the 1950s, virtually all universities had rallied 'round the banner of the New Criticism, regarding the *Kenyon* as their leader. Paradoxically, by this time the criticism published in

The Kenyon Review was almost anything but New Critical. With the publication of superior samples of all kinds of new approaches to criticism, from biographical to mythical, the magazine was once more ahead of its time. The creative writing appearing in its pages was of the same high quality as its literary criticism; excellent drama and movie criticism added extra spice to this exciting salmagundi. It is indeed possible to show, then, that though the *Kenyon* of the 1950s is known as the epitome of the New Criticism, its content belies this assumption.

During the final years of Ransom's editorship, from about 1955 onwards, *The Kenyon Review* declined steeply. Several new literary reviews had been founded or would soon appear—*Chicago Review, The Georgia Review, The Massachusetts Review, The Minnesota Review, Shenandoah, Wisconsin Studies in Contemporary Literature*—and the market for criticism had reached its saturation point. The fight for a critical approach to literature had been brilliantly successful. Moreover, Ransom was tired out; he was nearing seventy, and while editing had once been his passion, it had now become mere routine. Unadventurous, conservative, anemic, and academic, the *Kenyon* barely coasted along on its reputation.

When Ransom retired in 1960, it was hoped that the new editor, Robie Macauley, would bring a much-needed fresh impetus to the magazine. Eric Bentley, for one, wrote to Macauley that he would have "like[d] to drag [the *Kenyon*] down from its academic height. . . . [A] sign of the victory of the critical approach in departments of literature is that even PMLA has become less arid. But as it moves toward KR, KR should back away fast! . . . As Chesterton said, nothing fails like success. . . . Things have been quietly going to sleep recently, not just at KR but 'at' all such reviews. Evergreen Review has grabbed a new audience but not in a fashion I'd like to see you copy. But what to do?"[8] Macauley had a number of answers to that question. He shifted the *Kenyon*'s focus from criticism—for which the literary review is a preeminently suitable vehicle—to fiction; he shifted its concentration from America to the world at large; and he shifted its appeal from highbrow to middlebrow. But in his zeal to move with his times, Macauley introduced so many new traits

8. Bentley to Macauley, September 9, [1959], in *KR* Papers.

that *The Kenyon Review* lost its personality. *Playboy,* admiring the stories Macauley had published, kidnapped him in 1966 and made him its fiction editor. Macauley's successor, George Lanning, pursued Macauley's editorial policies, but lacked his creativity and drive. Moreover, the social-literary weeklies and fortnightlies, including the newly founded *New York Review of Books,* could meet the urgent need for immediate information and opinion about political issues, but the *Kenyon* appeared only five times a year. In other areas, too, *The Kenyon Review* simply was out of touch and no longer of vital interest or consequence to the intellectuals, let alone to the middle-brow public it had hoped to reach.

When *The Kenyon Review* was killed off in 1970, the literary world did not mourn the passing of Macauley's and Lanning's magazine; though contemporaneous, it had been so nondescript as to fade from memory almost instantly. Ransom's magazine, on the other hand, which had had its halcyon days a literary generation earlier, had been so clearly and brilliantly present as to be unforgettable, and it was his magazine that was commemorated. Therefore, *The Kenyon Review* under the editorship of Macauley and Lanning will be briefly discussed as a postscript to and an elucidation of the magazine's golden years. This study, then, will put the emphasis where it should be, on the first fifteen years of *The Kenyon Review,* on a time when its contents formed a treasure house of critical and creative writing, on a time when it helped to define the literary culture because it tried, in Matthew Arnold's familiar words about the *Revue des Deux Mondes,* "to understand and utter the best that is known and thought in the world."[9]

9. Matthew Arnold, "The Function of Criticism at the Present Time," *Matthew Arnold: Poetry and Prose,* ed. John Bryson (London, 1967), 361.

1 Toward the First Issue

John Crowe Ransom, Fugitives, Agrarians

When Gordon Keith Chalmers was elected president of Kenyon College in early 1937, he became the head of a school that, if it was known at all, certainly was not famous for its intellectual distinction. At the time of his selection, Chalmers was president of Rockford College for women in Rockford, Illinois. Born in 1904, the son of a Baptist minister, he spent his boyhood in Philadelphia. After attending eastern private schools, he graduated from Brown University in 1925 and, as a Rhodes scholar, went to Oxford, where he received his B.A. in English literature in 1928. It was at Oxford that Chalmers met his future wife, Roberta Teale Swartz, an American poet, who, as Ransom recalled in 1963, "really founded the *Review*. During her college days a strong-minded old mistress had enrolled her in an Eighteenth Century course, and made her read the British quarterlies of the period; not without remarking that no Review of such quality had yet appeared in America. Roberta at once resolved to remedy this disaster, and it is now known . . . that she early came to an understanding with Gordon that he would bring it about if and when he could."[1]

Gordon Chalmers had taught English at Mount Holyoke College till 1934, when he became president of Rockford College. At Ken-

---

1. John Crowe Ransom, "The Gordon Keith Chalmers Memorial Library at Kenyon," *American Oxonian*, L (1963), 93.

yon, where he succeeded the sixty-nine-year-old William Forster Peirce, Chalmers' main task, as Wilbur L. Cummings, chairman of the committee to select the new president, wrote to him, was to raise the standards of scholarship.[2] He certainly lost no time in doing so: Chalmers was elected president at the trustees' meeting of May 1, and he wrote a memo referring to Ransom's visiting Kenyon on May 15 and 16 about a possible job as professor of philosophy and poetry. From the correspondence between Ransom and Chalmers during May and June of that year, it becomes clear that the former did not have an inkling that Chalmers was planning to found a review at Kenyon. As Ransom did not feel qualified to head the philosophy department, Chalmers offered him a high position in the English department only, and Ransom immediately worried that his advanced teaching would condemn the other members of the department to elementary teaching. He obviously thought that the greater part of his time would be spent in teaching, but there is every indication that Chalmers had already set his heart on a review with Ransom as its editor: he even went to Vanderbilt University in Nashville, Tennessee, to persuade Ransom to come to Kenyon College.

In fact it was Robert Frost, whose word the Chalmerses took as gospel, who had suggested that Ransom be offered the editorship. At first sight, why Frost proposed Ransom is a mystery. Allen Tate, Ransom's closest friend and literary associate, admitted: "Well, not even his old friends were sure that he would become one of the great modern editors. He had not been very eager to know contemporary literature, so I for one supposed that he might well get out a quarterly in which his own fastidious taste was illustrated, and in which he might occasionally issue gentle fulminations against modern errors."[3] He may have been Frost's choice because he was one of the few American men of letters whom Frost did not regard as a threat to himself. Ransom, after all, had not published a book of poetry since *Two Gentlemen in Bonds* (1927). Then, Roberta Chalmers'

2. Wilbur L. Cummings to Chalmers, April 1, 1937, quoted in Thomas Boardman Greenslade, *Kenyon College: Its Third Half Century* (Gambier, Ohio, 1975), 67.

3. According to Thomas Daniel Young, *Gentleman in a Dustcoat: A Biography of John Crowe Ransom* (Baton Rouge, 1976), 297, Chalmers had first tried to persuade Frost himself to come to Kenyon College. Allen Tate, "Teacher and Friend," in D. David Long and Michael R. Burr (eds.), *John Crowe Ransom: A Tribute from the Community of Letters,* supplement to the *Kenyon Collegian,* XC (1964), 18.

second-place prize in the 1923 poetry contest held by *The Fugitive*—a magazine Ransom had helped edit—may have also played a role in Chalmers' decision. But for all that, there is no obvious clue in Ransom's history that accounts for his becoming one of America's foremost editors.

John Crowe Ransom, a Methodist minister's son, was born on April 30, 1888, in Pulaski, Tennessee, and spent most of his childhood in small towns in that state. He entered Vanderbilt University at fifteen and studied philosophy and the classics. Because of his excellent record he was appointed a Rhodes scholar and studied Greats at Oxford—a program that included Greek, Latin, philosophy, and ancient history—from September, 1910, until July, 1913. Back in America, Ransom became an instructor in English at Vanderbilt. In Nashville, he also joined a group centered around the mystic Sidney Mttron Hirsch, and took part in their philosophical discussions. This group of friends, which grew in number and would come to be known as the Fugitives, met regularly after World War I. Soon their discussions shifted from philosophy to poetry, and even Hirsch came to acknowledge Ransom's "leadership and influence in the Fugitive group," at least in part because Ransom was the only member to have published a volume of poetry.[4]

In November, 1921, Donald Davidson, who also taught English at Vanderbilt, took one of his pupils, Allen Tate, along to a Fugitive meeting. Tate was in his early twenties then. Born in Winchester, Kentucky, in 1899, Tate had had a difficult youth and a haphazard education before he entered Vanderbilt in 1918, where he soon attracted Davidson's attention. Tate was the first undergraduate accepted into this group. His deep attachment to modernist poetry caused suspicion among his fellow Fugitives. Indeed, the only serious falling-out Ransom ever had with Tate during their lifelong friendship, which originated during this period, was over T. S. Eliot's *The Waste Land*. Tate immediately recognized the poem as a master-

4. The members of the Fugitive group were: John Crowe Ransom, Allen Tate, Robert Penn Warren, Donald Davidson, Merrill Moore, Jesse Wills, Ridley Wills, Laura Riding, Walter Clyde Curry, Sidney Mttron Hirsch, James Frank, Alec Stevenson, William Yandell Elliott, William Frierson, Stanley Johnson, and Alfred Stark. For a comprehensive and well-written history, see Louise Cowan, *The Fugitive Group: A Literary History* (Baton Rouge, 1959). Sidney Mttron Hirsch to Ransom, October 31, 1930, in Ransom Papers; John Crowe Ransom, *Poems About God* (New York, 1919).

piece, but Ransom at that time still regarded it as an interesting oddity at best. This difference of opinion may have been one of the reasons why Tate had his doubts about Ransom's becoming a great editor.

Ransom's subsequent involvement with the Agrarian movement made him an even less likely choice as the editor of a midwestern quarterly. By the late 1930s, Agrarianism was generally considered out of touch, reactionary, and, by some, racist. It is startling, therefore, that Chalmers should want one of its foremost spokesmen to be the editor of the review that was intended to bring his college prestige. Still, there are some indications, however slight, of Ransom's eventual success as an editor. For one thing, Ransom had not been appreciative of modernist poetry during his early Fugitive period, but he became more favorably disposed to it as he grew closer to Allen Tate through the years. Then, too, there was his editorial experience on *The Fugitive*. Even though the usual editorial procedure there was to "cling to an old-fashioned, roundabout method of group-action . . . with the very idea of securing the blessings of individual liberty against the possible suspicion of a tyrant," Ransom did some of the actual editing.[5]

It was also during this time that Ransom formed a close relationship with Robert Penn Warren, a relationship that was to prove reciprocally advantageous too. Indeed, ever since Warren attended his first Fugitive meeting in 1923 at the age of eighteen, Ransom, next to becoming a close personal friend, was the foremost influence on his development as a major American poet, novelist, and critic. Thus, as a Fugitive, Ransom acquired editorial experience and formed alliances with writers of stature, who became valuable contributors as well as advisors to *The Kenyon Review*. Both Tate and Warren, through their wide interests and their many contacts in the literary world, would

5. Alexander Karanikas, *Tillers of a Myth: Southern Agrarians as Social and Literary Critics* (Madison, Wis., 1966), contains much valuable information about the Agrarian movement. One should take this book with several grains of salt, however, as Karanikas is biased against the Agrarians. For a different view, particularly with respect to the shift to Southernism by Davidson, Ransom, Tate, and Warren, see Daniel Joseph Singal, *The War Within: From Victorian to Modernist Thought in the South, 1919–1945* (Chapel Hill, 1982), 200–201, 398. Singal argues that the importance of the Scopes trial has been overvalued. The first issue of *The Fugitive*, a magazine mainly devoted to poetry, appeared in April, 1922; its final number was published in December, 1925. The Fugitives found the magazine too time-consuming ("Announcements," *Fugitive*, II [1923], 34).

bring new writers to Ransom's attention or themselves secure contributions for the *Kenyon*. Furthermore, during their meetings the Fugitives discussed each other's poems, paying close attention to the text. Thus Ransom laid the groundwork for the critical theories that guided him when he came to edit *The Kenyon Review*.

As for his Agrarian beliefs, one must keep in mind that, in contrast to, for instance, Donald Davidson and John Gould Fletcher, Ransom was not really interested in the economic and sociological reality of Agrarianism. To him, an agrarian society was an ideal world in which man could value God, nature, and art in all their fullness and complexity; he was interested in "the aesthetic and social relationship of man to nature." A few weeks before the actual release, on April 30, 1936, of the second collection of Agrarian essays, *Who Owns America?*, Ransom, one of the contributors, had written to Tate that he was "signing off but a little by degrees." A few months later, again in a letter to Tate, Ransom expressed himself much more forcefully: "[P]atriotism has nearly eaten me up, and I've got to get out of it." As a way out of Agrarianism he proposed to found an "American Academy of Letters" with Tate—which never came about—since "we need an objective literary standard." He went on to reject as prospective members Agrarians like Andrew Lytle and John Gould Fletcher because he did not want "our list [to] be confused with a Fugitive or Agrarian organization."[6]

All this makes Ransom's eventual editorial success a little less unexpected, but his appointment nevertheless remains hard to explain. For one thing, Frost and Chalmers could not have known that Ransom had privately given up Agrarianism when the idea of his editorship was first raised. In any case, Chalmers' offer came at a good time, for though Ransom had earned his professorship at Vanderbilt without having obtained his Ph.D. and was highly esteemed by most of his colleagues and students, he was none too

6. Telephone interview with Warren, August 17, 1983. Warren called the Agrarians "very different animals . . . who agreed about practically nothing," and repeatedly stressed that Ransom was not interested in Agrarianism as politics. Herbert Agar and Allen Tate (eds.), *Who Owns America? A New Declaration of Independence* (Boston, 1936). Twelve Southerners, *I'll Take My Stand* (1930; rpr. New York, 1962), was the first Agrarian volume. The "Twelve Southerners" were, in order of appearance: John Crowe Ransom, Donald Davidson, Frank Lawrence Owsley, John Gould Fletcher, Lyle H. Lanier, Allen Tate, Herman Clarence Nixon, Andrew Nelson Lytle, Robert Penn Warren, John Donald Wade, Henry Blue Kline, and Stark Young. Ransom to Tate, April 6, 1936, September 17, [1936], both in Tate Papers.

happy. At Vanderbilt, Ransom remained identified with the Agrarian cause, was loaded with committee work, which he hated, and was continually being hounded to get his Ph.D. He refused on principle to pursue the degree: a true understanding of literature had nothing to do with the mainly biographical and bibliographical emphases that were the doctorate's usual basis. Moreover, at Kenyon College, Ransom would have a lighter teaching load, so that he could devote more time to his own writing. Finally, Ransom's annual salary at Vanderbilt was $3,820, out of which he had to pay $45 a month for rent; the Kenyon offer was for $4,500 in addition to the use of a house.[7] All these considerations must have played their part in Ransom's decision, wired on June 11, 1937, to accept Chalmers' proposal. He would be leaving the South and his alma mater for an old but undistinguished college in a midwestern village.

An additional motive is furnished by Allen Tate. He regarded Ransom's "leaving Tennessee . . . as [a] disaster," but found himself "partly to blame for it. I pushed him into Ohio." Although this is an exaggeration, the rumpus that Tate in particular created when he heard that Vanderbilt's most prestigious professor might leave, may have tipped the scales in Kenyon's favor. When Tate realized that Ransom was seriously pondering the Kenyon offer, he wrote an open letter to Vanderbilt's retiring chancellor, James H. Kirkland, which appeared in the Nashville *Tennessean* of May 26, 1937. Tate chided Kirkland for letting go "one of the most distinguished men of letters in the world today."[8] Donald Davidson, Lyle Lanier, Andrew Lytle, and other Agrarians immediately rallied to this worthy cause: letters were written to F. Rand, president of the Vanderbilt Board of Trustees; C. Cason, director of the Alumni Association; O. C. Carmichael, the chancellor-elect; and others, protesting Ransom's possible departure and urging Vanderbilt to match the Kenyon proposal. Vanderbilt students such as George Marion O'Donnell, Peter

---

7. David McDowell and John Nerber, for instance, left Vanderbilt for Kenyon College in 1937; Peter Taylor followed in 1938, as his parents initially did not want their son to leave the South. Robert Lowell left Harvard for Kenyon College instead of Vanderbilt in order to study under Ransom, and Randall Jarrell, a student of Ransom's at Vanderbilt, became an instructor in English at Kenyon through Ransom's intercession. A memo by Chalmers written in May, 1937, mentions these figures (Memo in KC Papers).

8. Tate to Lytle, November 28, 1940, in Lytle Papers; Tate's open letter to James H. Kirkland is quoted in Young, *Gentleman in a Dustcoat,* 274.

Taylor, Randall Jarrell, and David McDowell also championed Ransom. Jarrell, for instance, wrote a petition offered to Kirkland that celebrated Ransom as the university's best teacher for over two decades.

Although he realized that "John will not be pleased," Tate felt that if they did not put up a fight, the cause of literature in the South would suffer. He could only hope that Ransom would not be offended by his "high-handed methods" and would remain one of his "dearest friends." Next to writing petitions and angry letters to the literary world at large, Tate—who had actually returned his "diploma to the University because it is no longer an honor to be one of her alumni"—was the main organizer of a dinner given in Ransom's honor on June 10, 1937. This dinner, at which Ford Madox Ford presided, was sponsored by the *Southern* and *Virginia Quarterly* reviews, and the guests numbered over a hundred. They listened to the reading of letters and telegrams from distinguished men and women of letters such as T. S. Eliot ("Delighted add name Ransom testimonial"), Morton Dauwen Zabel ("Now that Vanderbilt is losing Ransom, another college will soon be mentioned enviously as a place where one goes for something better than a degree, a diploma, and a lifetime exemption from responsible thinking and productive curiosity"), and Katherine Anne Porter ("Do raise the devil of a row. . . . [M]y deep regard and respect to John Crowe Ransom").[9]

But all to no avail. At the dinner, Ransom, characteristically the only one to keep his head, who had remained aloof from all these hectic activities, announced his decision to leave the South. This conclusion cannot really have come as much of a surprise, for on June 4, Andrew Lytle had already written to Tate that "the chances of retaining John look slim. He has given up all hope of staying."[10]

Associates and Advisors

On October 29, 1937, Ransom informed his mother of a "profound secret," which was that "the President called me to talk about founding and editing a great *Review* here; that is more than I ever ventured

9. Tate to Lytle, May 29, 1937, in Lytle Papers; Tate to James H. Kirkland, June 7, 1937, T. S. Eliot to Tate, [June, 1937], Morton Dauwen Zabel to Tate, May 27, 1937, all in Tate Papers; Katherine Anne Porter to Lytle, June 6, 1937, in Lytle Papers.
10. Lytle to Tate, June 4, 1937, in Tate Papers. For an extensive account of the stir caused by Ransom's departure, see Young, *Gentleman in a Dustcoat*, 272–88.

to hope for, and the most interesting thing I could possibly get into."
When, on the same day, Ransom described this "very interesting
situation" to Tate, he added that Chalmers

thinks of its editing as a full-time one-man job, aside from secretarial and
business help. Doesn't want to withdraw me from all teaching, and pro-
poses to go out and get another man to be a co-editor with me, both of us to
teach half-time. . . . Wants to consider long and hard with me the choice of
the man. Names a name or two I don't know and therefore suspect, is much
impressed with the idea of [Mark] Van Doren. I held my peace but instantly
occupied my mind with the idea of: TATE. After Tate, Warren, of course.

Ransom realized that Kenyon was not the most intellectually exciting
place to live, but he wanted Tate, as "we could really found criticism
if we got together on it."[11]

Chalmers gave reasons for establishing a quarterly to the Trustees
of Kenyon College in a letter written at the end of December. He
tried to sell them the idea that a "successful quarterly if well subsidized and well edited and managed, turns out to be the best possible
publicity for the institution to which it is attached." Moreover, "the
general intellectual and creative activity of the place is much stimulated by the creative and original men who are attracted to it because
of the quarterly." Since a "quarterly stands or falls on the ability of its
editor," Kenyon College was "most fortunate to have Mr. Ransom
on the faculty, for his creative and critical experience certainly ranks
him with the most sound and penetrating editors in this country and
in England." Therefore, under his leadership Kenyon might "develop
a quarterly which will become a real influence in this country."[12]

Ransom meanwhile felt "greatly cheered" by Tate's immediate acceptance of Kenyon and the review project. He had already decided
"that our cue would be to stick to literature entirely," and not to try
to include politics. Soon after, in his determination "to make sure of
your connection with it," Ransom developed a plan to have Scribners, Tate's publisher, back the new review more or less in the way
that Faber and Faber was financing T. S. Eliot's *Criterion* in England.
Maxwell Perkins, however, Scribners' legendary editor, showed no
interest in a literary review.[13]

11. Ransom to Mrs. J. J. Ransom, October 29, [1937], in Ransom Papers; Ransom to Tate,
October 29, [1937], in Tate Papers.
12. Chalmers to Trustees, December 24, 1937, in KC Papers.
13. Ransom to Tate, November 4, 1937, and n.d., both in Tate Papers.

In late November, Ransom wrote apprehensively about "the latest catch: that . . . we make it a perfectly general Review, with all sorts of things, political and otherwise. . . . The distinction would be gone before we started." In spite of that threat, Ransom kept working toward his own kind of magazine. On December 8, he handed Chalmers a list of possible names for the new quarterly: *Letters, Literature, Arts and Thought, The American Critic, American Letters, The Kenyon Reviewer,* and *The Kenyon Review.* These titles suggest Ransom's continuing bias toward a literary review. Nevertheless, his report, two days later, of an extensive conversation with Chalmers shows that he had resigned himself: "Personally I don't so much mind the thought of political philosophy, religion, philosophy in general, having representation in the review if I . . . have an editorial veto . . . in exercise of a *literary* control; and if it is understood that this . . . at once enlarges the size and scale of the project and does not propose to reduce the pure literary exhibit." In this same conversation, Ransom proposed Tate to Chalmers; he had delayed mentioning Tate, hoping that the president would "see of his own accord the unsuitability of most people for the position and be all the more agreeable to my proposal." Although Chalmers had initially seemed somewhat diffident with respect to having two Agrarians as editors, Ransom could inform Tate that "the prospect is good."[14]

It soon appeared, however, that in spite of his enthusiasm for the review, which had also found expression in his letters to Scribners about their possibly backing the quarterly, Tate had more strings to his bow. He and his wife, the novelist Caroline Gordon, accepted an offer from the Woman's College at Greensboro, North Carolina, even though Tate would "prefer to be with Ransom." But had Tate not accepted the Greensboro proposal—"which asks of us almost no work . . . and gives in return an amount of money . . . perfectly incredible"—he still would not have become Ransom's co-editor. Apparently, Tate would have been too expensive. Ransom, thinking "that maybe in spite of your latest letter you were not irrevocably committed to Greensboro," had had a long talk with Chalmers, who "had been extremely anxious to get you here with me." But,

14. Ransom to Tate, November 22, [1937], in Tate Papers; Ransom to Chalmers, December 8, [1937], in KC Papers; Ransom to Tate, December 10, [1937], November 19, [1937], both in Tate Papers.

Ransom continued his New Year's Day letter, "things didn't work out right, a great disappointment of 1937 for me," as "the more we talked the more he felt that the financial prospect here wasn't of a kind to put up against the kind in hand there." [15]

Now that Tate was out of the running, another editor had to be found. Ransom realized that if Tate would have unbalanced the Kenyon budget, so would Robert Penn Warren, and he therefore left the search up to Chalmers. The latter immediately wrote to Philip Blair Rice to ask him, without as yet mentioning the review, whether he would be interested in "an appointment in philosophy." Chalmers had first met Rice at Oxford, where Rice too had been a Rhodes scholar from 1925 to 1928. He was born in 1904, in Martinsville, Indiana. There he was brought up by his mother and his maternal grandfather, his father having disappeared when Rice was only one month old. Rice got his B.A. from Indiana University in Bloomington, where his brilliant record led to a Rhodes scholarship. Already at that time his interests were philosophy and literature. From Oxford, where, in Chalmers' words, he would "quote page after page of Santayana" and talk about "almost everything of importance: The newest poets, political theory, and philosophy," Rice went to Paris to become a reporter for the Paris *Times*. His friends there included, among others, Vernon Venable, with whom he collaborated by mail on an unsuccessful play and who later taught philosophy at Vassar College; Joseph Sagmaster, also from Indiana, who became a reporter for the Cincinnati *Times-Star*; and Theodor Geisel, who became famous as Dr. Seuss, the author of children's books. In 1930, Rice returned to the United States and soon became an assistant professor in philosophy at the University of Cincinnati, which he was to leave for Kenyon College. He devoted his spare time to both leftist politics and literature. Rice regularly contributed to *The Symposium*—where he published an attack on *The Waste Land*—and to *The Nation, Poetry,* and *Partisan Review*. [16]

Indeed Rice was, as Ransom wrote, "a most competent philosopher, [who] wishes he were a literary man." Therefore, when it ap-

15. Tate to Lambert Davis, December 22, 1937, in *VQR* Papers; Ransom to Tate, January 1, 1938, in Tate Papers.

16. Chalmers to Rice, January 14, 1938, in Rice Papers; Gordon Keith Chalmers, "Philip Blair Rice" (TS, memorial speech, 1956, in Rice Papers); Philip Blair Rice, "Out of the Waste Land," *Symposium*, III (1932), 422–42.

peared during the interview Chalmers had with Rice that his prospects at Kenyon involved not only his heading the new philosophy
department but also spending half his time as the managing editor of
a literary review, Rice showed an immediate interest. But even a half-
time salary would burden the review's low budget too heavily, so
Chalmers, at the end of May, 1938, officially invited Rice to join the
Kenyon faculty on a one-quarter review and three-quarters philosophy basis.[17]

A week earlier, Ransom, who judged Rice to be "a good man
though not a great one" and "very capable," had contacted Rice on
his own initiative to tell him that he had "laid it down as a condition
with Chalmers that I'm unwilling to go it alone, that is, without
your distinguished help. It would be too much of a responsibility,
and would take up all my time." Ransom continued this letter with
an astonishing remark: "I need not enlarge on my own desire to see
you here, for the double purpose of founding a Review and of improving the intellectual quality of Kenyon life. As for the former, it
would be my pious expectation and hope that before long I would
retire to the Editorial Board and leave you holding the bag; assuming
of course that you found this move congenial."[18]

While the overall tone of this letter is honeyed, this last observation
seems not merely flattering, but seriously and honestly meant, in
which case Ransom's twenty-one years of editing *The Kenyon Review*
would indicate that his enjoyment of the work was greater than he
had initially expected. Besides, Ransom probably intended to give
up editing in order to devote himself to poetry, but when it appeared
that his vein of poetry had dried up, he continued the editorship of
the review. That Ransom wanted Rice is beyond doubt, as is again
apparent in his description of the Kenyon situation to Tate:

[Chalmers] was a little alarmed at your reference to Rice as a Leftist. He
knew that perfectly well, and Rice is as honest as a man can be . . . but I
guess he had hoped that Rice wasn't publicly known as a Leftist. . . .
Rice has already come in, though Chalmers confessed to me that he
would not have had Rice, except that I insisted on him, and that he thought
I might keep Rice straight. . . . Each time I have been with him I have liked

17. Ransom to Tate, May 28, [1938], in Tate Papers.
18. Ransom to Tate, May 28, [1938], in Tate Papers; Ransom to Lambert Davis, May 2,
1938, in *VQR* Papers; Ransom to Rice, May 20, [1938], in Rice Papers.

him better. His Leftism is not a literary matter; he only sees Collectivism as inevitable, he doesn't think it has anything to do with literature directly.[19]

Since Kenyon College was going to publish a general review, that is, one including politics, and since the wealthy trustees who backed *The Kenyon Review* were not of the society-improving kind, it is quite understandable that Chalmers, who had to answer to the trustees, was alarmed. Thus, Ransom's insistence on Rice must have put him in a difficult position. But Chalmers may well have reasoned that an editor with an Agrarian background and a leftist managing editor would likely give the review a balanced political section. It is also noteworthy that Ransom was not at all disturbed by Rice's leftism, which was only political and "not a literary matter." Clearly, Ransom, as in his Agrarian days, was not interested in everyday active politics.

Chalmers now had an editor and a managing editor; he had also found a "young and enterprising and admirable" secretary, Norman Johnson from Harvard, "who had the double role . . . of secretary to the Kenyon Review (3/4 time) and Instructor of one section of Freshman composition." This "principle of stability" would be "the office man, the man who opens and files every communication, and nags . . . till the proper answer is made to each one, provided it is a communication that he cannot answer himself."[20] It soon became apparent, though, that Johnson was not all that stable: he left Kenyon College and the *Kenyon* within two years, mainly because he could not get along with Rice.

The Scope of the Magazine

Ransom and Chalmers also disagreed about the nature of the review: Chalmers and the trustees wanted a general periodical along the lines of *The Yale Review;* Ransom vastly preferred a review like *The Dial,*

19. Ransom to Tate, June 22, [1938], in Tate Papers.

20. Ransom to Lambert Davis, May 2, 1938, in *VQR* Papers; Ransom to Charles W. Pipkin, Dean of the Graduate School at Louisiana State University, June 1, [1940], in *SoR* Papers; Ransom to Rice, June 4, [1938], in Rice Papers. Randall Jarrell wrote to Margaret Marshall, [January 4, 1946]: "I helped Ransom and [Philip] Rice with the *Kenyon Review* for its first year. . . . I read the manuscripts submitted, corrected proof, suggested reviewers, and so on" (in Mary Jarrell [ed.], *Randall Jarrell's Letters: An Autobiographical and Literary Selection* [Boston, 1985], 152). However, no other evidence exists to support Jarrell's claim.

devoted to arts and letters only. But since a general review was better than no review at all, Ransom had acquiesced and had drawn up a four-page proposal for Chalmers at the end of January, 1938. In spite of this serious attempt to outline a general review in which Ransom described politics as "of maximum interest with readers" and briefly referred to possible sections on the social sciences, religion, and economics, he made it quite plain where his priorities lay. Ransom stressed that the "first distinction of a new Review . . . might lie in its superior literary quality." Furthermore, his interpretation of his "Literature and the other Arts" section is clear: "In no field is there better room for a new periodical. . . . There are not Reviews enough to take care of the good literary critics who have emerged in this and the previous decade." He went on to describe the book review section and the foreign contributors, and emphasized that "the one art which a Review can exhibit in action is literature."[21]

On May 20, Ransom wrote to Tate that the review was "right on the edge of starting" and that it would be "a handsome thing, and of the most distinction I can make it, and prompt and regular" but, he again added, "my interest in it would be greater if it were a literary magazine." About a week later, the situation had changed drastically: Ransom had got his way because there was not "money enough to get out a real Review, I am glad to say. We've canvassed printers, who charge a lot of money hereabouts; and have finally dropped the notion of a skimpy publication trying to compete with the comprehensive article re[p]resented by 200-pagers like Yale and Southern Reviews, 170-pagers like Virginia Quarterly Review. We will get out 100-page issues and devote the pages exclusively to literature and the arts." In his report to Chalmers on "the present state of our periodical project," Ransom wrote more specifically:

We have turned, very naturally, to the idea of a Review devoted to literature and the arts. . . . Our dimensions are ample for a rich and substantial publication of this restricted character. At present there is nothing in America published under just this classification; but we would be a successor to several very brilliant periodicals which used to flourish in this field: SEVEN ARTS, THE DIAL, HOUND AND HORN. . . . Professionally, it is what I could edit best, better than the comprehensive kind of Review, and it is more according to my preference. I believe it is also closer to the interests of Professor Rice and

21. Ransom to Chalmers, January 20, 1938, in KC Papers.

Mr. Johnson, the other members of the Staff. . . . And, really, to me that sort of publication seems more becoming for the style of a periodical published under the auspices of a small college, whereas the general Review would seem rather to belong to an institution with large and diversified interests, to say nothing of a large war-chest, such as Yale University.[22]

Naturally, Chalmers was less pleased by this change dictated by lack of money and, on May 28, wrote that he regarded "the arts and letters as very generally related to all affairs and, consequently, will be inclined to interpret that phrase to include from time to time treatment of subjects not conventionally called literary or artistic."[23] It was on this same day, seven months after Chalmers had first broached the subject of a magazine to Ransom, that the Board of Trustees authorized the publication of the new review, the first issue to be out in December, 1938. *The Kenyon Review* was now a fact.

A fact, yes, but still a nameless one. Ransom reflected: "Kenyon might appear in the title . . . I don't dislike the term and it will mean a lot of subscriptions from dutiful though likely dumb Kenyon alumni." Soon he "had come to the name 'The Critic', or 'The American Critic'; but that scared [Chalmers] somehow; and I thought it mattered so little that I waived my insistence in view of more important concessions on his part. So it's THE KENYON REVIEW; with some sort of sub-title or qualification like, 'Devoted to Arts and Letters.'"[24]

And Chalmers certainly made concessions, particularly in the matter of advisory editors. This subject came up first in Ransom's letters to his literary confidant Tate. Ransom stated that "the last but not least item in our organization is a Board of Advisory Editors, of whom one shall be Tate; indeed the Chairman, if there is such an office. I fear it is an empty honor, at least it will not carry any compensation. . . . Be ready to name your accomplices." In Ransom's view, to have Tate as an advisory editor at the least—"Much better if I had you at Kenyon, and we were co-editors"—was of paramount importance. A few weeks later, when Ransom proposed Howard Baker, William Empson, Paul Rosenfeld, Allen Tate, Mark Van Doren, and Mrs. Chalmers, Gordon Chalmers wondered why he did not "refer to

22. Ransom to Tate, May 20, [1938], May 28, [1938], both in Tate Papers; Ransom to Chalmers, June 8, 1938, in *KR* Papers.
23. Chalmers to Rice, May 28, 1938, in Rice Papers.
24. Ransom to Tate, May 28, [1938], June 22, [1938], both in Tate Papers.

other members of the Kenyon Staff or to Kenyon Alumni." Ransom did not mind accommodating Chalmers somewhat by adding Philip Timberlake of the English department to the list, as "it is not in him to do us harm" and as this would probably facilitate the relationship with the English department. It was a good move, for the members of this department saw Ransom as a southern newcomer who earned more than they did and got the editorship of the new quarterly to boot. Ransom, however, did not want to "fill up our list with Faculty men regardless of their qualifications," and vetoing Rice's suggestion of Archibald MacLeish was his only other concession to Chalmers. On the final list of advisory editors, only Philip Timberlake and Mrs. Chalmers (R. T. Swartz) appeared as courtesy names representing Kenyon College. Frederic Torrence, a poet second only to Frost in Chalmers' opinion, was not on it, and neither was Gordon Chalmers, who in May had still asserted that "I, also, shall be an associate [advisory] editor." There were a few other names mentioned by Ransom himself that came to nothing: "Gilbert Seldes; he represents Movie-art (if any); . . . Marianne Moore; though I don't know if she would serve; [and] A painting man." [25]

The following names, then, appeared as advisory editors on the masthead of the first issue of *The Kenyon Review:* R. P. Blackmur, "for moral support and for advertising purposes," P. Rosenfeld, "a music man, the best writer in that field . . . and we should have one non-letters man; he used to be with Hound and Horn," R. T. Swartz, A. Tate, P. Timberlake, M. Van Doren, and E. Vivas, a philosopher friend of Rice's. As we have seen, Timberlake and Swartz were there mainly to placate the Kenyon community. Although Eliseo Vivas, "a Venezuelan, a professor of philosophy at Wisconsin, considered brilliant among the philosopher group, and a pretty good literary man," must have been chosen partly for his closeness to Rice, and Mark Van Doren for his name, Ransom sincerely hoped to be counseled not only by Tate but also by all non-Kenyon advisors. As Ransom wrote to Van Doren: "The duties of an Advisory Editor are whatever he

25. Ransom to Tate, May 28, [1938], in Tate Papers. Already on May 20, when the future of the *Kenyon* was still uncertain, Ransom had asked Tate to serve as an advisory editor. Chalmers to Ransom, July 19, 1938, Ransom to Chalmers, July 31, [1938], both in KC Papers; Ransom to Tate, June 22, [1938], in Tate Papers; Chalmers to Rice, May 28, 1938, in Rice Papers; Ransom to Tate, June 22, [1938], in Tate Papers. Both Seldes and Moore were closely associated with *The Dial.*

will make them; we want his advices, his contributions, and his name on our masthead. It is all in our favor, not his." He asked them, for instance, to send a frank critique of the first issue of the magazine and hoped that they would steer any contribution they thought well of, and supposed Ransom or Rice had not heard of, in the *Kenyon's* direction. As it turned out, Ransom had to tell Tate after some three years that he remained "the one whose advice I have constantly sought, the only one."[26] Consequently, for this and other reasons, which will be discussed later, this first board of advisory editors— who received complimentary subscriptions, but no financial compensation—was disbanded as of the Autumn, 1942, issue of *The Kenyon Review*. The job of the later advisory editors was not usually merely honorary; on the contrary, some of them, such as Robert Penn Warren, Cleanth Brooks, and Eric Bentley, helped influence the direction *The Kenyon Review* was to take. The importance of choosing the first group of advisory editors lies therefore not so much in the actual advice they gave, or, rather, did not give, but in the demonstration that from the very beginning, Ransom had the upper hand, even though Chalmers often tried to exert control.

Finances, Circulation, Promotion

In 1934, Ransom had written to John Gould Fletcher, impressionist poet and fanatic Agrarian, who had suggested that they publish an "unfashionable agrarian sheet," that he "would not care to be connected with a publication that did not promise to have a good run of life, to be soundly administered by a circulation department other than the poor editors, and to have some self respect by reason of a fairly full and presentable appearance." Now, in 1938, Ransom could be assured of nearly all these conditions. As for the budget, thanks to large gifts of $500 to $1,000 per annum by individual trustees and over a hundred smaller gifts from people who wished the new review well—among them were John Berryman, Richard Eberhart, Wallace Stevens, Eudora Welty, Paul Rosenfeld, the Fugitive poet Merrill

26. Ransom to Rice, August 10, [1938], in Rice Papers. Actually, Ransom is mistaken here: Rosenfeld used to be with *The Dial*. Ransom to Tate, October 1, 1938, in Tate Papers; Ransom to Mark Van Doren, September 14, 1938, in Van Doren Papers; Ransom to Tate, July 12, 1942, in Tate Papers.

Moore, and Frederick Dupee, one of the *Partisan Review* editors—
The Kenyon Review at the end of May, 1938, had $15,000 pledged.[27]

In December, 1937, on the basis of a conversation with Lambert
Davis of *The Virginia Quarterly Review,* Chalmers had announced to
the trustees that the average guaranteed annual subsidy necessary for
a Kenyon quarterly review would be about $6,000. When in spite of
extensive canvassing, it appeared that about $5,000 annually would
be all that they could count on, Chalmers had had to make the difficult decision to have a 100-page arts and letters review instead of
a 132-page general one. But the $15,000 eventually pledged to the
Kenyon was not meant to span three full years of publication, for a
fair amount had to be spent on, for example, the over four thousand
copies of the first issue sent out for promotional purposes to Kenyon's 2,700 alumni and others. The budget that Ransom sent to
Chalmers in June gives a detailed account of how the money was to
be spent. The Manufacturing Printers Company in nearby Mount
Vernon, Ohio, undertook to print two thousand copies of a 96-page
quarterly, including the cover, at $440 per issue. Envelopes and mail-
ing would come to about $35 per issue, so total printing and mailing
costs were $1,900 annually. Furthermore, it was decided to pay con-
tributors $5 per page for prose, and about $.50 per line for verse, thus
making a yearly amount of $1,800. The other items on the list were
Rice's salary of $800, Johnson's salary of $1,000, and office expenses,
covering postage, stationery, office supplies, additional printer's costs
for extra copies, circulars, and so on. Against a total outgo of $6,700,
income came from two sources only: the pledges and the sales in the
form of subscriptions at $2 per year and newsstand sales at $.50 a
copy.[28]

The budget statement of July 31, 1939, indicates that *The Kenyon
Review* had about six hundred subscribers, a number that almost

27. Ransom to John Gould Fletcher, March 7, 1934, in Fletcher Papers; minutes of the
meeting of the Board of Trustees of Kenyon College, March 19, 1938, in KC Papers. The lion's
share of the money came from Kenyon's trustees. It was decided at this board meeting that the
funds for the *Kenyon* would be "kept in a separate account and that no financial obligation
should be imposed upon the College." During Ransom's editorship, Kenyon College indeed
only subsidized the *Kenyon* to the amount of a few thousand dollars, that is, not counting
salaries.

28. Ransom to Chalmers, June 8, 1938, in *KR* Papers. Rice's salary was somewhat more
than one-quarter of the $3,000 he earned. Johnson's salary constituted two-thirds of his total
earnings.

doubled by September, 1941, reached two thousand by 1946, and remained more or less steady between two thousand and three thousand during Ransom's editorship. When Robie Macauley took over as editor, he prided himself on having boosted the number of paid subscriptions to over five thousand within a short period of time. One must note, however, that circulation figures may be misleading. Still, it would be going too far to agree with William Phillips, staunch editor of *Partisan Review,* who reasons that the number of subscriptions directly correlates with the amount of money spent on promotion. Thoroughly researched and consequently much more dependable is Richard Blackmur's "Literary Magazines Study" for the Rockefeller Foundation. In this study, which he submitted in 1944, Blackmur concludes that there is a "three thousand maximum paid circulation for a literary quarterly, ten thousand for a monthly, and twenty-three thousand for a weekly." Only through compromises in quality could these numbers be increased, Blackmur warned. Naturally, there are some links between circulation and the time and money spent on promotion, but one must keep in mind that regular, faithful subscribers, the ones that count, are only initially won over by advertising, but renew because of the quality of the periodical's contents. Also, Blackmur's figures are time bound: today they should probably be multiplied. Another indication that circulation figures are deceptive is that they do not reflect the number of readers, if only, as Monroe Spears noted, because "most of the quarterlies send almost half their copies to libraries."[29] In other words, circulation figures do not necessarily indicate influence.

Although too much promotion is liable to attract the May-fly type of reader, Ransom knew that some promotion was necessary to make the really interested reader aware of the existence of his quarterly, and he campaigned doggedly. Here is George Lanning's account:

[E]ach year before Christmas we did a mailing—usually to our own subscribers and recent lapses—in the hope that readers would not only send in

29. Budget statement, July 31, 1939, in *KR* Papers; William Phillips, "Poor and Pure," in Bill Henderson (ed.), *The Art of Literary Publishing: Editors on Their Craft* (Wainscott, N.Y., 1980), 184; Richard Blackmur, "Literary Magazines Study" (TS in LMS Papers). This 43-page report resulted in his less extensive "The Economy of the American Writer," *SR,* III (1945), 174–85. Monroe K. Spears, "The Present Function of the Literary Quarterlies," *Texas Quarterly,* III (1960), 40. In "Poor and Pure," Phillips notes that "readers are calculated differently, usually for our kind of publication, about eleven readers per copy" (184).

renewals but order gift subscriptions at (of course) a remarkable saving. Mr. Ransom either wrote the copy himself or extensively revised that done by other people; and I am sure there is at least one Ph.D. dissertation to be got from the Stately Subscription Letters of John Crowe Ransom. He began several of them "Dear Literate," which must have occasioned surprise as well as gratification in some of the recipients. The Dear Literates never responded in droves—except in the sense that the volume of manuscript submissions picked up for a month or two, each Dear Literate being persuaded that we would prefer his story, poem, or essay to his check.

Everybody dreaded and hated these campaigns. . . . The annual labor was gone through glumly, and when, weeks later, the last of those reply-paid envelopes came drifting in a euphoria seized the staff. We knew you had to do this kind of thing, and we had done it, but now we could forget the whole business for another year. . . .

Once in a while Mr. Ransom and Phil Rice would brood on possible features that might make the magazine more popular with the general reader. The only one I can recall Mr. Ransom suggesting—and he came up with it every time—was a crossword puzzle which would occupy the magazine's back page. It would be, of course, of the highest literary order, difficult and yet irresistible. . . . I suppose Mr. Ransom envisioned . . . addicts scattered about in our colleges and universities, all of whom would have to subscribe to the *Review* in order to work on the puzzle, rather than meanly reading a library or departmental copy.[30]

An example of a failed promotion campaign is Ransom's very first try: 2,700 free copies of the inaugural issue sent to Kenyon's alumni resulted in only a few one-year subscriptions; Ransom had expected them to come through in hordes. Others were more cooperative. In November, 1939, for instance, James Johnson Sweeney, one-time associate editor of the little magazine *transition* (1927–1939), offered Ransom "a list of names and addresses of Transition subscribers." He wrote: "It would be doing them a good turn to call their attention to The Kenyon Review if they have not seen it. For in four issues you have done a great job."[31] It is unclear, though, whether his offer resulted in new subscribers to the *Kenyon*. At any rate, Ransom tried hard, if not always effectually, to launch his magazine. He had asked relatives and friends to make up lists of prospective subscribers, and he gave his mother a subscription for Christmas.

Subsequently, in the course of the magazine's first year and a half,

---

30. George Lanning, "Ransom as Editor," in Thomas Daniel Young (ed.), *John Crowe Ransom: Critical Essays and a Bibliography* (Baton Rouge, 1968), 216–18.

31. James Johnson Sweeney to Norman Johnson, November 7, 1939, in *KR* Papers.

promotion became somewhat more efficient. This was mainly due to the efforts of Philip Blair Rice. He reported: "Our promotion methods so far have consisted principally in the following methods: circulars to selected lists, advertisements in other periodicals, club subscription offers, and personal contacts by the staff. We have sent out some 30,000 circulars, in most cases following them up at least once and often twice by other circulars. . . . We have received a considerable number of subscriptions from advertisements in other magazines. Most of these have been exchange ads and have cost us nothing except the space in the *Review*." Rice also noted that though the number of subscribers had increased satisfactorily, they had encountered difficulties with their newsstand sales. For one thing, the *Kenyon*'s price of fifty cents per copy was higher than customary for a magazine of its size.[32] All in all, however, one may conclude that, with respect to its circulation, *The Kenyon Review* did as well as might be expected from a magazine of its kind.

Promotional problems were not the only ones Ransom and his staff were up against. Although in September, Ransom had decided that the cover was to be printed on gray Strathmore Emissary, he still had to find a design for that cover. Finally, he enlisted Kenyon College, and Norris Rahming, "the painter here directing the art students," drew a "most unusual and . . . distinguished cover." That Ransom actually admired this parochial cover—the main part was a rather crude drawing of Bishop Philander Chase, the Episcopal founder of Kenyon College, on horseback—is hard to credit. Malcolm Cowley, one of the editors of *The New Republic*, voiced the feelings of most readers when he wrote to Rice that he could not have "my frank opinion of your cover because this letter is being dictated and there are certain words that I can't use. But if I translated my thoughts into respectable language, I'd say that it was God-awful."[33] After a second equally disastrous design by Rahming, it must have been Philip Blair Rice, much more sensitive to the visual arts than Ransom was, who finally persuaded Ransom to follow Cowley's suggestion and have the artist Moholy-Nagy design the cover. Consequently, from the 1942 autumn issue until Robie Macauley became

32. Philip Blair Rice, "Report of the Managing Editor" (TS, [April 5, 1940], in *KR* Papers).
33. Ransom to Tate, [early January, 1939], in Tate Papers; Malcolm Cowley to Rice, December 29, 1938, in *KR* Papers.

the editor, the *Kenyon's* cover was the simple, direct, two-color presentation that still comes most readily to mind when one thinks of *The Kenyon Review.*

The first person Ransom turned to for help with the contents of the maiden issue was, of course, Allen Tate, to whom he explained that it was not as difficult to find good critical articles as it was to maintain a high standard of writing. The circular sent out to hundreds of prospective contributors was an invitation to submit critical essays—book reviews were usually assigned—and contained this emphasis: "The KENYON REVIEW hopes to carry on literary and aesthetic discussion in language of rather severer economy than is usual, provided no sacrifice is required in the warmth of the style, or literary quality." Then both Ransom and Tate wrote personal notes to critics and poets they particularly coveted in order to make a splash with the first issue; among these were Ford Madox Ford, Ezra Pound, Delmore Schwartz, Edmund Wilson, and Philip Wheelwright, one of the editors of the former review *The Symposium.* "Thanks for the announcement," Pound wrote from Rapallo. "On the face of it, it wd. seem that you mean to fill a long felt want." But, he added, "I imagine I had better see the first issue before merely looking into my owne heart and typing."[34] Meanwhile, Tate also contacted writers in Britain such as William Empson, Dylan Thomas, and T. S. Eliot. But the writers Ransom had most dearly wanted to display in his first issue were Allen Tate, Robert Penn Warren, and Richard Blackmur, none of whom actually appeared in it. Blackmur had not yet secured permission from the Adams family to publish about Henry Adams; Warren had had to beg off because of other commitments; and Tate, though he had initially consented to do a review, also had to withdraw at the last moment because he was pressed for time.

Still, there also were people who needed no circulars, no urging at all. George Marion O'Donnell, for instance, had heard rumors about the new review and immediately sent a batch of poems and asked in the same breath about books he would like to review, what Ransom's policy was on critical articles, and whether he was interested in short stories. Similar submissions led Rice to lament to Kenneth Burke that they had received reams of poetry, but little that was worth printing,

34. Circular to prospective contributors, September 28, 1938, in *KR* Papers; Ezra Pound to Ransom, October 15, 1938, in D. D. Paige (ed.), *The Letters of Ezra Pound 1907–1941* (New York, 1950), 318.

and to ask Burke to submit something. The poetry that finally did appear in the first issue came from much closer quarters, from Randall Jarrell and Robert Lowell, both at Kenyon College.[35]

And so, though Ransom complained to Mark Van Doren "that the motions of a green editor are pitiful," the inaugural issue of *The Kenyon Review* took shape.[36] Most of the contributions were in by November 10, so that before the end of 1938, a little over a year after Chalmers had first mentioned the possibility of a quarterly to Ransom, the editor could send the very first issue of the magazine that came off the press to his mother. *The Kenyon Review* had been launched.

Characterizing the New Critics

Before the first issue was published, however, Ransom did not seem to have irrevocably lost his heart to editing *The Kenyon Review*. When in November, 1938, Tate wrote to Ransom about a possible position at the Woman's College in Greensboro, Ransom professed interest. The actual offer proved to be so attractive that Ransom wrote to his mother that "[i]t looks like 'Ca'lina' from here." Another very important consideration was that Tate was in Greensboro. Ransom foresaw a great career for both of them—they would "crowd" the North Carolina Press with "fine critical books" and would "get a foothold into educational conferences . . . and preach criticism and have fun."[37]

But there were some drawbacks, too. Although *The Kenyon Review* "probably costs me more than it is worth," Ransom's "principal hesitation" was that he might be "letting [Chalmers] down." Therefore, during the initial negotiations with the Greensboro administrators, Ransom specified that he wanted to see the *Kenyon* through its two trial years. Ransom's Kenyon contract stipulated no length of tenure, but Ransom gave Chalmers "every opportunity to talk me out of the [Greensboro] thing" and to procure money from an outside source. This money was both to relieve the Kenyon budget of

35. George Marion O'Donnell to Ransom, September 30, 1938, in O'Donnell Papers; Randall Jarrell, "The Winter's Tale," *KR,* I, 57–59; Robert Lowell, "The Cities' Summer Death" and "The Dandelion Girls," *KR,* I, 32–33.

36. Ransom to Mark Van Doren, October 20, [1938], in Van Doren Papers.

37. Ransom to Mrs. J. J. Ransom, March 5, 1939, in Ransom Papers; Ransom to Tate, April 15, [1939], in Tate Papers.

the heavy burden of Ransom's salary—which far exceeded those of his colleagues—and to meet the Greensboro offer. Chalmers secured a ten-year Carnegie grant of $60,000 in total; and meanwhile Tate had resolved to leave Greensboro for Princeton. So Ransom decided to stay at Kenyon College after all. He explained: "The job here is at least equivalent to the Greensboro offer in every respect, and in fact a little better."[38] *The Kenyon Review* was saved, since, basically, Ransom was *The Kenyon Review*. This is not to say that Rice, Tate, and some of the other advisory editors were without influence with respect to editorial policies, but Ransom was in command: their power was based on his respect for their judgment. This autocratic control worked only to the good of the *Kenyon*.

Ransom's special interests were mirrored in *The Kenyon Review* and gave it its personality. Reading Greats at Oxford had made philosophy one of Ransom's durable interests. In a 1983 interview, Robert Penn Warren recalled that when he was a student at Vanderbilt, Ransom read Plato and Kant all the time, and that Ransom kept struggling with Kantian problems throughout his life. In Warren's opinion, Ransom took philosophy as seriously as literature, perhaps even regarding philosophy as "more of a profession," because it was something you had to "bite into."[39]

However, Ransom always treasured poetry most. Even if his own poetry suffered under the strain of editing the magazine, his interest in poetry remained intense; to this the careers of Randall Jarrell, Robert Lowell, and James Wright bear witness. Fiction, on the other hand, never won his heart. "I have the idea there is nothing to modern fiction but its ideology," Ransom wrote to George Marion O'Donnell in 1939. "The Marxists have done that for us, and all the critics are ideologizing now."[40] Ransom's preference is also clear in his own critical articles, most of which deal with poetry. It must be added, however, that Ransom's opinion of fiction became more favorable over the years.

In the late 1930s, Ransom was no longer concerned with Agrarianism. In December, 1937, he explicitly told Chalmers that he "would not like to see the Review pinned to any economic or political pro-

38. Ransom to Tate, April 15, [1939], in Tate Papers; Ransom to Mrs. J. J. Ransom, March 5, 1939, in Ransom Papers; Ransom to Tate, May 13, [1939], in Tate Papers.
39. Telephone interview with Warren, August 17, 1983.
40. Ransom to George Marion O'Donnell, December 25, 1939, in O'Donnell Papers.

gram," and in soliciting material from his old friend Donald Davidson, he stipulated that "we won't be in the field for patriotic and agrarian things." Higher education now took the place Agrarianism had formerly occupied in Ransom's mind. There is a clear link between his interest in education and his preoccupation with criticism. Basically, Ransom's pedagogical ideas were the methodological elaborations of his critical theories. In early October, 1937, he had written to Tate that "we certainly need some close modern critical studies; I mean modern as based on some close modern work as object of study; and we rarely get it." A few weeks later, Ransom foresaw "so much future for critical studies that my own are just beginning; it's the biggest field that could possibly be found for systematic study, almost a virgin field. I want to wade right into it."[41] And that is precisely what Ransom did with his *Kenyon Review*.

Initially, though, there was a danger that he would not be free to have his likes and dislikes determine the content of the *Kenyon*. Ransom conceded that Chalmers had some "responsibility in the matter; it's his project, and he is responsible to the donors and to the Board and to the Kenyon community." But when he realized that Chalmers intended to interfere with the actual content of the magazine, Ransom angrily informed Tate, "[I]t is clear that I won't have that." Apparently that threat soon passed, for in August, Ransom blithely told Rice that "Chalmers . . . is not disposed at all to offer directions." That Chalmers seemed to have every confidence in Ransom is also evident in his moving heaven and earth to avoid losing Ransom to Greensboro. However, in early 1940, Chalmers overrode Ransom's recommendation of Robert Lowell and appointed David McDowell the *Kenyon*'s secretary. Ransom felt that Chalmers had done so in order "to assert his authority," as "he is beginning to be afraid I am too highbrow an influence."[42] As a matter of fact, this uneasy, oscillating attitude was representative of Chalmers' relationship with the *Kenyon* to the end.

As Ransom's interest in criticism mainly determined the content of

41. Ransom to Tate, December 10, [1937], in Tate Papers; Ransom to Donald Davidson, September 28, 1938, in *KR* Papers; Ransom to Tate, October 10, [1937], October 29, [1937], both in Tate Papers. Ransom himself published few close readings of poetry. In an interview on October 11, 1982, Bentley voiced his admiration for the way Ransom scrutinized poetry in class and lamented that most of Ransom's essays were theoretical rather than practical.
42. Ransom to Tate, June 22, [1938], in Tate Papers; Ransom to Rice, August 10, [1938], in Rice Papers; Ransom to Tate, [spring, 1940], in Tate Papers.

his magazine, a closer look at the kind of criticism he believed in is in order. Just prior to his editorship of the *Kenyon,* in "Criticism, Inc."—virtually the one essay he endorsed throughout his life—Ransom had sought a definition:

What is criticism? Easier to ask, What is criticism not? . . . Professor Crane [of the Chicago school of criticism] excludes from criticism works of historical scholarship and of Neo-Humanism, but more exclusions are possible than that. I should wish to exclude:

1. Personal registrations, which are declarations of the art-work upon the critic as reader. The first law to be prescribed to criticism, if we may assume such authority, is that it shall be objective, shall cite the nature of the object rather than its effects upon the subject.

2. Synopsis and paraphrase. . . .

3. Historical studies. . . .

4. Linguistic studies. . . . Acquaintance with all the languages and literatures in the world would not necessarily produce a critic, though it might save one from damaging errors.

5. Moral studies. . . . [T]he moral content is not the whole content, which never should be relinquished.

6. Any other special studies which deal with some abstract or prose content taken out of the work.

After having extensively described what criticism is not, Ransom, in trying to define what it is, only gets as far as the following:

However the critic may spell them, the two terms are in his mind: the prose core [or "structure," in Ransom's later terminology] to which he can violently reduce the total object, and the differentia, residue, or tissue [later: "texture"], which keeps the object poetical or entire. The character of the poem resides for the good critic in its way of exhibiting the residuary quality.[43]

It is not surprising that such a pronouncement, one worked out in Ransom's book *The New Criticism,* in which he again stressed that "the distinction . . . especially of DM [Determinate Meaning, a refinement on "structure"], and IM [Indeterminate Meaning, a refinement on "texture"] is the vocation *par excellence* of criticism," would come under fire. This emphasis on technique was branded "academic" and lacking "gusto"; this kind of criticism had become "a science" and was "monstrous—an obsession with skill . . . that made

43. John Crowe Ransom, "Criticism, Inc.," *The World's Body* (1938; rpr. Baton Rouge, 1968), 342–49. This essay was first published in *Virginia Quarterly Review,* XIII (1937), 586–602. Lambert Davis wrote to Ransom on October 20, 1937, that "Criticism, Inc." had excited much comment and had gained the magazine sixty new subscribers (Letter in *VQR* Papers).

criticism larger than life . . . and never touched it"; in short, it was "mere barbarism." One must remember, however, that Ransom paid so much attention to texture and structure—to form—because the reigning approaches to literature in the 1930s, from Humanism to Marxism, ignored them. He uses such expressions as "a change of policy" and "strategy" in "Criticism, Inc." In addition, once his battle was won, Ransom was the first to stress that the prose content of a poem is as important as its texture, and that historical studies can be useful. Ransom was not being inconsistent; he merely changed emphasis. In "Criticism, Inc." he added to his extensive description of what criticism is not: "[T]he critic may well inform himself of [all] these materials as possessed by the artist, but his business as critic is to discuss the literary assimilation of them."[44]

Surely, Cleanth Brooks, Allen Tate, R. P. Blackmur, William Empson, and Ransom himself are New Critics: they in fact labeled themselves as such in 1948. But here we strike a snag, for both Cleanth Brooks and Robert Penn Warren have repeatedly argued that Ransom is *not* a New Critic. And in "A Burden for Critics," Blackmur describes the New Criticism as "facile," finds it too exclusively technical and only suitable for a very restricted kind of poetry. In his turn, Brooks is condemned by Ransom for paying too much attention to detail "in the manner of the bee who gathers honey from the several blossoms as he comes to them, without noticing the bush which supports all the blossoms." And Ransom criticizes Empson for his overindulgence in ambiguity for ambiguity's sake. If these New Critics, for all their superficial likenesses, are so much at variance with each other, less prototypical New Critics such as Robert Penn Warren, Austin Warren, Arthur Mizener, and, especially, such critics as Eric Bentley, Francis Fergusson, Eliseo Vivas, and F. O. Matthiessen, who are only infrequently classified among them, reinforce Tate's observation that the "New Critics look alike as Mongolians look alike to me; as Mr. Ransom might look, to them, like the late Babe Ruth."[45]

44. John Crowe Ransom, "Wanted: An Ontological Critic," *The New Criticism* (Norfolk, 1941), 301; Howard Mumford Jones, "The Uninfluentials," *SRL,* October 11, 1941, p. 20; Alfred Kazin, "Criticism at the Poles," *On Native Grounds* (New York, 1942), 446, 440; Joseph E. Baker, "The Philosopher and the 'New Critic,'" *SR,* L (1942), 171; Ransom, "Criticism, Inc.," 345.

45. In a letter of July 8, [1948], to his wife, Richard Chase describes a conversation that took place during the first session of the Kenyon School of English when Ransom and others tried to

In spite of the differences and disagreements among the New Critics, the term does have a characterizing significance. All three of Ransom's archetypal New Critics—I. A. Richards, Yvor Winters, and T. S. Eliot—he commends for their emphasis on the literary text. Richards is an "astute reader" whose "most incontestable contribution . . . is in developing the ideal or exemplary readings, and in provoking such readings from other scholars"; Winters' "distinction is his skill in analyzing structure"; and "it is likely that we have had no better critic than Eliot," who is an even "closer" reader than Dryden or Johnson. In 1979, Cleanth Brooks confirmed this view of the New Critics as truly essential by pointing out that a critic can emphasize the reader, the writer, or the writing, and that the New Critics chose the third option.[46]

The emphasis on the text itself led to a concern with the technical aspects of the text, and terms like *wit, paradox,* and *irony* became the fashion. It is easy to see that this kind of detailed analysis is more readily applicable to poetry than to prose, and more suitable to dense, complicated metaphysical and modernist poems than to sprawling, less tight and complex romantic poems, which indeed the New Critics neglected. George Core's opinion that "[t]he New Criticism was created in part as a means of coping with . . . modernism" is shared by many other critics. Also, the emphasis on technique sometimes led to excesses—for some critics, obscurity became an essential characteristic of good poetry. This moved William Barrett to object to the New Critical "use of an elaborate apparatus to reach a point which I find usually very trivial, even banal."[47]

Most frequently the New Criticism is linked with reactionary poli-

answer the question, Who are the New Critics? (Letter in Chase Papers). An unknown person has dated this letter 1949, but Chase served at the school in 1948 only. For example, during the interviews with Brooks (August 17, 1982) and with Warren (August 17, 1983), they both made this point. Richard Blackmur, "A Burden for Critics," *Lectures in Criticism,* Bollingen Series, XVI (New York, 1949), 187–209; John Crowe Ransom, "Poetry: I. The Formal Analysis," *KR,* IX, 436; Ransom, *The New Criticism* (part of the chapter on Richards is devoted to Empson, Richards' "pupil," and his overemphasizing ambiguity [128–32]); Allen Tate, "The Critic's Business," *KR,* XI, 16.

46. Ransom, *The New Criticism,* 45, 212, 140; B. J. Leggett, "Notes for a Revised History of the New Criticism: An Interview with Cleanth Brooks," *Tennessee Studies in Literature,* XXIV (1979), 1–35.

47. George Core, "The Dominion of the Fugitives and Agrarians," in Louis D. Rubin, Jr. (ed.), *The American South* (Baton Rouge, 1980), 300; "American Scholar Forum on the New Criticism [Part Two]," *AS,* XX (1951), 221.

tics. The Agrarian background of most of the southern New Critics, the contributions of some of them to Seward Collins' eventually fascist *American Review,* and T. S. Eliot's political conservatism probably all account for this association. In contrast to the Marxist critics, most of the New Critics consciously avoided political implications in their discussions of literature, and that too could be—and has been—interpreted as evincing a reactionary political stand. But in fact Ransom became a New Dealer in the early 1940s, and Empson, Bentley, Rice, and F. O. Matthiessen had always held leftist political views. Besides, it is less to the point to attack the New Critics for their alleged reactionary views than to call them to account for their literary misinterpretations.

Other frequent complaints are that the New Criticism feels a "strong antipathy to . . . the historical method of studying literature" and has "at least a limiting or negative influence on much of the [creative] work produced." Further, it is "narrow and dogmatic and also erratic," is "too much like an intellectualized version of art for art's sake," and is, in effect, the "equivalent of the scientist's escape from life into the laboratory." These critics "take in each other's washing and listen to each other's disputations with admirable gravity and seem to themselves to be of the first importance in moulding literary opinion in the United States. . . . For them, your people, sir, is a great beast; and they therefore retreat upon . . . the impression that Mr. Eliot's essays have somehow profoundly revolutionized the literature of the age."[48] What is noteworthy is that the torrent of adverse comments was turbulent in the late 1930s and early 1940s, quieted down during the mid-1940s, and gained strength again toward the end of that decade and into the 1950s and 1960s. The growth in influence of the New Criticism may be seen to account for this fluctuation.

The broad definition of the New Criticism, with its emphasis on the writing rather than on the reader or the writer, certainly fits *The Kenyon Review* during the first ten years of Ransom's editorship. Next

48. Frederick A. Pottle, "The New Critics and the Historical Method," *Yale Review,* XLIII (1953), 15. Further on in this essay, Pottle admits that the New Critics are not totally lacking in historical scholarship, but then disapproves of their too-selective application of it. R. G. Davis, "The State of American Writing," a symposium held by *PR,* XV (1948), 867; Douglas Bush, "The New Criticism: Some Old-fashioned Queries," *PMLA,* LXIV (1949), 19–20; Jones, "The Uninfluentials," 20.

to Ransom and Rice themselves, R. P. Blackmur, Cleanth Brooks, Robert Penn Warren, Arthur Mizener, Eliseo Vivas, and Eric Bentley, all of whom may fairly be called New Critics, were the main contributors to the *Kenyon* during this period. Most of these critics also contributed to *The Hound & Horn* and *The Southern Review*. But both these magazines were of a more general nature than *The Kenyon Review*. And since the *Kenyon* appeared at exactly the right moment in history—at a time when there was a critical vacuum waiting to be filled—it was *The Kenyon Review* that came to be known as the epitome of the New Criticism.[49]

The New York Intellectuals

The Kenyon Review was never limited to the New Criticism only. Already during the first years of its existence, the editors gave ample space to the writings of the New York intellectuals. It is quite as hard to characterize them as it is to pin down the New Critics. Sometimes, in fact, the groups are interchangeable. Delmore Schwartz, for instance, who was labeled a New York intellectual by his biographer James Atlas, wrote to Tate in 1938: "[W]hen I do write good criticism I am merely extending something I have learned from Eliot or yourself." Even Lionel Trilling, whom Grant Webster described as "the Intellectuals' Representative Man" and whom Alfred Kazin has called "an Emersonian teacher of the [New York intellectual] tribe"—even Trilling was convincingly ranked among the New Critics by Cleanth Brooks in "The Formalist Critics."[50]

Nevertheless, as in the case of the New Critics, the term *New York intellectual* is not an empty one. General characteristics of the New York intellectuals are that, obviously, most of them were born New Yorkers; that they had close connections with *Partisan Review*; that nearly all of them had an interest in politics, an interest that, very broadly, moved away from the Left through the years; that many of them were Jewish; and that they so often met, praised, and abused

49. Not completely objective, but still a good defense of the New Criticism is Cleanth Brooks, "The Formalist Critics," *KR*, XIII, 64–81.

50. James Atlas, *Delmore Schwartz: The Life of an American Poet* (New York, 1977), 142; Delmore Schwartz to Tate, March 14, 1938, in Tate Papers; Grant Webster, *The Republic of Letters: A History of Postwar American Literary Opinion* (Baltimore, 1979), 252; Alfred Kazin, *Contemporaries* (Boston, 1962), 497.

each other that Norman Podhoretz dubbed them "the Family." Also, while the New Critics gave most of their attention to poetry, the New York intellectuals more generally concerned themselves with fiction. Another common characteristic is that in their criticism they often considered the relation of art to culture; Ransom therefore named them "cultural critics." The following critics showed most of these characteristics: Lionel Trilling and Diana Trilling, Philip Rahv, William Phillips, Dwight Macdonald, William Barrett, Isaac Rosenfeld, Delmore Schwartz, Robert Warshow, Elizabeth Hardwick, Mary McCarthy, Alfred Kazin, and Irving Howe. In *A Margin of Hope,* Howe also includes Sidney Hook, Meyer Schapiro, Harold Rosenberg, Saul Bellow, and even Randall Jarrell and John Berryman.[51]

The New York intellectuals and the New Critics shared a deep concern for literature as literature and a belief in the value and necessity of literary criticism. This formed a strong if uneasy bond between them, a measure of agreement often obscured by the disproportionate attention paid to their disagreements and differences. The antipathies that existed were mainly political and rather one-sided to boot: the New York intellectuals found grave fault with the alleged conservatism of the New Critics; most of the time, the New Critics could not care less about the political beliefs of the New Yorkers. In general, there was more that drew these two groups together than kept them apart. The common concern for literature proved such a firm bond that when the "Protofascists" actually met the "Communists," they recognized "with almost ludicrous rapidity that they were very close together indeed in literary matters and felt alike on an astonishing number of social issues."[52]

Many of the New York intellectuals were published in *The Kenyon Review* from its very beginning. Ransom's ability to recognize the genius of critics like Lionel Trilling, Rahv, and Schwartz, even if their emphases differed from his, was to be characteristic of his editorial career and one of the reasons for his success. Rice's part in the prominence of *The Kenyon Review* will be discussed later. Still, it must be stressed here that Rice rather than Ransom—"whom they

51. Norman Podhoretz, *Making It* (New York, 1967). Richard Chase mentions that Ransom called Trilling and others "cultural critics" (Chase to his wife, July 8, 1948, in Chase Papers). Irving Howe, *A Margin of Hope: An Intellectual Autobiography* (New York, 1982).

52. Arthur Mizener to James Atlas, 1975, quoted in Atlas, *Delmore Schwartz,* 158.

probably suspected of lynching a nigger every week"—got the New York intellectuals actually to submit their work to the *Kenyon*.[53]

So we find that the early *Kenyon Review* fulfills Eliot's criteria for an ideal literary quarterly: the influx of the New Yorkers prevented it from becoming too "narrow," and there clearly remained "a residue of a common [New Critical] tendency, in the light of which many occasional contributors, otherwise irrelevant or even antagonistic, may take their place and counteract . . . sectarianism." Many readers, however, were not alive to the broader, non–New Critical aspects of the *Kenyon*. John Marshall, an officer of the Rockefeller Foundation, voiced a widely shared attitude toward the *Kenyon* when he wrote that it was "a journal representative of an exceedingly small and exceedingly advanced group." R. P. Blackmur, on the other hand, found *The Kenyon Review* too much of a "miscellany" and wanted Ransom to "choose his contributors more strictly; neither taste nor standards can exist without a continuous element of decisiveness—which is the vital risk in the cultural enterprise that, successively taken, becomes a policy."[54]

The discussion of the first volumes of the *Kenyon* will show that both these opinions were biased and that Ransom admirably realized Eliot's criteria, which corresponded to his own explicitly stated editorial policies:

We should not wish to be construed as representing some "school" or theory of literature or art, unless a very broad one. Within the limits of our taste we take the best writing we can find, or commission writing from the best writers that we can approach.

But I hope we are not without character. . . .

As for the substantial part of our character, I must plead guilty to having an "aesthetic," or philosophy of art, though not a narrow one; and I am more serious about that than about nearly anything else in the world. . . . But we do not print our own and similar views exclusively.

Are we then too "highbrow," or are we too "arty"? I cannot tell. I should prefer to answer the question by recalling, for the purpose, four distinguished quarterlies which might be said to be in some sense our predecessors: the *Dial*, the *Symposium*, the *Hound and Horn*, and the *Criterion* of T. S. Eliot's in England. I should say that we are much less heavy and dogmatic

53. Interview with David McDowell, December 4, 1981.

54. T. S. Eliot, "The Idea of a Literary Review," *Criterion*, IV (1926), 3; John Marshall to David Stevens, October 19, 1943, memo in LMS Papers; Blackmur, "Literary Magazines Study," 20.

than the last of these; less technically philosophical than the Symposium and with more soundness in the writing and less irresponsible and faddish than the other two.[55]

The First Issue

Although Ransom described the first issue of *The Kenyon Review* to Tate as "good not great," it did reflect most of his interests and intentions. It is primarily a critical issue, representing New Critics and New York intellectuals; it discusses education, publishes young poets, and includes contributions dealing with the other arts. As expected, we do not find any fiction or discussions of political questions. The issue is unusual, though, in that philosophy is not represented. The contributions by the New Critics—Ransom, Rice, Blackmur, and Winters—all appeared in the book review section. Following the tradition of the literary magazines that Ransom acknowledged, the reviews were substantial; Ransom emphasized that "it should not be taken for granted that, in being smaller than the essays, the reviews are critically inferior. Good reviews are likely to hold to an extreme economy, but sometimes are all the more wonderful in their easy deployment of critical principles and methods answering to the purpose."[56] He generally chose to publish few, long reviews rather than short, superficial ones; and though the reviews in *The Kenyon Review* were sometimes too heavy, or too indecisive, they are vastly superior to the puffs and invectives that generally went by the name of book reviews in the literary and cultural weeklies.

Ransom did not write an introductory editorial for the first issue to state his policies, but his review of *Understanding Poetry* (1938) by Cleanth Brooks and Robert Penn Warren leaves the reader in no doubt about his priorities: "But now it is the Age of Criticism. I need only cite: Eliot, Richards, Empson, Tate, Winters, Blackmur—a list of intensive critics the like of which has certainly not been furnished in literary history at one time before. The living art decays, for that must be the impression of an editor reading faithfully through the

---

55. "Report of Mr. John Crowe Ransom, Editor" (TS, [April, 1940], in *KR* Papers).
56. Ransom to Tate, October 18, [1938], in Tate Papers; John Crowe Ransom, "Introduction," in Ransom (ed.), *The Kenyon Critics: Studies in Modern Literature from The Kenyon Review* (Cleveland, 1951), x.

manuscripts on the desk. . . . We shall have other ages in which criticism relaxes, and poetry spontaneously increases, but not now. Our age is critical, and it has its own passionate enjoyments."[57]

Ransom's other—rather dull—review deals with *Shakespeare's Philosophical Patterns* by Walter Clyde Curry, a Fugitive and a Vanderbilt colleague. He disagrees with Curry's thesis that Shakespeare—not a favorite of Ransom's at that time anyway—was a profound philosopher and suggests that Curry apply his considerable scholarly intelligence more appropriately, more critically.[58]

Blackmur's review of Claude Colleer Abbott's edition of *Further Letters of Gerard Manley Hopkins* constitutes a New Critical manifesto. He had enjoyed reading Hopkins' letters "as a lesson in the direct operation of mature intelligence," but "emphatically" insists that the letters cannot "affect the poetry or understanding of it as poetry so far as the poetry was successful in its own right." Rice's review of James Laughlin's *New Directions 1938* is noteworthy for the perspicacity with which he singles out for praise its most gifted writers, namely, John Berryman, Delmore Schwartz, and Eleanor Clark. Yvor Winters highly commended *The Complete Collected Poems of William Carlos Williams, 1906–1936,* thereby refuting the myth that the New Critics only discussed poets in the Pound-Eliot tradition. The review was not a characteristic example of Winters' brand of New Criticism: close structural analyses are practically absent. Still, since Williams' collection numbered 313 pages and Winters had only 3 pages at his disposal, it is astonishing how to the point, especially with respect to Williams' use of free verse, most of Winters' remarks were. Also to the point was his prediction that "the end of the present century will see [Williams] securely established, along with Stevens, as one of the two best poets of his generation." Ransom was in high feather about this review; he found it "exhilarating" that Winters had proved "that an alleged whizbang like Williams is a great classical artist."[59]

57. John Crowe Ransom, "The Teaching of Poetry," *KR,* I, 81–82.
58. John Crowe Ransom, "Was Shakespeare a Philosopher?" *KR,* I, 75–80. Ransom had published "Shakespeare at Sonnets" in *SoR,* III (1938), 531–53, in which he argues that Donne's poems are to be preferred to Shakespeare's sonnets, as they are much more logical and systematical. In a "Postscript" to the 1968 edition of *The World's Body,* Ransom admits to a "bad lapse of judgment" with respect to "Shakespeare at Sonnets."
59. Richard Blackmur, "Mature Intelligence of an Artist," *KR,* I, 96, 97; Philip Blair Rice,

Delmore Schwartz's "The Two Audens," a "pretty good model of effectiveness by condensation," proves how blurred the dividing line between the New Critics and the New York intellectuals sometimes was. After having applied the terms *Ego* and *Id* to the Marxist and the private aspects of Auden's poetry, respectively, Schwartz remarks that "the proof that these terms are relevant . . . is to be found where all proof of judgment awaits us, in the text itself," and goes on to suit the action to the word. Another masterly essay by a New York intellectual is Philip Rahv's "Franz Kafka: The Hero As Lonely Man." Realizing that "the application of Freudian ideas to literature has often been gratuitous," Rahv finds that Kafka could not "be explained adequately by a strictly literary analysis" and considers "the methods of Freud . . . superior . . . to the metaphysical flights which he had inspired in his German critics."[60] By extensively applying both psychoanalysis and biography to the text, Rahv indeed sheds new light on Kafka's works.

The best critical article in this maiden issue, the beautifully written lead essay on the recently deceased novelist Thomas Wolfe, was contributed by John Peale Bishop, who was neither a New Critic nor a New York intellectual. Ransom thought the essay "swell" and included it in *The Kenyon Critics,* the *Kenyon Review* anthology published in 1951. At a time when Wolfe stood extremely high in the estimation of both critics and common readers, Bishop unabashedly points out that, genius though Wolfe was, he was incapable of making his novels cohere. Since "the meaning of a novel should be in its structure," according to Bishop, this was severe criticism indeed.[61]

Ransom's preoccupation with education is apparent from his review of *Understanding Poetry,* in which he refers to "the authorized distortions of pedants who are placed over the courses in literature by the colleges" and whose learning is "peripheral." Ransom wants to see this textbook with a New Critical approach adopted in all colleges, but fears that this may take ages because of the ignoramuses in

---

"Twenty-five Directions," *KR,* I, 109–11; Yvor Winters, "Poetry of Feeling," *KR,* I, 106; Ransom to Tate, May 23, [1941], in Tate Papers.

60. Ransom to George Marion O'Donnell, January 31, 1939, in O'Donnell Papers; Delmore Schwartz, "The Two Audens," *KR,* I, 39; Philip Rahv, "Franz Kafka: The Hero As Lonely Man," *KR,* I, 67.

61. Ransom to John Peale Bishop, December 4, 1940, in Bishop Papers; John Peale Bishop, "The Sorrows of Tom Wolfe," *KR,* I, 9.

charge of the English departments.[62] As it turned out, *Understanding Poetry* became the vade mecum of nearly every student of English within a few years.

The first issue also contained Robert Lowell's dense, complex, and ironic "The Cities' Summer Death" and "The Dandelion Girls," his first published poems. Although they are definitely minor, Ransom, by printing them, publicly showed his confidence in his pupil. Jarrell's less conventional "The Winter's Tale" does stand on its own, even if it is not one of his best early poems.

As for the other arts, Paul Rosenfeld, the advisory editor, published the first part of "The Advent of American Music," the second installment of which appeared in the spring issue. The impressionistic and voluble style of his essay clashes with Ransom's wish for clarity and economy. Ford Madox Ford's "Parish Letter," a hymn to Paris as the eternal seat of international culture, also belongs to the "arts" part of *The Kenyon Review*. Ransom praised the first draft for its "warmth of style," but asked Ford to cut it because "we are 112-pages big, a very poor dimension" and "want to practice economy." Ford willingly complied: he could not "bear to think of taking up too much of your space and crowding out a lot of young things who are panting to appear." The eventual result, "a beautiful thing," was Ford's only contribution to the *Kenyon*; he died in June, 1939.[63]

In the book review section, attention was paid to the arts, too: B. H. Haggin, the former music critic of *The Hound & Horn* who now regularly wrote for *The Nation,* reviewed *George Gershwin* by Merle Armitage, and Seldon Cheney discussed a book on Toulouse-Lautrec. This review was Cheney's sole contribution to the *Kenyon,* as was Vernon Venable's hostile review of Bertrand Russell's *Power: A New Social Analysis.* Howard Baker acclaimed Allen Tate's only novel, *The Fathers.* He found it "symbolic . . . [and] organically significant," but "not in the least lacking in flesh and blood." This was an illuminating review, even though Baker overemphasized Tate's "determinism" and his "essential religious belief in the innate evil

62. Ransom, "The Teaching of Poetry," 79.
63. Paul Rosenfeld, "The Advent of American Music (I)," *KR,* I, 46–56; Ford Madox Ford, "A Paris Letter," *KR,* I, 18–31; Ransom to Ford Madox Ford, October 13, [1938], in F. M. Ford Papers; Ford to Ransom, October 21, 1938, in *KR* Papers; Ransom to Ford, November 2, 1938, in F. M. Ford Papers.

of man." In a letter to Tate, though, Ransom apologized for the review as "just a so-so job," and it was Baker's only contribution during Ransom's editorship. The two remaining, rather unremarkable reviews are H. M. Chevalier on Jules Romains' *Death of a World* and C. A. Millspaugh on books of poetry by Kay Boyle, Frederic Prokosch, and Ben Belitt.[64]

All in all, it was a good first issue. Press reactions, which were on the whole restricted to the Ohio area, were extremely favorable. Most of the reviewers understood Ransom's intentions: "Judged by its initial number, the new quarterly rates the sort of serious attention given the Yale Review, Southern Review and other university periodicals aimed at the discriminating in the national audience." The reviewer in the Cleveland *Plain Dealer* was positively euphoric: "[I]f 'The Kenyon Review' could come out once a week, it wouldn't be too often for me." From outside the state came the apposite *Vanderbilt Alumnus* editorial: "It offers a diet that is sternly intellectual, and though the style of its articles is distinguished and interesting, no effort is made anywhere to appeal to popular taste."[65]

64. B. H. Haggin, "Genius Limited and Yearning," *KR*, I, 107–108; Seldon Cheney, "Painter of the Half-World," *KR*, I, 93–96; Vernon Venable, "Russell's Theory of History," *KR*, I, 102–104; Howard Baker, "The Shattered Door," *KR*, I, 90–93; Ransom to Tate, [December, 1938], in Tate Papers; H. M. Chevalier, "Gallic Pageant," *KR*, I, 84–86; C. A. Millspaugh, "Private and Public Verse," *KR*, I, 87–89.

65. "Kenyon and the Arts," Cleveland *News*, December 27, 1938; Ted Robinson, "Philosopher of Folly's Column," Cleveland *Plain Dealer*, December 27, 1938; Richard Croom Beatty, "The Kenyon Review," *Vanderbilt Alumnus*, [XXV?] (1939), n.p.

2 A Multiplicity of Interests

1939–1942

Criticism

The editorial direction was etched more clearly still in the following issues. One of the key theoretical essays on the New Criticism was Ransom's review, in the second issue, of Cleanth Brooks's *Modern Poetry and the Tradition*. It honors Brooks as "very likely, the most expert living 'reader' or interpreter of difficult verse." Although he has no equal with respect to explaining the texture of a poem, his understanding of its structure, its framework, is deficient. Ransom stresses that "the logic is . . . more organic to the imaginative effects than Mr. Brooks will admit." Still, Ransom considered it a "magnificent" book. Brooks was "very well satisfied with the review as a whole," though he did agree with Donald Davidson "that John is out on a limb in his emphasis on 'logic.'" Austin Warren's reaction to this essay was representative of that of many readers: he was "surprised," as he "had been in the habit of assuming that the critical performances of Penn Warren & Brooks were orthodoxly Ransomic."[1]

In his winter, 1941, editorial "Ubiquitous Moralists," Ransom discusses an important book by another New Critic, Blackmur's *The Expense of Greatness*. And, again, Ransom finds fault: Blackmur "has no theory of poetry which is comparable in distinction with his spe-

1. John Crowe Ransom, "Apologia for Modernism," *KR*, II, 248, 249; Ransom to Tate, October 11, 1939, in Tate Papers; Brooks to Donald Davidson, May 29, 1940, Austin Warren to Ransom, April 20, 1940, both in *KR* Papers.

cific judgments." Worse, when Blackmur feels "it incumbent upon him to declare a critical position in order to have somewhere officially to stand," it turns out to be a moralist position. Although both the Marxists and the Humanists have also taken this stand, "coming from him it is particularly depressing." However, "when he is going properly," that is, when Blackmur is a practical critic, he "is not really a moralistic critic at all." In his capacity as practical critic, Blackmur receives the highest praise: "[F]ew, if any critics live who write better criticism than Mr. R. P. Blackmur . . . and his judgments . . . are close enough to infallible." In this essay, Ransom also touches upon the "violent disagreements among the new critics," but concludes that they do form a group because "any one of these critics shows the influence of the others, and the total effort amounts to a sort of collaboration."[2]

Of paramount importance was a joint review of Ransom's *The New Criticism,* Tate's *Reason in Madness,* and *The Intent of the Critic,* a collection of essays by Edmund Wilson, Norman Foerster, W. H. Auden, and Ransom. Realizing that the objectivity of such a review would be easily doubted, Ransom had initially vetoed it. However, Rice insisted, Ransom yielded, and, astonishingly, I. A. Richards, one of the critics discussed in *The New Criticism,* was asked to review. Had Richards accepted, objectivity would have been all the more questionable. Fortunately, Richards declined: "Mr. Ransom seems to me to have just simply *mistaken* so much of the point and aim of my early books that to me it's as though he were shooting into a pool, not at me. And I do not think the attempt to clear these mistakes up publicly could be profitable to anyone." Ransom himself was the most severe critic of his own book, in which he had in fact only repeated, elaborated, and applied positions he had taken more persuasively in *The World's Body.* He described it to Kenneth Burke as "a laborious book without any grace about it" and wrote to Tate that he had "sacrificed the critics in order to get my own oar in; in view of a systematic book on poetic theory I found myself using the given critics to point to one." A few years later, Ransom even began to doubt the value of this poetic theory: "I should never have

2. John Crowe Ransom, "Ubiquitous Moralists," *KR,* III, 95–100.

proposed structure and texture till I could put the case much more fully."[3] It is telling, too, that *The New Criticism* was the only book Ransom would not allow to be reprinted, though David McDowell, when he turned publisher, repeatedly tried to get Ransom's consent to do so.

Kenneth Burke had a much higher opinion of *The New Criticism*. He had agreed to review the three books, which were, he stated, "written by some of the best men writing literary criticism in America today." He goes on to discuss succinctly *The Intent of the Critic,* omitting Ransom's contribution, "since it gives a curtailed version of his thesis in *The New Criticism*"—which Burke then proceeds to review. Burke finds great virtue in Ransom's use of structure and texture, for these terms "keep us fully aware of the fact that a good poem is not just one steady over-all concentration, but a constant succession of minor concentrations, each with some stylistic virtue of its own." But, Burke adds astutely, "Mr. Ransom could profitably round out his terminology by some such third term as the 'structure of texture' . . . a general tenor discernible among the heterogeneities, something that limits the range of variations, or that points them thematically in the same direction." Burke also pointedly discusses *Reason in Madness,* noting that Tate's "best work here is done on the specific analysis of texts . . . but in his general articles he is more given to pursuing the enemy . . . visiting upon them such scorn as would cause them to pine and wither."[4]

When he asked Burke to review these books, Ransom had thought of Burke as a Marxist critic, but had assured him that he "needn't worry over attacking the Editor. We'd take pride in going out of our gang, if there is a gang, to get a severe reviewer." The actual review made Ransom realize that Burke was critically much closer to him than he had assumed; so he immediately annexed him to the New Critics, and even suggested to Burke that they "write a joint book." This does not imply, of course, that Ransom now was in complete agreement with him—Ransom was temperamentally incapable of complete critical agreement with anybody—but he admitted to Burke: "I would have treated Burke as my critic of structure [in

3. I. A. Richards to Rice, July 11, 1941, in *KR* Papers; Ransom to Burke, March 29, 1941, in Burke Papers; Ransom to Tate, May 23, [1941], February 27, [1943], both in Tate Papers.
4. Kenneth Burke, "Key Words for Critics," *KR,* IV, 130, 131, 132.

The New Criticism] if I had known your work at that time better," especially since Winters had made "some heavy borrowings from you." Ransom's interest is apparent in his "An Address to Kenneth Burke," which appeared in the next issue. In this article, Ransom discussed the title-essay of Burke's latest book, *The Philosophy of Literary Form* (1941). He finds much to praise, but, as was to be expected, disagrees with Burke's purely dramatic, structural approach to literature.[5]

As usual with writers whom Ransom praised, the object of his tribute felt censured. Burke complained to Tate: "The most astounding thing to me about Ransom's piece was his complete refusal to let me build up a single point of mine in my own words. . . . In strict accordance with my firm belief in the saying that no editor ever lost a controversy in his own columns, I am not asking him for a chance to rebut. . . . I am asking him simply to let me publish there my analysis of the Keats Ode. . . . But will he?"[6] Ransom would not, yet Burke became a regular and valued contributor to the *Kenyon,* though he never quite convinced himself that Ransom truly held him in high esteem.

These and similar theoretical articles representing a New Critical point of view regularly appeared in *The Kenyon Review* and attracted much attention. The New Critics would not have had so large an impact, however, if their theories had not been supported by an abundance of excellent practical criticism, part of which was published in the early *Kenyon.* Truly seminal was George Marion O'Donnell's "Faulkner's Mythology." Published in the summer issue of the first volume, this essay gave the impetus to a full-fledged revaluation of Faulkner in the United States. His early insight into Faulkner was unparalleled. A few years later, Tate told O'Donnell that Malcolm Cowley, the editor of *The Portable Faulkner,* "thought your Faulkner essay the best thing ever written about him. I think so too."[7]

A prime example of close New Critical analysis is Randall Jarrell's brief essay "Texts from Housman." In this article, also in the first summer issue, Jarrell discusses every aspect of two short Housman

5. Ransom to Burke, September 8, 1941, November 17, [1941], December 5, 1941, all in Burke Papers; John Crowe Ransom, "An Address to Kenneth Burke," *KR,* IV, 219–37.

6. Burke to Tate, April 28, 1942, in Tate Papers.

7. George Marion O'Donnell, "Faulkner's Mythology," *KR,* I, 285–99; Tate to George Marion O'Donnell, January 24, 1945, in O'Donnell Papers.

poems in a generally appreciative way. This essay invalidates Irving Howe's classification of Jarrell as a New York intellectual in his *A Margin of Hope,* as does Jarrell's later, better-known practical criticism. Despite Jarrell's famous denunciation of the New Criticism in his *Poetry and the Age,* his inimitable, cataloging criticism in the 1950s remained grafted on to the literary text itself.[8]

In 1940, upon the intercession of I. A. Richards and Richard Eberhart, Ransom published a radio talk by William Empson on the use of Basic English in analyzing poetry. Empson defends using Basic English because "it lets [the reader] get more grip on what he is reading." To prove this, Empson uses some lines by Wordsworth that he turns into Basic English, ingeniously showing that doing so "makes you put the right questions" and, consequently, makes you understand the poem. This well-written essay also exemplifies the importance of close analysis for understanding poetry.[9]

More seminal than the pieces by Jarrell and Empson is Robert Penn Warren's essay on Katherine Anne Porter, another southern writer whose distinction had not yet received sufficient notice. By discussing Porter's method of composition, her style, by paraphrasing, by quoting, by closely analyzing, Warren firmly places Porter among "the relatively small group of writers . . . who have done serious, consistent, original, and vital work in the form of short fiction."[10] This essay abundantly proves that New Criticism could also be fruitfully applied to fiction, and that Robert Penn Warren was a master at it.

Other New Critical articles that are worth mentioning are Ransom, "Yeats and His Symbols"; Vivas, "Lawrence's Problems"; and Austin Warren, "Edward Taylor's Poetry: Colonial Baroque." Certainly outstanding, if only because of its controversial nature, is Yvor Winters' discussion of T. S. Eliot. Because of its length, the essay was among the few published in two parts in the *Kenyon.* Winters does not leave his readers in suspense about his opinion of Eliot's failings as a critic and a poet. His essay starts: "T. S. Eliot is probably the most widely respected literary figure of our time; he is known primarily as the leader of the intellectual reaction against the romanticism of which he

8. Randall Jarrell, "Texts from Housman," *KR,* I, 260–71; Randall Jarrell, "The Age of Criticism," *Poetry and the Age* (New York, 1953), 63–86.
9. William Empson, "Basic English and Wordsworth," *KR,* II, 447, 452.
10. Robert Penn Warren, "Katherine Anne Porter," *KR,* IV, 29.

began his career as a disciple. It is my purpose to show that his intellectualism and his reactionary position are alike an illusion." Winters goes on to find fault with Eliot's theories about autotelic art, the objective correlative, thought and emotion in poetry, poetry and belief, and tradition. In the second installment, he accuses Eliot of being both determinist and anti-determinist, and contends that it is impossible to find out what Eliot means by the dramatic element in lyric poetry. But he is at his most famously vitriolic with respect to Eliot's poetic practice. Winters finds the treatment of the subject matter of *The Waste Land* trivial; its meter "a broken blank verse interspersed with bad free verse and rimed doggerel"; its method "the death of the mind and of the sensibility alike."[11]

No wonder the literary world was scandalized. Delmore Schwartz was one of many to vent his anger in a letter to Tate: "But really that man's become a kind of small-time Lucifer. His reading of Eliot, when it is not pretty close to dishonesty through distorted quotation, reminds me of myself translating French [badly]. . . . Eliot ought to be examined very carefully right now; but of course not with Winters' stupidity." The *Kenyon* also received reactions. In the autumn issue, Ransom published one of the more reasonable letters, by Louis Coxe, and even "edited some matter out of his communication which seemed slightly abusive." But Winters was furious: he regarded Coxe's letter as "immature," "abusive," and "downright mendacious." When Ransom refused to "print any editorial retraction on behalf of [Winters'] fancied injury" or to publish Winters' venomous reply to Coxe, Winters exploded. He requested the return of his already accepted essay on Wallace Stevens, stated that he would never send a submission to *The Kenyon Review* again, and even canceled his complimentary subscription, given in 1938 "in view of our admiration for your criticism and our hope that you will be a frequent contributor." Winters kept his word; his last contribution was a book review on Theodore Roethke, which appeared in the very issue in which Coxe's letter was published.[12] Ransom's attempt to

11. John Crowe Ransom, "Yeats and His Symbols," *KR,* I, 309–22; Eliseo Vivas, "Lawrence's Problems," *KR,* III, 83–94; Austin Warren, "Edward Taylor's Poetry: Colonial Baroque," *KR,* III, 355–71; Yvor Winters, "T. S. Eliot: The Illusion of Reaction (I)," *KR,* III, 7; Yvor Winters, "T. S. Eliot: The Illusion of Reaction (II)," *KR,* III, 238.

12. Delmore Schwartz to Tate, January 27, 1941, in Tate Papers; Ransom to Yvor Winters, November 18, 1941, Winters to Ransom, October 5, 1941, Ransom to Winters, December 1, 1941, Norman Johnson to Winters, October 8, 1938, all in *KR* Papers; Yvor Winters, "The

make a stir by publishing Winters on Eliot had succeeded beyond his expectation.

But in those early years, it was the book reviews rather than the articles that spread the New Critical gospel in the *Kenyon*. The second issue contained an excellent review section, in which the lead essay was by Tate on George Whicher's critical biography of Emily Dickinson. Tate shows that Whicher is scholarly and thorough with respect to Dickinson's biography and background, but he is not worthy of the label "critic": "Not towards a single poem by Miss Dickinson does Mr. Whicher behave as if it were a whole, substantial object, the focus and the final test of the quantity and quality of its background; the poems (few are even quoted entire) appear to exist as illustration of Mr. Whicher's commentary." Then Jarrell discusses Winters' *Maule's Curse*. He points to Winters' "absolute moral dogmatism" which produces "occasional judgments that a tactful admirer might characterize as trembling on the brink of absurdity," such as ranking Bridges above Hopkins, and T. Sturge Moore above Yeats. But Jarrell also notes admiringly that Winters "reads each writer as if he had never been read before; he is a critical instrument completely uninfluenced by any fear of ridicule or consideration of expediency," and concludes that "*Maule's Curse* [is] the best book on American literature I ever read." And Robert Penn Warren reviews *Matthew Arnold* by Lionel Trilling. He calls it "admirable . . . well written, thoughtful and dispassionate," but he deplores Trilling's not having undertaken the task "of analyzing very closely the poems as poems and of relating their specific poetic method and quality to the body of Arnold's ideas." So Warren does this himself and succeeds in showing, in short compass, Arnold's strengths and weaknesses. In Ransom's estimate, it was "about the best review ever written."[13]

Almost as perspicacious is Ransom's treatment of *M: One Thousand Autobiographical Sonnets* by Fugitive turned Boston psychiatrist, Merrill Moore. Ransom characterizes Moore's sonnets as charming and technically satisfactory, but not mature and intense enough; and

Poems of Theodore Roethke," *KR*, III, 514–16; Louis Coxe, "Winters on Eliot," *KR*, III, 498–500.

13. Allen Tate, "The Poet and Her Biographer," *KR*, I, 203; Randall Jarrell, "The Morality of Mr. Winters," *KR*, I, 213–14; Robert Penn Warren, "Arnold vs. the 19th Century," *KR*, I, 217, 219; Randall Jarrell to Warren, n.d., in *SoR* Papers.

he suggests that Moore write fewer but more condensed sonnets. This review is representative of the objective way in which Ransom viewed his friends' works. Somewhat naïvely, Ransom never expected them to take even his severest criticisms personally. In this case, by way of exception, the victim was warned in advance: "I shan't ever overpraise anybody, even my best friends, you understand," Ransom wrote to Moore in November, 1938. And Moore's lavish donations to the *Kenyon* did not—properly—make any difference either. Perhaps Ransom undervalued Moore's poetry, because, as he himself admitted, he was "a high-brow and intellectualist . . . poet and critic."[14]

Being "high-brow and intellectualist" was definitely to Ransom's advantage in his review of the 1941 New Directions publication *Young American Poets,* which included Mary Barnard, W. R. Moses, George Marion O'Donnell, Jarrell, and Berryman. By paying attention to structure, texture, and meter, as well as by quoting extensively, Ransom argues convincingly that "Jarrell is quite the most brilliant of the five," and that while both Berryman and O'Donnell are "the most technically proficient," Berryman is the greater poet. These two reviews prove that Ransom was not only a theoretical but also a fine practical New Critic with a generally keen eye for the qualities of young poets. This trait led him to publish many of the most talented in his magazine. Ransom's judgment was not infallible, of course. In this same issue appeared Winters' review of Theodore Roethke's *Open House,* the first serious, laudatory review in Roethke's career. But Ransom was "disgusted" with Winters for trying to prove Roethke "a great classical artist" and did not publish Roethke until 1950, in spite of Roethke's bombarding him with poems from 1938 onwards.[15]

One of the *Kenyon*'s best reviewers was Cleanth Brooks. Already in 1939 he pointed out what other critics would come to much later, that Robert Frost's "'directness'" and "'simplicity'" had been overemphasized in contrast to the "'tortured obscurity'" of other modern poets. Without wanting to assign him "to one of the modern

14. John Crowe Ransom, "One Thousand Sonnets," *KR,* I, 229–31; Ransom to Merrill Moore, November 14, [1938], in Moore Papers. Moore had donated $100 and had pledged $100 annually for the next three years.

15. John Crowe Ransom, "Constellation of Five Young Poets," *KR,* III, 378, 380; Winters, "The Poems of Theodore Roethke," 514–16; Ransom to Tate, May 23, [1941], in Tate Papers.

schools of Donne," Brooks shows that Frost's best poetry "is in reality sophisticated, not naive." In the winter, 1941, issue Brooks discusses Housman, another poet who does not belong to the New Critical canon. In his review of the recently published *Collected Poems,* Brooks describes Housman as "essentially a romantic poet," but one whose best poems are in flat contradiction to Housman's explicitly stated distrust of the obscurity of metaphor, of irony and wit "as smacking of the unpoetic intellect." Comparing this extremely fair and balanced review, which was reprinted in *The Kenyon Critics,* to the earlier *Kenyon* article on Housman by Jarrell, one finds that Brooks gives a better overall portrait of the poet, and that Jarrell's article is too clearly part of a larger whole, his master's thesis on Housman.[16]

Brooks's review of Auden's *The Double Man* and John Peale Bishop's *Selected Poems* was also both New Critical and just. Bishop has often been accused of writing poetry about poetry, of being merely concerned with form, but Brooks reminds us that "form . . . is not a coating applied to the mass of content" and that in Bishop's poems the "problems of writing poetry and the problems of a formless and chaotic age become at many points identical." Less attention is paid to Auden, not because Brooks rates him the lesser poet, but because Auden had already had recognition. Although he considered himself an "admirer" of Auden's and felt attracted to his honest and intelligent mind as revealed in "New Year Letter," which was to him "the most interesting item in his new volume," Brooks's characteristic criticism of this poem is that "the logic of the discourse tends to override the texture."[17]

The contributions of the New York intellectuals lent additional distinction to the criticism and book review departments of the early *Kenyon Review.* Philip Rahv's second article, reprinted in *The Kenyon Critics,* is the classic "Paleface and Redskin," an essay that does not stand in need of discussion, since the terms in the title have become literary household words. Another seminal article is Delmore Schwartz's 1939 MLA speech, "The Isolation of Modern Poetry," which Ransom had solicited for the *Kenyon* after hearing Schwartz's lecture. However, when Ransom read the paper, he was disappointed:

16. Cleanth Brooks, "Poet or Sage," *KR,* I, 325, 326; Cleanth Brooks, "The Whole of Housman," *KR,* III, 106, 107; Jarrell, "Texts from Housman," 260–71.
17. Cleanth Brooks, "Form and Content," *KR,* IV, 244, 246.

it was too "encyclopedic" and not representative of Schwartz at his "highest *written* power." But the *Kenyon* had "been running a year without a piece from [Schwartz]," and Ransom knew that Schwartz needed the money, so he left the decision up to him.[18] The essay was published in *Kenyon's* spring, 1941, number, and though it is indeed somewhat discursive for a dense quarterly like *The Kenyon Review,* the reasons Schwartz gives for the obscurity of modern poetry and for its being limited to the lyrical form are signally stimulating.

Lionel Trilling contributed two excellent essays on Sherwood Anderson and E. M. Forster. In the first, which was included in his *The Liberal Imagination* (1950), Trilling takes a retrospective look at Anderson's literary career on the occasion of his death. One could not mistake this essay for New Criticism: Trilling starts out with personal impressions and shows that Anderson was a victim of his early success and of the cultural situation in general. The essay on the British novelist E. M. Forster constitutes the first chapter of Trilling's *E. M. Forster* (1943), which heralded a Forster revaluation. Trilling sees Forster as a passionate naturalist. In contrast to Anderson, with whom he has much in common—they dislike the middle class and celebrate love, passion, and the liberated personality—Forster never writes vaguely and abstractly, but roots his ideals in the particulars of reality.[19] Again, Trilling does not closely analyze separate passages from Forster's novels: his remarks deal with the interrelations of history, biography, culture, and, very broadly, the content of the texts. In short, in these essays Trilling honors Ransom's description of him as a "cultural critic."

As a regular reviewer, Trilling discussed books by Dorothy Richardson, John Dos Passos, Waldo Frank, and Sinclair Lewis. His major review in these early years was of *Let Us Now Praise Famous Men* by James Agee with photographs by Walker Evans. David McDowell, who was the *Kenyon's* secretary at that time, and part of whose job it was to make a preliminary choice from among the piles of books sent in by publishers, remembers how he enthusiastically told Ransom that this wonderful book simply had to be reviewed. Leafing through

18. Philip Rahv, "Paleface and Redskin," *KR,* I, 251–56; Delmore Schwartz, "The Isolation of Modern Poetry," *KR* III, 209–20; Ransom to Delmore Schwartz, September 30, 1940, in *KR* Papers.

19. Lionel Trilling, "Sherwood Anderson," *KR,* III, 293–302; Lionel Trilling, "E. M. Forster," *KR,* IV, 160–73.

Evans' photographs, however, Ransom decided against it, supposing the book to be a leftist tract about the South. But within a week, Trilling wrote to say that he very much wanted to review it. Ransom held Trilling in such esteem that he did not refuse and he thought so highly of the actual result that he made it the lead review of the winter, 1942, issue. The review was one of the few Agee was pleased with, not because it was favorable, but because Trilling understood Agee's agonizing sense of impropriety in intruding upon the share-croppers' lives. Trilling also sees that *Let Us Now Praise Famous Men* "is full of marvelous writing which gives a kind of hot pleasure that words can do so much"; he shows that Agee's one failure lies in his "inability to see [the sharecroppers he describes] as anything but good." [20]

Another excellent review, reprinted in *The Kenyon Critics,* was young John Berryman's "The Loud Hill of Wales," an analysis of Dylan Thomas' *The World I Breathe.* Although Howe labels Berry-man without reservation a New York intellectual, on the basis of Berryman's admiration for Blackmur and on the basis of much of his criticism he may, with equal reason, be regarded a New Critic. His New Critical bent is clear in his review of Thomas, published in the autumn of 1940, in his defense of Thomas against allegations, in *Kenyon*'s winter, 1940, issue, made by the leftist British critic Julian Symons:

I have not time to notice any considerable part of Mr. Symons's nonsense; one quotation must serve. "What is said in Mr. Thomas's poems is that the seasons change; that we decrease in vigour as we grow older; that life has no obvious meaning; that love dies. His poems mean no more than that. They mean too little." Evidently it is necessary to point out to Mr. Symons, what is elementary, that a poem means more than the abstract, banal statement of its theme; it means its imagery, the disparate parts and relations of it, its ambiguities, by extension the techniques which produced it and the emotions it legitimately produces. [21]

Berryman goes on to show that much of Thomas' creativity goes into his technique, but admits that, perhaps as a consequence, many of his poems are obscure.

20. Interview with David McDowell, December 4, 1981; Lionel Trilling, "Greatness with One Fault in It," *KR,* IV, 102.
21. Julian Symons, "Obscurity and Dylan Thomas," *KR,* II, 61–71; John Berryman, "The Loud Hill of Wales," *KR,* II, 482, quoting page 71 of Symons' article. Two other reviews pub-

The publication of Berryman's review on Dylan Thomas to counterbalance Symons' Marxist article reflects Ransom's dislike of Marxist critics, whom he once compared to "the bull in the china shop, the swine that eats the pearls; so simplified is their strategy for art." H. M. Chevalier's essay "André Malraux: The Return of the Hero," which highly praises *Man's Fate* because it heralds the beginnings of a heroic literature as opposed to novels with an alienated main character, met a similar demurrer. In his "Editorial Notes," Ransom recorded "a personal apprehension" because Malraux's "ardor for the [leftist] ideas strikes me as having displaced some of the interest in the art."[22]

No less clear was the editorial line with respect to Humanist-inspired criticism. Two reviews of books by Van Wyck Brooks reflect this. One of them, Delmore Schwartz's completely destructive discussion of Brooks's *New England: Indian Summer,* was reprinted in *The Kenyon Critics.* In his letter to Ransom asking to review the book, Schwartz wrote that he first simmered with anger at "seeing Henry James and Henry Adams abused and misunderstood and misrepresented by Brooks' impressionism, which pretends to be above literary criticism." Then he "more or less boiled over" when he came to Brooks's passages on T. S. Eliot and Wallace Stevens. The tone of this letter was continued in the review, which ends tartly: "If a masterpiece is a book many people read and enjoy for a long time, Mr. Brooks has produced a masterpiece. But one is profoundly mistaken, if one takes it for literary criticism, literary history, or anything close to those difficult arts." Robert Penn Warren's review of *The Opinions of Oliver Allston* is no less derisive. Warren takes the position of a longtime admirer of Van Wyck Brooks's persona, Oliver Allston, who thinks Allston's "untimely death" was "a real loss to American letters." However, his seemingly innocuous praise of Brooks's intellectual biography of Allston is devastating.[23]

---

lished in the autumn, 1940, issue were reprinted in John Crowe Ransom (ed.), *The Kenyon Critics: Studies in Modern Literature from The Kenyon Review* (Cleveland, 1951): Eleanor Clark, "The Myth of Sainthood," 485–88; and Richard Eberhart, "Q's Revisions," 496–99.

22. Ransom to Eliseo Vivas, June 10, [1940], in *KR* Papers; H. M. Chevalier, "André Malraux: The Return of the Hero," *KR,* II, 35–46; John Crowe Ransom, "André Malraux' Novels," *KR,* II, 93.

23. Delmore Schwartz to Ransom, August 18, 1940, in *KR* Papers; Delmore Schwartz, "Neither Historian Nor Critic," *KR,* III, 122–23. James Atlas, *Delmore Schwartz: The Life of an*

The Kenyon Review was not the only literary magazine to condemn Van Wyck Brooks's middlebrow denunciations of Joyce, James, Proust, Eliot, and others as coterie writers who were merely interested in form and not in celebrating the great themes of life such as love, courage, and justice. In the January, 1942, issue of *Partisan Review,* Ransom himself lined up with Tate, Trilling, and four others to condemn Brooks's nationalistic, moralistic ideas about literature as exposed in Dwight Macdonald's article, "Kulturbolschewismus Is Here." Ransom admitted that hardly any successful fiction and poetry were being written, but argued "bitterly in defense of the greatness of a few moderns, such as James, Yeats, and Proust." He found it "as incredible as it is cynical" that Brooks "blame[d] the tendency of the literature upon the vanity of the writers or their misanthropy," and he praised the moderns for not "evad[ing] their difficulties by denying them," calling Brooks's "idea of doing so . . . dogmatic, and . . . Christian Science."[24]

Of course, there also are contributions that are neither indicative of strong editorial preferences nor readily pigeonholed as New Critical or New York intellectual. An example is Daniel Aaron's fine tribute to F. O. Matthiessen's *American Renaissance.* Robie Macauley, who had just graduated from Kenyon College, made his first appearance in 1942 with a superficial review of novels by Mark Schorer and Robert Paul Smith. His was not the only review to come out of Kenyon College: Paul A. Palmer, of the department of political science, contributed twice; Chalmers sang the praises of Irving Babbitt's *Spanish Character and Other Essays.* Fortunately, this remained the president's only literary contribution to the *Kenyon.* As for the articles, a few deserve special mention: in "On Rereading Balzac," William Troy gives an excellent analysis of Balzac's novels; Lawrence Thompson's "Bert Brecht" is an early American evaluation of the German poet and playwright in exile; and in "Poet on Horseback," Justin O'Brien convincingly shows up Roy Campbell as a banal plagiarist of Baudelaire, Rimbaud, and Valéry.[25]

American Poet (New York, 1977), 298–300, quotes a disturbed letter dated February 8, 1952, in which Schwartz asks Brooks's forgiveness for this review. Robert Penn Warren, "Homage to Oliver Allston," *KR,* IV, 259.

24. Dwight Macdonald, "Kulturbolschewismus Is Here," *PR,* VIII (1941), 442–51; John Crowe Ransom, "On the Brooks-MacLeish Thesis," *PR,* IX (1942), 40.

25. Daniel Aaron, "Parrington Plus," *KR,* IV, 102–106; Robie Macauley, "Good-bad Nov-

Of special interest are two articles on foreign literary magazines. Both appeared in the autumn, 1939, issue. Delmore Schwartz wrote a glowing article on the recently discontinued *Criterion,* the bound volumes of which he deferentially described to Ransom as constituting "a permanent fund of awareness." *The Criterion* was also mentioned in Rice's more general survey, "Foreign Periodicals." James Atlas calls Schwartz's essay "a masterly . . . résumé of *Criterion*'s history, taking issue with Eliot's political views, his editorial choices and the inconsistent ideas put forth in his commentaries." Atlas also quotes part of a letter by T. S. Eliot, Schwartz's hero at that time, in praise of this essay and adds that "no single event in Delmore's career was more significant to him than this letter." In Rice's opinion, too, the demise of *The Criterion* was a great loss to letters: "[N]o British periodical has yet arisen to take its place. . . . *Scrutiny* . . . perhaps is closest, although it falls wide of the mark. Its contributions lack the brilliance and the philosophical incisiveness of *The Criterion* in its best days, the tone is often academic, and there is a more persistent concern with pedagogical than with larger aesthetic issues."[26] Here emerges an image of Rice's ideal literary quarterly, which is further adumbrated by his admiration for *La Nouvelle Revue Française* and the Mexican *Taller* and *Abside.*

So, with respect to criticism, which constituted the bulk of the magazine during these years, *The Kenyon Review* featured very many New Critical, quite a few New York intellectual, and a good many unclassifiable literary articles and book reviews. As the preceding discussion makes clear, the abundance, the distinction, and the variety of the criticism are all representative of *The Kenyon Review* during its first, epoch-making decade. The majority of the early *Kenyon*'s main critics—R. P. Blackmur, Cleanth Brooks, Robert Penn Warren, Kenneth Burke, Randall Jarrell, Philip Rahv, Lionel Trilling, and, of course, Ransom and Rice—all remained devoted contribu-

---

els," *KR,* IV, 124–26; Paul A. Palmer, "History without Philosophy," *KR,* III, 383–86, and "The Hero as Judge," *KR,* IV, 247–50; Gordon Keith Chalmers, "Rediscovery of a Radical," *KR,* III, 388–92; William Troy, "On Rereading Balzac: The Artist as Scapegoat," *KR,* II, 333–44; Lawrence Thompson, "Bert Brecht," *KR,* II, 319–29; Justin O'Brien, "Poet on Horseback," *KR,* IV, 75–86.

26. Delmore Schwartz, "*The Criterion,* 1922–1939," *KR,* I, 437–49 (this article appeared simultaneously in *Purpose,* XI [1939], 225–37); Delmore Schwartz to Ransom, April 25, 1939, in *KR* Papers; Atlas, *Delmore Schwartz,* 153–54; Philip Blair Rice, "Foreign Periodicals," *KR,* I, 472.

tors to the *Kenyon* in their common battle for the recognition of serious criticism in the universities and the literary world at large.

Pedagogics, Philosophy, Politics, Psychology

Although Ransom's *Kenyon Review* is generally known for its criticism only, other interests were represented too. For instance, during
its infancy, the *Kenyon* paid considerable attention to pedagogical
issues. For all Rice's objections to *Scrutiny*'s pedagogical bent, education was in fact one of Ransom's hobbyhorses. This interest was exemplified by the symposium "Literature and the Professors." Already in August, 1939, Ransom had asked Cleanth Brooks for a
contribution on the teaching of English; as a working title Ransom
suggested "Lit. Intelligence of the Teachers of Lit." Brooks replied
that he had thought of that subject entirely in terms of a book, and
that he was not at all sure whether he could handle it convincingly in
an essay. A few months later, Ransom's enduring enthusiasm for the
project made him try again to kindle Brooks's interest. Did Brooks
not feel "driven to take up that essay-project on the English professors?"[27] But only after Tate had delivered his inflammatory paper
"Miss Emily and the Bibliographer" at Princeton on April 10, 1940,
did Brooks feel sufficiently stirred to respond warmly to Ransom's
suggestion of a symposium on the state of teaching in America to be
published simultaneously in the *Southern* and *Kenyon* reviews.

In "Miss Emily and the Bibliographer," Tate had accused the literary profession of burying literature under a mass of biographical details, of having "lost confidence in literature," and of "The Great Refusal . . . to judge." He also cited their "insincerity" and their having
created a situation "in which it is virtually impossible for a young
man to get a critical, literary education." Tate's attack weakened his
position at Princeton, and it did not further his cause when Blackmur
started intriguing against him. Tate fell from grace and had to leave
Princeton, where he had been poet in residence, as soon as his three-
year contract expired, and Blackmur fell heir to his place. Of course,
Ransom was wholeheartedly with Tate and, in his summer, 1940,
editorial "Mr. Tate and the Professors," explained that Tate had

27. Ransom to Brooks, August 8, [1939], January 11, [1940; wrongly dated 1939], both in
SoR Papers.

"helped crystallize some editorial intentions," which would result in the symposium "Literature and the Professors." Ransom continued that he had decided upon a symposium because "combined essays . . . have a more formidable effect than that of those single studies that find publication now and then, and here and there." Ransom had initially suggested that the *Southern* and *Kenyon* reviews duplicate the essays, but Brooks came up with an alternative:

[W]e might get four or six people lined up . . . and allocate two or three of the articles to THE SOUTHERN and two or three to THE KENYON. We could act jointly to see that the balance in quality and in subject matter and so on was maintained, so that one magazine got as fair and powerful a set as the other. The essays in THE SOUTHERN could make explicit reference to the KENYON and vice versa, and each magazine would call attention very prominently to the other part of the Symposium in the other. This plan . . . might get heavier gunfire on the subject than the first plan.

Ransom agreed, but also suggested that two graduate students be asked to contribute and that Brooks and Ransom appear as symposiasts in their own reviews. Although Brooks foresaw possible trouble for the students, who, by putting themselves on record as being against their professors, might jeopardize their careers, he was pleased with the provocative aspects of the first suggestion. But he disagreed with Ransom's second suggestion, as that would certainly invite local hard feelings; therefore they compromised and appeared in each other's reviews.[28]

By the time the summer, 1940, issue appeared, Ransom had approached Tate, Arthur Mizener, Willard Thorp, Morton Dauwen Zabel, I. A. Richards, Harry Levin, Lionel Trilling, and Joe Horrell, a Louisiana State University graduate student. Except for Richards and Thorp, professor of English at Princeton, who had been asked to write about the political side of the issue, all accepted, though Zabel finally did not contribute. There also were volunteers. In July, 1940, Philip Wheelwright told Rice that he would like to write an essay for the symposium, and Blackmur confessed to Tate that he was sorely tempted to contribute, but in the end neither participated. John Gould Fletcher submitted an article, but his essay was so far below the mark

28. Allen Tate, "Miss Emily and the Bibliographer," *Essays of Four Decades* (London, 1970), 150, 153, 143, 148; Russell Fraser, *A Mingled Yarn: The Life of R. P. Blackmur* (New York, 1981), 194–95; John Crowe Ransom, "Mr. Tate and the Professors," *KR*, II, 350; Brooks to Ransom, April 13, 1940, in *SoR* Papers.

that it was not accepted. Finally, in the autumn of 1940, Ransom, Tate, Horrell, Levin, and Wright Thomas appeared in *The Southern Review,* and Brooks, Trilling, Mizener, Sidney Cox, and Hade Saunders in *The Kenyon Review.* Over 4,000 circulars announcing this symposium were sent out by the *Southern,* and the *Kenyon* sent announcements to 7,500 people, including all college English teachers and the MLA membership. Still, Ransom feared that "many who needed most to read it will never see it."[29]

Apart from his "Strategy for English Studies," which appeared as the lead essay in *The Southern Review* and which was actually only a tepid rewriting of "Criticism, Inc.," Ransom devoted a brief editorial to the symposium. In the essay in his own magazine, he frowns upon a Professor Gulette, who had complained about the quality of the student body. Ransom lectures the professor for not perceiving that "college students of all ranks seem entitled to the real creativeness of the professor," pointing out that it is not "to the credit of the professors if the studies which interest them are of no possible interest to the young men at large."[30]

The well-expressed arguments in Brooks's and Mizener's essays in *The Kenyon Review* part of the symposium are also close to those set forth in "Criticism, Inc.," and consequently do not need reiteration. In effect Trilling's paper, "Literature and Power," does not differ much either. According to Trilling, "[A]ny method which can bring enlightenment to literature is appropriate," but what should be avoided is "that all the multifarious processes which necessarily go on about literature . . . substitute themselves for literature itself." John L. Stewart, who in 1965 would publish *The Burden of Time: The Fugitives and Agrarians,* contributed "The Graduate Student in English" under the pseudonym Hade Saunders. His jeremiad ends with the lament that the only thing the graduate student, "poor devil," is being taught about the literature of the past is that a poem is "'Exhibit A' in an elaborate detective mystery. He reads lines for literary debts and sources. He can tell you all about the background of Webster's plays but is totally unmoved by their great dirges and secretly wonders what the real difference between blank verse and prose is anyway. Of such is his knowledge of literature."[31]

29. Ransom to Arthur Mizener, November 19, [1940], in Mizener Papers.
30. John Crowe Ransom, "Concerning the Symposium," *KR,* II, 477.
31. Cleanth Brooks, "Literary History vs. Criticism," *KR,* II, 403–12; Arthur Mizener,

It is unclear why Ransom included "If We Care Enough," an un-solicited article by Sidney Cox, professor of English at Dartmouth College. Although indeed quite different from the academic historical-biographical approach with which the symposium took issue, Cox's impressionism hardly accords with the ideal the other symposiasts stood for. Cox holds that "the only way to know a poet is to flow and form with him, and, after, by oneself." His ideal teacher "work[s] like hell to keep [the students'] common experiences open to the emergence of memories and feelings. . . . Without violating his own or the student's privacies, he will exert all his energy to keep his own and the student's dark and dangerous impulses in play."[32]

The Kenyon Review received mainly positive reactions to "Litera-ture and the Professors." Philip Wheelwright and Justin O'Brien, for instance, had greatly "enjoyed" the symposium, and even Winters found it "all very interesting." About the only dissenting voice was Trilling's. He noted in his own paper "an insufficient sincerity" and was dissatisfied with the other articles "partly because their tone did not . . . seem just," since "the subject is somehow more important than I—and the others—made it." Nevertheless, Trilling was "glad it is being noticed, for of course the tendency of the pieces is right enough." Although little had been said that was startling or un-usual—especially to readers of Ransom's earlier essays—the sym-posium certainly added fuel to the fire Tate had lit at Princeton. Be-cause it was a concentrated and well-promoted effort, it had the desired "formidable effect." The symposium tapped sources of sim-mering discontent among young teachers and graduates, and it proved one of the most potent impulses toward a radical change in the teach-ing of literature in the universities. Eric Bentley overemphasized the *Kenyon*'s pedagogical side in describing this symposium as taking up a "central position" in the review, but "Literature and the Professors" did represent the highpoint in the *Kenyon*'s interest in education.[33]

"Scholars as Critics," *KR,* II, 412–22; Lionel Trilling, "Literature and Power," *KR,* II, 439, 440; John L. Stewart [Hade Saunders], "The Graduate Student in English," *KR,* II, 432, 433.

32. Sidney Cox, "If We Care Enough," *KR,* II, 426, 427. Most of the essays in the *Southern* were also directed against that approach, but their overall quality was perhaps somewhat higher.

33. Philip Wheelwright to Rice, October 14, 1940, Justin O'Brien to Rice, November 16, 1940, Yvor Winters to Ransom, November 12, 1940, all in *KR* Papers; Lionel Trilling to Rice, November 17, 1940, in Rice Papers; Eric Bentley, "Editors in Person: Little Magazines," *KR,* IX, 285.

That Ransom set store by the possibilities symposia offered his magazine was apparent in the *Kenyon*'s second issue. This was largely devoted to the symposium "The New Encyclopedists" and reflected Ransom's and Rice's partiality for philosophy. They regarded "philosophy as a strong second fiddle to arts and letters"; and, indeed, at the end of the trial period discussed here, Ransom had reason to feel that "we have been slightly overplaying the heavy philosophical and aesthetic side of the publication." Next to the symposia on the new encyclopedists and naturalism are philosophical articles by, for instance, Virgil C. Aldrich, one of Rice's friends, and Marten ten Hoor, who in 1941 exposed the "philosophy" of the Nazis, as well as contributions by such well-known philosophers as Ernest Nagel, who briefly discussed the theories of, among others, Whitehead, Eddington, Russell, and Carnap. Both Ransom and Rice wrote editorials on philosophy and contributed to the symposia; and along with numerous reviews of books on philosophy, Rice also published a lucid, admiring article about Santayana, whose poetic theories he much preferred to Cleanth Brooks's. Ample and serious attention was also paid to philosophy in the book review section.[34]

"The New Encyclopedists," which appeared in the *Kenyon*'s second issue, exemplified its main philosophical interest: the opposition of poetry and science, or of a metaphysical versus a naturalistic philosophy. This symposium consisted of a discussion of *The International Encyclopedia of Unified Science,* a few volumes of which had just appeared under the editorship of Otto Neurath. The *Encyclopedia* was based on the belief that the physical sciences are fundamentally identical with biology, psychology, and the social sciences. Charles W. Morris' *Foundations of the Theory of Signs* was the volume that the contributors scrutinized most sharply, as it set forth the theoretical

34. Ransom to Philip Wheelwright, October 3, 1939, in *KR* Papers; Ransom to Burke, September 24, [1942?], in Burke Papers; Virgil C. Aldrich contributed "Beauty as Feeling," *KR*, I, 300–307, and "The Ivory Tower on Wheels," *KR*, II, 445–48; Marten ten Hoor, "The Nazis Purge Philosophy," *KR*, III, 335–43; Ernest Nagel, "Recent Philosophies of Science," *KR*, III, 303–19; Philip Blair Rice, "George Santayana: The Philosopher as Poet," *KR*, II, 460–75. A small but representative selection from the book reviews includes Austin Warren, "Humanism Ten Years After," *KR*, I, 336–39, on *Humanism and the Imagination,* by G. R. Elliott; Philip Blair Rice, "Dewey and His Critics," *KR*, II, 121–24, on *Logic: The Theory of Inquiry,* by John Dewey, as well as on critiques of Dewey by Sidney Hook and Paul A. Schilpp; Justus Buchler, "The Naturalism of Santayana," *KR*, III, 249–53, on both Schilpp's *The Philosophy of George Santayana* and Santayana's *The Realm of Spirit;* and Philip Wheelwright, "The Lonely Philosopher," *KR*, IV, 112–15, on two books about Nietzsche.

underpinnings of this naturalistic, in places positivistic movement. Eliseo Vivas, the advisory editor, was for the new encyclopedists; Howard Dijkema Roelofs, the head of the philosophy department at the University of Cincinnati, was against them. Rice added "Considerations," and Ransom devoted his "Editorial Notes" to his ideas on the opposition between poetry and science.

Vivas ends his extremely appreciative essay with a strong statement of faith: "[I]f our civilization is to perdure, the movement must triumph. For in a world in which science is freely applied to the material aspects of living there can be no place, in the long run, for antinaturalistic mysticism and for habits of mind which belong to an age of magic." Roelofs' attempt at popularization resulted in an atrociously written article in which he accuses the encyclopedists of presenting "verbal manipulations for real solutions." Worse, he says, they supply scientific so-called knowledge, which cannot lead to the "right moral choice, the personal character which resists evil and holds fast to liberty, justice and love"—in short, does not lead to what Roelofs regards as genuine knowledge. Roelofs' conclusion: "Today we have science and scientists aplenty. We lack saints." Rice looks at the issue from both sides: he strongly approves of the encyclopedists' efforts at a philosophical synthesis, but feels that its actual elaboration leaves much to be desired.[35]

Although Ransom in his private correspondence with Tate mentions Roelofs' "injustice to Morris" and describes Morris' *Foundations of the Theory of Signs* as "really brilliant," his publicly expressed sentiments are downright critical. His editorial "The Arts and the Philosophers" is a continuation of the main thesis of *The World's Body*. In his book, Ransom argued that science, generally regarded as providing real knowledge, merely gives pragmatic and consequently only partial knowledge of the world. Art, though considered decorative or cathartic at best, provides detailed, concrete, complete knowledge, "the world's body." In his editorial, Ransom asserts that art "fixes a kind of knowledge of which science has no understanding, and which gentlemen too confined within the scientific habit cannot approach intelligently." However, Charles Morris' rebuttal,

35. Eliseo Vivas, "The New Encyclopedists: I. Pro," *KR*, I, 168; Howard Dijkema Roelofs, "The New Encyclopedists: II. Contra," *KR*, I, 171, 175; Philip Blair Rice, "The New Encyclopedists: III. Considerations," *KR*, I, 176–82.

which appeared in the autumn, 1939, issue, reveals that he closely approximated Ransom's view of poetry as "the world's body." He argued that art "denotes the value properties [elsewhere in this essay defined as the "objectively relative properties of objects"] of actual situations," and that art "is a primary form of discourse, irreducible to the scientific." In contrast to Ransom, however, Morris emphasized that "the recognition that art has a semantical aspect need not make art a quasi-science, nor a metaphysical rival to scientific knowledge." He went on to describe a work of art as "an iconic sign, and not a statement, and this distinguishes . . . the aesthetic experience from scientific knowledge." Therefore, Morris argued, art as such cannot be included in *The International Encyclopedia of Unified Science,* but aesthetics is scientific discourse and should be incorporated. In spite of his admiration for Morris, Ransom continued to wage a battle against science's monopolistic position and, using his privilege as editor, had the final, though rather ineffectual say in this controversy.[36]

The general discussion of science versus poetry continued to fill the *Kenyon*'s pages. In "On the Semantics of Poetry," Philip Wheelwright asserts that poetry consists of "plurisigns," connotative words that have more than one meaning, while science uses words that are denotative and invariant, "monosigns." In her first appearance in prose, the young poet Josephine Miles contended that all words are plurisignificant and that science and poetry only differ in their selection from this plurisignificance; her contribution formed a useful complement to Wheelwright's otherwise excellent article.[37]

Wheelwright also took part in a more direct debate about poetry and science: the ongoing controversy about naturalism. Rice described this topic as "inescapable for a magazine with this Review's commitments. Not only does it have a profound if indirect bearing upon the standards of aesthetic criticism; it is of special moment to all who are concerned with the general reorientation of our culture which is being forced upon us by the tragic events of our time." Rice proudly adds that because of the "basically philosophical" character

36. Ransom to Tate, April 14, [1941], March 29, 1939, both in Tate Papers; John Crowe Ransom, "The Arts and the Philosophers," *KR,* I, 198; Charles Morris, "Science, Art, and Technology," *KR,* I, 416, 421, 422; John Crowe Ransom, "The Pragmatics of Art," *KR,* II, 76–87.
37. Philip Wheelwright, "On the Semantics of Poetry," *KR,* II, 263–83; Josephine Miles, "More Semantics of Poetry," *KR,* II, 502–507.

of this issue, the editors had called upon professional philosophers instead of men of letters.[38]

Eliseo Vivas opened the discussion, in the autumn, 1941, issue, with an essay in favor of the new naturalism. Although he rejects the nineteenth-century materialistic version of naturalism, as well as the related positivistic and pragmatist philosophies, Vivas emphasizes the necessity of a scientific approach to philosophy. He sincerely believes that such a "new naturalistic" approach "rather than killing or alienating our sense for conduct and for beauty, irrigates and fertilizes the soil in which these values germinate." At Ransom's request, Wheelwright belligerently replied in "The Failure of Naturalism." This theist philosopher points out that he is not against science, but against naturalism, which "declares scientific procedures to be the only ultimately valid means by which truth may be sought." Religion, he claims, is at least as legitimate an alternative in the search for truth. The controversy continued in William Barrett's review of *The Nature and Destiny of Man* (Volume I) by Reinhold Niebuhr, which also reflects an anti-naturalistic point of view. Barrett regrets that Niebuhr has tried to prove not that naturalism is an incorrect philosophy, but only that the naturalistic view is less interesting and less emotionally significant than the Christian's. Then, in his reply, published in the winter, 1942, issue, Vivas, his blood up, confronted Wheelwright with several misreadings and now spoke out even more boldly: "[I]f the claim is made by poet and prophet that they possess methods of verification different from the empirical, these gentlemen must be pitilessly shown up as muddlers."[39]

Invited by the editors, Wheelwright duly submitted a rebuttal. But when Rice informed him that, on reflection, the editors preferred to pass it up, as Vivas would insist on a counter-counterreply, Wheelwright exploded: "Why the devil, if you didn't want me to reply to Vivas, did you announce at the end of his letter ["Reply to Mr. Wheelwright"] that I'd be invited to continue the discussion '*with*' him in the next issue? . . . I wouldn't have cared a hang about continuing the I-didn't-say-you-said-what-I-said-was game, but now if I

38. Philip Blair Rice, "A Word About Naturalism," *KR*, IV, 87.
39. Eliseo Vivas, "The New Naturalism," *KR*, III, 459; Philip Wheelwright, "The Failure of Naturalism," *KR*, III, 462; William Barrett, "Christianity and Modern Man," *KR*, III, 503–508; Eliseo Vivas, "Reply to Mr. Wheelwright," *KR*, IV, 93.

don't yap back people will think I wouldn't meet your challenge." He was somewhat mollified by Rice's asking him to write a definite, constructive statement of his faith instead, but found the proposed length of four thousand words stingy: "You allowed me 6000 words or slightly more on poeto-semantics; can I deal with God in less?"[40]

He evidently could, for the result was "the most important [essay] I have written." In "Religion and Social Grammar," which was five thousand words long, Wheelwright called for a reacquisition of the religious perspective. But Bertrand Russell's well-argued, crystal clear counterthrust, which appeared in the next issue, turned the scales so much in favor of the naturalists that Ransom considered balancing it with an editorial necessary. Russell disposes of God and religion by pointing out that cosmic history has shown that God "has purposes quite different from ours," and that therefore "His existence, if He does exist, should afford us no comfort."[41]

Wheelwright found Russell's article "hackneyed and superficial," but Ransom wrote admiringly: "How that man can come to the point. But it needs offsets as he doesn't express our religio-aesthetic point of view at all. I'm getting down to a rather longish editorial, easy-chair-ish item which would go into that and other things and sort of define our attitude by implication. But it may not quite come off." Indeed, it did not. In his shallow two-page editorial, which included a discussion of Mark Schorer's anti-naturalistic article "Mythology (For the Study of William Blake)," Ransom did not get beyond such platitudes as "writers of opposing schools ought to learn from each other," and "when the total event of a sunrise is defined astronomically most of its phenomenal content is lost; when it is translated into myth it is defined very loosely, but the terms have a breadth of meaning proportionate to the object." Perhaps Ransom's gradual acceptance of naturalism was responsible for his inability to answer Russell effectively. Within a few months, Ransom publicly acknowledged his new philosophical faith: "[I]t has grown more and more upon me, at the expense of the strong prejudices which my old-line education drilled into me, to conceive human activities natu-

40. Philip Wheelwright to Rice, December 18, 1941, in *KR* Papers.
41. Philip Wheelwright to Ransom, January 21, 1942, in *KR* Papers; Philip Wheelwright, "Religion and Social Grammar," *KR*, IV, 202–16; Bertrand Russell, "Non-Materialistic Naturalism," *KR*, IV, 364; John Crowe Ransom, "Mr. Russell and Mr. Schorer," *KR*, IV, 406–407.

ralistically."[42] Ironically, Eliseo Vivas, who had been one of the staunchest defenders of naturalism in the early *Kenyon*, completely reversed his position in his *The Moral Life and the Ethical Life* (1950).

As we have seen, Ransom had never been in favor of editing a general magazine including politics, and he had explicitly warned his friends that the *Kenyon* was not in the market for essays with an Agrarian bias. The veto on political issues also applied to articles from Rice's friends, many of whom were politically to the Left. A case in point is an early draft of Vivas' essay on D. H. Lawrence in which he had implied that the "Leftist position [was] . . . a sort of official one with the Review." Ransom fumed: "We are not in politics. And that I say with an easy conscience. . . . [A]rt has no more to do with politics now than it ever had in its life." But history interfered with Ransom's nonpolitical stance. World War II made Ransom desire to have "K.R. . . . renounce its virginity and pitch into the world crisis." His momentary dissatisfaction with the anti-topicality of his magazine only led to the rather shallow symposium on American culture. The plans for this symposium probably sprang as much from the lecture committee at Kenyon College as from Ransom's desire to contribute to the war effort. The participants were invited by the committee to read their papers in Gambier in the spring of 1941, and the double pay (for the combination of speech and paper) was an added inducement. In his editorial in the 1941 spring issue, Ransom explains that the "symposium on 'The American Culture' . . . is by way of tribute to a sense of a crisis imperilling all." Yet, Ransom, once again, warns against the danger of turning art into propaganda. He emphasizes that *The Kenyon Review* will remain "constitutionally devoted to 'arts and letters,'" because "it is just as much a patriotic duty . . . to keep the arts going . . . as to attend to . . . the state of public opinion."[43]

In their optimistic predictions for the postwar world, the historian Rushton Coulborn and the poet John Peale Bishop virtuously follow

42. Philip Wheelwright to Ransom, October 18, 1942, in *KR* Papers; Ransom to Rice, August 4, [1942], in Rice Papers; Mark Schorer, "Mythology (For the Study of William Blake)," *KR*, IV, 366–80; Ransom, "Mr. Russell and Mr. Schorer," 406, 407; John Crowe Ransom, "The Inorganic Muses," *KR*, V, 284.

43. The final version was Eliseo Vivas, "Lawrence's Problems," *KR*, III, 83–94. Ransom to Eliseo Vivas, June 10, [1940], in *KR* Papers; Ransom to Burke, January 4, 1941, in Burke Papers; John Crowe Ransom, "Muses and Amazons," *KR*, III, 242, 241, 240.

Ransom's suggestion that "our proceeding becomes pointless if the parts are turned over to pessimists who can't prove anything." The anthropologist Clyde Kluckhohn is more realistic. He convincingly claims that the American frontier spirit has led to a "'deification of selfishness'" and regards "a scientific humanism . . . [as] the only hope for American culture," that is, "a society in which the lot of the common man will be made easier and his life enriched and ennobled." As Kluckhohn also speaks up for urban as opposed to Agrarian values, and for "assimilation . . . [as] the only solution to the Negro problem," viewpoints that must have seemed revolutionary to Ransom at that time, it is surprising that Ransom calls him "a brilliant young chap."[44]

Even before Ransom had expressed his ambition to "pitch into the world crisis," two articles dealing with the war and literature had appeared in *The Kenyon Review*. One was a succinct essay by Julian Symons about London, in which he predicts an increase in bad, propagandist writing in accordance with the rise of the emotional temperature. In the other, the lead essay of the 1940 autumn issue, Klaus Mann, Thomas Mann's son and the editor of the anti-Nazi magazine *Dissension*, contends that the brutal westerns of the "petty criminal" Karl May heavily influenced Adolf Hitler. This essay fitted only uneasily in the *Kenyon*. An anonymous writer for the Mount Vernon (Ohio) *News* was utterly surprised: "Kenyon Review Goes Tabloid in War Froth," he exclaimed. And though the philosopher Virgil Aldrich found "the content of the article . . . interesting and important and the general position of the author easily sympathized with," he was also shocked by the style of, especially, the last paragraph of the article: "The Third Reich is Karl May's ultimate triumph, the ghastly realization of his dreams. . . . [Hitler's] murderous minions are perverted romanticists, infantile, criminal, irresponsible. They are hopelessly estranged from both reality and art, sacrificing all civilization and all common sense on the altar of a brutish 'heroism,' but stubbornly loyal, to the foul substitute for poetry and culture repre-

44. Rushton Coulborn, "The American Culture: I. The Polity," *KR*, III, 143–60; John Peale Bishop, "The American Culture: III. The Arts," *KR*, III, 179–90; Ransom to John Peale Bishop, December 4, 1940, in Bishop Papers; Clyde Kluckhohn, "The American Culture: II. The Way of Life," *KR*, III, 178, 175, 162; Ransom to Bishop, December 20, 1940, in Bishop Papers.

sented by Karl May." Aldrich wrote that "such phrases may have a place in a pink-sheet bit of inflammatory recrimination, but not in the pages of literary construction and criticism." His reaction indicates that the gravity of the situation in Europe had not yet sufficiently permeated America. "The Nazis Purge Philosophy" by Marten ten Hoor was the only other direct result of the *Kenyon*'s renunciation of its political virginity.[45]

The editors' favorable attitude toward symposia is also apparent in "The Present State of Poetry" and "The Legacy of Sigmund Freud." In the 1939 autumn issue, the state of poetry in Great Britain, France, and the United States was discussed by Herbert Read, Justin O'Brien, and Robert Penn Warren. Read had initially hesitated about submitting: "I tend to value personal relations more than critical forthrightness. I know most of our poets . . . but in some cases my estimate of the poetry has declined in inverse ratio to the increases of friendship. And I haven't been honest enough or brave enough to confess it." Since Read simultaneously felt "a need to clarify the situation . . . in general, aesthetic terms," and since Ransom had no objection to such an approach, Read contributed a very broad account. He detests the lax rhythms and poverty of texture he finds in Britain's most prominent poets, Auden, MacNeice, and Spender, who use poetry as a vehicle for their political beliefs; Dylan Thomas and George Barker are the country's only true poets. In his mainly informative, perhaps too didactic essay on French poetry, Justin O'Brien takes the opposite stand: he endorses the "move away from the hermetic and the gratuitous" toward a poetry that has "greater communicability" and comes "into closer contact with life." Warren, finally, felt "pretty bad" about his essay. Indeed, he tries to do too much: in fifteen pages, he discusses nearly every living American poet.[46]

45. Julian Symons, "A London Letter: The Wartime Literary Situation," *KR*, II, 253–56; "Kenyon Review Goes Tabloid in War Froth," Mount Vernon (Ohio) *News*, October 9, 1940; Klaus Mann, "Karl May: Hitler's Literary Mentor," *KR*, II, 397, 400; Virgil Aldrich to the editors, October 25, 1940, in *KR* Papers; Marten ten Hoor, "The Nazis Purge Philosophy," *KR*, III, 335–43.

46. Herbert Read to Ransom, April 11, 1939, in *KR* Papers; Herbert Read, "The Present State of Poetry: I. In England," *KR*, I, 359–69. Although Auden was living in America at that time (he acquired American citizenship in 1946), Read regarded him as a British poet. Justin O'Brien, "The Present State of Poetry: II. In France," *KR*, I, 384, 378; Warren to Tate, December 14, 1939, in Tate Papers; Robert Penn Warren, "The Present State of Poetry: III. In the United States," *KR*, I, 384–98.

Clearly, "The Present State of Poetry" was not one of the *Kenyon*'s outstanding symposia.

As a memorial to Freud, in whom the *Kenyon* maintained a lively interest through the years, the editors "set about on a symposium of pieces trying to give a ripe and finished estimate of his final achievement. We thought of a paper by a first-rate philosopher . . . a paper on his therapeutic; and a paper on the application of his doctrines to the arts and to aesthetics." Although the advisory editors were asked for suggestions, Ransom and Rice mainly pursued their own ideas. They initially wanted Lovejoy or Whitehead to write the philosophical paper, but the former declined, and, on reflection, Ransom found "Whitehead . . . too old . . . from what I hear of his now doddering state."[47] Ernest Nagel also declined; and at long last Vivas accepted. Edmund Wilson, whom editors and advisory editors strongly favored for the literary paper, begged off. Since Ransom feared that Joseph Wood Krutch would do the same, he reluctantly asked Lionel Trilling, who accepted eagerly. Karen Horney refused to write the therapeutic paper; so the editors had no choice but to accept Alexander Reid Martin, whom she had recommended. All this goes to show that it often is practically impossible for an editor to realize his image of the ideal symposium. Even though in this case the contributors were to be handsomely paid, as the symposium was also sponsored by the lecture committee, not one of the initially invited scholars accepted.

Despite these difficulties, the Freud symposium was a resounding success. In his editorial, Rice pinpoints Freud's main achievement by emphasizing that he "was more concerned with opening an unknown country to adventure than with . . . blueprinting it for future settlement." Rice regards Vivas' essay as "very nearly a pioneer effort" in that most "[p]rofessional philosophers to their great loss have almost entirely ignored the potential contributions of Freudism to the worldview which they are trying to construct." Vivas' essay is the least laudatory one. He grants the therapeutic value of Freud's doctrine, but denies a logical connection between clinical practice and theory. He regrets, though, that Freud's influence on philosophy had been nil: Freud's "conception of human nature is much more fruitful . . .

47. Ransom to Tate, October 11, 1939, November 9, [1939], both in Tate Papers.

than any other available at the moment. For all its defects it helps make sense of our experience in its private range." [48]

Alexander Reid Martin, head of psychiatry at the Children's Aid Society in New York City, first gives a clear survey of the history of psychoanalysis. He praises Freud for the discovery of the concept of the unconscious, the free association technique, and the importance of transference in the analyst-patient relationship. But after having paid his respects to Freud as the founding father of psychoanalysis, Martin pledges his allegiance to the new wave of culturally oriented analysts such as Erich Fromm, Karen Horney, and Abram Kardiner. Lionel Trilling's essay is a hymn to Freud. He describes Freudian psychoanalysis as "one of the culminations of the romantic literature of the 19th Century," which was "passionately devoted to . . . the knowledge of the self." In its turn, the influence of Freudian thought on modern literature has been "so pervasive that its extent is scarcely to be determined." Although not the symposium the editors had envisaged, "The Legacy of Sigmund Freud"—supported by a book review of his *Moses and Monotheism* and Auden's poem "For Sigmund Freud"—bears witness to not only Freud's but also the *Kenyon's* great distinction. [49]

Poetry

The poetry section of the early *Kenyon Review* also significantly contributed to its distinction. In 1941, Ransom sketched the ideal poetry editor: "An editor who is reasonable is not pre-committed for or against a given mode or kind or style of poetry. On the contrary, he is wholly averse to giving advices which would try to shift the substance of a poet's own poetry; he conceives the poet's originality as a function of the substance, and he does not propose to play God, if he could, at that level of the undertaking." But Ransom himself did not quite fit this portrait and gave a much more realistic picture of

---

48. Philip Blair Rice, "Psychoanalysis: The Second Wave," *KR*, II, 226, 227; Eliseo Vivas, "The Legacy of Sigmund Freud: III. Philosophical," *KR*, II, 185.

49. Alexander Reid Martin, "The Legacy of Sigmund Freud: I. Therapeutic," *KR*, II, 135–52; Lionel Trilling, "The Legacy of Sigmund Freud: II. Literary and Aesthetic," *KR*, II, 153, 156 (reprinted in Trilling's *The Liberal Imagination: Essays on Literature and Society* [New York, 1950]); Robert P. Casey, "Exodus: Freudian Version," *KR*, II, 239–42; W. H. Auden, "For Sigmund Freud," *KR*, II, 30–34.

his activities as a poetry editor when he wrote, rejecting poems by Charles Henri Ford, "I just have to publish that which comes up to my own taste." Indicative of Ransom's taste is his statement in the June, 1939, issue of *Poetry*: "[W]e take only work that seems to us very finished and rather intellectual." Ransom's rejection letters also reflect his preferences. He often returns poems because they are not lyrical enough, or too obscure, or too negative. In fact, the remainder of the 1941 editorial reinforces the impression that Ransom as a poetry editor was not without his prejudices. He was unfavorably disposed toward "the verse written upon burning contemporary issues, moral or political. Poetry with this substance is hardly eligible whether with connoisseurs or with aestheticians, the reason being that it does not seem to them to be exactly the poetic substance. It produces glowing moralisms, but moral glow is different from poetic illumination, and usually excludes it; or it produces satire, which is a negative thing and not really the creative art." He told aspiring contributors that "poetic texture without logical structure" was "not the right strategy" and that the editors preferred "poems which are metrically proficient, that is, close and careful; and the adjectives do not necessarily indicate at all those metrical effects that are regimented into monotony."[50]

Clearly, Ransom best liked the kind of poetry he wrote himself. But he hardly closed his eyes to young, original talent. He wrote to Muriel Rukeyser that it was "much better to find younger writers than to call on the old tired ones, and in fact there is no use in a journal that doesn't have a strong set of younger contributors." Consequently, he created the "Younger Poets" series for poets who, usually, had not yet published whole books of verse. And as these poets were paid at the prose rate—which was only half the poetry rate—Ransom could publish a fair selection of new talent. No fewer than twenty-four pages of the autumn, 1941, issue are devoted to the first installment of this series. There are poems by Jean Garrigue, John Ciardi, John Nerber, Reed Whittemore, Howard Nemerov, Howard Moss, John Parker, Elizabeth Lee, and Ruth Herschberger. Herschberger's three poems were her first appearance in print, as was

50. John Crowe Ransom, "The Younger Poets," *KR*, III, 492; Ransom to Charles Henri Ford, March 25, 1939, in C. H. Ford Papers, and quoted in Amy Bonner, "The Poetry Market: A Survey of American Periodicals," *Poetry*, LIV (1939), 167; Ransom, "The Younger Poets," 492–93.

Nemerov's "Notes on a New England Winter." In general, the poems are perhaps "rather thin, though pretty sophisticated," but in selecting these very poets, most of whom became distinguished, Ransom had shown that he possessed a superior eye for poetic talent. The second installment of the series substantiates this: the autumn, 1942, issue contains a second batch of poems by Jean Garrigue, as well as poems by John Thompson, a Kenyon College graduate, and Marguerite Young, a *Kenyon Review* discovery. The third installment consists of Thompson's second contribution and Robert Lowell's "Satan's Confession," which Ransom found "awfully spirited, an unusual very real 'enthusiasm' for poetry in these days." The discussion of the remainder of this series in later chapters will further corroborate the *Kenyon*'s significance as a discoverer of new talent and a place where promising poets were assured of repeated publication, and consequently could experiment and develop.[51]

Many young but poetically more mature poets were published at the usual poetry rate. Although it was not until 1946 that Lowell reappeared in the *Kenyon*'s pages, Jarrell remained one of its main poetry contributors from the first issue onwards. His "The Long Vacation" and "The Skaters" appeared in the winter, 1942, issue; and the singling out of the Emigrant poems led Jarrell to jubilation:

[T]his is overwhelmingly the best judgment any editors have ever had about my poems; I hope God rewards you. . . . I'm not being vain, but (I think) making an objective judgment when I say you're unlikely to get much poetry it would be better to use. After all the poetry I've been reviewing, mine seems charming. . . . Did you notice the way the Emigrants is written? Like an enormous rondo: there are several themes that keep coming round and round, to be treated differently, more seriously that is, each time. . . . It's the best constructed big poem I've done; I've never seen a poem constructed in at all the same way.

Although Jarrell cannot be called immoderately modest here, "For an Emigrant" is a splendid early war poem indeed; it appeared in a subdued version in his *Selected Poems* (1955).[52]

51. Ransom to Muriel Rukeyser, July 3, 1939, in *KR* Papers; "Younger Poets," *KR*, III, 397–420; Howard Nemerov, "Notes on a New England Winter," *KR*, III, 408–10; Ruth Herschberger, "Poems," *KR*, III, 416–20; Philip Rahv to Ransom, October 17, 1941, in *KR* Papers; "New Verse by Brave Poets," *KR*, IV, 352–56 (note that the "Younger Poets" appeared under different headings); "Verse by Two Poets," *KR*, V, 376–83; Ransom to Tate, May 16, 1943, in Tate Papers.
52. Robert Lowell, "Winter in Dunbarton" and "Mr. Edwards and the Spider," *KR*, VIII, 63–65; Randall Jarrell, "The Long Vacation" and "The Skaters," *KR*, IV, 45–47; Randall Jar-

John Berryman's gifts were also recognized at an early stage of his poetic career. He contributed one of his more personal early poems, "Letter to His Brother," the extremely topical "Nineteen Thirty-Eight," and "At Chinese Checkers," which is partly about his friend Delmore Schwartz. All of these are preliminary exercises: Berryman had not found his true personal voice yet. A blossoming Marguerite Young contributed four more poems, and Josephine Miles three; Muriel Rukeyser published the longish title piece of her third volume of verse, "A Turning Wind"; Weldon Kees and Frederic Prokosch contributed two poems each; "Colorado" by Robert Fitzgerald appeared; and Peter Taylor, at that time still a student at Kenyon College, published one of his very few poems, "The Furnishings of a House."[53]

If most of these poems conformed to Ransom's preference for short, lyrical, technically proficient poems, his ability to recognize and his wholehearted willingness to publish great poems that did not, accounts for the appearance of Delmore Schwartz's verse play "Shenandoah, or, The Naming of the Child." Over twenty pages in length, the play is about finding a name for an infant that is to be circumcised; all the action is in prose, the rest is in blank verse. "[I]t hit me so hard I wrote to see if we could get it. It's slated for [the] June number of Laughlin's Poet-a-Month; so Delmore's writing to see if Jay [James Laughlin] could use it a little later and we use it first. Intensely appealing and amusing—a new sort of thing. . . . I think Delmore is giving us something here which is very original and our readers will lap up."[54] So highly did Ransom value this verse play

rell, "For an Emigrant," *KR*, II, 190–94; Randall Jarrell, "The Winter's Tale," *KR*, I, 57–59; Randall Jarrell to Rice, n.d., in Rice Papers. "For an Emigrant" first appeared in book form in Jarrell's portion of *Five Young American Poets*. He included only one other poem from this 1940 New Directions publication in his *Selected Poems*.

53. John Berryman, "Letter to His Brother" and "Nineteen Thirty-Eight," *KR*, I, 257–59; John Berryman, "At Chinese Checkers," *KR*, III, 191–95. Delmore Schwartz wrote to John Berryman on May 8, 1940: "I think 'At Chinese Checkers' is easily your best poem; that is, if I am not too much flattered to say" (Letter in Robert Phillips [ed.], *Letters of Delmore Schwartz* [Princeton, 1984], 96). Marguerite Young, "Earth's History" and "Death by Rarity," *KR*, II, 443–44; Marguerite Young, "Summer Day" and "The Pattern," *KR*, III, 320–21; Josephine Miles, "Quiet and Firmer," "On Page," and "Wading," *KR*, III, 352–54; Muriel Rukeyser, "A Turning Wind," *KR*, I, 399–404; Weldon Kees, "For My Daughter" and "Poem," *KR*, II, 194–95; Frederic Prokosch, "Two Poems," *KR*, II, 309–11; Robert Fitzgerald, "Colorado," *KR*, IV, 177–78; Peter Taylor, "The Furnishings of a House," *KR*, I, 308.

54. Delmore Schwartz, "Shenandoah, or, The Naming of the Child," *KR*, III, 271–92; Ransom to Tate, April 14, [1941], in Tate Papers. From Phillips (ed.), *Letters of Delmore Schwartz*, 107–10, it appears that Schwartz had first offered "Shenandoah" to *Partisan Review*.

that even though Laughlin's edition could well have been out before the *Kenyon*—which it was—he nevertheless decided to print "Shenandoah." His usual policy was to reject contributions that were to be published simultaneously elsewhere in the United States.

Not all poets published in *The Kenyon Review* were young and in need of editorial support: Mark Van Doren, Marianne Moore, and Wallace Stevens also appeared. Nor were all the poets Americans. At Eleanor Clark's suggestion, Louis MacNeice submitted "Picture Galleries" and "The Dowser"; spurred by Allen Tate, Dylan Thomas sent his "If my head hurt a hair's foot. . . ." The publication of two poems by Federico García Lorca also bears witness to the poetic range of the *Kenyon*.[55]

Ransom did not mindlessly favor everything his friends submitted, but he was glad to publish their competent contributions. Tate's "first serious poem since 1935," the witty, metaphysical "Trout Map," appeared in the autumn, 1939, issue. Another metaphysical, conscious artifact is Robert Penn Warren's "Love's Parable." Two years later, "Original Sin: A Short Story," the "most signal example among the early poems that points to the possibility of development and continued risk-taking in Warren's work," appeared. Less successful were Richard Blackmur's too ingenious "Before Sentence Is Passed" and, especially, Ransom's own Harvard Phi Beta Kappa poem, "Address to the Scholars of New England." He had first offered this poem to *The Southern Review*, which had provisionally accepted it, but he had it printed in his own *Kenyon* when there were not enough poems for the autumn, 1939, issue. In asking Tate's reaction to the poem, Ransom remarked: "I enclose my PBK effort. I *mean* effort. What started out as a lark became a burden, and I could have written several free poems out of the energies I spent on this one occasional poem. . . . The way that . . . poem looks in print to me, perhaps even more to my friends, will determine my future avocations, pretty much." Ransom soon realized that it was only a poor poem, and he did not return to his poetry until old age. Much the worst poem

55. Mark Van Doren, "The Seven Sleepers," "Latter Day," "Northern Philosopher," and "Northern Minstrel," *KR*, IV, 174–77; Marianne Moore, "Four Quartz Crystal Clocks," "What Are Years," and "A Glass-Ribbed Nest," *KR*, II, 284–88; Wallace Stevens, "Variations on a Summer Day," *KR*, II, 72–75; Louis MacNeice, "Picture Galleries" and "The Dowser," *KR*, III, 31–33; Dylan Thomas, "If my head hurt a hair's foot . . . ," *KR*, I, 283–84; Federico García Lorca, "Walking Asleep" and "The Interrupted Concert," trans. Rolfe Humphries, *KR*, I, 144–47; William Carlos Williams, "Federico García Lorca," *KR*, I, 148–58.

to appear during this period was Mrs. Chalmers' religious "To the Regent (On the Late Secessions)"; it is only noteworthy as one of Ransom's very few attempts to ingratiate himself with the president.[56]

Altogether, though in these first years the editors often complained about the lack of good poetry, and consequently had actually to solicit it, the *Kenyon*'s record is surprisingly good. Poems that were not up to par, even if they were solicited or submitted by friends or established poets, were uncompromisingly rejected: "I should say that you don't let go enough, the poems lack exuberance; they have a good deal of depth certainly for poems which start out like trifles." More often, the rejections were worded in a typically Ransomian manner: "I like the occasion, and the feel, of the poem on the old church; but I'm [not] taken with it quite enough, and I don't know why," or "Probably a man just married is in no shape to write poetry; they don't (I mean the poems don't) come out of his deep places."[57]

Not all editorial plans worked out. There was, for instance, the failure to execute Jarrell's "best suggestion of his whole career. We [Ransom and Jarrell] were talking of Nobel and Pulitzer literary awards. He says: Why not have the Kenyon Review crown the best book of poetry annually? . . . We are feeling out the advisability of setting up a Poet's Prize (not a big one in money, say $100) and a Committee to consist of Tate, Blackmur, Marianne Moore, Burke, and the Editor."[58] Although Ransom and Jarrell intended this award to become a permanent feature of *The Kenyon Review,* the plan did not materialize.

Fiction and the Fine Arts

Another plan that misfired was a "fiction (or at least fiction-ish) number . . . to include Tate on critique, [the American author of well-

56. Tate to Mark Van Doren, September 18, 1939, in Van Doren Papers; Allen Tate, "The Trout Map," *KR*, I, 404–405; Robert Penn Warren, "Love's Parable," *KR*, II, 186–88; Robert Penn Warren, "Original Sin: A Short Story," *KR*, IV, 174–80; James Justus, *The Achievement of Robert Penn Warren* (Baton Rouge, 1981), 54; Richard Blackmur, "Before Sentence Is Passed," *KR*, III, 63–68; John Crowe Ransom, "Address to the Scholars of New England," *KR*, I, 406–408; Ransom to Tate, [summer, 1939], in Tate Papers; Roberta Teale Swartz, "To the Regent (On the Late Secessions)," *KR*, II, 189.

57. Ransom to Winfield Townley Scott, May 29, 1939, in Scott Papers; Ransom to John Gould Fletcher, July 3, 1939, in Fletcher Papers; Ransom to Robert Wooster Stallman, March 26, 1940, in Stallman Papers.

58. Ransom to Tate, January 7, [1939], in Tate Papers.

known mystery novels, Ruby Lorraine] Radford on detective fiction, [Robert Penn] Warren on the American short story, and two short stories or at any rate one (since we have one by [Paul] Goodman and will have one by Delmore)." The stories by Goodman and Schwartz were indeed published, but the promised essays were not handed in. Only one other story, "The Ball," by Eleanor Clark, had appeared earlier in the *Kenyon*. Ransom's interest in fiction was limited, and the scanty size of the magazine itself had initially prohibited the publication of short stories. But in 1940, in order to "have the 'rich variety' of the Southern Review," Ransom asked President Chalmers' permission to enlarge *The Kenyon Review* from 128 to 144 pages, so that "we could carry one or two more essays, or . . . some piece of fiction having both technical and imaginative distinction." At about the same time Ransom told Tate: "You know we officially want to print an occasional story: if it is experimental in technique at all, seems to extend the possibilities of fiction. We've had fine reactions on the Clark story in the summer. Have you any stories doing? Or can you direct us to stories of our sort? (Caroline [Gordon Tate], Katherine Anne [Porter], Andrew [Lytle].)" Thus, though Ransom did not think fiction "our forte as editorial critics," he did realize that short stories would enliven his compact and complex magazine. As the *Kenyon* was not enlarged until Volume V, it only added "Give Me Time" by Walter Southard to the fiction department during this period.[59]

The selection of these stories shows a much better editorial judgment with respect to fiction than Ransom thought. All four of them are technically indeed out of the common run: Clark's story is surrealist, Goodman's a mixture of interior monologue and plain narration, and Southard's a child's interior monologue. "An Argument in 1934," "[o]ne of Delmore's best stories," gives a good portrait of the intellectual climate of its time in "the grandiose style [Delmore] and his friends affected, in what he called 'Biblical prose.'"[60] However, one of the main functions of a literary magazine is to discover and

59. Ransom to Tate, April 25, 1941, in Tate Papers; Paul Goodman, "Frances," *KR*, III, 473–78; Delmore Schwartz, "An Argument in 1934," *KR*, IV, 62–74; Eleanor Clark, "The Ball," *KR*, II, 289–95; Ransom to Chalmers, June 13, 1940, in KC Papers; Ransom to Tate, [summer, 1940], in Tate Papers; Ransom to Ruth Herschberger, March 27, 1942, in *KR* Papers; Walter Southard, "Give Me Time," *KR*, IV, 195–201.
60. Atlas, *Delmore Schwartz*, 56.

publish new material. And Schwartz's story had been published in the 1937 New Directions anthology. Four stories in four years is not enough to go by, and the further history of *The Kenyon Review* will better show the editorial sensitivity to fiction.

Although *The Kenyon Review* was subtitled "A Quarterly of Arts and Letters," it only paid marginal attention to film, dance, and drama in the early years. Gilbert Seldes reviewed two books on the American theater and the movies in the second issue, and three years later Arthur Mizener discussed Elizabethan elements in film. In this essay, Mizener points out that it is shameful that movies are not being criticized seriously; by way of example, he himself gives an excellent analysis of several scripts. Ransom found Mizener's essay "good not only in itself but as varying our ordinary literary diet; it's as hard as it's desirable to get off the beaten track in our subject matter, style of presentation, and point of view." Even less attention was paid to dance. For seven years, Lincoln Kirstein's superficial review of Lillian Moore's *Artists of the Dance* was the sole contribution. Further, Francis Fergusson wrote an unremarkable review of Joseph Wood Krutch's *The American Drama Since 1918,* and in George Beiswanger's first "Broadway Letter," he labeled 1941 "the least productive [year] since American playwriting got under way some twenty years ago."[61]

While these arts would receive far more attention later on, music and the visual arts were featured prominently during the *Kenyon*'s first years. In spite of Ransom's dislike of Paul Rosenfeld's style, Rosenfeld wrote the "Music Chronicle" section for the review as long as he was an advisory editor. Another regular music critic was the young American composer Henry Woodward, whose way of criticizing music—in contrast to Rosenfeld's—corresponded very well to the New Critical way of analyzing poetry: "One cannot extract the 'content' of a piece of music anymore than one can extract the 'meaning' of a poem. This is not to say that it is futile to discuss the meaning of a work of art; it is only to remind us that the content or meaning of a piece of music or a poem can only be expressed adequately and completely by the work itself; that any attempt to con-

61. Gilbert Seldes, "Stage and Film," *KR,* I, 205–208; Arthur Mizener, "The Elizabethan Art of Our Movies," *KR,* IV, 181–94; Ransom to Arthur Mizener, December 15, 1941, in Mizener Papers; Lincoln Kirstein, "About Dancers," *KR,* I, 222–23; Francis Fergusson, "The Modern Temper in an Aisle Seat," *KR,* II, 376–79; George Beiswanger, "Broadway Letter," *KR,* IV, 264.

vey that meaning through another medium must proceed in a sort of paraphrase or parable, and must be inadequate and incomplete."[62]
It is remarkable that the British music and literary critic W. H. Mellers also recurrently appeared in the *Kenyon* in the 1940s. His theories differed so greatly from Ransom's that the latter devoted an editorial to Mellers' first contribution in order to refute his unsuitable assertions that "[n]o one can claim to be 'musically' educated who is not emotionally educated as well" and that the "cult of objectivity in music criticism . . . too often amounts to a refusal . . . to make first-hand judgments at all." *The Kenyon Review* paid considerable attention to music, but there is some justice in Eric Bentley's remark that Ransom accepted "poor stuff in fields he is little acquainted with especially politics, music, and painting."[63]
With regard to the visual arts, however, Bentley's judgment was too severe. The articles by the main contributors to this department, James Johnson Sweeney, Jerome Mellquist, and Nicolas Dorantes, who was a specialist in Mexican art, were usually sensible and solid. Much more brilliant, however, were the essays by occasional contributors. Dazzling, stimulating, if fundamentally wrong is Wyndham Lewis' illustrated article on Picasso, which Ransom solicited on the occasion of the November, 1939, Picasso exhibition in New York City. Lewis regards Picasso as an "interpretative executant musician as opposed to the creator, or original composer," as "nothing *but* periods," and "a *destructive* force . . . a 'decadent' principle, to promote decay," by whom he is "[b]ored—but nicely, amusingly, bored." It was not until the autumn of 1941 that Fairfield Porter's letter protesting this article was published. Porter tries to dispose of Lewis' article by characterizing it as "very bad" and "ignorant," and Lewis' "boredom with abstraction . . . [as] a boredom with the limitations of his own impotence." Porter may be generally right; still, Lewis on Picasso is much more engaging than Porter on Lewis.[64]

62. Paul Rosenfeld, "Music Chronicle," *KR,* II, 125–28, 380–83, and *KR,* III, 260–63; Henry Woodward, "The Changing Ethos of Contemporary Music," *KR,* II, 51.
63. W. H. Mellers, "On Writing about Music," *KR,* III, 444, 443; John Crowe Ransom, "The Aesthetics of Music," *KR,* III, 494–97; Bentley to Jacques Barzun, September 18, [1944], in Barzun Papers.
64. Wyndham Lewis, "Picasso," *KR,* II, 197, 204, 203, 201; Fairfield Porter, "Wyndham Lewis on Picasso," *KR,* III, 500, 501, 502. The publication of Porter's letter was a last-minute decision. A few days before the issue in which it appeared was to go to press, Ransom had written to Rice on August 16, [1941], that they were short on reviews. He therefore suggested a

Beaumont Newhall's article, "The Photography of Moholy-Nagy," called forth a reaction from Ransom himself. In "The Mimetic Principle" (1938), Ransom had regarded the photograph as a "mechanical imitation," and the act of photographing as "characterless." Newhall's article and the accompanying examples, however, made him realize the art of these photographs: "The functional use disappears; they become at once remarkable, in shape, in light-effect, and even in texture; they are pure particularity now, not function. This is one answer to the useful or non-aesthetic aspect of machinery, of which we are all terrified."[65] Moholy-Nagy soon designed the *Kenyon*'s characteristic cover, and Ransom eventually lost his fear of the functional aspects of the machine.

Paul Goodman and Percival Goodman published a lavishly illustrated article on Frank Lloyd Wright in which they trace both the principles of and contradictions in his theories on architecture. In this well-written lead article, the Goodmans compare Wright's "Organic Architecture" to Le Corbusier's "International Style" and conclude that these two strong and original architects are complementary adversaries.[66]

Finances, World War II, and The Southern Review

As in the case of the *Kenyon*'s early criticism, the *Kenyon*'s symposia, its philosophical interests, the kind of poetry published, and the relatively moderate interest in the other arts during these early years indicated the editorial lines of its first decade. And again, many of its early contributors in these fields, such as Eliseo Vivas, Philip Wheelwright, John Berryman, Robert Lowell, Josephine Miles, Delmore Schwartz, and Marguerite Young, continued to be familiar presences. Conspicuous by his absence is Allen Tate. In spite of Ransom's constant clamoring for contributions, Tate sent only four poems, his

---

"communications section" as a stopgap. The futility of such a section in a quarterly is proven here: topicality, essential in a correspondence column, is hard to achieve. Ransom realized, moreover, that the *Kenyon* generally was too cramped for space anyway, and so the communications section never became a regular feature (Letter in Rice Papers).

65. Beaumont Newhall, "The Photography of Moholy-Nagy," *KR*, III, 344–51; John Crowe Ransom, "The Mimetic Principle," *The World's Body* (1938; rpr. Baton Rouge, 1968), 209; John Crowe Ransom, "Moholy-Nagy's New Arts," *KR*, III, 374.

66. Paul Goodman and Percival Goodman, "Frank Lloyd Wright on Architecture," *KR*, IV, 7–28.

first article appeared in 1949, and his discussion of Whicher's biography of Emily Dickinson was his only review.[67] Not unwillingness to write for the *Kenyon,* but dilatoriness and unforeseen circumstances usually kept Tate from actually delivering the promised contributions. It must have broken Ransom's editorial heart that the contributor he coveted most so often let him down; still, he never held it against Tate, who remained his close friend and literary confidant.

Press and private reactions show that the *Kenyon's* excellence did not go unnoticed, and that within these four years, *The Kenyon Review* had gained a prominent place in literary circles at home and abroad. Howard Nemerov recalled that from "the first of my wish to write, my interest in writing, *The Kenyon Review* was there—so solidly there, in fact, that when I turned up at Harvard College I easily assumed it had been publishing since at least the Civil War; it was maybe twenty years before I learned the *Review* began only the year before I saw my first copy." In 1947, George Dillon, editor of *Poetry: A Magazine of Verse,* observed that "[d]uring the war . . . the American reviews that were read ragged by the young writers in England and Europe were the *Kenyon* and *Partisan* and *Poetry.*" As early as 1941, Justin O'Brien wrote to Ransom that the *Kenyon* had "made a place for itself in our literature that is not challenged by any other publication. For the first time since the death of the *Dial,* I feel that its job is again being done." He added that André Maurois and Paul Hazard, who were in exile in America, "were planning to launch here a quarterly in French and . . . they wanted to approximate your achievement both for content and for physical appearance." But not everybody held so high an opinion of *The Kenyon Review*: Jarrell reported with glee to Ransom that the other members of the English department at the University of Texas regarded the magazine as "*popularization.* There, that will put you in your place."[68]

More predictable was the reaction of R. A. Weaver, one of Ken-

---

67. The poems by Tate are: "The Trout Map," *KR,* I, 404–405; "Jubilo" and "More Sonnets at Christmas (Ten Years Later)," *KR,* V, 184–88; and "Seasons of the Soul," *KR,* VI, 1–9. His first article is "A Note on Autotelism," *KR,* IX, 13–16. The review is "The Poet and Her Biographer," *KR,* I, 200–203.

68. Howard Nemerov, in D. David Long and Michael R. Burr (eds.), *John Crowe Ransom: A Tribute from the Community of Letters,* supplement to the *Kenyon Collegian,* XC (1964), 24; George Dillon, "The 'Little Magazine' Gimmick," *Poetry,* LXXI (1947), 43; Justin O'Brien to Ransom, February 1, 1941, in *KR* Papers; Randall Jarrell to Rice, [summer, 1941], in Rice Papers.

yon's trustees, who found the *Kenyon* "entirely too 'highbrow.'" Weaver's reaction was typical of the answers Chalmers received when he asked the trustees to sponsor the magazine privately. The initial $15,000 was nearly gone, and though the *Kenyon*'s earnings from subscriptions and advertising sales totaled over $5,000, new outside support was needed for long-term survival. But Weaver regarded the *Kenyon*'s weak financial situation in wartime as "a good excuse for dropping the Review," and most of the other trustees also refused financial support.[69]

Chalmers also approached the Carnegie Corporation again, asked for $25,000, but was turned down. Somewhat earlier, Blackmur, on his own initiative, had spoken to his friend John Marshall, Associate Director of the Humanities Section of the Rockefeller Foundation. Blackmur was not successful either: "[W]e seldom if ever can consider support for a magazine. . . . Certainly there would be no chance of our considering help for a magazine of this type no matter how meritorious." Ransom "had not attached much weight" to Blackmur's writing to the foundation, but when, about three years later, the Rockefeller Foundation became the *Kenyon*'s mainstay until Ransom's retirement, Ransom wrote Tate that Blackmur's early letter "must have been the prime cause of our success."[70]

In November, 1941, the future of *The Kenyon Review* still seemed relatively safe, even if the contributors' prose rate had to be cut back from five to four dollars. Two months later, however, the war had caught up with the review:

There is . . . a possibility that we have to discontinue. . . . President Chalmers . . . has invited the faculty to elect a committee to study the actual college budget with him. . . . So a committee is doing that, and inevitably they will come to the question whether the Review—which no one at all ventures to oppose openly—is not a luxury rather than an "educational necessity" and might not be cut off "for the duration." Faculty men whom I have talked with about the matter are opposed to such a stand, and I don't really expect such a thing. But the President, who seems to be behind us with all his might, has said that he doesn't know whether he could afford to go against a powerful faculty opinion in the matter; and that's the possibility of our discontinuing, right there.

69. R. A. Weaver to Chalmers, December 11, 1941, in KC Papers.
70. Chalmers to Robert Lester, Secretary of the Carnegie Corporation, October 1, 1941, in KC Papers; John Marshall to Blackmur, January 23, 1941, in KC Collection; Ransom to Tate, April 24, 1944, in Tate Papers.

I am sure that presently we'll have a little card for use with our contributors . . . to the effect that we'll pay just half of what we formerly did. And we'll shorten our office expenses, and after this spring go along on a student secretary rather than a graduate secretary. And I believe we'd better come down to an "occasional" publication, which in fact would mean three times a year, rather than a quarterly.

Ransom actually had to carry out all these economy measures. The summer, 1942, issue was skipped not only because of a lack of money but also because Ransom had no time and energy left for editorial tasks, since he had to devote himself to the hateful job of serious and active campaigning. The spring, 1942, editorial informed readers that "the *Kenyon Review* very soon will have to find outside patronage to the amount of about $2,500.00 annually. The alternative is to suspend publication. Meanwhile we shall be grateful if we may hear from our readers of anything that would seem to our interest."[71] Form letters were sent to contributors, asking for names of likely patrons. Possible angels were written to, telephoned, and visited, either by Ransom himself or by Robert A. Weaver, Jr., student at Kenyon College and son of the stone-hearted trustee, who also secured $300 in publishers' advertisements.

In February, 1942, the situation had become "worse than ever." Ransom feared "that we can't last beyond the fiscal year without outside aid." In desperation he turned to Henry Church. Church had financed and edited the magazine *Mesures* in France before he returned to the United States at the outbreak of the war. Ransom now offered him a stake in *The Kenyon Review* and laid at his feet "a 12-page department of FOREIGN LETTERS or FOREIGN LITERATURE in each number," as Ransom wrote to Tate, adding in the margin "more space if [Church] can put in more money."[72] Church had—temporarily—lost his editorial enthusiasm, and this plan failed; Church eventually gave $500 with no strings attached. Altogether, the actual results of the extensive fund-raising campaign were very poor. The editors had aimed at ensnaring a small number of angels who would each donate at least $500 annually. In effect, they found only one new patron, Henry Church, and one of the old-time supporters of the

71. Ransom to Tate, January 28, 1942, in Tate Papers; John Crowe Ransom, "War and Publication," *KR*, IV, 218.
72. Ransom to Tate, February 6, [1942], in Tate Papers.

Kenyon, a trustee of Kenyon College, George Frazer, now contributed $1,000.

Another rash proposal that foundered, in spite of much initial excitement, was Ransom's suggestion to New Directions publisher James Laughlin: "Why not subsidize us (in part if not altogether) and in return have the right to a running commentary on New Directions books regularly, the *exclusive* right to our advertising pages; with some nomenclature or some acknowledgment to the effect that you were as a publishing house behind the periodical. . . . You couldn't possibly get to a better audience for your own sales." Realizing that this was not a very attractive offer from Laughlin's point of view, Ransom threw himself into the bargain: "I would personally work for you; I'd read for you or write (anonymously) for you. While I couldn't take a job with you for my own gain, I can do it for the mag. . . . To make it go I'd be glad to hire myself out in some special manner if it would do any good."[73]

But it was the demise of *The Southern Review* that turned the financial scales in favor of the junior magazine. The considerable anti–*Southern Review* faction at Louisiana State University in Baton Rouge had seized upon the war to point out that at a time when severe economies were required, this expensive magazine was an extravagance. Cleanth Brooks recalls:

It was devastating because we knew that the real reason we were being suspended was not lack of money, was not the war. That was a pretense. I found out later . . . that the Louisiana State University had made over a million dollars . . . from government contracts of teaching students for the army. They had a pet tiger for the football team to live in a steam-heated cage. What happened was that we had angered most of the powers in the administration of the university. . . . They could not understand the poetry we were printing. They could not understand the fiction. They did not know what the essays were talking about. To them it was purely a waste of money and . . . a way for these two young men to build up their own careers.[74]

Although Brooks and Warren did their utmost to save *The Southern Review* by suggesting extensive cuts and by applying to every possible foundation, they met with refusals all around. On December

73. Ransom to James Laughlin, April 6, 1942, in KC Papers.
74. Interview with Brooks, August 17, 1982.

20, 1941, the decision was made to suspend *The Southern Review* indefinitely.

When Ransom heard "about that momentous and heroic casualty," he immediately made a "lurid suggestion" and proposed a merger that, he thought, might be the saving of both magazines. His plan came down to a review with combined contents, with both names on the cover, financed mainly by Kenyon College, based at Gambier, and staffed by *Kenyon* and *Southern Review* editors. A "noble" proposal indeed, as Warren and Brooks wrote to Tate, "noble because it is one-sided with John giving nearly everything and LSU getting full share of the credit merely by giving some editorial time. We have felt that he was largely swayed by personal friendship in making us the offer." But Tate was not so sure. He saw Ransom's proposal partly as a friendly gesture to perpetuate the name of *The Southern Review,* but he also regarded it "as a way of boosting the subscription list of the KR by about 1000 and as also a talking point to raise money. All of which is perfectly legitimate, but there's no reason not to see it realistically."[75]

Although Tate exaggerated the number of eventual subscribers, which actually came to about three hundred, he was right about Ransom's interest in the *Southern's* subscription list. But Ransom had never denied or concealed his wish to gather *Southern Review* readers into the *Kenyon* fold. It seems, then, that self-interest rather than a laudable concern for *The Southern Review* may have been at the bottom of Tate's insinuating remarks. For Tate had been asked to become the editor of a new quarterly that was to take over the name and the subscription list of *The Southern Review* and be subsidized by Agnes Scott College, the University of Georgia, and Emory University. Brooks and Warren, fearing that the LSU administration would block a merger with *The Kenyon Review,* wrote Tate that they "would

75. Ransom to Warren and Brooks, January 7, 1942, in KC Papers. LSU basically was to pay for the completion of the *Southern's* subscriptions only. This proposal was made exactly two weeks before the date mentioned in A. J. Montesi, "*The Southern Review* (1935–1942): A History and Evaluation" (Ph.D. dissertation, Pennsylvania State University, 1955), 305, and G. A. M. Janssens, *The American Literary Review: A Critical History 1920–1950* (The Hague, 1968), 261. Both works give comprehensive reports on the relation between the *Kenyon* and *Southern* reviews. Thomas W. Cutrer, *Parnassus on the Mississippi: The "Southern Review" and the Baton Rouge Literary Community, 1935–1942* (Baton Rouge, 1984), concentrates on the community rather than on *The Southern Review.* Warren and Brooks to Tate, February 18, 1942, in Tate Papers; Tate to Lytle, March 2, 1942, in Lytle Papers.

be proud and happy . . . to see the name carried on under *your* editorship" and were "anxious to see your proposition at Georgia go through." Initially the money for the Georgia magazine had seemed "virtually secure," but on March 2, 1942, Tate had to inform *The Southern Review* editors that the "magazine is not going through. Money, of course; and beyond that I don't know much."[76]

The *Kenyon* and *Southern Review* editors then worked out a detailed merger plan very favorable for LSU, but even when its board "unaccountably refused to sanction the merger," Ransom was not inconsolable. Brooks had telegraphed him, as he told Tate, that "he was still sure we could have the official right to take over their subscription list and fill it out, also take over their remainder money for the expense of doing so." Consequently, Ransom felt entitled to call the *Kenyon* the "literary heir" to the prestigious *Southern Review,* which he had described in 1940 as "close to being the best thing in the history of American letters."[77]

Although Ransom was genuinely distressed about the demise of *The Southern Review,* the nearly $600 LSU paid for the completion of its subscriptions, together with the gifts by Frazer and Church, and small ones by some 130 *Kenyon Review* readers, brought the total budget for 1943 just below the $2,500 minimum necessary to continue publication.[78] Offsetting this deficit was the $300 in publishers' advertisements secured by Robert Weaver, Jr., for the autumn, 1942, issue. And so the *Kenyon's* first and perhaps most severe financial crisis had been successfully weathered.

The tragic demise of *The Southern Review,* which entailed both cash and subscribers for the *Kenyon,* also meant the eclipse of its main competitor. "With the So. Rev. gone," Kenneth Burke noted, "the importance of the Kenyon's function was proportionately increased." The *Southern* and the *Kenyon* had had so many interests in common that though the editors had agreed upon "steering stuff to each other," Ransom had also admitted to Warren that "[o]ne of our embarrassments is not too obviously following in the footsteps of the Southern

76. Warren and Brooks to Tate, February 18, 1942, Tate to Warren and Brooks, February 16, 1942, both in Tate Papers; Tate to Warren, March 2, 1942, in *SoR* Papers.

77. Ransom to Tate, [June 2, 1942], in Tate Papers; Ransom to Brooks, April 19, [1940], in *SoR* Papers.

78. Budget statement sent to the Rockefeller Foundation at the end of 1943 (Statement in KC Collection). It appears that readers gave $334.

Review."[79] Many of the contributors to *The Southern Review* also wrote for the *Kenyon*. But it was true, too, that *The Southern Review* was a broad quarterly, both physically and figuratively, with political and regional articles and a generous amount of fiction, features lacking in the *Kenyon*. With *The Southern Review* out of the way, the *Kenyon* did not lose those readers who might otherwise have opted for its more comprehensive and perhaps more controversial competitor.

At the end of March, the influential, prestigious New York *Herald Tribune,* which mistakenly assumed that both magazines had suspended publication, put its finger on the importance of these two "highly respected and highly literary publications":

> The value and the influence of both these magazines were not to be measured by numbers. Their circulation was, by any standard, small. What made them important was that they reached a new group of readers. They had a real following among writers, teachers and humanistic scholars. They combined the erudition and literary excellence of the best of the older English quarterlies. They had, in addition, a sharp eye to the fresh, the experimental, the significant novel movements in literature and art, and a genuine sense of basic ideas and of traditional values.[80]

It was not until the middle of July that a relieved Ransom could inform the *Herald Tribune* that "the report of our demise is 'exaggerated'" and that *The Kenyon Review* "hope[d] to survive even the present war." In his letter Ransom also mentioned the defunct *Southern's* bequest of its subscription list and good will, honors that he felt obliged him to "enlarge our periodical somewhat. We are planning a department of fiction, a larger coverage of important current books in our review section and something like a coverage of the several arts in departmental commentaries." The *Kenyon's* readers were assured of its continuation in the autumn, 1942, editorial, which was succinctly entitled "We Resume." Ransom confessed that "[i]t was altogether likely that a discontinuation would have been permanent and would have amounted to not merely a war casualty but a mortality, and a kind of victory for the enemy," but now he felt "as secure in the prospect of entering upon and completing another volume . . . as a merely literary enterprise has the right to feel in these times. Nor do

79. Burke to Ransom, February 7, 1942, in *KR* Papers; Warren to Ransom, October 22, 1938, Ransom to Warren, October 17, 1938, both in *SoR* Papers.
80. "Cultural Priorities," New York *Herald Tribune,* March 29, 1942, Sec. 2, p. 6.

we expect to discontinue after that." And, in fact, in the first few years following this severe crisis, *The Kenyon Review,* by adopting some of the *Southern*'s characteristics, was to become, in Ransom's own words, "better as well as bigger." [81]

81. John Crowe Ransom, "'Kenyon Review' to Continue," letter dated July 17, 1942, to the New York *Herald Tribune*; John Crowe Ransom, "We Resume," *KR,* IV, 405; Ransom, "'Kenyon Review' to Continue."

3 A Flowering of Criticism

1942–1947

Philip Blair Rice, Advisory Editors, Rockefeller Fellows

Even during the *Kenyon*'s trial years, Rice had played a larger part than had been anticipated at its founding. Initially, Chalmers characterized the managing editor as "the man who does the routine work of considering manuscripts, who cultivates new writers, and carries on the correspondence." Since Ransom very soon came to respect Rice highly, the latter never had to restrict himself to mere "routine work." As early as September, 1938, Ransom described Rice as "a natural-born editor . . . [who] knows all the young writers and has executive force." Ransom reaffirmed this when he found Rice "entirely capable of carrying on" while he was deliberating the Greensboro offer. And in early 1943, in a letter to Tate, he ranked Rice "almost Joint Editor, not Managing Editor," adding that "[w]e both together perform about every editorial action that takes place in our office." Indeed, their editorial relationship was one of cooperation rather than of subordination—there are numerous letters in which Ransom makes remarks such as "we conferred ceaselessly," "I want to argue that with Mr. Rice," and "Rice and I have deliberated a lot about the . . . essay."[1]

1. Chalmers to the Trustees of Kenyon College, December 24, 1937, in KC Papers; Ransom to Tate, September 22, [1938], in Tate Papers; Ransom to Mrs. J. J. Ransom, March 5, 1939, in Ransom Papers; Ransom to Tate, February 27, [1943], in Tate Papers; Ransom to John Gould Fletcher, October 2, 1939, in Fletcher Papers; Ransom to Josephine Miles, March 30, 1940, in Miles Papers; Ransom to Justin O'Brien, January 27, 1941, in *KR* Papers. Moreover, Ransom dedicated *The New Criticism* (Norfolk, 1941) to Rice.

Rice brought some important writers to *The Kenyon Review*, though David McDowell somewhat overstated the case when he said, "[t]hat thing that changed the literary climate . . . on . . . particularly the critical level was that odd merger [of New York intellectuals and New Critics] that would never have happened if Rice had not come." Still, it was Rice who made the actual connection between his friend Lionel Trilling and the *Kenyon*. And in Trilling's wake came most of the other intellectuals, though it must be added in fairness that Allen Tate's friendship with Philip Rahv was important, too. Anyway, once enticed by Rice, Trilling soon became such "a tremendously ardent friend of the Review" that when Rice wrote him about its probable demise, Trilling grieved: "to me it's a great personal loss not to have the Kenyon to write for. . . . I felt as if I had a personal part in it; when your letter came I was . . . planning to write you some ideas I had for the improvement of the magazine."[2] Yet, understandably, he was not interested in Rice's ill-considered plan to found a new kind of *Kenyon Review* at Columbia University with Trilling at its head.

Rice also brought in Eliseo Vivas. Vivas was one of the *Kenyon's* most enthusiastic advisory editors during its pre-merger period and held naturalistic philosophical views that were quite close to Rice's. In addition, Rice kept abreast of national and international developments in philosophy; had a wide circle of philosopher friends—from Henry David Aiken, Charles Morris, and Van Meter Ames to Jean Wahl and Jean-Paul Sartre; was acquainted with many young American poets; and had a lively interest in French literature and modern art. These interests supplemented Ransom's and broadened the *Kenyon's* horizon.

Rice's temperament also differed from Ransom's. Rice was extroverted, rash, emotional, and capable of great outbursts; Ransom remained a "mystery" to many of his friends. Although Tate detected "[u]nder [his] surface of moderation and urbanity . . . about the completest violence I've seen in human nature," outwardly Ransom was calm and collected. But Ransom's love of a good argument, and his "valu[ing] and even relish[ing] the differences of temperament" between him and his friends, made for a continuous discussion of problems at the editorial office that was all to the good of the *Kenyon*.[3]

2. Interview with David McDowell, December 4, 1981; Ransom to Chalmers, December 16, 1941 (Memo in KC Papers); Lionel Trilling to Rice, March 15, 1942, in Rice Papers.
3. Donald Davidson to Tate, March 10, 1938, in Tate Papers; Tate to Mark Van Doren,

Ransom's confidence in Rice came to the fore in early 1944, when Rice's Kenyon contract came up for renewal. Ransom wholeheartedly seconded Rice's request for a continuation of his devoting one-quarter of his time to *Kenyon* matters and explained why Rice was indispensable: "At the present time I am doing without him, and finding the going pretty heavy at times. . . . Where I need Rice the most is in constantly having his literary impression to compare with mine. . . . Beyond that, however, he is peculiarly valuable in being better posted than I in current literary discussion, and especially in that which concerns the foreign writers." Rice's contract was renewed on the old basis. Ransom proved his "perfect confidence" in Rice's editorial qualities when he gave him "the sole charge" for the spring, 1945, issue before leaving Gambier for a brief sabbatical from October, 1944, to mid-February, 1945. Rice did not let Ransom down: with contributions by Eric Bentley, Bertolt Brecht, Richard Chase, Philip Rahv, Arthur Mizener, and Richard Blackmur, this issue certainly was up to par and paved the way for Rice's editing *The Kenyon Review* on his own during the academic year 1949–50 when Ransom taught at Indiana University in Bloomington.[4]

After the demise of *The Southern Review,* Ransom had taken on Cleanth Brooks and Robert Penn Warren as advisory editors partly "for political reasons": the presence of their names on the masthead would confirm that the *Southern*'s good will had gone to *The Kenyon Review.* But as was the case with Rice, they too came to influence the *Kenyon*'s editorial line because of Ransom's high opinion of them. Cleanth Brooks now views Rice's relationship to Ransom in the same light as he does his own to Warren during their joint editorship of *The Southern Review:* that of a respected and admired working partner to a genius.[5] But Brooks is overly modest. His careful editing alone of the Hopkins issues for the sixth volume of the *Kenyon* con-

December 21, 1937, in Van Doren Papers; Ransom to Arnold Stein, June 22, 1956, in *KR* Papers. In an interview with Helen and Elizabeth Forman, October 19, 1981, Helen Forman said: "If there is one thing Pappy [as Ransom was called by most of his intimates] liked, it was a good argument."

4. Ransom to Chalmers, February 25, 1944. Rice was on a Guggenheim in New York City (Letter in KC Papers). Ransom to Rice, September 11, [1944], in Rice Papers. In *KR,* VII:2, are Eric Bentley, "The Drama at Ebb," 169–84; Bertolt Brecht, "Gedichte aus dem Exil," 198–207; Richard Chase, "The Sense of the Present," 218–31; Philip Rahv, "Modernizing James," 311–15; Arthur Mizener, "Mr. Auden's Tennyson," 315–18; and Richard Blackmur, "Notes on Eleven Poets," 339–52.

5. Ransom to Tate, July 12, 1942, in Tate Papers; interview with Brooks, August 17, 1982.

vincingly shows that he is not a mere plodder. Another first-rate special issue, which will be extensively discussed later, is the one on Henry James, guest edited by Warren. Had Brooks and Warren only edited these two specials, they would have amply shown their value as advisory editors. But we shall see that their advice did not remain thus restricted; Warren's intimate knowledge of modern short stories, for instance, helped make the *Kenyon's* turn to fiction, which Ransom had chosen to inherit from *The Southern Review,* a propitious one.

Taking on Brooks and Warren made the list of advisory editors too long, and Ransom thus had a great opportunity to "make a clean sweep, have about five names new altogether—not to hurt the feelings of Rosenfeld and probably Vivas." Trilling, Burke, and Jarrell were "pretty good persons," Ransom thought; and he wanted Thomas Munro of the Cleveland Art Institute, Philip R. Adams, or Jerome Mellquist to represent painting. Most members of the first board easily acquiesced in their dismissal; Eliseo Vivas, for instance, was "sensitive of the fact that my connection with Kenyon Review has all been to my advantage." As Ransom soon came to prefer a few advisory editors to a mere list of impressive names, only Brooks and Warren appear as advisory editors on the masthead of the autumn, 1942, issue. When Rice strongly urged Ransom to add Trilling to the list, Ransom yielded. He admired Trilling as a critic and realized that the addition of an energetic New York editor might bring in a whole range of new writers and manuscripts. Trilling took his advisory editorship so seriously that he actually felt hurt and worried when the editors did not consult him continually.[6] Finally, though Tate's name was struck from the list, Ransom continued to seek his support and advice.

Another important influence on *The Kenyon Review* was a consequence of an initiative of the Rockefeller Foundation, which, in spite of its earlier firm refusal to support the *Kenyon,* had gradually become interested in literary magazines. In December, 1943, David

6. Ransom to Tate, July 12, 1942, in Tate Papers; Eliseo Vivas to Ransom, September 8, 1942, in *KR* Papers. On February 23, [1945], Bentley wrote to Rice: "Trilling wrote me that he had patched things up with KR; so much to the good. I think one of his worries was . . . that you didn't consult him on policy or submit material to him. He felt, for example, that he might have contributed to keeping P. Magg out of K.R." (Letter in Rice Papers). P. Magg published "Education for the Age of Labor," *KR,* VI, 632–44, in which he severely criticizes the New School for Social Research.

Stevens, Director of the Humanities Section, informed Chalmers of his plan to appoint young critics as Rockefeller Fellows to *The Kenyon Review*. Sounding Paul Engle on whether he was interested, Ransom included Stevens' description of the position: "[T]he Fellow to assist editorially; and the Fellow to confer endlessly with the Editor about Poetry & Criticism, etc. . . . to their mutual advantage; and the Fellow then to go away to spread light in darkness." Since Ransom preferred a meeting of minds to assistance with routine editorial jobs, he suggested that the foundation send short-term but "mature" Fellows, "so that the Editor may receive *great* benefit from the association and improve his own critical foundations."[7] But Engle had to decline because he could not disentangle himself from earlier commitments. Other names that ran through the editors' heads were Cleanth Brooks, Kenneth Burke, Lionel Trilling, Meyer Schapiro, and Jacques Barzun.

Harold Whitehall, a British critic who had come to the United States to take his doctoral degree at Iowa State University and who had gone on to teach at Indiana University, became the *Kenyon*'s first Rockefeller Fellow, from May to August, 1944. His stipend of $185 a month was the first money ever to be—indirectly—paid by the Rockefeller Foundation to a literary magazine. Ransom was not particularly impressed by Whitehall's gift for writing, but found him "a fine linguistic and phonetic scholar, not a dry crabbed one, and the best prosodist I know," and labeled his first contribution to the review a "bang-up article." Ransom, who had expected to "exchange . . . mental wares [with Whitehall] . . . to my advantage," actually found him "adaptable . . . [and] good company" but rather lacking in initiative. Whitehall hardly influenced the *Kenyon*'s editorial line.[8]

The second Fellow, Eric Bentley, was a man of different stature. Like Whitehall, Bentley was born in Great Britain, but was in the

7. Ransom to Paul Engle, January 11, [1944], in Engle Papers.
8. Ransom to Brooks, November 22, [1939], in *SoR* Papers. Harold Whitehall's first contribution was a review of Volume I of W. A. Craigie and J. R. Hulbert (eds.), *A Dictionary of American English on Historical Principles*, entitled "America's Language: A to Dew," *KR*, II, 212–25. Ransom to Rice, December 13, [1943], September 11, [1944], both in Rice Papers. Thomas Daniel Young (in *Gentleman in a Dustcoat: A Biography of John Crowe Ransom* [Baton Rouge, 1976], 380) assumes wrongly that the *Kenyon*'s first Fellow was Bentley, followed by Whitehall, Riker, and Warren.

process of becoming an American citizen at the time of his application. He went to Oxford, earned a Yale Ph.D., taught English at UCLA, and spent two years teaching cultural history at Black Mountain College. Although still young—he was born in 1916—Bentley had published two books and numerous articles in such prominent literary magazines as *The Nation, Antioch Review,* and *Partisan Review.* He had come to Ransom's attention "through the kind offices of Lionel Trilling . . . who was so enthusiastic about him that he called . . . up from New York . . . to talk about him."[9] Ransom recommended him for an appointment, but Bentley failed the foundation's obligatory medical examination. At Ransom's insistence, however, Kenyon College received a "Grant-in-Aid" of $1,000 that was to be Bentley's stipend for four months with the *Kenyon.*

A letter Bentley wrote to his friend and advisor Jacques Barzun soon after his arrival in Gambier in September, 1944, shows that he already identified himself with *The Kenyon Review* and testifies to his intelligence, energy, and imagination. Even though Bentley warned Barzun that he "should not imagine that I am very important here," Bentley's "pushing the things I believe in" often bore fruit. "I have suggested that the KR run two series of articles each of which would be a book later. The first is a survey of the liberal arts at the moment: The Present State of Poetry, Drama, Fiction, Music etc. The second is a series of Reconsiderations of classics. . . . I am also trying to make our book reviews come out more promptly."[10] The surveys of the liberal arts eventually appeared as a series entitled "Post-War Stock Taking"; and "Reconsiderations" became a very successful series of high-quality articles that continued into 1949 with contributions by, among others, F. R. Leavis, Robert Penn Warren, Richard Chase, and Bentley himself.

Ransom "found him so useful" that he made Bentley an advisory editor, and from the summer, 1945, issue, Bentley's name adorns the masthead. Soon he became, in Ransom's words, "the most active member of our Advisory staff." Bentley's interest in Bertolt Brecht

9. Eric Bentley, *A Century of Hero-Worship: A Study of the Idea of Heroism in Carlyle and Nietzsche, with Notes on Other Hero-Worshipers of Modern Times* (Philadelphia, 1944); Bertolt Brecht, *The Private Life of the Master Race,* trans. Eric Bentley (New York, 1944); Ransom to John Marshall, March 25, 1944, in KC Collection.

10. Bentley to Jacques Barzun, September 18, [1944], in Barzun Papers.

and in drama in general, and his many suggestions for contributors and books he thought should be reviewed, all left their mark on the *Kenyon*. As an advisory editor, Bentley continued to feel close to the magazine and, until the early 1950s, submitted most of his usually first-rate articles and book reviews to its editors, who almost invariably published them. Ransom's report on Bentley for the Rockefeller Foundation demonstrates both Bentley's special gifts and Ransom's keen eye for young talent:

Bentley is a brilliant specimen of a certain tough-minded sector of the younger generation which is likely to play an important part in our future culture. He is learned academically but scornful of the academic style; he is capable of most intensive thinking but determined not to inhabit an ivory tower; and incidentally, or rather significantly, he is in politics decidedly to the left. So thorough is his political commitment that it gives him this advantage: he does not bother much about the current political issues but can put his whole energy into literature. His principal literary interests do not involve any political bias. In the discussion of drama, for example, his interest is very pure, and his intelligence and information are alike most unusual. . . .

[H]e writes with exceptional clarity and force. . . . I might remark that he has also a keen interest in music. He is going to produce many vital books, on a variety of subjects, if I am any prophet; his energy and facility seem to make that inevitable.[11]

In his turn, Bentley wrote the foundation that he had gone "daily to the Review office . . . to help with editorial work. This consisted chiefly of two things: the consideration of such MSS. as had come in and discussions of plans for the future. . . . I helped in preparing the Winter and Spring issues. . . . I was especially eager to help the editors find contributors outside the field where the Review already excels. Accordingly I suggested the names of certain music, art, and foreign literature critics."[12] It may seem as if the *Kenyon* had much more to gain by its association with Bentley than vice versa, but Bentley still was a relatively unknown critic, and his career was decidedly fostered by his connection with the prestigious *Kenyon Review*.

David Stevens, who had become more and more interested in the

11. Ransom to Chalmers, December 14, 1948, Ransom to David Stevens, February 22, 1945, both in *KR* Papers.
12. Bentley to David Stevens, January 13, [1945], in *KR* Papers.

Kenyon, asked Bentley for information and recommendations, and Bentley came up with some large-scale plans for the magazine. He aimed "at 10,000 readers," at a *Kenyon* with "musical, artistic, linguistic, political . . . as well as literary interests" and "representatives in New York, London, and Paris." He thought "commercial slickness was required" to beat the *Partisan* and *Sewanee* reviews, edited by "very canny slicksters like . . . Tate and . . . Rahv." Hearing of Bentley's suggestions, Ransom wrote to the Rockefeller Foundation that he "felt morally impelled" to dissociate himself from these "high-powered plans" and, particularly, from Bentley's commercialism. He preferred "making the Review *good*" to going to any length to increase circulation, "otherwise we are just journalists." Ransom need not have worried about the impact of Bentley's remarks, for R. P. Blackmur's findings in his "Literary Magazines Study" for the foundation supported his views. Ransom's tolerance for and confidence in talented, if dissentient newcomers are clear: despite his horror at Bentley's wild plans, he subsequently made him an advisory editor.[13]

Much less influential was the next Fellow, Charles Riker, who had graduated from Kenyon College in 1927. Riker, who taught at the Eastman School of Music in Rochester, New York, was chosen in order to stimulate the arts section of the *Kenyon,* and he spent the summer of 1945 in Gambier. He did not bring in any new, valuable, regular contributors; at his suggestion, Roger Sessions was made an advisory editor, but since Sessions never advised, his name did not long remain on the masthead. Riker got Alexander Calder to illustrate Robert Penn Warren's revaluation of *The Ancient Mariner* for the *Kenyon,* and that may have been his best venture, also because Warren and Calder subsequently became good friends.[14]

Robert Penn Warren was the foundation's fourth and final grantee. Like Bentley, Warren received not the title of Rockefeller Fellow, but the lump sum of $1,000. In Warren's case, however, the sum was meant for three months, as opposed to Bentley's four; and the foundation's reason was flattering. "[A]ssistance in some other form than a fellowship" was "more appropriate . . . since Warren is a . . . more mature and established scholar than candidates for fellowship appointments

13. Bentley to David Stevens, February 27, 1945, Ransom to David Stevens, March 5, 1945, both in *KR* Papers; Richard Blackmur, "Literary Magazines Study" (TS in LMS Papers), 5.
14. Robert Penn Warren, "A Poem of Pure Imagination," *KR,* VIII, 391–427.

usually are." It is hard to point to directly demonstrable results of the summer of 1946 that Warren and his wife spent in Gambier. But in Ransom's eyes, Warren had been the ideal Fellow: they had "an almost continuous literary conversation," a true meeting of minds, refreshing and stimulating to both of them. And, of course, as Ransom reported to Chalmers, Warren "advised us editorially, and it is public knowledge that he is an able and veteran editor."[15] Finally, it must be emphasized that Warren's editorial suggestions never took the form of cut-and-dried advice, but, rather, were part of his personal, informal conversation and correspondence with Ransom.

So Rice, who became associate editor in 1945, the advisory editors, and the Rockefeller Fellows crucially influenced *The Kenyon Review* in all its aspects. From fiction to philosophy, and, above all, in literary criticism, they made their presence felt. Criticism was definitely the *Kenyon*'s most prominent department and its main claim to well-deserved distinction during these years. It drew particular attention in the *Kenyon*'s special issues. In *The Republic of Letters* (1979), Grant Webster regards the *Kenyon*'s issues on Henry James, Gerard Manley Hopkins, Dante, and "English Verse and What It Sounds Like" as "Ransom's central achievements," but Ransom himself actually had had charge of only the issue on prosody. The others were composed, at the editors' request, by Robert Penn Warren, Cleanth Brooks, and Francis Fergusson, respectively.[16]

Special Issues, "Reconsiderations," New Critical Articles

Commemorating James's hundredth birthday, the Henry James issue also marked the end of the *Kenyon*'s fifth year of publication, a feat that was "a little bit exhilarating" to Ransom, who felt that *The Kenyon Review* now had "got safely by [its] most infant and most mortal years." Although Ransom had been "growing steadily in the opinion that James was pretty near the principal literary figure in the language for the latter half of the 19th century," the James issue may have re-

---

15. John Marshall to Ransom, January 16, 1946, Ransom to Chalmers, December 14, 1948, both in *KR* Papers.
16. Grant Webster, *The Republic of Letters: A History of Postwar American Literary Opinion* (Baltimore, 1979), 105. *KR*, V:4, is the James issue; *KR*, VI:3, and VI:4, are the Hopkins issues; *KR*, XIV:2, is the Dante issue; and *KR*, XVIII:2, is the special issue, "English Verse and What It Sounds Like."

sulted indirectly from Warren's suggestion. The idea was originally Morton Dauwen Zabel's, but Warren had proposed a 1943 centenary special on Henry James for *The Southern Review* as early as April, 1941, as "such issues may easily take a year or a year and a half to prepare properly."[17] So, in this very particular respect too, the *Kenyon* was the *Southern's* "literary heir."

Although both *The Little Review* and *The Hound & Horn* had paid homage to Henry James in 1918 and 1933, respectively, Warren felt that this subject had not yet been worn out, especially since "we have a lot of new critics about these days." In September, 1942, Robert Penn Warren reluctantly—"I'm certainly not a James expert"—agreed to become guest editor for the *Kenyon's* James issue and "to take over the correspondence on the subject." He drew up a tentative list of contributors including Tate, Burke, Blackmur, F. O. Matthiessen, Edmund Wilson, David Daiches, Joseph Warren Beach, and Howard Baker. Beach and Baker are not on a later list, made in collaboration with Ransom and Rice, on which the names of Francis Fergusson, Katherine Anne Porter, Lionel Trilling, Eliseo Vivas, and Austin Warren also appear. Warren asked these twelve to write for the James issue and to send him statements about the subjects they were interested in so there would be no duplication. In due course, other possible contributors were mentioned. Trilling, for instance, proposed Jacques Barzun and Andrew Chiappe. Warren threw himself into an extensive and convoluted correspondence and on December 15, 1942, blithely reported to Ransom: "The people now signed up are Austin Warren, Zabel, K. A. Porter, Kazin, Matt[h]iessen, Trilling, Daiches, Vivas, Blackmur, Fergusson, Tate, and Rahv. That makes twelve. Would it be possible to stretch things a little more? At 5000 words a head, this would account for 60,000 words. But Schwartz would be good, and I would like to see Marianne Moore represented and Edel (the man who is editing the James plays)."[18]

17. Ransom to Chalmers, August 27, 1943, in *KR* Papers; Ransom to Tate, May 16, 1943, in Tate Papers; Warren to Henry Moe of the Guggenheim Foundation, October 17, 1941, in *SoR* Papers. Warren mentions a *Southern Review* James issue in his letter of April 15, 1941, to the other editors of the *Southern* (Letter in *SoR* Papers). However, according to Delmore Schwartz, it was Blackmur's "essay on *The Sacred Fount,* which seemed to have suggested to [Ransom] a James number in 1943" (Schwartz to Blackmur, August 16, 1942, in Robert Phillips [ed.], *Letters of Delmore Schwartz* [Princeton, 1984], 127).

18. Warren to the other editors of *The Southern Review,* April 15, 1941, in *SoR* Papers; Warren to Ransom, September 16, December 15, 1942, both in *KR* Papers.

But three months later, Warren had to inform Ransom that Kazin had had to welsh on his acceptance because the army wanted him and that, because of a misunderstanding, Trilling was no longer on the list either. By the end of May, Porter, Tate, and Zabel had still not sent him the subjects of their essays, and Warren became worried. His letters were in the following vein: "And what has happened to your James piece? . . . Two people have already dropped off the list and we couldn't stand another piece of perfidy." They seem to have had some effect, for both Zabel and Porter hurriedly sent in their titles. But at the last moment, not only Zabel and Tate but Rahv, too, let Warren down. Rahv was afraid that Ransom would be "fuming," he wrote his fellow shirker Zabel, but he had been unable to finish his essay, as "the departure of the Macdonalds (male & female) has put the magazine [*Partisan Review*] into a phase of convulsive re-organization."[19] And Warren himself was also too busy to fall in with Ransom's suggestion that he write an overview essay.

In spite of these disappointments, the James issue was outstanding and diversified, though perhaps somewhat heavy. Its density may be partly due to the concentration of many contributors on James's less accessible novels, *The Golden Bowl* and *The Ambassadors*. The lead essay was an exception: Porter's "magnificent James piece" dealt with "James as a child and boy . . . almost altogether notes on his autobiographies, with side glances at the children in his works." Fergusson wrote that James's "ideas of form and of techniques of presentation throw at least as much light upon drama as upon fiction."[20]

His article links up nicely with Barzun's, which contends that James "is a writer of melodrama," that is, "the endless battle of God and Satan." The author of the illustrated article that follows Barzun's, John L. Sweeney, is not mentioned at all in Warren's letters to Ransom about this issue; so Ransom or Rice must have brought him in. Deal-

19. Warren to Tate, [spring, 1943], in Tate Papers; Philip Rahv to Morton Dauwen Zabel, August 10, 1943, in Zabel Papers.
20. Ransom to Katherine Anne Porter, September 27, 1943, in Porter Papers; Porter to Ransom, June 3, 1943, in *KR* Papers; Katherine Anne Porter, "The Days Before," *KR*, V, 481–94; Francis Fergusson, "James's Idea of Dramatic Form," *KR*, V, 498. The Henry James issue, *KR*, V:4, also includes: Jacques Barzun, "James the Melodramatist," 508–21; John L. Sweeney, "The Demuth Pictures," 522–32; F. O. Matthiessen, "James and the Plastic Arts," 533–50; Austin Warren, "Myth and Dialectic in the Later Novels," 551–68; David Daiches, "Sensibility and Technique (Preface to a Critique)," 569–79; Eliseo Vivas, "Henry and William (Two Notes)," 580–94; and Richard Blackmur, "In the Country of the Blue," 595–617.

ing only indirectly with James, Sweeney discusses in detail a group of water colors painted by Charles Demuth under the literary spell of *The Beast in the Jungle*. The careful editing of this issue appears not only in its minimal overlap but also in the arrangement of the articles: after Sweeney's is Matthiessen's on the influence of the plastic arts on James.[21]

Austin Warren's article was reprinted in *The Kenyon Critics*. In this intricate essay, he claims that James distinguished between a dialectic and a mythic way of knowing. Dialectic knowledge is a conscious, social, and cerebral process; the mythic truth can only be arrived at intuitively, subjectively, through images and symbols. The doubts Robert Penn Warren had had about Daiches, whose critical articles at that time often dealt with social or socialist concerns, proved to be wholly unfounded. Daiches argues that with James, "unless one begins a study of any individual work with an examination of the technique . . . one will run the danger either of interpreting the novel in too limited and specific a manner, or of misinterpreting it completely." Vivas uses the philosophical-biographical approach: he first contrasts Henry's and William's "moral conceptions" of the world, which he defines as principle against expedience, but then points to "the resemblance . . . in which they conceive . . . the process . . . through which the mind enters into relations with its world." Blackmur points to still another aspect of James, discussing those tales in which the protagonist or narrator is an artist and claiming that these tales "look both ways, to the social novels that preceded them and to the fiction of fate that came after them."[22]

Although not exactly pioneering, the issue certainly was timely: it helped launch the James revival in the 1940s and stimulated critical concentration on James's final period. That this special James number was not superfluous appears in, ironically, some remarks made by Ransom. In this very issue, he writes shortsightedly that James merely recorded "the fastidious transactions of . . . the finished and Olympian society." And though he acknowledges that James "came to this stock fiction with an improved technical facility," Ransom thinks

21. Barzun, "James the Melodramatist," 509.
22. Daiches, "Sensibility and Technique," 578–79; Vivas, "Henry and William," 581; Blackmur, "In the Country of the Blue," 597.

that "the modernity of his methods and the obsolescence of his materials are ironically at odds."[23]

Most reactions to the James issue were favorable. Marianne Moore, for instance, felt under "deep obligation" to the editors "for the good it does me to have . . . the Anniversary Number of THE KENYON REVIEW," and spoke of its "vivid and absorbing presentation." John Marshall was bowled over and wrote to David Stevens: "This certainly sets a high standard for contemporary criticism. If we can somehow help . . . I'm for it." This led to the Rockefeller Foundation's first direct gift of $7,500 to *The Kenyon Review*. But, of course, not everybody was pleased. Edmund Wilson, who had contributed to *The Hound & Horn*'s James number, fretted: "It does seem to me an extraordinary lack of something or other on Ransom's part to get up these symposia on these very subjects such as Henry James and Symbolism which have already been written to death, and induce a lot of writers, most of them mediocre, who have really nothing to say on the subject, to contribute articles about them—instead of finding out what people who are worth reading have written or want to write."[24] Wilson did not know that he was on the list of possible contributors, and his strange hostility toward the *Kenyon* was probably fed by his unjustified feeling that its editors regarded him as merely a journalist.

The editors had hoped to persuade a publisher to bring out the James issue in book form, but their efforts failed. They were more successful with Hopkins, when, in 1945, James Laughlin's New Directions published *Gerard Manley Hopkins* by the Kenyon Critics. As early as the autumn of 1942, that is, at about the same time that Ransom had asked Warren to edit the James number, Cleanth Brooks had agreed to guest edit a Hopkins centennial issue. Approximately one year later, Brooks set to work in earnest. He told Ransom: "I am writing at once to line up Hopkins essays. (I shall certainly write [Harold] Whitehall and should like to have more suggestions from you.) I agree that it is better to plan four or five papers rather than more. . . . [T]he smaller number certainly seems the sensible thing,

23. John Crowe Ransom, "E. M. Forster," *KR*, V, 620, 621.

24. Marianne Moore to Rice, October 1, 1943, in *KR* Papers; John Marshall to David Stevens, January 3, 1944, in KC Collection; Edmund Wilson to Tate, October 22, 1943, in Edmund Wilson, *Letters on Literature and Politics 1912–1972*, ed. Elena Wilson (London, 1977), 400.

and I heartily concur in that view."[25] It is clear from this letter and from further correspondence with Ransom that, though Ransom had given him a free hand, Brooks deferred much more to Ransom than Warren had done. Brooks's first choices were rather obvious ones, but not very likely to work out—as he himself realized: "I should like to have Red [Robert Penn Warren] in the number, and shall ask him, though I fear he is too busy to contribute. Blackmur is, of course, an excellent choice, and so, I think, would be Allen [Tate]— though here again I imagine that he is too busy to contribute." But by December 10, Brooks already had acceptances from four of the six eventual contributors: Josephine Miles, Arthur Mizener, Austin Warren, and Harold Whitehall. He had also received an analysis of "The Windhover" by a Father Schoder, S.J., about which he was none too enthusiastic, even though he thought it "well to have a piece . . . by one of the brethren."[26] But the Jesuits were not to be represented.

Jean Garrigue did not reply to Brooks's letters, but Brooks was cheered by Robert Lowell's promise to write about Hopkins after March 16, 1944, when he would be released from the penitentiary where he was serving his sentence as a conscientious objector. In May, however, it appeared that neither Lowell nor Mizener could make the summer, 1944, Hopkins issue. Aside from a brief editorial by Brooks, the issue therefore features only four Hopkins articles. But, as he wrote to Mizener, Ransom saw "a fine way out":

We are going to press with four (4) pretty good Hopkins pieces. Now suppose we have a follow-up in the Autumn number, of which deadline will be *August 1*: featured by your "letter" or "essay" . . . supplementing, perhaps also criticizing, the original papers. . . . I've often thought any symposium needed a follow-up, to fill in the gaps, and record the objections. I know this: What a symposium on a poet will generally lack most is the *general reader's* essay on the total impact of the poet; the less specialized, pure belles-lettres effect. So what about that? A piece positive or a piece negative, or both. I thought of you all along as the man who would be most likely to give the general effect of an unusual poet.

25. On October 12, [1942], Brooks wrote to Ransom: "I shall be happy to undertake the Hopkins number, if you would like for me to." The letter quoted in the text was written on September 22, 1943. Both letters in *KR* Papers.
26. Brooks to Ransom, November 5, 1943, February 18 [1944], both letters in *KR* Papers. Brooks mistakenly calls Schoder "Schoden" in his letters.

Mizener accepted this new deadline, Lowell again promised an essay, and Austin Warren gladly agreed to review *Gerard Manley Hopkins: A Life* by Eleanor Ruggles, which had been advertised in the summer issue. These three were in the autumn, 1944, Hopkins number.[27] Clearly, it had been altogether easier to compile the Hopkins issues than the one on James.

Brooks's editorial in the first Hopkins issue merely mentioned that the essays were a centennial tribute to Hopkins, and that Mizener and others would continue the discussion in the autumn issue. He also invited reactions from readers, but as usual, if these arrived at all, they were not considered good enough to be published. In one of his first published articles, the Catholic convert Herbert Marshall McLuhan—whose name is not mentioned in Brooks's letters about the issue to Ransom—defends his thesis that "Hopkins is not a nature mystic at all, nor a religious mystic either but an analogist. By stress and instress, by intensity and precision of perception, by analogical analysis and meditation he achieves all his effects." In a letter commenting on this issue, Lowell observed that McLuhan's essay was "good . . . but perhaps more an example of how critical analysis is improving than a brilliant essay." Whitehall contends that Hopkins' sprung rhythm is to be found in medieval dipodic poetry and that Hopkins, in order to "write sprung rhythm . . . was obliged to use alliteration, internal rhyme, assonance, and word repetition . . . [and that to] use these devices, he needed new compounds and syntactic shortcuts." Mizener, however, put his finger on the sore spot when he remarked that "[i]t seems to me an open question whether the necessities of Hopkins' sensibility, with its need for repetition, led to his adoption of Sprung Rhythm or the necessities of Sprung Rhythm, as Mr. Whitehall suggests, led to the repetitions."[28]

Josephine Miles looks at Hopkins from yet another angle. On the

27. Ransom to Arthur Mizener, May 13, [1944], in Mizener Papers. The contents of the Hopkins issues, *KR*, VI:3 and VI:4, are Cleanth Brooks, "Gerard Manley Hopkins," 321; Herbert Marshall McLuhan, "The Analogical Mirrors," 322–32; Harold Whitehall, "Sprung Rhythm," 333–54; Josephine Miles, "The Sweet and Lovely Language," 355–68; Austin Warren, "Instress of Inscape," 369–82; Robert Lowell, "The Hopkins Centennial: A Note," 583–86; Austin Warren, "Monument Not Quite Needed," 587–89; and Arthur Mizener, "Victorian Hopkins," 590–606.

28. McLuhan, "The Analogical Mirrors," 324; Robert Lowell to Ransom, July 10, [1944], in *KR* Papers; Whitehall, "Sprung Rhythm," 353; Mizener, "Victorian Hopkins," 601.

basis of many examples of Hopkins' favorite diction, she emphatically does not group Hopkins, as F. R. Leavis had done, with the metaphysicals, but with Milton and "the wordpainting poets" such as Keats. Austin Warren disagrees with both Miles and Whitehall. He points out that the early Hopkins indeed follows Keats but that the nearest parallel to the Hopkins of the terrible sonnets is Donne. He acknowledges Hopkins' acquaintance with Anglo-Saxon, but emphasizes that the poet was mainly influenced by Welsh poetry. Although Warren had written to Brooks about the "protruding 'facts'" of his essay, "its shaky hypotheses, its bad proportions, its incoherence," Brooks, in sending it on to Ransom, proclaimed it "one of the best pieces on Hopkins that I have seen in a long time." Warren's second contribution on Hopkins, a brief review of the Ruggles biography, was less sparkling and wide-ranging, but it affirmed the *Kenyon*'s line that it "is through literary studies like his own, not through more biographical detail, that we come to a richer understanding of his work." [29]

Lowell's note on Hopkins is not very valuable in itself and is mainly worth mentioning as one of the first and one of the very few pieces of criticism he ever published. In its emphasis on Hopkins' "heroic sanctity," the article is perhaps as much a portrait of Lowell's own preoccupations at that time—he had become a passionate Roman Catholic convert in 1940—as a note on Hopkins. Mizener had seen proofs of the first batch of Hopkins essays and he explicitly referred to some of them, but his main concern was to write the suggested general survey of Hopkins and his times. In this "masterpiece," as Ransom termed it, Mizener reasons with reference to specific poems that Hopkins does not belong with the modern poets at all, but is a true exponent of tradition and "obviously Victorian." [30]

In contrast to the James issue, the Hopkins issues, which total nearly ninety pages, are partly contradictory, but each separate essay is written so convincingly, alluringly even, that the reader's mind at times gets quite confused. Using Hopkins' own pronouncements on his poems, most of the symposiasts also closely analyzed the pro-

29. Miles, "The Sweet and Lovely Language," 359; Brooks to Ransom, May 2, [1944], in *KR* Papers; Warren, "Monument Not Quite Needed," 588.

30. Lowell, "The Hopkins Centennial," 583; Ransom to Arthur Mizener, August 23, 1944, in Mizener Papers; Mizener, "Victorian Hopkins," 606.

sodic, textural, and structural elements of Hopkins' poems, and quoted extensively. In short, they criticized him in New Critical fashion. The symposium was well timed, since not many full-fledged articles on Hopkins had yet appeared, Hopkins criticism having so far been largely restricted to reviews. Therefore, the symposium and its appearance in book form significantly contributed toward a serious placing of this poet. The editors, rightly considering that *The Kenyon Review* had given Hopkins his due, published only one more review on Hopkins.[31]

Although most of the separate critical articles during this period dealt with modern, mainly American writers, Eric Bentley's suggestion—probably inspired by "Revaluations," which had been appearing in F. R. Leavis' *Scrutiny* since 1933—to publish "Reconsiderations," "a series of fresh estimates of old authors by living critics," fell on fertile ground. Bentley unofficially opened this series in the autumn, 1944, issue with "The Theatres of Wagner and Ibsen" and closed it with his "Chekhov as Playwright" in the spring, 1949, issue. Most of the twelve "Reconsiderations" came up to the high standards Ransom set for this series. On April 18, 1945, he wrote to Mizener: "I think we have a big chance by planning to make something really good out of RECON.'s. Something perfect in its concision, overwhelming show of authority, and easy balance of learning and critical reaction. And the more balls there have been written about the man, the more importance the RECON. will have." A week later he added: "[T]hey ought to leave the common thing and the academic thing unsaid, and fix and focus on the bright meaning which makes the vision. . . . What we need very much is a new statement . . . and not a synthesis of [earlier] statements."[32]

Bentley concentrated on international drama, which he considered

31. In *Gerard Manley Hopkins* (Norfolk, 1945) by the Kenyon Critics, two new articles appeared. Austin Warren wrote a biographical introduction, "Gerard Manley Hopkins (1844–1899)," and F. R. Leavis contributed "Metaphysical Isolation," which had appeared in *Scrutiny*. Austin Warren's review of the Ruggles biography was left out. The final review on Hopkins was John Pick's "More About Hopkins," *KR*, XI, 155–59.

32. Editor's note to J. E. Hardy, "Lycidas," *KR*, VII, 99. On September 14, [1944], Bentley wrote to Jacques Barzun: "The second [suggestion] is a series of Reconsiderations of classics. In a way my Ibsen-Wagner article begins the . . . series" (Letter in Barzun Papers). Eric Bentley, "The Theatres of Wagner and Ibsen," *KR*, VI, 542–69; Eric Bentley, "Chekhov as Playwright," *KR*, XI, 226–50; Ransom to Arthur Mizener, April 18, 25, 1945, both in Mizener Papers.

to have been sorely neglected: "Look through any good critical journal and you will find stringent, zealous, and expert criticism of all
the arts with the single exception of drama, for there is at present no
significant theatre, and even the better dramatists of yesterday—
Strindberg, Chekhov, and Synge—are to a large extent forgotten, while their contemporaries in the novel and poetry—James,
Proust, the Symbolists—maintain and even enhance their reputation." Bentley's own outstanding drama criticism, much of which
appeared in *The Kenyon Review,* was soon to fill at least part of this
void. Although Bentley himself argued that "[e]ven more directly
than the other arts . . . drama is a chronicle and brief abstract of
time . . . hence the necessity of historical criticism," history is only
one of Bentley's critical tools. Each of his essays bears witness to his
wide reading, not only in drama but also in literature in general, in
philosophy, and in psychology. Bentley both places his dramatists in
their times and traditions, and analyzes particular plays in detail
by paying attention to their theatrical conventions, structure, character development, language, and stage directions. "The Theatres of
Wagner and Ibsen" and "Chekhov as Playwright," as well as "August
Strindberg," are cases in point.[33]

Volume VII of *The Kenyon Review* (1945) is adorned with three
more "Reconsiderations." John Edward Hardy, a graduate student at
the State University of Iowa, takes issue with Ransom's "A Poem
Nearly Anonymous"—Milton's *Lycidas*—and contends, by means of
detailed textual analysis, that "Lycidas is a poem *wholly* anonymous."
Julian Symons' exploration of Restoration comedy led Bentley, though
he was not uncritical, to comment that "much of the essay gives the
lie to my statement . . . that the literary magazines do not publish
dramatic criticism on the level of their poetic criticism." The third is
by Wylie Sypher. Although he finds "Pope . . . superficial," this
"superficiality is of a very special and significant kind" and is analo-
gous to rococo architecture. Pope is, finally, a master of the arabesque in verse.[34]

33. Bentley, "The Theatres of Wagner and Ibsen," 542, 544; Eric Bentley, "August Strindberg," *KR,* VII, 540–60. Some of Bentley's "Reconsiderations" appeared in his *The Playwright
as Thinker* (New York, 1946).
34. John Crowe Ransom, "A Poem Nearly Anonymous," *The World's Body* (1938; rpr.
Baton Rouge, 1968), 1–28; J. E. Hardy, "Lycidas," *KR,* VII, 100; Julian Symons, "Restoration

It is in the eighth volume of *The Kenyon Review* (1946) that the series reaches its culmination: Cleanth Brooks discusses Wordsworth's "Intimations Ode," Robert Penn Warren analyzes *The Ancient Mariner,* and F. R. Leavis examines Doctor Johnson. Brooks's contribution was reprinted as "Wordsworth and the Paradox of the Imagination" in his well-known *The Well Wrought Urn* and may be considered characteristic of his brand of New Criticism. Brooks sees the ode "as an independent poetic structure, even to the point of forfeiting the light which his letters, his notes, and his other poems throw on difficult points. (That forfeiture, one may hasten to advise the cautious readers, need not . . . be permanent.)" As Brooks himself had feared, many readers found this article "an attempt to fit the poem to a Procrustean bed—in fine, the bed in which John Donne slept comfortably enough but in which a Romantic poet can hardly be supposed to find any ease." In reviewing *The Well Wrought Urn,* even Ransom felt constrained to point out that Brooks had overemphasized the importance of paradox, perhaps because he realized that in the hands of lesser men, Brooks's methodology would lead to word juggling.[35]

In June, 1945, Warren had sent Ransom an eighty-page draft essay on *The Ancient Mariner.* Warren realized that with respect to publication in the *Kenyon,* there would be "a real problem in length," but begged Ransom to "hold off a final decision," as he intended to visit Gambier in September. "Then we could take a look together and work the thing out. And . . . I think I might want to do some dickering and juggling there on the spot with you at my side."[36] Ransom decided to publish three of the seven sections that eventually appeared as the introduction to the 1946 Reynal and Hitchcock publication of *The Rime of the Ancient Mariner.* These three central sections could well stand on their own; they were also delivered as a lecture at

---

Comedy," *KR,* VII, 185–97; Eric Bentley, "The Views of Mr. Symons," *KR,* VII, 477; Wylie Sypher, "Arabesque in Verse," *KR,* VII, 457.

35. Cleanth Brooks, "Wordsworth and the Paradox of the Imagination," *The Well Wrought Urn* (1947; rpr. New York, 1975), 124–50; Cleanth Brooks, "The Intimations of the Ode," *KR,* VIII, 80, 82. Robert Heilman, "Baton Rouge and LSU Forty Years After," *SR,* LXXXVIII [1980], 139) recalls, probably referring to *Understanding Poetry:* "Brooks told me that Warren had said that applying their method to Wordsworth was like 'manicuring an elephant.'" John Crowe Ransom, "Poetry: I. The Formal Analysis," *KR,* IX, 436–56.

36. Robert Penn Warren, "A Poem of Pure Imagination," *KR,* VIII, 391–427; Warren to Ransom, August 23, 1945, in *KR* Papers.

Yale University. They still ran to a respectable length by *Kenyon* standards: thirty-seven pages, not including the eight fascinating illustrations by Alexander Calder.

However, the essay was not a drain on the *Kenyon*'s budget. Reynal and Hitchcock paid the magazine a share of Warren's royalties "to amount at least to the cost of payments-to-contributors for critique and drawings," because of the editors' "equity in the matter, in the drawings which we secured, even in the critique which we accepted," as Ransom told Rice. In the *Kenyon,* Warren heavily emphasizes Coleridge's use of symbolism in *The Ancient Mariner* and finds that "the poem is, in general, about the unity of mind and the final unity of values, and in particular about poetry itself." The complete version of this "famous and controversial" essay displays "one of the few demonstrable principles of [Warren's] criticism: that every conceivable resource available to the critic is potentially a useful tool."[37]

Although F. R. Leavis had been asked to review Joseph Wood Krutch's *Samuel Johnson* in 1945, it was not until the end of April, 1946, that he sent "instead of a review, an article you probably wouldn't find room for." Krutch's book had seemed to Leavis "surprisingly good." Consequently, Leavis apologized, he had found himself "committed to an article" because he had not wanted to "merely assert or imply." But Ransom was only too delighted to be able to publish an article by F. R. Leavis at long last. Moreover, this "fresh statement of Johnson's whole achievement" perfectly fitted the "Reconsiderations" series. In his belligerent essay, Leavis labels Johnson "the supreme Augustan writer" who "discriminates with something approaching infallibility between what is strong and what is weak in the eighteenth century." But, Leavis argues, Johnson's limitations, such as his failure to understand Shakespeare's genius, also follow from his being so wholly a man of his time.[38]

The careful composition of the *Kenyon* is once more demonstrated by the publication in this same issue of a review of *Explorations* by L. C. Knights, one of Leavis' "most intimate collaborators" on the

37. Ransom to Rice, September 21, [1945], in Rice Papers; Warren, "A Poem of Pure Imagination," 421; James H. Justus, *The Achievement of Robert Penn Warren* (Baton Rouge, 1981), 121, 123.

38. F. R. Leavis to Ransom, April 25, 1946, in *KR* Papers; F. R. Leavis, "Doctor Johnson," *KR,* VIII, 637, 651, 655 (this essay was reprinted in *The Common Pursuit* [1952; rpr. Harmondsworth, 1976], 97–115).

critical magazine *Scrutiny*. Eric Bentley, Knights's reviewer, who was to edit *The Importance of Scrutiny* in 1948, described this magazine as "one of the best literary journals of today." In his turn, Leavis reviewed this very issue of *The Kenyon Review* in *Scrutiny*. He argued with Bentley's reservations about *Scrutiny,* but returned the compliment by calling the *Kenyon* "the best of those American reviews which, published from universities, give American criticism so marked an advantage over British."[39]

"[T]he most exciting of Victorian novels," *Jane Eyre* and *Wuthering Heights,* both published in 1847, were discussed in Richard Chase's essay in the "Reconsiderations" series. In this early article, Chase already quests for myth, regarding the "Brontë culture heroine as a mythical being" who fails in her purpose "to transform primeval society into a humane and noble order of civilization." Harry Levin, author of the only essay dealing with a French novelist, approaches his subject in a much more traditional, mainly biographical way.[40]

In sum, the distinguished sequence "Reconsiderations" showed a wide variety of critical approaches and concerned, especially, British authors and foreign drama. Whether they were mainly biographical, formalistic, mythical, or mixed critiques, most of these always well written articles succeeded in their purpose to shed new light on the authors discussed, or even to rescue them from oblivion.

One essay in the series must still be discussed, Ransom's own "The Literary Criticism of Aristotle," which was also read as an independent paper at a symposium, "The Great Critics," at Johns Hopkins University on April 13, 1948. It is the continuation and the conclusion of two articles that had appeared in the *Kenyon* nearly a year before. The first article in this sequence, "Poetry: I. The Formal Analysis," already briefly mentioned, is essential. It is of supreme importance in the history of *The Kenyon Review:* for the first time, Ransom publicly dissociates himself from the New Criticism.

For twenty or twenty-five years we have lived with a kind of literary criticism more intensive than a language has ever known. But a revulsion is set-

39. Eric Bentley, "This Is the New Criticism," *KR,* VIII, 672; F. R. Leavis, "'The Kenyon Review' and 'Scrutiny,'" *Scrutiny,* XIV (1946), 134. *The Importance of Scrutiny* is dedicated to Ransom.

40. Richard Chase, "The Brontës: A Centennial Observance," *KR,* IX, 488, 497; Harry Levin, "Flaubert: Portrait of the Artist as a Saint," *KR,* X, 28–43.

ting in against it. The new criticism probably is most at home today in the academy, where it flourishes as a lively "minority" movement. The literary enthusiasms of the academy are sometimes tardy, however, and it is common for a given taste to have run through its period among professional men of letters at about the time it establishes itself among the students and instructors. From these it receives a second start in life, and if the taste is an intelligent one this will doubtless be a long life. But at the moment the new criticism appears to have been slightly disappointing to the expectations it had aroused.

It has achieved a linguistic revolution in its reading of poetry. Its emphasis is upon the total connotation of words. . . . So poetry has waited for our age to recognize and publish a sort of irresponsible exuberance in the energy of its materials, which constantly imperils its sober order. In fact the new critics, careless of the theoretical constitution of poetry, have contrived to create a sense of its disorder. But at last this has become embarrassing. We have grown familiar with many exciting turns of poetic language, but we begin to wonder if we are able to define a poem.

Ransom then calls for a new theory that includes psychology to determine poetry's use and motive as well as formal analysis. These two approaches, Ransom cautions, "have to be in consultation together at every step." Indeed, Ransom has come a long way from "Criticism, Inc.": psychology is not a subsidiary method any longer but at least as important as unraveling a poem's texture. The reasons for Ransom's change of heart are not far to seek. At a time when hardly any attention was paid to texture, Ransom had found it "tactical" to emphasize that aspect of poetry; but now that a mechanical, narrow kind of formal analysis threatened to become prevalent in the academy, he felt that the scales had to be tipped again to create the necessary balance.[41]

So, in his second, rather vague essay "The Final Cause," Ransom looks anew at poetry with the help of the Freudian terms *Ego* and *Id*. Theoretically, this essay only obfuscates his earlier statements on poetry, but the excellent practical analysis of, among other things, a scene from *Hamlet* is very much to Ransom's credit. Ransom announced that he would continue this discussion in the winter, 1947, issue, but it was not until the summer of 1948 that his third and con-

41. John Crowe Ransom, "The Literary Criticism of Aristotle," *KR*, X, 382–402; Ransom, "The Formal Analysis," 436, 440. In a letter to Morton Dauwen Zabel, Ransom denigrates his own achievement when he describes "Criticism, Inc." as "too general and too merely tactical for your purpose" (Ransom to Zabel, March 8, 1949, in Zabel Papers). Zabel's "purpose" was the second, revised edition of *Literary Opinion in America,* published by Harper and Row in 1951. "Criticism as Pure Speculation" was Ransom's contribution.

cluding article appeared in the "Reconsiderations" series. In late April, John Palmer had asked Ransom to submit his lecture on Aristotle to *The Sewanee Review*. But Ransom refused and explained that "[w]e are overdue with Ransom's instalment, and this is it." His main reason was not that "the item is . . . publicly called for," but that "[w]hat goes in the KR of mine is without 'payment to contributor.'" This meant a "saving of $65 or $75 to the budget." The mediocre quality of the essay cannot account for Palmer's interest. Ransom's outright declaring himself to be an Aristotelian naturalist who is "[n]ot for one minute . . . tempted . . . to 'reject' the scientific achievement" may have been shocking to some, but there is nothing new in his discussion of Aristotle's treatment of *mimesis* and *katharsis*. Robert Fitzgerald found that Ransom sometimes was "carrying [his] courtesy to positivism too far," and described the essay as "patient and charming."[42]

Although Ransom in "The Formal Analysis" lashed out at an academic, narrow conception of the New Criticism, it was to a large extent his own publication of brilliant practical New Critical articles in *The Kenyon Review* that had made this kind of criticism so popular in the universities. Robert Penn Warren's lucid essays on, for instance, Eudora Welty and Melville as poet again stand out, as does his essay on Hemingway, which served as the introduction to Scribners' 1949 edition of *A Farewell to Arms*. More theoretical, but still firmly embedded in practical criticism, is Warren's classic, widely anthologized "Pure and Impure Poetry." In this essay, which appeared in the spring, 1943, issue, he attacks the notion that poems should include only certain areas of experience and, particularly, should not contain anything that seemingly contradicts the poet's main purpose. Ransom's reactions to "Pure and Impure Poetry" reflected both his personal intolerance of critical theories that differed from his own and his editorial acumen. On the one hand, he reprimanded Warren for not recognizing "that not all the relationships between items in the poems are structural ones"; on the other hand, he included this essay in *The Kenyon Critics*.[43]

42. John Crowe Ransom, "Poetry: II. The Final Cause," *KR*, IX, 640–58. John Palmer edited *The Sewanee Review* from 1946 to 1952. Ransom to John Palmer, April 24, [1948], in *SR* Papers; Ransom, "The Literary Criticism of Aristotle," 395; Robert Fitzgerald, "Critics on Criticism," *KR*, XIII, 138, 139.
43. Robert Penn Warren, "The Love and the Separateness in Miss Welty," *KR*, VI, 246–59; Robert Penn Warren, "Melville the Poet," *KR*, VII, 208–23; Robert Penn Warren, "Heming-

A survey of the *Kenyon's* important book review section during this period displays R. P. Blackmur's best and main contributions. Delmore Schwartz, for instance, regarded Blackmur's admittedly somewhat too laudatory discussion of his long poem *Genesis* (1943) as one of the few intelligent reviews of the book. Appearing two years later in the spring, 1945, issue, Blackmur's "Notes on Eleven Poets," however stimulating, was too severe at points. In particular, his opinion of Lowell's first volume of verse, *Land of Unlikeness,* was too low, though perhaps a good counterpoise to the overenthusiastic reviews it generally received. "In Lowell's *Land of Unlikeness* there is nothing loved unless it be its repellence; and there is not a loving metre in the book," Blackmur wrote. This led Ransom to confess to Lowell that he "felt violently let down by Blackmur's patronizing and superior remarks." Blackmur himself realized "that what I had to say about Robert Lowell may be too wide," but, as he told Tate, Lowell "had . . . invited it by publishing so much anathema himself." Yet, if this review shows Blackmur's inability to treasure poetry that was technically very different from his own, such as H.D.'s or William Carlos Williams', or his lack of charity toward poets, such as Lowell, with whose ideas he disagreed, it also shows his perfect phrasing with respect to poetry he felt empathy with, such as Tate's. Moreover, Blackmur stayed close to the texts he discussed; he had not yet yielded to the flights of critical fancy of his later years.[44]

Marianne Moore was particularly pleased with Randall Jarrell's review of her *What Are Years* (1941). Included in *The Kenyon Critics,* this essay acclaims Moore as "the greatest living woman poet," as "Henry James in pure crystalline form." No wonder that Moore felt "under a heavy debt to Randall Jarrell." Jarrell's own *Blood for a Stranger* came in for praise in an omnibus review by Arthur Mizener that appeared in the winter, 1943, issue. "[I]n desperation," Mizener had ranged his eleven poets—"a random selection" made by "[t]ime alone"—from right to left, "according as they were more or less con-

---

way," *KR,* IX, 1–28; Robert Penn Warren, "Pure and Impure Poetry," *KR,* V, 228–54; John Crowe Ransom, "The Inorganic Muses," *KR,* V, 288.

44. Richard Blackmur, "Commentary by Ghosts," *KR,* V, 467–71; Richard Blackmur, "Notes on Eleven Poets," *KR,* VII, 348; Ransom to Robert Lowell, December 12, [1945], in Lowell Papers; Blackmur to Tate, March 29, January [24?], 1945, both in Tate Papers.

ventional in manner." He found Jarrell's first solo volume "the most exciting of th[e] whole collection" and recognized in Berryman's *Poems* "a writer of considerable natural talent." Mizener remarked upon Blackmur's "incredible ingenuity," upon Mark Van Doren as "one of the most attractive poets . . . unpretentious and expert." He waved aside Hans Zinsser as "an example too derivative and insensitive to be of interest." All this and more made Ransom exclaim that the *Kenyon* had "never had a neater & more discriminating job."[45]

F. O. Matthiessen's omnibus review, which appeared about two years later, was also excellent. His condemnatory phrase about E. E. Cummings as "the experimentalist of one experiment" is memorable, but Matthiessen is as perceptive when he praises. He rightly notes, for instance, that Robert Penn Warren has, with his "Ballad of Billie Potts," entered "quite a new realm by accomplishing the fusion . . . between the poetry of the coteries and the poetry of the folk." Matthiessen's spring, 1943, article on Eliot's *Four Quartets,* which he analyzed in New Critical detail, is as penetrating. But Ransom disagreed with Matthiessen's admiration for Eliot's poetry and in an editorial used Matthiessen's article as a starting point for an attack on *The Waste Land,* the "structural unity [of which] . . . has been sought by [the] ablest and most generous scholars without conspicuous success." In the autumn, 1947, issue Mark Schorer discussed no fewer than fourteen novels by mainly minor talents in his omnibus review. This was a precursor of his more theoretical critical classic "Technique as Discovery," which appeared in *The Hudson Review*'s maiden issue. In "The American Novel," Schorer proves himself a New Critic in arguing that fiction deserves the same scrutiny that had been lavished on poetry. Contradicting the notion that the New Criticism had stunted the growth of young poets, Schorer suggests that "poetry has had the advantage of a large and excellent accompaniment in criticism," with the result that for "every six or seven men and women now writing distinguished poetry, one can name perhaps one man or woman who is writing distinguished fiction."[46]

45. Randall Jarrell, "The Humble Animal," *KR,* IV, 411, 410; Marianne Moore to Rice, October 11, 1942, in Rice Papers; Arthur Mizener, "Poetry from Right to Left," *KR,* V, 154, 158, 156, 157, 155, 154; Ransom to Arthur Mizener, September 20, [1943], in Mizener Papers.
46. F. O. Matthiessen, "American Poetry Now," *KR,* VI, 688, 692; F. O. Matthiessen, "Eliot's Quartets," *KR,* V, 161–78; Ransom, "The Inorganic Muses," 298–99; Mark Schorer,

Three years earlier, one of those excellent technical analysts of poetry, Cleanth Brooks, had extensively discussed *The Anatomy of Nonsense* by Yvor Winters, whom he described as "perhaps our most
logically rigorous critic; . . . certainly one of the most intelligent;
and . . . undoubtedly the most cantankerous." Winters had certainly
been cantankerous in his condemnation of Ransom's essay on him in
The New Criticism, which, as Brooks pointed out, actually "was
characterized by critical sympathy." But Brooks, not blinded by his
being "deeply indebted" to Ransom's criticism, argued that Winters
"searches some of the weaknesses in Ransom's position." Brooks
wrote to Ransom that he wished he "had been able to take more time
for the discussion of Winters' chapter on you" and "were surer of my
own position in relation to his and yours," but Ransom quite liked
the review. Ransom was pleased, too, with Harold Whitehall's very
flattering review—written in only four hours—of H. L. Mencken's
The American Language: Supplement One (1945). He included this review in *The Kenyon Critics.* As a professional linguist and an En-
glishman who had been living in the United States for many years,
Whitehall proved to be eminently suited for the job of reviewing the
amateur Mencken on the differences between British and American
English.[47]

Finally, among Eric Bentley's many excellent reviews in fields as
diverse as drama, psychology, and architecture, his discussion of *The
Little Magazine* (1947) by Frederick J. Hoffman *et al.* is of particular
interest. Somewhat unfairly, Bentley compares this historical and
bibliographical work, which he regards as "superficial and erratic,"
to the *Accent* and *Partisan* anthologies, which give a "much better notion of little magazines." In discussing the *Partisan Reader* (1946),
Bentley remarks that it "is in spite of the big political talk, and in
spite of the bad manners and ugly cruelties that mark its controver-
sies, that *Partisan Review* earns our admiration." He turns the most
common charge against *Partisan,* namely, that it is journalistic, into
praise: "The interest in the new is legitimate and necessary." More-

---

"The American Novel," *KR,* IX, 636; Mark Schorer, "Technique as Discovery," *HR,* I (1948),
67–87.

47. Cleanth Brooks, "Cantankerous and Other Critics," *KR,* VI, 283, 286; Brooks to Ransom, February 18, [1944], in *KR* Papers; Harold Whitehall, "Linguistic Patriot," *KR,* VIII,
156–60.

over, Bentley observes, "each magazine has the right to choose its own site and stick to it." He continues: "If *Partisan* . . . is to rid the word Journalism of its pejorative overtones, KR is to perform the same office for the word Academic." The function of the "'academic' magazine" is "to show that *all* the past is 'usable,'" Bentley argues, rather overemphasizing the *Kenyon's* interest in the past.[48]

Conspicuously absent from this presentation of excellent contributions by practical New Critics are Ransom and Rice. Although they often contributed to the book review section, their reviews are not so outstanding as to merit special attention. During the period under discussion, their main achievements were in the fields of aesthetics and philosophy, which will be dealt with later.[49]

The New York Intellectuals, Kenneth Burke

In these years, the New York intellectuals are not at all as prominently represented as they were during the earlier period and pale into insignificance beside the New Critics. Of the New York intellectuals, Lionel Trilling, the advisory editor, acquitted himself best. He, for instance, reviewed—and demolished—Theodor Reik's *Psychology of Sex Relations*. He also disagreed with Maxwell Geismar's main thesis in *Writers in Crisis*, that the function of the writer is to "provide the stipulated salvation of the moment." Although Ransom had initially credited only Kenneth Burke with the "necessary perspective" to handle both *Writers in Crisis* and two other books dealing with the same theme "coolly and ad[e]quately," Ransom was impressed with Trilling's treatment.[50]

48. Eric Bentley reviewed, for instance, Cleanth Brooks and Robert Heilman, *Understanding Drama*, in *KR*, VIII, 333–37; Hanns Sachs, *Freud, Master and Friend*, in *KR*, VII, 521; and Frank Lloyd Wright, *When Democracy Builds*, in *KR*, VIII, 160–63. Eric Bentley, "Editors in Person: Little Magazines," *KR*, IX, 280, 282, 284, 285.

49. From the autumn, 1942, issue to the autumn, 1948, issue, John Crowe Ransom reviewed eleven books—among them, Harry Levin, *James Joyce: A Critical Introduction*, in *KR*, IV, 430–32; Kenneth Patchen, *Memoirs of a Shy Pornographer*, in *KR*, VIII, 171; and Eudora Welty, *Delta Wedding*, in *KR*, VIII, 503–507. During this period, Philip Blair Rice reviewed eight books, including Muriel Rukeyser, *Willard Gibbs*, in *KR*, V, 310–12; and Vladimir Nabokov, *Nikolai Gogol*, in *KR*, VII, 355–56.

50. Lionel Trilling's review of *Psychology of Sex Relations* appeared in *KR*, VIII, 177–78. Lionel Trilling, "Artists and the 'Societal' Function," *KR*, IV, 425–30. In this review, he also discusses Philo Buck, Jr., *Directions in Contemporary Literature*, and N. Elizabeth Monroe, *The Novel and Society*. Ransom to Burke, June 28, 1942, in Burke Papers.

Trilling also reviewed the English translation of Denis de Rougemont's *La Parte du Diable*. But Charles Glenn Wallis had, in the
winter, 1944, issue, discussed the original so admirably that his review was included in *The Kenyon Critics*. And so Trilling's was redundant. (Ransom had eagerly published everything Wallis, "one of
the most brilliant of the young critics," ever submitted. Wallis died in
an accident in the spring of 1944.) Trilling "didn't quite like" his one
full-scale contribution during this period, a long review of *The Bitter
Box,* Eleanor Clark's first novel, which appeared in the autumn,
1946, issue. This piece is mainly remarkable in that in praising Clark
for dealing with the Communist party, "this subject that properly
should have attracted many novelists before," Trilling is, in effect,
praising himself: he was writing *The Middle of the Journey* (1947) at
that time. The main thesis of this review was worked out to perfection in his famous "Manners, Morals, and the Novel," which appeared about a year later in *The Kenyon Review;* here he describes the
ideal novel as "a perpetual quest for reality, the field of its research
being always the social world, the material of its analysis being always manners as the indication of the direction of man's soul."[51]

One of the few full-fledged articles by a writer whom Irving
Howe grouped with the New York intellectuals was John Berryman's
"F. Scott Fitzgerald." For some years, Fitzgerald had been buried
in oblivion and, as Ransom wrote Berryman, never had "had an
adequate highbrow treatment" anyway. So, on the occasion of the
publication of *The Crack-up* (1945), edited by Edmund Wilson,
Berryman undertook to rescue Fitzgerald from such an undeserved
fate. His discriminating essay heralded the Fitzgerald revival. In it
Berryman looks at Fitzgerald's background and argues that his living
among "the well-heeled infantile world of American popular writing," among "the formula boys," "cost him . . . the criticism that

51. Lionel Trilling, "A Derivative Devil," *KR,* VII, 497–502; Charles Glenn Wallis, "Satan and Denis de Rougemont," *KR,* VI, 150–56. Wallis also reviewed Isidore Ducasse
Lautréamont, *Les Chants de Maldoror,* trans. Guy Wernham, in *KR,* VI, 294–300; and Søren
Kierkegaard, *Either/Or,* in *KR,* VI, 464–69. Moreover, Wallis's article, "The Blood of a Poet,"
on Cocteau's film *Le Sang d'un Poète,* appeared in *KR,* VI, 24–42. "Contributors," *KR,* VI,
319; Lionel Trilling to Rice, April 25, 1947, in Rice Papers; Lionel Trilling, "The Life of the
Novel," *KR,* VIII, 659; Lionel Trilling, "Manners, Morals, and the Novel," *KR,* X, 17. Ini-
tially Trilling had wanted to call the latter essay "That Corpse Is Here Again" (Trilling to Rice,
April 25, 1947, in Rice Papers).

might have saved him," "his sense of reality," and "his faith in art."[52]

Philip Rahv reviewed relatively often for *The Kenyon Review.* His most controversial contribution appeared in the spring, 1944, issue and dealt with *Arrival and Departure* by Arthur Koestler. Ransom wholly disagreed with Rahv's exhortation to Koestler and his hero, a disillusioned political revolutionist, "to go on with the fight," and in his editorial "Artists, Soldiers, Positivists," stressed once again that propaganda is inimical to art. A collection of essays by Koestler, *The Yogi and the Commissar,* was the subject of the only review William Phillips, Rahv's fellow editor at *Partisan Review,* wrote for the *Kenyon.* In this review, Phillips shows up Koestler's "odd mixture of penetrating observation and glib generalization, of unusually perceptive writing and flashy, upper-case rhetoric."[53]

Koestler was the intellectuals' pet subject at that time. His *Insight and Outlook* was condemned by Isaac Rosenfeld in *Kenyon*'s spring, 1949, issue. Some of the radiance of *Partisan*'s "golden boy," as Irving Howe dubbed Rosenfeld, was reflected in the *Kenyon,* where he reviewed fairly often, too. Most important is Rosenfeld's treatment of Kenneth Burke's *A Grammar of Motives* in 1946. In this essay, which was included in *The Kenyon Critics,* Rosenfeld claims that *A Grammar of Motives* is "not a grammar at all, but a mixture of formal and material elements, comprising a metaphysics," and points out that metaphysics is particularly "ill-suited to the analysis of language." Burke's thought is "linguistic solipsism." Naturally, this angered Burke, who wrote to Allen Tate: "Ransom put me up to bat in Kenyon with two out, two strikes, and nobody on base (in giving the book to one of the stinks of the Phartisan, and a positivist)."[54]

Part of the final chapter of *A Grammar of Motives* entitled "The

52. Ransom to John Berryman, July 7, [1945], in Berryman Papers; John Berryman, "F. Scott Fitzgerald," *KR,* VIII, 110, 111.

53. Philip Rahv reviewed, for instance, Virginia Woolf's *The Death of a Moth* and books about her by E. M. Forster and David Daiches, in *KR,* V, 147–51; and F. O. Matthiessen, *Henry James: The Major Phase,* in *KR,* VII, 311–15. Philip Rahv, "Lost Illusions," *KR,* VI, 288–92, is on Arthur Koestler's *Arrival and Departure.* John Crowe Ransom, "Artists, Soldiers, Positivists," *KR,* VI, 278; William Phillips, "A Tract for the Time," *KR,* VII, 709.

54. Isaac Rosenfeld, "Aesthetics Without Experience," *KR,* XI, 321–25. Rosenfeld reviewed, for instance, Paul Goodman, *The Facts of Life,* in *KR,* VII, 709–12; and James T. Farrell, *The League of Frightened Philistines,* in *KR,* VII, 718–19. Irving Howe, *A Margin of Hope: An Intellectual Autobiography* (New York, 1982), 133; Isaac Rosenfeld, "Dry Watershed," *KR,* VIII, 315, 313; Burke to Tate, April 14, 1946, in Tate Papers.

Temporizing of Essence" had appeared in the autumn, 1945, issue of the *Kenyon*. Ransom had called this part "simply first-rate," "[c]lean and clear," and Burke's "books . . . evidence that no living critic has made steadier or further progress in the theory of literature." But added to Rosenfeld's offensive review in the *Kenyon* was the insult, as Burke saw it, of Ransom's unexpectedly condemnatory discussion of *A Grammar of Motives* in *The New Republic*. Here Ransom suddenly describes Burke's dialectic as cold, verbal manipulation. Moreover, he berates Burke for speaking disparagingly about "'scientism,'" and even speaks up for behaviorism.[55]

A long, involved correspondence followed. Burke, who in December, 1945, had written to Ransom that he was "delighted to learn that you intend inspecting the Grammar," was bitterly and furiously disappointed. Referring to Ransom's *New Republic* review, his own reaction, and Ransom's counterreply—both of which this weekly had promised to publish—Burke wrote: "You may manage in your letter to kick up a cloud of dust in the hopes of escaping before it settles. And you may succeed because, as you know, I will not have the opportunity to answer you publicly, unless you gallantly offer me the chance to do so in your own pages. . . . I am not asking for gentleness from anybody. I am asking only for a right to make my position clear, asking it of an opponent who has the space to offer me if he will. I won't get it." Ransom tried to conciliate Burke and asked *The New Republic* to return his own letter. In the end, however, *The New Republic* did not publish Burke's protest either, probably considering this controversy rather insignificant. Ransom then chivalrously offered to print a reply by Burke to Isaac Rosenfeld. But by that time, May, 1946, Burke had cooled down a bit and answered that he would "be happy, wholly happy, if you would merely give [Rosenfeld] [Charles] Morris' new book to review. Let him show how and why it is so good."[56]

Whether because not Rosenfeld but Rice eventually reviewed Morris' *Signs, Language and Behavior,* or because Ransom finally got

55. Kenneth Burke, "The Temporizing of Essence," *KR,* VII, 616–27; Ransom to Burke, May 29, 1945, in Burke Papers; "Contributors," *KR,* VII:4, n.p.; John Crowe Ransom, "Mr. Burke's Dialectic," *New Republic,* February 18, 1946, pp. 257–58.
56. Burke to Ransom, December 15, 1945, in KC Papers; Burke to Ransom, March 10, May 8, 1946, both in Burke Papers.

fed up with Burke's dictatorial, multipaged missives, or both, it was not until late 1948 that Ransom and Burke were on good terms again. After a long silence, Ransom wrote to Burke on August 25, 1948, "to propose that you keep a steady place on our list of contributors; not to have Burke is to argue ourselves out of the running; and personally you always exhilarate me and instruct me." By this mollifying letter, but even more by its enclosure, Ransom's admiring review of Burke's "The Imagery of Killing," Burke was wholly won over. Ransom had called his expository style, if cold, "a masterpiece of language" and suggested that "the kind of critic we need now is the synthesis of a Blackmur and a Burke." Burke then became a regular contributor to *The Kenyon Review* again.[57]

57. Philip Blair Rice, "The Semiotic of Charles Morris," *KR,* IX, 303–11; Ransom to Burke, August 25, 1948, in Burke Papers; Kenneth Burke, "The Imagery of Killing," *HR,* I (1948), 151–67; John Crowe Ransom, "The New Criticism," *KR,* X, 687.

4 Poetry, Fiction, and Other Interests

1942–1947

Other Critics, Philosophy, Politics

The Kenyon Review's main editorial line during its first decade was clearly represented by the New Critics, and the New York intellectuals played a supporting role. Of course, contributions from outside these critical circles also appeared, and, moreover, room was made for philosophy, creative writing, and the visual arts. The gifted Walter Southard, one of Ransom's protégés, published critical essays only during this period of the magazine's history. Southard's method is not the New Critical one. In his most important article, "The Religious Poetry of Robert Penn Warren," which appeared in the autumn, 1945, issue, Southard does not closely analyze Warren's poems: he quotes selectively and perspicaciously, and speculates about those themes of Warren's poems that interest him. And Southard's style is not the usual, formal *Kenyon Review* one: "Negro jazz is a real recovery, because it's a medium you can't kid yourself in . . . you've got to put out. Warren usually puts out." The final pages of his essay constitute a passionate plea for Agrarianism. His detecting an Agrarian ethos in *The Kenyon Review*, however, touched a raw nerve and led to Ransom's first public recantation of his Agrarian principles.[1]

One article and two book reviews published during this period

---

1. Walter Southard, "Speculation: I. The Religious Poetry of Robert Penn Warren," *KR*, VII, 655. In "Speculation: III. Art and the Human Economy," *KR*, VII, 683–88, John Crowe Ransom termed Agrarianism "a phantasy" and even "a heavy punishment." Walter Southard again took an Agrarian stand in "Escape to Reality," *KR*, VIII, 136–39.

were reprinted in *The Kenyon Critics* and consequently deserve brief mention. In the summer, 1947, issue, the young Irish critic Donat O'Donnell admirably discusses Evelyn Waugh's Catholicism, his snobbery, his adolescent cruelty, and his preoccupation with youth. Martin Lebowitz, one of Lionel Trilling's students, reviews Aldous Huxley's *Time Must Have a Stop* in the winter, 1945, number; Lebowitz points out that the amusing substance of the novel and its message are never properly integrated. Dudley Fitts argues that Robinson Jeffers' adaptation of Euripides' *Medea* "lacks insight and control" and that Jeffers is "in this poem incapable of tragic force."[2]

It is noteworthy that most of the articles by critics who do not fit into the New Critical or New York intellectual ranks are either about or written by French authors. "Three Portraits from Gide's Journal," for instance, selected, translated, and introduced by F. W. Dupee, and dealing with Paul Valéry, Paul Claudel, and Marcel Proust, appeared in the winter, 1944, issue. And in the spring issue of that same volume is Malcolm Cowley's translation of Gide's "An Introduction to Goethe's Theatre." This lead essay, in which Gide explains Goethe's key words *Entwicklung* and *Entsagung,* Ransom described to Cowley as "one of the very best things we have published." In the same letter Ransom asked Cowley to "let us have some other translation from the French. . . . I am convinced that there is a big field of interest there. I recall your talking about Valéry, for instance, and I wonder if you have tran[s]lated any of his recent things." But it was only at the end of Ransom's editorship that a Cowley translation of an article by Paul Valéry appeared.[3]

Soon after Valéry's death in 1945, Gide's classic funeral tribute to his friend appeared in *The Kenyon Review.* Ransom explained to his readers that Gide's "stature as a prose stylist leads us to break precedent and publish the present essay in the original [French]"; "Paul Valéry" was to remain the only article in a foreign language to appear in the *Kenyon.* Gide's moving memoir was accompanied, redun-

2. Conor Cruise O'Brien [Donat O'Donnell], "The Pieties of Evelyn Waugh," *KR*, IX, 400–11; Martin Lebowitz, "The Everlasting Mr. Huxley," *KR*, VII, 135–38; Dudley Fitts, "The Hellenism of Robinson Jeffers," *KR*, VIII, 682.

3. "Three Portraits from Gide's Journal," trans. F. W. Dupee, *KR*, VI, 91–100; André Gide, "An Introduction to Goethe's Theatre," trans. Malcolm Cowley, *KR*, VI, 161–79; Ransom to Malcolm Cowley, February 22, 1945, in Cowley Papers; Paul Valéry, "The Existence of Symbolism," trans. Malcolm Cowley, *KR*, XIX, 425–47.

dantly, by Jean Hytier's official funeral oration, which was translated by Jackson Mathews. Also in this issue Lawrence Leighton's rather rambling essay mainly shows that he himself is in favor of politically engaged writing: he can only honor Valéry as "the highest poet" after he has emphasized that Valéry was not as "remote from actuality" as is commonly assumed. Two years earlier, Edouard Roditi had also discussed Valéry's poetry and poetics, but without reference to Valéry's political engagement.[4]

The prolific French Catholic writer François Mauriac was discussed by Wallace Fowlie in the spring, 1943, issue. Fowlie assigned Mauriac "the first place of importance" among his generation, but only three years later, Jean Guiguet described Mauriac as a "[f]ormer great writer." Guiguet briefly discusses the postwar literary situation in France, paying special attention to existentialism and the growing interest in *la littérature engagée*. He also supplies an annotated bibliography of some twenty-five French reviews. In the same summer, 1946, issue, Adrienne Monnier, the first publisher of the French translation of James Joyce's *Ulysses,* gives "some of the essential summings-up of *Ulysses* by its French readers" and adds "a few personal views." Conspicuously clear and succinct, this appreciative essay found its place in *The Kenyon Critics.*[5]

These articles constitute only a small selection from the many critical essays dealing with French literature in the broadest sense that were published in the *Kenyon* during this period. It should be noted that Ransom had never felt much affinity for France, so Rice was responsible for the publication of most of them. Rice's six-month sojourn in Paris in the late 1920s had turned him into a Francophile, and, as he wrote to John Marshall in 1947, "French philosophy and French literature have continued to be among my chief sources of intellectual nourishment." Rice's letter to Marshall was in reply to the latter's asking him whether he was interested in going to France on a Rockefeller grant. Rice jumped at the chance, and spent September

4. André Gide, "Paul Valéry," *KR*, VIII, 277–90; "Contributors," *KR*, VIII, 346; Jean Hytier, "At Valéry's Funeral," trans. Jackson Mathews, *KR*, VIII, 274–76; Lawrence Leighton, "Valéry: La Poésie Engagée," *KR*, VIII, 295, 294; Edouard Roditi, "Paul Valéry: Poetics as an Exact Science," *KR*, VI, 398–408.

5. Wallace Fowlie, "François Mauriac," *KR*, V, 189; Jean Guiguet [Jean Isère], "Des Revues Françaises Après la Libération," *KR*, VIII, 510; Adrienne Monnier, "Joyce's *Ulysses* and the French Public," trans. Sylvia Beach, *KR*, VIII, 430.

till December, 1947, in that country; the very palpable consequences for the *Kenyon* of this second visit will be dealt with later.[6]

The high quality of the magazine during this period was only rarely marred by editorial mistakes. The two most prominent ones are John Rodell's "Maxwell Anderson: A Criticism," which appeared in the spring, 1943, issue, and D. S. Savage's "The Aestheticism of W. B. Yeats" in the winter, 1945, issue. Rodell does little more than harp on Anderson's not facing and solving the problems he poses, he who is "neither poet nor dramatist." Ransom thought that this article needed offsetting, and he promised the *Kenyon*'s readers more views on Anderson in the summer issue. He did not keep that promise, probably because the articles he had solicited were never actually submitted. The English poet and critic D. S. Savage dealt so sternly with Yeats that Ransom felt obliged to write a three-page editorial to temper Savage's severity. Contrary to custom, instead of being placed just before the book reviews toward the end of each issue, this editorial directly preceded Savage's essay, so that the reader would come upon Savage's strictures after Ransom's "protest against the attack upon a poet who seems to me more than any other to have recovered the old magnificence to the art in our bad time."[7]

Another serious editorial mistake of greater consequence was the introduction of short reviews. The editors' intention was to have a few regular reviewers such as Eric Bentley, Robert Lowell, and Robert Penn Warren send "a steady stream of 250 word reviews to the Kenyon Review." These very short reviews also had to be "equal in quality and authority to the longs."[8] Ransom and Rice had wanted to start this new feature in the 1943 winter issue, but in spite of their exertions hardly any shorts were submitted. So they decided to put the "Brief Comment"—or, as it was also called, "Brief Notices" or "Short Notices"—section off for a while. It was not until the spring, 1945, issue that the first short reviews were published. And it turned out that Ransom and Rice themselves, together with Arthur Mizener and Eric Bentley, had to write most of them. More important, it

6. Rice to John Marshall, March 4, 1947, in GF Papers.

7. John Rodell, "Maxwell Anderson: A Criticism," *KR*, V, 273; D. S. Savage, "The Aestheticism of W. B. Yeats," *KR*, VII, 118–34; John Crowe Ransom, "The Severity of Mr. Savage," *KR*, VII, 114.

8. Bentley to Arthur Mizener, July 25, [1945], Ransom to Arthur Mizener, August 11 [1945], both in Mizener Papers.

proved to be impossible to review other than journalistically in 250 words. This department was, therefore, dropped after five consecutive issues and was not taken up again until Robie Macauley became editor.

Failures too were the three planned special issues on Melville, on Symbolism, and on Faulkner, due not so much to editorial incompetence as to contributors' not producing the promised articles. "I wonder what you would think about our having a special exhibit of Melville pieces; and about your assuming editorial responsibility for it," Ransom wrote to Trilling in April, 1944. It is likely that Trilling refused to act as the guest editor; at any rate, the Melville feature never got beyond this embryonic stage. Much energy, however, was devoted to the other two issues by their guest editor Allen Tate. In September, 1943, Ransom had asked Tate to edit a special issue on the French Symbolist poets as well as to write an essay, preferably on Baudelaire. Ransom added that this issue was intended to please Henry Church, the *Mesures* editor, who by then had donated $1,250 to *The Kenyon Review*. Tate consented to guest edit the issue, but did not care to write on Baudelaire. He immediately sent off letters to, among others, T. S. Eliot, R. P. Blackmur, Delmore Schwartz, and Edmund Wilson. He explained that it seemed to him that the Symbolist movement was "about over" and that this was "a good chance to see it as a whole"; he also suggested to each of them a particular subject.[9]

Contrary to Tate's expectations, however, Blackmur had not been "pining away to write a big essay on Baudelaire"; he suggested Joseph Bennett instead and proposed Kenneth Burke on Rémy de Gourmont. Eliot simply wired Tate that he was too busy to write on Mallarmé. Edmund Wilson's rejection was downright rude: "It is difficult for me to think of anything that I should be less likely to write than an essay on the influence of Symbolist poetry. I will go even further and say that it seems to me absurd in the extreme for *The Kenyon Review* at this time of day to devote a special number to the subject. And I will even go on to explain that I would not write

9. Ransom to Lionel Trilling, April 11, 1944, in Thomas Daniel Young and George Core (eds.), *Selected Letters of John Crowe Ransom* (Baton Rouge, 1985), 314; Tate to Delmore Schwartz, September 23, 1943, in Tate Papers.

anything whatever at the request of *The Kenyon Review*. The dullness and sterility and pretentiousness of the *Kenyon*, under the editorship of Ransom, has really been a literary crime in this period when the market for serious work has been so limited." Delmore Schwartz wrote the only positive reply; he would "be delighted to write an essay for the Symbolist number," and proposed either to write on Joyce "as the logical conclusion to the movement" or to "use . . . Bowra's book, 'The Heritage of Symbolism.'" The correspondence between Tate and prospective contributors to the Symbolist issue dragged on, but the results were meager. Lawrence Leighton's reviews of C. M. Bowra and of two other Symbolist books are the only indications in the *Kenyon* that a Symbolist issue was ever considered.[10]

The proposed Faulkner issue, if it had succeeded according to plan, would have been a pioneering tribute to a writer who had not had nearly the critical recognition he deserved. Again, Ransom asked Tate—who had just had to give up the editorship of *The Sewanee Review* and now worked as an editor at Henry Holt—either to guest edit or to contribute an essay to this special issue. "Apparently F's *litterature* is not *engagee* enough for the New York critics," Ransom shrewdly remarked, "so that he is in the position of a prophet who will not be honored at home till the visible honors come from abroad." Ransom wanted to avoid parochialism, so he told Tate that he "wouldn't want too many Southerners to contribute" and greatly preferred an international tribute. Robert Penn Warren, who spent the summer of 1946 with the Ransoms in Gambier as a Fellow, was also very much involved in this project, which, indeed, had been partly his idea. On July 18, 1946, Warren wrote to Malcolm Cowley, whose *Portable Faulkner* had just come out, that *The Kenyon Review* intended to publish a Faulkner issue "as a kind of present for the gent's fiftieth birthday, which comes next year." He asked Cowley to contribute an essay, to suggest French and English critics, and, as

10. Tate to Blackmur, September 23, 1943, in Tate Papers; Edmund Wilson to Tate, September 28, 1943, in Edmund Wilson, *Letters on Literature and Politics 1912–1972,* ed. Elena Wilson (London, 1977), 399; Delmore Schwartz to Tate, September 29, 1943, in Tate Papers; Lawrence Leighton, "Criticism from Oxford," *KR,* VI, 146–50; Lawrence Leighton, "Roman Criticism and English Translation," a review of *Clowns and Angels* by Wallace Fowlie and *Coronal* by Paul Claudel, in *KR,* VI, 461–64.

Cowley knew Faulkner personally, to help procure a new Faulkner story "to lead off the issue."[11]

Meanwhile, Tate had written to Ransom that he was "all for the Faulkner number," but preferred to share the editorship with Warren, since he doubted his own "ability to do a good job." He was soon dissuaded, and hardly had he agreed to be the sole guest editor after all, when, at the end of August, Ransom sent him a letter packed with suggestions, which "were just that—you have the final decision at every point. We'll even splurge, spend money, as you require, in order to do . . . something of unusual distinction; though naturally I hope we can get out without shedding too much blood." Ransom suggested the following contributors:

For American writers who ought to be in the issue there are Red [Robert Penn Warren], Caroline [Gordon], Cowley, Katherine Anne Porter, [Francis] Fergusson, [William] Troy, and [F. O.] Matthiessen . . . all would be good. . . . Cowley we are pretty well committed to, and he has written about a piece he wants to do. . . . Then . . . there would need to be a biographical-bibliographical piece, for which you mentioned [Robert?] Daniel, and there is always Robert Stallman if we need him. . . .

   For French critics . . . Red and I both think there would be some advantage in getting either Camus or Sartre: though [Jean] Hytier is a more catholic critic and a very fine one. . . .

   For Italian critics there are [Elio] Vittorini (I think that's right) the novelist and translator of Faulkner, and also Mario Praz. . . . Incidentally, Auden might be considered as one of the English critics.[12]

Tate doubted that "Auden would write an article . . . for less than five hundred dollars," felt "some mild opposition to both Camus and Sartre who would certainly try to make an Existentialist party man out of Faulkner," and preferred Luigi Berti, "one of the editors of the excellent new magazine INVENTARIO," to the Italians Ransom had mentioned. But he was in general agreement with Ransom's suggestions and acted accordingly. Warren remained interested and in October proposed a few more names: Warren Beck, René Wellek, and Abram Fiskin, a Canadian instructor at Northwestern.[13]

   11. Ransom to Tate, July 17, [1946], in Tate Papers; Warren to Malcolm Cowley, July 18, 1946, in Cowley Papers.
   12. Tate to Ransom, July 22, August 30, 1946, Ransom to Tate, September 19, [1946], August 22, [1946], all in Tate Papers.
   13. Tate to Ransom, August 30, 1946, Warren to Tate, October 28, 1946, both in Tate Papers.

In spite of these combined efforts, not one of their ideas came to fruition, and Tate gave up. On September 12, 1947, Ransom concurred with Tate's "view that the Faulkner number is off; no use doing it with second rate critics." But he had not yet completely lost heart, having received a "very good" essay on Faulkner's technique by Lawrence Bowling. Accompanied by a new short story, a drawing, and a study of Faulkner's "poetic and philosophical attitudes" (preferably written by Tate), "a very good Faulkner *feature*" might yet be had, Ransom wrote. But not even a second letter in this vein could break down Tate's resistance: he had definitely washed his hands of the issue. Ransom tried to enlist Cowley's help once more. But to no avail. So, after two years of planning, the autumn, 1948, Faulkner feature came down to Bowling's essay and one Ransom had solicited from Richard Chase. Chase's essay, discussing the "symbolic texture" of *Light in August,* was reprinted in *The Kenyon Critics.*[14]

Ransom's interest in pedagogical effects had considerably waned after the 1940 symposium "Literature and the Professors." The almost immediate success of this symposium, and of Cleanth Brooks's and Robert Penn Warren's textbook *Understanding Poetry* (1938), may well account for this diminished interest. As early as February, 1942, Lionel Trilling noted "with satisfaction" that "although the archaeological and quasi-scientific and documentary study of literature is still the dominant one in our universities, it is clear to everyone that scholarship is on the defensive and is ready to share the rule with its antagonist." In this period of the magazine's history, we find no main articles on this topic, but only a few reviews—and a few shorts.[15]

Philosophy, on the other hand, remained very dear to both Ransom and Rice. So dear, in fact, that in 1944, Allen Tate told R. P. Blackmur that *The Kenyon Review* was "pretty dull and hopeless, most of the contributors being semi-philosophers whom John uses

14. Ransom to Tate, September 12, [1947], in Tate Papers; Lawrence Bowling, "Faulkner: Technique of *The Sound and The Fury,*" *KR,* X, 552–66; Richard Chase, "The Stone and the Crucifixion: Faulkner's *Light in August,*" *KR,* X, 539.

15. Lionel Trilling, "The Sense of the Past," *The Liberal Imagination: Essays on Literature and Society* (New York, 1950), 181; Horace Gregory, "Dr. Leavis' English School," *KR,* VI, 485–89, on Leavis' *Education and the University;* Lincoln Reis, "Pedagogue and Person," *KR,* VII, 487–90, on Barzun's *Teacher in America;* John Crowe Ransom, Review of José Ortega y Gasset's *Mission of the University,* in *KR,* VII, 524–25; John Crowe Ransom, Review of Fred B. Millett's *The Rebirth of Liberal Education,* in *KR,* VIII, 176–77.

every quarter as an excuse for one of his little homilies."[16] Tate had just become the editor of *The Sewanee Review* and was piqued that only the *Kenyon* had received a Rockefeller grant, so this remark should not be taken at face value.

The controversy about naturalism simmered on, and Ransom's editorials confirmed the earlier indications of his gradual acceptance of this philosophy. In the spring, 1943, editorial, "The Inorganic Muses," Ransom still calls himself "an objector" against the positivist-naturalist civilization he finds himself part of. Even so, he admits that "it has grown more and more upon me . . . to conceive human activities naturalistically." Sooner than Ransom himself, Tate it was who realized that his friend was close to embracing naturalism wholly. Tate was much upset by "The Inorganic Muses" and "let [Ransom] have it in the strongest terms." But Ransom was not to be moved. In his four-page reply to Tate's volley, he assured Tate that his editorial had been "thoroughly in tune" with *The World's Body,* and suggested that Tate's needless distress was based on Ransom's having "acquired a more flexible and accurate vocabulary."[17]

But Tate was proved right. Two years later, in his awkwardly titled editorial "Art Worries the Naturalists: Who in Turn Worry the Arts with Organism, Fusion, Funding," Ransom remarks that "[i]f there is anywhere a philosophy indigenous to our local climate, it is naturalism." Although he "used to regard naturalism as a specially malignant heresy, if not an abomination unto the Lord," Ransom now convicts it "at most of an immaturity." And by the time Ransom wrote about Aristotle in the "Reconsiderations" series, he had definitely become a naturalist. In this essay, Ransom traces his own development when he describes Aristotle, whose "theory of poetry when completed is my theory," as "a man of letters who had become a pedagogue, and . . . an idealist who had become a naturalist."[18]

Of course, Ransom was not the only one to write on naturalism

16. Tate to Blackmur, [early 1944], in Tate Papers.
17. John Crowe Ransom, "The Inorganic Muses," *KR,* V, 282, 284; Tate to Arthur Mizener, March 1, 1943, in Mizener Papers; Ransom to Tate, February 27, [1943], in Tate Papers.
18. John Crowe Ransom, "Art Worries the Naturalists: Who in Turn Worry the Arts with Organism, Fusion, Funding," *KR,* VII, 283; John Crowe Ransom, "The Literary Criticism of Aristotle," *KR,* X, 382; Ransom to John Palmer, August 24, [1948], in *SR* Papers.

and its subsumed philosophies pragmatism and positivism.[19] Nevertheless, in all, naturalism and related problems now were discussed less often and less heatedly than during the earlier period of the magazine's history. And once Ransom had, in his own mind, settled the controversy in favor of naturalism, the topic almost completely disappeared from the *Kenyon*'s pages.

Unlike Ransom, Rice did not need to write out his thoughts on this issue in order to clear his mind: he had always been, and remained, a convinced non-materialist naturalist. Rice's intense interest in France made him follow the development of existentialism both early and closely. Even before his trip to France at the end of 1947, Rice was the chief force behind the *Kenyon*'s publications about this movement. This is not to say that Rice ever enthusiastically advocated existentialism: he sympathized cautiously, with reservations. As in most matters of philosophy, Ransom followed suit slowly. Although he was initially wary of existentialism, he came to share Rice's open-mindedness toward it. True, unlike *Partisan Review,* the *Kenyon* hardly ever published the actual writings of French existentialists, but the *Kenyon* was one of the first American magazines to analyze the origins and principles of their philosophy.

Some attention was paid to existentialist philosophy as embedded in novels and plays, in essays and reviews by Eleanor Clark and Eric Bentley—but the *Kenyon*'s main interest was in explicit existentialist theories. There were two articles on Søren Kierkegaard, one of them written by Marjorie Grene. One of the few female critics in the *Kenyon,* Grene published two more expositions of existentialist philosophers, one on Heidegger and Sartre and one on Karl Jaspers and Gabriel Marcel. Since Grene was essentially critical of this movement, the editors would have done well to counterbalance her articles with a pro-existentialist view. But it was not until after Rice's sojourn in France that he took it upon himself to remedy this omission. In "L'Homme Est Une Passion Inutile," Grene criticizes Sartre for being too cold, too loveless, too nihilistic, and concludes: "If existen-

19. Eliseo Vivas, for instance, reviewed S. K. Langer, *Philosophy in a New Key,* in "On Symbolism," *KR,* V, 301–304; Philip Wheelwright acclaimed Werner Jaeger, *Paideia,* in "The Hellenic Ideal," *KR,* VIII, 154–58; and Sidney Hook admired Ernst Cassirer, *An Essay on Man,* in "Man and the Universe of Symbols," *KR,* VII, 335–38.

tialism suits us, it is as much our failure as existentialism's success."
For R. W. Flint, who regularly sent Ransom very welcome critiques,
and who had actively disliked Grene's essay on Kierkegaard, this was
the last straw. "Existentialism is not a synthetic philosophy of being;
it is a way of reviving an awareness of the essential difficulty of existence so that life may resume on a deeper level than heretofore," Flint
wrote, and accused Grene of being "vulgar" and "making a game out
of serious matters."[20]

Along with the articles for and against naturalism and existentialism, there are some incidental articles on aesthetics, the particular
branch of philosophy closest to Ransom's heart. But, of course, there
is a considerable overlap between the two. Ransom's laborious "The
Inorganic Muses," for instance, which Tate had attacked for its naturalism, was also the starting point for the poet Ruth Herschberger,
who took issue with Ransom's terms *structure* and *texture*. Her essay,
in turn, led to Ransom's summer, 1943, reply in which, ironically, he
accused Herschberger of selling poetry out to the positivists. In the
same issue, Ransom's theory of poetry as "the world's body," as
cognition, came under fire from Rice's philosopher-friend Virgil C.
Aldrich, who cleverly and convincingly differentiated between pictorial and cognitive aspects of (poetic) utterances. Next to these and
other articles on the aesthetics of language and literature, we also find
essays on the aesthetics of music, for instance by Arnold M. Walter
and George Hemphill, a Kenyon graduate. Helen Ransom Forman
remembers that her father was "enormously impressed" by Hemphill's article, which is not surprising, as Hemphill calls for a kind of
New Critical approach to music. Finally, in the spring, 1946, issue is
a comprehensive but not very convincing article on the past, present,
and future of the study of aesthetics by Stephen C. Pepper.[21]

20. Eleanor Clark, "Death of a Thinker: A Note on the French Novel 1925–1940," *KR*, III,
322–34; Eleanor Clark, "Existentialist Fiction," *KR*, VIII, 674–78; Eric Bentley, "Jean-Paul
Sartre, Dramatist," *KR*, VIII, 66–79; William G. O'Donnell, "Kierkegaard: I. The Literary
Manner," *KR*, IX, 35–47; Marjorie Grene, "Kierkegaard: II. The Philosophy," *KR*, IX,
48–69; Marjorie Grene, "L'Homme Est Une Passion Inutile: Sartre and Heidegger," *KR*,
IX, 185; Marjorie Grene, "Two More Existentialists: Karl Jaspers and Gabriel Marcel," *KR*, IX,
382–99; R. W. Flint to Ransom, [spring, 1947], in *KR* Papers.
21. Ransom, "The Inorganic Muses," 278–300; Ruth Herschberger, "The Structure of
Metaphor," *KR*, V, 433–43; John Crowe Ransom, "Positive and Near-Positive Aesthetics,"
KR, V, 443–47; Virgil C. Aldrich, "Pictorial Meaning and Picture Thinking," *KR*, V, 403–12;
Arnold M. Walter, "The Composer in Search of Freedom and Progress," *KR*, V, 100–13;

Pepper's essay was part of the "Post-War Stock-Taking" series initiated by Eric Bentley. Only four out of seven commissioned (and a larger number of planned) articles appeared in this series: Randall Jarrell, Walter Gropius, and Roger Sessions, the advisory editor on music, did not submit their promised articles on poetry, architecture, and music. The first contribution to this series of essays "taking stock of the human condition in various fields of activity in a postwar time" was by Bentley himself on his favorite subject, drama. In "The Drama at Ebb," Bentley remarks with great regret that "[t]oday it is almost inconceivable that any drama could satisfy the canons of the most exigent criticism and also be popular." But at the end of his long lament, Bentley neutralizes his own argument by standing up for the universally favored Bertolt Brecht, "young, definitely original . . . one . . . to keep your eye on." Taking stock of religion, in the autumn, 1946, issue, Horace L. Friess, a progressive professor of philosophy at Columbia and editor of *The Review of Religion,* points out that religious enlightenment "can be better served if sciences continually collaborate in trying to understand the significance of specific religious developments." After a one-year interruption, the series was concluded with a rather dull and vague article on political theory by Paul A. Palmer, teacher of political science at Kenyon College, who during these years wrote most of the sporadic papers on political issues in *The Kenyon Review.*[22]

The only political essay of consequence is Robert Foxx's solicited, searching "China Letter," which lovingly and poetically depicts the China scene. Foxx was the pseudonym of Walter Southard, who had left for China in 1945 as a naval intelligence officer, and who, of course, could not write under his own name for fear he would get "the bloodhounds" after him. "[I]n this sailorsuit I'm too easy game," Southard told Ransom, adding that he did not want to be paid for his contribution, that all he cared about was "to have somebody publish the truth about what is happening here, and best it should be you."

George Hemphill, "The Discourse of Music," *KR*, V, 413–32; interview with Helen and Elizabeth Forman, October 19, 1981; Stephen C. Pepper, "The Outlook for Aesthetics," *KR*, VIII, 179–87.

22. "We Announce," *KR*, VII:4, n.p.; Eric Bentley, "The Drama at Ebb," *KR*, VII, 174, 184; Horace L. Friess, "The Importance of Religion," *KR*, VIII, 630; Paul A. Palmer, "On the Agenda of Political Theory," *KR*, IX, 552–62.

William Carlos Williams' reaction to Southard's timely "China Letter" is representative of the enthusiasm with which it was received:

Who is this person, Robert Foxx, of whom you say next to nothing in your "Contributors" notes? . . . I am floored by the quality and the revelations of his writing. . . . Everything I know about prose, especially everything I know as rare and superlatively worth while about prose is at least indicated somewhere in this piece of work and most of it is shown in full. Add to this the critical quality of the thing in a connotative manner, it's a scythe in the grass of ordinary writing. . . . [I]t roars with an authority of expression nowhere forced but of that convincing finality of statement which leaves the mind satisfied and at rest after it: nothing more to be said.[23]

Publishers swarmed around Southard: Pelligrini & Cudahy, the Pilot Press, and Henry Holt were eager to publish this letter together with two promised ones on the Chinese people and the current head-on collision of the Chinese, American, and Russian world views in China. But this was not to be: China had taken so much out of Southard, mentally and physically, that he had to return to America to recuperate.

With the exception of a few reviews, the subject of the war was infrequently broached. Some stir was caused by Ransom's own "Artists, Soldiers, Positivists," which appeared in the spring, 1944, issue. Ransom quoted a letter sent by a soldier who found "the poetry in *Kenyon Review* lamentable in many ways because it is cut off from pain," and who called for a poetry promising "survival" and communicating "an overwhelming desire to go on." Ransom evaded answering this soldier's questions about the importance and usefulness of art in war and discussed the state of the arts in peacetime, complaining that even then "the arts are often held to account as if in war."[24]

Poetry and Fiction

The soldier, who remains unnamed, had attacked Wallace Stevens because he, though of "charming distemper," did not transcend "the

23. Walter Southard [Robert Foxx], "China Letter," *KR*, IX, 113–33; Walter Southard to Ransom, October 8, 1946, William Carlos Williams to Ransom, January 3, 1947, both in *KR* Papers.
24. The war is further mentioned in, for instance, C. G. Wallis, "Satan and Denis de Rougemont," *KR*, VI, 150–56; and Andreas Dorpalen, "Towards a Better World," *KR*, VI, 308–12. John Crowe Ransom, "Artists, Soldiers, Positivists," *KR*, VI, 276, 277.

aesthetic of poetry." Replying to Ransom's request for poetry—"I'd rather have you than anybody"—Stevens wrote that he had been "particularly interested" in the soldier's letter "about the relation between poetry and what he called pain." He was not quite sure what the soldier had meant by that, but thought that "it might be interesting to try to do an esthétique du mal. It is the kind of idea that it is difficult to shake off. Perhaps that would be my subject in one form or another." So, the soldier's dissatisfaction was the direct impulse to what Randall Jarrell called "the best of [Stevens'] later poems," "Esthétique du Mal," which appeared as the lead of the autumn, 1944, issue of *The Kenyon Review.* Ransom, too, thought it "truly magnificent." He wrote to Stevens that as "a sort of trustee of the interests of this Review," he could not "pass up" his generous offer to waive payment for the poem. "But we would have paid double or triple for it if we had had to, and thought it sound business." [25]

It may seem as if Ransom had decided to give the soldier no more cause for complaint, for in contrast to the nearly complete disregard of World War II in the *Kenyon's* critical department, many of the poems that appeared from about the summer of 1944 onwards dealt with the war. This was not so much a result of a conscious shift in editorial policy, as of the many excellent unsolicited war poems that now crowded the *Kenyon's* mailbox. And truly creative non-propagandist writing dealing with the war had never met editorial objections. It was only that Ransom, his personal involvement and earlier rash resolutions "to pitch into the world crisis" notwithstanding, basically wanted the *Kenyon* to remain a literary and not a political review. Randall Jarrell submitted his war poems "The Germans Are Lunatics" and "Losses," both of which were accepted and appeared in the summer, 1945, installment of the "Younger Poets" series. Samuel French Morse also contributed two war poems to this installment, to which were added poems by Reed Whittemore and David Cornel DeJong. Ransom's editorial intentions with respect to poetry are reflected in his comment about this collection: "It may not

25. Ransom, "Artists, Soldiers, Positivists," 276; Ransom to Wallace Stevens, June 15, 1944, in Young and Core (eds.), *Selected Letters of John Crowe Ransom,* 316; Wallace Stevens to Ransom, June 17, 1944, in Holly Stevens (ed.), *Letters of Wallace Stevens* (London, 1966), 468; Wallace Stevens, "Esthétique du Mal," *KR,* VI, 489–503; Randall Jarrell, "Reflections on Wallace Stevens," *Poetry and the Age* (New York, 1953), 126; Ransom to Wallace Stevens, August 18, 1944, in Young and Core (eds.), *Selected Letters of John Crowe Ransom,* 317.

be immortal verse but it's live and I'd rather have it than poor stuff by the big names." But even though Ransom preferred fostering future "big names," he was not prepared to pass up good poetry by contemporary bigwigs and accepted, for instance, Mark Van Doren's "extremely fine" war poem "April, 1942."[26]

Randall Jarrell was the *Kenyon's* most frequently published poet during this period: he appeared at least once a year, usually with a small group of poems. The *Kenyon's* hospitality and confidence were mainly instrumental in gaining for Jarrell high stature as a poet by the end of the 1940s. Particularly impressive was his "The Rising Sun," another of his moving, unsentimental, sophisticated war poems, which appeared in the spring, 1947, issue. Its subject matter is unusual and complex: the protagonist is a Japanese boy who has to learn how to fight and die according to his country's traditions. Another young poet the editors cherished was Jarrell's Kenyon College companion Robert Lowell. After Lowell's first appearance in the *Kenyon's* maiden issue, Ransom had refused his submissions for four years, but then found Lowell ready for a further unfolding of his gifts in the magazine. Lowell repeatedly appeared in the "Younger Poets" series, but in the autumn, 1946, issue, three of Lowell's poems were especially honored—they were published as a separate group. "Mary Winslow," "At a Bible House," and "The First Sunday in Lent" were reprinted in Lowell's second book of verse, *Lord Weary's Castle* (1946). The volume received the Pulitzer Prize in poetry and placed him among the "few excellent contemporary poets America has produced," as Howard Moss pointed out in his *Kenyon* review of this book. Ransom could not agree more. As early as October, 1945, he had observed the remarkable development of Lowell's poetry since *Land of Unlikeness* (1944): "I don't know who has grown up in verse more than you, these last few years; mostly, I think by way of giving

26. As for Ransom's personal involvement, his son Reavill served in the war, and he tried to persuade his daughter Helen to become a WAC (Interview with Helen and Elizabeth Forman, October 19, 1981). Ransom to Burke, January 4, 1941, in Burke Papers; Randall Jarrell, "The Germans Are Lunatics" and "Losses," *KR*, VII, 442–43; Samuel French Morse, "Soldier Sewing on Chevrons" and "Another Soldier, . . . From the Aleutians," *KR*, VII, 443–46; Reed Whittemore, "Home Abroad," "On the Death of Someone Close," "This Is It," and "Hester Prynne," *KR*, VII, 447–49; David Cornel DeJong, "State of Soul in Grand Rapids" and "Sentimental Theme," *KR*, VII, 454–55; Ransom to Arthur Mizener, May 14, [1945], in Mizener Papers; Mark Van Doren, "April, 1942," *KR*, V, 182–84; Delmore Schwartz to Mark Van Doren, April 8, 1943, in Van Doren Papers.

up the effort to communicate more than was communicable, and by consulting the gentle reader's traditional range of intelligence rather than your own private article."[27]

Another poet who had an early chance in the "Younger Poets" series and who rose to independent publication during this period was Jean Garrigue. Ransom grew to appreciate her poems so highly that soon he "could not forbear inserting two of yours in order to improve the general impression [of the winter, 1944, "Younger Poets" section]." In this particular case, however, the "Younger Poets" installment, which included Jarrell's "The Carnegie Library, Juvenile Division" and Muriel Rukeyser's excellent "Dream-singing Elegy," needed no strengthening. The publication of Garrigue's longish poem "False Country of the Zoo," though, deservedly constituted her solo appearance in the autumn, 1946, issue: less complicated and more concrete than her former poems, it is her finest achievement in *The Kenyon Review* during this period. Josephine Miles, whom Ransom had called "a sister of Laura Riding," remained a favorite, too. The summer, 1944, and the autumn, 1947, issues contained altogether fifteen of her very short sophisticated poems.[28]

Although both Delmore Schwartz and Karl Shapiro appeared only once, their contributions were highlights in the *Kenyon*'s history. Schwartz's biographer James Atlas regards the often anthologized "The Starlight's Intuitions Pierced the Twelve" as "Delmore's most accomplished poem since the work collected in *In Dreams [Begin Responsibilities* (1938)]." It remained Schwartz's own favorite poem—"the best lyric I've written"—till the end of his life. As for Shapiro's "Essay on Rime," when Ransom saw a small part of this long poem, he found it so "th[o]roughly up to my expectations" that he suggested to the author that the *Kenyon* publish "twice or three times the

27. Randall Jarrell, "The Rising Sun," *KR*, IX, 260–61; Robert Lowell, "Mary Winslow," "At a Bible House," and "The First Sunday in Lent," *KR*, VIII, 613–16; Howard Moss, "Ten Poets," *KR*, IX, 294; Ransom to Robert Lowell, October 5, [1945], in Lowell Papers.

28. Ransom to Jean Garrigue, November 3, 1943, in *KR* Papers; Jean Garrigue, "Conjectural Domain" and "Discourse," *KR*, VI, 66–68; Jean Garrigue, Review of Robert Penn Warren, *At Heaven's Gate*, in *KR*, VI, 135–38; Randall Jarrell, "The Carnegie Library, Juvenile Division," *KR*, VI, 64–65; Muriel Rukeyser, "The Dream-singing Elegy," *KR*, VI, 59–63; Jean Garrigue, "False Country of the Zoo," *KR*, VIII, 567–69; Ransom to Josephine Miles, March 30, 1940, in *KR* Papers; Josephine Miles, "Sonata from Above," "Confidence," "Funeral," "Nosce Te Ipsum," "None," "The Disturbed," "Look," and "Midwatcher," *KR*, VI, 394–97; Josephine Miles, "Aboriginal," "Kind," "Expectation," "An Apprehension," "Riddle," "Countenance," and "Yield," *KR*, IX, 569–73.

number of lines you have sent us, provided of course that they all make a single unit or series of units, as do those of 'Personal Systems.'"[29]

At long last, in the spring, 1943, issue, Allen Tate appeared again with "Jubilo" and "More Sonnets at Christmas"—additions to "Sonnets at Christmas" (1934). The absence of Tate from his friend's magazine was definitely not due to Ransom's reluctance to publish him, or to Tate's reluctance to be published there. But these poems were the first ones Tate had written "off the top of his mind in six years." Tate had given Ransom first refusal even though his meters would surely "drive him wild": Tate thought Ransom had "become a perfect neo-classicist and will have nothing to do with accentual versification." Tate had submitted these poems too late for inclusion in the Christmas issue, but Ransom was so taken with them that he was "not being diverted too much by the seasonal title," and accepted them for the spring. If Tate insisted on early publication, however, Ransom wrote to him, he would "get them off at once" to *The Nation, The New Republic,* or "anywhere you say." But, Ransom emphasized, "I don't like to get them out of sight." Tate was thrilled by Ransom's enthusiasm and vastly preferred publication in the *Kenyon.*[30]

Tate's classic "Seasons of the Soul" made an even deeper impression. Ransom thought it Tate's "best yet with the possible exception of Confederate Dead" and called it "mighty fine," about the highest praise to be found in his vocabulary. He remarked on its "perfection," "cleanness," and its "finished" quality. The only thing he did not like was Tate's title "Seasonal Confessions"; he therefore suggested "something bigger, statelier," like "The Soul Amidst the Ele-

29. Delmore Schwartz, "The Starlight's Intuitions Pierced the Twelve," *KR,* VI, 383–85. This poem appeared in the not very successful *Vaudeville for a Princess* (New York, 1950) under the title "Starlight Like Intuition Pierced the Twelve." James Atlas, *Delmore Schwartz: The Life of an American Poet* (New York, 1977), 291; Delmore Schwartz to Ransom, December 10, 1954, in Robert Phillips (ed.), *Letters of Delmore Schwartz* (Princeton, 1984), 296; Karl Shapiro, "Essay on Rime: Confusion of Personal Systems (From Part III)," *KR,* VII, 378–81; Ransom to Karl Shapiro, April 14, 1945, in *KR* Papers. It is not clear from the correspondence whether the 121 lines that were eventually published constitute Shapiro's first or a second, extended submission.

30. Allen Tate, "Jubilo" and "More Sonnets at Christmas (Ten Years Later)," *KR,* V, 184–88; Tate to Arthur Mizener, February 5, 1943, in Mizener Papers. Tate is exaggerating his period of poetic aridity, though: his "Trout Map," for instance, had appeared in *KR,* I, 404–405. Tate to Donald Davidson, February 3, 1943, in Davidson Papers; Ransom to Tate, December 10, [1942], in Tate Papers.

mental Seasons," or "Annus Miserabilis." Ransom soon decided that
these were not simple enough and he came up with, among others,
"The Soul to the Seasons," all but the eventual title. He told Tate that
this poem "ought to lead off" the winter, 1944, number, that "the
other poetry look[ed] slight and tame . . . after yours," and would
therefore "be lumped together." Indeed, "Seasons of the Soul" stands
head and shoulders above Jean Garrigue's "Conjectural Domain" and
"Discourse" and, too, above Jarrell's "The Carnegie Library, Juvenile
Division." It led Robert Penn Warren to write to Tate: "You've never
done better, nor has anybody else writing today." Wallace Stevens
was one of the few competent readers to voice dissatisfaction with
"Seasons of the Soul": he pointed out that it was "like poetry written
under glass," adding, though, that the poem "doesn't in the least im-
pair one's sense of Tate's power." [31]

So during this period *The Kenyon Review* published the best poems
by some of America's best poets—Stevens, Tate, Jarrell—as well as
excellent work by poets who would soon find wide recognition:
Lowell, Shapiro, and Miles. Add to this the publication of promising
poets such as John Malcolm Brinnin, Jean Garrigue, and Marguerite
Young, as well as the sporadic translations of important foreign poets
such as Louis Aragon and Bertolt Brecht, and the conclusion is clear.
Even if it has had little critical attention, the *Kenyon's* poetry section
was well matched with its famous critical department. [32]

It was inevitable that some poets who belonged to the Ransom-
Kenyon circle were published elsewhere. Robert Penn Warren's famous "Ballad of Billie Potts," for instance, appeared in the winter,
1944, issue of *Partisan Review*. There is some evidence that Warren
submitted this poem to the *Kenyon*, and Ransom turned it down because of its naturalism. More to Ransom's discredit is his rejection of

31. Ransom to Warren, July 7, 1943, in Young and Core (eds.), *Selected Letters of John Crowe Ransom*, 311; Ransom to Tate, September 21, [1943], November 1, [1943], both in Tate Papers; Allen Tate, "Seasons of the Soul," *KR*, VI, 1–9. The dates on the November letters to Tate and to Garrigue suggest that only after Ransom had decided to publish "Seasons of the Soul" separately did he resolve to include Garrigue's poems in the poetry section. Warren to Tate, April 2, 1945, in Tate Papers; Wallace Stevens to Henry Church, January 21, 1944, in Holly Stevens (ed.), *Letters of Wallace Stevens*, 461.
32. For instance: John Malcolm Brinnin, "With a Posthumous Medal" and "Gunnery Practice," *KR*, VI, 198–99; Marguerite Young, "Of Deed, Love, Death," *KR*, VII, 69–70; Louis Aragon, "Lancelot," trans. Sally Wood, *KR*, VIII, 238–41; Bertolt Brecht, "Poems of Exile," trans. H. R. Hays, *KR*, VII, 198–207.

Robert Duncan's "Sections toward an African Elegy." Initially, Ransom had accepted this "very brilliant" poem, intending it to lead off the 1945 winter issue. However, after Ransom had read Duncan's article "The Homosexual in Society" in Dwight Macdonald's *Politics,* the poem suddenly seemed "to have an obvious homosexual advertisement, and for that reason not to be eligible for publication." Duncan pointed out to Ransom that "once the aesthetic choice had been made," an editor is morally obliged to accept a poem "regardless of its agreement or opposition to one's own convictions." Although this was an article of Ransom's editorial faith, he nevertheless returned Duncan's poem because of its homosexual overtones, with his "deepest apologies."[33] Finally, two other promising poets who had been given a chance during the *Kenyon* trial period, Howard Nemerov and John Berryman, now were not published either, for the simple reason that Ransom did not think their present poems merited publication.

However, the *Kenyon* recognized Berryman's talent for fiction and published two of his short stories. This was thanks mainly to Rice and Robert Penn Warren, on whose judgment with regard to fiction Ransom strongly depended. Anyway, Ransom's "considered determination . . . to strive for a greater warmth in the content . . . [which] would take the form of giving more space to creative work" bore fruit. During the first three and a half years of the *Kenyon's* existence, only four stories were published; from the demise of *The Southern Review* up to 1947, the amount of space devoted to fiction increased sevenfold: over forty stories appeared. And the increase in quantity was not at the expense of quality. Paul Robert Stewart, chronicler of *Prairie Schooner,* remarked that this little magazine,

33. In *The Achievement of Robert Penn Warren* (Baton Rouge, 1981), 335, James H. Justus mistakenly assumes that "The Ballad of Billie Potts" was published in the 1944 *Kenyon.* The "Ballad" appeared in *PR,* XI (1944), 56–70. In "The Inklings of 'Original Sin,'" *SRL,* May 20, 1944, pp. 10–11, John Crowe Ransom remarks that Warren's poetry is superior to his fiction, which is too "naturalistic." He adds that this same naturalism mars "Billie Potts." Ransom to Robert Duncan, October 26, 1944, in Duncan Papers; Robert Duncan, "The Homosexual in Society," *Politics,* I (1944), 209–11; Robert Duncan to Ransom, n.d. [draft], Ransom to Duncan, December 6, 1944, both in Duncan Papers. In Jack R. Cohn and Thomas J. O'Donnell, "An Interview with Robert Duncan," *Contemporary Literature,* XXI (1980), 524, Duncan refers to this incident. Twelve years later, Ransom had forgotten all about this and returned some of Duncan's poems with the note that though they seemed "a little heavy, a little contrived," Duncan was a "good prospect." Ransom to Duncan, August 14, 1957, in Duncan Papers. Robert Duncan never published poetry in the *Kenyon.*

which was best known for its fiction, "was shaded . . . in the '40's by *Story,* the *Kenyon Review,* and the *Partisan Review.*"[34]

Yet, even more than with its poetry, the bold fighting spirit of the *Kenyon*'s criticism obscured its very real achievement in fiction, namely, its introducing unknown writers of merit to publisher and public. But if the *Kenyon*'s competent and finished fiction cut a fine figure in comparison to that of other little—and not so little—magazines, technically it was not very innovative or spectacular. The reason was that such stories were not to Ransom's liking. "A story has to have a *meaning,* I believe—unless it's for the New Yorker," he wrote in 1953. His preference for traditional forms is also illustrated in his rejection of three stories solicited from William Carlos Williams. "The stories you sent us I admire very much in their method—absolutely clean, stripped and adequate," Ransom explained, "but I don't think they are stories, but rather episodes or anecdotes, if there is such a distinction."[35] It was the absence of plot that he objected to. Still, Ransom's lack of understanding of experimental fiction was not really damaging: the majority of submitted stories were traditional anyway—and he had Rice and Warren to advise him.

The "greater warmth in the content," which was to result from more fiction in *The Kenyon Review,* did not come about effortlessly. For one thing, it was necessary to spread the word that the *Kenyon* was now in the market for creative as well as for critical writing; for another, the editors did "not wish to sacrifice too much of our critical staple in order to publish creative work more fully" and therefore had to "increase the size of the periodical as a standard thing." It was Rice who solved both mainly pecuniary problems with one blow. He made a deal with the New York publisher Doubleday, Doran, and Company, whereby, beginning with the winter, 1944, issue, as Ransom told Tate, "each year for three years we hold a SS [short story] contest for $750.00 of prizes, which they pay, and whereby also we receive $500.00 worth of annual advertising by DD in KR." In return, the *Kenyon* happily committed itself to judge the manuscripts, "fix the number and value of the prizes . . . and publish the

34. Ransom to Chalmers, November 24, 1943, in *KR* Papers; Paul Robert Stewart, *The Prairie Schooner Story: A Little Magazine's First 25 Years* (Lincoln, Neb., 1955), 169.
35. Ransom to Priscilla Heath, December 19, 1953, Ransom to William Carlos Williams, June 3, 1941, both in *KR* Papers.

prize stories." Only authors who had never published a book of fiction were eligible, and Doubleday, Doran acquired the exclusive "privilege of reading in advance of publication any manuscript . . . submitted for the contest." [36]

So *The Kenyon Review* came to be "very much in the SS game"— so much so, the announcement of "The 1944 Short Story Prizes" in the winter issue brought an avalanche of over eleven hundred manuscripts between April and June. Ransom, Robert Penn Warren, who visited Gambier during the first week of June, and Harold Whitehall, the Rockefeller Fellow at that time, judged these entries and "arrived at some pretty fine ones though not world classics." The first prize went to Jean Garrigue. "Robert Penn Warren was particularly enthusiastic about your story," Ransom told Garrigue, "though hardly more than the other two of us": it had been a "unanimous" decision. Nevertheless, Ransom suggested some revisions and, off his own bat, substituted "The Snowfall" for Garrigue's proposed titles "The Dead" and "Choice of Loss." Garrigue gladly acquiesced, set to work, made many minor revisions, and even completely altered the conclusion, which Ransom had disliked. Ransom, however, "went into a huddle over the revised story": many of the revisions were much too "'literary,'" the new conclusion was "just naturalism." Whitehall agreed that the original story was better, and the first version went to the printer. "The Snowfall," a story about a woman painter who is loved by several men, and falls in love with the most superficial, egotistical of them all, is indeed rich, poetic, and perhaps even "Jamesean" (as Ransom had it), yet technically it is rather conventional. [37]

Subtle, southern, competent, but also conventional was the second-prize story, "A Piece of Bread" by Frances Gray Patton, another promising newcomer to the field of fiction. John Berryman's partly autobiographical entry "The Lovers," which appeared in the winter, 1945, issue, was as finished as both prize-winning stories, but more moving and involved without becoming sentimental. In a letter almost begging Berryman to participate again in the 1945 contest,

36. Ransom to Chalmers, November 24, 1943, in *KR* Papers; Ransom to Tate, November 22, [1943], in Tate Papers; Chalmers to Doubleday, Doran, and Company, Inc., December 4, 1943, in KC Papers.

37. Ransom to Tate, November 22, [1943], June 9, [1944], both in Tate Papers; Ransom to Jean Garrigue, June 15, August 17, July 5, 1944, all in Garrigue Papers; Jean Garrigue, "The Snowfall," *KR*, VI, 505–30.

Ransom admitted that "[s]ome people have said that *your* story . . . was better than our Prize 1944 story. Maybe it was." Berryman's "The Imaginary Jew" deservedly won first prize in 1945. Initially, though, the prize went to an author who, as it turned out, had already published a book of fiction and consequently had to be disqualified. Annoyed, the editors sent out a circular letter on May 12, 1945, in which they announced that after reading the six hundred entries, they were "not satisfied as to having two stories of sufficient distinction to secure the prizes."[38] With the consent of Doubleday, Doran, they therefore decided to hold the contest open, for new entrants only, for three more months.

Mona Van Duyn, whom Ransom had informed that her sensitive story about a young girl who is introduced to sin and sex had won second prize on May 7, 1945, received this form letter, too. In a covering note, Ransom hastened to assure her that her award was "in no way imperilled," and that she even might win first prize if no "bigger" stories came in. But Berryman's affecting story, sent in in the second round, based on a street brawl that had badly shaken him four years earlier (and that he had unsuccessfully tried to render in poetry at that time) won hands down. "The Imaginary Jew" deals with a Catholic who protests against a half-drunk Irishman's fascist pronouncements. In spite of the protagonist's vehement if clumsy denials, he is taken for a Jew, jeered at and hunted down. Only much later does he realize: "My prosecutors were right: I was a Jew. The imaginary Jew I was was as real as the imaginary Jew hunted down, on other nights and days, in a real Jew." Erich Kahler, a Jewish refugee, was so moved by this story that he translated it for *Die Neue Rundschau*: this marked Berryman's first appearance abroad. In her memoir *Poets in their Youth*, Eileen Simpson, Berryman's first wife, mentions that others who were as impressed also urged Berryman to continue writing stories, but that Berryman felt that his talent was for poetry, not for fiction. So, "The Imaginary Jew," "The Lovers," and a late story, "Thursday Out," were the only stories published during Berryman's lifetime.[39]

The 1946 Short Story Prize Contest ended in a tie between "You

38. Frances Gray Patton, "A Piece of Bread," *KR*, VI, 531–41; John Berryman, "The Lovers," *KR*, VII, 1–11; Ransom to John Berryman, May 12, 1945, in Berryman Papers; circular letter by the editors of *The Kenyon Review*, May 12, 1945, in Van Duyn Papers.
39. Ransom to Mona Van Duyn, May 23, 1945, in Van Duyn Papers; Mona Van Duyn, "The Bell," *KR*, VII, 598–615; John Berryman, "The Imaginary Jew," *KR*, VII, 539; Eileen

Can Wreck It," a story about double morals and racial discrimination in a "liberal" town by Walter Elder, a Kenyon graduate studying philosophy at Harvard, and Arthur Mizener's too academic, too Fitzgeraldian "You Never Go Back to Sleep." Ransom wrote to Mizener that the judges—Ransom, Rice, and Robert Penn Warren— "thought one story (yours) excelled in form and quality of style. . . . The other story does not excel in that way . . . and rather is a powerful story on the prime (maybe primitive) human level; it excels in the appeal of the content, we think. And for a prize story we don't want to put one of these requirements above the other." Both stories had to be substantially revised. Elder simply "followed Red's suggestions to the letter," but Mizener struggled with Ransom's foolish advice to introduce plot and external action into a story that showed a young man's awakening to the reality of an adored, formerly legendary writer. (Of course, the parallel with Mizener and Fitzgerald leaps to mind.) In the end, the published version of Mizener's story was only slightly different from the original one.[40]

Walter Elder's and Arthur Mizener's prize-winning stories marked the end of the Doubleday, Doran deal, which Ransom, for reasons unknown, was "loath to renew." His attempts to interest Henry Holt and the Cleveland World Publishing Company in a similar arrangement failed. Although the loss of a sponsor was unfortunate, the editors decided to continue to publish at least one story per year. And since the short-story contest had definitely called attention to *The Kenyon Review* as a market for fiction, droves of unsolicited stories kept coming in.[41]

Looking at the fiction the *Kenyon* published during this period, we find that the magazine does well. Stories by southern writers, such as Andrew Lytle's long, mysterious "Alchemy" and Peter Taylor's subtle, impressive "Allegiance," appeared side by side with Boris Pasternak's early "Aerial Ways" and Mary Lavin's "A Wet Day"; the latter two stories were included by Robie Macauley in his *Kenyon Re-*

Simpson, *Poets in their Youth* (New York, 1982), 106. "Thursday Out" was written in 1958 and published in Saul Bellow's short-lived journal *The Noble Savage* in the spring of 1961.

40. Walter Elder, "You Can Wreck It," *KR*, VIII, 571–92; Arthur Mizener, "You Never Go Back to Sleep," *KR*, VIII, 593–612; Ransom to Arthur Mizener, July 2, [1946], in Mizener Papers; Walter Elder to Ransom, November 8, [1946], in *KR* Papers.

41. Ransom to Tate, August 2, [1946], in Tate Papers.

view anthology, *Gallery of Modern Fiction* (1966). Women were not as badly represented in the *Kenyon*'s creative departments as in its critical and philosophic sections. Over one-third of the stories published during this period were written by women.[42]

It is thus apparent that the widespread belief that southern writers dominated the *Kenyon*'s fiction department is at least partly untrue. New York intellectual fictionists alone appeared nearly as frequently as did their southern colleagues. Isaac Rosenfeld, for instance, had as many as three stories published. Ransom preferred the extremely clever "The Party," which he described as "a gentle but satirical and delicious account of the human insides of a Communist local" by "our very good man Isaac Rosenfeld," to part of Katherine Anne Porter's novel in the making, *Ship of Fools* (1962), as well as to Arthur Mizener's "Discard," as the autumn, 1947, fiction selection. Delmore Schwartz's attempt to come at least to fictional terms with anti-Semitism is expressed in "A Bitter Farce," "the only thing [he had] brought to a successful conclusion in almost a year of trying." It appeared in the spring, 1946, issue. Ransom admired its "true tone" and "the casual development of the very real topics." Although Elaine Gottlieb did not belong to the New York intellectuals proper, she was a New York–based Jewish writer who contributed two stories.[43] These and other nonsoutherners, such as Jean Stafford, Sidney Sulkin, Meridel Le Sueur, and David Cornel DeJong, made up the varied roster of mostly young, technically proficient fiction writers in *The Kenyon Review*.

Drama and the Fine Arts

An entirely new venture in creative writing was the publication in the *Kenyon* of "The Key," a short tragedy by Spanish refugee Ramón

42. Andrew Lytle, "Alchemy," *KR*, IV, 273–327; Peter Taylor, "Allegiance," *KR*, IX, 188–200; Boris Pasternak, "Aerial Ways," trans. Robert Payne, *KR*, VIII, 463–76; Mary Lavin, "A Wet Day," *KR*, VI, 10–23; Robie Macauley (ed.), *Gallery of Modern Fiction: Stories from the Kenyon Review* (New York, 1966). See, for example, Olivia Manning, "A Visit," *KR*, VI, 418–24; and Anaïs Nin, "The Mouse," *KR*, VIII, 266–73. The latter story verges on the feminist.

43. Isaac Rosenfeld, "The New Egypt," *KR*, VIII, 376–90; Isaac Rosenfeld, "The Railroad," *KR*, IX, 235–47; Isaac Rosenfeld, "The Party," *KR*, IX, 572–607; Ransom to Katherine Anne Porter, September 9, [1947], in Porter Papers; Delmore Schwartz, "A Bitter Farce," *KR*, VIII, 245–61; Delmore Schwartz to Ransom, October 28, 1945, in Phillips (ed.), *Letters of*

José Sender, and of Act Five of the classic "The Caucasian Circle of Chalk," by German refugee Bertolt Brecht. These two pieces were eminently suited for magazine publication: they are both poetic and rich in action. Such a happy combination is hard to find, and so Sender's and Brecht's plays remained the only drama contributions to the *Kenyon* for a long time.[44]

Drama criticism continued to flourish, thanks to Eric Bentley. Besides the drama criticism in the "Reconsiderations" department, distinguished drama critic Francis Fergusson reviewed Granville-Barker and also compared Wagner and Eliot. At Bentley's request, Berthold Viertel, another refugee from Nazi Germany, contributed two discerning articles on Bertolt Brecht and a review of *The Fervent Years* by Harold Clurman. Bentley and Jacques Barzun, whom he much admired, paid tribute to George Bernard Shaw. Barzun concentrated on defending Shaw as a dramatist—"He is in the great tradition, not in the little routine"—and Bentley discussed him as a propagandizing socialist. Barzun's 1943 tribute was timely, lucid, and well written. And Ransom was effusive: "[W]e have never been more grateful to a contributor than we were to you when you delivered the very fine critique upon Shaw at our request." This is, however, a diplomatic prelude to his rejection, in the same letter, of Barzun's article on education, which Bentley had solicited.[45]

Starting in 1942, George Beiswanger contributed three annual letters bewailing Broadway, until his replacement by Quentin Anderson in the summer of 1946. Anderson was a better critic but, in the eyes of the *Kenyon* editors, still too pessimistic about the state of the theater, so his letters appeared only twice. After an interval brilliantly tided over by Bentley's "*Monsieur Verdoux* as 'Theatre,'"

Delmore Schwartz, 220; Ransom to Delmore Schwartz, June 19, 1945, in *KR* Papers. "A Bitter Farce" was collected in his *The World Is a Wedding* (1948). Elaine Gottlieb, "Where Are You Roaming," *KR*, VI, 260–74; Elaine Gottlieb, "The Norm," *KR*, VII, 246–60.

44. Ramón J. Sender, "The Key," *KR*, V, 201–18; Bertolt Brecht, "The Caucasian Circle of Chalk, Act Five," trans. James Stern and W. H. Auden, *KR*, VIII, 188–202.

45. Francis Fergusson, Review of *The Use of the Drama* by H. Granville-Barker, in *KR*, VIII, 171–73; Francis Fergusson, "Action as Passion: *Tristan* and *Murder in the Cathedral*," *KR*, IX, 201–21; Berthold Viertel, "Bertolt Brecht: Dramatist," *KR*, VII, 467–75; Berthold Viertel, "The Brecht Performance," *KR*, VII, 690–92; Berthold Viertel, "The Group Theatre," *KR*, VIII, 302–309; Jacques Barzun, "Bernard Shaw in Twilight," *KR*, V, 338; Eric Bentley, "Bernard Shaw's Politics (A Birthday Tribute)," *KR*, VIII, 347–71; Ransom to Jacques Barzun, October 7, 1944, in *KR* Papers.

George Nobbe was given an opportunity to become the *Kenyon's* regular theater critic in the summer, 1949, issue. But his sloppily written, inordinately laudatory letter failed to please the editors; he did not get a second chance.[46] The editors' efforts to enliven their magazine by means of a regular theater chronicle had failed signally so far.

As for the remaining performing arts, dance was hardly mentioned during this period, but music received some attention. The *Kenyon's* coup in this field was T. W. Adorno's prescient "A Social Critique of Radio Music." Roger Sessions contributed a laudatory review of two books by D. F. Tovey to the summer, 1945, issue. In the same issue, Leo Balet published "The Nuisance of Music 'Re-Creations,'" which dealt with Walt Disney's *Fantasia,* and a badly reasoned review of Alfred Einstein's *Mozart.* In his regular music column for *The Nation,* B. H. Haggin wrote about this review: "What I think of the method, the purpose, the complete, detailed piece of writing, I have not been able to find polite language for." Bentley wrote to Barzun that he thought Haggin had "Balet looking more of an ass than he really is" and that he had consequently written "to both gents on KR notepaper asking why they don't write something further explaining their points of view." Bentley enclosed their answers as "Literary Documents of Our Time." Haggin, who was under the false impression that he would not be paid, had refused angrily: "Believing as I do that editors publish what they think worthy of publication, I was amazed that *Kenyon Review* published Balet's pieces, but am even more amazed that after their publication an outsider should be invited [quoting Bentley] 'to send a communication about Balet's strange article on re-creations.' I don't think 'strange' is the word I would use about Balet's writing; but I certainly would apply it to *Kenyon Review's* procedure in connection with that writing. . . . I do no *unpaid* speaking at all. I can't afford it; and I disapprove of it, and in particular of solicited unpaid 'communications.'" Balet simply remarked that Haggin's "'attack' was such as not deserving further thought."[47]

46. George Beiswanger's letters on Broadway appeared in *KR,* IV, 264–71, *KR,* V, 114–17, and *KR,* VI, 318–20; Quentin Anderson's letters appeared in *KR,* VIII, 477–83, and *KR,* IX, 481–86. Eric Bentley, "*Monsieur Verdoux* as 'Theatre,'" *KR,* X, 705–16; George Nobbe, "Theatre Letter," *KR,* XI, 533–38.

47. T. W. Adorno, "A Social Critique of Radio Music," *KR,* VII, 208–17; Roger Sessions,

So Bentley's attempt at stirring up a spicy controversy went up in smoke. But this episode shows that Bentley was given rather a free hand and that he made enthusiastic use of it.

As before, architecture, sculpture, and especially painting took up the bulk of the art section, which continued even though the *Kenyon*'s subtitle, "A Quarterly of Arts and Letters," had been dropped. Remarkable in all respects are "Cities' Renaissance," a combined effort by Walter Gropius and Martin Wagner, and "Renaissance and Renascences" by Erwin Panofsky, articles that appeared in the winter, 1943, and spring, 1944, issues. Walter Gropius, Bauhaus founder working at Harvard, had responded warmly to Rice's request to contribute an article—as Rice wrote, "partly because we are very much in need of a feature on one of the non-literary arts in the Winter issue, but mainly because we are especially eager to number you among our contributors." The gist of this article, written in collaboration with another refugee, Martin Wagner, professor of regional planning at Harvard, was given in Gropius' answer: "My opinion is that the future of the Architectural Profession will greatly depend on the ability of the architects to handle planning problems, for every house and building is part of a larger unit, the town."[48]

Erwin Panofsky was concerned with the Italian Renaissance, which he lucidly compared and contrasted to renascences that had come before, such as the Carolingian in the eighth century and the Ottonian in the tenth century. The correspondence between Panofsky and Ransom about this lavishly illustrated essay was most gentlemanly: they seem to try to outdo each other in politeness. When Panofsky hesitantly inquired whether the *Kenyon* might be interested in his writing up an address he had given to students at the Graduate School of Fine Arts at New York University, Ransom assured him that he would accept such an essay unseen, a gesture far from his common practice. Panofsky soon sent the essay, but feared that Ransom would regret his confidence in him as the address was "not overwhelmingly

"Sir Donald Tovey," *KR*, VII, 504–507; Leo Balet, "The Nuisance of Music 'Re-Creations,'" *KR*, VII, 382–98; Leo Balet, "The Humanity of Mozart," *KR*, VII, 494–97; B. H. Haggin, "Music," *Nation*, August 11, 1945, p. 142; Bentley to Jacques Barzun, [September, 1945], enclosed in which are B. H. Haggin to Bentley, n.d., and Leo Balet to Bentley, September 12, 1945, all in Barzun Papers.

48. Walter Gropius and Martin Wagner, "Cities' Renaissance," *KR*, V, 12–33; Rice to Walter Gropius, September 30, 1942, Gropius to Rice, October 13, 1942, both in *KR* Papers.

interesting." He gave Ransom "*carte blanche*" in all matters of "phrasing, spelling and punctuation," and added that he was "*still* free to return it." Ransom, however, was so impressed that he spontaneously placed at Panofsky's disposal twelve pages for expensive illustrations (instead of the eight agreed on), an offer Panofsky snapped up. Ransom had another pleasant surprise in store: the Rockefeller Foundation had hinted that they would subsidize the *Kenyon,* and Ransom intended to raise the contributors' rates to what they had been before the war, which had forced them down to about $2.50 per page. Panofsky, extremely pleased with his four extra pages, renounced the extra Rockefeller money "so as to lessen the expense for the plates."[49]

Over a year later, Panofsky wrote "Dear Mr. Blair": "Surprisingly, I have received a request for my article . . . from the Warburg Institute of London University . . . and you would greatly oblige me by sending them the number of the *Kenyon Review* . . . at my expense." *The Kenyon Review*'s reputation had indeed spread worldwide. Partly as a consequence, probably, of the postwar export of and international interest in American culture, soon after the war about 130 of its 2,400 copies went to foreigners. International, too, was the *Kenyon*'s coverage with respect to the fine arts. To name a few examples: the all-knowledgeable Walter Southard reviewed *Paul Klee* edited by Karl Nierendorf; in his summer, 1943, "Art Letter," Philip R. Adams tellingly described Salvador Dali as "one of the most curious mixtures of charlatan and authentic craftsman that the arts have ever produced"; Jean Charlot wrote a timely article on Mexican murals; and Louis Graff misapplied Hegelian philosophy to Van Gogh's *Ravens Flying Over Cornfield.*[50]

Finances and the Rockefeller Foundation

In spite of the *Kenyon*'s high standing, its circulation had dropped considerably during the war. The rise in the price of annual subscrip-

---

49. Erwin Panofsky, "Renaissance and Renascences," *KR,* VI, 201–36; Erwin Panofsky to Ransom, January 8, 29, 1944, both in *KR* Papers.

50. Erwin Panofsky to Rice, May 1, 1945, circulation report, October 1, 1947, both in *KR* Papers; Walter Southard, "Images with Abstract Titles," *KR,* V, 464–67; Philip R. Adams, "Art Letter," *KR,* V, 477; Jean Charlot, "Pre-Hispanic Quota in Mexican Murals," *KR,* VIII, 1–13; Louis Graff, "Pictorial Tragedy," *KR,* IX, 96–109.

tions from $2 to $3, the "many . . . subscribers . . . in the services," and the Kenyon's "white-collar constituency" being "the class hardest hit by war finance" caused a drop in sales from about 1,400 in the autumn of 1942 to about 1,100 in the autumn of 1944. And there were other debits: the gradual enlargement from about 140 pages per issue in 1942 to approximately 175 by 1944 also unbalanced the budget. Then there was the falling away of private sponsors. George Frazer and Henry Church gave $1,750 during the budget year 1942–1943, but the year after only Frazer was left, Church having become an advisory editor and sponsor of The Sewanee Review, now edited by his friend Allen Tate. After July, 1944, Frazer backed out, too. Only a year after the demise of The Southern Review, the Kenyon was in financial straits again. Although the Doubleday, Doran deal, which was to become effective in 1944, would clear up some clouds, the editors took such a bleak view of the Kenyon's future in Gambier that Rice went prospecting for other sites.[51]

But Rockefeller Foundation money rendered further searching redundant. Not only did the foundation provide stipends for the Fellows (Harold Whitehall, Eric Bentley, Charles Riker, and Robert Penn Warren), who came to The Kenyon Review "on a basis of mutual service through literary and editorial associations," it also gave the Kenyon a three-year grant of $7,500 in total, beginning January, 1944. Even if Ransom had, at Chalmers' insistence, applied for the rather outrageous sum of about $9,000 per year, Ransom was thoroughly satisfied. His August, 1947, report to the foundation shows that Ransom made excellent use of their grant. Although this report is dressed up a bit—Ransom was trying to obtain a new Rockefeller grant—its basis is sound. Indeed, without this foundation's "generous benefactions," the magazine might have folded. Ransom wrote:

The addition of $2,500.00 to our annual revenue for three years made a great difference in the magazine. We employed a professional secretary and put our business office in order. We paid a little better rates to our contributors. We increased the size of the issues, so that they might have a more rounded

51. Ransom to Tate, March 20, [1943], in Tate Papers; circulation reports, September 29 (on autumn, 1942, issue) and September 22 (on autumn, 1944, issue), both in KR Papers. Stanford is mentioned as a possible base for the Kenyon in a letter written by Rice from New York, January 20, 1944, to Charles Coffin, professor of English at Kenyon College, in Rice Papers.

content. We brought up to the highest current standard, as I have been pretty well informed, our department of original fiction, and we printed new verse on a more liberal scale. As for the critical essays which are our staple, I am confident that we raised our standard steadily, and at the end of the period had come to be accepted in the academic world, and with some outside readers, as perhaps offering the best examples of what literary criticism should be. . . . But all these scattering items come to saying that with your help the Review made a great qualitative improvement within the three years.[52]

In a letter to Chalmers amplifying this statement, Ransom emphasized the link between a rise in standards and an increase in the rate paid to contributors: "It is obviously a great advantage for a periodical to be able to pay its contributors decently; the existing contributors work for us the more cheerfully and punctually, and new contributors volunteer (or can be successfully solicited) who might not previously have cared to write for us." In an earlier interim report to the foundation, Ransom had diplomatically pointed to another "great but intangible benefit": "You came to us saying that you thought we were 'educationally important' with what we were doing as a critical organ. You restored our courage when we must have been conscious that we were fighting a losing battle. I am not prepared to say that we were operating 'weakly' in our shaky financial condition, but I [am] sure that knowing our lack of capital we lacked the editorial incentive, since we could not make the improvements that were most obviously called for. You placed a responsibility upon us, and at the same time gave us the means to discharge it; the combination being a wonderful morale-builder."[53]

By the mid-1940s, the confidence the Rockefeller Foundation had shown in *The Kenyon Review*—which was described as "virtually the only critical journal of first quality under control of a college or university," in its report of January 10, 1944—was shared by almost the entire American literary community. The *Kenyon's* fame had even come home to popular weeklies such as *Time* and *Newsweek,* which paid tribute to the *Kenyon* as "one of the most distinguished of U.S.

52. Ransom to John Marshall, August 13, 1947, in *KR* Papers.

53. Ransom to Chalmers, December 14, 1948, Ransom to David Stevens, August 30, 1945, both in *KR* Papers.

little magazines" and "one of the most revered in that esoteric field."
"Esoteric" perhaps to their millions of readers, yet within ten years
of its inception, *The Kenyon Review* with its circulation of less than
2,500 had managed to become "virtually required reading for everyone concerned with contemporary literature." [54]

54. "Grant in Aid to Kenyon College" (TS, January 10, 1944, in KC Collection); "The
Fugitive," *Time,* May 10, 1948, p. 70; "Professor on a Hill," *Newsweek,* August 2, 1948, p. 73;
John Marshall to Ransom, April 3, 1947, in *KR* Papers.

5 Recognition and New Directions
1947–1955

Academic Influence, the Bollingen Prize,
the Rockefeller Foundation

The subsidy given by the Rockefeller Foundation, that bulwark of respectability, put the seal of approbation of the literary establishment on *The Kenyon Review*. The foundation's action reflected the high standing the magazine and the New Criticism, the kind of criticism most consistently represented therein, had attained in the literary and academic world. It simultaneously paved the way for the New Criticism in those institutions that still regarded this kind of criticism as verbal jugglery or unscholarly impressionism. Prestigious universities such as Princeton and Yale were among those already won over to the New Criticism. Richard Blackmur, for instance, was the most influential critic at Princeton, and Cleanth Brooks expounded his branch of the New Criticism at Yale, where, in his own words, a "palace-revolution" had taken place.[1]

The enormous influence on the academy of *The Kenyon Review* and of other literary quarterlies emphasizing serious criticism, such as *The Sewanee Review, Partisan Review,* and, from its founding in 1948, *The Hudson Review,* is also apparent in the very number of articles about them in the periodical press during the late 1940s and early 1950s. In most of these articles, the links between magazine and academy are explicit and positive. The subsidies by academic institu-

---

1. Interview with Brooks, August 17, 1982.

tions are seen to account for, or at least to contribute to, the longevity of the magazines, to their handsome appearance, and to the securing of excellent contributions. Moreover, most of the contributors to and readers of these magazines were in the university. In Theodore Peterson's words: "[L]iterary quarterlies . . . huddle in the warmth of academic shelter." Meanwhile, the fame of the American literary reviews had spread to Europe. In Great Britain especially, many articles dealt with their influence and importance, often revealing a certain jealousy with respect to the academy's encouragement. A 1954 British article noted enviously that the "close connection with the universities . . . is one reason why these periodicals present such a glossy surface to the world. . . . They have kept a place for the intellectual to talk about his problems; they have preserved a sphere for free discussion."[2]

In a letter to Edward D'Arms of the Rockefeller Foundation, Ransom himself emphasized that "some 90 per cent of our contributors depend for their livelihood upon the academic economy," and described *The Kenyon Review* as "very largely an academic product."[3] He realized that such a close academic association also had its dangers and disadvantages. But whether for better or worse, the tide could not be turned. By the 1950s, the critical quarterlies had become institutionalized, had lost much of their fighting spirit because they needed it less, and had become legislators in the university.

A telling indication of the influence of—and the growing antagonism toward—the critics who appeared regularly in the literary reviews was the battle about the 1948 Bollingen Prize, which divided the literary world into two fiercely hostile camps and in which *The Kenyon Review* became closely involved. In 1948 the Library of Congress received from the Bollingen Foundation a sum of $10,000 to be used for an annual award of $1,000 for the best book of verse by an

---

2. A prime example is William Elton's "Glossary of the New Criticism," *Poetry*, LXXIII (1948–49), 151–62, 232–45, 296–307; another is the *American Scholar* forum, "The Misery and Necessity of the Quarterly," with contributions by John Crowe Ransom, Paul Bixler, Delmore Schwartz, and Irwin Edman, which appeared in *AS*, XV (1946), 550–54. Theodore Peterson, "The Role of the Minority Magazine," *Antioch Review*, XXIII (1963), 67; William J. Newman, "The American Literary Reviews," *Twentieth Century*, CLV (1954), 342, 350. Other examples of British articles mainly devoted to American literary reviews are "The Serious Literary Review," *TLS*, September 17, 1954, lviii, and "The American Scene," *TLS*, August 24, 1951, xxxiv–xxxv.

3. Ransom to Edward D'Arms, December 17, 1951, in KC Collection.

American author. The Fellows in American Letters of the Library, advisors on the development of the Library's collection of American literature, were to be the jury of selection. Serving on the jury in 1948 were Conrad Aiken, W. H. Auden, Louise Bogan, Katherine Garrison Chapin, the 1948 Nobel laureate T. S. Eliot, Paul Green, Robert Lowell, Katherine Anne Porter, Karl Shapiro, Theodore Spencer, Allen Tate, Willard Thorp, and Robert Penn Warren, as well as Leonie Adams, the Library's Consultant in Poetry in English for that year. As the committee's secretary, Leonie Adams received from the jury members the preliminary letters of nomination, which clearly foreshadowed the final ballot: eleven of the fourteen Fellows cast their votes for Ezra Pound's *Pisan Cantos*.

Pound was at that time in St. Elizabeths Hospital in Washington, D.C., the federal asylum for the insane, where he had been committed before he could stand trial for the treasonable, Fascist radio broadcasts he had made in Italy during World War II. The *Pisan Cantos,* the first draft of which Pound had written when he was kept as an American prisoner of war near Pisa, contained pronounced anti-Semitic statements. The Fellows, of course, knew that awarding the first Bollingen Prize to such a clearly controversial poet would, to say the least, raise a storm. With the announcement of the award, therefore, was a diplomatically worded statement by Shapiro (who had in fact voted against Pound), Adams, and Lowell:

The Fellows are aware that objections may be made to awarding a prize to a man situated as is Mr. Pound. In their view, however, the possibility of such objection did not alter the responsibility assumed by the Jury of Selection. This was to make a choice for the award among the eligible books, provided any one merited such recognition, according to the stated terms of the Bollingen Prize. To permit other considerations than that of poetic achievement to sway the decision would destroy the significance of the award and would in principle deny the validity of that objective perception of value on which any civilized society must rest.[4]

At first, there was only relatively mild opposition. One of the most violent reactions was by William Barrett, who, in an editorial in *Partisan Review,* accused the jury of a nearly inhuman insensitivity

4. Library of Congress Press Release No. 542, February 20, 1949: "The *Pisan Cantos* Wins for Ezra Pound First Award of Bollingen Prize in Poetry," included in Fellows of the Library of Congress *et al., The Case Against the Saturday Review of Literature* (Chicago, 1949), 29–30.

and suggested that, as no other book of verse had met their critical standards, they should have decided not to award the 1948 Bollingen Prize in consideration of the feelings of the Jews and other victims of fascism. Allen Tate read into this editorial the accusation that the jury had been swayed by anti-Semitism and, characteristically, challenged Barrett to a duel, which Barrett refused. In the national press, too, the exchange of enmities was moderate until suddenly, in June, Robert Hillyer reopened the controversy with two devastating attacks on the award in the *Saturday Review of Literature*. The editors of the *Saturday Review,* through an intermediary, A. D. Parelhoff, had first vainly tried to get the dissenter Karl Shapiro to denounce the award. The editors then approached Hillyer, who had jumped at the chance.[5]

In his long, demagogic articles "Treason's Strange Fruit" and "Poetry's New Priesthood," by perverting facts and violating the truth, and by means of guilt by association, Hillyer attacked C. G. Jung, the Bollingen Foundation, Eliot, and indeed all advocates of modernist poetry and the New Criticism. He denounced them, first, as agents of a Fascist conspiracy and, then, paradoxically, as politically naïve, irresponsible aestheticists: "An uncompromising assault on this new estheticism is long overdue. The award to Pound made it inevitable. In a spiritual morass where language, ethics, literature, and personal courage melt into something obscure and formless, a guided impulse has stirred the amorphous haze into something approaching form, something shaped out of stagnant art by *Fascism*."[6]

It is easy to find reasons for Hillyer's antipathy. A writer of romantic, pastoral poetry, such as *The Death of Captain Nemo* (1949), Hillyer found himself outside the main Pound-Eliot tradition of American poetry. Moreover, John Marshall had just refused to fund "The Poetry Society of America," of which Hillyer was president. Hillyer attributed Marshall's refusal to Marshall's having "pour[ed]

---

5. William Barrett, "A Prize for Ezra Pound," *PR*, XVI (1949), 344–47. There has been much discussion about the Bollingen award to Pound: Irving Howe, *A Margin of Hope: An Intellectual Autobiography* (New York, 1982), 151–56; William McGuire, *Bollingen: An Adventure in Collecting the Past* (Princeton, 1982), 208–18; E. Fuller Torrey, *The Roots of Treason: Pound and the Secret of St. Elizabeths* (New York, 1984); and Thomas Daniel Young, "The Little Houses Against the Great," *SR*, LXXXVIII (1980), 320–30.
6. Robert Hillyer, "Treason's Strange Fruit," *SRL*, June 11, 1949, pp. 9–11, 28; Robert Hillyer, "Poetry's New Priesthood," *SRL*, June 18, 1949, pp. 7–9, 38 (quotation).

money into those wretched New Criticism publications, probably because of his friendship with Dick Blackmore [*sic*]."[7] While the award to Pound was made to measure for a controversy involving questions about the relation between art and moral values, Hillyer's vicious, false, personal attacks were surely contemptible. And cowardly, too. For Hillyer had been Ransom's colleague as a visiting professor of English at Kenyon College for the last term of the academic year 1948–1949. He had been high-handedly and underhandedly reappointed for a two-year period by President Chalmers to serve as a corrective to Ransom's literary opinions. Cunningly, Hillyer had planned his attacks during the summer holidays of 1949; that is, before his return to Kenyon College in October, 1949, which he had timed to occur just after Ransom's departure for Indiana University in Bloomington, where he had been invited to spend the academic year 1949–1950.

Hillyer's assaults caused a violent outbreak of hostilities at the local as well as at the national level. In Gambier, Rice led the troops against "Nemo" and company. Nationally, Tate, who this time had reason to feel provoked, took command. Part of the local battle was fought in the *Kenyon Collegian*. A Kenyon College sophomore, D. H. Lobdell, clearly in Hillyer's camp, set off a bomb by denouncing not only "mad Ezra Pound, T. S. Eliot and other high priests of incomprehensibility worshipped by the 'new critics'" but also "John Crowe Ransom, archdeacon in Poetry's New Priesthood, and home bailiwick for the ultra avant-garde *Kenyon Review*." The blast was felt all over Gambier. "We did everything . . . but dig trenches," George Lanning, in those days a student at Kenyon College, remembers. Vituperative letters calling Lobdell's article "muddled," "hysterical," "sordid," and even "fascistic" poured into the *Collegian*'s editorial office. Chalmers tried to pacify both parties by emphasizing Ransom's "honored place among us," but conceding that the "explicit intention of [Lobdell's] article—to rehearse and summarize a current dispute among the critics—is of course a proper one." Chalmers concluded this letter to the *Collegian* with a paean to free speech. Chalmers' statement was partly written under pressure from Rice and Charles Coffin and Denham Sutcliffe of the English depart-

7. Robert Hillyer to S. Foster Damon, March 22, 1949, in Hillyer Papers.

ment. Somewhat appeased by Chalmers' letter, they decided to hold their fire for the time being and "not [to] publish anything except in event of further aggression by the other side," as Rice wrote to Ransom in Bloomington, adding with glee that Hillyer was "almost completely ostracized." But Roberta Chalmers, who guided her husband's thinking in literary matters as before, still cherished and defended Hillyer, whose ideas about poetry were much closer to hers than Ransom's had ever been.[8]

Meanwhile, Tate had rallied his troops. With the help of John Berryman and others, Tate had drafted a letter to be sent to the editors of the *Saturday Review*. This letter protested their sanctioning and guiding "a prepared attack on modern poetry and criticism, impugning not only the literary reputations but the personal characters of some of its foremost writers" as well as "the methods of [their] attack, which . . . has violated the standards of responsible literary controversy, and thus has dealt a blow to American culture."[9] About eighty of the hundred writers asked to sign this letter did so gladly. Among them were Philip Rahv, Clement Greenberg, and Arthur Mizener. These writers had violently disagreed with the awarding of the Bollingen Prize to Pound, but found Hillyer's charges sickening. Many of America's preeminent writers, including James Agee, R. P. Blackmur, Cleanth Brooks, Malcolm Cowley, E. E. Cummings, Randall Jarrell, Alfred Kazin, Howard Nemerov, J. F. Powers, Mark Schorer, Delmore Schwartz, Peter Taylor, Diana Trilling, Lionel Trilling, and Mark Van Doren, signed the group statement. Others, such as John Dos Passos and Katherine Anne Porter, sent their own letters of protest. But the editors of the *Saturday Review,* who had backed up Hillyer's attacks in flaming editorials, refused to print the group protest, arguing interestingly if not convincingly that the controversy had long since been brought to a close. John Berryman then

8. In an undated, late September or early October, 1949, letter to Ransom, Rice refers to Hillyer as "Nemo" (Letter in Rice Papers). D. H. Lobdell, "Hillyer Sets Off Poetry Powder Keg with Pound Attack," *KC,* September 30, 1949, pp. 2, 4; interview with George Lanning, October 21, 1981. The adjectives "muddled," "hysterical," "sordid," and "fascistic" are all from the one letter actually published in *KC,* October 7, 1949, p. 2. Its author was Richard Thomas Gibson, a student at Kenyon College. Gordon Keith Chalmers, "Controversy Unfortunate But Necessary," *KC,* October 7, 1949, p. 2; Rice to Ransom, [late September or early October, 1949], in Rice Papers.

9. "A Prepared Attack," letter to the editors of the *Saturday Review of Literature,* published in *Nation,* December 17, 1949, pp. 598–99.

sent the statement on to the editors of *The Nation,* who published it in their December 17 issue.

In the meantime, at Tate's suggestion, *Poetry* magazine, edited by Hayden Carruth, had published a fat pamphlet, *The Case Against the Saturday Review of Literature,* which contained, among other things, letters criticizing Hillyer's position, reprints of denunciatory articles by Malcolm Cowley, the editors of *The Hudson Review,* Aline B. Louchheim, and Hayden Carruth himself, as well as explanatory statements by the Fellows of the Library of Congress, including a well-considered point-by-point refutation of the "facts" in Hillyer's articles. Less cool and collected but nonetheless noteworthy, as they reflect the heat of the battle, were Yvor Winters' and Robert Penn Warren's reactions. Winters wrote to the editors of the *Saturday Review*: "Your group is the lowest group of cheap punks I have ever seen in action; to save my soul I cannot imagine your motives. . . . To hell with all of you." And Warren hoped Rice would give Hillyer "whack for whack" in Gambier.[10]

Although Rice, Coffin, and Sutcliffe did nothing to hide their disgust of "Nemo" in private, Chalmers pressured them not to vent their anger in print. About the only thing Rice could do without fear of repercussion was to ask Pound to contribute poetry to *The Kenyon Review* in order "to show that the opinion of Pound's poetry expressed by our new colleague, Mr. Hillyer, does not represent the attitude of Kenyon as a whole toward Pound, and particularly not the attitude of the *Kenyon Review,*" as Rice informed William Carlos Williams, whom he had asked to act as an intermediary. But Pound had to refuse: "Yr. sentimungs, sir, as forwarded by . . . B. Willyums do you credit. But after more than 4 years, cage-birdee no sing." So Rice's covert gesture of rebellion came to nothing, but Tate's resounding national campaign—the group letter to the *Saturday Review* and the *Poetry* pamphlet—reverberated on the local front and made Chalmers "sit up and take notice." Rice kept Tate posted: "A violent reaction of some sort is going on in the presidential—should I say mind?—but the outcome as always is totally unpredictable."[11]

10. Fellows of the Library of Congress *et al.*, *The Case Against the Saturday Review of Literature;* Yvor Winters to Harrison Smith of the *Saturday Review of Literature,* December 10, 1949, in Tate Papers; Warren to Rice, September 21, 1949, in Rice Papers.

11. Rice to William Carlos Williams, September 20, 1949, in *KR* Papers; Ezra Pound to

Chalmers vacillated indeed. Ransom, who had met him at a conference in Chicago, in December wrote to Rice that Chalmers seemed "deeply *committed* to Hillyer" but had told Ransom "almost with tears that Hillyer felt no opposition to me or the KR at all. . . . I think [Chalmers] is so blind . . . that he may believe that. . . . Of course in every general meeting he shows his deep ignorance about literary matters and contemporary attitudes." Ransom concluded: "Let Hillyer dry up in his own ineptitude, or float and bloat in his own romantic stew, or whatever figure is appropriate." But within a week, it became clear that there was "no peace at Gambier" yet, and in January, 1950, Chalmers was again making "wild charges" against Ransom, Rice, and Sutcliffe. From Bloomington, Ransom could suggest they let the issue "just wear itself out," but as Rice's letters indicate, not until April did the battle in Gambier more or less definitely die down: "Locally, Hillyer's influence has been nullified, [and] Chalmers is on the defensive, though we haven't won a total victory yet."[12]

All in all, however, Hillyer and his fellow Philistines had lost the war: the congressional investigation that Hillyer and the *Saturday Review* had tried to instigate misfired; Hillyer did not get tenure at Kenyon College; and, even though the Library of Congress barred the Bollingen Prize, the funds were transferred to the Yale University Library, and in 1951 they awarded the Bollingen Prize to Ransom. In 1951, Ransom was also asked to become the Library's consultant in poetry, an honor and a mark of confidence he had to decline for financial reasons. The officers of the Bollingen Foundation itself reaffirmed their confidence in Ransom and company, too: in 1951, Rice received a two-year Bollingen grant to relieve him from summer teaching, and when the Carnegie funds for Ransom's Kenyon Chair of Poetry had been used up, Paul Mellon, founder of the Bollingen Foundation, donated $8,000 toward that endowment. Of course, there were also a few losses. Hayden Carruth was forced to resign as editor of *Poetry* and Karl Shapiro succeeded him, most likely because of their respective involvement with the prize to Pound. The

---

Rice, n.d. [postmarked September 26, 1949], in Rice Papers; Rice to Tate, November 15, [1949], in Tate Papers.

12. Ransom to Rice, December 3, [1949], December 14, 1949, January 20, [1950], all in Rice Papers; Rice to Tate, April 18, 1950, in Tate Papers.

last shot—and the one that perhaps hit Tate hardest, as he had championed Shapiro—was fired about ten years after hostilities had ceased: "I voted against giving Pound that prize, but I believed all the same that the jurors acted in good faith. The methods used by the *Saturday Review* were unspeakable (calling the prize a Fascist plot), but now it seems to me that the jurors, led by Eliot himself, acted in a distinctly underhanded manner."[13]

The battle about the Bollingen Prize had in no way daunted the Rockefeller Foundation. It remained a staunch supporter of Ransom and *The Kenyon Review* and, as a matter of fact, gradually extended its philanthropic activities to other critical reviews, thereby strengthening their joint position in the literary world. Richard Blackmur's 1944 study of literary magazines, which had shown that no highbrow magazine could operate without a large deficit, had resulted in the foundation's first direct gift of $7,500 to the *Kenyon,* thanks mainly to John Marshall's exertions. Marshall initially had not believed Blackmur on the necessity of financial assistance to noncommercial magazines, being inclined instead to impute their deficits to the editors' total lack of business acumen. But interviews he conducted with editors, publishers, and writers made him change his mind. It seemed "evident" to him that, besides rendering a great service by the publication of new and noncommercial writing, the literary magazines were "representative of the most advanced critical thinking in the country." In a memo of September 11, 1946, he therefore pointed out that assisting these reviews financially would "constitute an opportunity for the RF to encourage further literary growth," and recommended grants to provide for "more adequate payment" to contributors.[14]

Marshall's memo found favor with the foundation, and Richard Blackmur, Malcolm Cowley, and Lionel Trilling were appointed as members of an advisory committee to review the whole field of magazines, their problems and their potentialities, and to submit recommendations. This triumvirate drafted a form letter inviting suggestions and comments and asking for a comparative rating of the

13. Karl Shapiro, *In Defense of Ignorance* (1960; rpr. New York, 1965), 268.
14. Richard Blackmur, "Literary Magazines Study" (TS in LMS Papers); John Marshall, "Possible RF Assistance to the So-called Literary Magazines," September 11, 1946, memo in LMS Papers.

literary reviews. The letter went out to nineteen eminent writers, half of whom, to be sure, had almost exclusively published their work in little and literary magazines: W. H. Auden, E. Bentley, L. Bogan, V. W. Brooks, K. Burke, G. Hicks, F. T. Hoffman, A. Kazin, R. Jarrell, F. O. Matthiessen, G. Mayberry, Marianne Moore, W. Stevens, A. Tate, R. P. Warren, W. C. Williams, E. Wilson, Y. Winters, and M. D. Zabel. No wonder, then, that nearly all of them greeted enthusiastically the announcement of possible support for these reviews.

William Carlos Williams was the only one to react almost wholly contrarily:

> To hell with them all with their scholarly editors each with his prejudices and predilections, Kenyon, Sewanee and Partisan: each with some sort of axe to grind. . . . A magazine of the arts cannot be confined by juvenilia, by region, by politics or philosophic fencing. . . .
>
> I used to be for a Little Magazine Clearing House with a banking and clerical center in say, St. Louis or if you prefer, Colorado Springs—provided the climate wasn't TOO salubrious to make us all over sanguine. Any mag that wanted any money . . . could present its case and ask for support. But who, in God's name would be the judges? There is no one, including myself, that I'd trust. . . .
>
> I give it up.[15]

Williams did not quite "give it up," though, for in the next two pages, he inveighed against committees, colleges, and commercialism. Edmund Wilson was more selectively antagonistic. Although he regarded the extinct *Dial* and *Little Review,* as well as the still-bouncing *Partisan Review,* as "immensely valuable," he wrote off *The Kenyon Review* as "indescribably awful," and was, if possible, even more offensive about *The Sewanee Review*: "All[e]n Tate, before he left the *Sewanee,* never succeeded in lifting the shadow of the influence of J. C. Ransom or being able to refuse filling its space with the writings of his cousins and aunts." *Accent* was "perfectly piffling," and *Poetry* "as dead as Hull House." What Wilson did want was "a new first-rate magazine that would serve both as a critical review and as a vehicle for new creative writing."[16]

But the others were satisfied with the existing possibilities and

15. William Carlos Williams to Blackmur, November 11, 1946, in LMS Papers.
16. Edmund Wilson to Blackmur, November 6, 1946, in LMS Papers.

were only too glad to give their preferences and advice. On the basis of their answers, the advisory committee concluded that *Partisan Review* was most deserving of support, that *The Kenyon Review* came a close second, that *The Sewanee Review* came third, followed at a distance by *Accent, Poetry, The Western Review,* and a few others. *Partisan* took pride of place because Frederick Hoffman, Jarrell, Kazin, and Stevens, while emphasizing the *Kenyon's* incontestable importance, had nevertheless put *Partisan* first, whereas most of the others had found these two reviews equally indispensable. But Bentley voted unqualifiedly for the *Kenyon:* "Being one of the editors [*sic*] of the Kenyon Review I am prejudiced as a witness."[17] Finally, those who gave advice about specific methods of financing the literary reviews agreed with Marshall, perhaps not altogether altruistically, that a substantial increase in their payments to contributors would increase their services to literature. This suggestion was endorsed by the committee.

The *Partisan, Kenyon,* and *Sewanee* reviews, then, clearly had a head start on the others, and Marshall consequently recommended them for Rockefeller grants. But the foundation decided to subsidize only *The Kenyon Review* and in April, 1947, donated $22,500 to Kenyon College to be used up in five years. The money was to increase the rates for contributors to two and a half cents a word for prose and fifty cents a line for verse. Cowley commented that "[i]t was the best choice of the lot, Kenyon, for the sort of help you can give," but hoped that the experiment would be broadened. Trilling reacted likewise: he was "disappointed that the Foundation did not, right off, cut a wider swathe," but his "commitment of affection" for the *Kenyon* made him "happy that the Kenyon has new resources."[18] So *Partisan Review,* even though it topped the list, was passed over. Fortunately, its editors soon received such a sizable contribution from Allan Dowling, poet and partner in the City Investing Company, that they could publish *Partisan Review* as a monthly and still pay writers far better than they had before. Early in 1948, *The Sewanee Review,* finally, received a five-year Rockefeller grant of $27,600 in order to raise its rates to the *Kenyon's* new level.

17. Bentley to Blackmur, November 10, 1946, in LMS Papers.
18. Malcolm Cowley to John Marshall, April 28, 1947, Lionel Trilling to John Marshall, March 25, 1947, both in LMS Papers.

The foundation's deliberate passing over of *Partisan Review* was undoubtedly inspired by that magazine's Marxist origins, even though the review had already in 1937 deemed it necessary to "disclaim obligation" to Party politics.[19] This is not to say that by 1947, *Partisan Review* had become another *Kenyon*. True, both were highbrow reviews that published distinguished fiction and critical prose, and were hospitable to all kinds of promising serious writing. But the cosmopolitan *Partisan* gave much more space to European writers and published considerably less poetry and drama than the *Kenyon*. Furthermore, to generalize broadly, the New York intellectual *Partisan* still had a definitely cultural-ideological-political slant, was more radical and polemical, and, consequently, more lively, if more journalistic and faddish than the *Kenyon*. In light of its past as a fellow traveler, all this must have made the Rockefeller Foundation decide not to support *Partisan Review*.

Closer to the *Kenyon* was *The Sewanee Review*. This is apparent in its editors from 1942 onwards: Andrew Lytle (1942–1944), Allen Tate (1944–1946), and John Palmer (1946–1952), who had been managing editor of *The Southern Review*. Although his editorship lasted only two years, Tate—much more than Lytle, who had been a reluctant, temporary editor—left so strong a mark on the *Sewanee* that his successor hastened to reassure its readers that "[i]f under my editorship there should appear to be a break in editorial continuity from the pattern established by Mr. Tate, it will be the result not of intention but of failure of intention." Like Ransom, Tate explicitly modeled his review on *The Dial* and claimed kinship with *The Southern Review*.[20]

The *Sewanee*'s closeness to the *Kenyon* is apparent in its list of regular contributors during Tate's editorship, which included Berryman,

19. "Editorial Statement," *PR*, IV (1939), 3. For interesting material about *Partisan Review*, see Lionel Abel, *The Intellectual Follies: A Memoir of the Literary Venture in New York and Paris* (New York, 1984); William Barrett, *The Truants: Adventures among the Intellectuals* (Garden City, N.Y., 1982); Howe, *A Margin of Hope;* and William Phillips, *A Partisan View: Five Decades of the Literary Life* (New York, 1983).

20. J. E. Palmer, "Editorial," *SR*, LIV (1946), 732. In "The State of Letters," *SR*, LII (1944), 609, Allen Tate writes: "Since World War I the only American literary magazine (in the tradition in which *SR* will continue) that had a large circulation, was *The Dial*." In a form letter *ca.* summer, 1944, announcing his forthcoming editorship, Tate mentions as a specific editorial aim "to continue . . . the recent service to letters performed by *The Southern Review* from 1935 to 1942" (Letter in Cairns Papers).

Blackmur, Burke, Fergusson, Jarrell, Mizener, and Wallace Stevens. And, of course, there were the close personal bonds between Tate and Ransom, reflected in their continuous, mainly literary correspondence. Nevertheless, the differences between these two reviews, however minor, should not be disregarded. Philosophy, drama, and the arts, for instance, played only a negligible part in the *Sewanee*. Moreover, due to both the regional situation of the *Sewanee* and Tate's deep-rooted interest in the South, the *Sewanee* was more southern-oriented and somewhat more cliquish and reactionary than the *Kenyon*.

The Kenyon School of English
and the Kenyon Review Fellows

In 1947 the differences between the plucky, cultural-political *Partisan* and the more serene and perhaps at times somewhat academic *Kenyon* and *Sewanee* reviews were still so striking that the Rockefeller Foundation decided to fund only the latter two. Paradoxically, it was another grant by this very foundation that caused the differences between *Partisan* and the other reviews to diminish. Since 1944, when the Rockefeller Foundation gave $7,500 to *The Kenyon Review,* David Stevens and Ransom had been talking informally, off and on, about setting up a summer school of criticism for graduate students. In the summer of 1945, plans were made in earnest. At Ransom's suggestion, Rice discussed the school with Lionel Trilling and Robert Penn Warren. Rice's memo to Ransom of these conversations touched upon aspects that would be important in the years to come: the aversion of returning veterans to resuming their literary studies at the existing graduate schools, which mainly provided historical-bibliographical scholarship, and the beneficial collaboration among the school's teachers with their varied views about literary criticism. Rice had no doubt whatsoever that a foundation would back such a scheme and, in his turn, asked Ransom to draft an extensive prospectus. Four months later, in January, 1946, Ransom approached the Rockefeller Foundation armed with a provisional plan.

If in his proposal Ransom emphasized the benefits for the students, his correspondence shows that he set more store by the benefits for the school's staff—the "meeting . . . of contrary and even cantankerous minds" and "the approach to amity and to common views insofar as community is possible among the teaching fellows." In one of the drafts submitted for approval to the Rockefeller Foundation, Ransom, in agreement with his editorial policy, emphasized strongly that the school would "not permit itself to be identified exclusively with any one critical 'position.' . . . A staff of teaching Fellows may be generally of high intelligence and skill, yet their several doctrinal convictions may be widely at variance. It would be improper for a School of Criticism to deny or suppress this variance, and such a school would be evading its responsibilities and its opportunities if it failed to make some provision for displaying and if possible 'clarifying' the basic critical issues." In the proposal proper, subtitled unequivocally "A Plan for an Educational Project in the Humanities," Ransom once again pointed to the limitations of the customary English courses devoted to scholarship and once again made the familiar points about the great importance of critical studies for the understanding of literature, but he now went on to stress strongly the absolute necessity of these studies for the "men and women who are preparing for a career in English teaching." [21]

There was initial hesitation about the project because the foundation thought it would be "essentially a one man show centering around John C. Ransom." John Marshall, who in September, 1946, had commented that "the value of the plan hinged on Ransom," wondered a year or so later whether it was advisable to be "putting all our critical eggs in the Kenyon basket." However, the sincerity of Ransom's emphasis in his proposal on the desired diversity of critical points of view is amply demonstrated by his choice of his two associate Senior Fellows, F. O. Matthiessen and Lionel Trilling. In 1972, Trilling described the "founding of the School . . . as a notable event of my personal past." Ransom's letter asking Matthiessen to become a member of the proposed school's "executive council" reflects his striving after critical diversity: "I have thought for some time of you and Trilling and myself as constituting this council. We are quite dif-

---

21. Ransom to Burke, October 21, 1948, in Burke Papers; Ransom to Rice, December 10, [1949], in Rice Papers; John Crowe Ransom, "The Kenyon School of Criticism: A Plan for an Educational Project in the Humanities" (TS in *KR* Papers).

ferent from each other and that ensures a catholic view; and I should say we respect each other enough to put up with a majority ruling gracefully."[22]

But when, after many letters, explanations, and reassurances, the hurdle of the foundation's fear of Ransom's possible monopoly of critical studies in the United States had been taken, another obstacle came in sight: the Rockefeller Foundation decided that the proposed school was much too expensive. In September, 1947, after a great deal of haggling, David Stevens proposed recommending an experimental grant for one year only; should Ransom not be satisfied with this, he warned, "the question of help [would] be unanswered." But both Chalmers—who played a major part in the negotiations, as Kenyon College was to be the school's site and liable to pay for its possible deficits—and Ransom unhesitatingly turned this offer down. They had already changed their original proposal of five years to three years, but a one-year school would, as Ransom pointed out, "rate along with . . . conferences, and would not attract the right people for staff or for students." He added that Trilling would surely withdraw from such a slight undertaking unworthy of the name "school." The foundation's officers reconsidered and, contrary to expectation, decided to grant $40,000 for a three-year period: the school fitted in too neatly with their cherished project of aiding "promising methods for improving the teaching of humanities."[23]

The staffs of the 1948, 1949, and 1950 Kenyon School of English, as the school came to be officially called, have probably never been equaled for genius or for critical and personal diversity. They are a gauge of the brilliance, exhilaration, geniality, and glory of these three summers that briefly turned Gambier into "the literary capital of the nation."[24] The staffs were as follows: in 1948, Bentley, Brooks, Richard Chase, F. O. Matthiessen, Ransom, Tate, Austin Warren, and

22. Edward D'Arms, "Comments on Proposed Grant for School of Criticism Kenyon College," July 31, 1947, John Marshall, interview with Blackmur, September 18, 1946, and John Marshall, dated August 22, 1947, memos all in KC Collection; Lionel Trilling to Newton P. Stallknecht, May 8, 1972, in Stallknecht Papers; Ransom to F. O. Matthiessen, November 26, [1946; wrongly dated 1948], in Matthiessen Papers.

23. Memo by David Stevens of an interview with Chalmers, September 5, 1947, Ransom to David Stevens, September 4, 1947, resolution by the Rockefeller Foundation to grant $40,000 to Kenyon College for a School of English, October 17, 1947, all in KC Collection.

24. "Kenyon School of English," *Kenyon Alumni Bulletin*, VI (1948), 11.

William Empson, who was flown in from China; in 1949, Ransom, Tate, and Bentley served again, Herbert Read came over from Great Britain, and Rahv, René Wellek, Mark Schorer, and Yvor Winters completed the team; and in 1950, Empson and Ransom participated for the second and third time, respectively, L. C. Knights fortified the British ranks, Coffin and Rice the home front, and Burke, Lowell, Mizener, and Schwartz brought the staff up to strength.

Approximately seventy-five students were selected annually out of hundreds applying mainly from schools to the west of Gambier, as the critical way of teaching literature had already penetrated the major eastern schools. One student's rapturous reaction is indicative of the boundless enthusiasm the sessions evoked: "I have never before associated with eight men of such brilliance. . . . I honestly believe that I received sufficient inspiration from attending the 1948 session to sustain me in my study of English throughout the rest of my life. I could envision no higher personal honor than the opportunity to return to the school as teacher—say in 1970 or thereabouts." The Kenyon School of English did not only inspire and inspirit its students, attending the School also paid off in job prospects. The School simultaneously drew attention to the existing critical void and prepared its students to fill this void. Soon the new-style teacher-critics were in such great demand all over America that Charles Coffin, the dean of the Kenyon School of English, complained that he seemed to head an "employment agency."[25]

The same mixture of worldly and spiritual benefits fell to the School's staff: Richard Chase, for example, was appointed at Columbia University mainly because he had been a teaching Fellow during the 1948 session. The staff was struck by the often unsuspected brilliance of colleagues holding controversial critical opinions. Outlooks were expanded, friendships were formed—or, at least, enmities were buried. Superlatives abound in the staff's descriptions of the meetings, too. Matthiessen, who in 1947 had threatened to resign when he heard that Ransom asked Rahv to participate, wrote to Tate that the 1948 "session at Kenyon was very rewarding for me, especially through the opportunity of getting to know better your 'Southern

---

25. Howard Babb to John Marshall, Thanksgiving, 1948, in KC Collection. In a letter to Chalmers, December 14, 1948, Ransom quotes Charles Coffin's remark that "his office seemed to be becoming an employment agency" (Letter in *KR* Papers).

agrarian poets and critics.'" Rahv "found teaching more to my taste than I would have thought possible." Even irritable, thin-skinned Yvor Winters, whom Ransom had come to dislike almost as much as Matthiessen loathed Rahv, but whom he had invited nevertheless— "I should welcome a Stalinist if there were a good one in the literary sense"—even Winters turned out to be "[m]ost helpful" and companionable.[26]

It would be wrong to conclude from all this that because of the Kenyon School of English, the teaching Fellows hastily abandoned their critical views and enthusiastically embraced those of former opponents. There is a story of Empson drunkenly yet brilliantly attacking Burke's views at four in the morning, at which a devoted student of Burke's got so upset that he woke Burke and pleaded with him to get dressed and let Empson have it; however, when Burke arrived, Empson had passed out, so Burke returned to his pajamas and bed. Nevertheless, the close association, the social gatherings, games, and charades at the School prevented dogmatic isolation and bred tolerance and a broadening of views.[27]

In 1958, reporting once more to the Rockefeller Foundation, Ransom emphasized the great importance of the School of English for *The Kenyon Review*: its impact was "momentous . . . so much did it expand our outlook." And, of course, as Ransom remarked to Chalmers, "the kind of interest taken in the Review and the kind of interest taken in the School are almost identical; they have to do with articulating the literary judgment. Our teaching Fellows are also identical, so far as numbers permit, with our contributors to the Review;

26. F. O. Matthiessen to Tate, September 11, [1948], in Tate Papers; Philip Rahv to Morton Dauwen Zabel, September 16, 1949, in Zabel Papers; Ransom to F. O. Matthiessen, December 1, 1947, in Matthiessen Papers; memo by David Stevens of an interview with Chalmers, October 26, 1949, in KC Collection. The gossipy, sometimes malicious running commentary on the 1948 session by "'Trilling's star-pupil,'" as Richard Chase was known at the School of English, clearly indicates the change from initial mistrust to friendship. "The kind of close moral awareness . . . the liberal criticising liberalism, the political sagacity etc etc which one associates with Lionel are foreign to the Southerners and others. I am much distressed by the political innocence of the Fellows here this summer. . . . It is indeed difficult, apparently, to be a good literary critic *and* a good moralist. On the evidence offered by the New Critics in general I do believe if I had to choose I should want to be a moralist," Chase wrote to his wife on July 3, [1948; wrongly dated 1949]. But by July 18, [1948; wrongly dated 1949], he had come to speak of "my friends the Southern writers," who in practice "lean to the left" politically and "see in capitalism no power at all of establishing any kind of coherent culture in which individual life can have meaning" (Both letters in Chase Papers).

27. Interview with Helen and Elizabeth Forman, October 19, 1981.

while the students of the School are our potential contributors." The help of Matthiessen and Trilling notwithstanding, Ransom was the vital, visionary force behind the School. He was the one to come up with suggestions for staff members and to write numerous letters begging coveted Fellows to teach—often in vain, as in the case, for example, of T. S. Eliot, F. R. Leavis, Robert Penn Warren, and Randall Jarrell. He was the one to suggest courses from Donne to modern drama, and, during the sessions themselves, the one to "plea[d] for cooperation and harmony in the collective enterpri[s]e." So, as with the *Kenyon,* it was Ransom's critical knowingness and open-mindedness that made the School a "great success." [28]

But the School's success could not guarantee that it would continue. The Rockefeller Foundation decided to refuse Chalmers' request for a renewed, more extensive three-year grant because "the recognition that the School has won indicates its very real accomplishment in demonstrating the importance of a truly critical approach to the study of literature. . . . [I]ts wider acceptance means that from now on it can make its way on its own in the United States." But other considerations were at least as important: there was the Hillyer business, which had got Kenyon College talked about, and there was Chalmers, who, while requesting a grant, had hinted in several interviews with foundation officers that the Kenyon School of English constituted mere New Critical nepotism. Together with the retirement of David Stevens, the School's guardian angel, this worked against the foundation's acceding to a second $70,000 plan for what amounted to a more expensive version of the existing Kenyon School of English. [29]

"I tell you frankly, sir, that the failure of Kenyon College to keep the School of English will probably go down in history as one of the anomalies of academic statesmanship," an enraged Tate wrote to Chalmers. Ransom and Trilling were deeply disappointed, too, and

28. Ransom to John Marshall, [summer, 1958], Ransom to Chalmers, December 14, 1948, both in *KR* Papers; Richard Chase to his wife, July 15, [1948; wrongly dated 1949], in Chase Papers; Austin Warren to Lytle, July 27, 1948, in Lytle Papers.

29. John Marshall to Chalmers, March 13, 1950, copy in Tate Papers. Chalmers also had at first made the Senior Fellows and the foundation enthusiastic for a plan in which one teaching Fellow was to stay at Kenyon College during the entire year, so that exceptionally bright students could get their master of arts degree in Gambier. But when Ransom made it very clear that he was not going to stand for Chalmers' appointing such a Fellow single-handedly, Chalmers huffily withdrew the resident-Fellow proposal.

offended by Chalmers' insistence that the School stood for "'one thing'" only. Ransom did not "to save my life know what is the 'one thing' we stand for," and Trilling found the School "'one thing' only insofar as it is good and insofar as it is humanistic," and pointed to the religious, political, temperamental, and critical differences among the Fellows.[30] Other foundations were approached determinedly, but in vain: the Kenyon School of English was lost to Kenyon College. But not lost completely, because Indiana University, where Ransom was teaching during the academic year of 1949–1950, was so impressed by the School's record that it adopted the School integrally, merely changing its name to the School of Letters at Indiana University.

By 1950, a critical approach to literature had become part of the regular university curriculum; this rendered the School of Letters (partly) redundant. Moreover, after the first years when many of its students were subsidized by the GI Bill, the School's enrollment dropped drastically; besides, most of its twenty-odd students came from Indiana University. This, and the retirement of its director, Newton P. Stallknecht, led to the School's being closed in 1972. Meanwhile, Ransom's remaining an active Senior Fellow had staved off the complete severance of the link between the School and *The Kenyon Review*. Nevertheless, as Ransom only sporadically taught at the School of Letters, the bonds between the new Bloomington teaching Fellows and Ransom, and consequently the *Kenyon,* were never as close as during the School's provocative, convivial, conciliatory years at Kenyon College.

Although the officers of the Rockefeller Foundation refused to subsidize the Kenyon School of English again, they had not washed their hands of *The Kenyon Review*. When the five-year grant for raising the contributors' rates came to an end in 1952, the *Kenyon* was once more in very real danger of being suspended. More writers had been able to dedicate more of their time to writing of the quality the *Kenyon* required, but the foundation's officers were disappointed that there had been no notable increase in the *Kenyon's* circulation and no improvement in its general financial situation. Consequently, Charles Fahs, who succeeded Stevens as Director of the Humanities

---

30. Tate to Chalmers, October 25, 1950, in Tate Papers; Ransom to Chalmers, December 6, 1949, Lionel Trilling to Chalmers, December 18, 1949, both in KC Papers.

Section and who was no friend of the reviews, wrote to Chalmers that a request for renewal would be refused. Chalmers, according to Ransom, once again was "wonderfully 'for' the Review just as it stands, considering that he doesn't and can't read it." He and Ransom and Rice were in sackcloth and ashes, since they read Fahs's letter as "a final brushoff." But Edward D'Arms, recently appointed Associate Director and "a former Oxonian chum of Phil's," gave them "a broad hint" to make the foundation a new proposition that took into account the officers' feeling that "greater opportunity lay in directly encouraging the new-found writers of already-evident ability."[31]

Out of this came the first three-year program of literary fellowships, inaugurated in 1952 and involving $41,400; this grant was renewed and increased to $52,200 in 1956. *The Kenyon Review,* though the first, was not the only beneficiary: *The Sewanee Review* received a similar grant in 1953, which was also renewed in 1956. Moreover, *The Hudson Review* and now *Partisan Review,* too, benefited from this second round of fellowships, an extension Ransom was "happy" with. The terms of the first grant to *The Kenyon Review* show the advantages for the magazine:

The proposed grant is for provision for the award by the editors of the *Review* of three fellowships annually, one each in fiction, poetry, and criticism, and for editorial expenses, including overhead expenses involved in these appointments, the latter item admittedly to assist the *Review* to some extent in maintaining present rates of payment during a period of transition to other sources of support. These fellowships, which would carry stipends of approximately $2,000 for unmarried fellows and $3,000 for married fellows, are to be awarded to individuals in each field whose work in the judgment of the editors of the *Review* merits such encouragement.[32]

The fellowships not only benefited *The Kenyon Review* financially, they had the same effect as the Kenyon School of English had had: they infused fresh blood into the *Kenyon,* vitally broadening its scope. Although these Fellows, as opposed to the *Kenyon* Rockefeller Fellows of the mid-1940s, were free to live where they wanted and were under no obligation to the *Kenyon* whatsoever, they eagerly and

31. Ransom to Tate, April 9, [1952], in Tate Papers; "Literature and the Little Magazines" (TS, Rockefeller report, November 1, 1955, in KC Collection), 12.
32. Ransom to Blackmur, January 1, [1956; wrongly dated 1955], in Blackmur Papers; Rockefeller Foundation resolution to grant $41,400 toward *Kenyon Review* fellowships, June 20, 1952, in KC Collection.

gratefully submitted the work written during their fellowships on their own initiative. Their work almost invariably was of such high quality that it was enthusiastically accepted and paid for at the regular rates. Again we find a sort of interaction. The grant required Ransom to exert himself and to look for new talent; his keen eye for coming writers, and his intimate knowledge of the literary world because of his editorship, ensured a varied list of gifted Fellows.

Even though a few writers, such as Walter Elder, Kaj Klitgaard, Robie Macauley, and Robert Wooster Stallman, inquired about their possible eligibility after reading the announcement about the fellowships in the autumn, 1952, issue, the selection procedure was not based on open application, which would have involved an exorbitant amount of work for the editors. Ransom and Rice generally wrote to the *Kenyon's* advisory editors and other literary friends and asked for suggestions. Marianne Moore, for example, proposed Ernest Jones, fiction critic of *The Nation,* R. P. Blackmur, Leonie Adams, Louise Bogan, and Ralph Hodgson; Arthur Mizener proposed Howard Nemerov, Reed Whittemore, and Clay Putman; Francis Fergusson also proposed Leonie Adams as well as Joseph Frank, William Merwin, Robert Fitzgerald, and Leslie Fiedler. The eventual list of *Kenyon Review* Fellows contains many writers who soon came to achieve national acclaim. The Fellows for 1953 were: in poetry, Edwin Watkins; in fiction, Flannery O'Connor; in criticism, Irving Howe. For 1954: in poetry, William Merwin; in fiction, George Lanning and Flannery O'Connor; in criticism, Richard W. B. Lewis. For 1955: in poetry, Edgar Collins Bogardus and Douglas Nichols, both from Kenyon College; in fiction, Howard Nemerov; in criticism, Richard Ellmann. For 1956: in poetry, Ruth Stone; in fiction, Andrew Lytle; in criticism, Leslie Fiedler and the drama critic Theodore Hoffman. For 1957: in poetry, to prop up rather than to encourage, Delmore Schwartz; in fiction, James F. Powers and Elizabeth Spencer; in criticism, Francis Fergusson. And for 1958: in poetry, James Wright and Theodore Henry Holmes; in fiction, Robie Macauley; and in criticism, Thomas Henry Carter.[33]

A number of these Fellows had published in the *Kenyon* before, but

33. "Kenyon Review Fellowships," *KR,* XIV:4, n.p.; Marianne Moore to the editors, November 8, 1952, Arthur Mizener to Ransom, November 19, 1952, both in KC Papers; Francis Fergusson to Rice, October 21, [1952], in *KR* Papers. The appointment of four Fellows instead

now they belonged to Ransom's elect. They benefited greatly from their appointments. Their literary abilities were now manifestly recognized by the prestigious *Kenyon Review,* and the money bought them time to devote to serious work instead of hack writing. A selection of the Fellows' reactions confirms this. Irving Howe, who compared his acceptance as a critic in New York intellectual circles to "gaining applause for a recitation at a family party," did not feel acknowledged as a serious critic until "a letter arrived . . . from John Crowe Ransom . . . saying I had been chosen for a Kenyon Fellowship in Criticism. For all one's New York cockiness, one still wanted a word, a glance, from those distant spaces beyond the Hudson." And Flannery O'Connor, working away lonely and ill in Milledgeville, Georgia, wrote to John Marshall that the fellowships had been "a great help . . . financially and in the way of encouragement." In a later letter, she elaborated: "Generally you expect to make a thousand or two dollars from a novel but nothing from a book of stories, and not much from the individual story published in a quarterly, so that if you don't have much money, you can't well afford to write stories. . . . You will probably agree that my stories are better than my novel [*Wise Blood* (1952)]—anyway, at the time that I wanted to write stories and had stories to write, I felt free to write them, thanks to the fellowship." Edwin Watkins "cried like a Frenchman" when he heard that he had been elected the *Kenyon's* first Fellow in Poetry.[34]

Challenging the New Criticism

The battle over the Bollingen Prize, the great amount of money given both directly and indirectly by the respectable Rockefeller Foundation to *The Kenyon Review,* the monopoly position the New Critics had built up in the universities: all this indicates the consolidation and institutionalization in the late 1940s and early 1950s of the New Criticism and the critical quarterlies, among which *The Kenyon Review* was foremost. Paradoxically, while academics warmed to the

---

of three is easily explained: the majority of the chosen Fellows were unmarried and therefore cheap, and the unused money went toward the appointment of the extra Fellows.

34. Howe, *A Margin of Hope,* 148; Flannery O'Connor to John Marshall, August 28, September 14, 1955, both in KC Collection; Edwin Watkins to Ransom, December 19, [1952], in *KR* Papers.

New Criticism, Ransom grew cold to it, or, rather, grew cold to the academic version of the New Criticism as represented, for him, by Robert Wooster Stallman and others. He condemned the academic "cold-blooded critics of poetry working away at what sometimes appear to be merest exercises with words"; he damned the "doctrinal satisfactions" leading to "shallow judgements" that are "especially brutal when the critic is led to reject on the basis of supposed technical or formal requirements." As early as 1947, in "the Formal Analysis," Ransom had taken his distance from Cleanth Brooks's *The Well Wrought Urn,* feeling that the New Criticism had been "slightly disappointing to the expectations it had aroused." Even though a year later, in a review of Stanley Edgar Hyman's book on the New Critics, *The Armed Vision,* Ransom doubted whether it was "wise as yet to sell this criticism short," he did think that "actual production and merchandizing in this business are ready for a going over." [35]

Therefore, while at the turn of the decade *The Kenyon Review* was generally considered the epitome of the New Criticism, the essays contributed by the New Critics were, in fact, few compared to those written by new, vital talents such as Paul Goodman, Leslie Fiedler, Richard Ellmann, Stanley Edgar Hyman, and Richard Chase. This is not to say that the *Kenyon* ignominiously dropped the first generation of New Critics, for Empson, Mizener, and Tate all retained their critical vitality and wholeheartedly shared Ransom's dislike of dull New Critical academics. The second generation of methodological New Critics, however, though they were influential in the universities, hardly ever appeared in *The Kenyon Review.*

If in his reviews of *The Well Wrought Urn* and *The Armed Vision,* Ransom had indicated which way *The Kenyon Review* was to go, his editorial intentions became even more clear with "The Critic's Business," a symposium featured in the *Kenyon's* tenth-birthday issue. Ransom had invited about half a dozen critics to react to his "provocative" Hyman review and to give their opinions on the outlook for literary criticism. It is telling that all the eventual contributors—

35. John Crowe Ransom, "Poets and Flatworms," *KR,* XIV, 159; John Crowe Ransom, "Introduction," in Ransom (ed.), *The Kenyon Critics: Studies in Modern Literature from The Kenyon Review* (Cleveland, 1951), viii; John Crowe Ransom, "Poetry: I. The Formal Analysis," *KR,* IX, 436; John Crowe Ransom, "The New Criticism," *KR,* X, 682.

William Barrett, Tate, Blackmur, and Chase—seized this opportunity to look back on the New Criticism as past, albeit elusive, history. Barrett, "puzzled as to the unity that is supposed to connect [the New Critics]," suggested that "the term itself, 'the new criticism,' ha[d] outlived its usefulness and could . . . be safely dropped." The true New Critics, such as Blackmur, Empson, Ransom, and Richards, whose one common "initial point of departure" had been "close textual analysis," now "each in his own direction, ha[d] moved beyond this task." Tate, referring likewise to the "myth" of the New Criticism but nevertheless acknowledging its presence in *The Kenyon Review,* strongly repudiated the academy's attempt to turn myth into methodology. Blackmur, describing himself as "the hunter and the hunted, in *The Kenyon*'s pages," argued that "the New Criticism which Mr. Ransom has gathered and firmed in *The Kenyon Review*" had "restored . . . the *aesthetic* to good standing," but had done this "to excess." Still, Blackmur thought that the time had come to start applying this kind of criticism to the novel, too. Richard Chase, who, as the youngest of the symposiasts, never had been bound or hindered by the bibliographical-historical chains of the academy, was the harshest judge of the New Criticism. He compared and contrasted it to the kind of moralistic criticism Van Wyck Brooks stood for, and, finding both kinds wanting, saw "a mobile middle ground" as "the only possible habitat for the critic."[36]

By initiating the pivotal symposium "My Credo," which appeared in the autumn, 1950, and winter and spring, 1951, issues, the editors helped to put the New Criticism in its proper perspective. "We have meant to assemble a catholic and various statement of the critic's business without presupposing any single kind of thing as preferred," Ransom wrote, asking Van Wyck Brooks to contribute. "My Credo," a continuation of "The Critic's Business," was also and more important a direct consequence of the Kenyon School of English. Reporting on a meeting of its Senior Fellows, Ransom wrote to Rice:

36. "Statement" (TS, n.d., in Tate Papers); William Barrett, "The Critic's Business: A Present Tendency in American Criticism," *KR,* XI, 4; Allen Tate, "The Critic's Business: A Note on Autotelism," *KR,* XI, 13; Richard Blackmur, "The Critic's Business: For a Second Look," *KR,* XI, 7, 8. Only a few months earlier, though, in "A Burden for Critics," which appeared in the summer, 1948, issue of *The Hudson Review,* Blackmur had severely attacked the New Criticism for being facile and limited. Richard Chase, "The Critic's Business: New vs. Ordealist," *KR,* XI, 13.

During our session at New York I made the point, which I hold to rather strongly, that one of the benefits of the School of English has been the approach to amity and to common views insofar as community is possible among the teaching Fellows. Matthiessen backed this up strongly, and Trilling was at least sympathetic. But we were all aware that the Foundation would want to see objective evidence of this, and we knew of a little such evidence. Then it occurred to me that something might be done that would be very strong evidence, and of some value otherwise though it could not be improvised in a hurry. Suppose the Kenyon Review should ask the individual Fellows of the School, or a good many of them, to take 2500 to 5000 words apiece and write out their critical Credoes. I think it would be of interest in view of the many misrepresentations which enemies make of the new critics, and might surprise even the critics themselves. It would compel some of the critic-Fellows to search their hearts. KR could print them in instalments, and eventually the New Directions people would surely be delighted (or some other publisher if we preferred another) to publish them all in a book: My Critical Credo, by 15 Kenyon Critics, or something like that.[37]

Rice, the *Kenyon's* acting editor during Ransom's time in Bloomington, found this a perfect proposal and, together with Ransom, drafted a form letter that they sent out to the School's Fellows and to practically all prominent critics, mainly American, of every persuasion: from Bentley to Bush, Frye to Fiedler, Rahv to Richards, and Sartre to Spender. Part of this form letter said: "[I]t would be a public service if various well-known critics quite independently of each other should write out for publication their critical Credoes. . . . The occasion would seem to demand of each critic that he search his own heart afresh if need be, at any rate that he indicate the vital philosophy from which his way of criticism must have proceeded, and the personal and social responsibilities which it required him to assume."[38]

In spite of the absence of a few important, provocatively polemical critics who reneged on their acceptance of this invitation, such as F. R. Leavis and Philip Rahv, the symposium represented, as planned, a broad range of critical approaches.[39] Leslie Fiedler's ambitious, ar-

37. Ransom to Van Wyck Brooks, February 17, 1951, in Van Wyck Brooks Papers; Ransom to Rice, December 10, [1949], in Rice Papers.

38. Ransom and Rice to (among others) F. O. Matthiessen, December 27, 1949, in Matthiessen Papers.

39. The symposium "My Credo" consists of the following articles: in the autumn issue of Volume XII, we find Leslie Fiedler, "Toward an Amateur Criticism," 561–74; Herbert Read, "The Critic as Man of Feeling," 575–580; Richard Chase, "Art, Nature, Politics," 580–94; and

rogant, anti–New Critical plea, "Toward an Amateur Criticism," started off the symposium. Then the British critic Herbert Read declared: "Sympathy and empathy—feeling *with* and feeling *into*: these are the essential psycho-physical processes without which all criticism is null and dull." The next contributor, Richard Chase, did not yet stress the importance of myth in criticism, but proved himself to be truly Trilling's pupil in arguing that "the literary critic will find himself inescapably a political writer." William Empson spoke up for the New Criticism in the conclusion of the first installment of "My Credo": "There is room for a great deal of exposition, in which the business of the critic is simply to show how the machine is meant to work, and therefore to show all its working parts in turn." Ransom was more than agreeably surprised by the quality of these first four statements, which he described as "very *various* but all composed with great scruple and making philosophical (ethical, social, aesthetic, formal, etc) commitments about the demands which they make on literature and the proper and improper varieties of criticism."[40]

Meanwhile, Ransom had written to Tate that the symposium "very much need[ed] some old-line new-critic Credos, and most of all that means you." But Tate did not contribute and the editors had to be—and should have been—content with Cleanth Brooks's "The Formalist Critic," a level-headed, logical defense of the New Criticism. Although Brooks sympathized "with writers who are tired of reading rather drab 'critical analyses,'" he pointed to the dangers of Leslie Fiedler's "amateur" and Douglas Bush's "'human'" criticism. "The formalist critic knows as well as anyone that poems and plays and novels are written by men. . . . But the formalist critic is concerned primarily with the work itself," Brooks wrote decisively. Bush, sworn enemy of the New Criticism, emphasized that literature is "ethical" and "didactic." Given Brooks's excellent essay, Ransom's speaking of "some little let-down in the hands of Bush and Brooks"

William Empson, "The Verbal Analysis," 594–601; in the winter, 1951, issue of Volume XIII, we find Cleanth Brooks, "The Formalist Critic," 72–81; Douglas Bush, "The Humanist Critic," 81–92; and Northrop Frye, "The Archetypes of Literature," 92–110; finally, in the spring issue of Volume XIII, we find Stephen Spender, "On the Function of Criticism," 207–17; Arthur Mizener, "Not in Cold Blood," 218–25; and Austin Warren, "The Teacher as Critic," 225–30.

40. Read, "The Critic as Man of Feeling," 575; Chase, "Art, Nature, Politics," 591; Empson, "The Verbal Analysis," 597; Ransom to Arthur Mizener, September 7, 1950, in Mizener Papers.

shows that Ransom's own critical position was further from Brooks's than ever.[41] Northrop Frye's intricate, almost abstract credo was not exactly sparkling, but it did no damage to the *Kenyon*'s standards either, and was in fact a worthy conclusion to the second installment of credos.

Stephen Spender, Arthur Mizener, and Austin Warren were in the last part of the symposium. The British critic joined hands with the diverse group of anti–New Critics consisting of Fiedler, Read, Chase, Bush, and Frye; Mizener and Warren spoke in concert with the remaining few in favor of, or anyway not against, the New Criticism. Mizener's modest essay, which culminated in his tolerant statement that criticism "consists in getting hold of other people's insights, somewhere deep in the seriously idle, unawed, and affectionate part of the mind, and then, by whatever method serves the occasion best, trying to make them available," was perhaps the most sensible, but certainly not the most passionate, provocative opinion represented. Ransom was particularly satisfied with Warren's emphasis on the necessity and inevitability of tension and collaboration between historical scholarship and close reading, and hoped this essay would yet "stir . . . up" Tate "for our wind-up" in the summer, 1951, issue.[42]

But, as Rahv and Leavis failed to deliver the papers promised for that issue, Austin Warren's credo turned out to be the final one. Disappointing, too, was that though both Random House, where David McDowell now was an editor, and the University of Oklahoma Press had initially expressed an interest in "My Credo," the symposium did not appear in book form after all, probably because World Publishing Company in Cleveland was about to bring out *The Kenyon Critics* (1951), a selection of essays and book reviews that had appeared in the first twelve volumes of *The Kenyon Review*. A missed chance, nevertheless, for "My Credo" certainly was "something super in respect to timeliness & importance in the way of symposia": almost the whole gamut of contemporary critical approaches are represented in these three consecutive issues of *The Kenyon Review*.[43]

41. Ransom to Tate, September 6, 1950, in Tate Papers; Brooks, "The Formalist Critic," 77, 74; Bush, "The Humanist Critic," 86; Ransom to David McDowell, March 1, 1951, in Random House Papers.

42. Mizener, "Not in Cold Blood," 225; Ransom to Tate, April 3, [1951], in Tate Papers.

43. Ransom to Arthur Mizener, September 7, 1950, in Mizener Papers.

6 A Second Flowering of Criticism
1947–1955

The Donne Series and the Dante Symposium

"My Credo" illustrated that the New Criticism was wilting, and that some of the new theoretical approaches in criticism were fresh and stimulating. Nevertheless, in part of *The Kenyon Review*, particularly in its continued tradition of successful symposia and series, the old New Criticism was still alive. The sequence on John Donne, which the editors had organized "[i]n the belief that he deserves a new evaluation now that the controversial period has passed," is a case in point. This series was opened by William Empson's malicious review of Rosemond Tuve's *Elizabethan and Metaphysical Imagery* (1947) in the autumn, 1949, issue, and brought to a close by the same author's elaborate discussion, "Donne the Space Man," in the summer, 1957, issue.[1] As had become the usual *Kenyon* practice with a unified series of articles on one author, Ransom and Rice asked someone else to become guest editor. Charles Coffin, chairman of the Kenyon College English department, one of Ransom's "best friends," and, most

1. Editor's note to William Empson, "Donne and the Rhetorical Tradition," *KR*, XI, 571. The Donne series consists of the following articles: William Empson, "Donne and the Rhetorical Tradition," *KR*, XI, 571–87; Arnold Stein, "Structures of Sound in Donne's Verse," *KR*, XIII, 20–36; Josephine Miles, "A Language of the Donne Tradition," *KR*, XIII, 37–49; Arnold Stein, "Structures of Sound in Donne's Verse (continued)," *KR*, XIII, 256–78; D. W. Harding, "Coherence of Theme in Donne's Poetry," *KR*, XIII, 427–44; Marius Bewley, "Religious Cynicism in Donne's Poetry," *KR*, XIV, 619–46; Austin Warren, "The Very Reverend Dr. Donne," *KR*, XVI, 268–77; Robert M. Adams, "Donne and Eliot: Metaphysicals," *KR*, XVI, 278–91; Charles Coffin, "Donne's Divinity," *KR*, XVI, 292–98; L. L. Miller, "Communication," *KR*, XVI, 505; and William Empson, "Donne the Space Man," *KR*, XIX, 337–99.

relevant here, the author of the standard work *Donne and the New Philosophy* (1937), enthusiastically accepted the editors' invitation.[2] As had become the custom, too, the editors shouldered part of the burden: Ransom and Rice wrote for contributions and invited, among others, Burke, Tate, Robert Penn Warren, and Austin Warren. As usual, too, Tate initially accepted and finally reneged.

Arnold Stein's "Structures of Sound in Donne's Verse," totaling about forty pages, is based on the obvious thesis that sound in Donne's poetry is not merely ornamental but significant. The essay is sometimes strained and basically boring. Even longer, certainly strained, basically unsound, but not boring in the least was Empson's conclusion to the series, tacked on in 1957 after a three-year interval: "Donne . . . from a fairly early age, was interested in getting to another planet much as the kids are nowadays." For all of the essay's Empsonian ingenuity and deft handling, it is quite understandable that Parker Tyler, the *Kenyon's* regular movie critic from 1947 onwards, was led to "wonder audibly at [its] odd direction and perhaps deliberately specious air," and that he argued that the essay sounded "categorically the wrong note and, astronomically as well as aerially speaking, [was] badly irrelevant to the purposes of metaphysical poetry."[3] Empson's first effort on Donne had been less air-built: he vehemently but persuasively waged war upon Rosemond Tuve, whom he accused of not realizing that Donne's words may have more than one meaning.

As he had done with Hopkins, Austin Warren treated his subject biographically with an ecclesiastical slant and, in accordance with his own background and interests, concentrated on Donne's sermons. Promised in October, 1949, Austin Warren's article was not submitted to the *Kenyon* until February, 1954. By that time, Coffin had immersed himself in the just-published first two out of ten volumes of Donne's *Sermons* (1953–1962), edited by E. M. Simpson and G. R. Potter. So Coffin's essay, "Donne's Divinity," appeared simultaneously, and somewhat redundantly, with Warren's in the spring, 1954, issue. As in her essay on Hopkins, Josephine Miles concentrated on Donne's language, pointing out that it had only minimally influ-

---

2. Ransom to Randall Stewart, May 1, [1956], in Stewart Papers.
3. Empson, "Donne the Space Man," 338; Parker Tyler to the editor, October 14, 1957, in *KR* Papers.

enced T. S. Eliot; Robert M. Adams counterbalanced Miles by discussing Donne and Eliot as "the key figures of metaphysical analogy"; Adams was counterbalanced in his turn by L. L. Miller, who discounted Adams because of his judging these poets as if he were God. Marius Bewley set out to prove that Donne's two brilliant *Anniversaries* only superficially deal with the deceased Elizabeth Drury and at a much more profound level deal with Donne's apostasy from the Roman Catholic Church; and D. W. Harding emphasized the continuous theme of anticipation in Donne's poetry in an essay in which biography and close reading are in perfect harmony.[4]

If the Donne series was successful, even if too drawn out in time, the Dante issue was superb. The roster of contributors to the spring, 1952, issue is indicative of its brilliance: T. S. Eliot, Charles Singleton, Erich Auerbach, Tate, Robert Fitzgerald, R. P. Blackmur, Jacques Maritain, and the guest editor Francis Fergusson.[5] At the time of his election as guest editor, Fergusson had not yet published any of his epoch-making works on Dante. As a matter of fact, Eric Bentley had regarded it as his duty to warn Rice that, according to the Italian poet-critic Paolo Milano, "someone should question everything Fergusson does with Dante."[6] But in electing Fergusson, the editors made a happy choice. In fact, everything seemed to conspire to turn this symposium into one of the *Kenyon*'s best. It was the only time during the entire run of the magazine that the editors managed to snare T. S. Eliot and that most of the desired contributors accepted and, what is more, had their essays in so that it took only about half a year to organize the symposium; not even Tate went back on his word.

From correspondence it appears probable that both the symposium and asking Fergusson to be guest editor were Rice's ideas. Be

4. Adams, "Donne and Eliot," 286; Miller, "Communication," 505.

5. The contents of the Dante issue, *KR*, XIV:2, are: T. S. Eliot, "A Talk on Dante," 178–88; Charles Singleton, "The Other Journey," 189–206; Erich Auerbach, "Farinata and Cavalcante," trans. W. R. Trask, 207–42; Francis Fergusson, "Purgatorio, Canto XVIII: The Fruit of Philosophy," 243–55; Allen Tate, "The Symbolic Imagination: A Meditation on Dante's Three Mirrors," 256–77; Robert Fitzgerald, "The Style That Does Honor," 278–85; Richard Blackmur, "Dante's Ten Terms for the Treatment of the Treatise," 286–300; and Jacques Maritain, "Dante's Innocence and Luck," 301–23.

6. Bentley to Rice, January 7, [1950], in *KR* Papers. Among Fergusson's works on Dante are *Dante's Drama of the Mind: A Modern Reading of The Purgatorio* (Princeton, 1953); *Dante* (New York, 1966); and *Trope and Allegory: Themes Common to Dante and Shakespeare* (Athens, Ga., 1977).

that as it may, Ransom immediately collaborated enthusiastically and, at Fergusson's request, approached Eliot. Fergusson concentrated on pressing and prodding his Princeton colleagues Blackmur, Fitzgerald, Maritain, and Tate. But, of course, selecting, inviting, and prodding contributors were not Fergusson's only tasks; he had to take care that there would be no overlap in topics and points of view. He also suggested the order in which the essays appeared.

Organizing this symposium took an unusually short time. But then Eliot's "A Talk on Dante," a testimony to Dante's modern vitality, had already been delivered at the Italian Institute in London and had been published in *The Adelphi* (1951), a British magazine hardly read in the United States. Tate did not have to think up a new essay either, his having been read as a Candlemas Foundation lecture at Boston College in February, 1951. Auerbach's essay was part of his classic *Mimesis,* published in German in Berne in 1946, but not translated into English until 1954. Fergusson himself adapted part of his forthcoming *Dante's Drama of the Mind* for *Kenyon Review* publication. But the ease with which the symposium was brought about does not detract from the editor's and the issue's merits. In the prestigious *Mercure de France,* Jacques Vallette described it as "copieux, important"; those closer to the *Kenyon*—Ransom, Rice, and Tate—could only find superlatives such as "exceedingly good," "topnotch," "brilliant"; and the editor, Fergusson, admitted to being "pretty pleased."[7]

In his "Talk on Dante," T. S. Eliot reviewed the whole range of his own poetry, a unique event. There was also "his sly restoration of Shelley to the canon," as Tate commented in a letter to Ransom. Tate was "a little disappointed" by Charles Singleton, who taught courses on Dante and Italian literature at Harvard. He was also somewhat disappointed in his friend Robert Fitzgerald. Ransom, too, found Fitzgerald's essay "the only ordinary piece" in an otherwise "brilliant" issue. With respect to Blackmur's intricate explication and application of Dante's criticism, Tate had "no doubt that Dick is on the trail of something very useful." For Jacques Maritain "to have writ-

7. Jacques Vallette, "Lettres Anglo-Saxonnes," *Mercure de France,* July 1, 1952, p. 534; Ransom to Tate, March 19, [1952], Rice to Tate, November 19, 1951, both in Tate Papers; Tate to Ransom, April 12, 1952, in *KR* Papers; Francis Fergusson to Tate, April 16, 1952, in Tate Papers.

ten that essay in English, is a triumph," Tate went on. Again, however, in spite of his repeated emphasis on the brilliance—a word Tate did not use lightly—of the Dante issue, Tate managed to find fault with Maritain. The Catholic philosopher's argument was, he said, "a little obscure without the context of the book [*Creative Intuition in Art and Poetry* (1953)] of which it is a part." Fergusson, however, found Maritain's essay "significant not only for the light it sheds on Dante, but as completing his ripest thoughts on poetry," and placed the essay "at the end, because his piece feels to me like 'the last word', and because the end, like the beginning, is a place of honor." And in spite of his comments, Tate admitted that Maritain's "essay teaches me a good deal more than any of the others. His sense of the relation of Dante to Baudelaire and to our own climate is extremely enlightening."[8]

"Well, as for Tate," Tate modestly went on, "he seems in retrospect elaborately thin." He confessed that he felt "an amateur" in the Dante field, even though Fergusson had assured him that his essay, "The Symbolic Imagination," was "simply first rate. . . . I don't care what the Dantisti may think or say. They could not dispute your general view without a restudy of the Paradiso (at least)—and that takes more pep than they've got." Indeed, this essay and its antipode, "The Angelic Imagination," belong with Tate's best critical work. Opposing the "angelic imagination," of which Poe is a clear example and "which tries to disintegrate or to circumvent the image in the illusory pursuit of essence," to Dante's "symbolic imagination," which is rooted in action and in concrete experience, Tate, for all his fascination with Poe, clearly opts for Dante, for the "Poetic Way."[9]

Dante is still in Purgatorio in Fergusson's paper, which he had selected from his work in progress "partly because it deals with the middle of the whole poem, between Singleton and Auerbach on the Inferno and Allen on the Paradiso." Tate judged this essay "the best, from every point of view," but Fergusson thought that honor should go to Auerbach's "Farinata and Cavalcante." In Tate's opinion Auerbach had "a real critical intelligence," but had brought

8. Tate to Ransom, April 12, 1952, in *KR* Papers; Ransom to Tate, April 9, [1952], in Tate Papers; Francis Fergusson to Ransom, February 7, 1952, in *KR* Papers.
9. Tate to Ransom, April 12, January 14, 1952, both in *KR* Papers; Francis Fergusson to Tate, December 18, 1951, in Tate Papers; Allen Tate, "The Angelic Imagination: Poe and the Power of Words," *KR*, XIV, 455–75; Tate, "The Symbolic Imagination," 260, 261.

"too much learning to bear up on a small focus . . . cluttering up the exposition." Fergusson disagreed and labeled Auerbach's contribution "one of the very most important contemporary studies of Dante." Although Auerbach's "very fascinating workout on the Cavalcanti episode"—which demonstrates the underlying paradox of the poem, namely, that the "image of man eclipses the image of God"— was over ten pages longer than the second-longest essay (Tate's "The Symbolic Imagination"), Fergusson found it too fine to cut.[10]

Individual Approaches to Criticism

As with the Hopkins issues, the editors decided that they had devoted enough space to Dante to last a lifetime, and so Dante was laid to rest, only to be resuscitated briefly in Leslie Fiedler's "Green Thoughts in a Green Shade," published in the spring, 1956, issue. Fiedler, a protégé of R. P. Blackmur's, appeared frequently in the *Kenyon*'s pages before he became its Fellow in Criticism for 1956. Although Fiedler recalled in 1964 that he had first encountered Ransom "in the loveliest letters of rejection I have ever had," correspondence shows that their first transactions did not go quite so smoothly. On October 19, 1947, Fiedler burst out: "It requires on my part a stubborn act of faith to send you yet more of my stuff. Yours is the only publication from which in my year + a half of submitting material I have received nothing but the dumb rebuke of a formrejection slip. In most cases I get at least some acceptance—in all, decent + interested notes of rejection. I should be less than frank, if I did not say that these anonymous pale slips of yours irk, annoy (and even, tho I am a resilient fellow, discourage) me. I like, in general, your taste, but I am equally fond of my own pieces. What is it?" Ransom's detailed, scrupulous reaction to the story submitted with this blast "pleased [Fiedler] greatly," as did Ransom's asking him to review for the *Kenyon*. Ransom regularly made this offer to authors whose submissions he did not yet find up to par, but of whom he expected so much that he wanted to tie them to his magazine.[11]

10. Francis Fergusson to Rice, January 25, 1952, Tate to Ransom, April 12, 1952, memo by Fergusson on the Dante issue, n.d., all in *KR* Papers; Francis Fergusson to Tate, November 19, [1951], in Tate Papers; Auerbach, "Farinata and Cavalcante," 242.
11. Leslie Fiedler, "Green Thoughts in a Green Shade: Reflections on the Stony Sestina of Dante Alighieri," *KR*, XVIII, 238–62; Leslie Fiedler, in D. David Long and Michael R. Burr (eds.), *John Crowe Ransom: A Tribute from the Community of Letters*, supplement to the *Kenyon*

Fiedler's first contribution to *The Kenyon Review* was a spring, 1948, review of *The Stature of Thomas Mann,* edited by Charles Neider, in which Fiedler took issue with a "general unwillingness to close with the problem of *evaluation*" with respect to Mann. Ransom was impressed and entrusted Fiedler with an omnibus review on the novel. Fiedler proved himself equal to the task. Among novels such as *The Mote and the Beam* by Percy Winner, *A Flask for the Journey* by F. L. Green, and "one of the most grotesquely melancholy books ever written," *Raintree County* by Ross Lockridge, Fiedler singled out for praise Saul Bellow's second novel *The Victim,* which he described as "one of the most complexly moving books of the past ten years," as "a novel that establishes in a single gesture its structure and its meaning." He faulted Trilling's *The Middle of the Journey,* though the "noblest version of the liberal position," as "a schedule" of its ideas, rather than a unified, felt novel. In the winter, 1951, issue, Fiedler's second omnibus review concerned fourteen collections of short stories, an even harder nut to crack, but one Fiedler himself had requested. Again, he exercised exceptional critical judgment: Irwin Shaw and Christopher Sykes are found wanting; William Carlos Williams' stories "are not sufficiently *written,* not enough re-realized in the passage through sensibility to language." Although Fiedler finds Paul Bowles "a pornographer of terror," in the end, the "astonishing ease and rhythmical beauty of [Bowles's] style" win him pride of place. Fiedler's emphasis on style is particularly striking in light of his later, better-known emphasis on myth, sociology, and psychology in his often eccentric but lively critiques.[12]

Sociology and psychology are, however, prominently present in the two essays Fiedler contributed during this period, besides his "Credo" and the article on Dante. In "Italian Pilgrimage," the lead essay in the summer, 1952, issue, Fiedler looks at the influence of America on Italy and Italian writing, and in passing praises Cesare Pavese, the main subject of his other article. Altogether, Fiedler was an important contributor of criticism before he became the *Kenyon*'s

---

Collegian, XC (1964), 13; Leslie Fiedler to the editors, October 19, 1947, Fiedler to Ransom, November 4, 1947, both in *KR* Papers.

12. Leslie Fiedler, "Mann and His Critics," *KR,* X, 349–54; Leslie Fiedler to Ransom, November 8, 1947, in *KR* Papers; Leslie Fiedler, "The Fate of the Novel," *KR,* X, 524, 527, 526; Leslie Fiedler, "Style and Anti-Style in the Short Story," *KR,* XIII, 161, 170.

Fellow in Criticism for 1956. His application outlined "a fullscale book on archetypal themes in the American Novel," which was to become his best-known work, *Love and Death in the American Novel* (1960). Ironically, his 1956 essay on Dante remained his only critical contribution to the *Kenyon* after his election as Fellow during Ransom's editorship.[13]

Irving Howe had been the *Kenyon*'s first Fellow in Criticism. This New York intellectual felt obliged to warn Ransom—"surely the *nicest* editor . . . I ever dealt with"—that he was "a Marxist of sorts, though an anti-Stalinist, of course, and a most heterodox Marxist at that." But Ransom was undaunted. He had read Howe's publications and knew that Howe did not often fall into the trap of political parochialism. Moreover, in outlining his fellowship project on the political novel, Howe had written that the "dangers of such a study are clear: that a consideration of ideology eliminates the matter of art, making one forget that one is dealing with a work of the imagination; or that an excessively narrow esthetic point of view does not allow one to see how the coarse and recalcitrant materials of political reality do enter the works of such writers. Of the latter danger one need not be quite so frightened as the former; perhaps, in reality they are not dangers so much as poles of perspective by which one orients oneself."[14]

Like Fiedler, Howe had already proven his worth in his contributions to the *Kenyon* before his election. He had written an article on the pervasive and ultimately tragic influence of the *Zeitgeist* on Sherwood Anderson, as well as a few reviews. His first was the spring, 1949, review of *The Collected Essays of John Peale Bishop,* edited by Edmund Wilson. Ransom was so impressed by this review, in which Howe shed light on Bishop's alienated life and excellent, epigrammatic criticism, that he included it in *The Kenyon Critics.* Howe's contributions after he was elected, two essays on Conrad and one on Dostoevsky, all stemmed from his fellowship project. The essays on Conrad happened to fall in beautifully with Ransom's plan to

13. Leslie Fiedler, "Italian Pilgrimage: The Discovery of America," *KR,* XIV, 359–77; Leslie Fiedler, "Introducing Cesare Pavese," *KR,* XVI, 536–53; Leslie Fiedler to Ransom, n.d., in *KR* Papers.

14. Irving Howe, *A Margin of Hope: An Intellectual Autobiography* (New York, 1982), 181; Irving Howe to Ransom, June 9, 1953, December 8, 1952, both in *KR* Papers.

"start a long series of Conrad studies." As it turned out, however, in spite of promises by—once again—Morton Dauwen Zabel and others, Howe's essays were two-thirds of the series: an essay by Vernon Young, *Hudson Review* Fellow for 1957, on the three Lingard novels was the only other contribution.[15]

In the lead essay in the autumn, 1953, issue, Howe focuses on the relation between literature and ideology, and discusses *Under Western Eyes*. Neglected in the United States at that time, *The Secret Agent* and *Nostromo* were treated in Howe's second installment. These personal, intelligent essays throw new light on Conrad's political nightmares. Howe could not, "short of emasculation," prevent his political views from coming into play, but this was all to the good, as he successfully applied the "trick" of letting "one's political ideas and knowledge enter into a view of the novels, without allowing them to distort." The same is true of his essay on Dostoevsky's *The Possessed*, which appeared one year later.[16]

The first contribution to the *Kenyon* by the next Fellow in Criticism, R. W. B. Lewis, also stood out. In sending Lewis' essay "Casella as Critic" to Ransom, Trilling commented: "R. W. B. Lewis, whom perhaps you know, and, if you know, probably admire as a remarkably gifted young critic, has sent me . . . the enclosed piece on R. P. Blackmur. . . . Lewis seems to write on the assumption that I am a working editor and I am explaining to him that I shall have no part in . . . acceptance or rejection of the essay. But I imagine you will like to have my opinion of it, which is very good." And indeed, even if Lewis' emphasis on Blackmur as a theologically oriented critic is somewhat farfetched, in general his remarks defending and explaining Blackmur's often intentionally intricate poetic narrative technique show an early and intelligent appraisal of the workings of Blackmur's mind. Blackmur's own "*Madame Bovary*" was chosen by

15. Irving Howe, "Sherwood Anderson: An American as Artist," *KR*, XIII, 193–203; Irving Howe, "The Cost of Distraction," *KR*, XI, 336–42; Ransom to David McDowell, June 12, 1952, in Random House Papers; Vernon Young, "Joseph Conrad: II. Lingard's Folly: The Lost Subject," *KR*, XV, 522–39.

16. Irving Howe, "Joseph Conrad: I. Order and Anarchy: The Political Novels," *KR*, XV, 505–21; Irving Howe, "Joseph Conrad: III. The Political Novels (cont.)," *KR*, XVI, 1–19; Irving Howe to Ransom, June 9, 1953, in *KR* Papers; Irving Howe, "Dostoevsky: The Politics of Salvation," *KR*, XVII, 42–68. Irving Howe's *Politics and the Novel*, one of the fruits of his fellowship, was published in New York by Horizon Press in 1957.

the editors to follow immediately upon "Casella as Critic." Its first five pages, which mainly deal with theoretical problems, are so complex as to need Lewis' preceding exegesis. But when Blackmur goes on to discuss *Madame Bovary* in detail, his scrupulous attention to the text, his insight into and explanation of "Bovarysme," which he defines as "an habitual, and infatuated practice of regarding, not the self, but the world as other than it is; . . . an attempt to find in the world what is not there," are all voiced with such lucidity as to render superfluous even so discerning an essay as Lewis'.[17]

In his second contribution, on William Faulkner's *The Bear*, Lewis' use of Christian symbols, giving rise to such empty ingenuities as "it requires only the slightest twist of the tongue to convert the story's title into 'The Birth,'" becomes too emphatic. Less fanciful was "Fiction and Power," which was "the first fruit" of his fellowship and "an unusually hard essay to put together." Lewis also wrote some reviews for the *Kenyon*, the most important and the best of which was "Poetry's Chevalier," on Randall Jarrell's provocative *Poetry and the Age*, "the soundest introduction available to modern American poems; and . . . the most irresistable." Possibly infected by Jarrell's "lyrical" criticism, by his "cunning rhetoric," Lewis' language here makes lighter and more pleasant reading than usual. Altogether, Lewis amply fulfilled Ransom's expectations as "holding great promise for the future."[18]

Ransom's favorite Fellow in Criticism was Richard Ellmann, who started his tenure in 1955. From 1948 to 1958, Ellmann contributed nine regular articles to *The Kenyon Review*, which gave him a position of authority if one considers that on average only some thirteen full-scale articles appeared in the magazine annually. Even though Ellmann was only in his early thirties when his first essay, "Robartes and Aherne," became the lead of the spring, 1948, issue, he was al-

---

17. R. W. B. Lewis, "Casella as Critic: A Note on R. P. Blackmur," *KR*, XIII, 458–74; Lionel Trilling to Ransom, March 9, 1951, in *KR* Papers; Richard Blackmur, "*Madame Bovary*: Beauty Out of Place," *KR*, XIII, 485 (reprinted in Richard Blackmur, *Eleven Essays in the European Novel* [New York, 1964]).

18. R. W. B. Lewis, "The Hero in the New World: William Faulkner's *The Bear*," *KR*, XIII, 649; R. W. B. Lewis, "Fiction and Power: Some Notes on Ignazio Silone," *KR*, XVII, 23–41; R. W. B. Lewis to Ransom, October 4, 1954, in *KR* Papers; R. W. B. Lewis, "Poetry's Chevalier," *KR*, XVI, 130, 129; Ransom to John Marshall, December 17, 1951, in KC Collection.

ready an accomplished critic; this first of his three essays on Yeats was included in *The Kenyon Critics*. In it Ellmann's trademark of ignoring the contemporary critical practice, which tended to be either purely biographical or purely critical, is already apparent.[19]

The discerning essay immediately following "Robartes and Aherne," W. H. Auden's "Yeats as an Example," was also included in *The Kenyon Critics*. Since Auden considers Yeats's influence on other poets, including himself, the essay tells us as much about Auden as about Yeats. Ellmann's and Auden's essays were part of a Yeats feature that was concluded by Bentley's "Yeats as a Playwright," in which he compares and contrasts Yeats and Eliot as dramatists. During these singularly successful years, the editors had once again composed a sequence that was not only harmonious and varied but brilliant as well. It is satisfying, too, to find that the poetry in this issue, "A Group of Irish Poems," including works by Roy McFadden, Donagh MacDonagh, and others, harmonized well with the emphasis on Yeats.[20]

Besides his work on Yeats, Ellmann is, of course, best known for his massive, definitive biography *James Joyce*. His first *Kenyon* article solely on Joyce, "The Backgrounds of *Ulysses*," led off the summer, 1954, issue. In a letter to Ransom, Ellmann emphasized that the essay was "more than a source-hunt—it's also a way of showing how the master's hand alters what his memory supplies—it's the first investigation of Joyce's methods of composition which has been able to start from something like the raw materials." And he described his autumn, 1958, essay "The Backgrounds of 'The Dead,'" as "a new interpretation of [Joyce's] story at the same time as it tries to relate the story to his other work and to his life." His "A Portrait of the Artist as Friend" was partly the result of Ransom's having sent him William Empson's article, "The Theme of *Ulysses*," a radio talk held

19. Richard Ellmann's articles are "Robartes and Aherne: Two Sides of a Penny," *KR*, X, 177–86; "The Ductile Universe of Henri Michaux," *KR*, XI, 187–98; "Joyce and Yeats," *KR*, XII, 618–38; "The Doctor in Search of Himself," *KR*, XIV, 510–12; "The Art of Yeats: Affirmative Capability," *KR*, XV, 357–85; "The Backgrounds of *Ulysses*," *KR*, XVI, 337–86; "A Portrait of the Artist as Friend," *KR*, XVIII, 53–67; "Wallace Stevens' Ice-Cream," *KR*, XIX, 89–105; and "The Backgrounds of 'The Dead,'" *KR*, XX, 507–28.

20. W. H. Auden, "Yeats as an Example," *KR*, X, 187–95; Eric Bentley, "Yeats as a Playwright," *KR*, X, 196–208. The contributors to "A Group of Irish Poems" were Valentin Iremonger, George M. Brady, Donagh MacDonagh, Roy McFadden, and Patrick MacDonogh.

for the BBC on Bloomsday, 1954. "Although I think Empson is obviously wrong," Ellmann reacted in a four-page letter, "his article is lively and worth printing," adding that if Ransom "would be interested in a quite different 'psychoanalysis' of Joyce's writings, based upon the same materials but reaching quite other conclusions, I have a paper which I gave last month before the English Institute which I should be glad to have you read." Ransom found Ellmann's "A Portrait of the Artist as Friend" a good corrective to "The Theme of *Ulysses,*" and placed it right after Empson's essay. In answer to Ransom's question whether Empson would mind coming out with Ellmann, Empson wrote that that "would be wildly unreasonable." But in a later letter, Empson commented that Ellmann's "scholarly background picture" was "clearly right as far as it goes," but it made "Joyce look so neurotic, not to say nasty, that he could not have been liberated into writing *Ulysses* at all."[21] This closed the discussion.

Ellmann found the fellowship, which he had received for his Joyce studies, "a tremendous help." In October, 1955, he was "well into [his] book without the distractions of teaching," and intended "to spend the summer [of 1956] in Trieste and Zurich . . . to check facts and add more information." Clearly, then, some of the luster of *James Joyce* reflects on the *Kenyon* and on Ransom, who, as early as 1956, had predicted that this biography in the making was "surely going to be author[it]ative." Apart from his essays on Joyce and Yeats, Ellmann also contributed essays on subjects that have a less obvious connection with him, such as William Carlos Williams and Henri Michaux. Ellmann's piece on Williams' autobiography was published together with an essay by Vivienne Koch on the same subject. This time, simultaneous publication had not been planned. Ransom was determined to have *The Autobiography of William Carlos Williams* reviewed, and when Vivienne Koch—whom he had asked "in desperation" after "five refusals"—kept on stalling, he had approached Ellmann, "whom I think well of, though totally foreign in background to Williams." Koch's and Ellmann's essays arrived at the

21. Richard Ellmann, *James Joyce* (1959; rev. ed., New York, 1983); Richard Ellmann to Ransom, January 25, 1954, July 3, 1958, both in *KR* Papers; William Empson, "The Theme of *Ulysses,*" *KR,* XVIII, 26–52; Richard Ellmann to Ransom, October 7, 1955, William Empson to Ransom, October 25, 1955, February 10, 1956, all in *KR* Papers.

same time and Ransom felt honor bound to accept both of them, even though both reflected disappointment with the autobiography. Finally, Ellmann's sensitive and intelligent essay on Michaux, accompanied by his expressive translation of Michaux's entrancing, fluid prose poem "In the Land of Magic," testify to Ellmann's versatility. Part of the credit for these last gems, incidentally, goes to Rice, who, during his trip to France in 1947, had learned about and become an admirer of this neglected Belgian-French poet.[22]

The selection of Fiedler, Howe, Lewis, and Ellmann as Fellows in Criticism, an idiosyncratic, a cultural, a Christian, and a biographical critic, clearly indicates Ransom's and Rice's catholicity. In a different way, this is also apparent in their refusing Robert Wooster Stallman a fellowship, even though this academic New Critic of the second generation kept applying for one from 1954 until the last round for 1958. Since his politely worded refusals apparently did not register, Ransom wrote pointedly: "We have in view for our next fellowship two candidates or so of almost equal rank with [Lewis, Howe, and Ellmann], so I leave it to you. We will send an application blank if you like." Stallman nevertheless tried again the year after. But the infusion of new kinds of spirited criticism in *The Kenyon Review* did not occur solely because of those lucky enough to become Fellows in Criticism. Very gifted, many-sided writers such as Howard Nemerov, Randall Jarrell, and Paul Goodman also frequently published critical articles in the *Kenyon*. During these years, Nemerov contributed several sparkling poetry reviews and one excellent short story, "Tradition." From 1956 onwards, he would contribute more fiction and more full-scale articles, but, strangely enough, no poetry at all. In 1954, Ransom wrote to John Marshall that he was not sure whether Nemerov "excell[ed] most at fiction or verse or criticism." He was sure, though, that Nemerov was "one of the most deserving writers of his age." By awarding Nemerov the fellowship in fiction for 1955 and by frequently publishing his criticism, the editors, ironically, helped to further Nemerov's career in all directions but the one on

22. Richard Ellmann to Ransom, October 7, 1955, in *KR* Papers; Ransom to Robert Wooster Stallman, January 31, 1956, in Stallman Papers; Ransom to David McDowell, March 13, 1952, in Random House Papers; Vivienne Koch, "The Man and the Poet," *KR*, XIV, 502–10; Ellmann, "The Doctor in Search of Himself," 510–12; Henri Michaux, "In the Land of Magic," trans. Richard Ellmann, *KR*, XI, 173–86; Ellmann, "The Ductile Universe of Henri Michaux," 187–98.

which Nemerov himself had set his heart, poetry. "It's been . . . during the last year, I think, that I realized writing poems to be what I most wanted to do in this world, and realized, too, that I'd go on even if it could be rationally & geometrically demonstrated to me that I was the worst poet in the world."[23]

If the editors did not show ostensible confidence in Nemerov's talent as a poet, they did make him the *Kenyon's* regular poetry reviewer from 1948 to 1956.[24] In his first review, the lead of the summer, 1948, book review section, Nemerov discussed C. Day Lewis, Ruth Herschberger, Norman Macleod, Jarrell, and Tate. Although Nemerov was only twenty-eight, he did not suffer from youthful timidity, and scrutinized each and every one of these poets severely, only Tate and Jarrell coming off well. As in his other omnibus review, "Poets in the Dark," Nemerov quotes a bit here and there, but in the end he has not enough room to prove his case. He merely, though convincingly, asserts. Seven pages, however, proved sufficient for his persuasive discussion of *The Collected Poems of Dylan Thomas* (1953), which punctured Thomas' inflated reputation. Nemerov shows, by quoting and explaining a few representative, complexly vaporous stanzas, why he is no admirer of Thomas, but in all fairness also closely reads and quotes from the "few poems, and few poets have more, which strike . . . as perfected results and very beautiful."[25]

Good writing, close reading, a few comments on his personal prejudices and on the kind of sterile, prescriptive criticism that takes itself more seriously than poetry are again the main ingredients of "Three in One," on Theodore Roethke, Karl Shapiro, and Yvor Winters, and of "A Wild Civility," on Stephen Spender, W. H. Auden, and Randall Jarrell. His review of Robert Graves' *Collected Poems, 1955* departs somewhat from this recipe. Nemerov, an excellent close reader himself, starts off with a diatribe against the "dominant criticism of the day . . . which explains things." His object in discussing Graves,

23. Ransom to Robert Wooster Stallman, January 31, 1956, in Stallman Papers; Howard Nemerov, "Tradition," *KR,* XVII, 408–24; Ransom to John Marshall, November 29, 1954, Howard Nemerov to Ransom, November 20, 1952, both in *KR* Papers.
24. Nemerov's poetry reviews are "The Poets," *KR,* X, 501–507; "Poets in the Dark," *KR,* XII, 165–72; "The Generation of Violence," *KR,* XV, 477–83, on Dylan Thomas; "Three in One," *KR,* XVI, 144–54; "A Wild Civility," *KR,* XVII, 476–84; and "Just a Good Poet," *KR,* XVIII, 131–36, on Robert Graves. He also wrote a review of three novels by William Sansom, "Sansom's Fictions," *KR,* XVII, 130–35.
25. Nemerov, "The Generation of Violence," 478.

Nemerov continues, "is appreciation, which is something like advertisement; benign descriptions and free samples. How undignified!" But he manages beautifully.[26]

Randall Jarrell, of course, is the past master at the kind of appreciative criticism Nemerov speaks up for. Fortunately, Jarrell could keep the "[s]omething in me [that] does not *want* me to write criticism" sufficiently at bay to write the combative or laudative, but always exciting and refreshing essays that made him one of America's major critics. Two of his very best essays, "Walt Whitman: He Had His Nerve" and "To the Laodiceans" on Frost, appeared in the 1952 *Kenyon Review.* Although Ransom could not refrain from inserting a Ransomian modifier, his description of these essays as "almost epoch-making in establishing for the first time securely the position which Robert Frost and Walt Whitman occupy in American poetry" is unprecedentedly laudatory.[27]

Earlier, Ransom and Rice had been so taken with Jarrell's criticism as it had appeared in different magazines that they suggested that Jarrell write "a literary column of Views and Impressions" every other issue beginning with the winter, 1952, one. This proposal, the most generous they ever made to anybody, reflected their utter confidence in Jarrell's critical abilities. Jarrell accepted this honor enthusiastically and sent in his essays on Whitman and Frost. But, with his 1938 New Critical piece on Housman, these turned out to be his only articles in *The Kenyon Review.* Perhaps they cost him too much. Jarrell wrote: "Here's my article—a piece about Whitman over which I've labored like a hermit horse; for a number of days I've eaten, slept, and written my Whitman article and done no other

26. Nemerov, "Just a Good Poet," 131, 133.
27. Randall Jarrell to Ransom, n.d., in *KR* Papers; Randall Jarrell, "Walt Whitman: He Had His Nerve," *KR,* XIV, 63–79; Randall Jarrell, "To the Laodiceans," *KR,* XIV, 535–61; John Crowe Ransom, "The Rugged Way of Genius," in Robert Lowell, Peter Taylor, and Robert Penn Warren (eds.), *Randall Jarrell 1914–1965* (New York, 1967), 159. Randall Jarrell wrote to Mary Von Schrader, [January, 1952], that he had felt "right distressed" when he found out that "Mr. Ransom, dear sweet idiot that he is, had *changed* the title without telling me. My 'Some Lines from Whitman' had become (a quotation from later in the article) 'Walt Whitman He Had His Nerve.' . . . He meant well, but gee, gee!" (Letter in Mary Jarrell [ed.], *Randall Jarrell's Letters: An Autobiographical and Literary Selection* [Boston, 1985], 315). Robert Lowell, in "Randall Jarrell," in Lowell, Taylor, and Warren (eds.), *Randall Jarrell,* 104, wrote: "[E]ulogy was the glory of Randall's criticism. . . . He left many reputations altered and exalted. I think particularly of his famous Frost and Whitman essays."

thing, not one." And: "This is a letter from a really exhausted man, but from one that feels awfully good; I'm hopeful that I've really done the best I could with Frost."[28]

The *Kenyon's* preference for wide-ranging, independent thinkers rather than specialized, methodological critics is also apparent in its frequent publication of Paul Goodman at the time when he wrote his best work, long before he became fashionable in the 1960s. The 1942 article on Frank Lloyd Wright was followed by one on Freud, which in style resembled a psychoanalytical session; by an excerpt from his impressionistic, perhaps best book of literary criticism, *Kafka's Prayer* (1947); and by an informative, partly psychological explanation of the importance and construction of Japanese Noh plays. He also contributed a psychological-sociological description of the relation between the avant-garde artist and his audience. His convincing thesis is that the avant-garde artist does not dwell in an ivory tower but, in contrast to the "integrated" artist "taking the environment for granted," is "essentially concerned with the immortal perfection of the particular society of which he is a member." These five essays, though widely varied in subject and style, have in common the prevalence of sudden, sharp flashes of insight over logically built-up trains of thought. Also, in nearly every essay, Goodman's essentially optimistic, perhaps even romantic conception of human nature emerges.[29]

From 1947 to 1955, Goodman also contributed eight book reviews on subjects ranging from Le Corbusier to psychiatry, and from Elizabethan England to modern short stories. His 1948 review of *Oscar Wilde* by Edouard Roditi was included in *The Kenyon Critics*. Although Goodman considered this biography to be of real value, he only partly agreed with Roditi's view of Wilde and spent half of his review giving his own ideas, and the other half quarreling with

28. The editors' suggestion is apparent in an autumn, 1951, promotion leaflet, in KC Collection. Randall Jarrell, "Texts from Housman," *KR*, I, 260–71; Randall Jarrell to Ransom, n.d., Jarrell to Ransom, n.d., both in *KR* Papers.

29. Paul Goodman and Percival Goodman, "Frank Lloyd Wright on Architecture," *KR*, IV, 7–28; Paul Goodman, "The Father of the Psychoanalytic Movement," *KR*, VII, 628–44; Paul Goodman, "Kafka's Prayer," *KR*, IX, 225–33; Paul Goodman, "Notes on a Remark of Seami," *KR*, XX, 547–53; Paul Goodman, "Advance-Guard Writing, 1900–1950," *KR*, XIII, 378.

Roditi about details. In a letter to the editors, written from Germany, where he lectured, Roditi showed that most of Goodman's quibbles were based on misinterpretation.[30]

Goodman's deprecatory, unjust review of *In Search of Theater* by Eric Bentley, which appeared in the autumn, 1953, issue, called forth reactions from angry readers, too. Bentley's own reaction was relatively moderate: "An author is obviously the most biased witness of reviews of his books. But it had seemed to me Goodman was not merely unfavorable but arrogantly ignorant—he said he knew nothing of Brecht and then proceeded to explain him to me." Because Goodman's review had seemed to him "to make a painful little spectacle," Lionel Trilling ventured the following piece of advice: "[M]ake it a policy not to review books of your advisory editors." Ransom disagreed: "I should think the general understanding . . . is that we leave all to the reviewer, and pick the best reviewers we can though with the reservation: not the friends, in any close sense, of the authors. . . . Isn't it good to seek the impression that we are willing ourselves to take the chances that other writers do?" Theodore Hoffman, a protégé of Bentley's, enclosed in a letter to Ransom "a sort of jeremiad against Paul Goodman's review of *In Search of Theatre*. I'd meant to submit it as a letter to the editor but my wrath never subsided enough for me to condense or temper it, so I suppose I must offer it for your private amusement or annoyance." In fact, Ransom somewhat regretted having published Goodman on Bentley and in the next issue he used Hoffman's indeed ferocious letter to offset the review.[31]

If two of Goodman's many contributions provoked polemics, absolutely all of Stanley Edgar Hyman's arrogant pieces did. For a while, Hyman also was one of the *Kenyon*'s cherished critics. Ransom

---

30. Paul Goodman, "French Uncle," *KR,* IX, 477–80, on Le Corbusier; Paul Goodman, "Jurisprudence vs. Psychiatry," *KR,* XI, 700–702; Paul Goodman, "An England Without Compromise," *KR,* XIII, 714–19; Paul Goodman, "They've Been Good Enough Long Enough," *KR,* XVII, 144–48, on short stories; Paul Goodman, "Tardy and Partial Recognition," *KR,* X, 340–46 on *Oscar Wilde*; Edouard Roditi, "Communications: Wilde, Goodman, and Roditi," *KR,* X, 699–700.

31. Paul Goodman, "Bentley on Theater," *KR,* XV, 662–68; Bentley to Ransom, December 19, [1953], Lionel Trilling to Ransom, October 12, 1953, both in *KR* Papers; Ransom to Lionel Trilling, October 20, 1953, in Thomas Daniel Young and George Core (eds.), *Selected Letters of John Crowe Ransom* (Baton Rouge, 1985), 372; Theodore Hoffman to Ransom, November 28, 1953, in *KR* Papers; Theodore Hoffman, "Communication," *KR,* XVI, 166–68.

particularly admired his writing "with documentation and forceful style" and his "many original insights" in folk literature. But Hyman's career as a *Kenyon Review* critic did not last long. In 1954, after Ransom had published three articles and two extensive reviews by Hyman, he "closed [the *Kenyon*'s] pages against him," because Hyman had been "poisonous to the people he didn't approve." Hyman's first article turned out to be his only commendatory one. It was the anti–New Critical but laudatory chapter on Caroline Spurgeon from his generally combative *The Armed Vision* (1948). This provoked only one, rather mild letter: G. Wilson Knight denied Hyman's claim that he had been deeply influenced by Spurgeon. Hyman's "Some Bankrupt Treasuries," an abusive review article about some ten books on folklore, did not get off as lightly. Paul R. Beath, whose *Febold Feboldson* Hyman had slaughtered, found Hyman's treatment "a classic misstatement of facts and deliberate misreading of plain language" and accused him of being, at best, "a mere pamphleteer."[32]

Hyman's devastating review of *Funk and Wagnalls Standard Dictionary of Folklore, Mythology, and Legend* (Volume I), a "seriously and essentially flawed" book, "almost to the point of becoming a joke," caused an avalanche of acrimonious letters. Half a year after the autumn, 1950, publicaton of this review, three of these reactions were published together with Hyman's reply. Erminie Voegelin, one of the contributors to the *Dictionary,* took Hyman to task for "several misstatements of fact," and M. J. Herskovits wondered at Hyman's hatred of anthropologists. In answering, Hyman sweetly suggested that Voegelin "might better spend her time seeing that some of the worst absurdities and deficiencies of the book are corrected for a second edition," and assured Herskovits that he did not intend to "drive anthropologists out of folklore study," but only wanted "to see them pulled off its back." A. C. Morris, editor of *Southern Folklore Quarterly,* had the last word: "[T]his dictionary in spite of its shortcomings is too valuable a beginning to be treated with . . . captiousness."[33]

32. Memo by Ransom concerning the appointment of his successor, November 23, 1957, in KC Papers; Ransom to Tate, November 23, 1957, in Tate Papers; Stanley Edgar Hyman, "The Critical Achievement of Caroline Spurgeon," *KR,* X, 92–108; G. Wilson Knight, "A Communication," *KR,* XI, 172; Stanley Edgar Hyman, "Some Bankrupt Treasuries," *KR,* X, 484–500; Paul R. Beath, "Communications," *KR,* XI, 313.

33. Stanley Edgar Hyman, "Dissent on a Dictionary," *KR,* XII, 722; Erminie Voegelin,

Hyman's other folk entry was a lively one, in which he submitted mildly that much modern Scottish poetry, such as Hugh Mac-Diarmid's, is disappointing. Although Bernard Landis felt obliged to rush to MacDiarmid's defense, the article was in fact not very belligerent. Hyman's "Myth, Ritual, and Nonsense," which appeared in the summer, 1949, issue and butchered books about myth, "the new intellectual fashion," provoked very different reactions. James Dickey was one of what must have been very few readers to be positively affected by it: he regards Hyman's quoting of Van Gennep's concept of "rites de passage" as the "literary or mythological precedent for *Deliverance*." Richard Chase, whose *Quest for Myth* was cut to pieces in the article, was not at all "moved to reply. . . . [Hyman] may fulminate at will for all of me, in fact." But R. W. Flint, who did not want his letter to be published because he did not "think Hyman's tactics are worth bothering with in public," was "horrified by the nastiness and dishonesty of it." Further, "it is not only superficial but senselessly malicious," he wrote, and concluded that he really did not "see why the prestige of the *Kenyon Review* need be put behind [Hyman's] bursts of venom."[34]

The editors, however, continued to appreciate Hyman's vitriolic articles until he went beyond civilized bounds with what Ransom termed his "'wild interpretation'" of Robie Macauley's first novel, *The Disguises of Love* (1952). Hyman tried to "defend and explain" this review because of his "enormous respect and admiration" for Ransom: "As for your general charges of immoderation and belligerence, I would agree that I have written harshly about many books, sometimes in your pages, but would argue that these attacks have been reserved for incompetence and dishonesty, particularly rife in my chosen field of folklore. Whether a critic ought to devote any substantial part of his efforts to exposing this trash is debatable, and

"Communications: Mr. Hyman and the Dictionary," *KR*, XIII, 315; M. J. Herskovits, "Communications: Mr. Hyman and the Dictionary," *KR*, XIII, 319–20; Stanley Edgar Hyman, "Communications: Mr. Hyman and the Dictionary," *KR*, XIII, 321, 322; A. C. Morris, "Communications: Mr. Hyman and the Dictionary," *KR*, XIII, 322.

34. Stanley Edgar Hyman, "The Language of Scottish Poetry," *KR*, XVI, 20–37; Bernard Landis, "Communications: Hugh MacDiarmid," *KR*, XVI, 334–35; Stanley Edgar Hyman, "Myth, Ritual, and Nonsense," *KR*, XI, 455; James Dickey in L. S. Dembo (ed.), *Interviews with Contemporary Writers: Second Series, 1972–1982* (Madison, Wis., 1983), 83; Richard Chase to Ransom, June 24, 1949, R. W. Flint to Ransom, July 4, 1949, both in *KR* Papers.

in the last few years I have in fact decided to concentrate on more constructive matters, but I do not agree that the effort is unfair or misguided, or the result of any personal belligerence. I just wish someone else were doing it." Not until 1957 was Hyman allowed to appear in the *Kenyon* again.[35]

New Critics and New York Intellectuals

Howe, Fiedler, Lewis, Ellmann, Nemerov, Jarrell, Goodman, and Hyman. Beyond dispute, *The Kenyon Review* was genuinely receptive to young talents in criticism. This does not mean, though, that the earlier contributors to the magazine were shelved: William Empson and R. P. Blackmur, for instance, contributed more articles during this period than they had before, and Tate's essays, compared to his earlier contributions, actually crowded the *Kenyon*. Burke, Matthiessen, and Trilling also continued to figure in its pages.

Empson, besides his contributions on Donne and Joyce and his "Credo," wrote five more articles and two reviews for the *Kenyon* from 1948 till Robie Macauley became its editor. Empson was, in fact, mainly a Kenyon School of English addition to the ranks of regular writers for the magazine. His first *Kenyon* article in years, "Emotion in Words Again," which appeared in the autumn, 1948, issue, was an outgrowth of the course he gave as a Fellow that summer, and it inaugurated a whole series of his essays in the *Kenyon*. In "Emotion in Words Again," which became part of his *The Structure of Complex Words* (1951), Empson, in the words of Cleanth Brooks, "works through, and loose from, the limitations of [his teacher I. A.] Richards' earlier theory about emotive words in poetry. Empson is admirably firm in refusing to make a 'flat separation of Sense from Emotion.'" Brooks found Empson on Richards "most interesting and rewarding," but Empson's overingenious treatment of the word "all" in *Paradise Lost*—he links "all" and "F*all*," for instance—was "pointless and quite unrewarding." The editors' opinion of Empson's article is apparent: they included it in *The Kenyon Critics*. But not all readers were pleased. F. R. Leavis, who had an ongoing feud with

35. Stanley Edgar Hyman's review of *The Disguises of Love* was not submitted to the *Kenyon*, but appeared in *The Hudson Review*, VI (1954), 417–22, and was entitled "Some Notes on the Albertine Strategy." Stanley Edgar Hyman to Ransom, March 12, 1954, in *KR* Papers.

Empson, wrote a furious letter from Cambridge. He was outraged because Empson had suggested that Leavis' own "*very* scrupulous and responsible criticisms of Richards [were] to be explained by personal hostility," and even went so far as to attribute Empson's "daring to be so irresponsible in print" to "his more alcoholic moments." A much subdued version of this letter was published in the spring, 1949, "Communications" section. Following Leavis' letter was one by Gerald Smith who, in his turn, jumped at Empson for attacking Richards. Empson's reply was diplomatic. He showed Smith that they did not "really disagree," and, though he was justifiably angry about some of Leavis' slurs on his character, Empson's statement that "his convictions about Leavis . . . [were] on the whole greatly in his favor" was conciliatory.[36]

"Sense in the Prelude," a spring, 1951, essay in which Empson contends that Wordsworth depended on an undeveloped theory about how the mind interprets what it gets from the senses, is one of Empson's weaker essays; it is clever but implausible. Empson's 1952 and 1953 essays on Shakespeare, on the other hand, were not only witty but convincing, too. Jarrell, for one, "enjoyed the[se] Empson pieces very much, though often he out-Holmes Sherlock by many miles." Empson gave Dover Wilson a hard time. He took issue with and partly refuted Wilson's interpretations and editing of *Macbeth*; and in his detailed fifty-page analysis of Falstaff, he showed that Wilson's sanctioning only one possible view of Falstaff and Prince Hal does not do them justice. To Murray Krieger, whose essay on *Richard III* he returned, Ransom explained his preference for Empsonian, unconventional criticism: "[W]e have always been especially skittish about papers on Shakespeare. I guess if we have used them, it has been when they were very comprehensive and radical too, like Empson's long piece on the Falstaff-Prince Hal relation." Sending to Monroe Spears, the editor of *The Sewanee Review*, the companion piece to "Falstaff and Mr. Dover Wilson," "*Hamlet* When New," Ransom voiced the same sentiments and added a personal

36. William Empson, "Emotion in Words Again," *KR*, X, 579–601; William Empson, *The Structure of Complex Words* (London, 1951); Cleanth Brooks, "Hits and Misses," *KR*, XIV, 672, 673; F. R. Leavis to Ransom, November 19, 1948, in *KR* Papers; F. R. Leavis, "Communications," *KR*, XI, 315–16; Gerald Smith, "Communications," *KR*, XI, 316–20; William Empson, "Communications," *KR*, XI, 672.

note: "It is very good writing, and good thinking, with just enough controversy and meanness in it to make it exciting to the literary mind; and the typography is as always in execrable shape. We'll try our luck with Falstaff, which is the less good of the two. . . . I hope you'll find a place for yours; if not just return it to me. Empson is so important, I think, and has been so handicapped alone in China, removed even from any sort of library, that I very much like to serve him if possible."[37]

Empson's two book reviews also dealt with Shakespeare. In the spring, 1949, issue, he discussed Robert Heilman on *King Lear* in *The Great Stage,* and in the winter, 1954, issue, he violently disagreed with many of the points G. R. Elliott had made about *Othello* in *Flaming Minister.* As a victim, Elliott proved to possess admirable resilience: "[M]y enjoyment of [Empson's] really remarkable essay is impaired by the sensation of partial (but not unbloody) decapitation. He . . . discusses only the first word of my main topic, 'pride and self-esteem' . . . ignoring the distinction . . . between false pride and . . . right self-esteem." Empson's final contribution dealt with *Tom Jones* and took up about one-fifth of the space in the spring, 1958, issue, which was much less than his articles on Falstaff and on Donne as spaceman. Those essays had each taken up more than one-third of an issue, a privilege granted to the select few in this magazine committed to concision. In "Tom Jones," Empson set about rescuing Fielding from being "under-rated" and from being read "as a cynical aristocrat." The essay, "one of his best," as Ransom wrote to Richard Blackmur, certainly was a worthy conclusion to Empson's brilliant critical career in *The Kenyon Review.*[38]

Ransom continued his letter to Blackmur by emphasizing that, his admiration for "Tom Jones" notwithstanding, he would "certainly

37. William Empson, "Sense in the Prelude," *KR,* XIII, 285–302; William Empson, "Dover Wilson on *Macbeth,*" *KR,* XIV, 84–102; William Empson, "Falstaff and Mr. Dover Wilson," *KR,* XV, 213–62; Randall Jarrell to Ransom, n.d., Ransom to Murray Krieger, January 28, 1957, both in *KR* Papers; Ransom to Monroe K. Spears, November 19, 1952, in *SR* Papers. "*Hamlet* When New" appeared in two parts in *The Sewanee Review,* LXI (1953), 15–42 and 185–205.
38. William Empson, "The Errors of King Lear," *KR,* XI, 342–54; William Empson, "The Pride of Othello," *KR,* XVI, 163–66; G. R. Elliott, "Communications: Othello Is Saved," *KR,* XVI, 335; William Empson, "Tom Jones," *KR,* XX, 217–49; William Empson to Ransom, January 25, [1958; wrongly dated 1957], in *KR* Papers; Ransom to Blackmur, February 14, [1958], in Blackmur Papers.

not prefer it to yours by any means." Ransom referred to Blackmur's
"Ara Coeli and Campidoglio," which Blackmur had promised as his
"'big essay'" for the spring, 1958, issue in October, 1957, but which
he eventually submitted only just in time for the summer, 1958, one.
Ransom regarded Blackmur as "the best critic in America," a judgment that was, of course, reflected in *The Kenyon Review*. Besides
some book reviews, the number of Blackmur's essays comes second
only to those by Ransom himself. Blackmur's biographer, Russell
Fraser, and his best critic, Robert Boyers, as well as many others emphasize that in the 1950s Blackmur was definitely not a New Critic
anymore. This change is apparent not only in Blackmur's attack on
the New Critics, "A Burden for Criticism," but also in his later articles dealing with particular novelists, poets, and essayists. Many of
these appeared in *The Kenyon Review*. Fraser and Boyers also agree
that the later Blackmur is not half as good a critic as the earlier, more
concrete, New Critical Blackmur had been.[39]

Since Ransom did not care about fashions in criticism and critics,
Blackmur's growing fame can hardly have seduced him into publishing so much of Blackmur's later, opaque criticism. One could specu-
late that Blackmur's extremely high standing with the Rockefeller
Foundation, the *Kenyon's* main sponsor, prevented the editors from
rejecting Blackmur's obscurer articles, but correspondence reveals
that such mercenary motives do not apply. In his letters to Blackmur,
Ransom constantly asks for more articles and reviews—"we don't
want to go through the Autumn number without another Blackmur
item in our pages"—and, when Blackmur delivers them (usually
late), finds them "distinguished" or simply "damned good." Moreover, Ransom also praised Blackmur in letters to others: "I think he
is a great man," Ransom told Arthur Mizener.[40]

Blackmur's contributions to "The Critic's Business," to the Dante

39. Richard Blackmur, "Ara Coeli and Campidoglio," *KR*, XX, 337–61; Blackmur to
Ransom, October 30, 1957, in *KR* Papers; Ransom to Franze Edward Lund, November 6,
1957, in *KC* Papers; Russell Fraser, *A Mingled Yarn: The Life of R. P. Blackmur* (New York,
1981); Robert Boyers, *R. P. Blackmur: Poet-Critic: Toward a View of Poetic Objects* (Columbia,
Mo., 1980).

40. Ransom to Blackmur, May 16, March 8, 1956, both in *KR* Papers. Richard Blackmur,
"Emily Dickinson's Notation," *KR*, XVIII, 224–37, was "one of your most distinguished
writings"; and Richard Blackmur, "*Anna Karenina:* The Dialectic of Incarnation," *KR*, XII,
433–56, was "damned good." Ransom to Blackmur, July 21, [1950], in Blackmur Papers;
Ransom to Arthur Mizener, February 3, [1953], in Mizener Papers.

symposium, and his essay on *Madame Bovary* have already been discussed. "Parody and Critique: Notes on Thomas Mann's *Doctor Faustus*," which appeared in the winter, 1950, issue, and "*Anna Karenina*: The Dialectic of Incarnation," which appeared two issues later, were published with "*Madame Bovary*: Beauty Out of Place" in *Eleven Essays in the European Novel* (1964). These three as well as most of the other essays Blackmur contributed to the *Kenyon* during this period are sufficiently well known and too idiosyncratic and resistant to summary for extensive discussion here. It is more to our purpose to look behind the scenes at the author's own notes and remarks, and at Ransom's and other readers' reactions as expressed in private correspondence.[41]

Blackmur's "Parody and Critique" was included in *The Kenyon Critics*. But R. W. Flint, faithful *Kenyon* reader, was "pretty much anti-Blackmur on *Faustus* by Mann." He objected to Blackmur's theological assumptions. Even Ransom, though he admired its "elevation" and "seriousness," found the essay "a little bit shrill." But Thomas Mann himself was unrestrictedly laudatory: "[T]he repeated perusal of the study has given me great satisfaction, and . . . quite apart from its topic, I admire Mr. Blackmur's work as a highly distinguished critical achievement."[42]

In "Ransom as Editor," George Lanning tells the following anecdote about Blackmur's essay on *Anna Karenina*:

Another time, one of the magazine's less enthusiastic supporters on the faculty brought in his copy of the latest issue and said, "John, read that first paragraph." (The piece in question was an essay by R. P. Blackmur on *Anna Karenina*.)
Mr. Ransom dutifully read the first paragraph.
"Now, tell me," said his colleague, "what the hell that *means*."
"I don't know!" Mr. Ransom replied cheerfully. "I don't know."

41. Richard Blackmur, "Parody and Critique: Notes on Thomas Mann's *Doctor Faustus*," *KR*, XII, 20–40; Richard Blackmur, "*Anna Karenina*: The Dialectic of Incarnation," 433–56; Richard Blackmur, "*Madame Bovary*: Beauty Out of Place," *KR*, XIII, 475–503. Blackmur's other essays for the *Kenyon* during the period under discussion are "The Politics of Human Power," *KR*, XII, 663–73; "In the Hope of Straightening Things Out," *KR*, XIII, 303–14; "Lord Tennyson's Scissors: 1912–1950," *KR*, XIV, 1–20; "Toward a Modus Vivendi," *KR*, XVI, 507–35; "The Substance That Prevails," *KR*, XVII, 94–110; "Reflections of Toynbee," *KR*, XVII, 357–70; and "Adams Goes to School," *KR*, XVII, 597–623.
42. R. W. Flint to Ransom, November 18, 1950, in *KR* Papers; Ransom to Rice, January 20, [1950], Thomas Mann to Rice, March 24, 1950, both in Rice Papers.

Anyway, Ransom had told Blackmur that he was much impressed by his "damned fine piece." And indeed, the first page and a half, in which he submits his vague thesis that "the dialectic of incarnation" is important in *Anna Karenina,* are unclear and unreadable, but Blackmur comes down to earth in his actual discussion of the novel. What he says makes sense, and the way in which he says it is lucid enough. Philip Rahv, an authority on Russian writers, however, did not think so: he "was somewhat exasperated by [Blackmur's] essays on Russian novels."[43]

Blackmur contributed an "admirable" essay on *The Liberal Imagination* by Lionel Trilling to the autumn, 1950, issue under one of his "fuzzy captions," "The Politics of Human Power." The ideologue in Blackmur was attracted by Trilling's cultural ideology, and he treated Trilling sympathetically. But Blackmur's lenience did not thrill everyone. He reported, "Fergusson . . . thinks I took too mild a policy towards Trilling; he thinks I ought to have attacked him directly with explicit disagreements." Predictably, T. S. Eliot's *Selected Essays* gave Blackmur more trouble. He reviewed them lovingly in an essay entitled "In the Hope of Straightening Things Out" in the spring, 1951, issue. In a letter to Ransom, though, about this "essay-review of the Possum," he spoke of "other lines" he might have taken "which will lead to a more formal assessment of this and of that. Eg: the failure to deal well with contemporary poetry, with the novel at all, and the general habit of dealing with all literature on the lines that belong appropriately only to lyric poetry. But I would rather give the man a chance." The editors enthusiastically accepted the article; it was one of the few laudatory articles on Eliot as a critic to appear in *The Kenyon Review.*[44]

The lead essay in the winter, 1952, issue, "Lord Tennyson's Scissors: 1912–1950," a failed poet's tirade against most of his fellow modern poets, understandably provoked hostile reactions. As a critic, Philip Rahv was not personally harmed by this diatribe, but he was appalled nevertheless: "Blackmur's article in the recent Kenyon did [strike] me

---

43. George Lanning, "Ransom as Editor," in Thomas Daniel Young (ed.), *John Crowe Ransom: Critical Essays and a Bibliography* (Baton Rouge, 1968), 216; Ransom to Blackmur, July 21, [1950], in Blackmur Papers; Philip Rahv to Tate, March 10, 1952, in Tate Papers.

44. Ransom to Tate, September 6, 1950, in Tate Papers; Blackmur to Ransom, October 13, 1950, January 23, 1951, both in *KR* Papers.

as a *ne plus ultra* of some kind . . . which kind I don't quite know. He was bent on telling everybody off, all but Eliot and Yeats; Pound just barely gets in under the wire. He is writing criticism now of a type all his own, neither 'new' nor old, just Blackmur on a bender." Tate took offense, too, not so much because in the "School of Donne" he and Ransom were presented as "models of the uncontrollable in pseudo-control," but because Blackmur had treated Yeats, Eliot, and Pound as some kind of "Holy Trinity." Tate described the essay as "brilliant, but awfully cranky and presumptuous." He wrote to Ransom: "There's a sort of Delphic pomposity, along with an arrogant frivolity, that really gets on my nerves," and enclosed a nearly four-page angry "Letter to the Editor," in which he took issue with Blackmur's attempt, as Tate saw it, to substitute literature for religion. But Tate, a recent Catholic convert, soon saw that his missionary zeal had taken him too far, and withdrew this profession of faith.[45]

Blackmur's concept of "the new illiteracy"—of those who can read but without the means or the skill to read well or the material that ought to be read—was set forth in his "Toward a Modus Vivendi." Unfortunately, neither Blackmur's own nor the editors' thoughts on this essay are in the files in Gambier.[46]

The *Kenyon* essay by Blackmur about one particular poet during this period was "The Substance That Prevails," about Wallace Stevens. The decrease in the number of essays on individual poets is, of course, another indication of Blackmur's break from the New Criticism. Discussions of individual poets require close reading, while in the essays on culture, criticism, and fiction, which Blackmur now preferred to write, he could content himself and others with sweeping statements and the abstract meanderings of his mind. But also in the essay on Stevens, Blackmur manages to substitute airy theories and muddled generalizations for close reading. Ransom, however, was convinced of the wisdom of Blackmur's words: "If it had not been Richard Blackmur who wrote recently about Stevens as a poet not only dandiacal but unphilosophical, I should have boggled at

45. Philip Rahv to Tate, March 10, 1952, in Tate Papers; Blackmur, "Lord Tennyson's Scissors," 14; Tate to Ransom, January 19, 1952, in *KR* Papers.
46. Blackmur, "Toward a Modus Vivendi," 520.

both ascriptions, and thought that Blackmur's own guard was down, most unaccountably. But it *was* Blackmur, and Blackmur as a critic is so far from having an impediment in his speech that he excels other critics in the plenitude of his contexts, so that I dare say there are intimations in the one on Stevens which amount to proper qualifications; or amount partly to them."[47]

Blackmur's next essay for the *Kenyon* was different in subject and, fortunately, in style too: in the summer, 1955, issue, he speculated informatively about Arnold Toynbee. Although Blackmur himself was not satisfied with this "undistinguished thing," its aphorisms and analogues make for pleasant, if not exactly consecutive, reading. His next essay, in the next issue, was quite different again. "Adams Goes to School" is part of the Henry Adams biography that Blackmur started when he was still in his twenties. In August, 1955, Blackmur had submitted about sixty pages on Adams, which he hoped Ransom would print as a unit, mainly because the publication of as many as sixty pages would yield a lot of money. Ransom sympathized with Blackmur's attempt "to keep the wolf (the alimony one) from his door," but he published only the first half, since that contained "more generality" and since the *Kenyon* did not "have room" for both parts. John Marshall was interested: "Incidentally, over the weekend I also got to read your piece on Henry Adams in the autumn *Kenyon,*" he wrote to his friend, and "[i]t makes me all the more eager to see the whole book." But Blackmur never finished the biography, and *Henry Adams* was published posthumously.[48]

We noted that the only one to outdo Blackmur in number of contributions to the *Kenyon* during its second flowering was Ransom himself. When we take a look at Ransom's critical development as demonstrated in his essays of this period, we understand better why he cherished Blackmur's sweeping proclamations. Ransom had always been a theoretical New Critic, the one who stimulated others to pay close attention to the text, rather than doing so himself, but his theories had been precise and clear-cut. Now, however, Ransom, like

47. John Crowe Ransom, "The Concrete Universal: Observations on the Understanding of Poetry. II," *KR,* XVII, 401–402.

48. Blackmur, "Reflections of Toynbee," 357–70; Blackmur to Ransom, March 18, 1955, in *KR* Papers; Richard Blackmur, *Henry Adams,* ed. Veronica A. Makowsky (New York, 1980); Ransom to Rice, July 4, [1955], in Rice Papers; Ransom to Blackmur, August 20, 1955, John Marshall to Blackmur, January 3, 1956, both in Blackmur Papers.

Blackmur, started to write vague, verbose essays. He was now liable to discuss intangibles like "the actual warmth and feel and the powerful psychic focus, with which poetry comes into our experience." Ransom's gradual disappointment with the practice of close reading showed in his dissentient review of *The Well Wrought Urn* and, especially, in his—and Rice's—selection of critics for the *Kenyon*. But a consideration of some of Ransom's particular pronouncements at this moment of the *Kenyon's* history will shed additional light on the turn his mind took. Indeed, Ransom and Rice were on the whole extremely discriminating in their acceptances and rejections of critical articles for their magazine, but Ransom was not so perceptive with respect to some of his own articles.[49]

Ransom's essay-review of *Image and Idea* by Philip Rahv in the spring of 1950 at first seems to contradict the argument that Ransom turned away from close reading. He writes that style is as important in fiction as it is in poetry, and contends that, in judging prose, a critic should apply the methods the New Critics apply to poetry. However, Ransom goes on to charge that these critics fail "to identify, or even suspect, the emotional need which causes the public to receive the poems," stresses that "the literary critic now has to be his own psychologist," and even puts in a word for Marxist critics whose "social conscience" has moved him "very deeply." Although far removed from Ransom's earlier, much more specific guidelines for critics, this essay is still free of Ransom's later, vague, philosophical digressions. Ransom himself found the essay "a bit tenuous," but Rahv was more than pleased. "You deployed your own critical categories and interests around mine in a way that leaves us both intact— and that, after all, is what is wanted in any effort at understanding. The questions you raise are very large; but your approach is so stimulating that I would like to write something that would in effect continue your discussion, particularly in reference to the possibility of applying the methods of modern poetry-criticism to the study of fiction." It was not until six years later, however, in the spring, 1956, issue, that Rahv replied to Ransom's "The Understanding of Fiction."[50]

49. John Crowe Ransom, "Poets and Flatworms," *KR*, XIV, 101. *The Well Wrought Urn* was reviewed in "Poetry: I. The Formal Analysis," *KR*, IX, 436–56.
50. John Crowe Ransom, "The Understanding of Fiction," *KR*, XII, 201–202, 209, 208;

Ransom's next article, "William Wordsworth: Notes Toward an Understanding of Poetry," was a paper delivered at Cornell on the occasion of the hundredth anniversary of the poet's death. The preceding article was by Lionel Trilling, "Wordsworth and the Iron Time," a paper read at the Princeton Wordsworth celebrations, which was later included in *The Kenyon Critics*. Suggesting to Rice that he ask Trilling to submit his Princeton paper on Wordsworth to the *Kenyon,* Ransom grumbled: "I think it's high time he sent us an essay." Trilling was quite willing and paid the *Kenyon* an indirect compliment when he replied that it would "be a real help to me in keeping the tone of the paper what I should like it to be if I know that it is going to be published in the Review." The two papers dealt with two very different aspects of Wordsworth: Trilling advanced the rather farfetched hypothesis that there is a kind of Judaic quality in Wordsworth's poetry that makes him unacceptable to many readers, and Ransom rather dully discussed Wordsworth's theories about poetry. The nature of the occasion did not allow Ransom to advance provocative theories of his own.[51]

"The Poetry of 1900–1950" was, according to Ransom, "an odd thing" and was also "dictated by an occasion." On April 6, 1951, Ransom had read this paper before the Ohio English Association. It appeared in the summer, 1951, issue in conjunction with Paul Goodman's "Advance-Guard Writing, 1900–1950." Ransom's list of major and minor poets in the period from 1900 to 1950 hardly bears out the accusations that the New Critics neglected and rejected the less difficult and obscure poets. His minor modern poets are Robert Bridges, Walter de la Mare, John Masefield, Vachel Lindsay, W. C. Williams, E. Pound, Marianne Moore, E. E. Cummings, Hart Crane, and Allen Tate. His major poets: Thomas Hardy, W. B. Yeats, Edwin Arlington Robinson, Robert Frost, and T. S. Eliot. He is not quite sure whether to place Wallace Stevens, W. H. Auden, Dylan Thomas, and A. E. Housman among the minors or the majors.[52]

Ransom to Rice, March 3, [1950], in Rice Papers; Philip Rahv to Ransom, April 19, 1950, in *KR* Papers; Philip Rahv, "Fiction and the Criticism of Fiction," *KR*, XVIII, 276–99.

51. John Crowe Ransom, "William Wordsworth: Notes Toward an Understanding of Poetry," *KR*, XII, 498–519; Lionel Trilling, "Wordsworth and the Iron Time," *KR*, XII, 477–97; Ransom to Rice, March 3, [1950], in Rice Papers; Lionel Trilling to Rice, March 10, 1950, in *KR* Papers.

52. Ransom to David McDowell, July 10, [1951], in Random House Papers; John Crowe Ransom, "The Poetry of 1900–1950," *KR*, XIII, 445–54; Paul Goodman, "Advance-Guard

Two 1952 papers, "Poets and Flatworms" and "Why Critics Don't Go Mad," give a better indication of Ransom's critical development in these years. In "Poets and Flatworms" he wholeheartedly sympathizes with those who are weary of the New Criticism. He writes: "How confidently, twenty years or so past, were some of us offering a new 'understanding of poetry'! I will not say, How brashly; for the innovation was real, it was momentous; but it was not complete, and now it has bogged down at a most embarrassing point. In the academy the verbal analysis has pretty well secured its place and tenure, but its end-products are only half-finished, and their ragged showing does not alleviate the original apprehensions of the opposition." He now finds that Max Eastman, a Marxist critic whose revised edition of *The Enjoyment of Poetry* he is reviewing, "belongs in the company of our superior critics."[53]

Ransom's friends and fellow New Critics of the first hour had realized that Ransom had turned away from the New Criticism long before anybody else grew skeptical. Tate had perhaps even been a bit overhasty. As early as 1943, on the occasion of Ransom's editorial "The Inorganic Muses," he had cried out in disgust: "To think that after the brilliant essays in The World's Body he has come down to something like Max Eastman!" In the early 1950s, Cleanth Brooks had become convinced that Tate's censorious view of Ransom's criticism was "entirely right":

In reading for the book [*Literary Criticism: A Short History* (1957), written with W. K. Wimsatt], I have been going over—among other things—John Ransom's later work. All honor to John as a man and as a friend, but I am really surprised at what the position adds up to: John has argued himself back, unless I utterly misread him, into the positions of Eastman, the earlier Richards, and of Matthew Arnold!—positions which he so ably castigated at one time. I have been reminded forcibly of what you [Tate] told me as far ago as 1936 of John's basic view of poetry.[54]

Brooks was the main subject of Ransom's playfully written "Why Critics Don't Go Mad." As in "The Formal Analysis," Brooks is

---

Writing, 1900–1950," *KR,* XIII, 357–80. Goodman did not read his paper before the Ohio English Association.

53. Ransom, "Poets and Flatworms," 159, 157; John Crowe Ransom, "Why Critics Don't Go Mad," *KR,* XIV, 331–39.

54. John Crowe Ransom, "The Inorganic Muses," *KR,* V, 278–300; Tate to Arthur Mizener, March 1, 1943, in Mizener Papers; Brooks to Tate, April 13, n.y., in Tate Papers.

Ransom's example of a critic he has grown away from. "The fact is that Brooks and I were about as like as two peas from the same pod," and "perhaps we were most like in the unusual parallel of our formal educations," Ransom observes. But, he continues, "[w]e have diverged a little. . . . I find I am more captious than I like when I confront some of Brooks's departures." Ransom softens this by adding that he feels that he is "contending with my *alter ego*." From here Ransom takes off to berate Brooks extensively for his neglect of a poem's argument, and goes on to describe the "Great Scholar"—"Is he the figment of a bad conscience?"—as a "Guide for the critics." In his reaction to this article, Brooks conceded to Tate that Ransom "as always" had been "amiable and handsome" toward him, but admitted also that he wished "John would change his critical direction."[55]

From "Humanism at Chicago," which appeared in the autumn, 1952, issue, one might gather that Ransom had answered Brooks's prayer: he finds the Chicago critics, whose *Critics and Criticism* had just been published, dogmatic Neo-Aristotelians and blames them for paying attention to a poem's argument only. Jarrell was amused: "[S]ome of the blandest sentences were the most crushing," he complimented Ransom. The Chicagoans, predictably, were not at all amused, and Wayne C. Booth rushed to their defense in a letter published in the spring, 1953, issue. But in his "Reply by the Author," Ransom easily broke through this defense, and then decided that the matter had been settled once and for all.[56]

Ransom's return to his earlier critical position in "Humanism at Chicago" turned out to be only a brief detour from the critical course he had taken in the late 1940s and early 1950s. With his two literary-philosophical essays "The Concrete Universal: Observations on the Understanding of Poetry," Ransom was back on track. "[T]he language of poetry is the language of feeling, not the language of epistemology," he asserted in the first installment, and went on to an uninspired description of Hegel's ideas on poetry. In the second installment, which is even harder to read than the first, Ransom com-

55. Ransom, "Why Critics Don't Go Mad," 333, 334, 335; Brooks to Tate, April 22, [1952], in Tate Papers.

56. John Crowe Ransom, "Humanism at Chicago," *KR*, XIV, 647–59; Randall Jarrell to Ransom, n.d., in *KR* Papers; Wayne C. Booth, "Communications: On the Aristotelian Front," *KR*, XV, 299–301; John Crowe Ransom, "Communications: Reply by the Author," *KR*, XV, 301–304.

pares and contrasts Hegel and Kant—"the most radical and ultimate spokesman for poetry that we have had"—and emphasizes that the "reading of technical philosophy is the critic's home work."[57] The philosopher in Ransom, until now kept in check by the advocate of practical criticism, had run away with him.

Rice, the second philosopher on the editorial board, also contributed his share of articles for *The Kenyon Review*. In the years 1948 to 1954, he wrote six essays and two reviews for the *Kenyon*. Most of these dealt with French themes and resulted from his Rockefeller-sponsored three-month sojourn in France at the end of 1947. In "A Letter from France," which appeared in the winter, 1948, issue, Rice discussed the chaotic political situation in what he regarded as a very sick country. Half a year later, in "A Letter to a Frenchman," Rice discussed the country's cultural situation and found "that all is not well" in France.[58]

Existentialism and other directions in French philosophy were the main subjects of Rice's two 1950 articles, "Children of Narcissus: Some Themes of French Speculation" and "Existentialism and the Self," the second of which was reprinted in *The Kenyon Critics*. In "Children of Narcissus," Rice points to the obstinate recurrence of the theme of awareness of the self in recent French philosophy. He contrasts this to American philosophy, which is only concerned with the self when it has become a problem, and then saddles theology and psychology with it. One rarely finds in philosophical papers the great clarity and ease that Rice brings to bear here on his elusive subject. This is equally true of the sequel, "Existentialism and the Self," which, as its title indicates, deals with the major development in contemporary French philosophy. Praise for both essays poured in. Even if one takes into consideration that Rice had sent out numerous offprints, the quantity as well as the quality of the tributes he received reflect the importance of these essays. Philip Rahv "enjoyed [the] piece on contemporary French philosophy. It was a job that needed

57. John Crowe Ransom, "The Concrete Universal: Observations on the Understanding of Poetry. I," *KR*, XVI, 554; John Crowe Ransom, "The Concrete Universal: Observations on the Understanding of Poetry. II," *KR*, XVII, 392, 384. In "The Concrete Universal (1970)," which appeared in *Beating the Bushes: Selected Essays 1941–1970* (New York, 1972), and which was partly a rewrite of the 1954 essay, Ransom changed his mind again.
58. Philip Blair Rice, "A Letter from France," *KR*, X, 143–53; Philip Blair Rice, "A Letter to a Frenchman," *KR*, X, 473.

to be done: very informative and well thought out and presented." Katharine Gilbert, chairman of the department of aesthetics, art, and music at Duke University, confessed: "As you know, one cannot—or at least I cannot—write letters about all the offprints that people are kind enough to send one. However, I found your paper extremely informing and light-giving." And she asked Rice to address the American Society for Aesthetics. Marten ten Hoor, Clyde Kluckhohn, and Jack Sweeney described the essays as "most distinguished" and "very helpful," or exclaimed over their "steady clarity and . . . appropriate wit." Jean Wahl's five-page reaction, which was mainly a long denial of many of Rice's points interspersed with remarks like "all my congratulations" and "warm thanks," testifies to the thought-provoking quality of the essays.[59]

Rice's 1949 essay on Thomas Mann's *Dr. Faustus,* his third *Kenyon* paper on Mann, whom he regarded as one of the world's greatest novelists, had been received similarly well. Mann, for one, congratulated Rice on "one of the most important contributions written about my work." William Gass, who had studied philosophy under Rice at Kenyon College, wholly agreed: "Your article is the only good thing I've read on that book so far." R. W. Flint again dissented. He found the essay "interestingly and intelligently, but profoundly wrong," mainly because Rice's boundless admiration for Mann permeated the essay, and Flint regarded Mann as definitely "second-rate."[60]

"[S]imply brilliant," according to Philip Rieff, was Rice's final summer, 1954, essay for the *Kenyon,* "The Intellectual Quarterly in a Non-Intellectual Society." This essay, which had served as a lecture at the annual meeting of the Michigan Academy of Science, Arts and Letters, again possesses all the qualities of Rice's writing: perspicuity,

59. Philip Blair Rice, "Children of Narcissus: Some Themes of French Speculation," *KR,* XII, 116–37; Philip Blair Rice, "Existentialism and the Self," *KR,* XII, 304–30; Philip Rahv to Rice, January 25, 1950, Katharine Gilbert to Rice, February 27, 1950, Marten ten Hoor to Rice, February 14, 1950, Clyde Kluckhohn to Rice, February 14, 1950, Jack Sweeney to Rice, April 19, 1953, Jean Wahl to Rice, February 20, [1950], all in Rice Papers.
60. Philip Blair Rice, "The Merging Parallels: Mann's *Dr. Faustus,*" *KR,* XI, 199–217. Philip Blair Rice's two other papers on Mann were a book review of *The Transposed Heads,* in *KR,* III, 508–10, and "Thomas Mann and the Religious Revival," *KR,* VII, 361–77. Thomas Mann to Mary Rahming, secretary of *The Kenyon Review,* April 22, 1949, William Gass to Rice, January 13, 1950, both in Rice Papers; R. W. Flint to Rice, December 14, [1949], in *KR* Papers.

precision, and poise. In light of Rice's position as an associate editor, this essay, his one major statement on literary reviews, deserves extensive consideration. Rice tries to justify "the egghead quarterlies," as the literary reviews were thought of by their ill-wishers, who described them as "cliquish, esoteric, wilfully obscure, pretentious, snobbish, faddish, anemic, jargonic, and even subversive." Rice finds the customary justification that the reviews "publish the fledgling Hemingways, Faulkners and T. S. Eliots" an acceptable argument, but not more than that. Much more important to him is that they "let writers write the way they want to write, and not according to some formula. Their only formula is to avoid writing that is made to a formula. Their more distinctive job, however," Rice continues, "is that of intensive criticism. Even the fiction and poetry they publish is assumed to reflect a considered critical judgment, and to be illustrative of, or at least compatible with, the standards elaborated in the critical sections of the magazines." This leads Rice to a discussion of different kinds of criticism. The New Criticism—"though this is no longer so new. It is getting middle-aged, and is acknowledged . . . to be somewhat respectable"—he defines as "aesthetico-linguistic-structural criticism," and the Old Criticism as "socio-ethico-psychological." Rice stresses that his bipartition is "at most a tendency and an emphasis," and that the Old and New Critics often "trespass on each other's territory," "supplement each other usefully," and even "manage to co-exist in the pages of the same reviews with reasonable amity."[61]

As noted earlier, it is to a considerable extent thanks to Rice himself that these two kinds of equally important critics co-existed in *The Kenyon Review*. Again, Rice met with critical acclaim all around. Jack Sweeney, for instance, asked for an offprint. "I was put on to it by W. Stevens who praised it greatly." He added in a footnote: "As you probably know W. Stevens doesn't give praise easily. He's a surety bond specialist for an insurance Co."[62]

Another important publication on literary magazines was Arthur

61. Philip Rieff to Rice, August 30, 1954, in Rice Papers; Philip Blair Rice, "The Intellectual Quarterly in a Non-Intellectual Society," *KR*, XVI, 423, 421, 426, 428, 429, 430. "Foreign Periodicals," *KR*, I, 472–75, is Rice's only other paper on literary magazines and restricts itself to annotating the most important highbrow periodicals abroad.
62. Jack Sweeney to Rice, October 15, 1954, in Rice Papers.

Mizener's 1948 essay on *Scrutiny*'s contributors, whom he discussed as British counterparts of the American New Critics: "In these writers at their best . . . we have a variety of the new criticism which has clung to the old criticism's desire to evaluate the experience which the poem is, as well as to analyse what it is." Ransom's admiration for Mizener arose rather slowly. In the early 1940s, Ransom had not yet been quite convinced of Mizener's critical qualities; he found Mizener too "academic," even though as early as 1943, Tate had described him as "the best reader of poetry" in America and soon asked Mizener to succeed him as the editor of *The Sewanee Review*. Gradually, Ransom came to share Tate's high opinion of Mizener, and by 1949, Mizener and he apparently saw eye to eye on many important issues. Mizener's lead essay for the winter, 1950, issue, "The Novel of Manners in America," roused Ransom, who styled himself "Old Man of the New Criticism," to a general "preachment" about the New Criticism:

You've got precisely to the point where . . . all the New Critics of poetry got and where they are still stranded: viz., the poem (or the novel) deals with the concrete or particular, and the more show of the concreteness or particularity by the New Critic . . . the better. . . .

I said concreteness and particularity so long and ritualistically that I finally came to see that I was saying nothing to the pragmatical or positivistical naturalists. I therefore began to ask myself, What's the good of particularity, pure particularity? If we are dealing with human uses why do we want to clog them with particularity? . . .

The next phase . . . for the New Critics, seems to me, is to show what concrete individuals are for; how they are the appealing factor for the reader; and *what they mean* for him. . . . It is my hunch that the critics of literature are going to recover for literature, perhaps incidentally for religion, such sanctions as these human behaviors can boast.[63]

63. Arthur Mizener, "The *Scrutiny* Group," *KR*, X, 357. Ransom wrote to Mizener on May 24, [1946]: "My feeling is that your short story ["You Never Go Back to Sleep," in *KR*, VIII, 593–612] . . . will presently get you out of an attitude which I have felt was academic; you have a career, a big one, which is less in the academic terms than we (I at any rate) have supposed." Tate to Arthur Mizener, February 5, 1943. Both letters in Mizener Papers. On February 22, 1946, Mizener wrote with respect to Tate's asking him to become the editor of the *Sewanee*: "I am not, by temperament, an editor; it bores me; I am a teacher and some not very well defined sort of writer by temperament." Besides, Mizener had committed himself to teach at Carleton College in Minnesota for several years and was earning far more than he could expect to get as the editor of *The Sewanee Review* (Letter in Tate Papers). Ransom to Mizener, March 14, 1949, in Mizener Papers.

Although Mizener regarded not Ransom but Blackmur as "really the Ancient of Days, the really patriarchal figure" among the New Critics, he found himself in general agreement with Ransom: "Of course your [sic] quite right about the New Criticism. I keep wishing so much Cleanth would emerge from the c[h]rysalis stage, for instance, and stop being stubborn about the whole thing so far as poetry is concerned. . . . [I]t is one thing to talk the new criticism in the atmosphere when THE WOR[L]D'S BODY came out; these ideas were . . . needed then and always will be by people in the state of mind I at least was then. But those ideas are as false a note in the present atmosphere of criticism as a lecture at a cocktail party."[64]

Mizener's contributions to the *Kenyon* reflect this thinking. Simultaneously, they are representative of the general direction of the New Criticism in the late 1940s and early 1950s in that they deal with fiction rather than with poetry. By 1957, Ransom had been completely won over to Mizener, a "first-rate fiction man." He had also acquired a taste for Mizener's reviews of poetry and criticism: "Your pieces on Harry Levin's *Marlowe,* Aiken, Blackmur, 3 in a row, entitle you to the highest compliments of the season," he wrote to Mizener on February 3, 1953. Ransom showed his profound confidence in Mizener as a reviewer by entrusting him with Marianne Moore's translation, *The Fables of La Fontaine.* She was a poet whom he "would never trust . . . to untender hands," and Mizener was a "Moore man." But her translation proved to be a great disappointment, and Mizener said so baldly in his review. Ransom valued both Mizener's and the *Kenyon*'s integrity: "M. M. is a wonderful gal, and I *do wish* she hadn't left her beautiful MUSEUM. It will cut her down 50%, this new thing. But AM & KR, we could do no other." But others found shocking the deflation of their favorite, and angry letters bombarded the editors. R. W. Flint, for instance, usually the kindest, most tolerant of men, wrote three irate, long letters about *The Fables,* a copy of which "stretche[d] its wounded and bleeding length" beside his typewriter and cried out "for vindication of some sort."[65] Generally, though, Mizener's essays and reviews were too well reasoned and too

64. Arthur Mizener to Ransom, March 16, 1949, in Mizener Papers.
65. Some of Mizener's contributions are "The Thin Intelligent Face of American Fiction," *KR,* XVII, 507–24; "Truth Maybe, Not Fiction," *KR,* XI, 685–88; "Amphibium in Old Ken-

moderate in tone to evoke much reaction. Perhaps that is why Ransom, who liked to stir up literary controversy in *The Kenyon Review,* preferred Mizener as a reviewer to Mizener as a full-fledged essayist.

Mizener's New Critical mentor, Allen Tate, appeared only four times as a critic in the *Kenyon* during this period, even though the editors had assured him that "[t]hree essays by Tate in a year, or five or six, would not be too much for us." His magnificent twin essays on Dante and Poe and his contribution to "The Critic's Business" were supplemented by a rather sloppy essay in which he defends the Metaphysicals against Dr. Johnson. "Johnson on the Metaphysicals" was meant as the *pièce de résistance* of the summer, 1949, issue, which the editors had intended as a tribute to Tate's fiftieth birthday, perhaps to reciprocate in a small way the handsome "Homage to John Crowe Ransom" summer, 1948, issue of *The Sewanee Review* that Tate had helped to edit. But the Tate issue was as much a failure as Tate's own contribution to it. Both T. S. Eliot and Austin Warren reneged after initially accepting an invitation to write on Tate; this left the editors with Vivienne Koch, who wrote a careful essay, "The Poetry of Allen Tate," later reprinted in *The Kenyon Critics.*[66]

Still, compared to other first-generation New Critics, such as Cleanth Brooks, Austin Warren, and Robert Penn Warren, Tate appeared frequently. Cleanth Brooks's essay was his "Credo"; he contributed only two book reviews on William Empson and Arnold Stein; and it was not until 1964 that Brooks reappeared in the *Kenyon.* Austin Warren supplemented his contributions to "My Credo" and to the Donne series with an essay, which proved to be his last, on Sir Thomas Browne. Finally, Robert Penn Warren's essays were absent

---

tucky," *KR,* XII, 697–701; and "A Large Fiction," *KR,* XIII, 142–47. Ransom to John Shuman, March 18, 1957, in *KR* Papers; Ransom to Arthur Mizener, February 3, [1953], in Mizener Papers. The "highest compliments of the season" applied to Mizener's "Brilliant and Exasperating," *KR,* XV, 162–67, on Aiken's *Ushant: An Essay,* and to "The Great Profession," *KR,* XV, 306–10, on Richard Blackmur's *Language as Gesture.* Mizener did not write on Levin's *Marlowe* for *KR.* Arthur Mizener, "Transformations," *KR,* XVI, 473–82; Ransom to Mizener, February 28, [1954], May 15, [1954], both in Mizener Papers; R. W. Flint to Ransom, July 18, 1954, in *KR* Papers.

66. Rice to Tate, October 25, 1949, in Tate Papers; Allen Tate, "The Critic's Business: A Note on Autotelism," *KR,* XI, 13–16; Allen Tate, "The Symbolic Imagination: A Meditation on Dante's Three Mirrors," *KR,* XIV, 256–77; Allen Tate, "The Angelic Imagination: Poe and the Power of Words," *KR,* XIV, 455–75; Allen Tate, "Johnson on the Metaphysicals," *KR,* XI, 379–94; "Homage to John Crowe Ransom," *SR,* LVI (1948), 365–476; Vivienne Koch, "The Poetry of Allen Tate," *KR,* XI, 355–78.

from the *Kenyon*'s pages for all of twenty-one years, from 1947 till 1968, not because they were not wanted, but because Warren's main focus was on his poetry and fiction rather than on writing criticism.[67]

Eliseo Vivas, another old-time contributor, deserves mentioning, too. His "Kafka's Distorted Mask," a New Critical defense that opposed the prevalent psychoanalytic and sociological explanations of Kafka's work, appeared in the winter, 1948, issue and was reprinted in *The Kenyon Critics*. Vivas contributed a review of recent books by Paul Roubiczek and Richard Weaver. This review is noteworthy because it illustrates the complete reversal of the naturalistic position Vivas had held when he defended the encyclopedists in 1939. His final contribution to *The Kenyon Review* was a review of René Wellek and Austin Warren's *Theory of Literature*. Vivas acknowledged its immense learning but blamed Wellek and Warren for not having an aesthetic theory of their own. Incidentally, for once the editors had not been completely sincere. On September 30, 1949, Rice wrote to Vivas: "We have been especially eager to have a philosopher review the book—and naturally, as our most literate philosopher, you are first choice." Over half a year earlier, however, Ransom had in vain asked Kenneth Burke to review this important theoretical inquiry into the New Criticism.[68]

Two New Critical patriarchs, Benedetto Croce and I. A. Richards, also contributed to the *Kenyon*, if only once. Croce's "Criticism in Italy," written for a symposium, "The Great Critics," held at Johns Hopkins University in the spring of 1948, appeared in the autumn, 1948, issue of *The Kenyon Review*. Although Ransom had solicited Croce's paper, he tried to foist it off on Palmer of *The Sewanee Review* when he found out that the university lecture committee would not allow him to publish both this and his own Johns Hopkins lecture on Aristotle in the *Kenyon*, as they permitted only one lecture per magazine. Ransom told Palmer that the Croce was "finished, elo-

---

67. Cleanth Brooks, "The Formalist Critic," *KR*, XIII, 72–81; Cleanth Brooks, "Hits and Misses," *KR*, XIV, 669–78; Cleanth Brooks, "Recovering Milton," *KR*, XV, 638–47; Austin Warren, "The Teacher as a Critic," *KR*, XIII, 225–30; Austin Warren, "The Very Reverend Dr. Donne," *KR*, XVI, 268–77; Austin Warren, "The Style of Sir Thomas Browne," *KR*, XIII, 674–87.

68. Eliseo Vivas, "Kafka's Distorted Mask," *KR*, X, 51–69; Eliseo Vivas, "Historian and Moralist," *KR*, X, 346–49; Eliseo Vivas, "The New Encyclopedists: I. Pro," *KR*, I, 159–68; Eliseo Vivas, "Theorists without Theory," *KR*, XII, 161–65; Rice to Eliseo Vivas, September 30, 1949, in *KR* Papers; Ransom to Burke, February 28, [1949], in Burke Papers.

quent; not new, except the fling he takes against the 'hermetic' critics, who are we." But Palmer wanted Ransom's lecture, "The Literary Criticism of Aristotle," or nothing, and so the *Kenyon* was stuck with "Criticism in Italy." Fortunately, the lecture committee relented, and the *Kenyon*'s editors were allowed to publish both papers, on the condition that they appear in different issues.[69]

I. A. Richards' "The Places and the Figures," in the winter, 1949, issue, was an essay-review on two books dealing with rhetoric, in which he used such outlandish rhetorical terms as "epenthesis, proparalepsis . . . metathesis . . . aphaeresis . . . synaloepha, and apocope." Richards was "disappointed" in what he had managed to write on rhetoric, that "horribly deep subject," but "very much liked the way [his] article was made up in the Review." He reported that "[q]uite a number of people . . . commented . . . mostly on the queer *names* of the figures," but he was glad at "how widely . . . and how thoroughly" his article had been read.[70]

Kenneth Burke had read it thoroughly, too, and felt bound to defend one of the books, Sister Miriam Joseph's *Shakespeare's Use of the Arts of Language,* which Richards had criticized. Besides two book reviews, the main contribution by Burke, an unclassifiable critic, was his "Three Definitions," which appeared in the spring, 1951, issue. "Mighty crowded, we are," Ransom wrote, "but this is good, & bears on a big public topic—VALIDITY OF K.B.—& takes care of our long review of [Burke's] *Rhetoric* in this issue. This last by Kermit Lansner, a bit informal, but respectful, but philosophically dissenting. So there." Kermit Lansner, who had been an associate professor of philosophy at Kenyon College from 1948 to 1950, and who had attended Burke's course at the Kenyon School of English in 1950, had written an excellent, balanced review of *A Rhetoric of Motives.* But in an interview, over thirty years later, Burke still vividly remembered and resented Lansner's review. His anger was sparked by the title, "Burke, Burke, the Lurk." Even if Burke called himself "the lurk," he disliked Lansner's having stolen his epithet. In fact, though, Burke

69. Benedetto Croce, "Criticism in Italy," *KR*, X, 629–37; Ransom to John Palmer, April 24, [1948], in *SR* Papers; John Crowe Ransom, "The Literary Criticism of Aristotle," *KR*, X, 382–402.

70. I. A. Richards, "The Places and the Figures," *KR*, XI, 25; I. A. Richards to Ransom, October 28, 1948, and n.d., both in *KR* Papers.

should have directed his anger about the title at the *Kenyon*'s editors, since they were the ones who made up the headlines. But the actual review pained Burke even more. He informed Ransom: "Wrote out a several-thousand word answer to Lansner. To prove to myself that I knew exactly how ailing his review is." He sent Ransom a copy, but refused permission to publish it. "Communications," unless solicited, usually were not paid for, and Burke was in no mood to provide the *Kenyon* with a free sample. Burke's bitterness came as a surprise to Lansner; in submitting his review, Lansner had explained that he had written perhaps too sympathetic a critique in order to balance a few unfairly bad reviews that had concentrated on Burke's supposedly Stalinist bias.[71]

Only a few of those *Partisan Review* critics who had also been regular contributors to the *Kenyon* remained: Lionel Trilling, Isaac Rosenfeld, and Hannah Arendt are the only New York intellectuals who contributed more than one paper during this period, and who remain to be discussed. To his essays on the novel and Wordsworth, Trilling added a graphic essay on *Little Dorrit* and a review of Simon Nowell-Smith's collection of anecdotes about Henry James. Trilling's Dickens essay was meant as the introduction to the Oxford edition of *Little Dorrit,* and in 1952, "feeling guilty" about his "long non-appearance in *KR,*" Trilling had offered it to make amends. The editors accepted it eagerly, but their ardor did not rouse Trilling to produce more essays for the *Kenyon*. Eric Bentley was probably right when he asserted in 1982 that Trilling came to feel that the *Kenyon* was not informal enough, that he had to "put on his best clothes" for it, something he found too tiresome and time-consuming when he could dash off a piece for *Partisan* in a trice. And so Trilling disappeared forever from the *Kenyon*'s pages. Before his untimely death in 1956, Isaac Rosenfeld wrote as many as six sound, shrewd reviews; five of them on novels by Arthur Koestler, Charles Williams, Henry Green, Ernest Hemingway, and Robie Macauley, and one on an omnibus edition of Stephen Crane's work. Hannah Arendt contributed

---

71. Kenneth Burke, "Communications," *KR,* XI, 310–11; Kenneth Burke, "Three Definitions," *KR,* XIII, 173–92; Ransom to Burke, February 7, [1951], in Burke Papers; Kermit Lansner, "Burke, Burke, the Lurk," *KR,* XIII, 324–35; interview with Burke, August 16, 1983; Burke to Ransom, May 23, 1951, in *KR* Papers; Kermit Lansner to Rice, January 1, 1951, in Rice Papers.

to *The Kenyon Review* before she made her reputation with the publication of *The Origins of Totalitarianism* (1951). In two review-essays, she applauded Bertolt Brecht and Hermann Broch.[72]

The *Partisan* philosopher William Barrett contributed only one review, in which he compared and contrasted *Notes Towards the Definition of Culture* by T. S. Eliot to *The Revolt of the Masses* by Ortega y Gasset. Eliot lost on all counts. "The loss of vigor in [Eliot's] prose reflects the loss of vigor in the mind" and the "snob and the Christian are obviously in conflict in Eliot and though he makes no decisive choice between them, his sympathies seem to lean toward the snob"— remarks like these exemplify the tone of the review. Cleanth Brooks was one of the many readers who were scandalized: "Why should J. C. R. have got Barrett to review Eliot's *Notes*? It's all very well to 'represent both sides,' etc., but there are certain basic distinctions that must be accepted if we are to talk about literature—or anything else, for that matter—at all." Given that the review had been published in the heat of the Bollingen battle, even Ransom soon came to see that he had been carrying broad-mindedness a bit too far. He therefore asked Vivas to write a second and more positive review of the book—something unheard-of in the *Kenyon's* history. Vivas obliged, but submitted his review "with some misgiving." He could not "take the book for what its author intended it—an analysis of an important sociological category of value." Ransom rejected his review and asked Vivas to write yet another review, one "'answering' Barrett." But Vivas gave up: "I do not see where I could find the time to start over again. . . . The second reason is that answering the first review would be such a weary and unrewarding job! . . . No, I am afraid I am not up to *that*." Ransom gave up, too. It is unclear, though, why Ransom, after having tried to procure a review in favor

72. Lionel Trilling, "Manners, Morals, and the Novel," *KR*, X, 11–27; Lionel Trilling, "Wordsworth and the Iron Time," *KR*, XII, 477–97; Lionel Trilling, "Little Dorrit," *KR*, XV, 577–90; Lionel Trilling, "The Legend of the Lion," *KR*, X, 507–10; Lionel Trilling to Rice, July 2, 1952, in *KR* Papers; interview with Bentley, October 10, 1982. During this period, Isaac Rosenfeld contributed: "Aesthetics without Experience," *KR*, XI, 321–25, on Arthur Koestler; "The Love of Zombies," *KR*, XI, 497–500, on Charles Williams; "The Case against Pure Sensibility," *KR*, XII, 543–47, on Henry Green; "A Farewell to Hemingway," *KR*, XIII, 147–55; "Liebestod," *KR*, XV, 147–50, on Robie Macauley; and "Stephen Crane as Symbolist," *KR*, XV, 310–314. Hannah Arendt, "Beyond Personal Frustration: The Poetry of Bertolt Brecht," *KR*, X, 304–12; Hannah Arendt, "The Achievement of Hermann Broch," *KR*, XI, 476–83.

of Eliot, selected Barrett's extremely hostile assessment as one of the fifteen reviews for *The Kenyon Critics.*[73]

Apart from the main contributors during these years, such as Paul Goodman, Stanley Edgar Hyman, the Fellows, the New Critics, and a remnant of the intellectuals, there were others who, though they did not appear often, nevertheless wrote memorably. In 1948, for instance, the *Kenyon* published a selection from Valéry's posthumous *Choses Tues,* translated by William Geoffrey. In 1953, Claude-Edmonde Magny contributed a polemical essay against biographical-historical criticism, and against posthumous publications of rejected, immature works such as Proust's *Jean Santeuil.* Closer to home were the Canadian critics Hugh Kenner and Northrop Frye, who, like Hannah Arendt and so many others, published in the *Kenyon* before they became the fashion. Kenner appeared in 1948 with his first "fresh, original, and . . . convincing" essay on Joyce, a revised version of which became part of his *Dublin's Joyce* (1955). Frye's expositions of his belief in myth appeared long before he created a furor with his *Anatomy of Criticism* (1957). Another critic on the threshold of his career, Irish this time, was Donat O'Donnell, who discussed two Catholic writers, François Mauriac and Georges Bernanos. The *Kenyon* was still keen on concision: a first draft of the essay on Mauriac, for instance, was returned to the author with the note that the *Kenyon* "could use [it] if cut 1/2." Which O'Donnell did. His final contribution was a review, solicited by Rice, on Seán O'Faoláin and Arland Ussher.[74]

F. O. Matthiessen's last essay, before his suicide in 1950, was a portrait of the minor poet Phelps Putnam (1894–1948). "In thinking

73. William Barrett, "Artistocracy and/or Christianity," *KR,* XI, 489, 495; Brooks to Tate, August 5, [1949], in Tate Papers; Eliseo Vivas to Ransom, July 15, August 12, 1949, both in *KR* Papers.

74. Paul Valéry, "Things Left Unsaid," trans. William Geoffrey, *KR,* X, 228–39; Claude-Edmonde Magny, "'Finally . . . ,'" trans. Elizabeth Hardwick and John McCormick, *KR,* XV, 552–70; Hugh Kenner, "The *Portrait* in Perspective," *KR,* X, 361–81; Northrop Frye, "Levels of Meaning in Literature," *KR,* XII, 246–62; Northrop Frye, "The Archetypes of Literature," *KR,* XIII, 92–110; Northrop Frye, "A Conspectus of Dramatic Genres," *KR,* XIII, 543–62; Conor Cruise O'Brien [Donat O'Donnell], "François Mauriac: Catholic and Novelist," *KR,* X, 454–71; Conor Cruise O'Brien [Donat O'Donnell], "The Faust of Georges Bernanos," *KR,* XI, 405–23. These two essays, together with "The Pieties of Evelyn Waugh," *KR,* IX, 400–11, appeared in expanded versions in his *Maria Cross: Imaginative Patterns in a Group of Modern Catholic Writers* (1952). Note by Ransom in the margin of an undated letter by Conor Cruise O'Brien [Donat O'Donnell] to the *Kenyon,* in *KR* Papers; Conor Cruise O'Brien [Donat O'Donnell], "The Unfallen," *KR,* XII, 172–77.

over where to try to print [it]," Matthiessen told Tate, "I'd instinctively like to send it to John." When Ransom received it, he tentatively suggested that they "would like it *half* the length." But Matthiessen refused to cut so drastically. Only when Tate had not submitted his promised paper on Putnam to *The Hudson Review,* so that Putnam would likely be without any public testimonials, and, more important, when *The Kenyon Review* "turned up short with copy for Winter after the defection of one or two people we thought were committed," did the editors decide to publish Matthiessen's essay in its entirety. A critical classic by Mark Schorer, "Fiction and the 'Matrix of Analogy,'" which had been delivered at the Kenyon School of English in the summer of 1949 before its appearance in the autumn, 1949, issue; the first full-fledged article by Robie Macauley on Ford Madox Ford, which inaugurated a Ford revival and which was reprinted in *The Kenyon Critics*; and a *Kenyon Critics* book review by R. W. Flint on William Carlos Williams exemplify as well the varied profusion of superior critical articles in *The Kenyon Review.*[75]

Indeed, to list the *Kenyon's* main critical contributors is to illustrate its catholicity: Leslie Fiedler, Irving Howe, Richard W. B. Lewis, Richard Ellmann, Howard Nemerov, Randall Jarrell, Paul Goodman, Stanley Edgar Hyman, William Empson, Richard Blackmur, Arthur Mizener, and, of course, Ransom and Rice frequented the *Kenyon's* pages during this period. Most of these critics were young and were newcomers to the field of criticism, and their individualistic, often subjective approaches reflect all possible colors of the critical spectrum. Moreover, those New Critics who still often appeared in *The Kenyon Review* stood in less awe of the autonomy of the text and had broadened their critical horizons, if at times, it must be said, with sad results. Nevertheless, it seems warranted to describe the period from 1947 to 1955 as the *Kenyon's* second critical flowering.[76]

75. F. O. Matthiessen, "Phelps Putnam (1894–1948)," *KR,* XI, 61–82; F. O. Matthiessen to Tate, September 11, [1948], Ransom to Matthiessen, November 18, [1948], both in Matthiessen Papers; Mark Schorer, "Fiction and the 'Matrix of Analogy,'" *KR,* XI, 539–60; Robie Macauley, "The Good Ford," *KR,* XI, 269–88; R. W. Flint, "I Will Teach You My Townspeople," *KR,* XII, 537–43.

76. Interestingly, Kermit Lansner pointed out that it was "too tiring to track down a set of KR in Paris . . . one finds KR nowhere except at the main library Americain. The bookstores do not sell it although PR is on all stands" (Lansner to Rice, January 1, 1951, in Rice Papers).

7 Literature and the Arts

1947–1955

Philosophy and Politics

The Kenyon Review also experienced a second flowering with respect to, notably, creative writing. There were, however, no further articles on education. Rice's interest in existentialism, as noted, for example, in his own articles and the discussions of Kierkegaard, Heidegger, Marcel, Camus, and Sartre, was continued. Other more purely philosophical examples of the *Kenyon*'s interest are Herbert Spiegelberg's discussions of the "social philosophies" of existentialism and Walter Kaufmann's review of some "unexciting books" by Kurt F. Reinhart and James Collins about an "exciting" philosophy.[1]

Although the discussion about existentialism was predominant in the philosophy department during this period, some other philosophical views received attention, too. In 1950, Ernest Nagel reappeared in the *Kenyon*'s pages with a paper in which he contends that in spite of Einstein's many courageous statements about social policy and morality, he was not a profound or systematic social thinker. This article circulated widely among philosophers; from Paris, Kermit Lansner reported that he "met [Jean] Wahl . . . [who] was . . . carrying the *Review* to read Nagel's Einstein piece." Henry David Aiken, a friend of Rice's, disagreed with another friend of Rice's, Eliseo Vivas, in a 1955 review of the latter's *Creation and Dis-*

1. Herbert Spiegelberg, "French Existentialism: Its Social Philosophies," *KR*, XVI, 446–62; Walter Kaufmann, "Existentialism Tamed," *KR*, XVI, 487.

covery; Aiken had earlier reviewed *An Examination of the Place of Reason in Ethics* by Stephen Toulmin. In 1953, Aiken discussed George Santayana, one of Rice's pet subjects, but found him a "'cold fish.'" This was one essay out of a series of three in the scraped-up symposium "Art and 'Symbolic.'" An editorial note explained that though these essays had been "done independently," the editors had "grouped [them] arbitrarily under the term 'Symbolic,' a great word at the moment in the discussion of literature." Richard Ellmann on Yeats was the second article in this series, and Walter Elder's laudatory essay-review on *Feeling and Form* by S. K. Langer was the last. Two less successful philosophical surveys, by Arthur E. Murphy and by Morton White, complete the *Kenyon's* philosophy department.[2]

Philosophy had indeed come to play a minor part. In January, 1952, Ransom remarked to Chalmers that Rice and he had published so many philosophical essays that they had sometimes said that the *Kenyon* was a "quasi-philosophical magazine," but this observation was in fact no longer applicable. Still, if the quantity of philosophical essays—and perhaps their belligerency—diminished, their quality usually left nothing to be desired. The philosopher Morton White wrote to Rice that the *Kenyon* was "a tower of integrity in a field where, God knows, that is rare." The magazine's philosophical integrity was a reflection of the integrity of its editors. In "The Philosopher's Commitment," for instance, originally a public address at the height of McCarthy's slanderous campaigns, Rice spoke unambiguously of "the hysterical atmosphere into which we are moving" and pointed out that the philosopher's highest priority should therefore be given to "honest learning, courageous thinking and conscientious teaching."[3]

2. Ernest Nagel, "Einstein's Philosophy of Science," *KR*, XII, 520–31; Kermit Lansner to Rice, January 1, 1951, in Rice Papers; Henry David Aiken, "Aesthetics on the Stretch," *KR*, XVII, 633–39; Henry David Aiken, "Commonsensical Ethics," *KR*, XIII, 519–26; Henry David Aiken, "George Santayana: Natural Historian of Symbolic Form," *KR*, XV, 340; editor's note to Aiken, "George Santayana," 337; Richard Ellmann, "The Art of Yeats: Affirmative Capability," *KR*, XV, 357–85; Walter Elder, "This May Be the Book," *KR*, XV, 386–97; Arthur E. Murphy, "American Philosophy at Mid-Century," *KR*, XII, 647–62; Morton White, "Philosophy in England," *KR*, XIV, 599–607.

3. Ransom to Chalmers, January 22, 1952, Morton White to Rice, March 27, 1950, both in *KR* Papers; Philip Blair Rice, "The Philosopher's Commitment" (Address delivered at the Western Division of the American Philosophical Association meeting, St. Louis, May 1–2, 1953; Offprint in Rice Papers), 39. It is unclear where this was originally published. Rice was vice-president of that Division of the association from 1948 to 1949 and from 1951 to 1952. He was its president from 1952 to 1953 and from 1954 to 1955.

Rice's political commitment was not mirrored in the *Kenyon*, where, as before, politics played a minimal part. This was not because Ransom did not share Rice's views. For instance, after he had barred Hyman from the *Kenyon*, he compared his usual reviewing style to "Sen. McCarthy . . . plunged into the literary arena." But Ransom remained convinced that politics had no place in a literary magazine. He therefore rejected a review by Thomas Henry Carter: "It doesn't quite suit our content, I think; we haven't gone into the segregation matter because that is a political and social question, not exactly a literary one; and yet politics and social views color one's own writing even as a literary man so much that I felt I needed to see how you would pronounce with your own convictions." In the same letter, he said that the literary quality of the rejected review was such that Carter would be the Fellow in Criticism for 1958.[4]

As politics indeed "color one's . . . writing even as a literary man," a few politically flavored articles stole into the *Kenyon*. Irving Howe's essays on Conrad and Dostoevsky and Richard Chase's credo, "Art, Nature, Politics," are cases in point. In fact, in his winter, 1949, essay entitled "Melville's *Confidence Man*," Chase's conviction that "the literary critic will find himself inescapably a political writer" had buried Melville under the weight of observations on liberalism. Two bold, cogent, political essays were written by the New Yorker Harold Rosenberg and appeared in *Kenyon*'s 1948 and 1949 autumn issues. "The Resurrected Romans," in which Rosenberg advances the seductive theory that historical figures, when unequal to the situations they have to face, assume clichéd attitudes, is particularly brilliant and became part of his *The Tradition of the New* (1959). In his summer, 1959, *Kenyon* review of this book, Lionel Abel remarked that Rosenberg set great store by "The Resurrected Romans," which was "much admired by men as keen as Jean Paul Sartre and Merleau-Ponty," but he himself had reservations about its soundness.[5]

4. Ransom to Arthur Mizener, March 20, 1954, in Mizener Papers; Ransom to Thomas Henry Carter, December 2, [1957], in Carter Papers.
5. Irving Howe, "Joseph Conrad: I. Order and Anarchy: The Political Novels," *KR*, XV, 505–21; Irving Howe, "Joseph Conrad: III. The Political Novels (cont.)," *KR*, XVI, 1–19; Irving Howe, "Dostoevsky: The Politics of Salvation," *KR*, XVII, 42–68; Richard Chase, "Art, Nature, Politics," *KR*, XII, 591; Richard Chase, "Melville's *Confidence Man*," *KR*, XI, 122–40; Harold Rosenberg, "The Resurrected Romans," *KR*, X, 602–20; Harold Rosenberg, "The Pathos of the Proletariat," *KR*, XI, 595–629; Lionel Abel, "Virile Sophistication," *KR*, XXI, 493.

One final political essay was written by none other than Ransom himself. Correspondence reveals that President Chalmers had pressed Ransom to pay attention to *The Conservative Mind,* written by Chalmers' friend, the arch-conservative Russell Kirk. When he saw that further resistance was useless, Ransom wrote to Chalmers resignedly: "As for Kirk's book, I've spent the week with it and find that I'd like to review it myself, in Autumn. At first I felt it might be more topical, more in the way of current politics, than we [the *Kenyon*] were in the habit of discussing. But the issue is really a big one, or can be made so, and I have come to think I have something to dish up there. After all, I'm at least an ex-conservative-Southern-agrarian." Should Chalmers after this note still have had the illusion that Ransom endorsed Kirk's views, he was to be severely disappointed. "The conservative mind," Ransom concluded his essay, "is not unable, as has been charged, to learn any lesson from the change of history. It is only unable to recite the lesson faithfully." It is improbable that Chalmers tried ever again to force Ransom to review his friends' books. Anyhow, the few political essays that were published in *The Kenyon Review* during this period were liberal, even leftist, rather than conservative.[6]

Poetry

Ransom's ideas about the kind of poetry he preferred to publish remained constant. As before, he rejected poems that were "too *direct and bare,*" "too sharp, and quick, and informal," too "unorganized," or lacking in "lyrical *intensity.*" His eye for a poetical *tour de force* remained as keen as ever, and when a great poem such as Robert Penn Warren's "Brother to Dragons" was submitted, Ransom threw all his editorial principles overboard and made room for it in his magazine.[7]

Edwin Watkins, William Merwin, Edgar Collins Bogardus, and Douglas Nichols were the young writers who were the Fellows in Poetry for 1953, 1954, and 1955. Watkins, one of the many southern-

6. John Crowe Ransom, "Empirics in Politics," *KR,* XV, 654; Ransom to Chalmers, May 16, 1953, in KC Papers. Chalmers himself wrote a laudatory review of Kirk's book for the *New York Times Book Review.*

7. Ransom to Winfield Townley Scott, April 3, [1948?], in Scott Papers; Ransom to Cid Corman, June 5, 1954, in Corman Papers; Ransom to Theodore Roethke, September 24, 1951, in Roethke Papers; Ransom to Vernon Watkins, October 15, 1950, in Watkins Papers; Robert Penn Warren, "Brother to Dragons," *KR,* XV, 1–103.

ers who had come to Kenyon College to study under Ransom, did not quite live up to Ransom's high expectations. He appeared only twice in the *Kenyon*. William Merwin, whose name had been put forward by Francis Fergusson, turned out to be a much more satisfactory Fellow. From London, where he lived during his fellowship, Merwin reported that "a picture & paragraph" on him had appeared "in the . . . English *Vogue* telling about the Kenyon Fellowship," regarding this as a tribute to the *Kenyon* rather than to himself. In 1954, Ransom had prophesied that Merwin was "certain to be a very brilliant figure" because he possessed "marvellous verbal ability," and he published eight of Merwin's poems. The autumn, 1951, issue was enhanced by his first *Kenyon* appearance, "Ballad of John Cable and Three Gentlemen," published in the still existing "Younger Poets" series—now entitled "A Group of Young Poets." Merwin's first book of verse, *A Mask for Janus* (1952), followed. To Lionel Trilling, Merwin's "Ballad" was a pleasant surprise. "I am, as perhaps you know," he wrote to Ransom, "rather indifferent and even hostile to a great deal of the new poetry I come across. But every now and then something emerges and hits me—this happened with W. S. Merwin's 'Ballad.' . . . I think he's an extra ordinarily fine poet."[8]

Edgar Bogardus was highly praised by Ransom in 1954: "His first volume [*Various Jangling Keys* (1952)] was published recently as the 50th in the Yale Series of Younger Poets, and received an unusual acclaim. We have no doubt about his future." But in 1958, Bogardus died of monoxide poisoning at the age of thirty-one. James Wright had been one of Bogardus' admirers. After a pleasant visit in Gambier, late in 1957, Wright wrote to Ransom that he was sorry to have missed Bogardus, who had joined the Kenyon College faculty in 1956: "I had hoped to tell Mr. Bogardus how much I have cherished his extraordinarily beautiful book, but perhaps you will tell him for me. Poem after poem returns to my mind as I write—AT THE GRAVE OF ROBERT INGERSOLL, PROTHALAMION FOR K., FROM AUTUMN'S THRILL-

---

8. Edwin Watkins, "The Flower" and "The Poet at Nightfall Surveys His Dominion," *KR*, XII, 297–300; Edwin Watkins, "A Monument for Norfleet," *KR*, XVI, 200–207; William Merwin to Ransom, March 6, 1954, Ransom to John Marshall, November 29, 1954, both in *KR* Papers; William Merwin, "Ballad of John Cable and Three Gentlemen," *KR*, XIII, 668–71; Lionel Trilling to Ransom, October 12, 1951, in *KR* Papers. Merwin's other poems included "Canso," *KR*, XV, 591–94; "The Nine Days of Creation," *KR*, XVIII, 367–69; and "A Wit in Age," *KR*, XIX, 196.

ING TOMB (which I have memorized and learned from), CORRUPTION IN HIGH PLACES, EASTWARD TO EDEN. And I haven't seen the book for at least a whole year. He writes as memorably as anybody going." Bogardus' "At the Grave of Robert Ingersoll" and "Prothalamion for K." were among the eleven generally gloomy, intense, mythical poems of his published in *The Kenyon Review*. Douglas Nichols, "an old Kenyon boy" like Watkins and Bogardus, was the 1955 Fellow in Poetry simultaneously with Bogardus. Nichols published nine poems in the *Kenyon,* none of them memorable. Altogether, with the exception of Merwin, who went on to be a reputable poet, the choice of Fellows in Poetry had so far been less fortunate than the choice of Fellows in Criticism.[9]

Two other Kenyon graduates, Anthony Hecht and James Wright (the Fellow in Poetry for 1958), brightened the *Kenyon*'s poetry section. A number of the thirteen technically virtuose poems that Hecht published in the *Kenyon* from 1947 to 1954 were included in his exceptional first volume of verse, *A Summoning of Stones* (1954), by which he became famous overnight, both in America and Great Britain. In 1968, Hecht recalled the odd way he broke into print in *The Kenyon Review*. Having commented on Ransom's tact, which often left his listeners in doubt whether their work had been blessed or damned, Hecht, who had submitted a poem, continued:

One day I went to call upon him in his office for some help and advice about a class I was teaching. It had something to do with Shakespeare, as I remember, and we were deeply and vigorously into it, when I looked past his head to the blackboard where he habitually wrote down the names of the contributors to the next issue of the *Review,* in the order in which they would appear. And there, to my astonishment, high on the list, and right between Trilling and Bentley, was my name. At this point Mr. Ransom was being very animated about Macbeth, and all for my benefit, but after a minute or two I could not contain myself, and abandoning all decorum, I interrupted him to ask whether this meant that I was to be in the next issue. He turned around to look at the blackboard, and in his very gentle southern voice said, "I seem to have made a slight mistake," whereupon he rose, went to the blackboard and erased the H in front of my name, and put down Br instead.

9. Ransom to John Marshall, November 29, 1954, James Wright to Ransom, January 4, 1958, both in *KR* Papers; Edgar Bogardus, "At the Grave of Robert Ingersoll," *KR*, XIII, 280–81; Edgar Bogardus, "Prothalamion for K.," *KR*, XV, 190–94. Among Douglas Nichols' poems are "The Girl of the Golden West," *KR*, XIV, 452–53; "Hermes in California," *KR*, XVII, 74; and "Roman Spring," *KR*, XVIII, 542. Ransom described Nichols as "an old Kenyon boy" (Ransom to Marshall, November 29, 1954, in *KR* Papers).

The fact is, he did actually publish my poem in the issue following this one; though it seems to me possible that simple embarrassment forced this upon him . . . I can't believe he could have been much taken with it. But at this period he was often preoccupied with Freud, and particularly with the essay on Wit and the Unconscious, and such slips could not be regarded as wholly insignificant.

But if Hecht's first appearance had been due to a Freudian slip, Ransom's interest in Hecht as a poet was aroused, and he encouraged Hecht to continue submitting poems to the *Kenyon*. Among Hecht's *Kenyon* poems that convinced Ransom of his talent are "The Song of the Beasts," "Upon the Death of Santayana," and one of his best poems, the erotic, elegant "The Gardens of the Villa D'Este."[10]

James Wright, who graduated from Kenyon College in 1952, also abundantly fulfilled Ransom's expectations. "Lonely" and "Father" in the autumn, 1951, *Kenyon* constituted his first appearance in print, and "Robert Sitting in My Hands," which had won the 1952 Robert Frost poetry award at Kenyon College, appeared in the winter of 1953. Considering that Wright was only in his early twenties and that his first book of verse, *The Green Wall*, which was selected in the Yale Series of Younger Poets, did not appear until 1957, it is not surprising that Wright's publication in the *Kenyon* at this time was still sporadic. More attention will be paid to him later, but he deserves being bracketed here with Merwin and Hecht as poets whose very different gifts Ransom recognized from the outset and whose careers he supported and fostered without turning these poets into poor copies of himself.[11]

Of slightly lesser stature is the poet Robert Mezey, also a member

10. Anthony Hecht, "A Little Note," *Kalamazoo College Review*, XXX (1968), 9. It is not clear whether Hecht is speaking of "Once Removed" or "To a Soldier Killed in Germany," both of which appeared in *Kenyon*'s spring, 1947, issue, actually four issues after the one in which Brecht and Bentley appeared. Besides, Bentley, Brecht, and Trilling did not appear together in one issue. Hecht must mean either the spring, 1946, or the autumn, 1946, issue, for Bertolt Brecht, "The Caucasian Circle of Chalk, Act Five," trans. James Stern and W. H. Auden, and Eric Bentley, "Who Understands Drama?," both appeared in *KR*, VIII:2, pp. 188–202, 333–37; Lionel Trilling, "The Life of the Novel," and Eric Bentley, "This Is the New Criticism," were in *KR*, VIII:4, pp. 658–67, 672–74. The spring, 1946, issue seems to be the most likely choice, as it was only in *KR*, XX, 393–98, that Brecht reappeared with "The Life of Confucius," a posthumous fragment translated by H. E. Rank. Anthony Hecht, "Two Poems," *KR*, IX, 222–24; Anthony Hecht, "The Song of the Beasts," *KR*, XIV, 325–26; Anthony Hecht, "Upon the Death of Santayana," *KR*, XVI, 75–76; Anthony Hecht, "The Gardens of the Villa D'Este," *KR*, XV, 208–12.

11. James Wright, "Lonely" and "Father," *KR*, XIII, 672–73; James Wright, "Robert Sitting in My Hands," *KR*, XV, 127–28.

of the generation of aspiring poets who came to Kenyon College to learn their trade under Ransom. Mezey, too, made his debut in *The Kenyon Review*, in the summer, 1954, issue. He appeared once more with three poems in 1957. John Woods's poems also first saw public light in *The Kenyon Review*; "Birth Day," "The Old Man is Dying," and "Melville Has Green Eyes" were published in its winter, 1950, issue. As in the case of Mezey, only three more poems of his appeared in the *Kenyon,* and Woods too vanished from the *Kenyon*'s pages after Ransom's retirement. Other poets such as James Merrill, Peter Viereck, and Isabella Gardner were discovered by *Poetry,* but they were published in the *Kenyon* soon after, at the outset of their poetic careers. We find four poems by Merrill in 1947, among them "The Drowning Poet" and "Cloud Country"; he was published again in 1949 and 1958. Peter Viereck's first two poems in *The Kenyon Review* in 1947, "Now Kindness" and "From Ancient Fangs," were included in his first volume of verse, *Terra and Decorum* (1948), which won the Pulitzer Prize. Viereck wrote to Ransom that Ransom was "one of the few who like my poem 'From Ancient Fangs,' the most bitterly tragic poem I've ever written, yet wrongly taken as flippant, breezy, humorous by most readers." Over the years, Viereck continued to send, as he told Ransom, "new poems I feel excitement about to you before anyone else." Four of these found favor in Ransom's eyes, and he accepted them for publication. Isabella Gardner appeared once, in 1953.[12]

Other poets who appeared only once were Walter Southard and Helen Ransom Forman. Helen Forman remembered in 1981 that her father usually had the final say about the poems to be published in *The Kenyon Review,* but he made her submit her poems under a pen name in order to obtain Rice's unbiased opinion. Rice approved, and Helen Forman made her debut, and her finale, with "Ophelia" and "Mother and Child" in the "New Poets" section of the spring, 1951,

12. Robert Mezey, "Pakim Pond, New Jersey" and "An Acquittal," *KR,* XVI, 416–19; Robert Mezey, "Verse," *KR,* XIX, 109–12; John Woods, "Birth Day," "The Old Man Is Dying," and "Melville Has Green Eyes," *KR,* XII, 81–85; John Woods, "Two Poems," *KR,* XIV, 40–42; John Woods, "The Deaths at Paragon, Indiana," *KR,* XVI, 442–45; James Merrill, "Four Poems," *KR,* IX, 378–81; James Merrill, "Transfigured Bird," *KR,* XI, 108–12; James Merrill, "Dream and Waking," *KR,* XX, 436–39; Peter Viereck, "Now Kindness," *KR,* IX, 186–87; Peter Viereck, "From Ancient Fangs," *KR,* IX, 567–68; Peter Viereck to Ransom, July 28, 1951, [January, 1955], both in *KR* Papers; Isabella Gardner, "Sestina," "Timeo," and "The Minotaur," *KR,* XIV, 613–15.

issue. Other poets who published once in the *Kenyon* and hardly ever elsewhere included William Belvin, Buddhadeva Bose, and Arthur Boyars.[13]

Of course, the editors did not always recognize a good new poet when they saw one. It was only in 1950, after he had been steadily submitting poems from October, 1938, onwards, that Theodore Roethke made his *Kenyon* debut with "A Light Breather" and "Elegy for Jane." In 1945 he wrote to Kenneth Burke that Tate's *Sewanee* and Ransom's *Kenyon* were "the only ones I care much about. The hell with *Chimera* or *Accent*: rather bury the piece in the garden." Although Ransom had been attracted by Roethke's poems from the very beginning and had usually returned them with careful comments and promises of future acceptance instead of a mere rejection slip, generally their lack of form had put him off. In March, 1945, for instance, some of Roethke's poems about greenhouses called forth the following reaction from Ransom: "I do like these things, this garden opera. . . . Perhaps I have not the right, but these excellent pieces seem to me not so much verse as fine prose. . . . It's the lack of relation between a language and its sound pattern that seems to me to avoid the intention of a lyric poem. . . . Professorial remarks like these are what I get into from wanting to go pretty far and still holding back from acceptance." About two years later, Ransom, again "deterred by the looseness of the composition," rejected Roethke's "The Long Alley," but, he hastened to assure Roethke, "[p]robably I must just take time to get used to literary effects of this kind." Half a year later, in reply to another letter of Ransom's, Roethke wrote: "Regarding your *becoming* a convert to my work: I console myself that those slow to faith are in the end, the firmest." He included "A Field of Light," which was "typed by Master Robert Lowell, who says you will recognize what a labor of love his typing is. He thinks you might break down on this one."[14]

---

13. Walter Southard, "Winter Landscape, Tien Shan," *KR*, XVII, 111–12; Helen Forman, "Ophelia" and "Mother and Child," *KR*, XIII, 282–83; William Belvin, "Palermo, Mother's Day, 1943" and "Third Anniversary Poem," *KR*, XIII, 279–80; Buddhadeva Bose, "Two Poems," *KR*, XI, 289–90; Arthur Boyars, "Two Poems," *KR*, XI, 453–54.

14. Theodore Roethke to Burke, December 25, 1945, in Ralph J. Mills, Jr. (ed.), *Selected Letters of Theodore Roethke* (Seattle, 1968), 114; Theodore Roethke, "A Light Breather" and "Elegy for Jane," *KR*, XII, 475–76; Ransom to Theodore Roethke, March 1, 1945, December 5, [1946], Roethke to Ransom, July 28, 1947, all in Roethke Papers.

But it was not until June, 1949, that Ransom finally broke down. "I like this 'Light Breather', it is light and suited indeed to its title. Maybe you have another one to go with it? We'd rather publish a little group than a single poem, but we'll publish it anyhow, and thanks." Roethke did not "know when an acceptance has given me more pleasure" and enclosed "Elegy for Jane," which Ransom liked "even better." Both poems appeared in *Kenyon*'s summer, 1950, issue. However, Ransom was not yet completely won over to Roethke and rejected several new submissions. "Old Lady's Winter Words" appealed to him; it was in the winter, 1952, number. In 1954 he accepted "Words for the Wind" but returned it when he realized that the European magazines *Botteghe Oscure* and *Encounter* would publish it first: "Just a little while ago this general question of policy came up and we decided not to re-print from them; they both, but particularly *Botteghe,* have so much circulation in this country." In June, 1955, Ransom accepted a final batch, "I think the dead are tender . . ." and "I waited for the wind to move the dust. . . ."[15] Even if Ransom never embraced Roethke's often wild and whimsical poems as wholeheartedly as he did, for instance, James Wright's and William Merwin's more formalized work, he did come to realize Roethke's stature as a notable poet and asked him to be the Fellow in Poetry for 1957. Roethke had to decline regretfully, having just spent a year away from the University of Washington in Seattle as a lecturer in Florence in Italy.

Other established poets who had gotten regular rejections before being accepted were Babette Deutsch and Merrill Moore. The latter was so "deeply grateful" when, in 1951, Ransom asked him to submit some of his poems that he proposed to "pay your printer for inserting an extra number of pages," should Ransom wish to print as many as twenty or thirty of his poems. But Ransom only took five of Moore's elegant, proficient sonnets and printed them at the *Kenyon*'s expense. Like Moore, Babette Deutsch appeared only once, in 1948, with "Fountain and Unicorn," which Ransom thought was "awfully good" and the "most formal and studied poem" of hers that he had

15. Ransom to Theodore Roethke, June 16, 1949, Roethke to Ransom, June 22, 1949, Ransom to Roethke, June 24, 1949, all in Roethke Papers; Theodore Roethke, "Old Lady's Winter Words," *KR,* XIV, 60–62; Ransom to Roethke, June 18, 1954, in Roethke Papers; Theodore Roethke, "Two Poems," *KR,* XVIII, 120–21.

ever seen. Richard Wilbur also was in *The Kenyon Review* long after his fame had been established. When, in 1952, Ransom invited Wilbur to contribute, he was "much flattered" and made his one appearance in the winter, 1954, issue with "A Voice from under the Table."[16]

If particularly Theodore Roethke and the newcomers William Merwin, Anthony Hecht, and James Wright enhanced the *Kenyon's* poetry department, the poetic highlights of this period came from two cherished contributors of long standing, Wallace Stevens and Robert Penn Warren. Stevens contributed his classic poem "The Auroras of Autumn," which led off the winter, 1948, issue. In Ransom's view, this poem was "the best thing he ha[d] done for a long time." He told Stevens that he thought it "even better than . . . *Esthétique du Mal,*" because it had "a slightly warmer, more obvious humanism." With the publication of the first half of Robert Penn Warren's magisterial *Brother to Dragons* (1953), Ransom pulled off an even greater coup. The poem took up over a hundred pages of the winter, 1952, issue and is the longest piece of writing ever published in *The Kenyon Review.*[17] Considering Ransom's preference for technically proficient, short, dense, lyrical poems, and his dislike of the violence in Warren's fiction, his immediate fascination with and admiration for this long narrative poem full of passion and fury may initially come as a surprise.

Ransom thought the poem was "magnificent." It is very difficult, and perhaps undesirable, to keep up the fullest measure of lyrical intensity throughout such a long poem, and Ransom was struck by the

16. Merrill Moore to Ransom, November 6, 9, 1951, both in *KR* Papers; Merrill Moore, "Work in Progress (Five Sonnets)," *KR,* XIV, 80–83; Babette Deutsch, "Fountain and Unicorn," *KR,* X, 429–30; Ransom to Babette Deutsch, March 22, [1948], in Deutsch Papers. Actually, Babette Deutsch appeared twice: the second time, her translation of Ivan Goll, "Jean Le Fleuve," *KR,* XVII, 278–79, appeared side by side with the original. Richard Wilbur to Ransom, June 27, 1952, in *KR* Papers; Richard Wilbur, "A Voice from under the Table," *KR,* XVI, 79–80. Thomas Daniel Young and George Core (eds.), *Selected Letters of John Crowe Ransom* (Baton Rouge, 1985), 364–65, quote Ransom's letter of June 19, 1952, to Richard Wilbur in which he solicits poems. They note: "Ransom had lost a batch of poems from the manuscript for Wilbur's first collection of poetry, *The Beautiful Changes* (1947), and was here trying to make amends."

17. Wallace Stevens, "The Auroras of Autumn," *KR,* X, 1–10; Peter Viereck (quoting Ransom) to Ransom, October 21, 1947, in *KR* Papers; Ransom to Wallace Stevens, October 7, 1947, in Young and Core (eds.), *Selected Letters of John Crowe Ransom,* 337; Robert Penn Warren, *Brother to Dragons: A Tale in Verse and Voices* (1953; rev. ed., New York, 1979); Robert Penn Warren, "Brother to Dragons: A Tale in Verse and Voices," *KR,* XV, 1–103.

happy mean in style that Warren had found. "Stylistically you have
done a wonderful job; there's just enough High Poetry, while the
Mean Poetry is always vital and dramatic; what more could you
ask?" He admired Warren's ability "to manage a long poem, . . . all
the pace, variety, vitality, suspense, in the world." Yet Ransom added
some "piddling comments." Speaking of the poem's publication in
book form, he said: "I don't thin[k] the title is happy; and I don't
think it matters, as for that, that we have already given you a title in
KR—'twould make our version all the more attractive to the historian if it wasn't the authoritative title. BROTHER TO DRAGONS isn't eu-
phonious somehow; hard to say; hard to remember, as to which
noun is singular, which is plural, and why there's a distinction; and
it's a bit Tennysonian, isn't it?" Warren did not follow this suggestion, but he did take account of Ransom's comments upon his sometimes excessive use of repetition, and upon little matters such as
"shouldn't it be *sweated* for *sweat,* your p. 165? Elsewhere with a common speaker you can say *sweat* in the past, but this is Grand Style . . .
about how Hercules *sweat* in the Forum."[18]

Ransom did not stand alone in his opinion that *Brother to Dragons*
was "great" and would "make a great impression." Philip Rahv, for
instance, ranked the part published in the *Kenyon* among Warren's
"very best things." Randall Jarrell described it as "the best very long
poem in many many decades" and complimented *The Kenyon Review* on "printing that much of it. . . . I think it makes so much difference to do things like that; it would take a magazine like *Partisan* a
couple of years to find room for a couple of pages, since it's poetry."
As had remained the custom among Warren, Tate, and Ransom since
their Fugitive days, Warren had also sent Tate his poem in advance
for comment. "I have decided . . . that I don't at all like it," Tate
wrote bluntly, "but my reasons for not liking it would not be of
practical use to you now, if they would ever have been; so I will not
go into the questions of character and method. I suppose the first
snag I struck was your language. There are many fine things but I
kept saying to myself, when they appeared, that they didn't belong
here, but in some other poem of about 100 lines." And so on. Warren
was, to be sure, "distressed" by this letter, which Tate had hated

18. Ransom to Warren, December 22, [1952], in Warren Papers.

"like hell to mail," but he was not offended. "No, nothing would have been served had you been less than candid in your expression of opinion," Warren wrote to Tate, adding generously that he thought "The Buried Lake," which Tate had asked him to read, "very effective."[19]

In later years, Warren himself became dissatisfied with *Brother to Dragons* and, in 1979, brought out a substantially revised version; but Robert Lowell, who reviewed the first version for the *Kenyon* in the autumn, 1953, issue, felt "not only that Warren has written a successful poem but that in this work he most truly seems to approach the power of those writers one has always felt hovering about him, those poetic geniuses in prose, Melville and Faulkner. In Warren's case, it is the prose genius in verse which is so startling." "That Warren, one of the bosses of the New Criticism, is the author is as though Professor Babbitt had begotten Rousseau or a black Minerva dancing in Congo masks. Warren has written his best book, a big book; he has crossed the Alps and, like Napoleon's shoeless army, entered the fat, populated riverbottom of the novel."[20]

Lowell's own poem "Beyond the Alps," which had appeared in the summer, 1953, issue and which would introduce his *Life Studies* (1959), indicates that Lowell himself rather than Warren had just then broken free from his New Critical background. Describing both his renunciation of classical, formal poetry and his loss of faith, "Beyond the Alps," was Lowell's twelfth contribution to the *Kenyon's* poetry department. During this period, Lowell had already published three poems, "Falling Asleep Over the Aeneid," "Mother Marie Therese," and "The Mills of the Kavanaughs," which together made up about half of his book of verse, *The Mills of the Kavanaughs* (1951). When Lowell submitted "Falling Asleep Over the Aeneid"—Ransom being for Lowell "obviously the only editor . . . to send my Virgil poems to"—Ransom gladly accepted it for the winter, 1948, issue. Half a

19. Ransom to Warren, December 22, [1952], in Warren Papers; Philip Rahv to Tate, February 12, 1953, in Tate Papers; Randall Jarrell to Ransom, n.d., Jarrell to Ransom, n.d., both in *KR* Papers; Tate to Warren, November 9, 1952, Warren to Tate, November 13, 1952, both in Tate Papers.
20. Victor Strandberg, in *"Brother to Dragons* and the Craft of Revision," in James A. Grimshaw, Jr. (ed.), *Robert Penn Warren's Brother to Dragons: A Discussion* (Baton Rouge, 1983), 200–210, shows that Tate's suggestions for the revised edition "were manifestly efficacious" (204). Robert Lowell, "Prose Genius in Verse," *KR,* XV, 625, 621.

year later, Ransom published "Mother Marie Therese," which he found "gentle and good." Randall Jarrell was one among many who acclaimed these two poems—"'Mother Marie Therese' is the best poem Mr. Lowell has ever written, and 'Falling Asleep Over the Aeneid' is—is better"—but had mixed feelings about "The Mills of the Kavanaughs." R. W. Flint described "The Mills" as "magnificent in places and damned tiresome in others."[21] Unfortunately, Ransom's reaction has not been preserved, but his having this poem lead off the winter, 1953, issue indicates that he, for one, thought highly of it.

Ransom also continued to admire Randall Jarrell's poetry and published two long and three short poems of his during this period. "The Night Before the Night Before Christmas," the longest of all of Jarrell's poems, appeared in the winter of 1949. William Carlos Williams was "rouse[d]" by this "refreshing" meditation of a lonely, grieving girl to submit a few poems of his own—"not that they resemble his work or that I have any great confidence in them." Ransom, however, rejected Williams' work. Three of Jarrell's poems, full of feelings of despair and desolation, appeared in the spring, 1951, number. "The End of the Rainbow" was published some three years later and, like "The Black Swan" and many other of Jarrell's poems, combined dreams and elements of fairy tales and spoke of isolation and loneliness. Jarrell had submitted this last searching, painful poem instead of a piece on Yeats he had promised, in the belief that it was "considerably better than the Yeats piece would have been. Anyway, it was considerably more welcome to me, as you can imagine. . . . I wanted to give you the best things I had while I had them."[22]

Four of the poems William Carlos Williams submitted during this period did appear in The Kenyon Review; "Lesson from a Pupil's Recital" and "Voyages" in the summer of 1948, "The Host" in the sum-

21. Robert Lowell, "Beyond the Alps," KR, XV, 398–401; Robert Lowell, Life Studies (New York, 1959); Robert Lowell, "Falling Asleep Over the Aeneid," KR, X, 89–91; Robert Lowell, "Mother Marie Therese," KR, X, 403–406; Robert Lowell, "The Mills of the Kavanaughs," KR, XIII, 1–19; Robert Lowell, The Mills of the Kavanaughs (New York, 1951); Robert Lowell to Ransom, July 5, [1947], Ransom to Lowell, January 10, [1948], both in KR Papers; Randall Jarrell, Poetry and the Age (New York, 1953), 231; R. W. Flint to Ransom, January 31, [1951], in KR Papers.
22. Randall Jarrell, "The Night Before the Night Before Christmas," KR, XI, 31–42; William Carlos Williams to Ransom, January 15, 1949, in John C. Thirwall (ed.), The Selected Letters of William Carlos Williams (New York, 1957), 272; Randall Jarrell, "All or None," "The Tower," and "The Black Swan," KR, XIII, 204–206; Randall Jarrell, "The End of the Rainbow," KR, XVI, 600–10; Randall Jarrell to Ransom, n.d., in KR Papers.

mer of 1953, and "Of Asphodel" two years later. Williams was "eternally grateful" for Ransom's part "in seeing to the publication of ["Of Asphodel"]." He wrote: "When I saw the poem printed, I realized that the latter part of it is not quite up to what I could wish—but that is part of the game. The first part of the poem is thrilling to me and I am content." Ransom also was content, having after years of indifference come to appreciate Williams' unconventional, loosely metered poetry. Explaining to David McDowell, Williams' publisher, why he had only one extensive letter of Williams' in the *Kenyon* files for possible inclusion in the forthcoming *Selected Letters of William Carlos Williams,* Ransom wrote in 1956: "[I]t seems strange now, but . . . we were not printing him often. . . . It is only in recent years, and thanks to you, that I have really known Bill and got so much affection for him." Ransom's growing affection for the man had gone hand in hand with his growing admiration for the poetry, and in 1962 he mentioned Williams as one of America's six twentieth-century poets of world class.[23]

Another poet whose work had slowly grown upon Ransom was Richard Eberhart. Published only once during the preceding period, Eberhart's work now appeared no less than five times. Among his nine usually short poems appearing during these years are "A Legend of Viable Women," "Using the Meditative Means," and four poems grouped together under the title "The Seasons." Ransom's suggestions for changes and improvement could be extremely detailed, as Eberhart's answer to his comments on "The Seasons" indicates: "I think I will be coy about this now, argue meaning with you later if you like: I have consulted French experts and feel certain fort should not have an e. . . . I think I can explain voluptuary to the inner arm which is clear to me. . . . I debate a comma in Summer after Lost, the first word in line 3, only on time, to slow the movement—yet now I think not and leave it as it is." Eberhart was grateful for Ransom's confidence in his poetry and for his continued editorial support.

23. William Carlos Williams, "Two Deliberate Exercises," *KR*, X, 427–29; William Carlos Williams, "The Host," *KR*, XV, 404–407; William Carlos Williams, "Of Asphodel," *KR*, XVII, 371–82; William Carlos Williams to Ransom, n.d., in *KR* Papers. Internal evidence suggests that the unnamed poem Williams refers to is "Of Asphodel" rather than "The Host." Ransom to David McDowell, October 16, 1956, in *KR* Papers; Faith Corrigan, "Ransom Picks 6 Top U.S. Poets of This Century," Cleveland *Plain Dealer,* July 2, 1962. The other poets were T. S. Eliot, Robert Frost, Ezra Pound, Edwin Arlington Robinson, and Wallace Stevens.

"You have printed some of my best poems and you have stood by me for many years. My loyalty and devotion, as well as friendship is to you," he wrote in September, 1954.[24]

These sentiments were shared by Ruth Herschberger, three of whose poems appeared during these years. After not having "sent poems out in five years," she wrote to Rice in March, 1951, "[w]hat I did was sort out poems pre-'48 . . . in the Fall, because they happened to be there, and I sent what I thought were the best to Ransom. I am awfully glad he picked the Mink, and as to those he sent back—I have permanently discarded all but one. . . . So you can see how much it would mean to me if I could send you these culled from the last three years mainly, just for your [Ransom's and Rice's] judgment." "The Mink" appeared in the summer, 1951, issue, and "To S. R." and "My Dear He Dress in Scarlet" four years later. Another former contributor, Delmore Schwartz, whose poetic talent had long been in decline, published only two minor poems in the Kenyon, one in the spring of 1950 and the other in the autumn of 1955. John Berryman, Muriel Rukeyser, and Jean Garrigue appeared once during this period, but Josephine Miles remained a favorite contributor with nineteen of her short poems published. "I guess she is about as good as Marianne Moore," Ransom wrote to David McDowell in June, 1952. Moore herself appeared just once, in the winter of 1954, with her translation of two of La Fontaine's fables. As before, The Kenyon Review was wary of translations. But Lloyd Parks's translations of two of Jacques Prévert's witty poems and Gabriel Nahas' translations of three of Paul Eluard's somber ones deserve mention. Like Richard Ellmann's 1949 translation of Henri Michaux, they were a result of Rice's sojourn in France in 1947.[25]

24. Richard Eberhart, "A Legend of Viable Women," KR, XI, 83–86; Richard Eberhart, "Using the Meditative Means," KR, XVII, 447–48; Richard Eberhart, "The Seasons," KR, XIV, 327–30; Richard Eberhart to Ransom, January 30, 1952, September 22, 1954, both in KR Papers.
25. Ruth Herschberger to Rice, March 6, [1951], in KR Papers; Ruth Herschberger, "The Mink," KR, XIII, 425–26; Ruth Herschberger, "To S. R." and "My Dear He Dress in Scarlet," KR, XVII, 444–46; Delmore Schwartz, "The Early Morning Light," KR, XII, 243–45; Delmore Schwartz, "The First Morning of the Second World," KR, XVII, 575–80. On December 10, 1954, Delmore Schwartz wrote to Ransom that "The First Morning of the Second World" was "the first verse I've sent you (and almost anyone else) in over five years, and I hope you won't mind my saying that I feel, at the moment at any rate, that it's as good as the best lyric I've written, 'Starlight like Intuition Pierced the Twelve' [KR, VI, 383–85]" (Letter in Robert E. Phillips [ed.], Letters of Delmore Schwartz [Princeton, 1984], 296). John Berryman,

Clearly, the publication of established, important American poets—such as Richard Eberhart, Randall Jarrell, Robert Lowell, Theodore Roethke, Wallace Stevens, Robert Penn Warren, and William Carlos Williams—and, in particular, of a profusion of gifted debutants and relative newcomers to the field of poetry, such as Anthony Hecht, James Merrill, William Merwin, Robert Mezey, Peter Viereck, John Woods, and James Wright, shows *The Kenyon Review* to have championed talented poets during these years. In writing in 1950 that he was "grateful to the KENYON REVIEW for what it has done for me," Wallace Stevens voiced the feelings of many other poets published in the *Kenyon,* which had come to occupy a prominent place in the limited market for poetry in America.[26]

Fiction

The American market for short stories was better: in 1952, in *The Short Story in America, 1900–1950,* Ray B. West noted that "at least a few of the large-circulation periodicals," following the lead of the literary quarterlies, "have, during the 1940's . . . printed a high proportion of the first rate short fiction which has appeared." *The Kenyon Review* played an important part in discovering new fiction writers and, consequently, in furthering the development of the modern short story. It was harder for the editors to find good fiction than good poetry, however, and during the 1950s they often had to solicit short stories, something they hardly ever had to do with respect to poetry. This was not because fiction was not submitted. In 1952, Ransom wrote to Chalmers that the "largest fraction of material submitted in manuscript to us is fiction," but, he added, "sometimes in a

"A Winter-Piece to a Friend Away" and "Rock-Study with Wanderer," *KR,* X, 240–45. John Haffenden, *The Life of John Berryman* (Boston, 1982), 197–98, reports that Berryman became incredibly angry when he saw that Ransom had not followed his instruction to print "Rock-Study with Wanderer" first. Muriel Rukeyser, "Eyes of Night-time," *KR,* IX, 234; Jean Garrigue, "Invocation to Old Windylocks," *KR,* XIV, 616–18. Josephine Miles published, for instance, "Siege," "Son," "Idea of Joy," and "Bombay," *KR,* XI, 649–51; and "Barge," "Belief," "Find," "Bush," and "Height," *KR,* XVI, 76–78. Ransom to David McDowell, June 12, [1952], in Random House Papers; M. de La Fontaine, "The Cat and the Mouse" and "The Man and the Serpent," trans. Marianne Moore, *KR,* XVI, 71–74; Jacques Prévert, "Two Poems," trans. Lloyd Parks, *KR,* XI, 218–21; Paul Eluard, "Three Poems," trans. Gabriel Nahas, *KR,* XI, 222–25; Henri Michaux, "In the Land of Magic," trans. Richard Ellmann, *KR,* XI, 173–86.
26. Wallace Stevens to Rice, April 20, 1950, in *KR* Papers.

single quarter we will return several hundred manuscripts without finding one story that is satisfactory." Still, the editors kept on plowing through the piles of fiction manuscripts in the hope of discovering good writers. Sometimes their patience was rewarded: Robert Creeley, Ann Mitchner, and Stanley Sultan, for instance, made their fiction debuts in *The Kenyon Review*.[27]

The competition with the middlebrow magazines was strong. In 1946, for instance, *The Kenyon Review*—which paid better rates than both the *Sewanee* and *Partisan* reviews—paid its fiction writers $3.30 per page (about $.01 a word); *The Atlantic Monthly* paid a flat sum of about $200.00 per story and *Harper's* as much as $300.00. And over the years, the difference only became greater. In 1959 the maximum prose rate paid by the "Four Reviews" (*Kenyon, Sewanee, Partisan, and Hudson*) was about $8.00 per page (about $.025 a word); *The Atlantic Monthly* paid $300.00 to $750.00 per story, *Harper's* up to $500.00, and *The New Yorker* about $.20 a word.[28] It is quite natural, then, that many talented writers of serious fiction went over to the large-circulation magazines.

During this period, the *Kenyon's* fiction record is nevertheless outstanding. For instance, the first Fellow in Fiction was Flannery O'Connor. It was on the recommendation of Robert Fitzgerald, Allen Tate, and Peter Taylor that Flannery O'Connor received her first fellowship in 1953, but the renewal in 1954—O'Connor was the only Fellow ever to receive a renewal—was due to the brilliance of the stories she submitted to *The Kenyon Review*, which convinced Ransom that O'Connor was "probably the best short story writer in the country." The officers of the Rockefeller Foundation did not object in the least to the renewal, and in 1955 a wholly content John Marshall, also taking due account of *The Sewanee Review* fellowships, wrote to Flannery O'Connor that hers had been "the most

27. Ray B. West, *The Short Story in America, 1900–1950* (1952; rpr. New York, 1979), 118; Ransom to Chalmers, January 22, 1952, in *KR* Papers; Robert Creeley, "The Unsuccessful Husband," *KR*, XIII, 64–71; Ann Mitchner, "Invitation to Lunch," *KR*, XII, 602–17; Stanley Sultan, "The Fugue and the Fig Tree," *KR*, XIV, 418–31.

28. Most of these figures are taken from John Marshall to David Stevens, January 14, 1947, and G. Gillette to Marshall, February 18, 1947, both memos in LMS Papers. Some are from a leaflet attached to Frederick Morgan to Ransom, January 29, 1959, and from Ransom to Frederick Morgan, February 11, 1959, both in *HR* Papers.

complete success of the three years during which these fellowships have been granted."[29]

During Ransom's editorship, four of O'Connor's grotesque, sardonic, and tragic stories were published in the *Kenyon*. Ransom described "The Life You Save May Be Your Own," which appeared in the spring, 1953, issue, as "the best story I've seen in years." O'Connor also was pleased, if much too modest: "Mr. Martin at the University of Iowa wrote me that they were interested in 'The Life You Save, etc.' for the O. Henry collection. I've never had a story of mine used for any of these collections before and I find myself thinking that the Kenyon Fellowship has added enough distinction to my situation to get my stories reprinted." Indicative, too, of Ransom's admiration for O'Connor's stories is that he had "A Circle in the Fire" and "The Artificial Nigger" lead off the spring, 1954, and 1955, issues. "Greenleaf," which was published in *Kenyon*'s summer, 1956, issue, won the first prize in the O. Henry Memorial Awards for 1957 and was included in Robie Macauley's *Gallery of Modern Fiction* (1966). The sexual symbolism in this story about a woman pierced to death by the horns of a bull running wild was not lost on Kenneth Burke, who may indeed have read too much into this story. He wrote to Ransom: "I wholly agree with you in your admiration for it, though its sexually symbolic dimension puzzles me somewhat, beyond the obvious feature. . . . [O]ne suddenly realizes that, as regards the sheer pragmatics . . . there is the problem of a bull's having *two* horns, whereupon the membrum virile, as thus transformed, can make contact in two places. So if 'heart' takes the place of 'hymen,' as the euphemistic displacement of one stroke, 'side' might take the place of 'groin' as euphemistic displacement of the other. Or, because of the word 'grip,' we might rather assume that the second displacement involves connotations of *arms,* holding the body when initially pierced."[30] And so on.

29. Interview with Helen and Elizabeth Forman, October 19, 1981; John Marshall to Flannery O'Connor, August 26, 1955, in KC Collection.

30. Flannery O'Connor, "The Life You Save May Be Your Own," *KR,* XV, 195–207; Flannery O'Connor, "A Circle in the Fire," *KR,* XVI, 169–90; Flannery O'Connor, "The Artificial Nigger," *KR,* XVII, 169–92; Flannery O'Connor, "Greenleaf," *KR,* XVIII, 384–410; Ransom to Lytle, March 25, 1954, in Lytle Papers; Flannery O'Connor to Ransom, July 13, 1953 in *KR* Papers; Robie Macauley (ed.), *Gallery of Modern Fiction: Stories from The Kenyon*

George Lanning, who would be the last editor of the first series of *The Kenyon Review,* was the 1954 Fellow in Fiction along with Flannery O'Connor. He contributed only one story, the technically proficient "News about Miss Prince," which appeared in the autumn, 1951, issue, years before his election as a Fellow. In 1954, Ransom described Lanning as "a very young novelist . . . [with] a fine style and boundless resources of invention"; but it is as a writer of light novels, rather than as a writer of serious fiction, that George Lanning has made his mark. The Fellow in Fiction for 1955 was Howard Nemerov. Ransom had offered him the choice of a fellowship in fiction or criticism, but Nemerov left it to Ransom: "[J]ust at present I have no settled plan for my future work, and have been for some months past in a kind of crisis, arid and deserted by my images. I do not believe this means I will never write again . . . but it seems to me, and so it may to you, that right now I look like a mighty poor risk, fellowship-wise."[31] Ransom showed his confidence in Nemerov, who became the Fellow in Fiction on the basis of his past work. Richard Ellmann was made the Fellow in Criticism.

Nemerov's initial interim reports on his fellowship were hardly jubilant, but by the autumn of 1955, he had come to feel "its benign influence." "As to the Fellowship in Fiction," Nemerov then wrote, "I industriously set to work and broke my spirit on five starts at the same novel, which I incline to regard now as a total loss. Toward the end of summer, though, I began to write short stories, and think I have discovered some things and begun to see the light. . . . So:— I'm not out of the woods yet . . . but I feel the Fellowship has accomplished already part of its purpose—that is, it let me sit still for a while and consider what it was I wanted to do." The "total loss"

Review (New York, 1966); Burke to Ransom, [late January or early February, 1957], in Burke Papers. Another very sexual story, "The Comforts of Home," appeared during Macauley's editorship (in *KR,* XXII, 523–46) and marked O'Connor's final contribution to the *Kenyon.* Because mention is made of a female character in the nude, Macauley added a tiny illustration of a naked girl. This led Flannery O'Connor to write on January 2, 1961, that she was "disappointed and sick" when she saw the illustration and that Macauley "had lost a contributor" (Letter in *KR* Papers). Only long after O'Connor's death in 1965 did Macauley learn that "Flannery did not care one way or the other, but her mother was outraged . . . and . . . made Flannery write that letter" (Interview with Macauley, August 9, 1982).

31. George Lanning, "News about Miss Prince," *KR,* XIII, 624–40; Ransom to John Marshall, November 29, 1954, in *KR* Papers. One of George Lanning's most famous novels is *The Pedestal* (New York, 1966). Howard Nemerov to Ransom, October 10, 1954, in *KR* Papers.

eventually became Nemerov's witty novel about the academy, *The Homecoming Game* (1957), and three of his very fine, vivid, tragi-comic stories, "Tradition," "An Encounter with the Law," and "A Delayed Hearing," were published in *The Kenyon Review* and collected in 1959 in *A Commodity of Dreams and Other Stories*. Ransom came to regard Nemerov as "one of our most faithful and excellent contributors" and declared himself to be "grateful for any submissions of fiction" Nemerov would care to make. But "A Delayed Hearing," which appeared in the summer, 1957, issue and which Ransom described as "a nice piece of juggling between fantasy and the hard facts of life" and as "fine, good all round," turned out to be Nemerov's final short story for *The Kenyon Review*. His relatively few contributions to the *Kenyon* after Ransom's retirement were in poetry and criticism.[32]

Flannery O'Connor and Howard Nemerov were among the few fiction writers who published for the first time in *The Kenyon Review* during these years and who published more than one story. Others were Daniel Curley, now known for his children's books and his editorship of *Ascent*; Ruth Domino, a native of Austria; Priscilla Heath, wife of Denham Sutcliffe of the English department at Kenyon College; Edgar McGuire, a Kenyon graduate and later managing editor of *The Western Review;* and the British writer Wayland Young. Robert Creeley, Randall Jarrell, Wright Morris, and Richard Stern, who also published fiction twice, and Robie Macauley, who contributed three stories, are better known and deserve special attention.[33]

32. Howard Nemerov to Ransom, September 24, 1955, in *KR* Papers; Howard Nemerov, *The Homecoming Game* (New York, 1957); Howard Nemerov, "Tradition," *KR*, XVII, 408–24 (probably written just before Nemerov's fellowship); Howard Nemerov, "An Encounter with the Law," *KR*, XVIII, 212–23; Howard Nemerov, "A Delayed Hearing," *KR*, XIX, 448–62; Howard Nemerov, *A Commodity of Dreams and Other Stories* (New York, 1959); Ransom to Howard Nemerov, February 3, August 24, 1956, both in *KR* Papers.

33. Daniel Curley, "To Ask the Hard Question Is Easy," *KR*, XVI, 565–86, and "The Appointed Hour," *KR*, XVII, 543–74; Ruth Domino, "The Shared Bed," *KR*, X, 287–303, and "It Almost Happened," *KR*, XI, 397–404; Priscilla Heath, "The Mothers," *KR*, XIV, 406–17, and "The Other Woman," *KR*, XXI, 34–57; Edgar McGuire, "If a Man Die," *KR*, X, 273–86, and "The Tenant of the Room," *KR*, XI, 654–71; Wayland Young, "The Glass Trumpet," *KR*, XVI, 191–99, and "The Admirer," *KR*, XIX, 593–604; Robert Creeley, "The Unsuccessful Husband," *KR*, XIII, 64–71, and "The Boat," *KR*, XV, 571–76; Randall Jarrell, "Pictures from an Institution: Book I," *KR*, XV, 104–26, and "Pictures from an Institution: Book III," *KR*, XVI, 81–123; Wright Morris, "A Man of Caliber," *KR*, XI, 101–107, and "The Safe Place," *KR*, XVI, 587–99; Richard Stern, "Cooley's Version," *KR*, XVI, 257–67, and "The Assessment of an Amateur," *KR*, XXI, 250–59; Robie Macauley, "The Thin

Robert Creeley in later years spoke up for "'men who are trying to think in terms of contemporary realities, instead of being awfully-old-Southern-gentlemen,'" and spoke out against literary reviews, but it was in *The Kenyon Review* that he made his first breakthrough as a fiction writer with a wry story about a paranoid husband, published in the winter, 1951, issue. Ransom found this story "*extremely good*" and described Creeley to David McDowell at Random House as "an *unusually* able writer" and "a great prospect—provided he's got a certain toughness, and can rule himself, and take advice."[34] Creeley's second contribution, "The Boat," which appeared in the autumn of 1953, was another successful, painful psychological study of the miseries of married life.

Although Richard Stern had published fiction before his first appearance in the spring, 1954, *Kenyon Review*, "Cooley's Version" was one of his earliest short stories to be published. Stern's second story, which deals with the old theme of the American in Europe, appeared in the spring, 1959, number and won the Longview Foundation Literary Award. Stern also became a regular reviewer for the *Kenyon* from 1956. Robie Macauley, who had been reviewing irregularly for the *Kenyon* since 1942, appeared in 1951 for the first time in its fiction department with "The Thin Voice," a tale of war, an early, though not a first, story. Macauley's second story for the *Kenyon,* published in its spring, 1957, issue, "The Chevigny Man," an amusing exposure of academic pretense, was the best of Macauley's proficient, precise stories to appear in *The Kenyon Review* and won a Benjamin Franklin Magazine Award Citation for 1956. "I have such confidence in your gift as a fiction writer, and a man of letters generally, that I will not hold back from a little disparagement," Ransom wrote to Macauley with respect to his first version of another story, "The Legend of Two Swimmers," and he went on to give detailed criticism. Hoping that Macauley would not think his "advice . . . impertinent," Ransom concluded this letter by suggesting "humbly that you think through it again and see if you can get the best out of it."[35]

Voice," *KR,* XIII, 50–63, "The Chevigny Man," *KR,* XVII, 75–93, and "Legend of Two Swimmers," *KR,* XIX, 246–66.

34. Robert Creeley quoted in "Don't Bury the Hatchet," *TLS,* February 13, 1964, p. 127; Ransom to David McDowell, October 12, 1950, in Random House Papers.

35. Richard Stern reviewed, for instance, Marcel Proust, *Jean Santeuil,* and James Joyce,

The revised version was a penetrating story about hero worship and true heroes and appeared in *Kenyon*'s spring, 1957, issue.

Although Wright Morris had been writing and periodically publishing fiction for some ten years, he was hardly well known when he published his first *Kenyon Review* story, "A Man of Caliber," in the winter, 1949, issue. This partly autobiographical, compassionate story deals with Will Brady, the protagonist of Morris' novel *The Works of Love* (1952), as up and coming in the egg business in Calloway. "The Safe Place," one of Morris' most poignant stories, appeared in the autumn, 1954, issue. This story about disease and death, hope and hopelessness, became part of his novel *Ceremony in Lone Tree* (1960) and was reprinted by Robie Macauley in *Gallery of Modern Fiction*. Entirely different from Morris' deeply serious, sometimes seemingly nihilistic stories were Randall Jarrell's two hilarious *Kenyon* installments of his satirical chronicle of academe, *Pictures from an Institution* (1954). At the suggestion of his close friend Peter Taylor, himself a regular contributor to *The New Yorker*, Jarrell had first submitted his manuscript to that popular magazine in the hope of making a lot of money. Although its editors "liked the book in many ways and really wanted to be able to use a part, or parts of it," they regretted that they had to return the manuscript. The book's first chapter, which they had singled out for possible publication, had seemed to their legal advisor "to involve a libel." Jarrell hastened to forestall Ransom's fear of a possible libel suit, explaining that Harold Taylor, the young, progressive president of Sarah Lawrence College—where Jarrell had taught for a year—was like Dwight Robbins, the president of his fictional College Benton, "(except for a few particulars like curly hair, ingenuous sincerity) only insofar as he's like the general type of such Boy Wonder executives; he was mostly a point of departure for me, but I did take several firm steps before departing."[36]

Stephen Hero, in *KR*, XVIII, 486–96, and Saul Bellow, *Henderson the Rain King*, in *KR*, XXI, 655–62. Robie Macauley's first *Kenyon* appearance was his review of Mark Schorer, *The Hermit Place*, and Robert Paul Smith, *So It Doesn't Whistle*, in *KR*, IV, 124–26. Ransom to Macauley, December 3, 1956, in *KR* Papers.

36. Wright Morris, *The Works of Love* (New York, 1952); Wright Morris, *Ceremony in Lone Tree* (New York, 1960); Randall Jarrell, *Pictures from an Institution* (New York, 1954); K. S. White of *The New Yorker* to Randall Jarrell, September 14, 1951, in Jarrell Papers; Randall Jarrell to Ransom, n.d., in *KR* Papers.

Less cautious than the editors of *The New Yorker,* Ransom, who loved the novel, accepted Jarrell's first chapter for the winter, 1953, issue and Book III, which Jarrell had recommended as "the best of all the books, so far as printing by itself is concerned," for the winter, 1954, number. Most readers were delighted. After the publication of Book I, for instance, the *Kenyon* published a "Fan Letter" by an impatient reader, Isabel Hathorn, who found "'Institution' the funniest thing I ever hope to read" and begged: "Please, please, isn't there any way I can read the rest of it without having to wait?" Wallace Stevens regarded "'the parts of the novel that have been published . . . [as] of unusual interest and skill.'" And with that characteristic generosity of his toward authors he admired, William Carlos Williams wrote to Jarrell: "Before it is too late I want to compromise myself publicly by praising your recent book. . . . The book has a surface, a verbal quality, that attracted me. . . . Its humor reaches into regions seldom disturbed by most modern writing. Thank you for the privilege of reading it."[37]

Creeley, Stern, Macauley, Morris, and Jarrell, here were five very different and very distinguished writers of fiction who were given an early chance to prove themselves in *The Kenyon Review* during these years. Among other newcomers to the *Kenyon*'s fiction department, all of whom, for various reasons, published only once, were Elizabeth Hardwick and Leslie Fiedler. Hardwick's "Two Recent Travelers," an atmospheric story about two Americans in Turkey, was in the summer, 1953, issue. Robie Macauley reprinted it in his *Gallery of Modern Fiction* as one of the seven stories—among a total of twenty-four—selected from those published during Ransom's editorship. Ransom, however, initially had some doubts about "Two Recent Travelers," as it did not fit in easily with his rather traditional conception of the short story. He commented: "I want Phil and Peter Taylor and me to have one more conference about the story. It's a mighty nice piece but I think we're stuck in the categorical fallacy: we don't know what it is, since it doesn't appear to be all that a story is generally, and on the other hand is a good deal more than a descriptive sketch. . . . [W]e've been quite indecisive about it . . . you know

37. Randall Jarrell to Ransom, n.d., in *KR* Papers; Isabel Hathorn, "Fan Letter," *KR,* XV, 305; Wallace Stevens to Bernard Heringman, January 29, 1954, quoted in Sister Bernetta Quinn, O.S.F., *Randall Jarrell* (Boston, 1981), 128; William Carlos Williams to Randall Jarrell, March 5, 1954, in Jarrell Papers.

how luxurious it is to . . . postpone making up your mind." Leslie
Fiedler, in November, 1954, submitted, as he explained to Ransom,
"a story, quite different . . . from my naturalistic vein which has
given you so much pain." It was probably because this story was,
according to Fiedler, "rather antique" and "*un-fashionable,*" that is,
conventional and well written, that it was to Ransom's liking and appeared in the spring of 1955.[38]

William Goyen, Caroline Gordon, and Robert Penn Warren are
three notable southern writers who published fiction in *The Kenyon
Review* for the first time during this period. Goyen's "Old Wildwood," a subtle, poetic story about the importance of tradition, appeared in the summer, 1955, number. Both Gordon and Warren published parts of novels. Gordon's "The Feast of St. Eustace," in the
spring, 1954, number, was a section of her formidable novel about
religious salvation, *The Malefactors* (1956), and Warren's harrowing
"Portrait of La Grand' Bosse" was an excerpt from his *World Enough
and Time* (1950). The editors' opinions of the latter piece differed,
however. As usual, Ransom was critical of Warren's fiction: "I hope
Red's novel will be better in its general texture than this overblown
historic morsel." But Rice was so "delighted" with this "exciting"
fragment that he asked Warren whether he had another section "suitable for separate publication" for the forthcoming spring issue—a
request Warren could not fulfill.[39] Anyway, since Ransom was in
Bloomington and had left Rice in charge, Rice's judgment prevailed,
and "Portrait of La Grand' Bosse" was published in the winter,
1950, issue.

The eminent Irish novelist and biographer Seán O'Faoláin contributed a funny story about petty quarrels among Irish journalists to
the autumn, 1949, issue. Another coup was "The World's Fair," a
posthumous story by F. Scott Fitzgerald, which Arthur Mizener had

38. Elizabeth Hardwick, "Two Recent Travelers," *KR*, XV, 436–44; Ransom to Robert
Lowell (Hardwick's husband), December 13, 1952, in *KR* Papers. The date of publication,
about half a year after this letter was written, suggests that Hardwick submitted a revised version. Leslie Fiedler to Ransom, November 24, 1954, in *KR* Papers; Leslie Fiedler, "The Dancing of Reb Hershl with the Withered Hand," *KR*, XVII, 193–207.

39. William Goyen, "Old Wildwood," *KR*, XVII, 425–37; Caroline Gordon, "The Feast
of St. Eustace," *KR*, XVI, 234–56; Caroline Gordon, *The Malefactors* (New York, 1956);
Robert Penn Warren, "Portrait of La Grand' Bosse," *KR*, XII, 41–50; Robert Penn Warren,
World Enough and Time: A Romantic Novel (New York, 1950); Ransom to Rice, January 20,
[1950], in Rice Papers; Rice to Warren, September 27, 1949, in *KR* Papers. Robert Penn
Warren's second contribution in fiction, "It's a Long Way from Central Park to Fiddlersburg,"
is in *KR*, XXVI, 129–43.

dug up in the course of his research for his *The Far Side of Paradise* (1951). It was published in the autumn, 1948, issue together with a critical comment by Mizener. Ransom thought this story "masterly" and "very beautiful though painful like any tragedy." Others were not as enthusiastic. A sculptress from Baltimore wrote several letters to Ransom, "out of a very real and deep concern for the future of our country," lamenting "this trash" and its deplorable influence on "the young people that represent [the country's] future."[40]

Along with all these new arrivals in fiction, a few writers who had earlier published stories in *The Kenyon Review* put in one more appearance—Eleanor Clark, Elaine Gottlieb, Isaac Rosenfeld, Arthur Mizener, and Delmore Schwartz. Paul Goodman reappeared with two impressionistic stories, and Walter Elder had no less than three stories.[41]

In these eight years from 1947 to 1955, *The Kenyon Review* published over fifty stories, that is to say, some six or seven stories a year, or 10 to 15 percent of its content. Yet circumstances were such that the editors were often "rather desperately short of fiction." This problem was more general, as is apparent in the *Kenyon's* contract, in the early 1950s, with Random House. Thanks to editor David McDowell, this publisher paid the considerable sum of $1,000 in 1951, 1952, and 1953 for the *Kenyon's* service of referring young writers to Random House. This lucrative arrangement testifies to the *Kenyon's* reputation as a talent scout. In the course of these three years, Robert Creeley, Richard Gibson, George Lanning, Mortimer Slaiman, and Stanley Sultan were among those Ransom mentioned to Random House. He also referred writers whom he did not publish in

40. Seán O'Faoláin, "Persecution Mania," *KR*, XI, 588–94; F. Scott Fitzgerald, "The World's Fair," *KR*, X, 567–78; Arthur Mizener, *The Far Side of Paradise: A Biography of F. Scott Fitzgerald* (1951; rev. ed., Boston, 1965); Arthur Mizener, "A Note on 'The World's Fair,'" *KR*, X, 701–704; Ransom to Arthur Mizener, July 11, [1948], in Mizener Papers; Grace H. Turnbull to Ransom, January 3, 1949, in *KR* Papers.
41. Eleanor Clark, "The Head in the Parlor," *KR*, XVII, 208–54 (an excerpt from her novel *Baldur's Gate* [New York, 1970]); Elaine Gottlieb, "Give Her Roses," *KR*, X, 652–63; Arthur Mizener, "Undiscovered Country," *KR*, XV, 595–613; Isaac Rosenfeld, "In the Monastery," *KR*, XIII, 394–413. According to an editorial note, "In the Monastery" is an excerpt from "a novel, *The Enemy*, to be published in 1951 by the Viking Press," but this novel never came out. Delmore Schwartz, "The Fabulous Twenty-Dollar Bill," *KR*, XIV, 378–405. On March 17, 1952, Delmore Schwartz wrote to Ransom that he "thought it was the best piece of fiction [he] had written in years" (Letter in Phillips [ed.], *Letters of Delmore Schwartz*, 264). Paul Goodman, "Our School," *KR*, X, 445–53; Paul Goodman, "A Visit to Chartres," *KR*, XXI, 563–72; Walter Elder, "Roses Are Red," *KR*, IX, 353–77; Walter Elder, "The Divorce," *KR*, XIII, 563–80; Walter Elder, "The Unsayable," *KR*, XIV, 579–98.

The Kenyon Review, such as H. Louis Newell, whom he considered "[e]xtremely good, humorous, salty . . . though not exactly a high-brow for KR," and E. R. Karr. Random House decided not to renew the contract for 1954, since none of Ransom's suggestions had brought much profit. Moreover, Random House had expected monthly reports, and Ransom had been "neglectful" of this. Not without justification, Ransom said that he often just did not "have good prospects to report" and that he "couldn't think fiction [was] really flourishing."[42]

Yet fiction was "flourishing" in *The Kenyon Review.* Thanks to the editors' careful and time-consuming weeding out of manuscripts, they gathered a fine crop of writers. Although these writers' stories were very different, nearly all of them, as had been the case with the stories published in earlier years, were well written and technically proficient, but not experimental. In a 1952 report to President Chalmers, Ransom explained the current editorial line with respect to fiction:

In the annual collections of "Best Stories of the Year," we are sometimes remarked as a magazine devoted to "experimental" or "Advance Guard" fiction. I cannot think either term is quite correct. We are on the lookout for originality, it is true. We don't want the "well-made" story such as is manufactured by many writers in quantity; nor the story which is too imitative of another writer, or "school"; nor the story which depends on violence, horror, rejection, for its interest. I suppose we just look for good stories; stories that are not only contemporary but fresh, humanly wise, and beautifully written.

The editors used "just those value-judgements made in the critical writings . . . in their . . . selections of fiction and verse," Ransom continued, adding that creative writing ought to be related "to the body of the older literature," and that therefore an academic base might even be advantageous to the young writer.[43]

Again, as in earlier years, there were about as many southern writers as New Yorkers. Finally, where they had excelled before in the *Kenyon's* poetry department only, now quite a number of writers associated with Kenyon College were in its fiction department, namely,

42. Rice to Peter Taylor, January 17, 1950, in *KR* Papers; Richard Gibson, "Two Mortuary Sermons," *KR,* XIV, 432–45; Mortimer Slaiman, "Who's Bitter," *KR,* XVI, 405–13; Ransom to David McDowell, June 26, 1951, January 22, [1952], both in Random House Papers.
43. Ransom to Chalmers, January 22, 1952, in *KR* Papers.

Walter Elder, Richard Gibson, Priscilla Heath, George Lanning, Robie Macauley, and Edgar McGuire.

Drama and Film

The *Kenyon*'s tradition of reporting on drama and the theater, movies, painting, sculpture, and music continued. During these years, the attention paid to drama actually reached its culmination in the *Kenyon*'s pages—some thirty articles and book reviews focused on this subject. The driving force behind this emphasis on drama still was the advisory editor Eric Bentley, who suggested writers to Ransom and Rice and could take credit for writing nearly a third of the articles on drama and the theater. Besides "Yeats as a Playwright," "Chekhov as Playwright," and "*Monsieur Verdoux* as 'Theatre,'" Bentley wrote a review of Jean-Paul Sartre's *Théâtre* and brilliant, informative articles on Bertolt Brecht and contemporary German theater, on Eduardo de Filippo and contemporary Italian theater, and on Jean-Louis Barrault and contemporary French theater (preceded by an article by Barrault himself, procured and translated by Bentley). As for the contemporary American theater, Bentley wrote a severe but just critique of Eugene O'Neill as a victim of his times; entitled "Trying to Like O'Neill," it was published in the summer, 1952, issue of the *Kenyon*. He also contributed a laudatory, penetrating study of Stark Young, the former Agrarian and famous American theater critic, in the winter of 1950. With respect to this article, Bentley recalled in 1982 that Ransom had granted him permission to review Young's *Immortal Shadows* (1948) and, as Bentley had explained that he wanted Young's criticism to sink in, to take his time in doing so. Neither Ransom nor Bentley had probably reckoned that it would take him nearly two years to finish this review, "the most thoroughly prepared book review I've ever done," as Bentley told Jacques Barzun. The review had grown into a full assessment of Young's career, so Ransom waived the criterion of timeliness. One of the many readers pleased by the article was Stark Young himself, who showed or sent "that wonderful article . . . written by Eric Bentley, who knows more about modern drama than anybody in this country" to all his friends.[44]

44. Eric Bentley, "Yeats as a Playwright," *KR*, X, 196–208; Eric Bentley, "Chekhov as Playwright," *KR*, XI, 226–50; Eric Bentley, "*Monsieur Verdoux* as 'Theatre,'" *KR*, X, 705–16 (reprinted in *The Kenyon Critics*); Eric Bentley, "Sartre's Struggle for Existenz," *KR*, X,

These and earlier articles merited the high compliment Lionel Abel paid to Bentley in 1960, when he wrote that "the only functioning critic today, the only writer defending some general hypothesis of taste and testing that hypothesis in discussions of works past or contemporary is Eric Bentley." Unfortunately, after 1952, for reasons unknown, the *Kenyon* published hardly any articles or reviews by Bentley. In September, 1959, Bentley wrote to Robie Macauley, the *Kenyon*'s brand-new editor, that "while in earlier years KR published everything I sent, the magazine has rejected the last several things I've sent—is no longer, in short, the place where my own stuff most naturally appears." During Macauley's editorship, Bentley contributed only two more intelligent, well-informed articles, one in 1961 and the other in 1964.[45]

Since, as we have seen, George Beiswanger, Quentin Anderson, and George Nobbe had not been satisfactory chroniclers of the New York theater scene, Bentley suggested Henry Popkin, "one of last summer's [Kenyon School of English] students," who, as Bentley told Rice, "does not write too well but is well-equipped." Popkin accordingly contributed the "Theatre Letters" for 1950, 1951, and 1952. In June, 1952, however, Bentley wrote that he did not "think Popkin has worked out too well as a drama critic, though I believe I was responsible for his being tried out in the first place." He then advised Rice to give Theodore Hoffman a chance: "His writing is still a bit sloppy but he is more intelligent than Popkin." The editors promptly followed this suggestion too, and Hoffman wrote the "Theatre Letter" for 1953.[46]

328–34; Eric Bentley, "German Stagecraft Today," *KR*, XI, 630–48; Eric Bentley, "Eduardo de Filippo and the Neapolitan Theatre," *KR*, XIII, 111–26; Eric Bentley, "Jean-Louis Barrault," *KR*, XII, 224–42; Jean-Louis Barrault, "The Theatre and Its Instrument," trans. Eric Bentley, *KR*, XII, 219–23; Eric Bentley, "Trying to Like O'Neill," *KR*, XIV, 476–92; Eric Bentley, "An American Theatre Critic! (or the China in the Bull Shop)," *KR*, XII, 138–47; interview with Bentley, October 11, 1982; Bentley to Jacques Barzun, [April, 1950], in Barzun Papers; Stark Young to Ella Somerville, February 4, 1950, in John Pilkington (ed.), *Stark Young: A Life in the Arts* (2 vols.; Baton Rouge, 1975), II, 1136. See Pilkington (ed.), *Stark Young*, II, 1129–35, for Young's long and friendly letter to Bentley about the article.

45. Lionel Abel, "Eric Bentley's Classics," *KR*, XXII, 151; Bentley to Macauley, September 27, 1959, in *KR* Papers; Eric Bentley, "The Political Theatre Reconsidered," *KR*, XXIII, 75–90; Eric Bentley, "Bertolt Brecht's First Play," *KR*, XXVI, 83–92.

46. Bentley to Rice, January 7, [1950], in *KR* Papers. During these years, Bentley himself regularly contributed reports on Broadway to *The New Republic*. Henry Popkin, "Theatre Letter," *KR*, XII, 331–39; Henry Popkin, "Theatre Letter," *KR*, XIII, 504–11; Henry Popkin, "Theatre Letter," *KR*, XIV, 493–501; Bentley to Rice, June 18, [1952], in *KR* Papers; Theodore

The editors were thoroughly satisfied with Hoffman, and they made him a Fellow in Criticism for 1956. Since Hoffman lacked the time to continue to write up the Broadway season, Mary Hivnor wrote the next three "Theatre Letters." Hoffman's unsuccessful competitor for the 1956 fellowship, Hivnor had also been suggested by Bentley. Her successor, Gerald Weales, who wrote the "Theatre Letters" for 1958 and 1959, was not one of Bentley's favorites. "Weales is a student of mine at Columbia. Very bright but somewhat cantankerous, and I dont like cantankerous *tone*." He did think, though, that Weales was "rather better than Popkin."[47]

After Weales, the series of "Theatre Letters," fifteen of which had appeared over the years since 1942, was discontinued by Robie Macauley. Basically, the idea of using these reports to enliven the *Kenyon* had been a good one, but it proved to be impossible to fit accounts of something as fleeting as most Broadway productions to the format and intentions of a serious quarterly. This was not for want of trying. Usually receiving special attention were theater adaptations of books by distinguished writers and high- and middlebrow productions rather than box office successes. But the high demands put by the theater writers on the productions made for a generally glum tone, which did not contribute to the success of the "Theatre Letters." Neither did the fact that they were published only once a year. Numerous timely accounts of the theater appeared monthly or even weekly in such magazines as *The New Republic*. Clearly, Macauley's decision to discontinue this series was wise.

Francis Fergusson was the second important drama critic after Eric Bentley. His penetrating, enlightening, precise, if not thrilling, essays treated subjects as diverse as T. S. Eliot, Shakespeare, Federico García Lorca, and twentieth-century American drama; his equally well-informed, concise reviews treated books on French and American drama. In his summer, 1950, *Kenyon* review of Fergusson's "unusually suggestive, in fact excellent" *The Idea of a Theater*, Kenneth

---

Hoffman, "Theatre Letter," *KR*, XV, 293–98. Bentley wrote to Ransom, on December 19, [1953], that he had found himself "in hot water over the discontinuance of Popkin as drama critic. [Popkin] reported that he had been removed for personal reasons by me against the wishes of Ransom and Rice" (Letter in *KR* Papers).

47. Mary Hivnor, "Theatre Letter," *KR*, XVI, 463–67; Mary Hivnor, "Theatre Letter," *KR*, XVII, 294–99; Mary Hivnor, "Theatre Letter," *KR*, XVIII, 125–30; Gerald Weales, "Two Theatre Letters: Theatre I," *KR*, XX, 300–306; Gerald Weales, "Theatre Letter," *KR*, XXI, 327–33; Bentley to Ransom, April 1, [1957], in *KR* Papers.

Burke pinpointed Fergusson's kind of criticism: "For the most part, by centering on close analysis of particular texts, he can keep his observations well focussed; yet at the same time, since the theory of drama is so directly relevant to the theory of human motivation in general, the reader is continually getting glimpses down long corridors, vistas that reach far beyond whatever work happens at the moment to be under close scrutiny." Eric Bentley, Francis Fergusson, and the "Theatre Letters" constituted the core of the *Kenyon's* drama criticism during these years. As for drama proper, the editors published one play, Leslie Fiedler's "masque-poem," "The Bearded Virgin and the Blind God." Ransom was pleased with the play, Fiedler with his "kind words"—and with being paid in advance, contrary to customary *Kenyon* practice.[48]

As was true for drama and the theater, movie criticism took a great flight during this period. One would think that the imperfections in the *Kenyon's* "Theatre Letters" would also be generic to the "Movie Letters," which were published from 1947 onwards, but this was not the case. The success of the "Movie Letters" depended partly on biannual publication, but mostly on the *Kenyon's* having found one of the best American movie critics, Parker Tyler, to write them. A poet and a critic, and a regular contributor to numerous true little magazines, such as William Carlos Williams' *Contact,* Ronald Lane Mortimer's *Alcestis,* and Charles Henri Ford's surrealist *View,* of which he became an associate editor, Parker Tyler had in vain submitted poetry to *The Kenyon Review* from its very inception. He made his first appearance in the winter, 1946, number. Once in, Tyler stayed in; his second was a spring, 1946, review of Djuna Barnes's novel *Nightwood,* which he thought "overrated by Eliot and by the dubious clique which seems to have gotten it reprinted."[49]

Impressed by the quality of these contributions, Ransom asked

48. Francis Fergusson, "Action as Passion: *Tristan* and *Murder in the Cathedral*," *KR*, IX, 201–21; Francis Fergusson, "Philosophy and Theatre in *Measure for Measure*," *KR*, XIV, 103–20; Francis Fergusson, "*Don Perlimplin*: Lorca's Theatre Poetry," *KR*, XVII, 337–48; Francis Fergusson, "The Search for New Standards in the Theatre," *KR*, XVII, 581–96; Francis Fergusson, "The Tragedy of Passion," *KR*, XI, 148–52; Francis Fergusson, "A Memory for the Theatre," *KR*, XVIII, 310–11; Kenneth Burke, "Action, Passion, and Analogy," *KR*, XII, 532; Leslie Fiedler, "The Bearded Virgin and the Blind God," *KR*, XV, 540–51; Leslie Fiedler to Ransom, November 24, 1954, September 3, 1953, both in *KR* Papers.

49. Parker Tyler, "The Impressionism of Marcel Proust," *KR*, VIII, 46–54; Parker Tyler, "Pained Sex: Elizabethan Style," *KR*, VIII, 323–25; Parker Tyler to Ransom, January 19, 1946, in *KR* Papers.

254 / The Kenyon Review

Tyler to review a few recent movies, a request Tyler, a film fanatic and writer of two excellent books on film, could not resist. His first "Movie Letter" appeared in the spring of 1947 and produced evidence for his thesis that "artistic evolution in Hollywood takes more and more for granted the psychic premises of the dream." His second letter, two issues later, lamented Charlie Chaplin's development from the Little Tramp to the Chaplin of movies such as *Monsieur Verdoux, Modern Times,* and *The Great Dictator.* This letter grew into Tyler's *Charlie Chaplin: Last of the Clowns* (1948). These two letters, as did Tyler's later ones, constantly challenge the reader, who may often disagree but is always spellbound. They made Ransom, who relished provocative essays, invite Tyler to become the *Kenyon's* regular movie correspondent. Tyler enthusiastically accepted. In all his letters, usually refreshingly rebellious, Tyler exposes the recurrence of glib professionalism and the loss of artistic integrity; he often explains the movies under discussion in a psychoanalytic and moralistic way, bringing to them his knowledge of modern art and literature, and making no secret of his preference for artistic directors such as Sergei Eisenstein and Jean Cocteau. In later years, he noted: "I was delighted to become, in *Kenyon Review,* an interpreter of film to an elite interested primarily in literature."[50]

Tyler rejoiced over Ransom's including in *The Kenyon Critics* his condemnatory "Movie Letter" on the film adaptation of Robert Penn Warren's *All the King's Men.* He wrote in September, 1950: "It is the first time anywhere, I believe, that film criticism has been formally and signally recognized as of literary value." But within a year, Tyler had become very downhearted about the quality of movies and, concomitantly, movie criticism. In his summer, 1951, "Movie Letter," he explained: "In my ripened stage as a mythographer of the Hollywood product, I am suddenly oppressed by the consciousness of what I have written. It brings the faintly overwhelming thought that perhaps too much sadism is involved in my part amidst the great public. Furthermore, facing my seventh year of intensive and unflattering analysis, I have come to feel that my particular game is no

50. Parker Tyler, *The Hollywood Hallucination* (New York, 1944); Parker Tyler, *Magic and Myth of the Movies* (New York, 1947); Parker Tyler, "Movie Letter," *KR,* IX, 317; Parker Tyler, "Movie Letter: Charlie Verdoux," *KR,* IX, 457–64; Parker Tyler, *Chaplin: Last of the Clowns* (New York, 1948); Parker Tyler, quoted in Stanley J. Kunitz (ed.), *Twentieth Century Authors: A Biographical Dictionary of Modern Literature, First Supplement* (New York, 1967), 1013.

longer worth the candle of critical prose—at least, without danger of repetition."[51] Ransom promptly informed him of the decision to discontinue the biannual "Movie Letter." Although regular "Movie Letters" would never again be published in *The Kenyon Review,* Tyler continued to appear in its pages with imaginative film critiques, which were a credit to the *Kenyon,* in spite of the virtual absence of comments on editing, sequence, and sound, and in spite of—or perhaps because of—their usually impassionedly disapproving tone.[52]

Whereas some four articles and reviews on painting and sculpture had appeared annually, now the *Kenyon* published only one, or at the most two, and contributors usually appeared only once. The exception is Kermit Lansner. When a Fulbright scholar in France, Lansner submitted "Art Notes from Paris," which appeared in the winter, 1952, issue; later essays were on Georges Rouault and on the function of museums. Then a number of illustrated articles by different writers included Hudson Walker on Marsden Hartley, Frederick Wight on Edvard Munch, and Allyn Weisstein on Marc Chagall. Most successful of these was a study of Pierre Bonnard by Duncan Phillips of the Phillips Gallery of Modern Art in Washington, D.C. Robert Richman of the Washington Institute of Contemporary Arts was so impressed that he intended to send as many as three hundred reprints to members of his institute. Unfortunately, the type had already been broken up, so the cost of reprinting came too high and the project foundered. Besides writing this fine article, Duncan Phillips also made himself useful to *The Kenyon Review* in other ways; not only did he return his honorarium for the article, but from the late 1940s into the 1950s, he gave over $7,000 to the *Kenyon.* It is likely that Phillips indicated that he would like to see part of this money go toward including color reproductions of paintings in the *Kenyon.* These expensive reproductions of good quality on shiny paper were pasted to blank pages; they disappeared after 1954, just before Phillips stopped paying.[53]

51. Parker Tyler, "Movie Letter: Novel into Film: *All the King's Men,*" *KR,* XII, 370–76; Parker Tyler to Ransom, September 3, 1950, in *KR* Papers; Parker Tyler, "Movie Letter: Three Myths," *KR,* XIII, 542.

52. See, for example, Parker Tyler, "The Film Artist as Prometheus and Pantaloon," *KR,* XV, 155–59; Parker Tyler, "Movie Note: The 3-D's," *KR,* XVI, 468–72; Parker Tyler, "Lust for Lifelikeness," *KR,* XIX, 131–36; and Parker Tyler, "Film Letter: On the Cult of Displaced Laughter," *KR,* XX, 628–33.

53. Kermit Lansner was the *Kenyon's* editorial assistant from the middle of 1949 (or per-

Like the interest in painting, the interest in music in *The Kenyon Review* dwindled considerably. Only three articles and a few reviews about music appeared from 1947 to 1955. René Leibowitz's article in the autumn, 1949, issue, in which he tried to define a musician's responsibilities, had earlier appeared in *Les Temps Modernes*. Jacques Barzun's contribution in the winter, 1950, number was an excerpt from his *Berlioz and the Romantic Century* (1950). Ransom and Rice were sure that this would "not only be the 'definitive' work on Berlioz but set a new high in music criticism." The editors had solicited part of Barzun's book at Lionel Trilling's suggestion and had "feasted" on the chapters Barzun sent them, but selecting the right one for the *Kenyon* proved to be difficult. "Our particular problem . . . is to appeal to a generally literate reader without a specialized musical knowledge . . . but I am sure . . . that there must be many passages in the book which are very directly on the music itself, and yet not too 'technical' for the purposes of a magazine such as KR," Rice wrote to Barzun in September, 1949. Another important writer on music was B. H. Haggin, still on the staff of *The Nation*, who devoted a technical discussion to the music of Hector Berlioz, whom he, like Barzun, much admired. Before Ransom's retirement, Haggin published one more article and two reviews, which constituted almost the entire music department of *The Kenyon Review*.[54]

Dance criticism in the *Kenyon* had never amounted to much, partly because mature dance criticism did not yet exist in America. Be that as it may, during the period under discussion it was more prominent than ever in the *Kenyon*, which, however, is not saying much. Six articles on dance were published. In 1948, Walter Terry asserted that dance might mean the salvation of humanity; then Edwin Denby ex-

---

haps 1948) until sometime in 1950. Kermit Lansner, "Art Notes from Paris," *KR*, XIV, 141–47; Kermit Lansner, "Georges Rouault: As Seen in the Retrospective Exhibition at the Museum of Modern Art in New York," *KR*, XV, 455–60; Kermit Lansner, "Art Letter: Museum and Anti-Museum," *KR*, XVII, 160–68; Hudson Walker, "Marsden Hartley," *KR*, IX, 248–59; Frederick Wight, "Introduction to Edvard Munch," *KR*, XII, 457–69; Allyn Weisstein, "Iconography of Chagall," *KR*, XVI, 38–48; Duncan Phillips, "Pierre Bonnard," *KR*, XI, 561–66.

54. Two examples of music reviews are George Hemphill, "Negro Music," *KR*, IX, 299–303, and Robert E. Garis, "Sour Notes from Harvard," *KR*, XI, 325–30. René Leibowitz, "The Musician's Commitment," trans. Lionel Abel, *KR*, XI, 675–84; Jacques Barzun, "The Fetish of Form: An Example from Music," *KR*, XII, 86–98; Rice to Jacques Barzun, August 2, September 5, 1949, both in *KR* Papers; B. H. Haggin, "Berlioz," *KR*, XVII, 525–42; B. H. Haggin, "Musical Performance," *KR*, XVIII, 300–303; B. H. Haggin, "Concerning Opera," *KR*, XIX, 494–97; B. H. Haggin, "Harsh Notes among Music Critics," *KR*, XX, 317–22.

plained why dance criticism is almost impossible, which, incidentally, did not keep him from a lyrical discussion of ballet half a year later. Beatrice Gottlieb, who had been a student of dance at several studios as well as a student at the Kenyon School of English, wrote three articles on dance in 1950, 1951, and 1952. After 1952 until the *Kenyon*'s demise in 1970, only two or three more articles on dance appeared.[55]

Although the *Kenyon*'s contribution to dance, music, and painting was negligible, its movie and drama criticism, its poetry and its fiction, its sponsorship of new and original American critics, and its continued publication of the best of the established ones, certainly warrant describing the years from 1947 to 1955 as the *Kenyon*'s "second flowering." This success was thanks to Ransom's editorial genius, but Rice was hardly idle. Bearing his editorial mark were the many excellent articles on philosophy, and especially existentialism, those on France, and those about and by French writers. His importance for the *Kenyon* is confirmed by the continuing high quality of the magazine during Ransom's year in Bloomington when Rice was acting editor. His winter, 1950, issue, for instance, was much admired by *The Times Literary Supplement,* which noted that "the reader feels the vibration of profound minds investigating profound subjects; sometimes, indeed, the general impression of profundity is a little oppressive. The main effect of this issue, however, is inspiring. That so many literary lights can shine so far above the mundane level proves that creation and criticism in the United States are not yet enslaved by the mammon of the masses."[56]

Rice also edited the spring and summer, 1950, issues on his own. His issues can stand comparison with those composed by both editors. This is not to say that Rice had no help, for a lively correspondence sprang up between Bloomington and Gambier, with Ransom sending letters full of suggestions and advice. But Rice was in charge,

55. Walter Terry, "The Firstness of Dance," *KR*, X, 70–81; Edwin Denby, "Dance Criticism," *KR*, X, 82–88; Edwin Denby, "The American Ballet," *KR*, X, 638–51; Beatrice Gottlieb, "Dance Chronicle: New Trends in Modern Dance," *KR*, XII, 148–55; Beatrice Gottlieb, "A Year of Dance: Inventory vs. Invention," *KR*, XIII, 127–37; Beatrice Gottlieb, "Dance Chronicle: Significance and Insignificance in Technique," *KR*, XIV, 349–58. Examples of later dance criticism in the *Kenyon* are Selma Jeanne Cohen, "Not on Their Toes," *KR*, XXVII, 742–47, and Marcia B. Siegel, "The Year That Couldn't Happen," *KR*, XXXI, 533–45.
56. "Current Periodicals," *TLS*, April 21, 1950, p. 249.

and Ransom was always careful to add some such remark as "Do as you will," "I don't propose this for your policy, but I just want to let you know," or "I've told [Steven Marcus] *you* are the editor." Having to run *The Kenyon Review* on his own turned out to be "a big job," as Rice wrote to Lionel Trilling in November, 1949, in order to enlist his help. Therefore, though he had enjoyed being solely responsible, Rice was glad when Ransom came back to help shoulder the *Kenyon's* burden again.[57]

Finances and Foundations

Upon his return, Ransom again took most of the *Kenyon's* correspondence upon himself as well as the responsibility for its budget. Kenyon College stuck to its opinion that *The Kenyon Review*—which did more to put it on the map than any of its other achievements— should not be paid for out of college money, so finding sponsors to keep the *Kenyon* out of the red, alive, that is, remained a considerable and tiresome part of Ransom's job. The substantial grants from the Rockefeller Foundation together with the smaller gifts from other angels—Paul Mellon donating $8,000 toward Ransom's salary, Duncan Phillips giving over $7,000 in total, and Random House contributing $3,000—barely ensured the *Kenyon's* continued existence. "We have almost always been preoccupied in our minds with the problem . . . of survival with credit," Ransom wrote to Marshall in 1958, adding that at "various times there has been the problem of any kind of survival." For instance, in 1950, before Mellon came to the rescue, Ransom had almost made up his mind to stay on permanently at Indiana University, which would have been overjoyed, so his salary would not burden the *Kenyon's* budget. "Inflation and the necessary increase in salaries" had exhausted the 1940 Carnegie grant, which otherwise "would have proved adequate to pay for [Ransom's] chair to within a few months of Professor Ransom's reaching the retirement age."[58]

In late 1951 or early 1952, when the Rockefeller gift of $22,500 had

57. Ransom to Rice, October 10, [1949], March 3, [1950], both in Rice Papers; Rice to Lionel Trilling, November 16, 1949, in *KR* Papers.
58. Ransom to John Marshall, [April 17, 1958], in *KR* Papers; Gordon Keith Chalmers, "*The Kenyon Review*" (TS, undated report, dictated but not used by Chalmers for the October, 1952, meeting of the Board of Trustees, in KC Papers).

been nearly used up and the editors were certain that the foundation had decided to refuse further financial assistance, *The Kenyon Review* was again tottering on the brink of ruin. Ransom and even Chalmers searched for money in every nook and cranny. Ransom, for instance, exacted payment for the *Kenyon's* review copies from the library of Kenyon College, and Chalmers tried to "make an arrangement with a publisher to manufacture and distribute the magazine and handle its subscriptions and advertising and payment to contributors." "GKC has been quite fine in his recent dealings with us," Ransom wrote to Rice in April, 1952. "It's somewhat as a last resort . . . that the President talks about making a deal with [his publisher] Regnery; thinks it wouldn't be a good thing except as easing the financial worries of the College and the editors." But Regnery did not rise to the bait. Neither did Scribners, which was approached late in October of that year. Two other projects that Ransom mentioned in the same letter to Rice did, however, go through:

We stand to make a little money from [the reprint magazine] PERSPECTIVES USA that [James] Laughlin is about to put out with the backing of the Ford Foundation. . . .
    [James Laughlin] has suggested, or been given to understand, that Ford in his zeal to export American high-brow production will probably buy up a considerable quantity (maybe 900 copies) of KR to give to impecunious patrons abroad.[59]

As for *Perspectives USA,* the *Kenyon's* financial reports were generally none too accurate, and so it is not quite clear how much money *The Kenyon Review* made from reprinting *Kenyon* essays.[60] It is somewhat easier to track down the financial advantages for the *Kenyon* re-

59. Chalmers, "*The Kenyon Review*"; Ransom to Rice, April 16, [1952], in Rice Papers.
    60. For instance, for the academic year 1949–50, the *Kenyon* received $451.31 under the headings of "Royalties" and "Fees and Miscellaneous." For 1950–51, probably thanks to the publication of *The Kenyon Critics,* the *Kenyon* received as much as $1,500.58 under "Royalties." For 1952–53, the first year the *Kenyon* received royalties from *Perspectives USA,* "Royalties and Fees" amounted to $1,316.59—part of which may still be thanks to *The Kenyon Critics.* And for 1954–55, the amount under "Royalties and Fees" had collapsed to only $60.90. See the *Kenyon's* financial reports for 1947–48, 1949–50, 1950–51, 1952–53, 1953–54, and 1954–55. The reports for 1948–49 and 1951–52 are missing from the files. Reports in *KR* Papers. *Perspectives USA,* edited by James Laughlin and backed by the Ford Foundation, was published from the autumn of 1952 to the summer of 1956. Many authors, among them Richard Blackmur and Delmore Schwartz, were angered by the *Kenyon's* practice of keeping half of the *Perspectives*—and other—royalties for itself. Sometimes, as, for instance, with Delmore Schwartz, the *Kenyon* relented and gave the author more than half of the royalties.

sulting from the second project. In a letter to President Chalmers of July 9, 1952, James Laughlin, in his capacity as president of Intercultural Publications, Inc., wrote that his "little program of sending high level American Magazines to institutions abroad" would "mean at least a thousand subscriptions to the *Kenyon Review*." In the end, the *Kenyon* served only 468 foreign libraries, but the grant, which had initially been for only one year, was renewed twice. In a note of December 15, 1955, to Chalmers, Ransom explained that the "cost to Intercultural Publications was at the rate of $4.50 per annual subscription, or $13.50 for three years; and the total was at . . . $6,318 for the three years."[61]

Besides these two kinds of earnings, both of which came indirectly from the Ford Foundation, the Whitney Foundation gave $500 in 1953. This grant was, in fact, a severe disappointment, because the editors had earlier had "good hopes" of receiving an annual grant of $5,000 for three years. The *Kenyon's* application to the Whitney Foundation was dated October 1, 1952, that is, after the Rockefeller Foundation had promised to subsidize three years of fellowships, and involved ambitious plans for extension and improvement. Among other things, the money was to be used for "retaining two Foreign Editors," for "art-work," for "oversized numbers," for "extraordinary payments to contributors," and for "fees to Special Editors and advisers." The innovations formulated in this application show that Ransom and Rice still possessed a lot of editorial verve. But, as Chalmers reported on February 14, 1953, the Whitney Foundation only gave $500. "Professor Ransom proposed using the gift in additional activities of the *Review*," Chalmers added, "but . . . he [Chalmers] . . . could not recommend its use for anything but general operations, which would have the effect of reducing the accumulated deficit." The deficit at that time was over $9,000; it was reduced to $7,223 by June, 1953. Part of the money came from the Rockefeller Foundation and was used wholly against Ransom's wishes, who, as is apparent from his application to the Whitney Foundation, had wanted to use any surplus money to improve *The Kenyon Review*. In 1954 and 1955, Chalmers again insisted that any surplus be used to

61. James Laughlin to Chalmers, July 9, 1952, Ransom to [Chalmers], December 15, 1955, both in KC Papers.

decrease the deficit, so that in June, 1955, the *Kenyon*'s accumulated deficit had been brought down to $3,468.63.[62]

This may seem to contradict earlier assertions that the position of *The Kenyon Review* was very unstable, but it should be kept in mind that had not the Rockefeller Foundation decided to continue its help in 1952, the *Kenyon* would almost certainly have collapsed. "The REVIEW is saved," Charles Coffin wrote to Austin Warren in July, 1952, and "John and Phil are mightily well pleased." In January, 1955, when the 1952 Rockefeller grant had nearly run out, Ransom wrote to Chalmers that "the loss of the $4,800.00 from our operating budget would be a heavy one. Indeed it would probably be fatal to the continuance of the *Review.*" Angrily, and also anxiously, he added: "It has been my strong impression that our friends at the Rockefeller Foundation would not want to repeat their gift, now that it has come sharply to their attention that during the first two years of their grant more than half of their allotment of $4,800.00 for 'administrative and editorial expenses' has gone into the College treasury as a credit against the accrued deficit of the *Review.*"[63] It turned out that Ransom was too pessimistic, but his letter shows that without the support of the Rockefeller Foundation, *The Kenyon Review* was but a house of cards.

Duncan Phillips' gifts excepted, private gifts totaled less than $1,000 between 1947 and 1955. Advertising was a more reliable source of income, averaging $1,500 annually. The subscriptions and bookshop sales also remained regular sources of income, bringing in some $8,500 per year. Looking at the circulation reports of the autumn issues of *The Kenyon Review,* we find that the *Kenyon*'s circulation during all these years remained steady at just over 2,000. From these reports, it seems that bookshop sales dropped sharply: 681 copies of the autumn, 1947, issue were sold in this way, then 425 (in 1949) and 244 (in 1952). From 1953 to 1955, bookshop sales are no longer included in the reports. However, from a contradictory and perhaps

---

62. "PROPOSED BUDGET For present fiscal year beginning July 1, 1952, and ending June 30, 1953" (TS, October 8, 1952, in *KR* Papers); Ransom to Milton Rose, Secretary of the William C. Whitney Foundation, October 1, 1952, report by Chalmers for the meeting of the Board of Trustees, February 14, 1953, both in KC Papers.

63. Charles Coffin to Austin Warren, July 2, 1952, in *KR* Papers; Ransom to Chalmers, January 18, 1955, in KC Papers.

doctored report dated March 3, 1953, dealing with figures from 1944 to 1953, it appears that bookshop sales climbed rather steadily from an average of 250 in 1944 to an average of 950 in 1952.[64]

Even so, the Rockefeller Foundation—for whom the boosted report probably was meant—had changed its ideas about the optimum circulation of literary magazines and had become dissatisfied with the *Kenyon*'s figures. John Marshall and his fellow officers urged the *Kenyon* to raise its circulation, and on September 16, 1952, Rice sent a long letter to his friend Edward D'Arms, which contained and explained "the figures in which you expressed an interest, on the amount of increase in circulation which would enable the *Review* to become self-supporting." Summing up after considerable figure-juggling, Rice wrote rashly that it looked "as though a permanent increase in circulation of 1,500–2,000 copies (in addition to Magazines Abroad [Intercultural Publications] subscriptions) would make us self-sup[p]orting." The editors hoped that the prospect of their future independence would result in immediate financial assistance for extensive advertising campaigns, but the foundation was not fooled. So, by February, 1953, the editors again expressed "doubts . . . as to whether magazines like the *Kenyon Review* can be made wholly self-supporting from circulation and advertising." Continued financial assistance would remain indispensable, they now argued: magazines such as *The Kenyon Review*, "even though they are not *avant-garde* or wildly 'experimental', exist in order to be on the frontiers of literary and criticial effort; they must always be receptive to writing that appeals initially to a limited public."[65] Since it also seemed to the editors

64. During, roughly, the academic year 1951–52, John Nerber, Kenyon College graduate and former *Kenyon* contributor, living in New York, was the *Kenyon*'s advertising agent and received a $200 commission. The editors got fed up with Nerber, in particular since he boasted in the New York *Times* that he had been one of the founders of the *Kenyon*, whereas he had been a mere office boy for a little while. Nerber was replaced by George Lanning, among whose duties as the *Kenyon*'s part-time secretary at $38 per month was the securing of advertisements. In a hypocritical letter of January 31, 1952, to Ransom, John Nerber writes that he had only said to the editor of the *Times* that he had "helped to found" the *Kenyon,* and that he had "noted with horror" that he had been credited with being one of its founders. Letter in *KR* Papers. Taken into consideration are the circulation reports headed October 1, 1947, October 5, 1948, October 3, 1949, October 6, 1950, October 1, 1951, Autumn, 1952, Fall, 1953, Autumn, 1954, and Autumn, 1955. The contradictory report is dated March 3, 1953. All in *KR* Papers.

65. Draft of a letter by Rice to Edward D'Arms, September 16, 1952, Ransom to Charles Fahs, February 24, 1953, both in *KR* Papers.

that an increase in circulation would decrease the deficit, they whole-heartedly welcomed the willingness the foundation had expressed to help with their promotional activities.

The foundation felt it would be more sensible and economical to aid a group of magazines jointly, so officers convened a meeting with the *Hudson, Partisan, Sewanee,* and *Kenyon* reviews on March 12, 1953. Afterwards, the editors of the "Four Reviews" continued the discussion on their own, and Rice was delegated to report their conclusions to the Rockefeller Foundation. Their projected promotion campaign involved $12,000 per magazine, and the foundation promptly decided not to pursue this plan any further.

Their decision was made notwithstanding Rice's references to *The Times Literary Supplement,* which had repeatedly commented with envy upon the major role of the serious literary magazines in America. Indeed, the attention lavished on the American literary reviews in the foreign and especially the British press was unprecedented. For instance, in 1952, *The Times Literary Supplement* reported that "[t]oday there is a remarkable body of criticism in America and the work of the youngest generation which finds its way into such journals as *Partisan Review,* the *Kenyon Review* and the *Sewanee Review* is of a very high level." A year later, the same paper lamented that there was "no equivalent . . . in this country for American literary magazines like *The Kenyon Review* or *Hudson Review.*" And in 1954 it noted that if "by numbers of subscribers" and "[j]udged commercially," these reviews were "negligible," they were indispensable in that "[l]acking the outlets they provide, the unconventional poet or story-writer, who, as it is, meets difficulty and delay enough in getting a hearing, would find the attainment of that hearing harder still." In that same year, 1954, in the British periodical *Twentieth Century,* William Newman stated that "America . . . can . . . be proud of its literary reviews. . . . In one respect at least the American reviews live up to the standard of the French: their approach is cosmopolitan and catholic." The interest in the foreign press was more than equaled at home. In 1950 the New York *Herald Tribune* called *The Kenyon Review* "the literary quarterly that is one of the most respected in the field"; in 1958 the Nashville *Banner* noted that the *Kenyon* had "achieved an international reputation as a journal of the arts";

and in that same year, *Time* described it as "one of the nation's best and healthiest quarterlies."[66] Within twenty years of its birth, *The Kenyon Review* had left an indelible mark on letters and learning at home and abroad.

66. "The American Scene," *TLS*, August 24, 1951, xxxv; "The Younger Critics," *TLS*, August 29, 1952, ii; "The Serious Literary Review," *TLS*, September 17, 1954, lviii; William Newman, "The American Literary Reviews," *Twentieth Century*, CLV (1954), 343; "1950 Bollingen Prize in Poetry Awarded to John Crowe Ransom," New York *Herald Tribune*, January 22, 1950; "Macauley Succeeds Ransom As Kenyon Review Editor," Nashville *Banner*, March 28, 1958, p. 23; "Ransom Harvest," *Time*, May 12, 1958, p. 75.

8 Decline

1955–1960

The Institutionalization of the Quarterlies

The encomiums for the *Kenyon* and other literary reviews were temporarily free from false notes. After the battle about the Bollingen Prize had been won, the highbrow magazines confidently and as a matter of course further consolidated their grip on the literary world. Foundations now seemed to gain prestige from the reviews they subsidized, rather than the other way about. The reviews no longer had to defend themselves against the charges of the early 1940s when their New Critical contributors were accused of "new barbarism" and were challenged to demonstrate that they were "of real importance in the literary life of the nation." They had become the acknowledged leaders of the literary world. The times worked very much in their favor. Much of the criticism these magazines published was not politically oriented and therefore safe and ideally suited to the cold war atmosphere of the 1950s. Criticism, and particularly the New Criticism, had never had it so good.[1]

However, the monopoly position the reviews and their critics held in the literary world, which had now become largely centered in the universities, turned out to be self-destroying. Respectability, institutionalization, and a concomitant professionalism generally made for staid and academic rather than for fresh and vital criticism. The first

1. Joseph E. Baker, "The Philosopher and the 'New Critic,'" *SR*, L (1942), 171; Howard M. Jones, "The Uninfluentials," *SRL*, October 11, 1941, p. 20.

grumblings in the 1950s against the reviews no longer came from the middlebrows, but either from original writers inside the universities, such as Randall Jarrell, or from independent writers outside the academic world, such as Kenneth Rexroth. Primarily a poet, but also a critic out of the common run, Jarrell complained, in his comic but contentious "The Age of Criticism," about the overpowering predominance of criticism and the quarterlies. A great deal of the criticism published in the reviews, Jarrell wrote, "might just as well have been written by a syndicate of encyclopedias for an audience of International Business Machines. It is not only bad or mediocre, it is *dull*; it is, often, an astonishingly graceless, joyless, humorless, long-winded, niggling, blinkered, methodical, self-important, cliché-ridden, prestige-obsessed, almost-autonomous criticism." Kenneth Rexroth, rugged individualist and anti-academic to the core, concentrating on the sorry state of poetry in America, commented in 1952 that "[o]nly some aged crone . . . telling her beads would read anybody like the people who appear in the Kenyon & Partisan Reviews."[2]

By the late 1950s, the reviews came in for severe criticism from all sides once again, but now for the last time, as their rapidly waning influence subsequently kept them out of the literary limelight. In a 1960 article in *The Nation,* Barry Spacks slated "the Great Apathy of the Moment," described the *Kenyon* as one of the "bulwarks of respectability," noted the diminishing influence of the literary reviews, and blamed this on their having become "'robust academic playthings.'" Granville Hicks also was bothered by "the stamp of the academy" on the literary magazines. The impression Robert Phelps had was that the reviews in 1963 were "tutored, tame, and shaved at the armpits. The tone is middle-aged, proper, sober, professional." Phelps too thought that the "most obvious reason for this situation" was "the proximity of ivy-covered walls." As early as 1946, William Barrett had warned against the dangers of a close association with the

2. Randall Jarrell, "The Age of Criticism," *Poetry and the Age* (New York, 1953), 65. It appears that Jarrell had originally written this essay for the *Kenyon.* He writes: "Worked on my *Kenyon* piece . . . did well, too, except, alas! alas! I'm afraid they may think it an unkind tactless piece more or less directed at them, among others—as it is. It's about the Age of Criticism—takes a dim view of it" (Randall Jarrell to Mary von Schrader, [September 24, 1951], in Mary Jarrell [ed.], *Randall Jarrell's Letters: An Autobiographical and Literary Selection* [Boston, 1985], 270). Kenneth Rexroth to Babette Deutsch, June 16, 1952, in Rexroth Papers.

academy. Then in 1957 he wrote their somewhat premature epitaph, remarking that the academic "knows that Bohemia belongs to the past, that modern society has closed down on it, and that the literary review, which once drew its sustenance from that quarter, is no longer possible."[3]

Unlike earlier complaints, these charges contained more truths than untruths. In the case of *The Kenyon Review,* the change to dull and staid can be dated from about 1956. Like the other magazines, it had lost much of its individuality. The "Four Reviews" had grown more and more alike over the years, to such an extent that they were eventually written down, with some reason, as "a single clique" with "a very undesirable amount of inbreeding." One factor that caused the decline of the reviews is that there was little left to fight for. With respect to criticism, the quarterlies had so much capitalized on the "congenial literary spirit in the M.L.A.," which Ransom had detected in 1938, that they had rendered themselves almost redundant. Even *PMLA* now published criticism rather than biographical-bibliographical articles. Not scholarship but the publication of criticism had become the yardstick for a successful university career. And whereas in the late 1930s, hardly any outlets for serious criticism existed, from the mid-1950s, the market was overcrowded with new academic critical reviews. By 1956, *The Kenyon Review,* one of the "conventional quarterlies," had played out its role as a pioneer in the field of criticism; the battle against the old-style scholars had been won, and the defeated had enthusiastically become reconstructed and regenerate.[4]

But there were also internal reasons for the particular decline of the *Kenyon.* In 1949, when he was about to leave for Bloomington,

3. Barry Spacks, "Circulation 'Bloody Low,'" *Nation,* September 17, 1960, pp. 167, 168; Granville Hicks, "'Sewanee,' 'Partisan,' 'Kenyon' and 'Hudson' Reviews: A Brief Analysis," *New Leader,* December 9, 1957, p. 10; Robert Phelps, "The 'Little' Magazines," New York *Herald Tribune,* November 17, 1963, p. 25; William Barrett, "The Resistance," *PR,* XIII (1946), 479–88; William Barrett, "Declining Fortunes of the Literary Review: 1945–57," *Anchor Review,* II (1957), 158. The most severe attack, perhaps, on literary magazines is John W. Aldridge's caustic fictional account of an editor (partly modeled on Ransom) and his review, *The Party at Cranton* (New York, 1960).

4. C. B. Fahs, December 14, 1957, memo of a trip to Kenyon College, Alfred A. Knopf to John Marshall, October 30, 1957, both in KC Collection; Ransom to Tate, January 1, 1938, in Tate Papers; Theodore Peterson, *Magazines in the Twentieth Century* (1956; rev. ed., Urbana, 1964), 416.

Ransom had remarked to Robert Lowell that he wanted "to get away from KR completely for a while for fear I'm growing too stale." And when, about a year later, there was serious talk of his staying on at Indiana University, he confessed to Tate that he would not "mind dropping the editorship in favor of doing more writing at this stage," adding, though, that this was "not an objective."[5] Paul Mellon's gift of $8,000 secured Ransom's return to Kenyon College and *The Kenyon Review*. His sabbatical had been beneficial; for the next few years, the *Kenyon* maintained its standard of superior writing.

Slowly, however, cracks began to appear. Ransom reached his sixty-fifth birthday in 1953 and was getting tired of teaching and editing. The usual retirement age at Kenyon College was sixty-eight, and in July, 1955, Ransom admitted to Richard Blackmur to being "afraid my President won't carry on KR beyond my own tenure." In the same letter, however, Ransom mentioned that very early in 1955, Chalmers had asked him "to carry on for two years more if we get set up by the [Rockefeller] Foundation for another triennium starting in the fall." Replying to Chalmers' request on January 18, Ransom had insisted that he could not make a definite decision yet. In November, Ransom spelled out three conditions upon which his acceptance of a possible two-year contract hinged: secretarial aid was a "'must item'"; and the contributors' rates and the *Kenyon's* size should remain unchanged to "ensure that the Review [would] not be cheapened." Chalmers, who knew that the "secret of the *Kenyon Review* is John Crowe Ransom," was wholly willing to grant these three wishes.[6]

By this time, too, the Rockefeller Foundation had promised to renew its fellowship grants, so that financially at least the last few years of Ransom's editorship would be easy. As usual, the Rockefeller renewal had not been clear sailing. In September, after much to and fro, Ransom still had not heard from the foundation, so he tried a little blackmail. "I am obliged to say, in confidence," he warned Marshall, "that if this request fails, the Review will not continue beyond the Winter number now being planned." Although the trustees liked "the public notice which [the *Kenyon*] has given of the college,"

5. Ransom to Robert Lowell, August 10, 1949, in Lowell Papers; Ransom to Tate, June 27, [1950], in Tate Papers.
6. Ransom to Blackmur, July 3, [1955], in Blackmur Papers; Ransom to Chalmers, November 16, [1955], Chalmers to Hugh Kenner, August 20, 1955, both in KC Papers.

they were "pinching pennies very tightly" and, Ransom predicted, would not subsidize the magazine beyond "paying the salaries of the Editor and Associate Editor, as always, and supplying us with offices and some perquisites for the job." He had "some writing projects long overdue," but was "accustomed to work so much out of [his] editorial experience, with the constant stimuli which come in there," that he would "like to keep that up." Since, as Louis D. Rubin, Jr., so aptly put it, Marshall was "the honeycomb and Mr. Blackmur . . . the lion," Ransom's final, diplomatic argument may have been decisive: "[W]e are publishing authors like Richard Blackmur who depends on us as his outlet, and we are keeping a number of valuable balls in the air by way of some topics of artistic and cultural interest which we revert to again and again. This will explain why I should wish most of all if I keep on professionally for a few years to keep to the old base of operations."[7]

At the end of 1955, the Rockefeller Foundation decided to grant $52,200 to *The Kenyon Review*. The stipends for married and unmarried Fellows were raised to $4,000 and $2,700 respectively, but the *Kenyon* received only $4,000 instead of $4,800 a year for expenses. In accordance with a request by Chalmers, who pointed out that Ransom had decided to retire at the end of the academic year 1957–1958, the foundation fixed on June, rather than on December, 1958, as the termination date of the fellowships. With Ransom doing almost no teaching from June, 1956, onwards, it looked as if *The Kenyon Review,* now financially safe, could sail smoothly until Ransom's retirement.

But soon the first blow fell. On January 3, 1956, Rice, having left home in an overwrought state of mind, was seriously injured in a traffic accident. He seemed to be recovering, but suffered a sudden relapse and died on January 25 at the age of fifty-two. In numerous letters, Ransom wrote of his grief and despondency about Rice's death. *Kenyon*'s spring, 1956, number contained Rice's epitaph, written by Ransom:

PHILIP BLAIR RICE, Associate Editor of the *Kenyon Review,* died on January 25 last, in his fifty-second year. He had helped in the launching of the periodical, and his wisdom and energy had been invaluable throughout its history. . . .

7. Ransom to John Marshall, September 22, 1955, in KC Collection; Louis D. Rubin, Jr., to Tate, n.d., in Tate Papers.

At Kenyon he organized and administered the philosophical curriculum so well that his department became one of the best in the nation at the collegiate level; and his pupils often went on to be welcomed in the best graduate schools, and at length to be philosophers themselves. There was a wonderful scruple in his intellectual handling of ideas, and a grace and clarity almost unmatched among his contemporaries in philosophy when it came to expressing them. . . .

His interest in aesthetics was both cause and effect, perhaps, of a certain breadth of view which will have appeared, as I imagine, in these pages. There were not many persons who knew so much about so many arts. But unquestionably his favorite art was literature, and in literature his favorite genre was fiction. He wrote well and freely for the *Review*. But there were many other functions which he performed superbly. Probably the best working rule ever adopted in this office was the one prescribing that a manuscript had to be approved by both the Editor and the Associate Editor before it could be accepted for publication.

So the Editor of this Review, and its readers too, have suffered a loss indeed.[8]

Ransom was not the only one to grieve. Lifelong friends, such as Joseph Sagmaster, philosophers such as Henry David Aiken and Van Meter Ames, and many of his former students, such as Walter Elder, Kermit Lansner, Robie Macauley, David McDowell, Walter Southard, and Edwin Watkins, sent their sincere condolences to Kathryn Rice. Robert Lowell, also a former student, wrote to her of Ransom's "talking about the 'High-powered' man he had discovered to edit the Review with him." He recalled "handing in a paper, wild, illegible and foolish, which proposed that the different philosophies differed only poetically and were all equally valid, like Shakespeare's plays. And Phil despaired and gave me an A— for time spent, his time, I guess, trying to decypher my handwriting and lack of logic." Lowell also remembered his last meeting with Rice, in 1955, when they "talked over all the old subjects . . . Phil's growlers and joking subjects: President Chalmers, Hillyer, Thomist philosophers . . . and so on." Chalmers himself, Rice's opponent in many heated arguments, spoke of "the force of his strong feeling, whenever he fought for principles in which he steadfastly believed, and whenever he though[t] a

8. Ransom wrote, for instance, to William Empson on May 10, 1956: "I do not think Rice can be replaced"; to Blackmur on May 16, 1956: "I don't think he could be replaced"; and to Arthur Mizener on June 22, 1956: "I dare say he is irreplaceable" (Letters in *KR* Papers). John Crowe Ransom, "Philip Blair Rice," *KR*, XVIII:2, n.p.

friend had been wronged," of "the speed of his distinguished and brilliant mind," but also of his "abrupt and sometimes curt manner."[9]

Within months of Rice's death, Chalmers died of a cerebral hemorrhage on May 8, 1956, also at the age of fifty-two. After Chalmers' death, Austin Warren wrote to Ransom: "About him, I felt—like you, I dare say—quite mixed. He held the right principles, but held them too lightly and slickly."[10] Indeed, in most of the numerous disagreements between the editors and Chalmers, the former had had justice on their side. But then Chalmers had constantly found himself in a dilemma. On the one hand, the trustees were after him because he spent too much money and secured too little from foundations and such; and on the other hand, the editors—and others—found him mean and close-fisted. Chalmers may have evoked mixed feelings in most of the people he dealt with, but his accomplishments are undeniable. In the less than twenty years of his presidency, he had increased the reputation of Kenyon College, not least by his creation and continued, if sometimes not quite halfhearted, support of *The Kenyon Review*.

Chalmers' death came as a shock to Ransom, but it was not one that deeply touched his inmost self. Charles Coffin's sudden death, on July 20, 1956, did. Over the years, Coffin, Ransom's nearest neighbor, had become his "best friend," who shared not only his passion for literature but also his delight in gardening and bridge. "Within six months we lost Rice, Chalmers, and Coffin, a very dreary record," Ransom wrote to Robert Penn Warren in one of those characteristic emotional understatements of his. "I can't feel that the place is quite the same without them. And I guess of the three that I was closest to Charles."[11] But these losses were not all. Ransom himself had been in ill-health for some time. He suffered from vertigo, which forced him to give up golf and made traveling very unpleasant. Quite apart from the purely practical fact that Ransom now had to do all the *Kenyon* work on his own, he clearly had little energy and enthusiasm left for editing his magazine creatively.

9. Robert Lowell to Kathryn Rice, February 13, 1956, in Rice Papers; Gordon Keith Chalmers, "Philip Blair Rice" (TS, memorial speech, 1956, in Rice Papers); Gordon Keith Chalmers, "Philip Blair Rice" (TS, press release, January 25, 1956, in *KR* Papers).
10. Austin Warren to Ransom, June 3, 1956, in *KR* Papers.
11. Interview with Helen and Elizabeth Forman, October 19, 1981; Ransom to Warren, August 28, 1956, in Warren Papers.

The Search for a Successor

In 1946, Ransom had sensibly declared that when "the editorial impulse is spent, it seems altogether a mistaken piety to try to 'keep the magazine alive,' as if there were a virtue in the business. It is time then to let nature take its course." But he did not obey his own credo. At his retirement, the *Kenyon* could have died an easy, natural death, but desperate attempts were made to keep it alive artificially. The new president of Kenyon College, Franze Edward Lund, who had been appointed because of his financial acumen rather than because of his scholarship, understood the magazine's promotional value for the college and was all for its continuance. Ransom himself was of two minds about terminating *The Kenyon Review*. He told Robert Penn Warren and other friends that this was "the time to discontinue the magazine"; but when the *Kenyon*'s final hour drew near, he could not stand by and watch it die, and he sedulously searched for an editor to succeed him.[12]

Initially, this had seemed to be easy enough. In 1953, Ransom had made Peter Taylor an advisory editor in fiction. He was a Kenyon graduate, he had left Tennessee to study under Ransom, and he had already made a name for himself as the writer of subtly ironic, extremely well made Tennessee stories when he became a member of the English department at Kenyon College in 1952. In a 1981 telephone interview, Taylor emphasized that he had been made an advisory editor because of his easy accessibility and that Ransom had hardly ever consulted him—in short, that this position had been merely honorary. He remembered having read only a dozen stories or so during the five years he lived in Gambier. Unknown to Taylor, Ransom was interested in more than just the benefit of Taylor's advice. A memo written by Chalmers in June, 1953, reveals that Ransom already had Taylor in mind as his successor. As a member of the staff, Taylor could familiarize himself with the *Kenyon,* and its readers could get used to his name on the masthead.[13]

12. John Crowe Ransom, "These Little Magazines," in "American Scholar Forum: The Misery and Necessity of the Quarterly," *AS,* XV (1946), 551. Warren wrote to Tate on December 8, 1957: "John Ransom is right, I guess, in saying that now is the time to discontinue the magazine" (Letter in Tate Papers).

13. Telephone interview with Peter Taylor, December 19, 1981; memo by Chalmers, June 19, 1953, in KC Papers. From the conversation this memo records, it appears that Ransom had recommended Rice in addition to Taylor. In February, 1955, however, Chalmers told

After Rice's and Chalmers' deaths, Ransom offered the editorship, as planned, to Peter Taylor. On March 17, 1957, Taylor confided to his friend Randall Jarrell that he had "agreed to become the editor of The Review when Mr. Ransom retires" and revealed Ransom's preference for a change in editorial policy. "Please don't laugh," Taylor wrote. "Mr. Ransom and everyone else concerned has urged me to take it over and . . . to make a different sort of magazine of it—which means one devoted almost entirely to fiction and poetry *and* plays. . . . I really tried to get out of doing this. . . . But their pressure and my own vanity and ugly ambition and the thought that a lot of it would be really fun decided me finally to do it."[14]

Soon Taylor "decided that editing The Review would interfere with [his] own writing" and declined after all, perhaps partly because he was "more or less turned out of his house by the Acting President" of Kenyon College, Frank Bailey. Weary of it all, Ransom, on July 3, 1957, wrote a letter to Robert Penn Warren that once again shows his contradictory feelings about the *Kenyon*:

I believe it means that KR will go out after the Spring issue next year, just before my final retirement. No use going on just to be going, especially in a field (more or less "new" criticism, which has now decayed in the editorial sense, its fight being won and tucked away) that doesn't have the interest or urgency it had 19 years ago. What we would have done would have been to make Peter the editor . . . of a KR devoted to new fiction, theatre, and poetry, with just enough reviews and essays to keep the reader up; I think it might have been something very distinguished.[15]

Edward D'Arms that Rice was not regarded as Ransom's successor. This must have been one of Chalmers' arbitrary ideas, for it is inconceivable that Ransom would have agreed to Rice's elimination. Whether Rice himself knew of Chalmers' intentions is not quite clear, though his frantic search for a new job at the end of 1955 seems to indicate that he did.

14. Peter Taylor to Randall Jarrell, March 17, [1957], in Jarrell Papers.

15. Peter Taylor to the author, February 1, 1983; Ransom to Tate, October 2, 1957, in Tate Papers. Thomas Boardman Greenslade, *Kenyon College: Its Third Half Century* (Gambier, Ohio, 1975), 208, writes: "From the early days of Kenyon College it had been traditional for the College to furnish housing for its faculty. Just as traditional was the constant friction between administration and faculty caused by . . . inadequacies and inequities in housing. Moving from house to house was almost a yearly affair. Since the choice of a house was based on seniority, a vacated residence resulted in a complete movement of household goods, all down the line, and usually on the same day." Ransom to Warren, July 3, 1957, in Warren Papers. Mary Jarrell writes: "In an exchange of letters with Peter Taylor at this time [February, 1959], Jarrell learned that . . . Peter had been given a Ford grant that not only provided him and the family with a year in London for the 1960–1961 season of the Royal Court Theatre but also offered him a welcome release from the prospect of editing the *Kenyon Review*" (*Randall Jarrell's Letters*, 437–38). But it is clear from Ransom's July and October, 1957, letters to Warren and Tate that Taylor had refused the editorship long before the date Mary Jarrell mentions.

Yet, remarks such as "I'd rather it broke up, than be inferior" notwithstanding, Ransom had been "casting up accounts" of competent people in a restless search for a successor and had consulted friends whose literary judgment he trusted, such as Eric Bentley, R. P. Blackmur, Francis Fergusson, Allen Tate, and Robert Penn Warren. He asked Tate, whose advice, as always, he valued most, what he thought of Murray Krieger, indicating that his own "fear would be that he might have still too academic a mind." On October 2, 1957, he told Tate that he was "very gr[ate]ful" for Tate's confirmation of his fears about Krieger and for his suggestion of Robie Macauley. He added that Taylor, whom he had telephoned in the meantime, had seconded Tate's suggestion of Macauley, his fellow student at Kenyon College. He had also agreed with Ransom that John Thompson, another fellow student and a close friend of Robert Lowell's, "would be quite a fine stroke." Ransom confessed, "And my feeling is a little more for Jack [John Thompson] than for Robie."[16]

Thompson, who had contributed five poems to *The Kenyon Review,* had "a better critical head . . . than Robie," Ransom explained two weeks later. "I have always felt that Robie is one of the best technical critics, but commonplace . . . in the categories to which he submits the arts in the last resort. I'd look for a little more elevation (and style) in Jack's judgments." But he would "back either one of them" over and above two other writers Tate had recently mentioned, Howard Nemerov and William Jay Smith. Ransom did not really know Smith and he "thought Howard . . . a little foolish in finding his praise for *Lolita,* Nabokov's naughty novel that I had found pretty pointless (Howard reviewed it for us)."[17]

Ransom met Thompson for an interview, but, Ransom wrote to Tate in October, "he wasn't as impressive on the intellectual level as I had hoped." He mentioned Karl Shapiro, whom Robert Penn Warren had suggested as early as 1955, and Joseph Frank, but confessed that he was not happy with these two either. He concluded with a remark that was a complete contradiction of his earlier opinions. "Most of all I would like to feel that a real critic, having force, would

16. Ransom to Tate, September 24, October 2, 1957, both in Tate Papers.
17. Ransom to Tate, October 18, [1957], in Tate Papers. A selection of John Thompson's contributions to the *Kenyon* includes "Horses, Romantic Beasts," *KR,* IV, 356–58, and "Homecoming" and "The Deluge," *KR,* XII, 472–75. Howard Nemerov's in fact excellent review of *Lolita* and *Pnin* appeared in *KR,* XIX, 313–21.

be in charge," Ransom now wrote. "I suppose there is a good place for a merely 'literary' Review, especially centered upon the actual printing of much contemporary fiction, theatre, and verse, edited by a man who knows his literature; i.e. one with very high 'standards'. But I can't think that's the best; I wonder if it would even be the most interesting thing."[18] Ransom was to change his opinion about a critical as opposed to a literary *Kenyon Review* time and again.

Meanwhile President Lund had left Ransom a message saying that he was determined to let the *Kenyon* continue. The first thing Ransom did on receiving this note was to send a letter to Newton P. Stallknecht, director of the School of Letters, who, on behalf of Indiana University, had expressed an interest in taking over *The Kenyon Review,* informing him of the president's decision. There were other interested parties. Immediately after his official installment on October 4, 1957, Lund had received unsolicited advice from Russell Kirk, who wrote that he would be sorry to have *The Kenyon Review* "vanish utterly" and that, should "dissolution be imminent, perhaps some consolidation with *Modern Age* [a quarterly review he had just started] might be effected, *Modern Age* completing existing subscriptions and continuing some Kenyon connection."[19]

Lund assured Kirk that he was "firmly determined not to let the publication die," and invited his suggestions. He confessed: "I have tried to read two or three copies and . . . it is quite incomprehensible to me. Naturally I am terrifically impressed, but I have also the sneaking impression . . . that what we may have is a case of the 'emperor's clothes.'" Kirk subsequently sent Lund an extensive letter about every two weeks. Ransom's adverse review of his *The Conservative Mind* (1953) explains, perhaps, Kirk's vengeful description of the *Kenyon*'s content: "Kenyon Review in its present form . . . represents a literary vogue of twenty years since—and so is something of a bug in amber. . . . Rather an acid note has crept into the Kenyon Review these several years past; and though Ransom tries to be liberally-minded, the odds are that an essay representing his own present left-liberal sentiments will obtain preference over one representing his

18. Ransom to Tate, October 25, 1957, in Tate Papers.

19. Ransom to Newton P. Stallknecht, October 25, [1957], in Stallknecht Papers. As early as 1956, other institutions, such as Dartmouth College in Hanover, New Hampshire, had expressed interest in taking over *The Kenyon Review*. Russell Kirk to Franze Edward Lund, October 16, 1957, in KC Papers.

earlier agrarian and theistic views." Kirk's first two candidates for the editorship were both southerners, Thomas Henry Carter, the founder and first editor of *Shenandoah,* and Richard A. Weaver, the author of the conservative treatise *Ideas Have Consequences* (1948).[20]

Lund found the succession "too important a matter to accept just one man's [Ransom's] recommendation," so he had set up a committee consisting of Ransom, Denham Sutcliffe of the English department, and himself. They consulted regularly, but it is clear from memos and the extensive relevant correspondence that Ransom dominated these meetings and had the final say. Moreover, he took suggestions from his literary friends, and Tate in particular, much more seriously than those made by the other two members of the committee. Ransom wanted Tate's considered opinion of every possibility he proposed. On November 5, 1957, for instance, in a letter to Tate again expressing his doubts about Joseph Frank, who was recommended wholeheartedly by Richard Blackmur, Francis Fergusson, and others, as well as about Robie Macauley, he came up with a new name, Randall Jarrell, the only candidate after Taylor he endorsed, if with reservations:

I have said to the old President, and the present one too, that Jarrell is too polemical and stylistically too journalistic and personally too fond of his enemies (of having enemies) to be acceptable. But right now I'm inclined to think he might be the right man for our unusual situation. His way of life in a small community would make a riffle, and there would be many incidents, but . . . I have yet to find in Jarrell a lack of courage or of principle. I've always respected him for the way he will pitch into a question which puts the Jew at a disadvantage; even though he might pass for a Gentile if he kept quiet; and of course for his readiness to fight for unpopular causes, which indeed, being aggressive on principle, he rather enjoys. Now Randall has a great journalistic or publicist flair, and in the main it is directed against the Philistines. He is more or less sensational. And yet he showed enormous scruple and loyalty to a going institution during that year when he replaced Miss M[a]rshall on the Nation. . . . I hate to pester you with our problem so much, but you are the statesman and strategist for us all in these matters.

A November 23 memo of conversations Ransom had with Lund and Sutcliffe lists Macauley and Jarrell, but not Frank, and suggests that Tate, too, had doubted the latter's editorial abilities. Other new pos-

20. Franze Edward Lund to Russell Kirk, October 28, 1957, in KC Papers; John Crowe Ransom, "Empirics in Politics," *KR,* XV, 648–54; Russell Kirk to Franze Edward Lund, November 3, 1957, in KC Papers; Richard A. Weaver, *Ideas Have Consequences* (Chicago, 1948). This book was reviewed by Eliseo Vivas, "Historian and Moralist," *KR,* X, 346–49. Weaver

sibilities mentioned in this memo were the established novelist and critic of fiction Albert J. Guerard; the poet Donald Hall, whom Ransom found too young and too little known; and Stanley Edgar Hyman, "enfant terrible," but of "prodigious energies and (increasingly) learning." Howard Nemerov, whom Tate had proposed in October, also appears on this list. It is apparent from a letter written to Tate on this same day that Tate had disapproved not only of Frank but of Jarrell too. It also is clear from this letter that Jarrell was Ransom's favorite still, even if Ransom submitted for Tate's consideration the new possibilities of Guerard and Hyman, as well as, again, Macauley and Nemerov.[21]

Ransom had expected Lund to be pleased with Jarrell, but, initially, this was not the case at all. In giving his ideas about the two candidates who were most seriously considered at this point, Macauley and Jarrell, Lund wrote to Ransom on November 26, 1957, that because of Ransom's "high regard" for Jarrell, he had "tried to stifle [his] original hostility," but had not been able to "escape the conclusion that he must be at least personally, a very silly fellow." In an attempt to be helpful, Lund further mixed up matters by mentioning Carlos Baker and John W. Dodds, as well as Kirk's suggestions of Thomas Henry Carter and Richard A. Weaver. Meanwhile, at Lund's request, Jacques Barzun and Lionel Trilling had also discussed "persons and qualifications"; they suggested Joseph Frank, Robert Lowell, Leslie Fiedler, and Richard Chase. Kirk had been contemplating further and, on December 10, recommended Monroe Spears, the editor of *The Sewanee Review*; Anthony Harridges, "an experienced editor . . . and an intelligent conservative"; Louis D. Rubin, Jr., founder and editor of "the late lamented" *Hopkins Review*; Nicholas Joost, former managing editor of *Poetry* and "a good critic"; and Edward McClellan, who had helped Kirk with *Modern Age*. Kirk also included a detailed description of the general policy *The Kenyon Review* should follow; his ideal *Kenyon* came down to a very conservative foil to *Partisan Review*.[22]

had studied under Brooks and Warren at Louisiana State University in Baton Rouge. Thomas Henry Carter's *Kenyon* contributions had been "Ezra Pound the Critic," *KR*, XVI, 490–97, and "Rationalist in Hell," *KR*, XVIII, 326–36.

21. Franze Edward Lund to Russell Kirk, October 28, 1957, in KC Papers; Ransom to Tate, November 5, 1957, in Tate Papers; memo by Ransom, November 23, 1957, in KC Papers; Ransom to Tate, November 23, [1957], in Tate Papers.

22. Franze Edward Lund to Ransom, November 26, 1957, Jacques Barzun to Franze

The reader of the president's correspondence has the definite sense that the matter had already taken up too much of Lund's valuable time, but Kirk continued to submit new names, among them Donald Davidson and Allen Tate: "Either would make an admirable editor, but I doubt if you could detach them from their present haunts." To nominate Davidson and Tate was an afterthought to Kirk's mentioning them as possible informants about Joseph Frank, whom Kirk hardly knew. On reconsideration, on February 9, Kirk had come to the rather paranoid conclusion that Barzun, Blackmur, and Trilling, having concurred in commending Frank, a regular contributor to *Partisan Review,* might be trying "to establish two Partisan Reviews, one at Kenyon College." Having earlier described the "Partisan Review set" as "a tight and sour coterie intent upon setting up an intellectual hegemony in America," and as "disillusioned, disappointed, bitter, and substantially nihilistic," Kirk clearly meant to sound a serious warning.[23]

All this advice, however, was no longer needed. Ransom had already sent invitations to Jarrell, of whose worth he apparently had been able to convince Lund, and, against all expectations, to Nemerov, asking them whether they wanted to be considered for the editorship. Both were willing, and Nemerov immediately wrote to Tate, who had first proposed him, that he was "much moved, as well as honored, that you and Ransom should think of me in this connexion." Although it now seemed to be merely a matter of choosing between Jarrell and Nemerov, Ransom felt obliged to give Lund his reaction to the men Barzun and Trilling had lately proposed. "Does Joseph Frank know how to address himself, or his periodical, to the *general* reader?" he wondered, implying that Frank did not. And if Leslie Fiedler had "magnificent qualifications," he also was an "egotist, to a pathological extent" and therefore not suitable. Ransom also objected to Richard Chase, who was "a good literary man without any disqualifications" except that he was "not *extremely* good." This left Robert Lowell, who, "but for the question of his [mental] health," would be "the very best man living for the Review."[24]

Edward Lund, December 6, 1957, Russell Kirk to Franze Edward Lund, December 10, 1957, all in KC Papers.

23. Russell Kirk to Franze Edward Lund, January 19, February 9, 1958, both in KC Papers.

24. Howard Nemerov to Tate, December 5, 1957, in Tate Papers; Ransom to Franze Edward Lund, December 12, 1957, in KC Papers.

On January 3, 1958, Lund told Kirk that "out of respect to the very real father of the *Review,* John Ransom," he had committed himself "to a joint decision." He continued that they had "met Nemerov and eliminated him." To his surprise, Randall Jarrell, whom he had just interviewed, "while eccentric, . . . [had] lacked being either a *poseur* or a terrible-tempered Mr. Bang. . . . He was soft-spoken, reticent even, earnest, erudite, and sweetly reasonable." Some three weeks later, Ransom wrote apologetically to Tate:

I hope you won't be too much dismayed at our settling finally for Randall Jarrell as the man. . . . He has far more personal force than Nemerov, though we thought Nemerov would do a good job. . . .

I'd better add that the President takes the line that we have got a man whom we have confidence in, and will not interfere with; and that was certainly my own line. It is not expected that Randall will run the Review as it has been run, but as he wants to run it, and his ideas indicate that he has a good idea of how that will be. . . . I think that after our 20 years it is time for the Review to drop the technical emphasis on criticism and put forward the poems and bits of theatre and the fictions that come up in our time for themselves, with a critical background of general humanism. . . . There will be in the content perhaps a little more the sense of addressing the general but literate reader.[25]

It took Jarrell nearly two weeks to make up his mind, and then he declined. Although he was very much aware "what an honor and responsibility it would be to try to take Mr. Ransom's place," he had "a good many reasons" to refuse. "[I]t would interfere too much with my own writing and general peace of mind," Jarrell wrote to Lund on February 5, 1958. "I shouldn't be able to do the right kind of job because I don't feel enough sympathy with most of the criticism and poetry I would have to like, I'm afraid."[26] As Ransom and Lund now had set their hearts on Jarrell, Ransom telephoned him and wrote to him, begging him to reconsider. But Jarrell stuck to his rejection.

On February 14, Ransom, who had had enough and just wanted to get the succession over with, proposed Macauley to Lund in a letter airily waiving his former serious objections.

I think Robie Macauley is the best next man perhaps. Tate and others suggested him right off, when I first began to write round. He is wise and thor-

25. Franze Edward Lund to Russell Kirk, January 3, 1958, in KC Papers; Ransom to Tate, January 27, 1958, in Tate Papers.
26. Randall Jarrell to Franze Edward Lund, February 5, 1958, in KC Papers.

oughly experienced, an excellent critic (not given to extreme commitments but forceful and knowing); a pretty good fiction writer who has just begun to get a lot better; and a person universally admired and liked. He is a fine man, and he has a fine wife (from Memphis) and small son. He is a very tall lean dark man (from Michigan originally) with a mighty bright eye. You can't make him say or agree to foolish things. And he is a Kenyon man, as much as Taylor or Lowell or Jarrell. . . . I think he would be glad to come to Kenyon as an editor.[27]

Lund was in no mind to argue anymore either, and Macauley was invited to come up to Gambier for an interview. "Would you be interested in succeeding this editor on the *Kenyon Review*?" Ransom wrote to him on February 20. Because "the new criticism is the old criticism," Ransom suggested that the "saving course" for the *Kenyon* might be "a halfway-between position . . . with . . . criticism . . . along with a larger body of creative writing." Ransom, Lund, and Sutcliffe met Macauley at the beginning of March. The matter was settled at once. On March 11, 1958, Lund offered him "the combined position of Associate Professor of English and Editor of the *Kenyon Review*—to succeed Mr. John Crowe Ransom on or before July 1, 1959. This appointment will be effective June 30, 1958, and you would be on technical leave-of-absence from Kenyon July 1, 1958 to July 1, 1959—during which time Mr. Ransom will carry on."[28] Macauley's beginning salary would be $8,000 per year, in addition to housing at the expense of Kenyon College, that is, $1,000 less than Ransom was earning. Macauley accepted by return of post. The hitch in Macauley's appointment was that he was the Fellow in Fiction for 1958 and had already made arrangements to spend that year abroad by the time he was approached for the editorship. President Lund therefore had to give him leave of absence, and Ransom wearily consented to keep the *Kenyon* going for another year.

In *Kenyon*'s spring, 1958, issue, it was announced that Robie Macauley was elected the *Kenyon*'s next editor and that Edgar Bogardus was to assist him as managing editor. Bogardus, Kenyon graduate and Fellow in Poetry for 1955, had been an instructor in English at Kenyon College since September, 1956. Charles Coffin and Ransom had recruited him with the notion of having him appointed manag-

27. Ransom to Franze Edward Lund, February 14, 1958, in KC Papers.
28. Ransom to Macauley, February 20, 1958, in Thomas Daniel Young and George Core (eds.), *Selected Letters of John Crowe Ransom* (Baton Rouge, 1985), 398; Franze Edward Lund to Macauley, March 11, 1958, in KC Papers.

ing editor after Ransom's retirement, provided he suited the new editor, of course. Eventually Macauley had no choice but to be satisfied with Bogardus. The selection procedure took much longer than expected, and Bogardus had been employed in his new job since February. "They should make a good team," Ransom informed John Marshall on April 17, 1958. "They are knowing about literature generally, and versed in contemporary letters. Both write criticism, and Macauley is a writer of novels and short stories, while Bogardus is a poet, so that their special interests should complement one another." At any rate, Ransom would have Bogardus, whom he thought highly of, to help him out during Macauley's absence. Moreover, Bogardus would come to know the ropes of editing, so that he, in his turn, could break in Macauley. But this was not to be: Bogardus died on May 11, 1958. A week later, Irving Kreutz, another member of the English department and, as the writer of two plays, particularly interested in the theater, was hurriedly appointed managing editor. "His duties on the magazine," the Kenyon Alumni Bulletin reported, "include acting as first reader, soliciting advertising and new subscriptions, and collaborating with the editor, John Crowe Ransom, on policy and production matters."[29] Ransom's opinion of Kreutz as managing editor may be gathered from his preference for Bogardus, though Kreutz had been at Kenyon longer and was Bogardus' senior.

Ransom's correspondence at this time shows, with crystal clarity, that he was fed up and worn out by all the troubles and misfortunes and simply served out his sentence of an extra year. "This is my last year in the harness, and I am getting mighty willing to take to the pasture," Ransom had written to Andrew Lytle in August, 1957, before he knew he would have to shoulder the Kenyon's burden for another year. The last few months of that year were the heaviest. When it appeared that Macauley would not be on duty till late August, 1959, Ransom complained in uncharacteristically strong language that he was "mighty fagged out" and that keeping "the home fires burning about seven weeks after my retirement waiting for Robie . . . was a chore."[30]

29. Ransom to John Marshall, April 17, 1958, in KR Papers. The titles of Irving Kreutz's plays are Inconstant Moon and Teddy Bear, Teddy Bear. "New Managing Director," Kenyon Alumni Bulletin, XVII (1959), 13.

30. Ransom to Lytle, August 31, 1957, in Lytle Papers; Ransom to Warren, July 22, [1959], September 2, 1959, both in Warren Papers.

Ransom was now completely lacking in editorial initiative, and not only because he was weary. Knowing that Macauley was going to edit the *Kenyon* along different lines, he did not see any point in looking for new contributors or in developing new projects. Moreover, every time Ransom had thought the next few issues were to be his last, he had felt obliged to use up the accepted manuscripts indiscriminately, so as not to prejudice the performance of the next editor. For this reason alone, Ransom had been rejecting many excellent unsolicited poems, stories, and essays. When it seemed that Ransom would indeed have to get out the summer, 1958, issue, too, he asked Blackmur and other contributors of long standing to submit some "very choice things to leaven the rather indifferent items, at least several in number, which I stirred up from the bottom of the barrel."[31] Finally, when Macauley returned later than planned from Europe, Ransom even had to get out the autumn, 1959, issue.

This issue marked the definitive end of Ransom's twenty-one years of editing *The Kenyon Review*. For its five final issues, rather than overexert himself looking for new blood and also because he did not want to break the editorial continuity of the *Kenyon*'s "Old Phase," Ransom again turned to faithful contributors such as Blackmur and Burke. On November 10, 1958, before Ransom knew he would have to edit the autumn, 1959, issue too, he had written to Blackmur: "We'd like RPB in Winter, Spring, and Summer if we can; after that I'm a retired man. I speak casually, but you know how strongly I want this, desiring to leave the office with a bang not a whimper."[32] Blackmur and Burke appeared no less than three times each in these five issues, as did Paul Goodman and Richard Stern. Yet it was with a whimper rather than resoundingly that Ransom's *Kenyon* ended.

Criticism

For years, *The Kenyon Review* had been the leading magazine among the critical quarterlies, all of which, partly because of their having become institutionalized, had gradually grown flat and vapid. Now the *Kenyon* suffered from additional troubles—sudden deaths, age, re-

31. Ransom to Blackmur, November 1, [1957], in Blackmur Papers.
32. Ransom to Blackmur, February 4, November 10, 1958, both in Blackmur Papers.

tirement, and the time-consuming problem of finding a successor—and it actually started to lag behind its competitors. To discuss its content during this period is to expose its spiritless state. Most of the important critical articles that loyal contributors had submitted in the last years before Ransom's retirement have been treated earlier, including all of William Empson's essays. Richard Ellmann, Francis Fergusson, Paul Goodman, Stanley Edgar Hyman, Richard W. B. Lewis, and Arthur Mizener each submitted only one or two more pieces that deserve consideration.

Richard Ellmann's illuminating though in parts too ingenious essay "Wallace Stevens' Ice-Cream" appeared in the winter, 1957, issue. According to Ellmann, the essay differed "from previous work in that it re-interprets some of his more famous poems and tries to penetrate his work through his conception of death rather than of imagination." The lead article in this same issue was Fergusson's critical credo, which served as the introductory essay to his book *The Human Image in Dramatic Literature* (1957). Paul Goodman acclaimed Marius Bewley's important book *The Eccentric Design* (1959) and his "A Visit to Chartres" appeared in Ransom's final issue. Kenneth Burke thought Hyman's long autumn, 1957, review of *Literary Criticism* (1957) by Cleanth Brooks and William K. Wimsatt "quite a good job," and Ransom found R. W. B. Lewis' winter, 1957, essay on Graham Greene "first rate." Arthur Mizener contributed an omnibus fiction review to that year's summer issue.[33]

There is more to tell about two other old-time contributors, Richard Blackmur and Kenneth Burke. Blackmur published an article on Emily Dickinson in *Kenyon's* spring, 1956, issue. In September, 1955, Ransom had asked him with respect to the winter, 1956, number: "If it's a final issue, or otherwise, we'll want Blackmur in it. . . . I know what I'd like: a long note or essay on the new

33. Richard Ellmann, "Wallace Stevens' Ice-Cream," *KR*, XIX, 89–105; Richard Ellmann to Ransom, July 28, 1956, in *KR* Papers; Francis Fergusson, "The Human Image," *KR*, XIX, 1–14; Paul Goodman, "The American Writer and His Americanism," *KR*, XXI, 478–82; Paul Goodman, "A Visit to Chartres," *KR*, XXI, 563–72; Kenneth Burke to Ransom, October 10, 1957, in *KR* Papers; Stanley Edgar Hyman, "Palpable Designs," *KR*, XIX, 647–57; Ransom to Newton P. Stallknecht, January 3, [1957; wrongly dated 1956], in Stallknecht Papers; R. W. B. Lewis, "The Fiction of Graham Greene: Between the Horror and the Glory," *KR*, XIX, 56–75; R. W. B. Lewis, "Poetry and Change," *KR*, XVIII, 318–26; Arthur Mizener, "Spring Fiction," *KR*, XIX, 484–93.

Johnson performance [*The Poems of Emily Dickinson,* ed. Thomas H. Johnson (1955), and Thomas H. Johnson, *Emily Dickinson: An Interpretive Biography* (1955)] with Dickinson." He added persuasively: "Won't you have to post yourself on that anyhow, in deference to your profession?" Blackmur could not "resist the trap" Ransom had set. As usual, though, he was late in submitting copy and therefore had to be put off until spring. Blackmur did not mind at all and suggested that he write an essay instead of a review. "Please give me as much time as you can . . . and let me know the date," he wrote on January 11, 1956, adding that he very much wanted to see the piece on Dickinson that Ransom was writing for James Laughlin's magazine *Perspectives USA.* "My own thought has been running on Emily as the archetype and usufruct of all New-England shut-ins," he continued. Ransom, knowing Blackmur's bent for procrastination, feared that his thoughts would run loose forever and repeatedly pressed him to submit the promised essay in time for the spring issue. When Blackmur did, Ransom felt that he had wronged him "in being so peremptory about getting . . . that Dickinson essay," but also thought that he had been proved "right, because it came through in good order" and had turned out to be one of Blackmur's "most distinguished writings." Ransom's praise was unwarranted. If "Emily Dickinson's Notation" is slightly less abstruse than many other of Blackmur's later writings and in parts perceptive, the essay does ramble and is full of high-flown, meaningless phrases.[34]

Blackmur's next contribution was a winter, 1958, review of F. A. C. Wilson's *W. B. Yeats and Tradition* and was entitled "Obscuris Vera Involvens," which, contrary to *Kenyon* custom with reviews, was probably of his own invention. Blackmur's essay "Ara Coeli and Campidoglio," which appeared in the summer of that year, was an impressionistic, sometimes snobbish account of his recent travels in Europe and Japan. For the next issue, Blackmur pledged an essay on the plight of the modern intellectual. When he did not finish a satisfactory draft in time, Ransom speculated that the early versions must have seemed "too bold and plain" to Blackmur.

34. Richard Blackmur, "Emily Dickinson's Notation," *KR,* XVIII, 224–37; Ransom to Blackmur, September 13, [1955], in Blackmur Papers; Blackmur to Ransom, September 22, 1955, in KC Papers; Blackmur to Ransom, January 11, 1956, in Blackmur Papers; John Crowe Ransom, "Emily Dickinson: A Poet Restored," *Perspectives USA,* XV (1956), 5–20; Ransom to Blackmur, March 8, 1956, in *KR* Papers.

The essay was ready for *Kenyon's* winter, 1959, issue, by which time Blackmur had managed to obfuscate it to his heart's content. Yet "The Logos in the Catacomb" contained some intelligent, provocative pronouncements.[35]

Blackmur's final article for Ransom's *Kenyon* also was late. He had promised an essay on the poet Edwin Muir for spring, 1959, but by the end of February, he still had not handed it in. As nearly always with Blackmur, Ransom was forgiving, apologetic even, rather than angry about his tardiness. "If there's any point in it," he wrote to Blackmur on February 27, "we can happily pay for the essay upon receiving it, any time. And we wouldn't a bit mind having you twice in our pages in one issue if you'd concur." Both payment upon reception instead of upon publication and a contributor's double appearance in one issue were unusual for *The Kenyon Review.* Obviously, Blackmur was a very special case. Ransom himself suggested that Blackmur review the forthcoming paperback edition of Leon Edel's *The Psychological Novel: 1900–1950* to appear simultaneously with his Muir essay. The next day, Ransom came up with "another possibility for a review," *The Literary Works of Matthew Prior,* "which should be a delicious book."[36]

Since Edel was a friend of his, Blackmur declined to review his book, but he gladly took up Ransom's second offer. It was to be expected that he would submit his Prior review too late for inclusion in the summer issue with his Edwin Muir essay. Blackmur sent his glowing but abstract defense of a poet, who at that time was still underestimated, on April 29, 1959, with a covering note in which he complained: "I think my quotations are good but I am sorry there are so many of them since you have the abominable policy of not paying for them." Still, he was grateful for Ransom's promise to pay upon reception. "Homo Ludens," Blackmur's laudatory review of the H. Bunker Wright and Monroe K. Spears edition of Prior's verse was the very last piece of writing to appear during Ransom's regime. Blackmur was second only to Ransom himself in the quantity—and

35. Richard Blackmur," Obscuris Vera Involvens," *KR,* XX, 161–68; Richard Blackmur, "Ara Coeli and Campidoglio," *KR,* XX, 337–61; Ransom to Burke, September 2, [1958], in Burke Papers; Richard Blackmur, "The Logos in the Catacomb: The Role of the Intellectual," *KR,* XXI, 1–22.

36. Ransom to Blackmur, February 27, [1959], February 28, [1959], both in Blackmur Papers.

most likely, in Ransom's opinion, in the quality too—of his writings for the *Kenyon,* so it was fitting that "Homo Ludens" was the conclusion to Ransom's *Kenyon.*[37]

If Kenneth Burke's contributions to Ransom's *Kenyon Review* only numbered less than half of Blackmur's, and if Ransom did not constantly think quite as highly of Burke as of Blackmur, Burke, too, remained a valued contributor. His sometimes tortuous journeys into the labyrinths of symbolic action, logology, and rhetoric now attracted Ransom keenly, then seemed to him to go much too far, yet invariably inspired his respect. And if, in his turn, Burke could not always make out Ransom's true opinion of his work, he so prized his judgment that he often tried out new writings on him, awaiting his verdict "with trepidaysh."[38] Their voluminous correspondence confirms this—even though few of Ransom's letters to Burke have been preserved. To listen to Burke thinking out loud in his long letters is fascinating and fun; to see how, over the years, Ransom comes more and more to understand Burke and to agree with him and even, clearly influenced by Burke, comes to write more jauntily is engrossing and exciting.

For example, there is enjoyment and enlightenment to be found in the correspondence dealing with Burke's autumn, 1957, masterpiece "The Anaesthetic Revelation of Herone Liddell." This unclassifiable work is part fantasy, part philosophy, part poetry, full of double and treble meanings or, in Burke's description, an "Erziehungsnovelle" about a "palpably autobiographical figure . . . who felt as though he had got his balls cut out, and meditated accordingly." Not knowing "whether to love this thing or loathe it," Burke had submitted his account of Herone's harrowing hospitalization. It is "a grand thing," Ransom enthusiastically replied, "and confirms my idea that either I have been growing up to your philosophical problems, or my mind basically is much closer to your mind than I had known." Burke "o'ernipped at the bottle in celebration" and in July, 1957, wrote to Ransom: "I am more than happy at your re-assurance that my dear friend Herone's shaydevver [chef d'oeuvre] is to appear this Autumn.

37. Richard Blackmur, "Edwin Muir: Between the Tiger's Paws," *KR,* XXI, 419–36; Blackmur to Ransom, April 29, 1959, in Blackmur Papers; Richard Blackmur, "Homo Ludens," *KR,* XXI, 662–68.
38. Burke to Ransom, July 29, 1957, in *KR* Papers.

The poor guy's ego badly needed patching up, John—and your authoritative charity was just what the doctor ordered. God bless John C. R. and his Kenyon, that may help get Ken out of his canyon." About a month later, Ransom informed Burke that the printer had "Herone in charge now. (I think of him as a curious compound, extremely *organic,* of Hero and Heroin and Tyrone, etc. etc.) But I want to ask you about Liddell, his family moniker. I confess that, getting him packed off to the printer the other day, I finally crossed out the accent on the *e,* but realize fully that it is necessary only for you to express your wish and it will be restored in the proof. It feels like a small affectation to me. Probably you want to stress the possibility of an *L* or *ell* or *dell* in his make-up. I have felt, myself, that this name stands for his learning, as in Liddell and Scott; he's a highbrow. But you tell me, if you want the accent restored." Burke did not have "strong feelings in the matter" and consented to "leave it so," without the accent. Yet, at length had he pondered this and other seemingly small matters. Burke explained:

Originally I put [the accent] there because I heard someone pronounce "Liddell" on the first syllable—and I didn't know how prevalent this practice might be. So, just to be safe, I *indicated* the stress. Later, I began to think that it might have a certain advertising value, like commercial spellings of brand names, such as kreemee and taystee. Eventually I began to suspect also that perhaps it could be psychoanalyzed. In any case, you are right in your notion that I had the Liddell and Scott Bible in the back of my mind. . . . I also had in mind a remote pun on "little" (so that the name wd. have connotations of "little hero")—and, as I once wrote to Nemerov on this point, I thought that, in going out of my way to put the accent on the second syllable, I'd be in the position of one who doth protest *too* much. Yep, all that was involved in that hickey-madoodle; but at times the fate of empires has depended upon less.[39]

The very simple accompanying illustration, the only illustration to go with fiction during Ransom's editorship, received less extensive consideration. Working from a sketch by Burke, Ransom's daughter Helen Ransom Forman had drawn a plain wrenchlike bone to eluci-

---

39. Kenneth Burke, "The Anaesthetic Revelation of Herone Liddell," *KR,* XIX, 505–59; Burke to Ransom, March 28, 1957, in *KR* Papers; Burke to Tate, September 9, 1957, in Tate Papers; Burke to Ransom, March 4, 1957, Ransom to Burke, March 18, 1957, Burke to Ransom, March 28, July 11, 1957, Ransom to Burke, August 23, 1957, Burke to Ransom, September 1, 1957, all in Burke Papers.

date one of Herone Liddell's nightmares. Burke's enthusiasm seems a bit out of proportion. "The combination of strength and roughness is perfect," he wrote. "I feel exactly as a novelist might if an illustrator drew the imaginary portrait of his main character, and it turned out looking exactly as he had seen it with his inner eye."[40] "The Anaesthetic Revelation of Herone Liddell," published as the lead in *Kenyon*'s autumn, 1957, number, is wonderfully witty, but also curiously serious, and shows that, for Burke, creativity and criticism often merge. Poking fun at Freudians, Jungians, symbol hunters, New Critics, and what have you, Burke is his own skillful anatomist here.

Burke's next contribution appeared one year later and was a discerning review of Paul Valéry's *The Art of Poetry,* introduced by T. S. Eliot, in which Burke also managed to render clearly and concisely some of his own involved theories. Ransom "thought so highly" of Burke's analysis of Valéry that he "sent it to the printer to be set up in 12-point, for the front part," instead of incorporating it, as planned, into the book review section. Although Ransom had reasoned about a year earlier that he had gradually grown closer to Burke's ideas, he now saw it as the reverse process. "I think you have come over to my sober responsible conservative reactionary [literary] position, though you have done it mighty brightly and gracefully, not stodgily. . . . I think there has been a new springtime and widening in your views here these last few years, which (to whatever extent it exists) pleases me very much." Burke balked at this reading and, on September 20, 1958, pointed out that, writing the Valéry review, he had been "thinking continually of my early essay on Rémy de Gourmont." In his eagerness to convince Ransom that, though he had perhaps "somewhat altered" his "tactics in expressing" his ideas, he had not "essentially altered" his "position on litry matters," Burke sent him several explanatory letters in quick succession, but it is doubtful whether he succeeded in changing Ransom's mind.[41]

In early February, 1959, Burke submitted a paper on catharsis, part prose, part poetry, in good time for *Kenyon*'s summer number. Ran-

---

40. Burke to Ransom, September 1, 1957, in Burke Papers.
41. Kenneth Burke, "Towards a Post-Kantian Verbal Music," *KR,* XX, 529–46; Ransom to Burke, September 3, [1958], Burke to Ransom, September 20, 1958, both in Burke Papers. Burke discussed Rémy de Gourmont in "Three Adepts of 'Pure' Literature," *Counter-Statement* (1931; rpr. Berkeley, 1968), 1–28.

som and Burke did not quite agree about the actual publication of this "magnifique" essay. Initially, Ransom had written warmly: "You never wrote better than these days. And the Appendix, the Exercise of Disgruntlement, the Poem, must stay in." Soon he changed his mind and informed Burke that he preferred publishing the piece without its nearly seven pages of poetry. "Just so that my clumsy readers won't boggle over the PHILOSOPHY because there is an appendage of POETRY by the same hand. That's my Puritanism, Purism, however Freud might name it." Burke was crushed: "Oef! Helndamnaysh! . . . If that's how you think it had better be, then so it should be—and punctum. However, in keeping with the sound Aristotelian principle of *enargeia* (bringing the sorrow before one's eyes, making the judges weep by making them see the very form and color of the wounds), let me at least relieve myself by these depositions . . ." And Burke argued so eloquently that Ransom replied immediately: "But you know I wrote: we'd accept *your* decision. And even if you're pretty wonderfully polite about it, you don't think you (or we) *ought* to give up the conclusion,—so, by Heck, I've written the printer to go ahead with it. Some contributors rate having their own way with a piece, and we'd be in bad order to try to stop 'em."[42] And so *The Kenyon Review* was once more enriched by one of Burke's sometimes farfetched, but always entertaining, sparkling critical-creative papers. In comparing, contrasting, and combining Aristotle's theories about catharsis and Freud's theories about purifying physical purges, in playing with and upsetting common notions about pity and fear, *hubris* and *hamartia,* and in concluding with "Poetic Exercise on the Subject of Disgruntlement" and the poetic "Litany of Laments," Burke once more showed himself to be an imaginative, wide-awake, wide-ranging thinker.

Meanwhile, Burke, realizing that "after that big chunk of Burke scheduled for Kenyon's hammock-literature number, a review by one K. Burke may seem a bit de trop," had hesitantly asked to be allowed to review Philip Rieff's *Freud: The Mind of the Moralist.* But since Burke and Freud—let alone a possible meeting of their minds—had

42. Kenneth Burke, "On Catharsis, or Resolution, with a Postscript," *KR,* XXI, 337–75; Ransom to Burke, February 21, [1959], May 10, 1959, Burke to Ransom, May 13, 1959, Ransom to Burke, May 18, [1959], all in Burke Papers.

become meat and drink to Ransom by this time, he greedily rose to the bait. Burke "went berserk during the reading" of Rieff's book, but nevertheless managed to come up with a review on July 30, 1959. Two days later, feeling that he had not done quite right by the book, he sent in "about the only thing" he was capable of in his "present state of disrepair," namely, an eleven-line addendum that emphasized the brilliance of the book. Burke's perceptive review, in which, as Ransom had hoped and expected, he entered into a dialogue with Freud, appeared with its addendum in the autumn, 1959, issue and marked his final contribution to *The Kenyon Review*.[43]

Other faithful contributors of long standing, such as Eric Bentley, Leslie Fiedler, and Irving Howe, were not published at all during these last years. Ransom himself had little gusto left and because of all his additional duties he was so pressed for time that an article on Milton and anthropology and an article on prosody were all he could manage. The first, a revision of a speech he had given in Williamsburg in 1957, appeared in *Kenyon*'s winter, 1959, number and was in part a reply to Roy Harvey Pearce's important "Historicism Once More," published in the previous issue. If, in his "beautifully perfected essay," Pearce "recommended to the critics a kind of historicism, the speech will be recommending a kind of anthropologism," Ransom explained in the prologue to his own piece. Pearce's keen yet cautious essay, appearing in Ransom's *Kenyon* some twenty years after Ransom's own seminal essay "Criticism, Inc.," which took virtually the opposite direction, fought against the prevalent mode of methodological, mechanical New Criticism, and argued that the historical-cultural context of a literary work should be taken into account too. It manifested once more the turnabout that had taken place in the academic literary world over the years.[44]

Ransom, of course, had never tolerated New Critical narrowness and had usually been at least one step ahead of the academy. But if Ransom now still was out of step with the academics, he was no longer a pioneer. His essay on *Paradise Lost* was, in fact, an un-

43. Burke to Ransom, March 23, July 30, August 1, 1959, all in Burke Papers; Kenneth Burke, "Democracy of the Sick," *KR*, XXI, 639–43.

44. John Crowe Ransom, "The Idea of a Literary Anthropologist: And What He Might Say of the *Paradise Lost* of Milton," *KR*, XXI, 121; Roy Harvey Pearce, "Historicism Once More," *KR*, XX, 554–91.

convincing though timely attempt to introduce into literary-critical studies the "literary anthropologist," who "must needs be a great humanist," "a scientist," "a good naturalist or economist, and his understanding of literature . . . must have to do with its adaptation to the natural economy." His other essay, "The Strange Music of English Verse," also was weak. It was part of the only symposium published in *The Kenyon Review* during these years, "English Verse and What It Sounds Like," which took up nearly half of the summer, 1956, number.[45]

Tedious and repetitious, "English Verse and What It Sounds Like" was the worst symposium Ransom published. In his introductory essay, which was actually published at the end of the symposium, Ransom noted that it was "strange that a generation of critics so sensitive and ingenious as ours should have turned out very backward, indeed phlegmatic, when it comes to hearing the music of poetry, or at least, to avoid misunderstanding, to hearing its meters." Even if "the authority of meters is passing, or is past" in modern poetry, he continued, the "old poetry is still vivid with us, and it is metered." The symposium was meant to break the long neglect of prosody. However, its opening essay, written by Harold Whitehall, *Kenyon*'s summer 1944 Rockefeller Fellow, was a reprint of his *Kenyon*, autumn, 1951, review of George L. Trager and Henry L. Smith, Jr., *An Outline of English Structure*, supplemented by some remarks on the book's section on prosody. Then Seymour Chatman offered a technical analysis of Robert Frost's "Mowing," combining its abstract metrical pattern and the ordinary intonation pattern of spoken English, and basing his discussion on the Trager-Smith approach to English. Stressing the close interplay of sound and meaning, and asserting that intonation helps understanding, Chatman tried to show, with the help of charted readings, that intonation prevails over meter.[46]

45. Ransom, "The Idea of a Literary Anthropologist," 122; John Crowe Ransom, "The Strange Music of English Verse," *KR*, XVIII, 460–77.
46. The symposium "English Verse and What It Sounds Like," in *KR*, XVIII:2, consists of the following essays: Harold Whitehall, "From Linguistics to Criticism," 411–21; Seymour Chatman, "Robert Frost's 'Mowing': An Inquiry into Prosodic Structure," 421–38; Arnold Stein, "Donne's Prosody," 439–43; Seymour Chatman, "Mr. Stein on Donne," 443–51; Arnold Stein, "A Note on Meter," 451–60; and Ransom, "The Strange Music of English Verse," 460–77 (quotations on 460). Whitehall's review of Trager and Smith appeared in *KR*, XIII, 710–14.

292 / The Kenyon Review

The next article, by Arnold Stein, was another *Kenyon* 1951 reprint and consisted of four and a half slightly sharpened pages on Donne's "Elegy" from the second installment of his essay on Donne's verse. Then Chatman refuted Stein's assertion that the ambiguity of Donne's "Elegy" lies in its meter. Since Stein had had "some small uneasiness about being specifically commented on without rebuttal," Ransom allowed him to submit an "independent little note" on "the *form* of meter, that asks the question: what does meter do in a poem?" Ransom was pleased with Stein's "admirable" and "imaginative" second paper, which was partly an attack on Chatman.[47]

Before publication, about a hundred advance orders for bound reprints of the symposium had reached the *Kenyon* office, justifying Ransom's diagnosis of the shortage of and need for studies in prosody. The interest in metrical studies was obviously very lively, so what had started out as a one-issue symposium was expanded into a series of papers published intermittently over three years. The first paper to follow the symposium issue was a "Communication" by Chatman, who was allowed to reply to Ransom's recapitulative essay. George Hemphill praised the "liveliness" of the symposium papers but at the same time, in the winter, 1957, issue, criticized and set out to remedy their neglect of the existing if somewhat hidden metrics in modern poetry such as written by Randall Jarrell, Robert Lowell, Josephine Miles, and Robert Penn Warren. In the winter, 1958, issue John Thompson published an intricate chapter from his Columbia University dissertation on the rise of modern English meters. Robert Beloof's discussion of Marianne Moore's prosody was the final article to appear before John Hollander's opaque essay closed this generally mechanical, spiritless series in the spring, 1959, issue.[48]

Arnold Stein, the contributor of two papers to the series on prosody, had over the years become the *Kenyon*'s favorite writer on met-

47. Arnold Stein's "Donne's Prosody" was an expanded version of pages 261–64 of his "Structures of Sound in Donne's Verse (continued)," *KR*, XIII, 256–78. Arnold Stein to Ransom, April 2, 1956, Ransom to Stein, May 9, 1956, both in *KR* Papers.
48. Seymour Chatman, "Communication," *KR*, XVIII, 648; George Hemphill, "The Meters of the Intermediate Poets," *KR*, XIX, 37; John Thompson, "Sir Philip and the Forsaken Iamb," *KR*, XX, 90–115; Robert Beloof, "Prosody and Tone: The 'Mathematics' of Marianne Moore," *KR*, XX, 116–24; John Hollander, "The Metrical Emblem," *KR*, XXI, 279–96. Beloof refers (on p. 116) to an April, 1953, *Kenyon Review* article by Randall Jarrell on Marianne Moore, "The Humble Animal." He must have meant Jarrell's review of Moore's *What Are Years*, which appeared under that title in *KR*, IV, 408–11.

rics. Besides those two essays and his two for the Donne series, Stein had published "Structures of Sound in Milton's Verse," which Ransom and Rice found "brilliant"; they thought that he had "made Milton uniquely interesting for his sound structure." Stein's final contribution was a lively and discriminating article on Shakespeare's *Antony and Cleopatra* for the autumn, 1959, number. This article and the four discerning, skillful reviews Stein published in the *Kenyon* over the years testify more convincingly to his critical intelligence than do his articles on prosody.[49]

All the critics discussed so far had regularly appeared in *The Kenyon Review* before it started suffering from exhaustion. If a number of their contributions, such as Francis Fergusson's "The Human Image," showed these authors at their best, hardly any of these articles signified a new and exciting point of departure. The four Fellows in Criticism elected during this period did not contribute much toward a sorely needed rejuvenation of the *Kenyon* either. The final contribution by Leslie Fiedler, Fellow in Criticism for 1956, was his pre-fellowship spring, 1956, article on Dante. Ransom was very disappointed by the result of Fiedler's fellowship, *Love and Death in the American Novel* (1960), and not until 1964 did Fiedler reappear as a critic in the *Kenyon*'s pages. Theodore Hoffman, nominated by his friend Eric Bentley, was the second Fellow in Criticism for 1956. His project was "a book of essays in drama, not at all confined to the modern period," but the *Kenyon* did not reap any fruits of this work. Hoffman's final, pre-fellowship contribution, appearing in the spring, 1955, issue, was an extremely critical but just review of Wisner P. Kinne's *George Pierce Baker and the American Theatre*. Ransom was so taken with his review, "47 Workshop," that he placed it at the beginning of the review section.[50]

49. Arnold Stein, "Structures of Sound in Donne's Verse," *KR*, XIII, 20–36; Stein, "Structures of Sound in Donne's Verse (continued)," 256–78; Arnold Stein, "Structures of Sound in Milton's Verse," *KR*, XV, 266–77; Mary A. Rahming, secretary of *The Kenyon Review*, to Arnold Stein, n.d., in *KR* Papers; Arnold Stein, "The Image of Antony: Lyric and Tragic Imagination," *KR*, XXI, 586–606; Arnold Stein, "Shakespeare Allegorized," *KR*, V, 448–51; Arnold Stein, "The Criticism of Wyatt," *KR*, XIII, 703–10; Arnold Stein, "The Business of Wonder," *KR*, XIV, 513–20; Arnold Stein, "The Criticism of Allegory," *KR*, XX, 322–30.

50. Francis Fergusson, "The Human Image," *KR*, XIX, 1–14; Leslie Fiedler, "Green Thoughts in a Green Shade: Reflections on the Stony Sestina of Dante Alighieri," *KR*, XVIII, 238–62; Leslie Fiedler, "A Kind of Solution: The Situation of Poetry Now," *KR*, XXVI, 54–79. Irving Kristol, "A Traitor to His Class?" *KR*, XXII, 505–509, highly praised *Love and Death in the American Novel*; Ransom to John Marshall, March 8, 1956, in *KR* Papers; Theodore

The Fellow for 1957 was Francis Fergusson. Like Fiedler's, his contributions during these years have already been discussed. Fergusson received his fellowship for "a series of critical introductions to plays of Shakespeare's," solicited by Dell Books. As *The Kenyon Review* had "always been especially skittish about papers on Shakespeare" unless they were "very comprehensive and radical too," it is not surprising that, if Fergusson did in fact submit his introductory essays, they were not published. The *Kenyon*'s final Fellow in Criticism was one of the southerners proposed by Russell Kirk for the editorship, Thomas Henry Carter. Since the early 1950s, Carter had been submitting suggestions for essays and reviews to the *Kenyon,* but though Ransom found him a promising critic, as late as 1955 he still thought that Carter had "one disability which is extremely honorable, youth rather than maturity." And, he pointed out to Carter, "you let it get you into a corner unnecessarily."[51]

If Carter felt cornered, Ransom himself was at least partly to blame, for more than once he accepted one of Carter's reviews, only to reject it when a better review turned up unexpectedly. This happened with Carter's "excellent" review of Malcolm Cowley's *The Literary Situation,* which, later, suddenly "wasn't solid" anymore and was returned to Carter indecorously. Carter was not cowed by this ungentlemanly and uncharacteristic behavior of Ransom's and managed to get three reviews published in the *Kenyon* before he applied for a fellowship in criticism in 1957. His proposed project was extremely ambitious, covering a book of essays on American culture, William Carlos Williams, Ezra Pound, Ford Madox Ford, Wyndham Lewis, William Faulkner, Flannery O'Connor, and more. Yet Carter was convinced that it would only "take from nine to twelve months to complete the book." By 1961, Carter, as might have been expected, had only written half of the planned book. None of the essays outlined in his appli-

---

Hoffman, "47 Workshop," *KR,* XVII, 300–304. Eric Bentley and Francis Fergusson had refused to review Kinne's book. It was not until 1969 that a book on the theater by Theodore Hoffman appeared (with Kenneth Cameron, *The Theatrical Response*), so Hoffman's fellowship project must have failed.

51. Francis Fergusson, application form for fellowships, October 20, 1957, Ransom to Murray Krieger, January 28, 1957, both in *KR* Papers. Fergusson was the general editor of *The Laurel Shakespeare* (New York, 1958–68). One of Fergusson's earlier papers on Shakespeare had appeared in the *Kenyon:* "Philosophy and Theatre in *Measure for Measure*," *KR,* XIV, 103–20. Ransom to Thomas Henry Carter, October 13, 1955, in Carter Papers.

cation appeared in *The Kenyon Review*. His only contribution after his election as the Fellow for 1958 was a short spring, 1963, review of the George Wickes edition of Lawrence Durrell and Henry Miller's letters.[52] So, in general, after their election, these Fellows contributed only a few occasional papers to the *Kenyon*.

Howard Nemerov, unsuccessful candidate for the fellowship in criticism in 1953 and 1954, but the Fellow in Fiction for 1955, so far had only published superior reviews, but Ransom now also wanted articles from him. Besides two reviews, one about a study of A. E. Housman, the other about Nabokov's *Lolita* and *Pnin,* during these final years Nemerov published three lively, intelligent articles, one on Shakespeare's aesthetics, one on the poet Reed Whittemore, and one on the difficulty for younger poets "of continuing to see lyric poetry as an art by itself, the preference . . . to see it as the expression of strong emotions or fashionable opinions, the insistence on communicating as *opposed* to making." In the correspondence dealing with his winter, 1958, essay, Nemerov disclosed his critical credo:

I am uneasily sensible that in our like of certain poems and dislike of others there is always much that is accidental and much that is arbitrary, nor can more than rather crude distinctions be made on any bases of "craft", which anyhow are usually afterthoughts. . . . I do think, though, that the critic's business when he is being professional, as on his reviewing occasions he is, is to make his judgments as unequivocal as he can, and even perhaps exaggerate them somewhat—let him be decently wrong, as he will be wrong in any event some of the time, but let him reveal that he is taking some sort of responsibility for his judgments.[53]

Another essay noteworthy for its intrinsic quality and for the attendant correspondence is Philip Rahv's "Fiction and the Criticism of

52. Ransom to Thomas Henry Carter, February 18, [1955], March 29, 1955, both in Carter Papers; Thomas Henry Carter, "Ezra Pound the Critic," *KR*, XVI, 490–97; Thomas Henry Carter, "Rationalist in Hell," *KR*, XVIII, 326–36; Thomas Henry Carter, "That Hard Sophoclean Light," *KR*, XIX, 658–61; Thomas Henry Carter, application form for fellowships, n.d., in *KR* Papers. Thomas Henry Carter to Macauley, February 7, 1961, shows that Carter had not yet written the projected papers on O'Connor, Ford, and Pound (Letter in *KR* Papers). Carter died in 1963 when he was still in his early thirties. James Boatwright (ed.), *Essays and Reviews by Thomas H. Carter,* was privately printed in 1968. Thomas Henry Carter, Review of George Wickes (ed.), *Lawrence Durrell and Henry Miller: A Private Correspondence,* in *KR,* XXV, 382–84.
53. Howard Nemerov, "Iniquity It Is; But Pass the Can," *KR*, XX, 642–45; Howard Nemerov, "The Morality of Art," *KR*, XIX, 313–21; Ransom to Tate, October 18, [1957], in Tate Papers; Howard Nemerov, "The Marriage of Theseus and Hippolyta," *KR*, XVIII, 633–41; Howard Nemerov, "The Poetry of Reed Whittemore," *KR*, XXI, 260–78; Howard

Fiction." This was to appear simultaneously with, and as Rahv's reply to, Ransom's spring, 1950, "The Understanding of Fiction," which, in its turn, was prompted by Rahv's collection of essays, *Image and Idea* (1949). Rahv procrastinated, forgot, and did not return to Ransom's essay until the summer of 1955 when he gave a lecture on the criticism of fiction at the School of Letters in Bloomington. On August 7, 1955, Rahv told Ransom that he had been "much encouraged by the response" to his lecture and was "planning to recast the piece somewhat before sending it on" for possible publication. "As I have a strong sense of the platform and of the direct communication it entails," he explained, "I can never get myself to write a lecture as I would an essay." Rahv added as a two-edged compliment that he "really env[ied] people like [Lionel] Trilling, who so seldom deviate from their settled literary tone even when facing a live audience." Although he had promised the essay "in good time . . . for the Winter number," it was only on January 26, 1956, that Rahv sent in, "all too belatedly," the "much-revised version" of his lecture.[54]

In his essay, Rahv rested his argument on the premise that "20th Century criticism has as yet failed to evolve a theory and a set of practical procedures dealing with the prose-medium that are as satisfactory in their exactness, subtlety and variety as the theory and procedures worked out in the past few decades by the critics of poetry." But after this indirect compliment, he started berating poetry critics, objecting forcefully to the "recent infection of the prose-sense by poetics" and particularly to the fallacy, as exemplified by Ransom's "The Understanding of Fiction," that style is "the 'essential activity' of imaginative prose." In his polemical essay, Rahv had deliberately overlooked Ransom's admittedly rather vague and ineffectual but, at any rate, not coldly mechanical emphasis on the "human importance of the art-work . . . [which] 'touches the heart'" as well as his recognition of the "great contribution of the Marxists to literary theory," namely, "their firmness in regarding literature as a public property and holding it socially responsible for its effects." Stridently con-

Nemerov, "Younger Poets: The Lyric Difficulty," *KR*, XX, 25; Howard Nemerov to Ransom, July 13, 1957, in *KR* Papers.

54. Philip Rahv, "Fiction and the Criticism of Fiction," *KR*, XVIII, 276–99; John Crowe Ransom, "The Understanding of Fiction," *KR*, XII, 189–218; Philip Rahv to Ransom, August 7, 1955, January 26, 1956, both in *KR* Papers.

tentious, too, were Rahv's concluding remarks about myth criticism. The "obsession with symbolization is at bottom expressive of the reactionary idealism that now afflicts our literary life and that passes itself off as a strict concern with aesthetic form," he stated peremptorily. Then, in the spring of 1957, Robert Wooster Stallman, who had written what Rahv called a "far-fetched religious exegesis" of Stephen Crane's *The Red Badge of Courage* and denounced as "mere *Zeitgeist* palaver," quoted Joseph Conrad's declaration that the "nearer a work approaches art . . . 'the more it acquires a symbolic character.'" Marvin Mudrick, a critic Stallman had bracketed with Rahv, had the final say. He and Rahv, he stated, do not "deny the value of the study of myth and symbol in fiction, but . . . suggest that an . . . exploitation of symbol, as practiced in some of Conrad's fiction and . . . reflected in some contemporary criticism (Mr. Stallman's, for example), does not produce valuable fiction or valuable criticism."[55]

With the exception of the articles on prosody, the contributions discussed so far might suggest that the *Kenyon* still had a good bit of life in it. In fact, it was the contributors of long standing who created what life there was, and while their writings were by and large skillful and intelligent, they had lost their provocative or spectacular quality. One would expect to find such revivifying aspects in essays by newcomers to the *Kenyon*. But most of their contributions further depleted the *Kenyon*. It is depressingly easy to find newcomers' contributions that are too academic, tedious, or lifeless: essays by James Hall, Henry Gifford, Murray Krieger, Albert Cook, Glenn Pedersen, and Peter Kline are cases in point. Newton P. Stallknecht, director of the School of Letters, and the critic William Van O'Connor were not altogether new to the *Kenyon*'s pages, as each had appeared once before this period of decline; in these few pages, they each had two essays published, and to little effect.[56]

55. Rahv, "Fiction and the Criticism of Fiction," 277, 280; Ransom, "The Understanding of Fiction," 202, 208; Rahv, "Fiction and the Criticism of Fiction," 287, 284; Robert Wooster Stallman, "Fiction and Its Critics: A Reply to Mr. Rahv," *KR*, XIX, 291; Marvin Mudrick, "Communication: Mr. Stallman's Remarks," *KR*, XIX, 483.

56. James Hall, "The Fiction of Henry Green," *KR*, XIX, 76–88; Henry Gifford, "W. D. Howells: His Moral Conservatism," *KR*, XX, 124–33; Murray Krieger, "Tragedy and the Tragic Vision," *KR*, XX, 281–99; Albert Cook, "Modern Verse: Diffusion as a Principle of Composition," *KR*, XXI, 199–220; Glenn Pedersen, "Forster's Symbolic Form," *KR*, XXI, 231–49; Peter Kline, "The Spiritual Center in Eliot's Plays," *KR*, XXI, 457–72.

A passage from Cook's piece illustrates the deadly tone that characterizes many of these essays:

Vaporization and centralization constitute poles of the same *Moi*. So poets who vaporize with diffusion of images, and poets who centralize through strict control over a single image, are approaching the same problem from two different directions. It is because of their centralization in the midst of a consciously resisted flux that the modern poem of severe control and exclusive statement seems far more airtight than its romantic or classic prototypes. . . .

One can triumph over flux and defeat mere stasis in a poem either by mastering flux through keeping time with it in diffuse images, or by banishing flux as utterly as possible from the total artifice of the work. Modernism in poetry is not so much a tradition of diffusion or concentration as it is a condition of living, of knowing, in which the poet . . . tries to come to terms with living and knowing in a fusion so faithful to both that it will not admit the finality of either classical rhetoric or romantic tonal (and mythic) unity.[57]

Some of the new contributors steered clear of the *Kenyon*'s academic course, but the results were often as disappointing. For instance, in his emotional summer, 1957, essay, Vivian Mercier, writing from a decidedly leftist point of view, mainly manifested his own limitations in describing Flaubert as a "sentimental bourgeois" who wrote "sentimental rubbish" and whose "implied contempt for almost all the characters in his novels may be a form of compensation for [his] sense of inferiority." And Frederick Hoffman, in an autumn, 1957, essay, which, though concordant with the current growth in psychological awareness, went too far in wanting literature to be "analysed in terms of the verbal and metaphorical equivalents of the psyche and its behaviour." Lucia Dickerson was equally in step with the spirit of the times in her essay in *Kenyon*'s winter, 1959, number. Dickerson's "sort of rough translation" of P. H. Newby's novel, *The Young May Moon* (1950), begins:

At the opening of the story, Alec (the libido, the creative, Dionysian element) is living at Number 7 Zion (sunny, hill) Terrace (suggests levels of, for instance, the Seven Storey Mountain) with his wife, Freda (the superego? the conscience in the form of early instilled maternal values?), whose only charity is the Salvation Army. His first wife, Laura (the feminine creative unconscious), has left him and their son Philip, and married Grainger.

57. Cook, "Modern Verse," 219.

(The anima has allied itself with the intellect, producing a mana figure, the wise man. From this alliance, disturbances in the unconscious inevitably follow.) The product of this union has died. (Sterility of intellectualism.)[58]

The writer continues in this vein for two more pages.

A new and in itself interesting and promising venture, the interview, also failed. In Philip Stratford's "One Meeting with Mauriac," the interviewer puts himself rather than Mauriac in the forefront, and the conversation does not rise above banalities. Unsuccessful, too, was an old and tried practice, the publication of letters from abroad, which was revived at the suggestion of the British writer Wayland Young. His spring, 1954, *Kenyon* story "The Glass Trumpet" had displayed sensitivity and elegance, but his three letters from London fell far short of his creative writing. Ransom described Young as "one of the best commentators going," but the first letter's characterization by Gertrude Buckman, Delmore Schwartz's first wife, as "freshman theme drivel" seems more to the point. Young's final summer, 1957, "Letter from London," which was, in large measure, an early and appreciative discussion of William Golding's works, was a marked improvement over his first two letters with their affected, insipid witticisms about the political and cultural situation in Europe.[59] These two letters, incidentally, constituted about all the attention the *Kenyon* paid to politics during these vapid years.

Although the *Kenyon*'s critical department was, on the whole, so disappointing during this period, new contributors who wrote refreshing, if not particularly bold or impassioned, articles should be mentioned: Ernest Borneman, Martin Green, Frank Kermode, and Barbara Watson.[60]

58. Vivian Mercier, "The Limitations of Flaubert," *KR*, XIX, 404, 410; Frederick Hoffman, "Psychology and Literature," *KR*, XIX, 608; Lucia Dickerson, "Portrait of the Artist as a Jung Man," *KR*, XXI, 81.

59. Philip Stratford, "One Meeting with Mauriac," *KR*, XXI, 611–22; Wayland Young, "The Glass Trumpet," *KR*, XVI, 191–99; Ransom to Wayland Young, January 8, 1957, Gertrude Buckman to Ransom, n.d., both in *KR* Papers; Wayland Young, "Summer Letter from London," *KR*, XVIII, 642–47; Wayland Young, "London Letter," *KR*, XIX, 284–89; Wayland Young, "Letter from London," *KR*, XIX, 477–82. Another story by Wayland Young is "The Admirer," *KR*, XIX, 593–604.

60. Ernest Borneman, "Credo Quia Absurdum: An Epitaph for Bertolt Brecht," *KR*, XXI, 169–98; Martin Green, "British Decency," *KR*, XXI, 505–32; Frank Kermode, "The Dissociation of Sensibility," *KR*, XIX, 169–94; Barbara Watson, "The Dangers of Security: E. E. Cummings' Revolt Against the Future," *KR*, XVIII, 519–37.

Poetry, Fiction, the Fine Arts

The philosophy department of *The Kenyon Review* had almost completely disappeared. Two articles, by Albert William Levi and Walter Kaufmann, on Søren Kierkegaard appeared in *Kenyon*'s spring, 1956, issue to commemorate the centennial of his death. Henry David Aiken wrote a memorial to Rice for the autumn, 1956, issue. The essay concentrated on Rice's lifework, *On the Knowledge of Good and Evil,* published shortly before his death. Rice's concise, clear survey of the contemporary diversity in ethics and value theory had been very well received. Ransom, for one, thought Rice's study showed "on every page a meticulous scruple in passing judgment on other philosophers, and on frail ordinary mankind too which could only belong to an author who was himself a good man" and thought it would mark him "as a leading contemporary philosopher." In his *Kenyon* essay, Aiken described Rice as "a fine philosopher," "a first-rate editor and a great teacher," and "first of all, a magnificent human being," but this did not mislead him into admiring Rice's book unqualifiedly. Apart from Walter J. Ong's confused essay on personalism, these few articles represent the sad remains of the *Kenyon*'s once proud and prominent philosophy section, of which not only the quantity but also the quality decreased considerably during these meager years.[61]

With respect to the *Kenyon*'s poetry section, we note a diminishment of energy. Again, as was the case with the *Kenyon*'s criticism, no exciting discoveries were made. Again, *The Kenyon Review* survived weakly on the reputation of its old-timers and did not really try to foster young talent. There are, for instance, two poems by Richard Eberhart, two by Jean Garrigue, one by James Merrill, three short poems by William S. Merwin, three by Robert Mezey, ten brilliant, witty, precise poems by Josephine Miles, and two by Theodore Roethke. Robert Penn Warren published three poems, one of which was "Ballad of a Sweet Dream of Peace," about which Ransom rhap-

61. Albert William Levi, "A Hundred Years after Kierkegaard: I. The Three Masks," *KR,* XVIII, 169–82; Walter Kaufmann, "A Hundred Years after Kierkegaard: II. Kierkegaard," *KR,* XVIII, 182–211; Ransom to Rice, n.d., in Rice Papers; Ransom to David McDowell, August 17, 1955, in Random House Papers; Henry David Aiken, "Philip Blair Rice and His Philosophy," *KR,* XVIII, 618; Walter J. Ong, "Personalism and the Wilderness," *KR,* XXI, 297–304.

sodized: "You are extending the genre of the art here, Red, it's a fantasy full of melody and history, and it progresses, and your reader feels good progressively."[62]

Although quite a few poetry contributors were indeed new to the *Kenyon*'s pages, *The Kenyon Review* could not take credit for discovering them. Such accomplished poets as John Ashbery, James Dickey, Irving Feldman, Donald Hall, John Hollander, and John Logan had been published in other literary magazines for some years before their first and often only appearance in the *Kenyon*. The same is true of somewhat less distinguished poets such as Margaret Avison, who was from Canada; the poet and critic Edwin Honig; the editor of *The Hudson Review,* Frederick Morgan; Landis Everson; Patricia Goedicke; and Arthur Gregor. Everson, Goedicke, and Gregor made their first *Kenyon* appearance in the company of six other even lesser known poets, Michael Fried, Alan Marshfield, R. S. Patton, John Pauker, Sheila Pritchard, and Margaret Tongue, in a winter, 1958, poetry section entitled "The Younger Poets Themselves." It was one of Ransom's rare sparkling editorial ideas during this period to have these younger poets speak for themselves in order to balance Howard Nemerov's "Younger Poets: The Lyric Difficulty" in the same issue.[63]

62. Richard Eberhart, "Sermon on the Amount of Love," *KR*, XVIII, 365–67; Richard Eberhart, "The Parker River," *KR*, XX, 20–24; Jean Garrigue, "For a Holy Day in Naples" and "For the New Come to Elysium," *KR*, XIX, 574–76; James Merrill, "Dream and Waking," *KR*, XX, 436–39; William S. Merwin, "The Miner," "A Wit in Age," and "Coal Barges," *KR*, XIX, 195–96; Robert Mezey, "Dusk Near a Mental Hospital," "Corinna in Vendome," and "The Groundkeeper's Complaint," *KR*, XIX, 109–12; Josephine Miles, "Panther," "Dog," "Fish," "Sheep," "Monkey," and "The Savages," *KR*, XVIII, 21–25; Josephine Miles, "Magna Carta," "Aim," "Deed," and "Voyage," *KR*, XX, 428–30; Theodore Roethke, "Two Poems," *KR*, XVIII, 120–21; Robert Penn Warren, "Ballad of a Sweet Dream of Peace," *KR*, XIX, 31–36; Ransom to Warren, October 16, 1956, in *KR* Papers; Robert Penn Warren, "Penthesilea and Achilles: Fatal Interview" and "Switzerland," *KR*, XX, 599–603.

63. John Ashbery, "A Long Novel" and "Two Scenes," *KR*, XVIII, 272–74; James Dickey, "Awaiting the Swimmer," *KR*, XXI, 609–10; Irving Feldman, "Works and Days," *KR*, XXI, 84–96; Donald Hall, "Christmas Eve in Whitneyville, 1955," *KR*, XX, 433–35; John Hollander, "The Sun Dial," *KR*, XIX, 569–71; John Logan, "Narcissus: Vision and Retrospect," *KR*, XVIII, 267–69; Margaret Avison, "From a Provincial," "The Apex Animal," "New Year's Poem," and "Knowledge of Age," *KR*, XVIII, 263–65; Edwin Honig, "Near Hope in Providence" and "Corrales 1948," *KR*, XX, 597–99. As early as 1948, Edwin Honig had published criticism in the *Kenyon:* "Hobgoblin or Apollo," *KR*, X, 664–81. Other articles by Edwin Honig during Ransom's editorship are "That Mutation of Pound's," *KR*, XVII, 349–56, and "In Defense of Allegory," *KR*, XX, 1–19. Frederick Morgan, "Scene," "Etude," and "The Last Days," *KR*, XIX, 560–63; Landis Everson, "Tiger Watch," "Diamonds in Summery Cities," and "Angels Who Have Suffered the First Forlornment," *KR*, XX, 57–59; Patricia Goedicke, "Circumnavigation," "Proudflesh," and "Calypso," *KR*, XX, 59–61;

The poet and translator Richmond Lattimore had also appeared regularly in other magazines such as *The Hudson Review* and *Poetry* before his spring, 1955, entry into *The Kenyon Review* with translations of verse by the Greek poet Konstantinos Kavaphes. Ransom's choice of Lattimore's own "Andritsaina Revisited" and "Poussin's World" for the summer, 1959, issue showed editorial perspicacity; they won the Longview Foundation Literary Award. The publication of early poetry by the versatile and productive novelist, translator, and poet David R. Slavitt, in the *Kenyon's* summer, 1956, number, also was meritorious.[64]

Less commendable from a critical and aesthetic point of view, though all to Ransom's credit from an ethical perspective, was the election of Delmore Schwartz, by then virtually burned-out, as the Fellow in Poetry for 1957. Edwin Honig and Karl Shapiro were among his competitors, and, in fact, Ransom first offered the fellowship to Shapiro. Only when the University of Nebraska in Lincoln, where Shapiro was teaching at that time, suddenly decided to refuse him a sabbatical year, did Ransom approach Schwartz. Informing Honig of his rejection, Ransom wrote on December 11, 1956, that the elected Fellow in Poetry was "a man pretty well established as a poet, but just now neglected and very much in need of assistance."[65]

Three days earlier, Schwartz had told Ransom that the possibility of a fellowship was "the nicest thing" that had happened to him since 1954 when Ransom had accepted his "The First Morning of the Second World" for the *Kenyon's* autumn, 1955, issue. His letter was sound and sensible, but the fellowship project he enclosed was incoherent, illegible, and frenzied, and it manifested Schwartz's struggle against encroaching madness. During his fellowship year, Schwartz sent no news of himself. His terrorized second wife Elizabeth Pollet

Arthur Gregor, "Dreams" and "The Old Canal at New Hope, Pa.," *KR*, XX, 70–72. In "The Younger Poets Themselves," *KR*, XX, 51–73, are Michael Fried, "The Fossil Indian," 65–68; Alan Marshfield, "Pilgrim," 61–64; R. S. Patton, "A City," "For Hart," and "Mishap," 68–69; John Pauker, "On the Beach," 73; Sheila Pritchard, "Point of Change," "The Shattered Air," and "Sang My Name," 53–56; and Margaret Tongue, "After a Painting by M. Vanka," 51–53. Howard Nemerov, "Younger Poets: The Lyric Difficulty," *KR*, XX, 25–37.

64. Konstantinos Kavaphes, "Waiting for the Barbarians" and "Loutsa Beach," trans. Richmond Lattimore, *KR*, XVII, 291–93; Richmond Lattimore, "Andritsaina Revisited" and "Poussin's World: Two Paintings," *KR*, XXI, 388–89; David R. Slavitt, "Partiti Da Cotesti Che Son Morti," "Great Grandfather," and "Warning," *KR*, XVIII, 370–72.

65. Ransom to Edwin Honig, December 11, 1956, in *KR* Papers.

left him, he suffered frequent spells of insanity, and, for a brief period, was committed to Bellevue. In March, 1958, Schwartz again sent Ransom a lucid, sober letter and enclosed a few poems he had managed to write in spite of his adversities. Ransom was "awfully glad" to hear from Schwartz, praised the "integrity" of his poems, and spoke out against the current cult of merely intellectually sophisticated poetry. "I don't hold with the intentional willed subtlety of the modern poets; they are just evasive, and awed by the 'ideas' of the age," he wrote. He thought that Schwartz had made "fine use of the Fellowship" and published six of the poems Schwartz had submitted in the summer of 1958. By mistake, a slightly different version of the first poem, "Poem," also was printed at the end of the group. This caused Schwartz to comment that he had "heard so many very pleasant things about the group—some of them so pleasant as to be implausible—that the errors were clearly unimportant, save for the repetition of the first poem. The repetition was interpreted as deliberate on my part and the whole group as a cycle and in general—this is partly what I mean by implausibility—the poems were interpreted as having all sorts of systematic but hidden philosophical meanings: I wish some of them had occurred to me when I wrote the poems."[66]

In an attempt to help Schwartz to some more money, Ransom suggested that he write an essay on the Symbolists. Since Schwartz felt "more indebted" to Ransom "than to any other poet" and since Ransom's proposal was "exciting" and "attractive in itself," he was very tempted to accept this offer, but he felt obliged to refuse. He was already up to his neck in all kinds of unfinished projects. In the autumn of 1958, Schwartz flooded the *Kenyon* with some of the results of these projects—with poems, a long short story, part of a play, and an essay. He was surprised by his own output. The "quantity is such," he wrote, "as to surpass even Merrill Moore [who wrote many thousands of sonnets] in any period of eight months." But Schwartz's writings did not come anywhere near Ransom's standards, so he tried to reject them as diplomatically as he could. He was

66. Delmore Schwartz to Ransom, December 8, 1956, in *KR* Papers; Delmore Schwartz, "The First Morning of the Second World," *KR*, XVII, 575–80; Schwartz to Ransom, March 12, 1958, in *KR* Papers; Ransom to Schwartz, March 18, [1958], in Schwartz Papers; Delmore Schwartz, "Poem," "The Sequel," "Once and For All," "'At a Solemn Musick,'" "Poem (The Foggy, Foggy Playboy)," "Sonnet," and "Poem," *KR*, XX, 440–45; Schwartz to Ransom, n.d., in Schwartz Papers.

"happy" at Schwartz's "immense literary activity," but did not "quite think these manuscripts . . . [were] quite up to [his] big things heretofore in the matter of gravity and concision . . . in the matter of the pace, the speed." And "considering the crowded condition under which I have to work to get out the remaining issues," Ransom added, he had to return Schwartz's writings, even though they contained "so many good things."[67] Although tactfully worded, Ransom's letter came down to a rejection of nearly all that Schwartz had written during the preceding year. The absence of further letters to Ransom suggests that, in addition to Schwartz's rapidly declining mental health, this discouragement hastened the end of a warm and mutually respectful relationship that had lasted for over twenty years.

The other Fellows in Poetry were Ruth Stone for 1956 and Theodore Henry Holmes and James Wright for 1958. Stone, blessed with, in Ransom's words, "the gift of poetic phrase, and great originality," had been publishing poetry in literary magazines since the early 1950s. In the summer of 1953, she placed her first poems with *The Kenyon Review*; after her election, she published four more poems there, but she has remained virtually unknown. Holmes, a protégé of R. P. Blackmur's, made his debut in the spring, 1956, issue. Admiringly, Ransom wrote to Blackmur, who, acting as an intermediary, had submitted Holmes's poems to the *Kenyon*: "You know my own prejudices, and that I'm hoping there will be a stage in his sophistication in which he will not be afraid to make his moments formal and eternal [?]. But as to the free verse, don't we now have the courage to take it without question as the inevitable form of the flux of the matter, when one is at a certain stage of civilization (or sophistication) and too advanced to harden and sterilize the experience by just formalizing it somehow? Holmes is completely alive . . . and there are not too many young poets you can say that for." This letter shows once again that in spite of Ransom's basic preference for formal, metered poetry, he actively disliked poems that were merely technically proficient, poems without life, without vitality. Over the years, Holmes published other long poems in the *Kenyon*. However, though Holmes has several volumes of poetry to his credit, he has not established much of a reputation as a poet.[68]

67. Delmore Schwartz to Ransom, March 29, November 10, 1958, Ransom to Schwartz, November 17, [1958], all in Schwartz Papers.
68. Ransom to John Marshall, March 8, 1956, in *KR* Papers; Ruth Stone, "The Parents"

James Wright, Holmes's co-Fellow in Poetry for 1958, found him "an original poet" but could not "quite understand what he is doing technically." Wright's own poetry at this time was still richly and brilliantly formal. He made his first appearance in *The Kenyon Review* in 1951, when he was still an undergraduate at Kenyon College, and his second in 1953; after that, he was not published for five years. After his graduation from Kenyon College, Wright kept up a regular, lively personal and literary correspondence with Ransom. These letters reveal that Ransom stimulated Wright to write formal, traditional poetry and tried to curb his tendency to write poems that were too personal and too unformed, a direction Wright was later to take in his loose and despairing poetry. For example, returning quite a number of Wright's poems in February, 1957, Ransom noted: "In all these present manuscripts . . . there is considerable care . . . and less of what used to look to me like a certain haste and blindness in your composition." Submitting a new group of poems in November, 1957, Wright replied obediently: "You know that fatal weakness in almost everything I have written: I tend to shriek when I ought to speak, to howl when I ought to sing, to be frantic when I ought to be modest, and to be vaguely grandiose when the true source of power in language . . . is its patient precision."[69]

Ransom was impressed by Wright's new poems and, when they met at Christmas, suggested that Wright himself choose five pages of verse from them for the *Kenyon's* autumn, 1958, issue. Wright selected four poems and added a new one, "Safety," of which he wrote: "In earlier versions it was overwritten (my old weakness, which you pointed out long ago, of violence in language where the true strength would be a quiet restraint). But now I am convinced that I have made a real lyric out of it: a beautiful scene and a human attitude toward

and "Speculation," *KR*, XV, 402–403; Ruth Stone, "When Wishes Were Fishes," "Ballet," "Confusion in the Occident," and "Memoir," *KR*, XVIII, 538–40; Theodore Holmes, "The Life of the Estate," *KR*, XVIII, 274–75; Ransom to Blackmur, January 1, [1956; wrongly dated 1955], in Blackmur Papers; Theodore Holmes, "A Prayer for Rain," *KR*, XVIII, 361–64; Theodore Holmes, "Journeys," *KR*, XIX, 106–108; Theodore Holmes, "The Lovers in the Graveyard," *KR*, XIX, 197–98; Theodore Holmes, "The Knowledge of Our Dream," *KR*, XX, 250–56. Theodore Holmes's first book of poetry was *The Harvest and the Scythe: Poems* (New York, 1957).

69. James Wright to Ransom, January 28, 1958, in *KR* Papers; James Wright, "Lonely" and "Father," *KR*, XIII, 672–73; James Wright, "Robert Sitting in My Hands," *KR*, XV, 127–28; Ransom to James Wright, February 4, 1957, Wright to Ransom, November 5, 1957, both in *KR* Papers.

that scene, both clearly sung—as clearly as I can do." It seems as if Ransom wanted Wright, more than any other poet he supported and advised, to write rather like he himself did, with "quiet restraint"; perhaps Ransom realized that Wright could succumb to hysteria in his poetry. And Wright, at least at this stage of his career, wholly agreed with Ransom. "If I could curb my personal hysterias, then perhaps by the same token I could purge my verses of their violence. Violence is weakness; it is precision and grace that are strength," he admonished himself on May 25, 1958. Wright's last publication in *The Kenyon Review* was in the summer, 1961, issue and was still formal but vibrant in style.[70]

Also on the credit side of the *Kenyon* is the publication of "Red Jacket (Lake Seneca)," the only one of Paul Goodman's poems to appear there, and two of I. A. Richards' rhythmically simplistic, almost didactically philosophical, but also witty poems. On the debit side are the reappearance of Roberta Swartz with "Why We Loved Her" and the publication of three poems by the Kenyon College graduate Albert Herzing. Ransom was not the only one to appreciate Herzing's "The Candy-Man's Art Is the Sweetest Art I Know." Unknown to Ransom, *Partisan Review* had already accepted it for publication, and the poem appeared simultaneously in both magazines. Rahv's reaction was extraordinarily gracious. "Herzing should be proud of his poem now that it has appeared in two of our leading reviews; . . . we are perfectly willing to let him have the whole of your payment [instead of *Partisan* receiving royalties], mainly because we pay so little for verse and feel terribly guilty on that account." Charles Coffin's "Evening at the Athenaeum," published in the *Kenyon*'s summer, 1957, number, is not particularly distinguished either; it should be seen as a memorial tribute to Ransom's best friend.[71]

70. James Wright to Ransom, January 4, 1958, in *KR* Papers; James Wright, "A Girl Walking into a Shadow," "All the Beautiful Are Blameless," "Safety," and "With the Gift of a Feather," *KR,* XX, 592–96; James Wright to Ransom, May 25, 1958, in *KR* Papers; James Wright, "President Harding's Tomb in Ohio," *KR,* XXIII, 390–91.

71. Paul Goodman, "Red Jacket (Lake Seneca)," *KR,* XX, 431–33; I. A. Richards, "Lighting Fires in Snow" and "Screens," *KR,* XXI, 221–27; Roberta Swartz, "Why We Loved Her," *KR,* XX, 278; Albert Herzing, "The Candy-Man's Art Is the Sweetest Art I Know," *KR,* XX, 279–80; Albert Herzing, "The Spent Substance" and "A Winter's World," *KR,* XXI, 607–609; Philip Rahv to Ransom, April 27, 1958, in *KR* Papers; Charles Coffin, "Evening at the Athenaeum," *KR,* XIX, 418–19. Allen Ginsberg submitted poetry more than once. Ransom rather liked his poems, but thought that the *Kenyon* needed "a more compacted thing" and that

Concomitantly with the staunching of the inflow of gifted new poets, there was a considerable decrease in the quantity, though not in the quality, of the fiction published in *The Kenyon Review*. Many unknown young fiction writers appeared in the *Kenyon*. About two out of the four stories published annually came from people new to its pages. The Fellows in Fiction, Andrew Lytle for 1956, James F. Powers and Elizabeth Spencer for 1957, and Robie Macauley for 1958, were seasoned writers, however. "Lytle has already done three novels, of which at least two are absolutely first-rate, and at his best he has enormous style. I have known him since my Fugitive and Agrarian days at Vanderbilt, and I have the greatest faith in his vitality and potential. I have thought it was a scandal to see his whole time taken up in his teaching," Ransom wrote to John Marshall, informing him of Lytle's appointment. Lytle submitted part of the novel *The Velvet Horn* (1957), his masterpiece and fruit of his fellowship, but Ransom, who, from the outset of the project, had been "feeling a little antipathy . . . to the novel on the subject of incest," rejected it. Later, after he had read the entire novel, he admitted: "I can see now how mistaken I was in not using the magnificent section we had a chance at . . . a good while back. I'd say that your novel is a series of lyrical & dramatic achievements, on a base of philosophical attitude founded on the sense of nature and the paradoxes of sex, and grounded firmly in history and the old (and maybe timeless) South. This is the same Andrew we have known so many years, maintaining himself over a big novel at the top of his powers." And in reviewing *The Velvet Horn* for the *Kenyon*'s autumn, 1957, issue, Robie Macauley concluded that this novel "should assure Mr. Lytle of his rightful place among the first rank of American novelists practising today."[72]

The southern writer Elizabeth Spencer, like Lytle, had published several novels before her election as a Fellow but did not, again like

Ginsberg's poems lacked "independent *argument,* or *narrative.*" But during neither Ransom's nor Macauley's editorship did the Beats make an impact on *The Kenyon Review*. In an interview (August 8, 1982), Macauley stated that Ginsberg had told him he "would never submit anything to *The Kenyon Review* because they were so establishment." That this had not always been the case is apparent from Ransom's unfortunately undated letters to Ginsberg (in Ginsberg Papers).

72. Ransom to John Marshall, March 8, 1956, in *KR* Papers; Ransom to Lytle, February 28, 1956, August 31, 1957, both in Lytle Papers; Andrew Lytle, *The Velvet Horn* (New York, 1957); Robie Macauley, "Big Novel," *KR,* XIX, 646.

Lytle, appear in *The Kenyon Review* after she had become a Fellow. However, in her case, there is no evidence that she actually submitted stories to the *Kenyon,* though one may assume that, like all the other Fellows, she did. It was only in the spring, 1962, issue that James F. Powers appeared in the *Kenyon.* His novel-project for the fellowship was part of his superbly witty, tragicomic study of a worldly priest, *Morte D'Urban,* which won the National Book Award in 1963. Robie Macauley was so "delighted" with "Sailing Against the Wind"—it had "all that grand involvement of understanding and misunderstanding" that he liked so well in Powers' fiction—that he reprinted it in *Gallery of Modern Fiction.* Macauley's own three contributions in fiction also all appeared before he became a Fellow. During his fellowship, Macauley intended to write a novel "built around arrivals and departures" in which "the journey's ends and journey's beginnings make the world of the book," a novel "meant to reflect American life in the 1940's and '50's," but he never finished it.[73]

Ransom's financial administration of the fellowships was not a success. On June 14, 1958, he wrote to Marshall that "[j]ust yesterday" he had realized "that the amount to be expended for the Fellows' stipends was precisely $40,200," whereas he "had wrongly supposed that the sum was $48,000, allowing for the appointment of Fellows who were all married, if it should turn out so." Since nearly all the appointed Fellows were married, Ransom had "over-expended" the grant by $5,200. "The blame is entirely mine," he admitted, but suggested nevertheless that the Rockefeller Foundation make up the deficit. Marshall agreed with Ransom "that the writers to whom these fellowships have gone are an admirable lot," but was "somewhat at a loss to know how to reply" to his letter. Meanwhile, fortunately, Ransom had also been negotiating with President Lund and, on July 22, could quote from a "nice note" he had just received from Lund: "My idea is to 'consolidate' the accumulated deficit of the *Kenyon Review* up to July 1, 1958, including this $5,200, then write it off. When Robie Macauley takes over, he should start with a

73. James F. Powers, "Sailing Against the Wind," *KR,* XXIV, 257–80; James F. Powers, *Morte D'Urban* (Garden City, N.Y., 1962); Macauley to James F. Powers, November 6, 1961, in *KR* Papers; Robie Macauley, "The Thin Voice," *KR,* XIII, 50–63; Robie Macauley, "The Chevigny Man," *KR,* XVII, 75–93; Robie Macauley, "Legend of Two Swimmers," *KR,* XIX, 246–66; Macauley, application form for fellowships, October 27, 1957, in *KR* Papers.

fresh budget."[74] Lund's generosity, incidentally, foreshadows his openhandedness toward the *Kenyon* during Macauley's editorship. At any rate, Ransom's problem was solved.

Returning to the *Kenyon*'s fiction in the late 1950s, we find John Wain, Anthony Ostroff, and David Antin among prominent writers who had not appeared in the *Kenyon* before. John Wain's amusing, atmospheric story, in the spring, 1957, issue, was reprinted in *Gallery of Modern Fiction*. Ostroff's moving tale, in which he interwove straight narrative with stream of consciousness technique, appeared in that year's summer issue. In the autumn, 1959, number was David Antin's early, grotesque, somber story about the protagonist's failure to create a microcosm in which each living thing feeds on some other in an endless circle. There were other newcomers to the *Kenyon*'s department of fiction, such as William Van O'Connor, whose first story in the autumn, 1956, issue was much too academic, and Elaine Zimbel, whose story probably remained her only attempt at fiction. They hardly enlivened the *Kenyon*'s pages with their well-made but commonplace stories.[75]

Among the stories by regular contributors in fiction, some are truly noteworthy. Peter Taylor's contribution in the spring, 1958, issue was a stylistically immaculate story about southern morals and incest, about society and manners. It was an O. Henry first-prize winner and was reprinted in *Gallery of Modern Fiction*. Taylor's second excellent recollective story, published in the summer, 1959, number, treated the slow and sadistic destruction of a Negro servant by his seemingly protective white employers. After an absence of fourteen years, David Cornel DeJong returned to the *Kenyon* in the summer, 1958, issue with a psychologically convincing, penetrating study of patronage. To the winter, 1959, issue, Priscilla Heath contributed a discriminating, feminist story tracing the turmoil and guilt feelings of a formerly self-sacrificing wife and mother, who, after her husband's death, frees the other woman in herself.[76] All in all, if there

---

74. Ransom to John Marshall, June 14, 1958, Marshall to Ransom, June 17, 1958, Ransom to Marshall, July [22?], 1958, all in KC Collection.

75. John Wain, "A Few Drinks with Alcock and Brown," *KR*, XIX, 233–45; Anthony Ostroff, "La Bataille des Fleurs," *KR*, XIX, 463–76; David Antin, "The Balanced Aquarium," *KR*, XXI, 577–85; William Van O'Connor, "The Retirement of Professor John Underhill," *KR*, XVIII, 576–82; Elaine Zimbel, "Margie, This Is Your Father," *KR*, XVIII, 583–94.

76. Peter Taylor, "Venus, Cupid, Folly and Time," *KR*, XX, 169–202; Peter Taylor,

was not much fiction in the *Kenyon,* it was generally intelligent, discerning, and polished.

Except for the "Theatre Letters" by Henry Popkin, Mary Hivnor, and Gerald Weales, the criticism of drama was much neglected during this period. There were a few good book reviews, such as Mary Hivnor on Antonin Artaud's *The Theatre and Its Double* (1936; translated by Mary C. Richards, 1958) and Gerald Weales on T. S. Eliot's *The Elder Statesman* (1959). There were also some important articles, such as the lucid 1955 Wood Memorial Lecture by the British critic D. W. Harding and another slightly revised, enlightening speech by the translator and poet H. R. Hays on the neglect of Ben Jonson's plays in the modern period. Ransom found Hays's piece "first-rate" as a "modern examination of Ben's art": so far the "academics exclusively," lacking in "modern tools," had written about Jonson. Apart from these few pieces of drama criticism, the *Kenyon* published two plays. In its winter, 1956, issue, Act One of Peter Taylor's successful comedy *Tennessee Day in St. Louis* appeared; and in its summer, 1958, issue, a wise, witty, posthumous fragment written by Bertolt Brecht for a theater of child actors.[77]

Criticism about the visual arts was as badly represented as drama criticism was. Only two noteworthy articles were published. In the autumn of 1958, Sidney Tillim described the recently deceased sculptor Constantin Brancusi as an opportunist and his work as "sentimentality dressed up to look like an idea." One year earlier, Alfred Werner had made his *Kenyon* debut with his first "Art Letter," in which he compared the shock the 1940 American Picasso exhibition—cynically criticized in the *Kenyon* by Wyndham Lewis—had occasioned to the sedate reception of the 1957 American Picasso exhibition.[78] Werner soon became the *Kenyon*'s perceptive and respon-

"Who Was Jesse's Friend and Protector?" *KR,* XXI, 395–418; David Cornel DeJong, "The Drowning," *KR,* XX, 362–72; David Cornel DeJong, "When It Thundered," *KR,* VI, 180–88; Priscilla Heath, "The Other Woman," *KR,* XXI, 34–57.

77. Mary Hivnor, "The Other Language," *KR,* XX, 634–37; Gerald Weales, "The Latest Eliot," *KR,* XXI, 473–78; D. W. Harding, "The Progression of Theme in Eliot's Plays," *KR,* XVIII, 337–60; H. R. Hays, "Satire and Identification: An Introduction to Ben Jonson," *KR,* XIX, 267–83; Ransom to H. R. Hays, October 27, 1956, in *KR* Papers; Peter Taylor, "Tennessee Day in St. Louis," *KR,* XVIII, 92–119; Bertolt Brecht, "The Life of Confucius," trans. H. E. Rank, *KR,* XX, 393–98.

78. Sidney Tillim, "The Pedestals of Brancusi," *KR,* XX, 620; Alfred Werner, "Art Letter: Dr. Picasso and the Toothache," *KR,* XIX, 620–25; Wyndham Lewis, "Picasso," *KR,* II, 196–211.

sible regular fine arts critic and appeared about once a year in its pages until its demise. Both the movie criticism and the music criticism of this period, covered by Parker Tyler and B. H. Haggin, have been discussed. In fact, *The Kenyon Review* no longer had a fine arts section to speak of.

Both the institutionalization of the quarterlies as a group and its own internal troubles had turned *The Kenyon Review* into a sadly spiritless publication. Ransom was too listless to seek out innovative writers, and his magazine barely survived on the reputation of contributors of long standing. Particularly with respect to its important criticism department, those few critics who were new were severely disappointing. And whereas the *Kenyon*'s extensive coverage of the arts and especially of drama had greatly contributed to its overall excellence, now these subjects were neglected. In all, following time-worn tracks, *The Kenyon Review* of Ransom's final years was as spent as its editor.

Aftermath

Ransom's Review in Perspective

Changeover

Ransom spent the rest of his life in Gambier and must have run into his successor almost daily, but he took scrupulous care not to interfere with Macauley's approach to the editorship. He announced in *Kenyon*'s autumn, 1959, issue: "This issue concludes Volume XXI. . . . Mr. Macauley the new Editor has returned from his year's leave of absence abroad, and is from now on in full charge. We commend him without reservation to the readers of this Review, and wish him a long and happy tenure of his office. We beg to advise contributors and correspondents that from our private residence in Gambier we shall have no official connection with the periodical." And he kept his word. When, for instance, in 1965, Vernon Watkins sent him a "beautiful poem," he replied: "I am rather overnice perhaps, but I take care not to make any suggestions to my successor . . . for fear he might think I was encroaching upon his freedom; and nobody ever interposed in my own freedom." And he handed the poem over to Macauley without comment.[1] It was not published. Since Ransom denied himself any influence on the running and the content of *The Kenyon Review* under his successors, it will be instructive to compare his editorial performance to the fortunes of the *Kenyon* under Macauley and Lanning. It will put the Ransom years in perspective.

The discussion of the final years of Ransom's editorship, during

1. John Crowe Ransom, "Announcement," *KR*, XXI:4, n.p.; Ransom to Vernon Watkins, October 30, 1965, in Watkins Papers.

which the *Kenyon* had reached a point of exhaustion, may leave a pejorative impression. There had been years of high achievement, celebrated in the glowing testimonies about Ransom as the "presiding genius" of the *Kenyon*'s "most influential years" and about *The Kenyon Review* as a "shaping influence" on the lives of many writers and critics. If, as Ransom was the first to realize and regret, "an issue never did measure up with anything like evenness to the perfection that ha[d] been dreamed for it," Ransom got from his writers "the best they had to give," so that the *Kenyon* was, in Arthur Mizener's words, "the best actual review . . . there could be." Mizener also commented:

It would be fine to see justice done [to] John Crowe Ransom as an editor. Mr. Ransom's distinction as a poet is widely recognized but not . . . his greatness as an editor. Even more than *The Southern Review* under Brooks and Warren or *The Sewanee Review* under Allen Tate . . . *The Kenyon Review* under Mr. Ransom was the focus of the literary energy of its time; and *The Kenyon Review* was John Crowe Ransom. He not only invented the magazine; he practically invented many of its writers, giving them a conception of their function they would not otherwise have had and providing an imaginative sympathy that could make you feel you simply had to do your best because here was an editor who would understand your best and appreciate what it cost you.[2]

In this same volume, John L. Stewart referred to *The Kenyon Review* as "our bible" and to Ransom as "Moses leading us through the deserts to the promised land of poetry." Malcolm Cowley wondered rhetorically whether "anybody else [had] been the teacher, friend, guide of so many talented writers" and had "done so much to establish a sound literary culture away from . . . the busy New York world of publishing and reviewing." Allen Tate was pleasantly surprised that Ransom had turned out to be "the most hospitable editor of his time to new talent." Howard Nemerov remarked on "Ransom's fine poetical gift, . . . undeceived intelligence, and . . . great generosity," which "made *The Kenyon Review* such a challenging paper to write for, and so stimulating a one to read." And Mark Schorer's opinion

2. George Core, "New Critic, Antique Poet," *SR*, LXXVII (1969), 515; Norman Podhoretz, untitled tribute, in D. David Long and Michael R. Burr (eds.), *John Crowe Ransom: A Tribute from the Community of Letters*, supplement to the *Kenyon Collegian*, XC (1964), 17; John Crowe Ransom, "Introduction," in Ransom (ed.), *The Kenyon Critics: Studies in Modern Literature from The Kenyon Review* (Cleveland, 1951), vii; Arthur Mizener, "Ransom as Editor," in Long and Burr (eds.), *John Crowe Ransom*, 15, 14.

was that "Mr. Ransom should receive some lavish award for his long and devoted stewardship. Through his efforts on *The Kenyon Review,* he brought to American letters a new kind of dignity, seriousness and style." One could object that these encomiums are questionable, as they appeared in a booklet published to honor Ransom on his seventy-fifth birthday. However, *John Crowe Ransom: A Tribute from the Community of Letters* was not an official, prestigious publishing venture, but the result of a sudden impulse of two undergraduates at Kenyon College. The willingness, even eagerness, of so many distinguished writers to contribute to this amateur project reveals their real admiration for Ransom's achievements. Many writers of very different plumage—among them, W. H. Auden, Jacques Barzun, Cleanth Brooks, Richard Eberhart, William Empson, Lawrence Ferlinghetti, Northrop Frye, Granville Hicks, Randall Jarrell, Robert Lowell, Marianne Moore, Elder Olson, Norman Podhoretz, W. D. Snodgrass, Stephen Spender, Louis Untermeyer, and Robert Penn Warren— testified to Ransom's greatness.[3]

Also eloquent are the spontaneous reactions that poured into the *Kenyon* office as soon as rumors of Ransom's retirement spread. Philip Rahv doubted whether Ransom's successor would "ever be able to beat [his] performance." Stanley Edgar Hyman sent Ransom "congratulations on eighteen years of a superb magazine." Kenneth Burke spoke of his having "contrived an exceptionally admirable combination of authority and pliancy." Delmore Schwartz felt "devoted and obliged to the K.R." And Douglas Nichols thought Ransom and his *Kenyon* had "made us all better readers, writers, poets." Ransom was not praised to his face only. Karl Shapiro told Robie Macauley that Ransom's *Kenyon Review* was "probably the best magazine in the country," and John Berryman confessed to the new editor that he was "a lifelong admirer, or rather *lover* of Mr. Ransom."[4]

There were also public tributes from his fellow editors. In 1968, Charles Newman, editor of *TriQuarterly,* called *The Kenyon Review*

3. The quotations are all from Long and Burr (eds.), *John Crowe Ransom:* John L. Stewart, "A Little Higher in Spirit," 9; Malcolm Cowley, untitled tribute, 17; Allen Tate, "Teacher and Friend," 18; Howard Nemerov, untitled tribute, 24; Mark Schorer, untitled tribute, 27.
4. Philip Rahv to Ransom, April 27, 1958, Stanley Edgar Hyman to Ransom, January 14, 1958, Burke to Ransom, March 28, 1957, Delmore Schwartz to Ransom, February 2, 1954, Douglas Nichols to Ransom, October 1, 1957, all in *KR* Papers; Karl Shapiro to Macauley, April 24, 1958, in Shapiro Papers; John Berryman to Macauley, June 6, 1963, in *KR* Papers.

"perhaps the most influential critical review in the country when under the editorship of John Crowe Ransome [*sic*]." And in 1978, Theodore Weiss, poet and founding editor of *Quarterly Review of Literature*, spoke of "the influential *Kenyon Review*, magisterially edited by John Crowe Ransom." In 1970, James B. Colvert, editor of *The Georgia Review*, told editors of similar critical quarterlies that they should stop trying to "aspire to the impossible," that is, "to the eminence of such paragons among quarterlies as Eliot's *Criterion*, Ford Ma[d]ox Ford's *English Review*, or Ransom's *Kenyon*," and be satisfied with the "humbler function" of being "wholeheartedly academic." The "great reviews," he pointed out, "are special phenomena. They rise with great literary movements, or even in some cases set them in motion. Their editors, though they may have academic connections, are first and foremost men of letters who possess extraordinary creative and intellectual powers. Their quarterlies are institutions in themselves, reflecting a powerful, coherent critical view of the world. . . . Such quarterlies occur at special historical moments when radical changes in the operating of the critical intelligence are germinating, and when men of unusual abilities are on the scene to command and shape them."[5]

If there was a general sense that the end of Ransom's *Kenyon* closed a historic episode, reactions to the election of his successor, Robie Macauley, to the editorship were, on the whole, positive. Although Philip Rahv had been "rather surprised to hear of Macauley's election," he thought Macauley would "acquit himself well in the post." Judging by Macauley's writing alone, Delmore Schwartz was sure that he was an "excellent" choice, and Karl Shapiro was "delighted" that Macauley was taking over and found him "one of the finest and delightful young men" and "certainly a talented writer." Born on May 31, 1919, in Grand Rapids, Michigan, Macauley had not yet turned forty at the time of his election. Although he had gathered some editorial experience over the years, this was negligible, even compared to Ransom's training as one of the editors of the short-lived *Fugitive*. Like so many other aspiring writers, Macauley had

5. Charles Newman, "Literary Quarterlies, the Modest Mediators," Chicago *Tribune*, February 13, 1968; Theodore Weiss, in "Friends of Promise: Four Editors Look Back at Outstanding Periodicals of Their Youth," *TLS*, June 16, 1978, p. 667; James B. Colvert, "The Function of the Academic Critical Quarterly," *Mississippi Quarterly*, XXIII (1970), 98, 99, 100.

come to Kenyon College to study under Ransom in 1938. He graduated in 1941 and was a special agent in the Counterintelligence Corps in Europe during World War II. In 1950 he received his MFA from the University of Iowa in Iowa City and went on to teach English at the Woman's College of the University of North Carolina in Greensboro. It is not quite clear what kind of work Macauley did between 1953 and 1958, when he became the *Kenyon Review*'s Fellow in Fiction, but a letter written by Ransom on August 11, 1953, gives an indication: "I'd say we'd have high hopes of making a Fellow out of Robie if he doesn't take a job with Central Intelligence, as I've heard he's going to." Whatever Macauley did, he found time to publish a collection of accomplished stories, *The End of Pity* (1957), the successor to his 1952 novel *The Disguises of Love*.[6]

When Macauley came to *The Kenyon Review,* his assistant, inherited from Ransom, was Irving Kreutz. Kreutz's duties were mainly routine office jobs such as "promotion and advertising, proof-reading, layout work." After one year as Macauley's managing editor, Kreutz went to Great Britain on a sabbatical for the academic year 1960–1961. George Lanning succeeded him. Lanning was only a few years younger than Macauley; he was born in Lakewood, Ohio, on July 30, 1925. He graduated from Kenyon College in 1952 and his first novel, *This Happy Rural Seat,* was published in 1953, a year after Macauley's. Lanning had been writing the first draft of this novel under Robert Hillyer in 1949 while he was simultaneously working as a "dogsbody" for *The Kenyon Review.*[7] Lanning remained with the *Kenyon* in this menial capacity until his graduation, when he became the college's director of publicity at $250 a month and, for a year only, an official *Kenyon Review* office assistant at the lordly sum of $38 a month. In 1960 he became assistant editor of *The Kenyon Review,* which took up three-quarters of his time. He was also the editor of the college's *Alumni Bulletin,* which he had singlehandedly de-

6. Philip Rahv to Ransom, April 27, 1958, Delmore Schwartz to Ransom, April 9, 1958, both in *KR* Papers; Karl Shapiro to Ransom, April 24, 1958, in Shapiro Papers. At first sight, Macauley's editorial experience seems considerable. He had edited the Kenyon College undergraduate papers *Hika* and *Gourmet,* read manuscripts for *The Western Review,* and worked briefly at Henry Holt. However, most of these jobs were short and consisted of merely mechanical editorial work. Ransom to David McDowell, August 11, 1953, in Random House Papers.

7. Irving Kreutz to the author, November 5, 1983; interview with George Lanning, October 21, 1981.

veloped from a circular into almost a full-fledged magazine during his appointment as director of publicity. In late 1964, Macauley left for a sabbatical year, and Lanning dropped the *Alumni Bulletin* and became the *Kenyon*'s acting editor at about $7,000 per year, in addition to housing. David Madden, a newcomer to Kenyon College, was appointed his assistant editor and lecturer in English at nearly the same salary. Madden held these jobs until the summer of 1966 when he left for Ohio State University in Athens.

Interviews with Macauley and Lanning indicate that soon the working relationship between Macauley and Lanning resembled the one between Ransom and Rice more than the one between Macauley and Kreutz. Robie Macauley remembers: "George was a . . . wonderful number two editor. . . . We each did first readings and then, if we liked something well enough, we would pass it across the desk. We had a partners' desk. . . . I would sometimes veto, but generally we got along very well, understood what each of us wanted." And Lanning agrees that it was "pretty equal."[8] Unlike Ransom and Rice, however, Macauley and Lanning, though a good team, never became close friends.

In 1982, Macauley recalled that "Kenyon College did not have to contribute an enormous sum of money" during his editorship, "because I found ways of making money that Mr. Ransom had never thought of. . . . It still did not close the gap, but it was . . . a better situation." This is a misinterpretation of the *Kenyon*'s financial state, which was, admittedly, extremely confused. During Macauley's editorship, Kenyon College contributed some $24,700 annually to *The Kenyon Review*. If we consider the devaluation of the dollar and the significant increase in production costs, and then compare the $85,000 the college spent on the *Kenyon* during Ransom's twenty-one years as its editor to the $170,000 during Macauley's seven years, we must conclude that Macauley was quite wrong in thinking that he made it "a better situation" financially for Kenyon College.[9]

Macauley tried hard to make good the *Kenyon*'s losses. In the autumn of 1962 he raised the subscription price, which had remained steady at $4 since 1949, to $5. He sold the subscription list to list bro-

8. Interview with Macauley, August 9, 1982; interview with Lanning, October 21, 1981.
9. Interview with Macauley, August 9, 1982; figures are from budget statements and minutes of the meetings of the Board of Trustees, in KC Papers.

kers, doubled the number of pages sold to advertisers from thirty in 1959 to sixty in 1966, and also raised advertisers' rates. He increased the *Kenyon*'s circulation from just over two thousand in 1959 to about six thousand in 1964, a level it maintained until its demise. Whereas in 1950 the magazine was sold in some thirty countries, by 1964 it had readers in nearly sixty countries. Macauley also made an arrangement with Seymour Lawrence, director of the Atlantic Monthly Press, which was similar to Ransom's contract with Random House. Furthermore, he sold the *Kenyon*'s back issues and, as Ransom had done, books received for reviewing.[10]

Ransom's only interference with Macauley's *Kenyon Review* had been his attempt to give it a comfortable financial basis; to this end he had applied, in vain, to the Rockefeller and Ford foundations. Macauley adopted Ransom's policy of approaching possible donors jointly with the other three literary quarterlies as the "Four Reviews." He played a leading role in these projects, which consolidated the connections among these reviews, but did not bring in money. Fortunately, there existed no danger to the *Kenyon*'s survival under Macauley, for President Lund had promised to "underwrite it for some years at least regardless of what Foundations may do."[11]

Without the help of foundations, Macauley managed to raise the *Kenyon*'s income from $11,280.00 in 1959–1960 to $22,607.21 in 1962–1963. These are the only exact figures Macauley gave with respect to the magazine's income, but one may safely assume that its overall annual revenue during his editorship did not rise beyond $25,000. Taking his few rough estimates of the *Kenyon*'s expenses into consideration, one finds that from about 1962, the magazine was short $2,000 or $3,000 a year, excluding salaries. But salaries were a major item

10. Figures and other information are from letters written by Macauley to Franze Edward Lund, December 12, 1962, October 1, and December 31, 1963, from a letter written by George Lanning to S. S. Lord, comptroller of Kenyon College, dated January 11, 1965, from an undated [*ca.* 1964] untitled memo, all in *KR* Papers; from "Report on *The Kenyon Review* 1965–1966" (TS in *KR* Papers); and from "Foreign Subscriptions *Kenyon Review*" (TS, report dated October 6, 1950, in *KR* Papers). It is highly likely, however, that Macauley embellished some of the reports he gave to Lund. John Lavelle, "Facts of Journal Publishing, IV," *PMLA*, LXXXI (1966), 11, says that in 1965, *HR*'s circulation was 2,180; *KR*'s was 4,070, and *PR*'s was 7,800. *SR* was not listed. Compare the figures given for *Atlantic* (291,467) and for *Harper's* (291,917). Besides, the *Kenyon*'s rise in circulation was not entirely to the financial good of the magazine. Whereas each new subscriber used to mean added income, now production costs surpassed the selling price per copy.

11. Ransom to Monroe K. Spears, August 9, 1958, in *SR* Papers.

and rose sharply over the years. Macauley was appointed at $8,000 a year; by February, 1966, he was earning $12,400. Lanning had started out with a part-time job at $4,350 a year and, in 1966, was making $10,600 as a full-time assistant editor. By 1969, the editors' salaries totaled as much as $27,000. Then there was the salary of the part-time secretary, which came to about $3,500 in 1966. Printers' salaries also went up and, concomitantly, printing costs, which boomed anyway, as paper had become much more expensive too. The number of the *Kenyon's* pages increased from 672 in 1959 to 784 in 1965, the highest ever, to drop again to 720 in 1966—now to be divided over five issues instead of four. This too added to the mounting expenses.[12]

The contributors' rates for poetry were as low during the *Kenyon's* last decade as they had been in the early 1940s, namely, $.50 a line. The rates for critical prose also remained virtually the same: the *Kenyon* still paid $10 per page; however, a second appearance was now rewarded with $17 per page. For fiction, *The Kenyon Review* usually paid its best prose rate of $17; in special cases, with big-name authors, a little more. In the early 1960s the *Kenyon* was, as Macauley noted, still "competitive" with respect to fiction; but in 1967, after the best-selling magazines had raised their rates of payment considerably, Lanning complained that the *Kenyon's* rates for fiction were "not good at all in the open market (where payments run from $750 to $3000 or more)." Two years later, he thought the *Kenyon* again "reasonably competitive . . . because the outlets for stories are steadily shrinking. But we are not competitive where non-fiction is concerned."[13] This indicates an interesting change in the literary marketplace.

Rates for illustrations were low, too, "$15 for a spot drawing . . . and $50 for a cover." Nevertheless, payment for illustrations took up a sizable part of the budget. From Macauley's first issue, the *Kenyon's* cover had been changed; Moholy-Nagy's simple, two-color, charac-

---

12. General figures are taken from Macauley to Franze Edward Lund, December 12, 1962, and October 1, 1963, both in *KR* Papers; and from Macauley to Franze Edward Lund, October 2, 1963, in KC Papers. Salaries are mentioned in the minutes of the meetings of the Board of Trustees, February 22, May 31, 1958, February 12, 1966, and February 1, 1969, all in KC Papers.

13. Undated [*ca.* 1964], untitled memo, in *KR* Papers; George Lanning, "Report on *The Kenyon Review*" (TS, [January 27, 1967], in *KR* Papers); "Supplementary comments on the 1969–70 KENYON REVIEW budget" (TS, January 6, 1969, in *KR* Papers).

teristic cover was rejected in favor of a new cover for every issue. And, from Macauley's second issue, illustrations accompanied each story. These changes were chiefly to "emphasize the somewhat different editorial direction." Macauley noted them in a letter of March 14, 1958, to Lund, stating "a few points of policy" he had in mind for his *Kenyon Review*. In this important letter, he also emphasized that he would "try to get as much fresh and original writing in poetry and fiction as possible"; "would try to include writing . . . outside the field of pure literary study"; and "would include some new writing from abroad."[14]

But if Macauley wanted to change *The Kenyon Review* considerably, he did not want to frighten away its faithful readers. Therefore he asked Ransom's advisory editors—Cleanth Brooks, Eric Bentley, Peter Taylor, Lionel Trilling, and Robert Penn Warren—to stay on. The presence of those familiar names on the masthead would imply their confidence in the new editor and help the transition from Ransom's volumes to Macauley's. Brooks and Taylor resigned, but the others yielded to Macauley's repeated requests to stay on. Besides Ransom's advisory editors, Macauley also invited new foreign advisors in order to keep in closer touch with writing from abroad. A young Brazilian critic, Leo Gilson Ribiero; the British writer Raymond Williams; and George Steiner, a naturalized American, born in France, at the time teaching in Great Britain, all served on Macauley's board of advisory editors.

Eric Bentley and, particularly, George Steiner showered Macauley with imaginative and shrewd suggestions. Steiner proposed, for instance, a novella contest; he proposed that Macauley publish a special issue on the relationship between modern literature and music, or one on the classics; he brought writers to Macauley's attention and suggested to British writers that they contribute to *The Kenyon Review*. He commented critically or admiringly on particular articles and issues, and also remarked acutely on the overall poor quality of the magazine's poetry, on the lack "of a certain unity, a certain presence of voice and manner," and warned against a growing "slickness." But if Macauley often asked his advisory editors specific questions, he seldom listened to their answers, let alone to proposals he had not solicited. Ransom, however, had hardly ever asked advice,

14. George Lanning to Mort Epstein, November 2, 1960, Macauley to Franze Edward Lund, March 14, 1958, both in *KR* Papers.

but had followed up many of the recommendations his advisors spontaneously submitted. The advisory editors during Ransom's and
Rice's days, in particular from about 1942 to 1950, had inspired and
enriched *The Kenyon Review*. Under Macauley, however, the advisory editors had no influence, though he had initially intended,
particularly with respect to his foreign advisors, to make liberal use
of their suggestions. Macauley's masthead looked impressive enough
with the illustrious names of Lionel Trilling and Robert Penn Warren, but was, in fact, a facade. George Lanning had never seen any
point in having a board. "It was a trend of the time. Everybody had
an advisory staff, so we had one too," he explained in 1981. "They
were no damn good at all."[15]

On December 26, 1962, Trilling handed in his resignation, and
Macauley seized this as an opportunity to disband the entire board of
advisory editors. Trilling had once regarded Macauley as "the great
white hope of the Quarterly world" and in September, 1959, was
"quite in accord with the general direction" Macauley had envisaged
for the *Kenyon*. Trilling had come to believe, however, that under
Macauley's editorship, the magazine did not represent "any particular intention or tendency" that engaged his "especial commitment or
interest." It was, therefore, "a kind of misrepresentation" to continue
to have his name associated with the magazine in an advisory capacity. In contrast to his 1959 letter, in which he had described Ransom's
Kenyon as "too special, too 'literary,' too technical, too nearly academic," Trilling now spoke of his "strong general sympathy with the
critical movement that John was undertaking to advance." Macauley,
who now saw his advisors as nuisances, was quick to find himself
"quite in sympathy" with Trilling's "remarks about the anomaly of
the situation" and agreed to omit his name from the masthead quietly.
He informed the other advisory editors that Trilling had resigned and
suggested that "perhaps it would be better . . . not to print the advisors' names on the masthead."[16] Their names disappeared from
Kenyon's spring, 1963, issue.

A new name, Ronald Berman, under a new title, "editorial associ-

15. George Steiner to Macauley, September 1, February 6, 1962, both in *KR* Papers; interview with George Lanning, October 21, 1981.
16. Lionel Trilling had resigned as an advisory editor of *Partisan Review* on February 13,
1961 (Letter in *PR* Papers). C. P. Snow wrote to Macauley on December 15, 1960: "[M]y literary friends (like Lionel Trilling) . . . all regard you as the great white hope of the Quarterly
world for the next decade" (Letter in *KR* Papers). Lionel Trilling to Macauley, September 14,

ate," appeared on that issue's masthead and stayed there until the magazine's demise. Ronald Berman had joined the Kenyon College English department in 1962. His *Kenyon* status was that of "a volunteer editor serving without compensation and working on his own time"; his duties were "finding reviewers for particular titles, suggesting possible projects, and serving as first reader on many manuscripts." He also wrote numerous reviews on subjects as diverse as Augustan verse, Max Eastman, and Leslie Fiedler, as well as a trendy, unimpassioned article on sex in the poetry of the Earl of Rochester. Berman's close association with the *Kenyon* did not improve the magazine's popularity among the other members of the English department. As recently as 1982, Gerrit Roelofs still flared up at mention of Berman, "a guy who was terribly ambitious and . . . on the make." During the editorship of Ransom and Rice, the relationship between *The Kenyon Review* and Kenyon College as represented by Gordon Keith Chalmers had not been ideal, but Ransom and Rice were active participants in the life of the college through their teaching, and were close friends with Charles Coffin, head of the English department. In addition, Ransom's extraordinary gift for diplomacy had kept friction and jealousy to a minimum. Macauley, however, had separated *The Kenyon Review* so totally from the Kenyon community that it, in Roelofs' view, "could have been edited in Timbuktu for all its connection with Kenyon College. . . . In fact, one of the standard jokes was to call it *The Kenya Review* edited by Nairobi Macauley."[17] The complete breach between the magazine and the college, the mutual dislike and distrust, led to the *Kenyon's* isolation. It had hardly any supporters in the college when it needed them sorely at the end of the 1960s, when its reason for being was called into question.

1959, December 26, 1962, Macauley to Trilling, December 28, 1962, Macauley to Bentley, March 7, 1963, all in *KR* Papers.

17. Macauley to Franze Edward Lund, September 7, 1965, in *KR* Papers. After three years at Kenyon College, Ronald Berman left gladly for the University of California at San Diego, but he remained interested in the *Kenyon* and secured a number of reviews for it. Ronald Berman, untitled review of *Poems on Affairs of State: Augustan Satirical Verse, 1660–1714,* in *KR,* XXXI, 708–14; Ronald Berman, "The Convert and the Heretic," *KR,* XXVII, 530–35, on Max Eastman, *Love and Revolution;* Ronald Berman, "Zion as Main Street," *KR,* XXVII, 171–75, on Leslie Fiedler, *Waiting for the End;* Ronald Berman, "Rochester and the Defeat of the Senses," *KR,* XXVI, 354–68; interview with Gerrit Roelofs, September 28, 1982. Macauley made one other unsuccessful attempt to add an advisory editor from abroad to the *Kenyon's* staff. William Webb, literary editor of the British *Guardian,* was the *Kenyon's* "Editorial Associate for the U.K." from March to November, 1966.

Macauley succeeded in his objective, expressed at the start, to include in his *Kenyon Review* "some new writing from abroad." He initiated the series "Through Foreign Eyes," which intended "to try to discover the concept of America and Americans as it is derived from [American] writing." But after only four essays—on Japan, Poland, Brazil, and Scandinavia—Macauley abandoned this series and turned down solicited articles because most of them were boringly similar. Another indication of his ambitious aim to make the *Kenyon* more international and cosmopolitan was the column "Excursion," which first appeared in January, 1966, and which George Lanning continued during his editorship. "Excursion" was to be a "section . . . that touched lightly, sometimes caustically on various matters."[18] In order to shake off the *Kenyon*'s stigma of being staid and academic, the editors invited for this series personal sketches from writers abroad, but if most of the nine articles that appeared were indeed speculative and meandering, they also made for insipid and superficial reading.

Besides these two series, random articles on foreign countries, from Germany to China, often written by foreign contributors, were regular features. The Irish got most attention: Frank O'Connor until his death in 1966 was a main contributor, and the spring, 1964, number was a special Irish issue. Macauley did succeed in giving *The Kenyon Review* a broader orientation than Ransom's had had, but this was not to the magazine's credit. One reader wrote to Andrew Lytle, then editor of *The Sewanee Review,* that the *Kenyon* had "slipped" under Macauley. "So many of his 'international spreads' seem not worth it to me."[19] The series "Through Foreign Eyes" and "Excursion" had quite miscarried; moreover, the articles on the different countries—with the exception of Ireland—were so incidental that if they were not superficial in themselves, they gave only a very partial image of the country in question.

Macauley was successful in adding an international flavor to the important fiction department of his *Kenyon Review.* Of the eighty-

18. Macauley to Franze Edward Lund, March 14, 1958, Macauley to the advisory editors, November 1, 1959, both in *KR* Papers; Edward Seidensticker, "I. Through Foreign Eyes: Redskins in Japan," *KR,* XXII, 374–91; Jan Blonski, "II. Through Foreign Eyes: Americans in Poland," *KR,* XXIII, 32–51; Leo Gilson Ribiero, "III. Through Foreign Eyes: Brazil: Between Dogpatch and Yoknapatawpha," *KR,* XXIII, 394–407; Elsa Gress Wright, "IV. Through Foreign Eyes: Almost in the Family," *KR,* XXIV, 282–303; George Lanning to Mary Hivnor, November 7, 1967, in *KR* Papers.

19. Martha McDowell [Mrs. David McDowell] to Lytle, February 22, 1965, in Lytle Papers.

some stories he published, about thirty had foreign settings or were written by foreign contributors. Whereas Ransom was a poet, Macauley was a novelist and short-story writer. Whereas most of Ransom's critical essays dealt with poetry or criticism, most of Macauley's essays dealt with fiction. Whereas Ransom published a *Kenyon Review* anthology of criticism, *The Kenyon Critics* (1951), Macauley published a *Kenyon Review* anthology of short stories, *Gallery of Modern Fiction* (1966).[20] And just as Ransom's main concerns had been mirrored brightly in the *Kenyon,* so was Macauley's love of fiction. On average, he devoted almost one-third of the magazine's pages to fiction, publishing twelve or thirteen stories a year, whereas Ransom at most had published seven, and his stories were usually shorter and took up about one-seventh of the *Kenyon's* contents.

Himself a good judge of fiction, Macauley rated Ransom's capacities as fiction editor decidedly too low when, in 1978, he remarked:

Fiction was always one of John Ransom's blind spots. He considered it an interesting semi-art, necessary but usually tedious, and he did not read it often. . . .

I respected criticism and wanted to keep up that *Review* tradition—but with rather more maverick critics than John Ransom had printed. I also wanted to do well by the poets, though knowing that my editorial insight could never equal his. But chiefly I hoped that the *Review* could display some of the new talents in fiction. The late 1950s and early 1960s were a promising time for fiction writers. . . .

Under Ransom's editorship, the *Review* had tended to favor southern fiction: Robert Penn Warren's, Flannery O'Connor's, or Andrew Lytle's. My theory was—and is—that a good literary magazine ought to be about ten years ahead of general acceptance, as experience has proved. . . .

So in the 1960s I hoped to find the unknown generation of the 1970s—or

20. The following writers and stories appeared in Robie Macauley (ed.), *Gallery of Modern Fiction: Stories from The Kenyon Review* (New York, 1966): John Stewart Carter, "The Keyhole Eye"; Turner Cassity, "Distances from Berlin"; Hilary Corke, "Someone with Whom to Converse"; Avram Davidson, "The Dragon Skin Drum"; Vincent G. Dethier, "Haboob"; William Eastlake, "What Nice Hands Held"; Nadine Gordimer, "Message in a Bottle"; James B. Hall, "Letters Never Mailed"; Elizabeth Hardwick, "Two Recent Travelers"; R. Prawer Jhabvala, "The Award"; Mary Lavin, "A Wet Day"; Doris Lessing, "One Off the Short List"; Georgia McKinley, "The Short Rope"; Wright Morris, "The Safe Place"; Flannery O'Connor, "Greenleaf"; Boris Pasternak, "Aerial Ways"; Nancy Potter, "We Have Seen the Best of Our Times"; J. F. Powers, "Sailing Against the Wind"; Thomas Pynchon, "Entropy"; Peter Taylor, "Venus, Cupid, Folly and Time"; Betty Wahl, "A Shorter History of the Irish People"; John Wain, "A Few Drinks with Alcock and Brown"; Jessamyn West, "The Picknickers"; and Leonard Wolf, "Fifty-Fifty."

at least some worthy part of it. Most literary magazine editors share this hope and almost all of us are doomed to half-success.[21]

This article clearly shows Macauley's priorities, but it is hardly an objective assessment of Ransom's *Kenyon Review*. Macauley had succumbed to existing prejudices, as is plain from his remarks that Ransom had not published "maverick" critics, that "[f]iction was one of his blind spots," and that what fiction he published was southern. In fact, during Ransom's editorship, many of America's best writers of fiction came from the South and Ransom published them not because they were southern, but because they were good.

Macauley did not discover any writers of fiction who have gone on to great fame, but he published many early stories by promising young or unknown writers. If they did not make a breakthrough in the end, Macauley's *Kenyon* at any rate fulfilled one of the important functions of a literary magazine, which is to encourage young talent by publication. Among the numerous American unknowns who got their chance in Macauley's magazine are Avram Davidson, Vincent G. Dethier, Harriett Gail, Elizabeth Paris, and James M. Stitt. The names of the southern writers Georgia McKinley and Nancy Huddleston Packer, as well as those of Nancy Potter and William Wiser, all of whom appeared more than once in *The Kenyon Review,* may sound more familiar, but they are not widely known. John Stewart Carter is an American *Kenyon* discovery who, with his richly textured and vividly imagined stories, rose to spectacular critical and popular fame. His novel *Full Fathom Five* (1965), which consisted mainly of two of Carter's long *Kenyon* stories, was a huge success: it received the Houghton Mifflin Award and a fiction prize from the Chicago Friends of Literature; it became the Book-of-the-Month Club selection for January, 1965, and a best seller.[22] Carter's fame proved transient, however. His fiction initially dazzled his readers into blind admiration, but after the first brilliancy had faded, it was too clearly imitation Fitzgerald. Among the few American writers who published early stories in *The Kenyon Review* and who have achieved fame are Thomas Pynchon and Joyce Carol Oates.

21. Robie Macauley, "*The Kenyon Review,* 1939–1970," in E. Anderson and M. Kinzie (eds.), *The Little Magazine in America: A Modern Documentary History* (Yonkers, 1978), 74–76.
22. John Stewart Carter, "The Keyhole Eye," *KR*, XXIV, 595–623, and "To a Tenor Dying Old," *KR*, XXV, 567–631.

Quite a number of the foreign writers of fiction Macauley introduced to the American reading public are Irish—for instance, Benedict Kiely, Julia O'Faolain, and Sheila Negig. The British writer Hilary Corke published both linguistically virtuose stories as well as
poetry and amusing criticism in the *Kenyon,* but this has not brought
him fame. However, many of the writers from abroad whom Macauley published early in their careers have become well known internationally—among them, Olivia Davis, Nadine Gordimer, Ruth
Prawer Jhabvala, Doris Lessing, Clarice Lispector, V. S. Naipaul,
and Christina Stead.

With few exceptions, the stories Macauley published underscored
his claim that "most of the possible range of the short story in our
particular time [has] more or less settled within the limits of traditional good prose and good structure. The 'experimental' story—
those elaborate games of language and sensibility so favored in the
preceding period—has little to offer but repetition and . . . sounds
dated and old-fashioned today." In his emphasis on "traditional good
prose and good structure" and in his dislike of the "experimental"
story, Macauley clearly follows Ransom.[23] It is plain, too, that though
the quantity of Macauley's fiction surpassed Ransom's, there was
little difference in quality. The themes and settings of the stories in
Macauley's *Kenyon* did differ; they were generally less restricted than
those in the earlier magazine. In step with the times, Macauley
thought no subject was taboo or could be too explicitly portrayed.
Paranoia, sex of all varieties, Jews, and blacks were depicted in settings ranging from Vernon, Indiana, to Africa and India. Also,
whereas, with respect to fiction, Ransom had usually kept from
making or suggesting extensive changes, Macauley edited freely,
usually to the satisfaction of his authors. As had been the case in Ransom's *Kenyon,* a considerable number of the contributors in fiction,
more than a third, were women.

Some of the stories were published in a new section, "Department
KR: A Section of Briefer Comment," which appeared for the first
time in the spring of 1961 and became a regular feature of the *Kenyon*
until its demise. In its intention "to be more informal than the rest
of the magazine" and "to publish topical pieces," "Department KR"

23. Robie Macauley, "Introduction," in Macauley (ed.), *Gallery of Modern Fiction,* ix.

did not differ much from "Excursion," but in its actual realization, "Department KR" was more varied. Nevertheless, Macauley's belief that "our Department in the back of the magazine" was "generally better read than the front" was a misconception; those replying to a 1965 questionnaire agreed on one thing only, namely, that this section should be abolished. The few stories and poems that appeared in "Department KR" form its most palatable part. Nearly 20 percent of the "Department" consisted of petty communications; the essays in this section also were trivial rather than timely. Macauley incorporated the *Kenyon's* film criticism into this department. William S. Pechter succeeded Parker Tyler in 1961, but his discussions pale beside the brilliant criticism of his predecessor, whom he discredited disdainfully as "not writing film criticism while allegedly writing film criticism."[24] After 1963, various other critics commented on the movies, but their work too remained far below the high standard Tyler had set in Ransom's *Kenyon*. There were also two or three articles on drama in this section. The few other articles on this subject appeared elsewhere in the magazine; the three essays by Ransom's contributors Eric Bentley and Ernest Borneman stand out. In contrast to movie and drama criticism, the articles on painting and sculpture in the later *Kenyon* could bear comparison with those published in Ransom's time. This was thanks to Ransom, however, for he discovered and first published Alfred Werner, who became the regular art critic for Macauley's and Lanning's magazine.

It is plain from the *Kenyon's* emphases on fiction and foreign cultures, and from new ventures such as "Excursion" and "Department KR," that Macauley was an active editor who tried hard to impress his personality on the magazine. The editorial column "Standpoint" was particularly meant to sound the *Kenyon's* new voice. Appearing for the first time in Macauley's second issue, the spring, 1960, number, this column commented on events in the literary world, such as Pulitzer prizes, visits from foreign authors, or books of great topical interest, and on contributors to and articles in the *Kenyon*. Its tone was highly informal, chatty even, emphasizing Macauley's wish for a more popular, less highbrow magazine than Ransom's had been. It

24. Macauley to Karl Shapiro, August 9, 1962, in Shapiro Papers; promotion leaflet, [1962], in *KR* Papers; Macauley to Tate, December 5, 1961, in Tate Papers; William S. Pechter, "Two Movies and Their Critics," *KR*, XXIV, 351.

was in "Standpoint" that Macauley stated his editorial policies explicitly. The first "Standpoint" announced that the new *Kenyon Review* would print "a larger variety and greater amount of fiction than in the past." Marking the first anniversary of Macauley's magazine, the winter, 1961, "Standpoint" was almost completely about editorial intentions, Macauley making much the same points he had made in his letter to President Lund some three years earlier. Besides being informative, "Standpoint" usually made for good reading, particularly when Macauley was much vexed. The column was discontinued after four installments. Macauley had sufficiently expounded his editorial beliefs; discussing irritant books took up too much of his time and it was hard to be witty always; moreover, the "short signed pieces" he had promised for this column never appeared. The "Standpoints" constituted about half of Macauley's contributions. Unlike Ransom and Rice, he figured but infrequently in his own pages. "'Let Me Tell You about the Rich . . .'" is his only full-length article; he also is the probable author of four reviews, one unsigned and three under the pseudonym Zoilus.[25]

Again unlike Ransom, Macauley did not cultivate a regular core of *Kenyon Review* writers of criticism and usually did not publish more than three or four articles by those critics he valued most. If the multitude of Macauley's critics with their widely diverging viewpoints, subjects, and styles gave the *Kenyon* the desired broadness of range, the magazine also became so miscellaneous in nature that it lost its character. Among those who appeared with relative regularity were Eric Bentley, Ronald Berman, Hilary Corke, Frank O'Connor, and Alfred Werner. Philip Young, a pupil of Austin Warren's, was Macauley's foremost and most frequent contributor in criticism. His "Fallen from Time" and "The Mother of Us All" are two classic examples of myth criticism at its best. Two of his articles dealt with Hemingway. In the autumn of 1964, Young first cheerfully demolished about all the criticism that had appeared on Hemingway since 1960 and then went on to an admiring discussion of Hemingway's own posthumously published *A Moveable Feast* (1964). In a very personal essay, Young faced the question whether his study *Ernest Hem-*

25. "Standpoint," *KR,* XXII, 312; "Standpoint," *KR,* XXIII, 158; Robie Macauley, "'Let Me Tell You about the Rich . . . ,'" *KR,* XXVII, 645–71.

ingway had been a factor in Hemingway's decision to commit suicide.[26]

The advisory editor George Steiner also contributed rather often. Among his major articles are a lively, early piece on the Hungarian Marxist critic Georg Lukács, which led off Macauley's inaugural issue; an article "in celebration" of Robert Graves's art; and one lamenting "the retreat from language to alternate expressive forms." Steiner ceased to appear in *The Kenyon Review* after Macauley abruptly informed him about having abolished the board of advisory editors. George P. Elliott deserves mention because his essays are characteristic of the informal tone of Macauley's *Kenyon Review*. His "A Brown Fountain Pen" and "A Piece of Lettuce" are fusions of (partly invented) personal recollections and straightforward discussions of writers such as William Blake and H. G. Wells. Nelson Algren's contributions, two installments of his impressionistic book of travels, *Who Lost an American?* (1963), likewise are representative of this informality of tone.[27]

Yet, with few exceptions, the handful of old-fashioned, more objectively critical articles Macauley published are at least as memorable as the experimental, subjective accounts he favored. This is particularly true of his Modern Authors Series, which was to "give the general reader an informal but comprehensive introduction to a man of letters who has made a secure place for himself in the literature of the twentieth century." In Macauley's maiden issue, Arthur Mizener opened this series of generally appreciative though not uncritical discussions of mainly British and American novelists. John A. Meixner and R. W. Lid each discussed Ford Madox Ford in Macauley's second issue; George Steiner wrote on Robert Graves in his third; and Jerome Thale treated C. P. Snow in his fourth. Marcus Klein's essay, leading

26. Philip Young, "Fallen from Time: The Mythic Rip Van Winkle," *KR*, XXII, 547–73; Philip Young, "The Mother of Us All: Pocahontas Reconsidered," *KR*, XXIV, 391–415; Philip Young, "Our Hemingway Man," *KR*, XXVI, 676–707; Philip Young, "Hemingway and Me: A Rather Long Story," *KR*, XXVIII, 15–37. The revised 1966 edition of Philip Young's *Ernest Hemingway* (1952) was entitled *Ernest Hemingway: A Reconsideration*.

27. George Steiner, "Georg Lukács and His Devil's Pact," *KR*, XXII, 1–18; George Steiner, "The Genius of Robert Graves," *KR*, XXII, 340–65; George Steiner to Macauley, October 31, 1959, in *KR* Papers; George Steiner, "The Retreat from the Word," *KR*, XXIII, 187–216; George Steiner to Macauley, January 8, [1960; wrongly dated 1959], in *KR* Papers; George P. Elliott, "A Brown Fountain Pen," *KR*, XXIV, 62–79; George P. Elliott, "A Piece of Lettuce," *KR*, XXV, 295–315; Nelson Algren, "The Peseta with the Hole in the Middle, Part One," *KR*, XXIII, 549–70; Nelson Algren, "The Peseta with the Hole in the Middle, Part Two," *KR*, XXIV, 110–28.

off the spring, 1962, number, has become a classic example of well-thought-out Bellow criticism. Jonathan Baumbach, appearing in the summer of 1963, pinpointed early and precisely Malamud's main concerns, though perhaps overemphasizing the father figures in his fiction. Although Josephine Herbst's essay in the autumn, 1961, issue was rather repetitious, and although Edward Hyams' piece in the summer, 1962, issue was full of generalizations, the Modern Authors Series was, on the whole, one of Macauley's better ventures. However, in his zeal to dissociate his innovative, modern *Kenyon* from Ransom's, Macauley stretched the truth considerably when he implied, as he did in promotion leaflets, that his predecessor had mainly published articles about "Yeats, Lawrence, Shakespeare, and Donne."[28]

Macauley "did not like special issues particularly" and published only two, one of them the Irish issue mentioned earlier. The other, the winter, 1964, number, marked the *Kenyon's* hundredth issue and its twenty-fifth anniversary; it was dedicated to Ransom, who had turned seventy-five, and to the memory of Rice. It was, perhaps, Macauley's greatest editorial triumph. In March, 1963, Macauley had sent invitations for contributions to many of Ransom's stalwarts, most of whom had not appeared in the *Kenyon* since his retirement. Many accepted gladly, partly because Macauley had promised them special high rates, but mainly because, as R. P. Blackmur put it, they wanted "very much to do something for the 100th number . . . more especially for the John Ransom than the mere 100th."[29] As before, some of those who accepted later reneged; as before, Tate was one of them, as were Francis Fergusson and Lionel Trilling.

Macauley's editorial read in part: "Literary journalists often repeat the falsism that the *Review* was solely an organ of the 'New Critics.'

28. Promotion leaflet, [*ca.* 1960], in *KR* Papers; Arthur Mizener, "A Dance to the Music of Time: The Novels of Anthony Powell," *KR*, XXII, 79–92; John A. Meixner, "Two Discussions of Ford Madox Ford: I. The Saddest Story," *KR*, XXII, 234–64; R. W. Lid, "Two Discussions of Ford Madox Ford: II. Tietjens in Disguise," *KR*, XXII, 265–76; George Steiner, "The Genius of Robert Graves," *KR*, XXII, 340–65; Jerome Thale, "C. P. Snow: The Art of Worldliness," *KR*, XXII, 621–34; Marcus Klein, "A Discipline of Nobility: Saul Bellow's Fiction," *KR*, XXIV, 203–26; Jonathan Baumbach, "The Economy of Love: The Novels of Bernard Malamud," *KR*, XXV, 438–57; Josephine Herbst, "Nathanael West," *KR*, XXIII, 611–30; Edward Hyams, "Peyrefitte," *KR*, XXIV, 484–99; promotion leaflet, [*ca.* 1962], signed by Elizabeth Browne, secretary of the *Kenyon*, in *KR* Papers.

29. Interview with Macauley, August 9, 1982; Blackmur to Macauley, March 19, 1963, in Blackmur Papers.

The truth is that in 1939 almost any kind of intelligent critic was new—and over the years the *Review* has been hospitable to all varieties of them. In honor of Mr. Ransom, we have brought together a collection of new writing by his old friends. Those represented here are some of the critics, poets, and fiction writers who helped make his volumes of the *Review* so illustrious. It is, in a way, a family reunion." Almost twice as thick as an ordinary issue, the Ransom issue had two parts—one, the "family reunion"; the other, a symposium about W. H. Auden's new poem "A Change of Air." The poetry section of the reunion part was truly reminiscent of the *Kenyon's* golden years—John Berryman, Robert Lowell, Randall Jarrell, and Howard Nemerov were all represented. Robert Graves and Richmond Lattimore, belonging to Macauley's *Kenyon* rather than to Ransom's, also contributed poetry. Jean Stafford, Peter Taylor, and Robert Penn Warren, all in the family, contributed fiction, as did the newcomer Nadine Gordimer.[30]

In the critical department of this anniversary issue are Eric Bentley's discussion of Brecht; Richard Blackmur's transparent treatment of *The Charterhouse of Parma*; and Richard Ellmann's condemnation of the current disproportionate search for Yeats's sources. Leslie Fiedler contributed a prejudiced yet sparkling survey of modern poetry, from Blackmur to the Beats, with, at Macauley's request, a laudatory paragraph about Ransom's poems. Cleanth Brooks's essay was the prologue to the Auden symposium, which was "part of a series of such symposia which ha[d] been appearing in *New World Writing*." George P. Elliott discussed "A Change of Air" by combining New

30. "To John Crowe Ransom," *KR*, XXVI, 23. The contents of the Ransom issue also include: Robert Lowell, "Five Poems for John Crowe Ransom," 25–29; Richard Ellmann, "Yeats without Analogue," 30–47; Randall Jarrell, "Woman," 48–53; Leslie Fiedler, "A Kind of Solution: The Situation of Poetry Now," 54–79; Robert Graves, "All I Tell You From My Heart," "To Myrto about Herself," "In Time," "In Disguise," "The Leap," and "Man Does, Woman Is," 80–82; Eric Bentley, "Bertolt Brecht's First Play," 83–92; Nadine Gordimer, "One Whole Year, and Even More," 93–115; Jean Stafford, "The Tea Time of Stouthearted Ladies," 116–28; Robert Penn Warren, "It's a Long Way from Central Park to Fiddlersburg," 129–43; Peter Taylor, "There," 144–70; Richmond Lattimore, "Late Alone," "Lord Bountiful's Raid," and "Begin Autumn Here," 171–72; Cleanth Brooks, "W. H. Auden as a Critic," 173–89; "A Symposium on W. H. Auden's 'A Change of Air,'" with essays by George P. Elliott, Karl Shapiro, Stephen Spender, and W. H. Auden, edited by Anthony Ostroff, 190–208; John Berryman, "Three Dream Songs," 209–10; Richard Blackmur, "The Charterhouse of Parma," 211–31; Howard Nemerov, "The Human Condition," 232; and John Crowe Ransom, "The Planetary Poet," 233–64.

Criticism and speculation; Karl Shapiro cautioned that "[n]obody in his right mind is going to horse around with an Auden poem," but nevertheless had a go at it; and Stephen Spender concentrated on problems of grammar in the poem. W. H. Auden, replying to his critics, confessed that he felt "a little sad . . . that none of them seems to have spotted the kind of poem it is—namely a parable," and analyzed his own poem. The issue was concluded by Ransom himself. As one of the "old and happy gang" of regular contributors to his *Kenyon,* Ransom discussed Wallace Stevens, "a major poet whose magnitude has been dawning only gradually upon us."[31]

The *Kenyon*'s twenty-fifth anniversary, Ransom's seventy-fifth birthday, and the overall brilliance of this special issue were noted in the press. At home, in a long article, *Newsweek* remarked that *The Kenyon Review* "was edited by Ransom with such distinction that both it and the college are associated with literary excellence by intellectuals throughout the English-speaking world." In Great Britain, *The Times Literary Supplement* recalled the *Kenyon*'s first years and showered compliments: "[T]he *Kenyon* has led the way in a revolution in American literary criticism" and the "*Sewanee* . . . the *Partisan* . . . and . . . the *Hudson Review* . . . have all broadened a tradition that is essentially the *Kenyon*'s creation."[32]

Most of the credit given in these and other articles went to Ransom's *Kenyon* only. Whatever Macauley tried, patchwork instead of personality characterized his magazine. His experiments in the review section corroborate this. In his first issue, he started the column "Once Over Lightly," a "section of brief reviews of books by *Kenyon Review* contributors or associates," only to abandon it after one appearance. In 1962 he revived Ransom's "Shorter Reviews," published them irregularly, and, after some two years, gave them up, as Ransom had done, because they usually were mere synopses. In January, 1966, Macauley started the "Bad Books Department." This column appeared only once under his editorship; its reviewers only railed, they did not analyze. And though Macauley proudly announced that

31. Editor's note to "A Symposium on W. H. Auden's 'A Change of Air,'" *KR,* XXVI, 190; Shapiro, "Symposium," 196; Auden, "Symposium," 204; Ransom, "The Planetary Poet," 233. Poet," 233.
32. "Culture and Gallantry," *Newsweek,* January 27, 1964, p. 65; "Don't Bury the Hatchet," *TLS,* February 13, 1964, p. 127.

his review department intended "to provide the reader with guidance not only in the book but in the record market," the addition of reviews of records could not eliminate the general futility of the section.[33]

Futile, too, was the poetry section—and doubly so, when one calls to mind the distinction of the poetry during the Ransom years. The poet most frequently published, five times in all, was David Posner, a Kenyon College graduate, but he never gained recognition beyond *The Kenyon Review*. James Dickey, Leonard E. Nathan, and William Stafford each appeared four times. Although Macauley did not discover any of these distinguished poets, he published them early. Their poems were the highlights of the *Kenyon*'s poetry section. Brewster Ghiselin is the only one to merit mention among those few poets who appeared three times; when Macauley first published him, in the winter of 1963, he had long since made a name for himself. If we leave aside the special Ransom issue, the most renowned among the fifteen or so poets who appeared twice are Jean Garrigue and Howard Nemerov, both faithful contributors to Ransom's *Kenyon*. Jack Gilbert is the only poet of this group whom Macauley published when he was still a long way from fame; others, such as Robert Pack and Lewis Turco, were familiar presences in the literary reviews and had books of verse to their names before they appeared in Macauley's *Kenyon Review*.

By far the majority of the poets in Macauley's magazine appeared only once. Consequently, as in his departments of fiction and criticism, continuity was virtually absent. And, as in the case of the poets he published more often, Macauley preferred those whose work had earlier been in other magazines. This suggests that, as he himself admitted, Macauley was not too sure of his own judgment of poetry. Again, most of the major poets among those who appeared only once—Richard Eberhart, Robert Lowell, Muriel Rukeyser, Delmore Schwartz, Robert Penn Warren—belong to Ransom's *Kenyon*. Ransom himself also contributed a poem, "Master's in the Garden Again," a heavily revised version of "Conrad in Twilight," which he had written some forty years earlier. And while the early publication of

---

33. Editor's note to "Once Over Lightly," *KR*, XXII, 166. It is possible that George Lanning started the "Bad Books Department," because Macauley was on sabbatical until September, 1965. Promotion leaflet, [*ca.* 1962], signed by Elizabeth Browne, in *KR* Papers.

John William Corrington and L. E. Sissman is to Macauley's credit, as a rule the few poems by hardly known poets that he published were poor. The verse is "downright feeble," George Steiner pointed out to Macauley in the summer of 1961; "[w]hy not swallow pride and ask the good poets for some work." In 1962 he still found the "verse very weak" and emphasized that "[p]oetry must always be the crown." But Macauley turned a deaf ear. Although he had set out to "get as much fresh and original writing in poetry . . . as possible," it is plain that, as a poetry editor, he was neither keen nor daring and usually followed fashions set by others.[34]

By the publication of criticism treating themes beyond the purely literary and of criticism written in a subjective or slickly sophisticated way; by initiating new sections such as "Department KR" and "Excursion"; and, particularly, by the publication of a large amount of creative rather than critical writing, Macauley had tried to give the academic and mechanically edited *Kenyon* of Ransom's last years a more lively, more popular personality. But in view of Macauley's notion that "a good literary magazine ought to be about ten years ahead of general acceptance," it is deplorable that the *Kenyon* was no longer actively shaping a literary sensibility, but was now to a large extent being shaped by the latest literary fashions. *The Kenyon Review* illustrated the way, by the late 1950s, as Irving Howe has put it, the "lines of separation that had defined intellectual life—lines between high and middle-brow, radical and acquiescent, serious and popular—were becoming blurred." Then, in the 1960s, political and social issues—the civil rights movement, Vietnam, the first stirrings of the feminist movement—far more than literary ones, which had made the *Kenyon* so central in its great days, came to engage the intellectuals. But, like Ransom, Macauley excluded politics from *The Kenyon Review*. "I felt that a quarterly was not very *au courant* as far as politics [are] concerned," Macauley explained in 1982. "[Y]ou have to be in London, Washington, Paris or whatever to be close to good political writers and good political thinking. So I didn't want to compete with magazines like *Encounter* or *Partisan Review* who did the

34. John Crowe Ransom, "Master's in the Garden Again," *KR,* XXIV, 439–40; George Steiner to Macauley, July 15, 1961, February 6, 1962, Macauley to Franze Edward Lund, March 14, 1958, all in *KR* Papers.

job probably much better than I could have."[35] Besides, Macauley himself was simply not interested in politics.

Change for the Worse

In 1966, A. C. Spectorsky, who "thought that the REVIEW was printing the best fiction in any American magazine," asked Macauley to become *Playboy*'s fiction editor at a salary more than double his present wages. Macauley decided to give this halfheartedly sophisticated girly magazine a try.[36] He got Lund to grant him a year's leave of absence, should he regret this step and want to return to Gambier.

The conclusion to Macauley's career as the editor of *The Kenyon Review* was in violent contrast to its auspicious beginnings. In 1960, everybody had wholeheartedly endorsed the changes Macauley made. Hilton Kramer, editor of *Arts,* had told Macauley that his "new editorial policy [was] sure to excite a much more urgent interest in the magazine than has been possible for a long time"; he particularly welcomed the *Kenyon*'s "new worldliness." Seymour Lawrence had expressed his "great pleasure and delight" in "a new Kenyon . . . concerned with contemporary creative work rather than the more scholarly articles and the New Critics school." Austin Warren, who revered Ransom, thought Macauley was "doing an admirable job of editing."[37]

However, the enthusiasm with which the literary world had initially greeted Macauley's new magazine had decreased drastically within a few years. His attempt to shake off the academic yoke had failed signally, as the trend in the universities—and in the other literary quarterlies—had likewise been to move away from criticism to creative writing, from serious to sophisticated writing, and from appealing to a highbrow elite to appealing to a middlebrow multitude. Paradoxically, then, Macauley's *Kenyon* was much more deeply branded by the academy than Ransom's and Rice's magazine, avant-

---

35. Robie Macauley, "*The Kenyon Review,* 1939–1970," in Anderson and Kinzie (eds.), *The Little Magazine in America,* 74; Irving Howe, *A Margin of Hope: An Intellectual Autobiography* (New York, 1982), 171; interview with Macauley, August 9, 1982.

36. Macauley to Richard West, October 6, 1976, in KC Papers.

37. Hilton Kramer to Macauley, February 8, 1960, Seymour Lawrence to Macauley, July 11, 1960, Austin Warren to Macauley, July 10, 1961, all in *KR* Papers.

garde almost in spite of itself, had ever been, excepting its last few years. Consequently it was heavily attacked, particularly by those inside the flourishing and outspoken counterculture during the 1960s and also by many who missed the wild and free spirit of the little magazines of the 1920s and 1930s. "Is it reasonable to expect these academic . . . editors, acquiescent signers of McCarthyite Loyalty Oaths, recipients of sweet manna from countless foundation cornucopias . . . to present in their magazines any semblance of progressive revolutionary writing?" Leslie Woolf Hedley, poet and editor at the Inferno Press asked rhetorically. Robert Bly, in a leaflet promoting his own magazine *The Sixties,* spoke of the *Kenyon* as a "museum," as "oddly unfitted for MODERN life"; and the critic Beverly Gross compared the "gut commitment" of the colorful littles to the timidity of the pale literary quarterlies she saw as cankerous outgrowths of the academy. Theodore Solotaroff, in his well-considered "The Red Hot Vacuum," praised the *Kenyon* and *Partisan* reviews for having "had an incalculable effect in strengthening literary thought in America and, to some extent, artistic performance" in the 1940s and 1950s, but found them "much changed" in 1964. "The former ideas and values linger on as vague dispositions, without the energy or clarity they once had."[38]

It is clear that not only *The Kenyon Review* but all literary quarterlies were damned and doomed. Macauley, not a brilliant, but certainly a hard-working, adventurous editor, had come to head the *Kenyon* at an unpropitious time. In his vivid cultural history of the 1960s, *Gates of Eden* (1977), Morris Dickstein pointedly sketched the diminishing role of the reviews:

[W]ith outlets for political action and practical change unavailable, the fifties had proved very congenial to reflection, to the long view of things. . . . But the sixties began . . . with . . . freedom rides in the South, lunch-counter sit-ins, and civil rights demonstrations. . . . The humanist vision and the democratic creed were already finely honed; the time had come to push again for their practical enactment. Thus it happened that newsprint broadsheets like the *Village Voice,* in closer touch with the ongoing tumul-

38. Leslie Woolf Hedley, in "Little Magazines in America: A Symposium [Part One]," *Mainstream*, XV (1962), 28; Robert Bly, promotion leaflet for *The Sixties,* n.d., in *KR* Papers; Beverly Gross, "Culture and Anarchy: What Ever Happened to Lit Magazines?" *Antioch Review*, XXIX (1969), 53; Theodore Solotaroff, "The Red Hot Vacuum," *The Red Hot Vacuum and Other Pieces on the Writing of the Sixties* (New York, 1970), 153.

tuous flow of the new culture, displaced the once-preponderant quarterlies like *Partisan Review* as key voices of the sixties. . . . [T]hroughout our culture journalism and political controversy took on an energy and immediacy that had belonged in the fifties to the world of art and criticism.[39]

The eagerness and excitement with which the reviews had once been awaited and read, had now completely disappeared; instead of a keen pleasure, reading a literary review was more often a dull duty. Some of the passion that they had inspired during the 1940s was generated in the 1960s by the reemergence of the little magazine. Kindled by dissatisfaction with the literary establishment and, often, with the political establishment too, this little magazine boom depended largely on the general accessibility of inexpensive means of production. Other competitors of the quarterlies were such different publications as *The New York Review of Books, Rolling Stone,* and *The Village Voice,* which offered a mixture of political and literary interests and reached a wide audience. Thus the sedate quarterlies were played out. Looking back from the vantage point of the late 1970s, Macauley himself gave similar reasons to explain his defection to *Playboy*:

In the mid-1960s, I began to have a sense that the purely literary review was becoming outmoded. . . . It arrived four times a year, two hundred pages heavy, and demanded some long evenings of attention. . . . Along with that, there was the plain fact that Americans . . . were concerned far less with imaginative writing than with politics, social questions, factual writing of all sorts. . . . Readers wanted to know immediately what Norman Mailer had felt at the peace march last week in Washington. . . .

The quarterly review . . . in its responsible role as culture-bearer, is constantly encroached on. Its news value is gone. Its function as a developer of new talent has been lessened by the quicker receptivity of the commercial press.

"For these reasons and some personal ones," Macauley left Kenyon College.[40]

39. Morris Dickstein, *Gates of Eden: American Culture in the Sixties* (New York, 1977), 135–36.

40. In the symposium "The Role of the Literary Magazine," *TLS,* June 6, 1980, p. 637, Irving Howe recalls how he used to wait eagerly for each issue of *Partisan Review.* Ellington White, in an October 21, 1982, interview, similarly recalled the excitement when *The Kenyon Review* arrived. Robert Heilman, in "Baton Rouge and LSU Forty Years After," *SR,* LXXXVIII (1980), 126–43, speaks of the "excitement" *The Southern Review* generated.

When he did, he put President Lund on the spot; the college had no other choice but to make George Lanning acting editor until Macauley decided whether his position with *Playboy* would be permanent. On February 1, 1967, he wrote that he would stay in Chicago. His major consideration was financial: Macauley mentioned "a monetary difference of about $250,000 over the next twelve years." Macauley suggested Lanning as his successor. But Lund, who had obediently followed Ransom's lead when choosing his successor, ignored Macauley's counsel. Feeling that Lanning lacked "(1) a comprehensive vision of policy, and the vigor to achieve it; (2) a sufficiently large circle of contacts within literary circles; and (3) recognized stature," he had consulted Robert Lowell as early as the autumn of 1966 when Macauley had only just left "for the He[f]ner circus." Lowell suggested the British writers Donald Davie and John Wain, and the president duly approached, first, Davie and, later, Wain. Although both had initially been "flattered" and "dazzled," each turned down the offer when he learned its financial terms—an annual salary of $12,500. Wain refused elegantly: "When, over twenty years ago, I first began to read the Kenyon Review, it would have seemed merely fantastic if anyone had told me that I should live to be invited to the post of editor." Nevertheless, he did "not want to leave Oxford" and could not "really reconcile the two occupations of writer and editor."[41]

The end of the academic year was swiftly approaching, and Lund realized that it would be well-nigh impossible now to find an editor from within the academic world. Consequently, he decided to make Lanning the *Kenyon*'s official editor for two years, at an annual salary of $13,000, starting July 1, 1967. Hearing of this plan, Macauley, though "glad" for his former assistant, whom he himself had put forward, nevertheless spoke of "all the old doubts about lack of firmness." The president too still lacked faith in Lanning's editorial abilities; the two-year contract was to give the college "time to take some careful soundings, later to invite consultation, and then to decide whether to kill [*The Kenyon Review*] off or the new direction we

Macauley, "*The Kenyon Review*, 1939–1970," in Anderson and Kinzie (eds.), *The Little Magazine in America*, 76–77.

41. Macauley to Franze Edward Lund, February 1, 1967, Lund to James Bellows, February 23, 1967, Donald Davie to Lund, April 20, 1967, John Wain to Lund, [late April or early May, 1967], all in KC Papers.

should take."[42] The writing was on the wall. Already before Lanning had taken up his post as the main editor, the thought of doing away with the *Kenyon* had surfaced and was not to disappear.

During the interim period when Lanning was the acting editor, the British writer Wallace Hildick had been offered $10,000 to be associate editor from November, 1966, till September, 1967. In his early forties, Hildick had published some twenty children's books, some novels for adults, books of criticism, and numerous articles. He was an imaginative, hard-working editor. Unfortunately, his and Lanning's personalities clashed so strongly that Hildick tendered his resignation after only three months. Lund managed to pacify them somewhat, and Hildick stayed on, doing most of his work at home. On April 23, 1967, however, Hildick resigned definitively. He gave Lanning his version of his own contribution and his opinion that Lanning was too timid and spiritless to be the editor of a literary magazine.

The magazine is now, for the first time in many issues, back on schedule, with prospects of the June number coming out at the advertised time and material for several subsequent numbers already in hand. Regarding the . . . strengthening of the European viewpoint, we have, as a direct result of my efforts, my experience, and the wideness of my contacts, been able to commission or attract first-time contributions from some of the most eminent writers across the Atlantic. These include:

Angus Wilson	Leonard Woolf
T. F. Powys	William Golding
Frank Swinnerton	C. H. Rolph
Christopher Ricks	Phyllis Bentley
Robert Liddell	H. E. Bates
Margery Fisher	Mario Picchi
Alan Burns	P. N. Furbank

. . .

On this side of the Atlantic I have also been active, inducing writers like William Saroyan and Geoffrey Wagner to make first-time contributions— quite apart from spotting a number of publishable manuscripts . . . and initiating projects like the forthcoming symposium on the short story.

That is the record. Naturally, I am proud of it. . . . But it has only been achieved because of a firm and passionate devotion to the highest possible international standards, and I have . . . been disturbed . . . by your own

---

42. Macauley to Franze Edward Lund, May 2, 1967, Lund to James Bellows, May 10, 1967, both in KC Papers.

willingness . . . to sacrifice these standards . . . for the sake of a purely local, purely parochial . . . peace and quietness.[43]

After Hildick had resigned, Lanning approached his former Kenyon College classmate Ellington White, who had edited the student publication *Hika*; he had received his master's degree from Johns Hopkins University. Lanning had first asked him in 1966, but White had not been able to leave his teaching post at Hollins College in Virginia on short notice. Now he approached White in time, offered a salary of $12,000, which was $2,000 more than the year before, and promised an appointment for two years instead of one. White accepted, and his name first appeared on the *Kenyon*'s masthead in September, 1967. Simultaneously, the British writer Michael Mott, instructor in English at Kenyon College, became poetry editor and was joined in this capacity, four issues later, by Jean Farley, a poet and White's wife. When, after two years, Mott left Kenyon College, his place was taken by Philip Church, also a member of the English department.

It was plain from the first that Lanning as the major editor lacked force and initiative; he did not at all desire to make the magazine his own, thinking "the direction we were going in was the direction we . . . should go in."[44] In practice, Lanning's inclination to play it safe led him to adopt Macauley's *Kenyon* integrally, but since he—and, for that matter, White—lacked Macauley's editorial drive, the decline of *The Kenyon Review* accelerated. Lanning continued or revived his predecessor's worst experiments—"Excursion," the "Shorter Reviews," and the "Bad Books Department." Macauley's "Standpoint," which he had used as a kind of stopgap, was renamed "Front Matter." Lanning dutifully published the column every issue, beginning with January, 1967, whether he had something to say or not. Lanning also took over "Department KR" and, again following Macauley, put topical, informal subjects first; memoirs and reminis-

43. Under his full name Edmund Wallace Hildick, he had published, for instance, the Jim Starling, Lemon Kelly, and Questers series for children. His novels for adults until 1966 were *Bed and Work* (1962), *A Town on the Never* (1963), and *Lunch with Ashurbanipal* (1965), all published by Faber in London. His major book of criticism was *Word for Word: A Study of Authors' Intentions* (1965), also by Faber. Many of his children's books have been translated into Dutch, French, German, Italian, and Polish. Wallace Hildick to George Lanning, April 23, 1967, in KC Papers.
44. Interview with George Lanning, October 21, 1981.

cences, preferably light in tone, came second. He kept Alfred Werner as the *Kenyon*'s art critic and continued Macauley's ban on politics in the magazine.

Fiction remained the *Kenyon*'s main section, though Lanning published fewer stories than Macauley had done. They now took up about one-fourth of the magazine's content rather than one-third. Like Macauley, he published well-written, conventional fiction, by realists rather than postmodernists and by traditional Europeans rather than innovative Latin Americans. Unlike Macauley, however, he published established authors. Mainly thanks to Mott and Farley, the poetry under Lanning's editorship was a shade better than what Macauley had published, yet it could not bear comparison to Ransom's selections. Lanning printed about forty poets in his seventeen issues, but he generally published only one short poem per poet. Clearly, continuity was still lacking; the poems were so incidental that the *Kenyon*'s readers could not get an informed sense of the poets. Ransom had devoted almost three times as much space to poetry, had given each poet far more scope, and had printed them regularly. Thus he had enabled promising writers to develop their talent and to become known and so had decisively fostered the careers of poets such as John Berryman, Randall Jarrell, Robert Lowell, and Josephine Miles.

Although Lanning, like Macauley, considered criticism less important than fiction, as always, critical articles and reviews took up most of the *Kenyon*'s content. While following the main lines of Macauley's policies in criticism, Lanning here had some practical ideas of his own. He tried, for instance, to have an annual roundup of mystery books and he planned a ghost issue. Both projects failed. The most ambitious project of his editorship, "The International Symposium on the Short Story," which treated "both the literary and economic health of the story in many parts of the world," was Hildick's idea and was effected after his departure. Famous authors from all over the world were asked to write about the state of the story in their countries—among those approached who refused were Kay Boyle, John Cheever, Graham Greene, Doris Lessing, and Alain Robbe-Grillet. In the end, fourteen countries were represented, most of them by more than one writer; in all, there were thirty articles. The contributors had received the same general statement to respond to, and since most of them were short-story writers, their answers are virtually identical. From Japan to Yugoslavia, they come down to a predictable defense of the vitality of the short story and to a lament about its near unsalability. No less than 15 percent of the *Kenyon*'s final eight issues was devoted to these repetitious, trivial articles, most of which, as even Ellington White acknowledged, were "very weak." The symposium, he admitted, "was not at all successful."[45]

Besides all the insipid pages taken up by the symposium, "Excursion," and "Front Matter," the deathblow to the magazine was its tame book review section, covering more than one-fifth of each number. The insignificance of this section under both Lanning and Macauley is in stark contrast to its distinction under Ransom, who believed that good reviews in their "extreme economy . . . sometimes are all the more wonderful in their easy deployment of critical principles." Lanning considered the review section "a pain in the neck," and his fear to abolish the one section "he was never really happy with" shows his weakness as an editor. Also, the *Kenyon* completely ignored the newest developments in American literary criticism—for instance, the fast-growing emphasis on theoretical speculation (from Europe), the nativist debate on the black aesthetic, and personalist confessional approaches found no room in *The Kenyon Review*. Whereas Ransom's magazine had determined the literary climate in America, publishing the best, often innovative critics, during its final decade the *Kenyon* hardly knew what was going on in this field and generally published mediocre conformists.[46]

In the end, Macauley's *Kenyon* failed, because he made it too much of a miscellany, so that it lost its decisive voice, and because he became its editor at an infelicitous time. But he had at least tried to wake up the sluggish *Kenyon* of Ransom's last years by vigorously changing its direction. By the time he left, his magazine had printed some good fiction, but it clearly was no longer influential and had become, in fact, an academic visiting-card. Yet, instead of sharply altering the *Kenyon*'s direction, Lanning had followed Macauley's editorial policies, but had emphasized the worst aspects because he lacked

45. Editor's note to "The International Symposium on the Short Story: Part One," *KR*, XXX, 443; interview with Ellington White, October 21, 1982.
46. Ransom, "Introduction," in Ransom (ed.), *The Kenyon Critics*, x; interview with George Lanning, October 21, 1981.

imagination, discernment, daring. Lanning published established names and deferred to middle-of-the-road preferences; the early *Kenyon* had published talented young writers and dictated its readers' tastes. Lanning looked for celebrities to endow his magazine with distinction; in Ransom's days, *The Kenyon Review* had conferred prestige upon its authors.

It is telling that Lanning quoted with approval a student who, after intensive study, had found that "'literary magazines . . . are not written just with highbrow professors in mind.'" Even more than Macauley, who had tried to direct his magazine toward the "average non-academic reader," Lanning tried to broaden the *Kenyon's* base, to move away from seriousness in order to enlarge the magazine's popular appeal, hoping to attract as many readers as possible. With Ransom, of course, "making the Review *good*" had come first; in 1945 he had felt "morally impelled" to reprimand Eric Bentley for his commercialism. Lanning, by contrast, was proud to report that subscriptions were coming in from high schools and that his magazine was used "in classroom work and not merely as supplemental reading." He was proud, too, that the *Kenyon* was representative "of only one of the fashions of the day: non-commitment." Boasting that the magazine was "[w]idely ranging" and "completely modern without being frenziedly fashionable," Lanning did not realize that he was fast spilling its lifeblood.[47]

The End of a Tradition

Lanning's *Kenyon Review* was criticized for its sad record in creative and critical writing. Wylie Sypher thought that the magazine had "not moved with the times," that it had been "too cautious about using avant-garde criticism." Robert Penn Warren thought it needed "to be more flexible and experimental." In Allen Tate's opinion, it needed "to find a great editor and let him make his own plans." Robert Lowell was most damning—and perceptive:

47. "Front Matter," *KR*, XXX, 583; promotion leaflet, [1962], Ransom to David Stevens, March 5, 1945, both in *KR* Papers; George Lanning, "Report on *The Kenyon Review*" (TS, [January 27, 1967], in *KR* Papers); promotion leaflets, [May, 1967], [spring, 1967], both in *KR* Papers.

The old Kenyon concentrated on criticism, printed too much as people said, yet set a very high standard, and was surely a much better magazine than the present Kenyon, very weak on criticism and reviews. It is a little difficult to know what the Review now stands for; not only in criticism, but in fiction and poetry. Values, a furrow, a consistency—these are what it lacks. Perhaps the times forbid much improvement, and surely the best editor in the world might have trouble at this moment. Still, I feel something might happen. It isn't the proportions, I think, or having pieces on current events, tho this might work. It's having a very keen-minded editor; such are so hard to find or attract.[48]

These are passages from some of the answers to a form letter sent out, in the summer of 1968, by Patrick Cruttwell of the English department. He asked a number of American writers and scholars to comment on the position of literary reviews in general and of *The Kenyon Review* in particular. Cruttwell was the head of a committee established by Lund "to study *The Kenyon Review* and its possible future." The president himself had long been thinking of "a review still literary but more particularly political and concerned with current social and intellectual interest as is the *Partisan Review*—only the point of view would be right-of-center." By February, 1968, he had come to the conclusion that "the *Review* should not be killed, but that a new direction . . . was in order."[49]

In the meantime, however, Lund's leadership had come under discussion. Weary of the recriminations and of the college, he resigned in April, 1968. Within a month, a new president, William Caples, a businessman to the backbone, was elected; he took office in August. Unlike Lund, Caples believed that *The Kenyon Review* "should be kept as a literary review or discontinued"; he was initially inclined to keep the *Kenyon* alive. However, after a few months, when he had a better sense of the hostility the Kenyon community felt toward its magazine and after he had read the report by Cruttwell's committee, Caples changed his mind. Although the committee had decided to offer the president options only and not to urge on him any particu-

48. Wylie Sypher to Patrick Cruttwell, August 23, 1968, Warren to Patrick Cruttwell, August 26, 1968, Tate to Patrick Cruttwell, August 14, 1968, Robert Lowell to Patrick Cruttwell, August 13, 1968, all in KC Papers.

49. Minutes of the meeting of the Board of Trustees, June 1, 1968, Franze Edward Lund to Max M. Fisher, December 22, 1967, minutes of the meeting of the Board of Trustees, Presidential Report, February 17, 1968, all in KC Papers.

lar line of action, the message between the lines was that the committee wanted the *Kenyon* to continue as "a unique asset to the College of such powerful value." The answers to the form letter commonly emphasized that the demise of the *Kenyon* would be regretted "very keenly" and that the *Kenyon* "could still perform a useful function for American letters." But the answers also showed a "sense of disappointment with the present condition of the Review" and noted a decline in quality "largely because of . . . loss of defined stance." The correspondents had suggested that the magazine "be more vigorous, more enterprising, and in closer contact with new developments in literature." On the other hand, they admitted that all literary quarterlies were "suffering from a slump"; indeed, some correspondents, the committee reported, thought that there was "something inherently old-fashioned, by now, in the 'literary quarterly.'" In February, 1969, severing passages from their context in the Cruttwell report, Caples spoke of the magazine's "present mediocre state" and stressed that "Kenyon could get a bad reputation from such association." Consequently he wanted to "[k]ill it, change it, or sell it" rather than follow the committee's fourth option, namely, to let the *Kenyon* continue as it was.[50]

Meanwhile, sensing the danger they were in, Lanning and White had submitted money-saving emergency proposals such as eliminating the *Kenyon*'s artwork and abandoning its fifth issue. In hopes of meeting Caples' wish that the magazine be connected to the college again, they even offered to teach a seminar on the writing of fiction. By this time, the probable suspension of *The Kenyon Review* had led to an unexpected initiative: two members of the English department proposed a project that came down to reducing their teaching loads so they could edit the *Kenyon* within a severely limited budget. This plan, which would have caused the magazine to degenerate even further, into a purely academic publication, was rejected outright.

On December 9, 1969, it was summarily "RESOLVED, That in order to eliminate the outgo of funds caused by the continued publication of *The Kenyon Review,* the Administration of the College be . . . charged with suspending publication of the magazine as expedi-

50. Minutes of the meeting of the Board of Trustees, October 5, 1968, in KC Papers; Cruttwell Committee, "*The Kenyon Review*" (TS, [early 1969], in *KR*ns Papers); minutes of the meeting of the Board of Trustees, February 14, February 1, 1969, both in KC Papers.

tiously as possible; the Administration to determine the manner in which suspension of the publication shall be handled, and further that Kenyon College will maintain ownership of *The Kenyon Review*."[51] The $40,000 or more the college now lost annually on a magazine that had declined rapidly and was surviving on its reputation was obviously at the bottom of the decision to discontinue the *Kenyon*. However, it is safe to speculate that the ill-will that had arisen at Kenyon College when Macauley took over and that had spread like wildfire when he left for *Playboy* had been instrumental too.

The abrupt demise of *The Kenyon Review* meant the immediate dismissal of its editors. Ellington White had more or less decided to leave Kenyon College anyway. Editing had left him no time for his own writing; furthermore, he was fed up with the interminable wars with the English department. "Thank God I'm back in Virginia," he wrote in November, 1970. "The last three years in Gambier were the worst I have ever spent." To Lanning, however, the magazine's termination came as a great shock. "I can recall when [Caples] called me in to tell me that the magazine was . . . 'suspended.' . . . [H]e said: 'Kenyon College has been supporting the arts for 32 years and I figure that is long enough.' . . . There were rumors before, but I . . . discounted those more than I should have, because from the time I was an undergraduate at Kenyon, it was said that the *Review* was imminently going to fold. . . . I was appalled, not simply at the prospect of another job, but . . . at such an off-hand way of dismissing 32 years of real achievement."[52]

To dismiss Lanning, who had devoted nearly two decades of his life to the college, so summarily was singularly inelegant. Equally inelegant, but less painful, was the way in which the final issue, number 128, was tacked on to the preceding volumes. Had the *Kenyon* ended with number 127, the final issue of Volume XXXI, it would have made a reasonably clear break. But by the time the administration decided to discontinue *The Kenyon Review*, issue 128 was already in press. It was distributed, because Kenyon College disliked waste. Readers learned of the demise of their magazine from an unsavory message the administration had written. Since the exorbitant costs of

51. Minutes of the meeting of the Board of Trustees, December 9, 1969, in KC Papers.
52. Ellington White to Howard Allen, November 3, 1970, in *KR*ns Papers; interview with George Lanning, October 21, 1981.

the *Kenyon* would "penalize areas in [the college's] excellent programs," it read, publication had been suspended. It ended: "We know you share our deep disappointment in this suspension. The loyalty and support you have given to the *Review* are sincerely appreciated by Kenyon College and the *Review* editors and staff."[53]

There was no mention of refunds. One of the reasons was that Kenyon College was busy trying to sell *The Kenyon Review*. In November, 1969, before the decision to stop had been made definite, Caples had suggested to Lanning that he contact people who might wish to buy the magazine. Lanning left no stone unturned. Many institutions, among them Ohio State University, the Swallow Press, and the University of South Carolina Press, were interested in taking over the *Kenyon* integrally and entered into negotiations with Kenyon College, but found the magazine too expensive.

After the dismissal of the editors, the college's administration approached literary magazines in the hope of selling only the *Kenyon's* subscription list at great profit. The college expected them, first, to pay a considerable amount of cash and, second, to fill the magazine's unexpired subscriptions, which came to over eight thousand single copies. Charles Newman, editor of *TriQuarterly,* one of the magazines interested in the list, pointed out that Kenyon College was "asking us to pay a minimum of $23,000 for the use of a list which we could have rented from you for several hundred dollars a year ago," adding that "as *Kenyon* was perhaps the most important literary review in this country for some time . . . it is a disservice to its memory to dispose of its list in such a way." In deference to "the continuity of the tradition of literary reviews to which the *Kenyon Review* contributed so mightily," Newman suggested that he either send one free issue of *TriQuarterly* to "all subscribers not duplicated on our list" or rent *Kenyon's* list "at the old rates."[54]

Kenyon College rejected Newman's proposals, for *December, Partisan Review,* and *The Yale Review* also had expressed interest in the subscription list. But, on learning the college's inordinate demands, they too withdrew. Indeed, the college's attempts to bleed the *Kenyon* white seem unrealistic; some thirty years earlier, *The Kenyon Re-*

53. Statement for *KR,* issue 128 (1970), in *KR* Papers. It is not clear from the AMS reprint of *The Kenyon Review* whether this statement was an insert or put on the cover.
54. Charles Newman to John Fink, February 27, 1970, in *KR*ns Papers.

view itself had received the subscription list of *The Southern Review* free of charge, in addition to $600 for filling its unexpired subscriptions. Meanwhile, Kenyon College had been discussing plans for a new *Kenyon Review,* run jointly, with East Texas State University. East Texas knew that *The Kenyon Review* would bring "tremendous prestige" to its new doctoral program and therefore was extremely accommodating, willing to pay for practically anything. However, realizing that Kenyon College wanted to retain total editorial control and was "just looking for a sugar daddy," East Texas retracted its offer.[55]

Kenyon College had been as careless about the quantities of mail the magazine kept receiving as it had been about everything else in connection with the *Kenyon's* discontinuance. Bills and requests for refunds, for back issues, for permission to reprint, but also new manuscripts and new subscription orders had been piling up since December, 1969; however, it was not until September, 1970, that someone was appointed to try to sort out this mess. It remains doubtful whether the magazine's outstanding bills were ever paid or whether its subscribers ever received a refund. Yet, in all, the college was quite pleased with the swift way in which, in the words of one alumnus, it had handled the "wilful destruction of Kenyon's only remaining claim to national attention."[56]

Kenyon's new president, William Caples, who had been responsible for the demise of *The Kenyon Review,* was pleased to report "very little unfavorable comment on suspension of publication, practically none from faculty and students." It is true, at Kenyon hardly anybody mourned, not even Ransom, who was not much interested in the outside world any longer. But elsewhere, others were "deeply sorry," "distressed," or "terribly upset." Howard Allen was "dismayed" and referred to the killing of the *Kenyon* as "an act of senseless vandalism," as "one more corrosive element in the deterioration of Kenyon's public image." David Madden was "enraged and shocked and saddened" that the college had "axed" *The Kenyon Review.*

THE KENYON REVIEW made literary history. Most writers write the way they do today (the good ones, that is) and most teachers teach literature as they

55. James Conrad, interview with Thomas Perry, September 28, 1983, James Conrad, interview with Rodger Brooks, October 4, 1983, both in East Texas Papers.
56. Howard Allen to William Caples, December 9, 1969, in *KR*ns Papers.

do today because of the essays, the poetry, and fiction in that small circulation magazine. . . .

No literary history of the United States can fail to account for the Kenyon Review; henceforth that history will note that the College's new president killed the Review. . . .

All the good writers in this country . . . will remember Kenyon from now on, not as the college that produced the Kenyon Review, but as the college that tossed it into the junk heap.

This letter is not intended to persuade you to change your mind; the mind that could conceive of such an infamy in the first place is not likely to be swayed; for that reason few writers will bother to write to you personally; thus, you will, quite possibly, feel none of the contempt I am talking about. But because I do not believe that any man is completely lacking in conscience, I am addressing yours. Although you won't change your mind, at least you can feel guilty.[57]

Nadine Gordimer, Russell Kirk, Jerome Mazzaro, and William Phillips were among those who, in private correspondence, expressed their regret in a less outspoken manner. Phillips, for instance, wrote: "Makes you feel that maybe an era has ended, which I suppose is the case." In public, in her foreword to *The Best American Short Stories* (1971), Martha Foley commented: "The *Kenyon Review*—one of the most important magazines this country has ever seen or will ever see—is no more. Infuriating as might have been some of its theories of the 'new criticism' (in my opinion), the magazine never faltered in its respect for the highest standards in literature, and the short stories it published were usually magnificent." Clearly, Caples' complacency about the virtual absence of anger at the demise of the *Kenyon* was misplaced. Yet the outrage was not as violent as one might have expected in the case of a review that has been called "perhaps the most prestigious literary magazine of the century." But, then, the times when the death of any literary review—now the academy incarnate—was deeply felt had long since passed; besides, the medi-

57. Minutes of the meeting of the Board of Trustees, January 31, 1970, in KC Papers; Phil Cooper to Ellington White, February 2, 1970, in *KR* Papers; Holly Stevens, Business Manager of *The Yale Review*, to the Business Manager of *The Kenyon Review*, April 3, 1970, Alfred Werner to George Lanning, November 28, 1969, Howard Allen to Pierre McBride, Trustee of Kenyon College, November 3, 1969, all in *KR*ns Papers. Allen sent copies of this letter to William Caples and George Lanning, adding in a note to the latter: "Should Caples . . . ask who the hell is Howard Allen—tell him I'm a millionaire and he'd better keep [the *Kenyon*] alive or I won't leave a damned cent to the College." David Madden to William Caples, November 9, 1969, in KC Papers.

ocrity of *The Kenyon Review* in its late years was not worth weeping over. Those who mourned, mourned the *Kenyon* of Ransom and Rice, not the *Kenyon* of the 1960s. Even Macauley, Lanning, and White, remembering *The Kenyon Review* in the 1980s, kept veering away from their own editorships and time and again reverted to the *Kenyon* of the 1940s and 1950s under Ransom.[58]

When *The Kenyon Review* was revived in 1979, four decades after its birth, the new editors referred to Ransom's and Rice's magazine as an ideal they hoped to approach, though not to copy.[59] The history of this new series will have to be written by someone else—if it ever deserves a history. This study has shown that the era for literary reviews proper passed in the mid-1950s. Fortune telling is risky, but in our age of chips, computers, and artificial intelligence, one is hard pressed to find indications that in the foreseeable future, literary reviews are again to become as powerful as they once were. It is not that literary reviews, even now, are useless. If they are at present, in a narrow sense, university publications, the review still is an important means of advertising and public relations for a small university or college; if of a decent standard, the literary review enhances it sponsor's image. It confers the same advantages on its contributors, who are mainly academics: to contribute an article to a reputable review means to have published an advertisement for oneself.

Nowadays, then, the function of a literary review is to be an academic trade journal. This falls poignantly short of the ideal, voiced by T. S. Eliot, that "a literary review should maintain the application, in literature, of principles which have their consequences also in

58. William Phillips to George Lanning, February 20, 1970, Nadine Gordimer to George Lanning, November 22, 1969, William Odell, assistant to Russell Kirk, to George Lanning, March 14, 1970, all in *KR*ns Papers; Jerome Mazzaro to Jean Farley, January 9, 1970, in *KR* Papers; Martha Foley, "Foreword," in Foley (ed.), *The Best American Short Stories* (Boston, 1971), xi; James Neff, "Rebirth: Kenyon Review Makes a Comeback," Cleveland *Plain Dealer,* December 26, 1978, p. 1-b. In interviews with Robie Macauley (August 9, 1982), George Lanning (October 21, 1981), and Ellington White (October 21, 1982), it seemed as if all three actually preferred to talk about Ransom's *Kenyon.*

59. "The New Kenyon Review: A Prospectus" (excerpts from an October 11, 1975, report of the special presidential committee to study the revival of *The Kenyon Review*) states: "*The New Kenyon Review* would seek to establish and occupy a literary mainstream rather than defensively to assume a reactionary or an avant-garde position. To do so the *Review* should be prepared to set up its own standards of value, and to revive and appropriate to itself certain past standards of value that have been allowed to decay. The establishment of recognizable, even provocative and polemical positions would, as it was for Ransom's *Review,* be part of its mission." Macauley's and Lanning's *Kenyon* is not mentioned. Report in KC Papers.

politics and in private conduct; and it should maintain them without tolerating any confusion of the purposes of pure literature with the purposes of politics or ethics. . . . It is the function of a literary review to maintain the autonomy and disinterestedness of literature—not to 'life,' as something contrasted to literature, but to all the other activities, which, together with literature, are the components of life." Explaining why great creative epochs are so rare, Matthew Arnold wrote that "for the creation of a master-work of literature two powers must concur, the power of the man and the power of the moment and the man is not enough without the moment."[60] When Ransom founded *The Kenyon Review,* man and moment met.

60. T. S. Eliot, "Notes: The Function of a Literary Review," *Criterion,* I (1923), 421; Matthew Arnold, "The Function of Criticism at the Present Time," *Matthew Arnold: Poetry and Prose,* ed. John Bryson (London, 1967), 353.

Index

Aaron, Daniel, 58
Abbott, Claude Colleer, 42
Abel, Lionel, 5, 164n, 225, 251
Abside, 59
Accent, 116, 162, 163, 231
Adams, Henry, 30, 57, 206
Adams, Leonie, 155, 173
Adams, Philip R., 94, 149
Adams, Robert M., 182
Adelphi, The, 183
Adorno, T. W., 147
Agee, James, 55, 56, 158
Agrarianism, 4, 13, 14, 15, 18, 21, 25, 32, 33, 37, 62, 69, 70, 122, 169, 226, 250, 307
Aiken, Conrad, 155, 215, 216n
Aiken, Henry David, 92, 223, 224, 270, 300
Alcestis, 253
Aldrich, Virgil C., 64, 70, 71, 132
Aldridge, John W., 267n
Algren, Nelson, 329
Allen, Howard, 348, 349n
Alumni Bulletin (Kenyon College), 181, 316, 317
American Review, 37
American Scholar, 154n
Ames, Van Meter, 92, 270
AMS Press, 347n
Anderson, E., 2n
Anderson, Maxwell, 125
Anderson, Quentin, 146, 251
Anderson, Sherwood, 55, 187
Antin, David, 309
Antioch Review, 961
Aragon, Louis, 139
Arendt, Hannah, 219, 221
Aristotle, 111, 113, 130, 217, 218, 289

Armitage, Merle, 44
Arnold, Matthew, 9, 52, 209, 351
Artaud, Antonin, 310
Arts, 335
Ascent, 243
Ashbery, John, 301
Atlantic Monthly, The, 240, 318n
Atlantic Monthly Press, 318
Atlas, James, 38, 59, 137
Auden, W. H., 43, 47, 54, 71, 73, 128, 155, 162, 190, 193, 208, 314, 331, 332
Auerbach, Erich, 182, 183, 184, 185
Avison, Margaret, 301

Babbitt, Irving, 58, 235
Bailey, Frank, 273
Baker, Carlos, 277
Baker, George Pierce, 293
Baker, Howard, 23, 44, 45, 100
Balet, Leo, 147
Balzac, Honoré de, 58
Barker, George, 71
Barnard, Mary, 53
Barnes, Djuna, 253
Barrault, Jean-Louis, 250
Barrett, William, 5, 6n, 36, 39, 67, 155, 156, 164n, 176, 220, 221, 266
Barzun, Jacques, 95, 96, 100, 101, 107n, 129n, 146, 147, 250, 256, 277, 278, 314
Bates, H. E., 339
Baudelaire, Charles, 58, 126, 184
Baumbach, Jonathan, 330
Beach, Joseph Warren, 100
Beath, Paul R., 197
Beats, 307n, 331
Beck, Warren, 128

Beiswanger, George, 80, 146, 251
Belitt, Ben, 45
Bellow, Saul, 39, 144n, 186, 245n,
Beloof, Robert, 292
Belvin, William, 231
Bennett, Joseph, 126
Bentley, Eric: as advisor, 8, 25, 94n, 96–98,
  107, 133, 146, 147–48, 163, 182, 250, 274,
  293, 320; contributions of, 63, 93, 107–108,
  111, 116–17, 146, 250–51; biography of,
  95–96; as Rockefeller Fellow, 95–98, 150;
  Ransom on, 96–98; mentioned, 33n, 35,
  37, 38, 81, 125, 131, 162, 167, 168, 177, 190,
  196, 219, 228, 229n, 252, 253, 290, 294n,
  327, 328, 331, 343
Bentley, Phyllis, 339
Berlioz, Hector, 256
Berman, Ronald, 321, 322, 328
Bernanos, George, 221
Berryman, John, 25, 42, 53, 56, 57, 76, 82,
  115, 118, 140, 142, 143, 158, 164, 238, 239n,
  314, 331, 341
Berti, Luigi, 128
Bewley, Marius, 182, 283
Bishop, John Peale, 43, 54, 69, 187
Bixler, Paul, 154n
Blackmur, R. P.: and Rockefeller Founda-
  tion, 27, 84, 157, 161, 268–69; and New
  Criticism, 35, 176, 201–207, 215; as ad-
  visor, 40, 274, 276, 278; contributions of,
  42, 114, 182, 183, 188–89, 283–86; Ran-
  som on, 46–47, 114, 121, 202, 203–204,
  205–206, 282, 284–85; mentioned, 24, 30,
  38, 41, 56, 59, 60, 61, 77, 78, 93, 98, 100,
  102, 104, 115, 126, 129, 153, 158, 165,
  173, 185, 199, 216n, 222, 259n, 270n, 304,
  330, 331
Blake, William, 68, 329
Bloom, Alexander, 5n
Bly, Robert, 336
Boatwright, James, 295n
Bogan, Louise, 155, 162, 173
Bogardus, Edgar C.: as KR Fellow, 173,
  226–28; death of, 280–81
Bollingen Prize, 153, 154, 155, 156, 158, 160,
  161, 174, 220, 265
Bonnard, Pierre, 255
Booth, Wayne C., 210
Borneman, Ernest, 299, 327
Bose, Buddhadeva, 231
Botteghe Oscure, 232
Bowles, Paul, 186
Bowling, Lawrence, 129
Bowra, C. M., 127
Boyars, Arthur, 231

Boyers, Robert, 202
Boyle, Kay, 45, 341
Brady, George M., 190n
Brancusi, Constantin, 310
Brecht, Bertolt, 58, 93, 96, 133, 139, 146,
  196, 220, 228, 229n, 250, 310, 331
Bridges, Robert, 52, 208
Brinnin, John Malcolm, 139
Broch, Hermann, 220
Brontë, Charlotte, 111
Brontë, Emily, 111
Brooks, Cleanth: and Southern Review, 3,
  60–62, 86–88, 313; as advisor, 25, 93–94,
  99, 103–106, 320; and New Criticism,
  35–36, 53–54, 109, 116, 178, 199, 209, 215;
  Ransom on, 35, 46, 109, 175, 178–79,
  209–210; and Understanding Poetry, 41,
  43–44, 109n, 129; and Well Wrought Urn,
  109, 175, 207; mentioned, 38, 59, 64, 95,
  117n, 153, 158, 167, 216, 220, 277n, 283,
  314, 331
Brooks, Van Wyck, 57, 58, 162, 176
Browne, Sir Thomas, 216
Buck, Philo, Jr., 117n
Buckman, Gertrude, 299
Burke, Kenneth: contributions of, 47–48,
  218–19, 252–53, 286–90; Ransom on,
  48–49, 117, 120–21, 286, 288, 289–90; and
  Kenyon School of English, 168, 169; mentioned, 30, 31, 59, 78, 88, 94, 95, 100, 119,
  126, 162, 165, 181, 199, 217, 231, 241, 282,
  283, 314
Burns, Alan, 339
Bush, Douglas, 177, 178, 179

Calder, Alexander, 98, 110
Cameron, Kenneth, 294n
Campbell, Roy, 58
Camus, Albert, 128, 223
Candlemas Foundation, 183
Caples, William, 344, 345, 346, 347, 348, 349
Carmichael, O. C., 15
Carnap, Rudolf, 64
Carnegie Corporation, 32, 84, 160, 258
Carruth, Hayden, 159, 160
Carter, John Stewart, 324n, 325
Carter, Thomas Henry: as KR Fellow, 173,
  225, 294–95; mentioned, 276, 277
Cason, C., 15
Cassirer, Ernst, 131n
Cassity, Turner, 324n
Cavalacanti, Cavalcante de', 184, 185
Chagall, Marc, 255
Chalmers, Gordon Keith: biography of,
  10–11; initiates KR, 17–26; and conflicts

with editors, 18, 20–24, 33, 157–60, 170–71, 271, 322; mentioned, 12, 13, 14, 15, 31, 32, 58, 79, 83, 84, 91, 95, 99, 150, 151, 167, 168*n*, 169, 172, 224, 226, 239, 249, 259, 260, 261, 268, 269, 270, 272, 273*n*, 276

Chalmers, Roberta. *See* Swartz, Roberta Teale

Chapin, Katherine Garrison, 155

Chaplin, Charles, 250, 254

Charlot, Jean, 149

Chase, Philander, 29

Chase, Richard, 35*n*, 36*n*, 39*n*, 93, 96, 111, 129, 167, 168, 169*n*, 175, 176, 178, 179, 198, 225, 277, 278

Chatman, Seymour, 291, 292

Cheever, John, 341

Chekhov, Anton, 107, 108, 250

Cheney, Seldon, 44

Chesterton, G. K., 8

Chevalier, Haakon M., 45, 57

Chiappe, Andrew, 100

Chicago Review, 8

Chicago School of Criticism, 34, 210

Chimera, 231

Church, Henri, 85, 88, 126, 150

Church, Philip, 340

Ciardi, John, 74

Cincinnati *Times-Star,* 19

Clark, Eleanor, 42, 77, 79, 118, 131, 248

Clarke, Donald Lloyd, 5

Claudel, Paul, 123

Cleveland *Plain Dealer,* 45

Clurman, Harold, 146

Cocteau, Jean, 118*n*, 254

Coffin, Charles: as guest-editor, 180–81; mentioned, 150*n*, 157, 159, 168, 261, 271, 280, 306, 322

Coleridge, Samuel Taylor, 109, 110

Collins, James, 223

Collins, Seward, 37

Colvert, James B., 315

Conrad, Joseph, 187, 188, 225, 297

Contact, 253

Cook, Albert, 297, 298

Cooney, Terry A., 6*n*

Core, George, 2*n*, 36, 233*n*

Corke, Hilary, 324*n*, 326, 328

Corrington, John William, 334

Coulborn, Rushton, 69

Cowan, Louise, 12*n*

Cowley, Malcolm, 29, 49, 123, 127, 128, 129, 158, 159, 161, 163, 294, 313

Cox, Sidney, 62, 63

Coxe, Louis, 51

Craigie, W. A., 95*n*

Crane, Hart, 208

Crane, R. S., 34

Crane, Stephen, 219, 297

Creeley, Robert, 240, 243, 244, 246, 248

Crews, Frederick, 5*n*

Criterion, The, 1, 17, 40, 59, 315

Croce, Benedetto, 217

Cruttwell, Patrick, 344, 345

Cummings, E. E., 115, 158, 208

Cummings, Wilbur L., 11

Curley, Daniel, 243

Curry, Walter Clyde, 12*n*, 42

Cutrer, Thomas W., 87*n*

Daiches, David, 100, 102, 119*n*

Dali, Salvador, 149

Daniel, [Robert?], 128

Dante Alighieri: special issue on, 99, 180, 182–85, 202, 216; mentioned, 186, 187, 293

D'Arms, Edward F., 154, 172, 262, 273*n*

Dartmouth College, 275*n*

Davidson, Avram, 324*n*, 325

Davidson, Donald, 12, 13*n*, 14, 15, 33, 46, 278

Davie, Donald, 338

Davis, Lambert, 26, 34*n*

Davis, Olivia, 326

December, 347

DeJong, David Cornel, 135, 145, 309

de la Mare, Walter, 208

Dell Books, 294

Demuth, Charles, 102

Denby, Edwin, 256

Dethier, Vincent G., 324*n*, 325

Deutsch, Babette, 232

Dial, The, 1, 4, 21, 22, 24*n*, 25*n*, 40, 83, 162, 164

Dickens, Charles, 219

Dickerson, Lucia, 298

Dickey, James, 198, 301, 333

Dickinson, Emily, 52, 60, 83, 283, 284

Dickstein, Morris, 336

Dillon, George, 83

Disney, Walt, 147

Dissension, 70

Dodds, John W., 277

Domino, Ruth, 243

Donne, John: series on, 180–82, 199, 201, 293; mentioned, 42*n*, 54, 106, 109, 170, 205, 292, 330

Doolittle, Hilda. *See* H. D.

Dorantes, Nicholas, 81

Dorpalen, Andreas, 134*n*

Dos Passos, John, 55, 158

Dostoevsky, Feodor, 187, 188, 225

Doubleday, Doran, and Company: and fiction contest, 141–44, 150
Dowling, Allan, 163
Dr. Seuss, 19
Drury, Elizabeth, 182
Dryden, John, 36
Duncan, Robert, 140
Dupee, F. W., 26, 123
Durrell, Lawrence, 295

Eastlake, William, 324n
Eastman, Max, 209, 322
East Texas State University, 348
Eberhart, Richard, 25, 50, 237, 239, 300, 314, 333
Eddington, Sir Arthur Stanley, 64
Edel, Leon, 100, 285
Edman, Irwin, 154n
Einstein, Albert, 223
Einstein, Alfred, 147
Eisenstein, Sergei, 254
Elder, Walter, 144, 173, 224, 248, 250, 270
Eliot, T. S.: and literary magazines, 1, 2n, 17, 40, 59, 315; 350–51; *Waste Land,* 12, 19, 51, 115; discussed in *KR,* 50–52, 115, 204, 205, 220–21; and Bollingen Prize, 155–61; mentioned, 16, 30, 36, 37, 38, 41, 42, 57, 58, 126, 146, 170, 182, 183, 190, 208, 213, 216, 237n, 252, 253, 288, 310
Elliott, G. P., 329, 331
Elliott, G. R., 201
Elliott, William Yandell, 12n
Ellmann, Richard: as *KR* Fellow, 173, 189–92, 242; mentioned, 175, 222, 224, 238, 283, 331
Elton, William, 154n
Eluard, Paul, 238
Emerson, R. W., 38
Empson, William, 23, 30, 35, 36n, 37, 41, 50, 168, 169, 175, 176, 178, 180, 181, 190, 191, 199, 200, 201, 216, 222, 270n, 283, 314
Encounter, 232, 334
Engle, Paul, 95
English Review, The, 315
Euripides, 123
Evans, Walker, 55, 56
Evergreen Review, 8
Everson, Landis, 301

Faber and Faber, 17, 340n
Fahs, Charles, 171, 172
Farley, Jean, 340, 341
Farrell, James T., 119n
Faulkner, William: *KR* issue on, 126, 127–29; mentioned, 49, 189, 213, 235, 294

Feboldson, Febold, 196
Feldman, Irving, 301
Fergusson, Francis: as advisor, 99, 173, 184–85, 227, 274, 276; as *KR* Fellow, 173, 294; mentioned, 35, 80, 100, 101, 128, 146, 165, 204, 252, 253, 283, 293, 330
Ferlinghetti, Lawrence, 314
Fiedler, Leslie: as *KR* Fellow, 173, 185–87, 192, 293; mentioned, 5n, 175, 177, 178, 179, 199, 222, 246, 247, 253, 277, 278, 290, 294, 322, 331
Fielding, Henry, 201
Filippo, Eduardo de, 250
Fisher, Margery, 339
Fiskin, Abram, 128
Fitts, Dudley, 123
Fitzgerald, F. Scott, 118, 144, 247, 325
Fitzgerald, Robert, 76, 113, 173, 182, 183, 240
Flaubert, Gustave, 188, 189, 203
Fletcher, John Gould, 14, 25, 61
Flint, R. W., 132, 198, 203, 212, 215, 222, 236
Foerster, Norman, 47
Foley, Martha, 349
Ford, Charles Henri, 74, 253
Ford, Ford Madox, 16, 30, 44, 222, 294, 295n, 315, 329
Ford Foundation, 259, 260, 273n, 318
Forman, Elizabeth, 93n, 136n
Forman, Helen Ransom, 93n, 132, 136n, 230, 287
Forster, E. M., 55, 119n
Foxx, Robert. *See* Southard, Walter
Fowlie, Wallace, 124
Frank, James, 12n
Frank, Joseph, 173, 274, 276, 277, 278
Frank, Waldo, 55
Franklin, Benjamin, 244
Frazer, George, 86, 88, 150
Frazer, Russell, 202
Freud, Sigmund: symposium on, 71–73; mentioned, 43, 112, 117n, 195, 229, 288, 289, 290
Fried, Michael, 301
Frierson, William, 12n
Friess, Horace L., 133
Fromm, Erich, 73
Frost, Robert, 11, 14, 24, 53, 54, 194, 195, 208, 237n, 229, 291
Frye, Northrop, 177, 179, 221, 314
Fugitive, The, 12, 13, 315
Fugitives: meetings of, 12–14; mentioned, 10, 25, 42, 52, 62, 234, 307
Furbank, P. N., 339

Gardner, Isabella, 230

Garis, Robert E., 256n
Garrigue, Jean, 74, 75, 104, 137, 139, 142, 238, 300, 333
Gass, William, 212
Gail, Harriett, 325
Geisel, Theodor. See Dr. Seuss
Geismar, Maxwell, 117
Geoffrey, William, 221
Georgia Review, The, 8, 315
Gershwin, George, 44
Ghiselin, Brewster, 333
Gibson, Richard Thomas, 158n, 248, 250
Gide, André, 123
Gifford, Henry, 297
Gilbert, Jack, 333
Gilbert, James, 5
Gilbert, Katharine, 212
Ginsberg, Allen, 306n, 307n
Goedicke, Patricia, 301
Goethe, Johann Wolfgang von, 123
Gogol, Nikolai, 117n
Golding, William, 299, 339
Goll, Ivan, 233n
Goodman, Paul, 79, 82, 119n, 175, 192, 195, 196, 199, 208, 209n, 221, 222, 248, 282, 283, 306
Goodman, Percival, 82
Gordimer, Nadine, 324n, 326, 331, 349
Gordon, Caroline, 18, 79, 128, 247
Gottlieb, Beatrice, 257
Gottlieb, Elaine, 145, 248
Gourmet, 316n
Gourmont, Rémy de, 126, 288
Goyen, William, 247
Graff, Louis, 149
Granville-Barker, H., 146
Graves, Robert, 193, 329, 331
Green, F. L., 186
Green, Henry, 219
Green, Martin, 299
Green, Paul, 155
Greenberg, Clement, 158
Greene, Graham, 283, 341
Greenslade, Thomas Boardman, 273n
Gregor, Arthur, 301
Gregory, Horace, 129n
Grene, Marjorie, 131, 132
Grimshaw, James A., Jr., 235n
Gropius, Walter, 133, 148
Gross, Beverly, 3n, 336
Guardian, The, 322n
Guerard, Albert J., 277
Guiguet, Jean, 124
Gulette, [?], 62

Haffenden, John, 239n
Haggin, B. H., 44, 147, 256, 311
Hall, Donald, 277, 301
Hall, James, 297
Hall, James B., 324n
Hamilton, Ian, 5n
Harding, D. W., 182, 310
Hardwick, Elizabeth, 39, 246, 247n, 324n
Hardy, John Edward, 108
Hardy, Thomas, 208
Harper's, 240, 318n
Harridges, Anthony, 277
Hartley, Marsden, 255
Hathorn, Isabel, 246
Hayes, H. R., 310
Hazard, Paul, 83
H. D., 114
Heath, Priscilla, 243, 250, 309
Hecht, Anthony, 228, 229, 233, 239
Hedley, Leslie Woolf, 336
Hefner, Hugh, 338
Hegel, Georg W. F., 149, 210, 211
Heidegger, Martin, 131, 223
Heilman, Robert, 109n, 117n, 201, 337n
Hemingway, Ernest, 113, 213, 219, 328, 329
Hemphill, George, 132, 256n, 292
Henderson, Bill, 2n
Henry Holt, 127, 134, 144, 316n
Herbst, Josephine, 330
Hercules, 234
Herschberger, Ruth, 74, 132, 193, 238
Herskovits, M. J., 197
Herzing, Albert, 306
Hicks, Granville, 162, 266, 314
Hika, 316n, 340
Hildick, Wallace, 339, 340, 341
Hillyer, Robert: and Bollingen Prize, 156–60, 170; mentioned, 270, 316
Hirsch, Sidney Mttron, 12
Hitler, Adolf, 70
Hivnor, Mary, 252, 310
Hodgson, Ralph, 173
Hoffman, Frederick J., 1n, 116, 162, 163, 298
Hoffman, Theodore: as *KR* Fellow, 173, 251–52, 293–94; mentioned, 196
Hollander, John, 292, 301
Holmes, Sherlock, 200
Holmes, Theodore Henry: as *KR* Fellow, 173, 304–305
Honig, Edwin, 301, 302
Hook, Sidney, 39, 131n
Hoor, Marten ten, 64, 71, 212
Hopkins, Gerard Manley: special issues on, 93, 99, 103–107, 181, 185; mentioned, 42, 52

Hopkins Review, 277
Horizon Press, 188*n*
Horney, Karen, 72, 73
Horrell, Joe, 61, 62
Houghton Mifflin, 325
Hound & Horn, The, 1, 4, 22, 24, 38, 40, 44, 100, 103
Housman, A. E., 49, 54, 194, 208, 295
Howe, Irving: as *KR* Fellow, 173, 174, 187–88, 192; mentioned, 5, 6*n*, 39, 50, 56, 118, 156*n*, 164*n*, 199, 222, 225, 290, 334, 337*n*
Hudson Review, The, 2, 3, 153, 159, 172, 176*n*, 188, 199*n*, 222, 240, 263, 301, 302, 318*n*, 332
Hulbert, J. R., 95*n*
Humanism, 34, 35, 47, 57, 210
Huxley, Aldous, 123
Hyams, Edward, 330
Hyman, Stanley Edgar, 175, 196, 197, 198, 199, 221, 222, 225, 277, 283, 314
Hytier, Jean, 124, 128

Ibsen, Henrik, 107, 108
Indiana University, 19, 93, 95, 157, 158, 160, 171, 177, 247, 257, 258, 267, 268, 275, 296, 297
Inferno Press, 336
Intercultural Publications, Inc., 260, 262
Inventario, 128
Iremonger, Valentin, 190*n*
Isère, Jean, *See* Guiguet, Jean

Jaeger, Werner, 131*n*
James, Henry: issue on, 94, 99–103, 105, 106; mentioned, 57, 58, 108, 114, 119*n*, 142, 219
James, William, 102
Janssens, G. A. M., 1, 87*n*
Jarrell, Mary Von Schrader, 194*n*, 273*n*
Jarrell, Randall: contributions of, 49, 52, 54, 75, 114–15, 135, 136, 194–95, 236, 245–46; Ransom on, 194, 276; as Ransom's possible successor, 276–79; mentioned, 7, 15*n*, 16, 21*n*, 31, 32, 39, 44, 50, 59, 76*n*, 78, 83, 94, 133, 137, 139, 158, 162, 163, 165, 170, 189, 192, 193, 199, 200, 210, 222, 234, 239, 243, 266, 273, 280, 292, 314, 331, 341
Jaspers, Karl, 131
Jeffers, Robinson, 123
Jhabvala, Ruth Prawer, 324*n*, 326
John Reed Club, 4
Johnson, Norman, 21, 23, 26*n*
Johnson, Samuel, 36, 109, 110, 216
Johnson, Stanley, 12*n*

Johnson, Thomas H., 283
Jones, Ernest, 173
Jonson, Ben, 310
Joost, Nicholas, 277
Joseph, Sister Miriam, 218
Joyce, James, 58, 117*n*, 124, 127, 190, 191, 199, 221
Jung, C. G., 156, 288
Justus, James H., 140*n*

Kafka, Franz, 43, 217
Kahler, Erich, 143
Kant, Immanuel, 32, 211
Karanikas, Alexander, 13*n*
Kardiner, Abram, 73
Karr, E. R., 249
Kaufmann, Walter, 223, 300
Kavaphes, Konstantinos, 302
Kazin, Alfred, 5, 6*n*, 38, 39, 100, 101, 158, 162, 163
Keats, John, 106
Kees, Weldon, 76
Kenner, Hugh, 221
Kenyon College: writers at/from, 7*n*, 136, 173, 218, 227, 229, 230, 243, 249–50, 262*n*, 274, 305, 316, 322, 333, 340; and *KR* budget, 16–21, 84–85, 87, 258–59, 261, 268–69, 272, 275, 317–19; and suspension of *KR,* 338–39, 344–49
Kenyon Collegian, 157
Kenyon Review, The: comparison with other literary magazines, 1–5, 8–9, 161–65, 265–67, 313, 332, 334–35, 336–37; scope of, 21–23; advisors of, 23–25, 93–99, 320–21; business aspects of, 25–29, 84–88, 141–42, 149–51, 163, 171–72, 240, 258–63, 268–69, 308–309, 317–20; cover of, 29–30, 319–20; and poetry, 30–31, 44, 73–78, 134–40, 226–39, 300–306, 333–34, 341; and politics, 32–33, 69–71, 133–34, 135, 225–26, 334–36; and New Criticism, 33–43, 46–54, 56, 59, 114–17, 122, 174, 179, 199–201, 206–211, 214–18, 221–22, 292–94; and New York intellectuals, 38–41, 43, 54–56, 59, 117–19, 122, 145, 219–21, 295–97; and criticism, 43, 57–59, 123–25, 174–79, 185–99, 201–211, 218–19, 221–22, 293–95, 297–99, 328–30; and pedagogics, 43–44, 60–63, 129; and arts, 44, 80–82, 147–49, 253–57, 310–11; and *Southern Review,* 60–63, 86–90, 100; and philosophy, 64–69, 129–32, 211–12, 222–24, 300; and psychology, 71–73; and special interests, issues, symposia, and series, 71–73, 99–114, 126–29, 132–33,

174–79, 180–85, 290–92, 323, 326–28, 330–33, 340–42; and fiction, 78–80, 140–45, 239–50, 306–310, 324–26, 341; and drama, 80, 107–108, 133, 145–47, 250–53, 310; and Rockefeller Foundation, 84, 94–99, 150–51, 153, 165–74, 258–63; international aspects of, 127–29, 323–24, 326, 341–42; and the academy, 153–54, 265–67, 335–36; and search for Ransom's successor, 272–80, 338

Kenyon School of English: founding of, 165–67; staff of, 167–70; demise of, 170–72; links of, with *KR*, 176, 177, 222; mentioned, 35*n*, 199, 251, 257

Kermode, Frank, 299

Kiely, Benedict, 326

Kierkegaard, Søren, 118*n*, 131, 132, 223, 300

Kinne, Wisner P., 293, 294*n*

Kinzie, M., 2*n*

Kirk, Russell, 226, 275, 277, 278, 279, 294, 349

Kirkland, James H., 15, 16

Kirstein, Lincoln, 80

Klee, Paul, 149

Klein, Marcus, 329

Kline, Henry Blue, 14*n*

Kline, Peter, 297

Klitgaard, Kaj, 173

Kluckhohn, Clyde, 70, 212

Knight, G. Wilson, 197

Knights, L. C., 110, 111, 168

Koch, Vivienne, 191, 216

Koestler, Arthur, 119, 219

Kramer, Hilton, 335

Kreutz, Irving, 281, 316, 317

Krieger, Murray, 200, 274, 297

Kristol, Irving, 293*n*

Krutch, Joseph Wood, 72, 80, 110

La Fontaine, Jean de, 238

Landis, Bernard, 198

Langer, Susanne K., 131*n*, 224

Lanier, Lyle, 14*n*, 15

Lanning, George: as editor, 9, 312, 316–17, 319, 321, 323, 327, 333*n*, 338–47, 350; as *KR* Fellow, 173, 242; biography of, 316; mentioned, 27, 157, 203, 248, 250, 262*n*, 349*n*

Lansner, Kermit, 218, 219, 222*n*, 223, 255, 270

Lattimore, Richmond, 302, 331

Laughlin, James, 42, 76, 77, 86, 103, 259, 260, 284

Lautréamont, Isidore Ducasse, 118*n*

Lavelle, John, 318*n*

Lavin, Mary, 144, 324*n*

Lawrence, D. H., 50, 69, 330

Lawrence, Seymour, 318, 335

Leavis, F. R., 96, 106, 107, 109, 110, 111, 129*n*, 170, 177, 179, 199, 200

Lebowitz, Martin, 123

Le Corbusier, 82, 195

Lee, Elizabeth, 74

Leibowitz, René, 256

Leighton, Lawrence, 124, 127

Lessing, Doris, 324*n*, 326, 341

Le Sueur, Meridel, 145

Levi, Albert William, 300

Levin, Harry, 61, 62, 111, 117*n*, 215, 216*n*

Lewis, C. D., 193

Lewis, R. W. B.: as *KR* Fellow, 173, 188–89, 192; mentioned, 199, 222, 283

Lewis, Sinclair, 55

Lewis, Wyndham, 81, 294, 310

Lidd, R. W., 329

Liddell, Henry George, 287

Liddell, Robert, 339

Lindsay, Vachel, 208

Lispector, Clarice, 326

Little Review, The, 100, 162

Lobdell, D. H., 157

Lockridge, Ross, 186

Logan, John, 301

Longstaff, S. A., 5*n*

Longview Foundation, 244, 302

Lorca, Federico Garcia, 77, 252

Louchheim, Aline B., 159

Louisiana State University, 61, 86, 87, 88, 109*n*, 277*n*, 337*n*

Lovejoy, Arthur, 72

Lowell, Robert: contributions of, 44, 75, 106, 136–37, 236–36; mentioned, 7, 15*n*, 31, 32, 33, 82, 104, 105, 114, 125, 139, 155, 168, 194*n*, 231, 239, 268, 270, 274, 277, 278, 280, 292, 314, 331, 333, 338, 341, 343

Lukács, Georg, 329

Lund, Franze Edward, 272, 275, 276, 277, 278, 279, 280, 308, 309, 318, 320, 328, 335, 338, 339, 344

Lytle, Andrew: as Agrarian, 14–16; as *KR* Fellow, 173, 307–308; mentioned, 79, 144, 164, 281, 323, 324

McCarthy, Joseph, 224, 225, 336

McCarthy, Mary, 39

Macauley, Robie: as editor, 8, 9, 27, 29, 126, 199, 242*n*, 251, 252, 274–82, 308, 312, 315, 317–38, 340–43, 346, 350; contributions of, 58, 222, 244–45, 331; and *Gallery of Modern Fiction,* 144–45, 241, 245, 246, 308,

309, 324; as *KR* Fellow, 173, 280,
307–308, 316; biography of, 315–16; men-
tioned, 198, 219, 243, 250, 270, 295*n*, 314
McClellan, Edward, 277
MacDiarmid, Hugh, 198
MacDonagh, Donagh, 190
Macdonald, Dwight, 4, 39, 58, 101, 140
Macdonald, Nancy, 101
MacDonough, Patrick, 190*n*
McDowell, David, 15*n*, 16, 33, 48, 55, 92,
179, 237, 238, 244, 248, 270
McFadden, Roy, 190
McGuire, Edgar, 243, 250
McGuire, William, 156*n*
McKinley, Georgia, 324*n*, 325
MacLeish, Archibald, 24
Macleod, Norman, 193
McLuhan, Herbert Marshall, 105
MacNeice, Louis, 71, 77
Madden, David, 317, 348
Magg, P., 94*n*
Magny, Claude-Edmonde, 221
Mailer, Norman, 337
Malamud, Bernard, 330
Mallarmé, Stéphane, 126
Malraux, André, 57
Mann, Klaus, 70
Mann, Thomas, 70, 186, 203, 212
Manning, Olivia, 145*n*
Marcel, Gabriel, 131, 223
Marcus, Steven, 258
Maritain, Jacques, 182, 183, 184
Marlowe, Christopher, 216*n*
Marshfield, Alan, 301
Marshall, John, 40, 84, 103, 124, 156, 161,
163, 166, 174, 192, 206, 240, 258, 262, 268,
269, 281, 307, 308
Marshall, Margaret, 21*n*, 276
Martin, Alexander Reid, 72, 73
Martin, [Carter W.?], 241
Marxism, 35, 37, 43, 47, 48, 57, 164, 187,
207, 209, 296
Masefield, John, 208
Massachusetts Review, The, 8
Mathews, Jackson, 124
Matthiessen, F. O.: and Kenyon School of
English, 166–67, 169–70, 177; mentioned,
35, 37, 58, 100, 102, 115, 119*n*, 128, 199,
221, 222
Mauriac, François, 124, 221
Maurois, André, 83
May, Karl, 70, 71
Mayberry, George, 162
Mazzaro, Jerome, 349
Meixner, John A., 329

Mellers, W. H., 81
Mellon, Paul, 160, 258, 268
Mellquist, Jerome, 81, 94
Melville, Herman, 113, 126, 225, 230, 235
Mencken, H. L., 116
Mercier, Vivian, 298
Mercure de France, 183
Merleau-Ponty, Maurice, 225
Merrill, James, 230, 239, 300
Merwin, William S.: as *KR* Fellow, 173,
226–29; mentioned, 232, 233, 239, 300
Mesures, 85, 126
Mezey, Robert, 229, 230, 239, 300
Michaux, Henri, 191, 192, 238
Milano, Paolo, 182
Miles, Josephine, 66, 76, 82, 104, 105, 106,
137, 139, 181, 182, 238, 239*n*, 292, 300, 341
Miller, Henry, 295
Miller, L. L., 182
Millett, Fred B., 129*n*
Millspaugh, C. A., 45
Milton, John, 106, 108, 290, 293
Minerva, 235
Minnesota Review, The, 8
Mitchner, Ann, 240
Mizener, Arthur: contributions of, 80,
104–106, 114–15, 143–45, 179, 213–16,
247–48; mentioned, 35, 38, 61, 62, 93,
107, 125, 158, 165, 168, 173, 175, 202, 222,
270*n*, 283, 313, 329
Modern Age, 275, 277
Moholy-Nagy, Laszlo, 29, 82, 319
Monnier, Adrienne, 124
Monroe, Elizabeth, 117*n*
Montesi, A. J., 87*n*
Moore, Lillian, 80
Moore, Marianne, 24, 77, 78, 100, 103, 114,
162, 173, 208, 215, 238, 292, 314
Moore, Merrill, 12*n*, 26, 52, 53, 232, 303
Moore, T. Sturge, 52
Morgan, Frederick, 301
Morris, A. C., 197
Morris, Charles W., 64, 65, 66, 92, 120
Morris, Wright, 243, 245, 246, 324*n*
Morse, Samuel French, 135
Mortimer, Ronald Lane, 253
Moses, 313
Moses, W. R., 53
Moss, Howard, 74, 136
Mott, Michael, 340, 341
Mount Vernon (Ohio) *News,* 70
Mozart, Wolfgang Amadeus, 147
Mudrick, Marvin, 297
Muir, Edwin, 285
Munch, Edvard, 255

Munro, Thomas, 94
Murphy, Arthur E., 224

Nabokov, Vladimir, 117*n*, 274, 295
Nagel, Ernest, 64, 72, 223
Nahas, Gabriel, 238
Naipaul, V. S., 326
Napoleon, 235
Nashville *Banner*, 263
Nashville *Tennessean*, 15
Nathan, Leonard E., 333
Nation, The, 19, 44, 96, 138, 147, 159, 173, 256, 266, 276
Negig, Sheila, 326
Neider, Charles, 186
Nemerov, Howard: as *KR* Fellow, 173, 192–93, 242–43, 295; as Ransom's possible successor, 274–79; mentioned, 74, 75, 83, 140, 158, 194, 199, 222, 287, 301, 313, 331, 333
Nerber, John, 15*n*, 74, 262*n*
Neue Rundschau, Die, 143
Neurath, Otto, 64
Newby, P. H., 298
New Criticism: characterization of, 33–39, 169*n;* New Critical contributions in *KR*, 41–43, 46–54, 56, 59, 105–107, 109–111, 114–17, 178–79, 180–82, 183–85, 199–201, 214–18, 221–22; Ransom's move away from, 111–13, 175, 206–211, 214; mentioned, 5, 7, 8, 40, 55, 58, 80, 92, 99, 122, 123, 132, 153, 154*n*, 156, 157, 170, 174, 176, 192, 194, 197, 202, 205, 213, 235, 265, 280, 288, 290, 330, 332, 335, 349
New Directions, 42
New Directions, 53, 76*n*, 80, 86, 103, 177
Newell, H. Louis, 249
Newhall, Beaumont, 82
Newman, Charles, 314, 347
Newman, William, 263
New Republic, The, 29, 120, 138, 251*n*, 252
Newsweek, 151, 332
New World Writing, 331
New Yorker, The, 240, 245, 246
New York *Herald Tribune*, 89, 263
New York intellectuals: characterization of, 38–39; contributions of, to *KR*, 43, 54–56, 117–19, 145, 187–88, 219–21, 295–97; mentioned, 7, 40, 41, 50, 58, 59, 92, 122, 123, 164, 174, 199
New York Review of Books, The, 9, 337
New York *Times*, 262*n*
New York Times Book Review, The, 226*n*
Nichols, Douglas: as *KR* Fellow, 173, 226–28; mentioned, 314

Niebuhr, Reinhold, 67
Nierendorf, Karl, 149
Nin, Anaïs, 145*n*
Nixon, Herman Clarence, 14*n*
Nobbe, George, 147
Nouvelle Revue Française, La, 1, 59
Nowell-Smith, Simon, 219

Oates, Joyce Carol, 325
O'Brien, Conor Cruise, 123, 221
O'Brien, Justin, 58, 63, 71, 83
O'Connor, Flannery: as *KR* Fellow, 173, 174, 240–43; mentioned, 294, 295*n*, 324
O'Connor, Frank, 323, 328
O'Connor, William Van, 297, 309
O'Donnell, Donat. *See* O'Brien, Conor Cruise
O'Donnell, George Marion, 15, 30, 32, 49, 53
O'Faolain, Julia, 326
O'Faoláin, Seán, 221, 247
O. Henry. *See* Porter, William Sidney
Ohio State University, 347
Olson, Elder, 314
O'Neill, Eugene, 250
Ong, Walter J., 300
Ortega y Gasset, José, 129*n*, 220
Ostroff, Anthony, 309
Owsley, Frank Lawrence, 14*n*

Pack, Robert, 333
Packer, Nancy Huddleston, 325
Palmer, John, 113, 164, 217, 218
Palmer, Paul A., 58, 133
Panofsky, Erwin, 148, 149
Parelhoff, A. D., 156
Paris *Times*, 19
Parker, John, 74
Parks, Lloyd, 238
Parris, Elizabeth, 325
Partisan Review: compared to *KR*, 2–5, 83, 116–17, 131, 141, 162–65, 222*n*, 234, 240, 318*n*, 332, 334, 344; mentioned, 19, 26, 27, 38, 58, 76*n*, 96, 98, 101, 119, 139, 141, 153, 155, 172, 219, 220, 263, 266, 277, 278, 306, 336, 337, 347
Pasternak, Boris, 144, 324*n*
Patchen, Kenneth, 117*n*
Patton, Frances Gray, 142
Patton, R. S., 301
Pauker, John, 301
Pavese, Cesare, 186
Pearce, Roy Harvey, 290
Pechter, William S., 327
Pederson, Glenn, 297

Peirce, William Forster, 11
Pelligrini & Cudahy, 134
Pepper, Stephen C., 132, 133
Perkins, Maxwell, 17
Perspectives USA, 259, 284
Peterson, Theodore, 154
Phelps, Robert, 266
Phillips, Duncan, 255, 258, 261
Phillips, Robert, 76n, 100n
Phillips, William, 5, 6n, 27, 39, 119, 164n, 349
Picasso, Pablo, 81, 310
Picchi, Mario, 339
Pick, John, 107n
Pilkington, John, 251n
Pilot Press, 134
Plato, 32
Playboy, 9, 335, 337, 338, 346
PMLA, 8, 267
Podhoretz, Norman, 5, 6n, 39, 314
Poe, Edgar Allan, 184, 216
Poetry, 19, 74, 83, 159, 160, 162, 163, 230, 277, 302
Politics, 140
Pollet, Elizabeth, 302
Pope, Alexander, 108
Popkin, Henry, 251, 252, 310
Porter, Fairfield, 81
Porter, Katherine Anne, 16, 50, 79, 100, 101, 128, 145, 155, 158
Porter, William Sidney, 241, 309
Posner, David, 333
Potter, G. R., 181
Potter, Nancy, 324n, 325
Pottle, Frederick A., 37n
Pound, Ezra: and Bollingen Prize, 155–61; mentioned, 30, 42, 205, 208, 237n, 277n, 294, 295n, 301n
Poussin, Nicolas, 302
Powers, James F.: as *KR* Fellow, 173, 307–308; mentioned, 158, 324n
Powys, T. F., 339
Prairie Schooner, 140
Praz, Mario, 128
Prévert, Jacques, 238
Prior, Matthew, 285
Pritchard, Sheila, 301
Prokosch, Frederic, 45, 76
Proust, Marcel, 58, 108, 123, 221, 244n
Putman, Clay, 173
Putnam, Phelps, 221, 222
Pynchon, Thomas, 324n, 325

Quarterly Review of Literature, 315

Radford, Ruby Lorraine, 79

Rahming, Norris, 29
Rahv, Philip, 7, 39, 43, 54, 59, 93, 98, 101, 119, 158, 168, 169, 177, 179, 204, 207, 211, 234, 295, 296, 297, 314, 315
Rand, F., 15
Random House, 179, 244, 248, 249, 258, 318
Rank, H. E., 229n
Ransom, John Crowe: biography of, 12; and Fugitives, 12–14; and Agrarianism, 14–15, 32–33, 37, 69–70, 122, 126; and Vanderbilt, 14–16; and politics, 21, 37, 226; and advisory editors, 23–25, 93–94, 320–21; and Greensboro offer, 31–32; and philosophy, 32, 64–66, 68–69, 129–31, 132; and poetry, 32, 73–78, 135–36, 226, 231–32; and education, 33, 60, 62, 129; and criticism, 33–35, 41–42, 46–48, 52–53, 58, 111–13, 174–75, 206–211, 280, 290–91, 296; *New Criticism,* 34, 47–49, 91n, 116; *World's Body,* 42n, 47, 65, 66, 130, 132, 209, 215; *Kenyon Critics,* 43, 54, 56, 57, 102, 113, 114, 116, 118, 119, 123, 124, 129, 179, 187, 190, 195, 199, 203, 208, 211, 216, 217, 221, 222, 254, 259n, 324; and fiction, 78–79, 140–41, 240–41, 246–47, 249, 324–25; and Bollingen Prize, 157, 158, 160; loses interest in *KR,* 267–68, 271–74, 279–82, 290, 311; special issue for, 330–32
Ransom, Mrs. J. J., 16, 28, 31
Ransom, Reavill, 136n
Read, Herbert, 71, 168, 178, 179
Regnery, 259
Reik, Theodore, 117
Reinhart, Kurt F., 223
Reis, Lincoln, 129n
Review of Religion, The, 133
Revue des Deux Mondes, 9
Rexroth, Kenneth, 266
Reynal and Hitchcock, 109, 110
Ribiero, Leo Gilson, 320
Rice, Kathryn, 270
Rice, Philip Blair: importance of, 7, 39–40, 91–93, 94, 99, 124–25, 129, 140, 141, 177, 182, 191–92, 214, 223, 246, 247, 257–58, 269–70; biography of, 19; Ransom on, 19–21, 32, 91, 93, 269–70, 300; and politics, 19–21, 37, 224–25; and philosophy, 19, 64, 129, 131, 211–12, 223–24; contributions of, 42, 59, 66–67, 211–13; and Bollingen Prize, 157–60; death of, 269–71, 272, 300, 330
Richards, I. A., 36, 41, 47, 50, 61, 176, 177, 199, 200, 209, 217, 218, 306
Richards, Mary C., 310
Richardson, Dorothy, 55

Richman, Robert, 255
Ricks, Christopher, 339
Riding, Laura, 12n, 137
Rieff, Philip, 212, 289, 290
Riker, Charles: as Rockefeller Fellow, 95n, 98; mentioned, 150
Rimbaud, Arthur, 58
Robbe-Grillet, Alain, 341
Robinson, Edwin Arlington, 208, 237n
Rochester, John Wilmot, Second Earl of, 322
Rockefeller Foundation: and "Literary Magazines Study," 27, 161–64; and Rockefeller Fellows, 94–99, 142, 150, 172; sponsoring *KR*, 103, 149–51, 258–63; and Bollingen Prize, 156, 160; and Kenyon School of English, 165–71; and *KR* Fellows, 171–74, 240, 268–69, 308–309; mentioned, 40, 84, 124, 130, 153, 154, 177, 202, 211, 318
Rodell, John, 125
Roditi, Edouard, 124, 195, 196
Roelofs, Gerrit, 322
Roelofs, Howard Dijjema, 64
Roethke, Theodore, 51, 53, 193, 231, 232, 233, 239, 300
Rolling Stone, 337
Rolph, C. H., 339
Romains, Jules, 45
Rosenberg, Harold, 39, 225
Rosenfeld, Isaac, 7, 39, 119, 120, 145, 219, 248
Rosenfeld, Paul, 23, 24, 25, 44, 80, 94
Rouault, George, 255
Roubiczek, Paul, 217
Rougemont, Denis de, 118, 134n
Rousseau, Jean-Jacques, 235
Rubin, Louis D., Jr., 5. 269, 277
Ruggles, Eleanor, 105, 106, 107n
Rukeyser, Muriel, 74, 76, 117n, 137, 238, 333
Russell, Bertrand, 44, 64, 68
Ruth, George Herman, 35

Sachs, Hanns, 117n
Sagmaster, Joseph, 19, 270
Samson, William, 193n
Santayana, George, 19, 64, 224
Saroyan, William, 339
Sartre, Jean-Paul, 92, 128, 131, 177, 223, 225, 250
Saturday Review of Literature, The, 156, 158, 159, 160, 161
Saunders, Hade. *See* Stewart, John L.
Savage, D. S., 125
Schapiro, Meyer, 39, 95
Schoder, R. V., 104

Schorer, Mark, 58, 68, 115, 158, 168, 222, 245n, 313
Schwartz, Delmore: contributions of, 43, 54–55, 57–59, 76–77, 79–80, 137–38, 145; as *KR* Fellow, 173, 302–304; mentioned, 30, 38, 39, 42, 51, 82, 100, 114, 126, 127, 154n, 158, 168, 238, 248, 259n, 299, 314, 314, 333
Scopes, John, 134
Scott, Robert, 287
Scribners, 17, 18, 113, 259
Scrutiny, 59, 60, 107, 111, 214
Seldes, Gilbert, 24, 80
Sender, Ramon J., 146
Sessions, Roger, 98, 133, 147
Seven Arts, 22
Sewanee Review, The, 2, 3, 98, 113, 127, 130, 150, 153, 162, 163, 164, 165, 172, 200, 201n, 214, 216, 217, 231, 240, 263, 277, 313, 318n, 323, 332
Shakespeare, William, 42, 110, 112, 200, 201, 218, 228, 252, 270, 293, 294, 330
Shapiro, Herbert Eugene, 5
Shapiro, Karl: and Bollingen Prize, 155–56, 160–61; mentioned, 7, 137, 138n, 139, 193, 274, 302, 314, 315, 332
Shaw, George Bernard, 146
Shaw, Irwin, 186
Shelley, Percy Bysshe, 183
Shenandoah, 8, 276
Simpson, Eileen, 143
Simpson, E. M., 181
Singal, Daniel Joseph, 13n
Singleton, Charles, 182, 183, 184
Sissman, L. E., 334
Sixties, The, 336
Slaiman, Mortimer, 248
Slavitt, David R., 302
Smith, Gerald, 200
Smith, Henry L., Jr., 291
Smith, Robert Paul, 58, 245n
Smith, William J., 274
Snodgrass, W. D., 314
Snow, C. P., 321n, 329
Solotaroff, Theodore, 336
Southard, Walter, 79, 122, 133, 134, 149, 230, 270
Southern Review, The: "Literature and the Professors," with *KR*, 60–63; merger with *KR*, 86–90; mentioned, 1, 4, 16, 38, 45, 77, 79, 82, 93, 94, 100, 140, 150, 164, 313, 337n, 348
Spacks, Barry, 266
Spears, Monroe K., 2n, 4, 27, 200, 277, 285
Spectorsky, A. C., 335

Spencer, Elizabeth: as *KR* Fellow, 173, 307–308
Spencer, Theodore, 155
Spender, Stephen, 71, 177, 179, 193, 314, 332
Spielgelberg, Herbert, 223
Spurgeon, Caroline, 197
Stafford, Jean, 145, 331
Stafford, William, 333
Stallknecht, Newton P., 171, 275, 297
Stallman, Robert Wooster, 128, 173, 175, 192, 297
Stanford University, 150n
Stark, Alfred, 12n
Stead, Christina, 326
Stein, Arnold, 181, 216, 292, 293
Steiner, George, 320, 329, 334
Stern, Richard, 243, 244, 246, 282
Stevens, David, 95, 97, 103, 165, 167, 170, 171
Stevens, Wallace, 25, 42, 51, 57, 77, 134, 135, 139, 162, 163, 165, 205, 206, 208, 213, 233, 237n, 239, 246, 283, 332
Stevenson, Alec, 12n
Stewart, John L., 62, 313
Stewart, Paul Robert, 140
Stitt, James S., 325
Stone, Ruth: as *KR* Fellow, 173, 304
Story, 141
Strandberg, Victor, 235n
Stratford, Philip, 299
Strindberg, August, 108
Sulkin, Sidney, 145
Sultan, Stanley, 240, 248
Sutcliffe, Denham, 157, 159, 160, 243, 276, 280
Swallow Press, 347
Swartz, Roberta Teale, 10, 11, 23, 24, 78, 158, 306
Sweeney, James Johnson, 28, 81
Sweeney, John, 101, 102, 212, 213
Swinnerton, Frank, 339
Sykes, Christopher, 186
Symons, Julian, 56, 57, 70, 108
Symposium, The, 1, 19, 30, 40, 41
Synge, John Millington, 108
Sypher, Wylie, 108, 343

Taller, 59
Tate, Allen: on Ransom, 11, 87, 129–30, 132, 138, 209, 313; biography of, 12–13; as Ransom's confidant, 14, 20, 22, 23, 65, 84, 85, 91, 114, 141, 268, 273n; and Vanderbilt University, 15–16; as possible associate editor, 17–19; as advisor, 23–25, 30, 77, 94, 126–29, 240, 274–79, 343; and Greensboro, 31–32; and New Criticism, 35, 52,

176, 209; *The Fathers,* 44–45; contributions of, 52, 82–83, 138–39, 176, 184, 216; and "Literature and the Professors," 60–63; and *Southern Review,* 87–88; as *Sewanee Review* editor, 98, 162, 164, 214, 231, 313; Ransom on, 138–39, 178; and Bollingen Prize, 155–61; and Kenyon School of English, 167–70
Tate, Caroline Gordon. *See* Gordon, Caroline
Taylor, Edward, 50
Taylor, Harold, 245
Taylor, Peter: as advisor, 240, 245, 246, 274, 320; as Ransom's possible successor, 272–73, 276; mentioned, 15n, 16, 76, 144, 158, 280, 309, 310, 324n, 331
Temps Modernes, Les, 256
Tennyson, Alfred, First Baron, 204, 234
Terry, Walter, 256
Thale, Jerome, 329
Thayer, Scofield, 1
Thomas, Dylan, 30, 56, 57, 71, 77, 193, 208
Thomas, Wright, 62
Thompson, John, 75, 274, 292
Thompson, Lawrence, 58
Thorp, Willard, 61, 155
Tillim, Sidney, 310
Timberlake, Philip, 24
Time, 151, 264
Times Literary Supplement, The, 257, 263, 332
Tolstoy, Count Leo, 203, 204
Tongue, Margaret, 301
Torrence, Frederic, 24
Torrey, E. Fuller, 156n
Toulmin, Stephen, 224
Toulouse-Lautrec, Henri, 44
Tovey, D. F., 147
Toynbee, Arnold, 206
Trager, George L., 291
transition, 28
Trilling, Diana, 39, 158
Trilling, Lionel: as advisor, 7, 92, 94, 96, 100, 126, 188, 196, 256, 277–78, 320–21; contributions of, 55–56, 62–63, 72–73, 117–18, 208, 219; and Kenyon School of English, 165–67, 170–71, 177; mentioned, 2n, 38, 39, 52, 58, 59, 61, 95, 101, 123, 129, 158, 161, 163, 169n, 178, 186, 199, 204, 227, 228, 229n, 258, 296, 330
TriQuarterly, 314, 347
Troy, William, 58, 128
Turco, Lewis, 333
Tuve, Rosemond, 180, 181
Twentieth Century, 263
Tyler, Parker, 181, 253, 254, 255, 311, 327

Uberti, Farinata degli, 184
University of Georgia, 87, 88
University of Oklahoma Press, 179
University of South Carolina Press, 347
Untermeyer, Louis, 314
Ussher, Arland, 221

Valéry, Paul, 58, 123, 124, 221, 288
Vallette, Jacques, 183
Vanderbilt Alumnus, 45
Vanderbilt University, 11, 12, 14, 15, 16, 32, 42, 307
Van Doren, Mark, 17, 23, 24, 31, 77, 115, 136, 158
Van Duyn, Mona, 143
Van Gennep, Arnold, 198
Van Gogh, Vincent, 149
Van Rossem, Maarten, 5n
Venable, Vernon, 19, 44
Viereck, Peter, 230, 239
Viertel, Berthold, 146
View, 253
Viking Press, 248n
Village Voice, The, 336, 337
Virgil, 235, 236
Virginia Quarterly Review, The, 16, 22, 26
Vittorini, Elio, 128
Vivas, Eliseo, 24, 35, 38, 50, 64, 67, 69, 72, 82, 92, 94, 100, 102, 131n, 217, 220, 223
Voegelin, Erminie, 197
Vogue, 227

Wade, John Donald, 14n
Wagner, Geoffrey, 339
Wagner, Martin, 148
Wagner, Richard, 107, 108, 146
Wahl, Betty, 324n
Wahl, Jean, 92, 212, 223
Wain, John, 309, 324n, 338
Wald, Alan M., 6n
Walker, Hudson, 255
Wall, Alan, 6
Wallis, Charles Glenn, 118, 134n
Walter, Arnold M., 132
Warren, Austin, 35, 46, 50, 100, 102, 104, 105, 106, 107n, 167, 179, 181, 216, 217, 261, 271, 328, 335
Warren, Robert Penn: and *Southern Review,* 3, 86–88, 313; Ransom on, 17, 99, 113, 233–34; as advisor, 25, 93–94, 99, 100–104, 140–44, 165, 274, 320–21, 343; *Understanding Poetry,* 41, 43, 44, 109n, 129; contributions of, 50, 52, 57, 71, 77, 109–110, 113, 226, 233–35, 247, 300–301; as Rockefeller Fellow, 95n, 98–99,

127–28, 150; mentioned, 5, 12n, 13, 14n, 19, 30, 32, 35, 36n, 38, 46, 59, 79, 96, 115, 122, 125, 139, 155, 159, 162, 170, 181, 216, 217, 239, 254, 271, 272, 273, 277n, 292, 314, 324, 331, 333
Warshow, Robert, 39
Watkins, Edwin: as *KR* Fellow, 173, 174, 226; mentioned, 270
Watkins, Vernon, 312
Watson, Barbara, 299
Watson, James Sibley, 1
Waugh, Evelyn, 123
Weales, Gerald, 252, 310
Weaver, Richard A., 217, 276, 277
Weaver, Robert A., 83, 84, 85
Weaver, Robert A., Jr., 85, 88
Webb, William, 322n
Webster, Grant, 38, 99
Webster, John, 62
Weiss, Theodore, 315
Weisstein, Allyn, 255
Wellek, René, 128, 168, 217
Wells, H. G., 329
Welty, Eudora, 25, 113, 117n
Werham, Guy, 118n
Werner, Alfred, 310, 327, 328, 341
West, Jessamyn, 324n
West, Ray B., 239
Western Review, The, 163, 243, 316n
Wheelwright, Philip, 30, 61, 63, 66, 67, 68, 82, 131n
Whicher, George, 52, 83
White, Frederick, 255
White, John Ellington, 337n, 340, 342, 345, 346, 350
White, Morton, 224
Whitehall, Harold: as Rockefeller Fellow, 95; mentioned, 103, 104, 105, 106, 116, 150, 291
Whitehead, Alfred North, 64, 72
Whitman, Walt, 194
Whitney Foundation, 260
Whittemore, Reed, 74, 135, 173, 295
Wickes, George, 295
Wilbur, Richard, 233
Wilde, Oscar, 195
Williams, Charles, 219
Williams, Raymond, 320
Williams, William Carlos, 42, 114, 134, 141, 159, 162, 186, 191, 208, 222, 236, 237, 239, 246, 253, 294
Wills, Jesse, 12n
Wills, Ridley, 12n
Wilson, Angus, 339
Wilson, Edmund, 30, 47, 72, 100, 103, 118, 126, 127, 162, 187

Wilson, F. A. C., 284
Wilson, John Dover, 200
Wimsatt, W. K., 283
Winner, Percy, 186
Winters, Yvor, 36, 41, 42, 49, 50, 51, 52, 53, 63, 116, 159, 162, 168, 169, 193
Wisconsin Studies in Contemporary Literature, 8
Wiser, William, 325
Wolf, Leonard, 324n
Wolfe, Thomas, 43
Woman's College at Greensboro, N.C., 18, 31, 32, 33, 91, 316
Woods, John, 230, 239
Woodward, Henry, 80
Woolf, Leonard, 339
Woolf, Virginia, 119n
Wordsworth, William, 50, 109, 200, 208, 219
World Publishing Company, 144, 179
Wright, Frank Lloyd, 82, 117n, 195
Wright, H. Bunker, 285

Wright, James: as *KR* Fellow, 173, 228–29, 304–306; mentioned, 32, 227, 232, 233, 239

Yale Review, The, 22, 45, 347
Yeats, W. B., 50, 52, 125, 190, 191, 205, 208, 224, 236, 250, 284, 330, 331
Young, Marguerite, 75, 76, 82, 139
Young, Philip, 328, 329n
Young, Stark, 14n, 250, 251n
Young, Thomas Daniel, 5, 11n, 16n, 95n, 156n, 233n
Young, Vernon, 188
Young, Wayland, 243, 299

Zabel, Morton Dauwen, 16, 61, 100, 101, 112n, 162, 188
Zimbel, Elaine, 309
Zinsser, Hans, 115
Zoilus. *See* Macauley, Robie